INGO WALTER, Ph.D., New York University, is Professor of Economics and Finance, and Associate Dean at the Graduate School of Business Administration, New York University. He previously taught at the University of Missouri, and serves as consultant to the United Nations Conference on Trade and Development and the Organization for Economic Cooperation and Development. Dr. Walter has written numerous books and articles in the field of international trade and commercial policy, and has held research grants from the Ford Foundation and the Rockefeller Foundation.

SECOND EDITION

INTERNATIONAL ECONOMICS

INGO WALTER

NEW YORK UNIVERSITY

THE RONALD PRESS COMPANY • NEW YORK

Library of Congress Catalog Card Number: 74–22548
PRINTED IN THE UNITED STATES OF AMERICA

For Jutta, Carsten, and Inga

PREFACE

Students often find international economics complex and difficult. But if it is presented well, they usually discover a great deal of satisfaction in the way it helps them to analyze past and present developments in the world economy and reach conclusions that make sense. Not least important, the subject is rarely boring.

In this edition I have continued the emphasis on an orderly and logical presentation of the principles of international economic relations. The discussion concentrates on basic concepts and analytical techniques that can readily be applied to external events. Institutional and historical detail is avoided, except where it is indispensable, in order to encourage the reader to relate *what* is happening in the real world to the reasons *why* it is happening that are offered by the theory.

The discussion begins with the "pure" theory of international trade and the theory of commercial policy. It then turns to international monetary economics with an examination of the balance of payments, foreign exchange, and the theory of international financial adjustment and liquidity. The book concludes with a consideration of international capital and technology transfers in the context of economic growth.

Those familiar with the first edition of this book will find the revisions quite extensive. Where necessary, the level of presentation has been made somewhat less difficult, and alternative ways of explaining important concepts are frequently provided. Analytical techniques of greater sophistication, as well as suggestions for assigned reading, are presented in the Extensions and Additional Readings sections at the back of the book.

There are more but shorter chapters reflecting several organizational changes. For example, the statics and dynamics of economic integration are treated as special applications of more general international commercial policy. Separate chapters are devoted to the political dynamics of trade-policy formation and multinational corporate operations—both intended to align more closely what is happening in the real world with the underlying conceptual foundations.

Students with a solid background in general economics should have no difficulty with this book. However, review is provided in Chapter 2 for those who need it.

The revision of a text always involves the collection and evaluation of experience with the previous edition, and much of that experience has come from my own students in undergraduate and graduate international economics courses. Many were not hesitant to offer suggestions for improvement, and they deserve recognition. For their help as originators and conduits of criticism, I am also indebted to my colleagues Bob Hawkins, Kaj Areskoug, and Holger Engberg, as well as Peter Gray, Hal Malmgren, Larry Krause, Ronald Sutherland, Jaleel Ahmad, Adrian Throop, Walter Salant, Charles Pearson, and Norman Mintz. Marion Epps was largely responsible for preparing the manuscript for publication, and deserves my sincere thanks.

INGO WALTER

New York City
May, 1975

CONTENTS

PART II   Theory of Commercial Policy

PART III International Payments and Foreign Exchange

PART IV International Monetary Theory

INTERNATIONAL
ECONOMICS

1

INTRODUCTION

A nation does not exist in isolation. Sovereign national states invariably maintain political, military, social, economic, and cultural ties with the outside world. International economics concerns only one of these many areas of international involvement: the economic relations between nations. Economic considerations often have a profound effect on international cultural, social, political, and military affairs as well. Indeed, the root causes of important events in any one of the latter areas is often found primarily to involve economics. Conversely, it would be impossible to view international economic relations as separate, distinct phenomena since they are continually influenced by a constellation of noneconomic factors.

International economics concerns itself with all transactions that transcend national political boundaries. In each instance, therefore, such transactions involve at least two national economies. While it is true that national political frontiers do not invariably coincide with national economic "boundaries"—as determined by transport costs tariff walls, and so on—the relationship is probably close enough for purposes of economic analysis.

International transactions may be classified into several categories. The international *movement of goods and services* is probably the most apparent and certainly the most important type. Second, the international movement of *factors of production,* although perhaps less immediately recognized than international trade, is certainly of great significance for the national economies of the countries involved. International transfers of productive factors involve both the inter-country flow of labor—migration—and the international flow of capital.

Third, and of substantial long-range importance, is the international *transfer of useful knowledge.* While this is obviously a very broad category, it may be conveniently narrowed to consider only international technological

3

transfers, which prove to be of major economic importance for both the recipient and the source countries when related to the process of economic growth. Finally, it would be difficult to overlook the international *movement of entrepreneurship,* the organization of production and distribution for maximum gain under conditions of uncertainty. The risk-assumers in most of today's highly developed market-oriented economies have long sought to extend their scope of operation beyond the limitations imposed by national frontiers. The vital role exercised by entrepreneurs—as individuals, multinational corporations, or governments—generally accompanies and supports the international flow of capital and technology. Entrepreneurial transfer, like international flows of labor, capital, and technology, proves to be of major significance for economic growth.

DEVELOPMENT OF THE INTERNATIONAL ECONOMY

Although this text is basically a study of concepts and ideas, a short developmental exposition of the history of international economic relations (which is presented far more adequately elsewhere) is now provided.[1]

International trade and exchange, in a strict sense, may be traced only to a point in history heralding the emergence of the true national state in the modern sense of the term. Prior to that time, trade and exchange most certainly occurred among a host of relatively autonomous political units, but these could not be considered to be truly "national" in character. National states in Europe began to evolve during the sixteenth century, with France, England, Spain, and the Netherlands being the most prominent examples. It was not until the late nineteenth century that such economically significant nations as Germany and Italy could be considered real national entities. The United States, of course, evolved as a nation during the late eighteenth and early nineteenth centuries.

Such trade as did occur (often on a relatively unrestricted basis) before this era of national consolidation was of substantial importance to the level of economic activity prevailing at that time. This was true even in ancient times. Yet the evolution of the modern international economy really began with the period of rapid industrialization that more or less coincided with the period of national consolidation. With the extensive development of economic activity in a variety of forms and the inevitable extension of specialization, international trade and exchange began to assume an increasingly important and often crucial role.

The significance of international economic relationships during one of the early periods of national and commercial development may be gauged by the policies adopted by governments during the *Mercantilist* era, which

[1] See references in Section E-1.

dates from about 1500 to the middle of the eighteenth century. The Mercantilists felt that the accumulation of precious metals in the national coffers was crucial to the welfare of the state, and that the prime function of international trade was to augment this monetary stock in the national treasury. Accordingly, their efforts were geared toward maximum exports and minimum imports, that is, toward maintaining the greatest possible excess of exports over imports. The difference naturally was to be settled by the importation of gold and other precious metals, thereby attaining the desired increase in the national stock of "wealth" in this form.

Necessarily, international trade and exchange under the Mercantilist system involved a great deal of government control. State trading monopolies were common, and both exports and imports were subject to innumerable administrative regulations. Duty charges were used extensively to reduce the volume of imports and, if possible, to prevent the importation of certain goods completely. Concurrently, subsidies and rebates were used equally extensively to encourage and stimulate exports.

While Mercantilist ideas and policies, particularly their concept of wealth, might seem foolish at first glance, the accumulation of precious metals did, in fact, serve the purpose of stimulating the growth of national economic activity. At the same time, this resulted in the opening of new trade routes and in the state-fostered growth of efficiency levels in maritime industries, thereby facilitating and sometimes creating new opportunities for international trade and exchange.

The early phases of the Mercantilist era were dominated by Spain and Portugal, who pioneered in exploring the Western Hemisphere, Africa, and Asia. It was not long before the British and the Dutch began to expand their operations, particularly at the expense of Portugal, with Spain consolidating its position in Central and South America. Early Mercantilist exports included cloth, metalwares, trinkets, and gunpowder, with imports comprising many commodities entirely foreign to the European culture plus, of course, the coveted shipments of gold and silver.

One institution developed to facilitate pursuit of Mercantilist goals was the *trading company*. These organizations consisted of consortia under which merchants would pool their resources and, under government charter, engage in long-term and often risky trading ventures. The Dutch East India Company operated in parts of Asia and Africa, while the British East India Company concentrated on India and the Hudson's Bay Company on North America. Numerous other trading companies evolved in several European states, but the British were probably most successful. Trading companies were not always sound business ventures, as John Law's famous South Sea Company amply demonstrated in the early 1700's.

Trading companies usually established and colonized enclaves in their respective trading areas, and this naturally contributed to the evolution of the colonial and imperial era, with Britain and France replacing Spain and the Netherlands as the dominant powers. Tobacco, gold, silver, furs, lumber, and fish, and the traditional guns, spices, and silks constituted the primary imports from the colonial areas. Simple manufactures were also included as colonial capabilities to provide such goods improved. Still, Mercantilist ideas continued to prevail throughout the early colonial period, with due emphasis on maximum imports of precious metals. The age of colonial and imperial expansion which took root at that time thus may be seen as merely another outgrowth of Mercantilist ideas and policies. Regions under colonial domination effectively supplemented the economy of the mother country and aided in its accumulation of gold and other precious metals.

Eventually, the Mercantilist era gave way to a more liberal conception of national and international economic activity. This coincided with equally important changes that resulted in a fundamental transformation of contemporary political and religious thought, as well as with the rise to power and prominence of the bourgeois classes. Perhaps the most important force in the liberalization of international economic transactions, however, was the Industrial Revolution. By the late nineteenth century, in fact, international trade and capital movements were proceeding among the then "advanced" countries of the world with relatively few restrictions, spurred by a viable international standard of exchange—gold.

It was not until the onset of World War I that the basically smooth operation of the international economy was disrupted. Even the wartime emergency proved to be only a temporary setback, however. The period after World War I was marked by rapid recovery and a surge of economic activity throughout most of the western world, hindered only by the disastrous inflations in such countries as Austria and Germany during the early 1920's. By 1928, the volume of international trade had gained enormously, and the flow of capital between nations had assumed sizeable proportions.

After the cataclysmic onset of the Great Depression of the 1930's, there followed a precipitous decline in international economic transactions, punctuated by the suspension of the international gold standard in 1932 by virtually every important trading nation. The demise of gold in international exchange, as well as the continuing problem of World War I reparations, precluded rapid and substantial recovery by the world economy. A period of marked international economic disintegration and fragmentation followed. Each nation geared its policies more and more toward economic self-sufficiency, or *autarky*. This development was not excessively painful for large nations such as the United States, but it had near-terminal consequences for small countries dependent upon international trade for the maintenance of an acceptably high level of living.

The apparent necessity of rampant economic nationalism during the late 1930's coincided with the cancerous growth of political nationalism that led to World War II. The year 1946 marked the beginning of an international economic resurgence which characterized Japan and the war-devastated nations of Europe, as well as the economic relations between nations. This resurgence led into a period of rapid economic growth that has continued until the present time. European and Japanese economic recovery and massive infusions of American aid were accompanied by notable efforts to achieve some degree of renewed liberalization of international trade and payments. The establishment of the International Monetary Fund (IMF), the International Bank for Reconstruction and Development (IBRD), and even the ill-fated negotiations for the International Trade Organization (ITO), from which only the General Agreement on Tariffs and Trade (GATT) was salvaged, serve as prominent examples of the efforts put forth in this direction. We shall concern ourselves with these institutions in greater detail later on.

A partial freeing of international trade and payments did occur during the early postwar years but it was a long, hard process. As long as the productive capacity of most of the western European nations and Japan had not been restored, and the period of "dollar shortage" prevailed, movement in this direction was slow and beset with difficulties. Once economic recovery was complete, international trade and payments liberalization was greatly facilitated, although the broad ideal of free trade and free mobility of productive factors has never been attained.

The 1950's saw the rise of a number of regional economic blocs, of which the European Economic Community (EEC) is certainly the best known. To a degree, the rise of regional economic unions points to the failure to achieve trade and payments liberalization on a global basis. Although considerable progress was achieved during the 1960's—particularly in the form of the "Kennedy Round" of trade negotiations—the concept of economic regionalism seems here to stay. And so the question for the future is whether we will have an essentially unified international economic system or one of rival economic blocs. All of the returns are not in. But the answer will have a critical bearing on the shape of things to come.

INTERREGIONAL AND INTERNATIONAL ECONOMIC RELATIONS

The kinds of transactions that are the stuff of international economics also occur on a large scale between different regions of a single nation: interregional trade in goods and services, and interregional flows of labor, capital, technology, and entrepreneurship. The fact that there are sovereign national states with distinct political and economic frontiers indicates a fundamental difference between *interregional* transactions and *international* transactions, although they are basically not dissimilar in nature or in their effects. Presumably, important man-made barriers to the movement of goods, services, productive factors, knowledge, and entrepreneurship do not normally exist between regions of a single country, that is, within a single national economy. But such is not the case with regard to similar flows between separate politically sovereign national states—between national economies.

Perhaps of equal significance are international differences in the general economic environment which are not ordinarily found interregionally. We would expect, for example, to find a relatively homogeneous taxation system apply to all parts of a given country. In addition, national economic policy considerations at an aggregate level tend to have a similar impact on substantially all regions of a nation. Education, transportation, the regulation of competition, unionization, and social insurance systems are likely to be uniform within a country, but they usually differ quite markedly between countries.

Certainly not least important, trade or exchange within a nation involves only one currency and one monetary standard. Clearly, this is not true internationally. Each nation possesses its own currency and its own monetary standard, and all international transactions requiring some form of monetary payment must of necessity involve the exchange of one currency for another.

The one major qualification to this type of distinction between international and interregional transactions involves economic distance (transportation cost), which must be reckoned with in trade and factor movements both within and between nations. It is clear that natural obstacles, such as mountain ranges and bodies of water, can and do impede the movement of goods between sections of a single country as well as between nations. In fact, for some countries internal trade proves to be more difficult than international trade. The questions of location and transportation, then, cannot be overlooked in the study of trade either within a country or between countries.

SUBJECT MATTER

The operation of economic forces is transmitted from one nation to another in many ways. Hence it is not possible to study international economic relations in the same way as one studies economic activity within a single economy, and a variety of methods have evolved over the past several centuries for the analysis of international economic relations. The theories of international trade, commercial policy, international payments, and economic integration are some of these methods. Each attempts to explain the nature of observed or anticipated phenomena in international transactions. They may be used both to analyze and interpret past events and to predict the course of future developments.

The pure theory of international trade attempts to delineate why nations trade with one another. It strives to predict the direction, volume, and composition of international trade, as well as its effects on the structure of national economies. "Which nation trades what goods and services with whom and in what quantities?" is a fundamental question to which the theory of international trade addresses itself. If it is to be successful in its search for answers to such queries, international trade theory must concern itself with factors affecting both supply and demand in the international economy.

An important corollary to this question is concerned with the impact of international trade on the economic structure and material welfare of the trading nations. The degree of national specialization and the required attendant reallocation of productive resources themselves pose important problems for the national economy. In addition, the enhanced world and national welfare resulting from international specialization—the "gains" from trade—requires careful theoretical analysis.

The theory of commercial policy, on the other hand, attempts to delineate the effects of barriers to international trade and exchange, to explain why such barriers are erected by nations in spite of the apparent welfare gains resulting from free trade and specialization. What specific functions do they fulfill? If it is true, as the pure theory of international trade will convincingly demonstrate, that world output of goods and services can be maximized only through freedom of international trade, then why are impediments deliberately set up which effectively reduce or eliminate the free movement of goods and services internationally?

Armed with a fundamental understanding of the principles which underlie international trade and commercial policy as well as the major problems involved in each area, the student will be able to relate this knowledge to a number of specific questions of current interest and long-range importance. One of these is economic integration, the process of creating a single regional economic entity from several national economies. The theory of commercial policy also has important implications for national economic welfare and for the welfare of myriad sub-components of the national economy: regions, firms, industries, labor groups, and so forth. In addition, it is of great significance to the developing nations of the world who must weigh the sometimes conflicting "gains from trade" and "gains from growth" in their struggle for rapid economic advance. The evolution of national commercial policies has been of determining importance in international economic relations in the past, and it will certainly continue to play much the same role in future years.

It will also be necessary to develop some general statements bearing on the forces which determine international flows of the factors of production, useful knowledge, and entrepreneurship. Simultaneously, the impact of these flows on the volume and direction of international trade, as well as upon the respective economic structures of the various national economies, must be determined. Perhaps of even greater interest, specifically to the less developed nations of the world, are the ramifications which international transfers of technology, entrepreneurship, and productive factors hold in store for the process of economic development.

While the causes and effects of international trade, commercial policy, and factor movements are basic, and deal with real (physical) flows of goods, services, and productive resources between countries, these flows also give rise to money payments and receipts. These corresponding flows of money, and the transfers they involve among national currencies, are the concern of the balance of payments and foreign exchange. Just as money exerts a critical influence over strategic national economic phenomena such as employment, growth, and prices, so too do money payments and receipts between countries provide an additional connecting link between national economies. In this way international monetary theory—and the impact of intercountry payments and receipts on the national economy—becomes an integral part of international economic relations. This gives rise to a host of other questions concerning the nature of national monetary standards, the means of settling imbalances in foreign payments and receipts—international reserves and liquidity—and alternative international monetary systems.

Perhaps the most crucial questions facing the international economy today revolve around the struggle for economic growth, which absorbs the interests and efforts of the majority of the world's nations. The so-called developing nations justifiably possess high aspirations for rapid advancement of the levels of living of their respective peoples. This requires a high rate of growth of both national product and product per capita. To some extent, internal measures, such as industrialization and the limitation of population expansion, will aid in the attainment of these objectives. But progress will also depend to a large degree on developments in the international economy, especially those areas of international trade and the flows of productive capital and technology.

The world's less developed nations face some major and largely unique problems in finding suitable and stable access to markets for their exports, and in attracting productive capital and various forms of aid which will enable them to achieve the desired high rate of physical and human capital formation. To a marked degree, international cooperation can be of assistance in the realization of successful solutions to some of these dilemmas. At the same time, the developing nation itself must gear its policies and programs in accordance with the attainment of these objectives. The study of international economics is useful in providing guidelines to the direction in which these development policies should move.

INTERNATIONAL ECONOMICS AS A COURSE OF STUDY

International economics has justified its existence as a co-equal branch of general economics, along with national income analysis, price theory, and other more or less distinct aspects of the subject. It is tied to these other aspects of economics in numerous ways. International economics makes extensive use, for instance, of the tools of price theory to arrive at salient theoretical conclusions. At the same time, the impact of international economic relations on the national level of economic activity is of substantial importance (the reverse is also true), especially for relatively small nations which depend on international specialization and exchange for a viable level of living and rapid economic growth. This is becoming increasingly important from a policy standpoint.

As is true of any field of behavioral knowledge, the development of international economics has been evolutionary in nature. Partly, the contributions have been original ones applied directly to international economic problems, and partly they have consisted of applications of concepts and methods developed in other branches of economics. It is not a monolithic block of knowledge. The complexity of the subject—the number of different external and internal variables bearing on international economic relations—is probably more pronounced than in, say, the theory of income determination. As a consequence, its structure is bound to be somewhat less clearly defined.

There is, of course, a pronounced lag between the development and the dissemination of new knowledge in this as in any other field of endeavor. New ideas and alternative ways of looking at international economic problems are constantly evolving. Some never attain widespread acceptance. Others gain attention and prominence very rapidly and, within a short period of time, fade into relative obscurity. Still others become generally acknowledged by specialists in the field and, after a certain amount of time, achieve a status of general knowledge among students and practitioners in the field.

The purpose of this volume is to present international economic theory and analysis—the "state of the art" at the present time—in as concise and systematic a manner as possible. Its fundamental aim is to provide the student with the tools needed for mature analysis, interpretation, and prediction with regard to matters dealing with international economic affairs. It is not an intended function to present an elaborate exposition of international economic and financial institutions, nor of the historical evolution of the international economy. This has been done very adequately elsewhere.[2] On the other hand, it is also not intended that elaborate models

---

[2] See the references cited in Section E-1.

and rigorous academic exercises be constructed as ends in themselves, without sufficient regard to their relevance to conditions as they exist in current international economic relations. It is, rather, a study in method of analysis, with emphasis on the applicability of the method to actual and significant problems.

The material presented in this volume is, of necessity, abstract and conceptual in nature. In order to be applicable to the maximum number and range of observed phenomena in the real world, analytical concepts must be as broad as possible. This required breadth of application can only be achieved in abstraction. At the same time, the usefulness of the analytical tools hinges largely on their degree of precision.

An attempt is made to present each individual concept in as simple a manner as possible, consistent with the desired level of abstraction and breadth of scope. Concurrently, it is desired that the analysis presented be operational to the greatest possible degree. As with any predominantly theoretical approach to a highly complex subject, it will shortly become clear to the reader that there are a host of problems involved in applying simplified and sometimes highly aggregative economic models to the international economy as it actually exists. Nevertheless, such an approaach does yield a systematic, orderly way of looking at problems encountered in the real world and offers at least a starting point for detailed and thoughtful analysis.

It does not follow that the theoretical and analytical concepts developed here are severely limited in their applicability to the formulation of international economic policies. On the contrary, intelligent policy decisions require a sound grasp of the theories and concepts involved. No policy is ever made without an underlying theory. And it is the soundness of the theory which will determine the success and validity of the policy decision. Everyone knows that a theory is only useful as long as it is supported to a reasonable degree by the facts. When empirical analysis fails to substantiate the theoretical conclusions, then the theory must be rejected and serves only as a guide in the search for a more applicable one. Consequently, throughout this volume a great deal of emphasis is placed wherever possible on the testing of fundamental concepts, as well as on the conclusiveness of the results regarding the validity of the theory.

ORGANIZATION

The organizational structure of this text follows a pattern dictated by the intended conceptual and analytical approach to the subject of international economics, as outlined above. There are two sections. A *Core* section comprises the main body of the text and covers the substance of international economics at an introductory level. The presentation relies heavily on verbal and geometric exposition in order to minimize complexity and confusion. The intent is to provide a full discussion of the subject accessible to students previously exposed only to introductory economics. An *Extensions* section comprises the latter part of the book, and contains theoretical and empirical elaborations of points covered in the *Core,* as well as restatements of major theses in more elegant—but sometimes more complex—terms. It also contains an annotated guide to reading and research keyed to each of the topics covered in the text.

Before proceeding, the reader should at this point review his or her background in the fundamentals of economic analysis. This can best be done by reading the following chapter, which covers some of the basic tools required for the understanding of many of the ideas and concepts presented in the book. Students well-versed in economic theory may find this review useful. Others, acquainted only casually with the principles of economics, would do well to achieve reasonable competence in the economic analysis surveyed there.

2

SOME BASIC TOOLS

International economic analysis makes use of a number of fundamental concepts that are normally associated primarily with other branches of economics. In order to employ such analytical methods for the purpose of gaining a clearer understanding of the complex forces which form international economic relationships, a sound grasp of these methods is a necessity. We shall review briefly in this chapter those concepts necessary for an understanding of the material presented in this text. Should a more comprehensive examination be required of any of the ideas presented here the reader would do well before proceeding, to turn to one of the references cited in Section E-1.

DEMAND

The concept of demand refers to the amount of a given commodity that consumers or users are able and willing to buy at each and every possible price. It may relate to a certain product category (automobiles), or simply to the output of a single producing entity (Chevrolets); the former is called industry demand and the latter, firm demand. The demand concept may concern goods categories of an infinite range of degrees of homogeneity. In fact, economists even talk about aggregate demand (the demand for all of the goods and services produced by an economy) and foreign demand—the demand originating in the rest of the world for the goods and services produced by a national economy.

When applied to a single good, or a relatively homogeneous group of goods, the quantity demanded is generally an inverse function or price. At high prices, very little will be bought and at low prices the quantity demanded is likely to be quite large. Why? Because at lower prices the consumer or user (a) finds that his money income will buy more units of that particular commodity and all other commodities as well, and (b) tends to substitute that commodity for other goods in his purchase decisions.

The linear demand function D in Figure 2–1 is a graphical illustration of this relationship between quantity demanded and price, everything else being held constant. At price P_1, quantity OQ_1 will be demanded, and at a lower price P_2, a larger quantity, OQ_2, will be demanded.

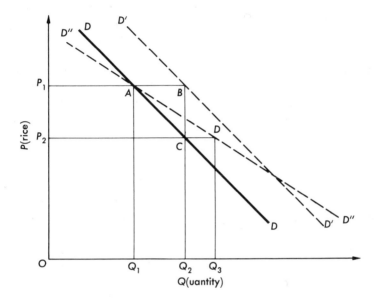

Fig. 2–1.   Demand.

Of course, the price of a good can be considered to be the sole determinant of quantity demanded *only* if we ignore all other factors which might influence consumer or user decisions to purchase. Clearly such elements as incomes, population, tastes and preferences, prices of goods that are considered substitutes or complements, and the available range of choice will also affect demand. A change in any one of these will cause a *shift* in the demand curve; that is, more or less will be demanded at any stipulated price. In Figure 2–1, we saw that a decline in price from P_1 to P_2 brought forth an increase in quantity from OQ_1 to OQ_2—it was a movement *along* the curve D. But the same OQ_1 to OQ_2 increase in quantity demanded could be achieved without any decrease in price if a factor such as incomes or tastes caused the entire demand curve to shift to the right. The relevant demand function is now D', with OQ_2 demanded at the original price P_1. Thus there is a crucial difference between changes in *quantity demanded* which result from changes in price, and shifts in *demand* which result from changes in variables other than the price of the commodity in question.

So far, we have talked about the position, or locus, of the demand curve. But what about its shape? If the price of oranges declines by 10 per cent, what will be the resultant response in the quantity of oranges demanded? Will it rise by 10 per cent, 15 per cent, 20 per cent, or more? This involves the concept of *elasticity*, a quantitative measure of the degree of response of quantity demanded to given changes in price, which defines the shape of the demand function.

Referring once more to Figure 2–1, with the original demand curve *D*, a decline in price of P_1P_2 brought forth an increase in quantity demanded of $OQ_1 - OQ_2$. Now suppose the demand curve had been D'' instead. The same P_1P_2 price reduction would have resulted in an increase in quantity demanded of $OQ_1 - OQ_3$. Clearly, $OQ_1 - OQ_3$ is greater than $OQ_1 - OQ_2$, and quantity demanded is substantially more responsive to price changes given demand curve D'' than under D. We say that the demand described by curve D'' is more *elastic* than that represented by curve *D*.

On the surface, it would seem that the elasticity of a demand curve is the same as its *slope*. It is not. Slope is measured in terms of absolute changes (e.g., price change in dollars and quantity change in units), whereas elasticity is measured in terms of relative changes (e.g., price change in per cent and quantity change in per cent). Whereas the slope of demand curve D would be defined as $\Delta P / \Delta Q$[1], the formula for the elasticity of the curve at, say, point A is given as:

$$e_p = \frac{\dfrac{\Delta Q}{Q}}{-\dfrac{\Delta P}{P}} = \frac{P\Delta Q}{Q(-\Delta P)} = \frac{\Delta Q}{-\Delta P} \times \frac{P}{Q}$$

Whereas the slope of a linear demand function, such as D in Figure 2–1, is constant, the elasticity changes throughout its length; the elasticity coefficient is large (elastic) at its upper end and small (inelastic) at its lower end. By applying some numerical figures to the example, the reader can verify this for himself. If the elasticity coefficient turns out to have a value of 1 at some point on the curve, we call it *unitary* elasticity; i.e., a 1 per cent decline in price will call forth exactly a 1 per cent increase in quantity demanded. Only if the demand function is a rectangular hyperbola, convex to the origin, will it have unitary elasticity throughout its length.

---

[1] We define Δ, the *delta*, as a "small change" in whatever variable is associated with it. Hence, this particular relation would read "a small change in price associated with a small change in quantity."

Usually we cannot talk about derivatives or infinitely small changes in price and quantity at a point on the demand curve, since they are not measurable in practice. Instead, we generally look at the elasticity of a demand curve between two points on that curve. This form of elasticity, called *arc elasticity,* may be written as

$$e'_p = \frac{\dfrac{Q_2 - Q_1}{Q_2 + Q_1}}{\dfrac{P_2 - P_1}{P_2 + P_1}} = \frac{(Q_2 - Q_1)(P_2 + P_1)}{(Q_2 + Q_1)(P_2 - P_1)} = \frac{(Q_2 - Q_1)}{(P_2 - P_1)} \times \frac{(P_2 + P_1)}{(Q_2 + Q_1)}$$

This will be recognized as being nothing more than a definitive, measurable percentage change in quantity demanded in response to a corresponding percentage change in price. The closer together the two points on the curve, the more useful will be this measure of elasticity. In terms of Figure 2–1, it defines the elasticity of the demand curve D between points A and C.

Finally, and of particular importance in our later discussion of balance of payments adjustment, is the response of total expenditure to changes in price. If the demand for a certain good is elastic, a decline in price will result in a rise in total money expenditure on that commodity, since the relative increase in quantity sold is by definition greater than the relative price reduction. Conversely, a price reduction in a commodity characterized by an inelastic demand will bring about a reduction in total money expenditure. Exactly the opposite holds true for price *increases* with elastic and inelastic demand functions, respectively; i.e., a price rise under inelastic demand conditions results in an expansion of total expenditures, while it causes a decline in total expenditures under elastic demand conditions.

There are other types of elasticities of demand, notably those measuring the response of quantity demanded to changes in variables other than the price of the good itself; *cross-elasticity of demand* and *income elasticity of demand* are two of these. If we let A and B represent two goods, then the cross-elasticity of demand for A can be defined as the responsiveness of the quantity demanded of good A to changes in the price of good B. Algebraically, this can be written as

$$e_{AB} = \frac{\dfrac{\Delta Q_A}{Q_A}}{\dfrac{- \Delta P_B}{P_B}}$$

If the two commodities are complements to one another, the cross-elasticity of demand will have a negative sign; if they are substitutes, the sign will be positive.

Income elasticity of demand, on the other hand, measures the degree of responsiveness of quantity demanded to a change in income, not price. Accordingly, this relation may be written as follows:

$$e_y = \frac{\dfrac{\Delta Q}{Q}}{\dfrac{\Delta Y}{Y}}$$

In the case of both income elasticity and cross-elasticity of demand, the arc form of the equation may be employed just as it was for price elasticity above. We need not dwell on elasticity any further at this point, although it will be mentioned several times later on in our study of international economics.

SUPPLY AND MARKET EQUILIBRIUM

An analysis similar to that just completed may be made of the factors affecting the supply of a given commodity or group of commodities. It seems natural that at low prices producers would be willing to provide the market with a smaller quantity of goods than at higher prices. Hence, we would expect the supply curve to be upward sloping, as, for instance, curve S in Figure 2-2. That is, quantity supplied is a *direct* function of price. But we do not have to rely on pure intuition to tell us that the supply curve should normally be upward sloping.

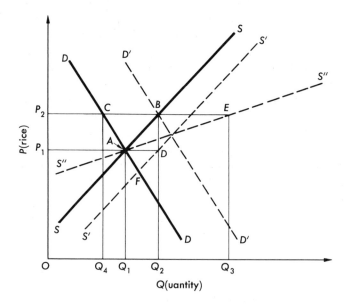

Fig. 2–2. Supply and equilibrium.

Without going unnecessarily deeply into production theory, we can say that the short-run supply curve of a given firm is based upon its *marginal cost*—the change brought about in its total costs as a result of a single additional unit of output. Up to a point, marginal cost falls with each additional unit of output because the efficiency with which variable inputs are utilized increases with increasing output, resulting in successively lower variable costs per *additional* unit of production. Thereafter, the degree of efficiency with which variable inputs are being used declines, and hence, variable cost per additional unit of production increases. We assume that most firms are operating under conditions of increasing marginal cost (on the upward-sloping part of the U-shaped marginal cost curve), and that the supply curve for a firm is therefore upward-sloping.

Whereas this justification for an upward-sloping supply curve is based only on the economics of a single firm and holds only in the short run, it can be demonstrated that it is a more general phenomenon, applying equally, but for different reasons, to the long-run cost behavior of a firm and to the output of entire industries. This does not mean that we can assume away the possible existence of constant costs or even decreasing costs (flat or downward-sloping supply curves) under certain circumstances, as we shall see later on.

Returning once more to the supply curve S presented in Figure 2-2, we must make the same distinction between changes in quantity supplied in response to price changes, on one hand, and shifts in supply made in the case of demand on the other. A price increase of P_1P_2 causes producers to supply an additional amount $OQ_1 - OQ_2$: a change in *quantity supplied*. The same $OQ_1 - OQ_2$ quantity increase could be achieved without any change in the price P_1, if the entire supply curve were to shift to the right, from S to S'. Supply shifts such as this could result from changes in the cost and availability of inputs, changes in the price of technical complements or substitutes, or perhaps from the introduction of cost-saving technological innovations.

The question of elasticity also enters into supply, just as it does in the theory of demand. If the market price of a good rises by 1 per cent, by what percentage are producers willing to increase their output?

Supply elasticity is defined as the degree of responsiveness of output offered by producers on the market to changes in price. Given the supply function S in Figure 2-2, an increase in price of P_1P_2 brought with it a rise in quantity supplied of $OQ_1 - OQ_2$. If, instead, the relevant supply function were S'', then the same P_1P_2 price rise would have caused quantity supplied to grow by $OQ_1 - OQ_3$. Clearly, $OQ_1 - OQ_3$ is very much greater than $OQ_1 - OQ_2$, and we say that S'' is substantially more elastic than S.

The coefficient of supply elasticity at a certain point on a supply curve may be stated by the relation

$$e_s = \frac{\dfrac{\Delta Q}{Q}}{\dfrac{\Delta P}{P}} = \frac{P\Delta Q}{Q\Delta P} = \frac{\Delta Q}{\Delta P} \times \frac{P}{Q}$$

This is the same formula given for point-elasticity of demand, although the supply elasticity coefficient will have a positive, instead of negative, sign; the supply curve generally has an upward slope while the demand curve normally is sloped downward. Again, the practical impossibility of measuring infinitely small changes in price and quantity leads us to a second derivation of the coefficient of supply elasticity: arc elasticity.

$$e'_s = \frac{\dfrac{Q_2 - Q_1}{Q_2 + Q_1}}{\dfrac{P_2 - P_1}{P_2 + P_1}} = \frac{(Q_2 - Q_1)(P_2 + P_1)}{(Q_2 + Q_1)(P_2 - P_1)} = \frac{(Q_2 - Q_1)}{(P_2 - P_1)} \times \frac{(P_2 + P_1)}{(Q_2 + Q_1)}$$

It measures the response of quantity supplied to changes in price between two points on the supply curve.

Given a linear supply function and a linear demand function, it is possible to determine a unique equilibrium price and quantity sold, since both supply and demand are functions of price. In Figure 2–2, this equilibrium is at point A, with a price P_1 and sales of OQ_1. Any price above P_1 will result in an excess quantity supplied over quantity demanded—a *surplus* on the market. The existence of a surplus causes sellers to strive for elimination of their unwanted, excess inventories, which drives the price downward. With a declining price, the quantity producers are willing to supply also declines, while the quantity demanded rises until equilibrium is reached at A. Conversely, if for some reason the prevailing price happens to be below equilibrium, quantity demanded exceeds quantity supplied and a *shortage* exists. Again, if prices are free to move, the shortage will cause consumers or users to bid up the price, and as the price rises the quantity producers are willing and able to supply increases, while some potential buyers drop out of the market and others reduce their demand for the commodity, thereby causing overall quantity demanded to fall. Again, the movement is toward equilibrium at A, the only point at which the system has no further tendency to change.

Of course, this model of supply and demand is greatly oversimplified, but it does give us an idea of market behavior which will serve as a tool in later analysis. We shall find later, for example, that price *can* be above or below domestic equilibrium if the resulting surplus is absorbed by exports or the domestic shortage is satisfied by imports.

Shifts in supply or demand may be easily applied to this simple model. If for any reason demand rises from D to D' in Figure 2–2, then equilibrium moves from A to B with attendant increases in price and output. If, on the other hand, supply rises from S to S', equilibrium moves from A to F and results in a reduced price and expanded output. The reader can work out for himself the effects of *decreases* in supply or in demand upon price and sales. Finally, demand *and* supply may shift simultaneously, and then the resultant equilibria are indeterminant unless we are given the precise extent of the respective shifts.

INDIFFERENCE ANALYSIS

Another important concept, which is frequently used as a tool in many branches of economics, is indifference analysis. Its application to international economics is quite extensive, particularly in the areas of international-trade theory and commercial-policy theory. An understanding of this particular analytical method is therefore basic to an understanding of what follows.

Presumably, the extra satisfaction that a person derives from obtaining one additional unit of a particular good declines as the number of units of that commodity in his possession increases. The satisfaction derived by obtaining the first automobile is generally considered to be greater than the additional utility derived from the fourth unit, for instance. This illustrates the classical notion of *diminishing marginal utility,* which is used to interpret the actions of consumers or users, as well as to explain the generally downward-sloping shape of consumer-demand curves. Since the consumer derives less and less extra satisfaction from each additional unit of a good, he is willing to buy additional units only at successively lower prices. Moreover, if it is assumed that the consumer at all times seeks to maximize his own material welfare, then utility theory tells us that he is, in fact, maximizing his welfare only when the utility derived from the expenditure of one extra unit of money is equal for each and every commodity under consideration.

The principle of diminishing marginal utility appeals to common sense, and many students of economics consider it to be intuitively obvious. It turns out to be highly useful in analyzing economic behavior, yet it is not readily quantifiable. In order to partly overcome this difficulty, indifference analysis was developed by economists such as Francis Y. Edgeworth, Vilfredo Pareto, and John R. Hicks. In its simplest and most easily explained form, sufficient for our purposes here, the indifference curve approach is limited to consumer choice between two distinct commodities.

An indifference curve is defined as depicting all possible combinations of two commodities which will yield a given, uniform level of satisfaction

for the individual consumer. Curve *IC* in Figure 2–3 represents a certain
level of satisfaction attained by consuming a variety of different combinations of commodities *X* and *Y*. The same satisfaction level can be maintained by consuming large quantities of *Y* and very little of *X* (in the
upper segment of the curve), or by consuming a great deal of *X* and
very little of *Y* (toward the lower right extremity of the curve), or at
any point in between. Indifference curves are generally convex to the origin
because as the consumer obtains more and more of *X*, he is willing to
give up less and less of *Y* in order to get one additional unit of *X*. We
say that the *marginal rate of substitution* of one good for the other diminishes throughout the extent of the curve.[2]

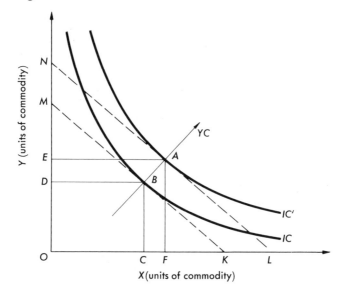

Fig. 2–3. Indifference analysis.

A little thought will quickly make clear that a diminishing marginal
rate of substitution of good *X* for good *Y* in Figure 2–3 means that the
indifference curve must necessarily be convex to the origin. The indifference curve becomes vertical when the consumer's demand is saturated with
Y; it becomes horizontal when his demand is saturated with *X*. These
are unlikely but not inconceivable situations. The degree of convexity of
an indifference curve is dependent upon the degree of substitutability of
the two commodities involved. If *X* and *Y* are perfect substitutes (e.g.,
two brands of flour), the curve would be a straight line and the marginal

[2] The marginal rate of substitution can thus be defined as the amount of *Y* the
individual is willing to give up in order to obtain one additional unit of *X*, without
incurring a loss of overall satisfaction as a result.

rate of substitution would be constant throughout. On the other hand, if X and Y are complements (e.g., nuts and bolts), where one cannot be used without the other, the indifference curve would approximate the form of a right angle.

In order to maintain a given welfare level, the consumer must substitute one good for another according to the ratios specified by his particular indifference curve. In Figure 2–3, he may consume anywhere along curve *IC* or along any other similarly shaped indifference curve. The precise consumption point can be determined only if we know his income and the relative prices of the two goods. Suppose the consumer's income suffices to buy *OK* of X or *OM* of Y, or any combination of X and Y along the *line of attainable combinations MK.* If he maximizes his level of material welfare, he will consume at point B, where the line of attainable combinations is tangent to one of his indifference curves, here curve *IC.* He cannot consume at any other point on *IC* or at any point *outside* of the area bounded by line *MK*, because his income would not suffice to do so. On the other hand, he would not want to consume at a point inside line *MK* because this would place him on a lower indifference curve and hence, on a correspondingly lower welfare level. All this means simply that the consumer can maximize his welfare only if he spends his income on X and Y in such a way that he attains the highest possible indifference level consistent with his available income. This is the tangency solution B in Figure 2–3.

How can the consumer better his welfare over and above the level represented by indifference curve *IC?* It is clear that this must involve a move to a higher indifference level such as that represented by *IC'.* One way this would be attainable is through a rise in real income, from *MK* to *NL*, with consumption of *OE* of Y and *OF* of X at point A, where *IC'* is tangent to *NL.* It should be equally clear that successively higher incomes will lead to successively higher levels of welfare along a line *YC* which connects the tangencies of all possible indifference curves and all possible lines of attainable combinations.

This permits us to define what is called the *income consumption curve.* Of course, a rise in real income may take the form of decreases in the price of commodities as well as increases in money incomes. If the price of good X fell and the price of good Y remained the same, the *YC* curve would be more horizontal; it would take on a more vertical shape, if the price of Y fell and the price of X remained constant. The former might be represented by a hypothetical attainable combinations line *ML*, and the latter by a line *NK* (not drawn).

Thus far, we have talked about indifference analysis only with reference to an individual consumer, and we have justified the construction of indifference curves on the basis of an assumption that the consumer is always in a position to judge clearly which combinations of two commodities yield him equivalent satisfaction. Conceptually, this is not an unreasonable assumption, although indifference analysis has often been criticized on the grounds that relative preferences are not readily quantifiable, and that any indifference curve derived would thus be nebulous at best. This criticism is somewhat softened by the notion of "revealed preference," developed by Paul A. Samuelson, which can be used to show that consumers do indeed indicate their relative preferences by their actions in response to price changes.

Indifference analysis as employed in this text will apply not to a single consumer, but to an entire nation. This will involve the idea of community indifference curves, referring to the combinations of two commodities which will yield a uniform level of satisfaction. Necessarily, the degree of abstraction here is even higher, and the analysis is even more vulnerable to attack and criticism than in the case of the individual consuming unit, especially with regard to drawing interpersonal welfare comparisons.[3] Nonetheless, it will become amply clear that it does furnish us an invaluable tool in the analysis of international trade as well as the impact of a variety of commercial policies upon the national level of material welfare.

TRANSFORMATION FUNCTIONS

Every beginning student of economics learns that a nation's economy possesses a certain maximum productive capacity, which is determined by the quantity of productive resources it has at its disposal—land, labor, natural resources, and capital—and that the efficiency or resource productivity is in turn contingent upon the level of technology and other forms of useful knowledge as well as upon climate, the character of the people, and so on. The student also learns that the nation may use this productive capacity in a variety of ways, and that it must make a number of choices regarding priorities in output. The standard, elementary "guns or butter" example offers a good illustration, in the simplest possible way, of the nature of the choices that must be made.

If we assume that a nation's production possibilities are limited to two types of goods, we can arrive at a so-called *transformation function*. The nation may choose, for instance, between private goods and public goods, war goods and peace goods, investment goods and consumption goods. In our example, we shall be a little more abstract, and conveniently call the two types of outputs *A*-goods and *B*-goods.

Referring to Figure 2–4, a typical transformation function (also known as the *production possibilities frontier*) might be represented by line *Y*. If

---

[3] We shall specifically delineate many of the limitations attending community indifference analysis later on when we begin to employ this particular analytical device.

all of the nation's productive resources were used to produce A-goods, then quantity Oa of A would be produced. Conversely, if all resources were applied to the production of B-goods, then Ob of B would be the maximum amount of that commodity that could be produced. Given the transformation function Y, then any combination of A and B could be produced at any point along its length. Production at a point inside the area bounded by curve Y would mean that the nation is not using its output capability to its fullest extent. That is, it would be operating with less than full employment of its various resources or is not using them as efficiently as is possible with existing technology. On the other hand, it would be impossible to produce at a point outside the production possibilities frontier, or transformation curve, because the latter is *defined* as presenting total productive capacity under conditions of full employment. Hence, if the nation fully used all of its productive capability, it would be producing somewhere along line Y.

Now suppose the production of A-goods for some reason became more efficient. By again fully employing its resources, the nation could produce Oa'' of A-goods instead of Oa. This would result in a new transformation curve ba'', somewhere along which would be the new production point. Obviously, curve ba'' is higher than line Y, and the nation can now raise its total output using the same quantity of resources because of a rise in the efficiency of production of A-goods. The same thing would be true if, instead, the production of B-goods became more efficient, or if the efficiency level rose in the production of both goods, or if additional productive resources became available.

With any transformation function such as those shown in Figure 2–4, the economy must give up some of one good in order to increase output of the other. The rate at which this substitution in production occurs is called the *marginal rate of transformation*. For example, if (under the transformation function ba'') in order to get one additional unit of the B-good, the economy had to give up two units of the A-good, the marginal rate of transformation of A-goods for B-goods would have a value of 2. The marginal rate of transformation is given by the slope of the transformation function at the particular point in question.

The two transformation functions described above (Y and ba'') are both linear. This means that the marginal rate of transformation is constant throughout their respective lengths. We must give up a certain number of units of A-goods in order to be able to produce one extra unit of B-goods, no matter which point along these curves we are talking about. Is it realistic, however, to assume that the marginal cost of producing a given good will be constant no matter how much of that good is produced, or how large a proportion of the nation's productive resources is devoted to it? If the concept of diminishing returns, or increasing costs, is applied here, as output of A-goods is increased beyond a certain point the economy would have to give up progressively more B-goods to get one extra unit of the A-good, and vice versa. This means the transformation function would be shaped as curve X in Figure 2–4, concave to the origin, and the marginal rate of transformation of one type of good for the other would be changing throughout its length. If the production of A-goods were to become more efficient in this case, the transformation curve would shift outward from X to some new position such as ba'.

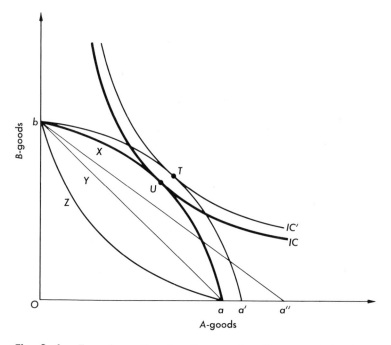

Fig. 2–4. Transformation functions and welfare maximization.

Instead of diminishing returns, or increasing costs, however, the condition of decreasing costs—*economies of scale*—might also apply. In this case the production possibilities frontier would be convex to the origin, and progressively less of one good would have to be given up as more of the other is produced. Such a case is depicted by curve Z in the figure. It is not possible to know the shape of a transformation function with respect to two types of goods until it is known whether constant, increasing, or decreasing costs prevail.

Given *any* type of transformation function, we will still be unable to determine precisely at which point on the curve the nation will in fact produce and consume. In order to make this determination, it is necessary that something be known about the nation's relative tastes or preferences for the two types of goods under consideration. This information is provided by the community indifference curve, developed in the preceding section of this chapter. In Figure 2–4, such community indifference curves are *IC* and *IC'*. If the transformation function *X*, embodying increasing costs, is given, then the nation will optimally produce and consume at a point along that transformation function where it is tangent to the community indifference curve *IC* (point *U*). Any other production point along transformation curve *X* will fall on a lower community indifference curve, and hence represent diminished economic welfare. At the same time, the nation cannot consume at any point other than *U* along *IC* because it does not have the productive capability to reach such a point. The point of tangency, where the marginal rate of transformation in production is exactly equal to the marginal rate of substitution in consumption, represents the highest possible material welfare level which the nation can reach in isolation (in the absence of trade) with the given transformation function and community indifference map. It is called a *Pareto Optimum*, maximizing both production and consumption.

If additional resources became available, or if it became possible to enhance the efficiency of production of one or both goods, it would be possible to move to a new, higher transformation function. In Figure 2–4, suppose that the country were able to increase output of the *A*-good only, because of some technological development. We could then shift to a new transformation function such as *ba'*. The new optimum would be at point *T*, where the new transformation curve is tangent to the community indifference curve *IC'*. Since *IC'* is higher than the original *IC,* the increased efficiency in the production of *A*-goods has resulted in an enhanced level of national economic welfare.

PRODUCTION THEORY: THE ISOQUANT–ISOCOST APPROACH

We saw in a previous section that indifference curves are of considerable assistance in explaining and analyzing consumption behavior. A similar approach is often used in portraying the optimum combination of inputs to achieve an intended level of output in production. Indifference analysis may be applied to an individual or to an entire community. Production theory also may be applied to an individual firm or to a nation as a whole. Indifference analysis deals with two alternative consumption goods combined to maximize something we call welfare or satisfaction. Here we are concerned with the use of two alternative inputs, or resources, combined to maximize output in the most efficient manner possible.

In order to produce a particular good, we assume that only two resources are needed, designated as *A* and *B*. We also assume that inputs *A* and

B are to some degree technically substitutable for each other, so that we can produce one unit of output by using either a great deal of *A* and very little of *B*, or a large amount of *B* and a small quantity of *A*, or any combination of *A* and *B* between the two extremes. The different combinations of inputs *A* and *B* that may be used in the production of a set number of units of output may be represented graphically in the form of a curve such as Q_2 in Figure 2–5. This is called an *isoquant,* meaning simply that a fixed quantity of output may be produced using the various different combinations of inputs represented by the curve.

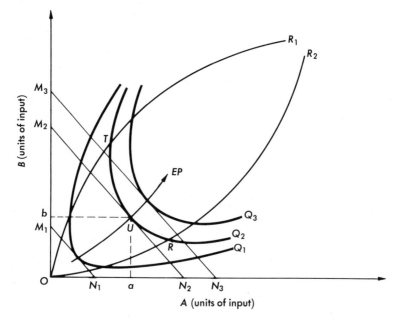

Fig. 2–5. Optimal input combinations.

The curve is convex toward the origin because as more and more of one input is used, it becomes increasingly difficult to substitute it for the other input. This involves a decreasing *marginal rate of substitution* of inputs in production. Beyond points *T* and *R*, the isoquant bends backward, and more of *both* inputs must be used to produce Q_2 of output—hence, the combination of inputs would logically never exceed those defined by these two points.

The lines R_1 and R_2, called *ridge lines,* connect these points for each and every level of production and therefore bracket the logical possibilities for input combination. Increasing output, of course, is represented by successively higher isoquants Q_1, Q_2, Q_3, and so forth.

Suppose, now, that the desired output of the commodity in Figure 2–5 is Q_2. Given a choice of two inputs, A and B, in its production, how much of A should be used and how much of B? We know that we would logically not use more of A than the quantity defined by point R, and that no more of B should be used than the quantity corresponding to point T. Within these limits, how does the producer combine resources A and B (say, labor and capital) to optimally produce Q_2 of output?

Necessarily, the answer depends upon the relative cost of A and B. If A is more expensive than B, then relatively more of input B should be used, and vice versa. The ratio of the price of input A to the price of input B is given by the slope of the *isocost* function, represented here by line $M_2 N_2$. If the price of a unit of input A were \$2.00 and the price of a unit of input B were \$4.00, then the ratio of the prices of the two inputs would be $1:2$ and the slope of the isocost line would be drawn accordingly.

In order for Q_2 of the commodity to be produced using an optimum input combination, quantity Oa of A should be used and an amount Ob of B should be employed. This combination of inputs A and B occurs where isoquant Q_2 is tangent to isocost M_2N_2 at point U.

Why would the production point not lie somewhere between U and T instead? Because at any such point the marginal rate of substitution of B for A is *greater* than the ratio of the price of B to the price of A, and it would thus pay the producer to substitute A for B until point U is reached, resulting in lower total production costs. Similarly, a production point anywhere on Q_2 between U and R is suboptimal because the marginal rate of substitution of D for A is *less* than the ratio of the factor prices, and total input costs could be reduced by substituting B for A until the factor combinations represented by point U are attained.

It is clear, then, given the intention to produce a quantity Q_2 of this particular commodity, that the factor combinations resulting in lowest input cost can occur only where the isoquant is tangent to the isocost line; i.e., where the ratio of input prices exactly equals the marginal rate of factor substitution. Each conceivable output level, represented in Figure 2–5 by successively higher or lower isoquants (Q-curves), will possess an optimum production point, and the line connecting all of these optimum points (EP) is called the *expansion path* of the firm. Assuming that a firm continues to optimize its use of factor inputs as its output grows and that the relative prices of the two factors of production do not change, then the expansion path traces the optimal use of the two inputs through successively higher levels of output.

A final word should be said about the shape of the isocost and isoquant functions, upon which this entire analysis is based. Isocosts will always be linear as long as the factor price ratios remain constant no matter how much of a given input is used, so that they pose no problems in this regard. Isoquants, on the other hand, are by no means as simple. If two inputs are nearly perfect substitutes for each other, the isoquant will be only slightly convex with a marginal rate of substitution in production nearly constant between the two productive factors. Conversely, if two factors of production are perfect complements to each other so that one cannot be used without a set quantity of the other, then the isoquant takes the form of a right angle, and the optimum production point is uniquely determined by the required, fixed factor combinations even without the aid of an isocost function, given the quantity of output to be produced.

Most factor inputs, of course, lie somewhere between these two extremes with respect to their substitutability for each other. We can be virtually certain that an isoquant will possess some degree of convexity. For instance, it is almost inconceivable, given the present state of the art, to use only capital in production without at least some labor, just as it is virtually impossible to employ only labor with no capital at all under conditions as they exist in our society. Between these two extremes, it is clear that labor is substitutable for capital, and vice versa, to a considerable degree. Whether labor or capital is used more extensively depends on their relative costs which, in the last analysis, is in turn contingent upon the relative abundance of these two productive factors.

Later, our use of this approach to production theory will deal not with an individual firm or producing entity, but with an entire nation. The factor inputs employed will be of the broadest possible classifications: land, labor, capital, and natural resources. In this connection, is sometimes useful to build a simplified model of an economy producing two types of goods using two factors of production, particularly in discussing international trade and specialization and its impact on domestic product and factor prices and economic structure. The tools necessary for this type of analysis are discussed in section E-2.

INCOME DETERMINATION REVIEWED

Recall the rudiments of national income determination. An equilibrium level of income is attained only whenever earned income precisely equals desired aggregate spending. If we assume a closed economy composed of three sectors, consumption (C), investment (I), and government (G), the sum of the desired spending in these three sectors must equal earned income at equilibrium (Y_e), illustrated in Figure 2–6A. At this point, earned income is precisely equal to aggregate demand, and desired savings, S, equal desired investment, so that

$$Y = C + I + G$$
$$Y = C + S + G$$
$$I = S.$$

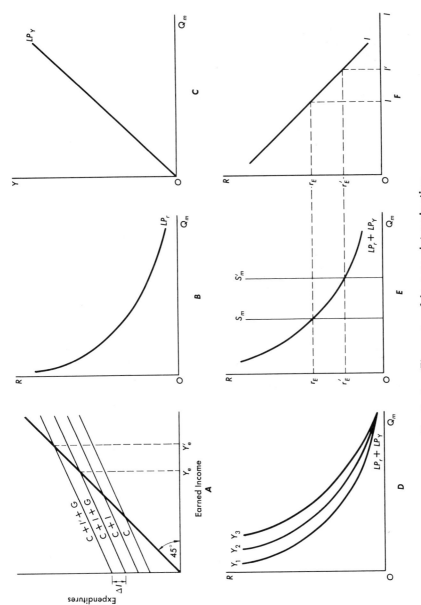

Fig. 2–6.   Elements of income determination.

The shape of the $C + I + G$ line in Figure 2–6A is determined by the consumption function, C, the slope of which is the marginal propensity to consume (MPC). Every increase in income causes consumption to rise, but not by as much as the causative income change; hence, the value of the marginal propensity to consume is normally less than one. Whatever is not spent must be saved, and hence the marginal propensity to save (MPS) is that part of every increase in income not spent on consumption. Algebraically, all of this can be summed up as follows:

$$MPC = \frac{\Delta C}{\Delta Y}$$

$$MPS = \frac{\Delta S}{\Delta Y}$$

$$MPS + MPC = \frac{\Delta S}{\Delta Y} + \frac{\Delta C}{\Delta Y} = 1$$

If any one of the components of spending is increased, income will rise to a higher equilibrium as a result of the *multiplier effect*. Suppose investment spending rises by $20 and the marginal propensity to consume is $\frac{3}{4}$. Initially, $20 would be added to national income. Three-fourths of the $20 would then be respent, adding another $15 to national income. In the next stage, three-fourths of the $15 would be respent and, in turn, added to national income, and so forth. In all, the initial $20 injection calls forth an increase in national income of $80. At that point, savings will also have increased by $20, so that savings will again equal investment.

In Figure 2–6A, the increased investment spending raises the aggregate demand function from $C + I + G$ to $C + I' + G$ and, via the multiplier effect, causes the equilibrium income to rise from Ye to $Y'e$. The geometric progression involved in the spending and respending process may be summed up and the multiplier (k) derived as follows:

$$k = \frac{1}{1 - \dfrac{\Delta C}{\Delta Y}} = \frac{1}{\dfrac{\Delta S}{\Delta Y}}$$

or

$$k = \frac{1}{1 - MPC} = \frac{1}{MPS}$$

The value of the multiplier clearly depends upon the marginal propensity to consume—the higher the marginal propensity to consume (and the lower the marginal propensity to save) the greater will be the effect of an initial change in spending on the level of income, and the higher the value of the multiplier.

Any autonomous increase in aggregate demand will tend to raise equilibrium income via some version of the multiplier, whether its origin is a higher level of investment, consumer purchases, or government spending.

If the level of aggregate demand determines the equilibrium level of national income, then how are the various individual components of total spending determined? *Government* spending can be treated as an autonomous factor, subject to manipulation directly by the central authorities. Government can also affect the level of *consumer* spending by varying tax rates, transfer payments, and so forth. The level of *investment* spending, on the other hand, tends to be largely determined by the level of interest rates. Specifically, this takes the form of the *investment demand* (*marginal efficiency of capital*) function, which links the interest rate to the desired investment level (see Figure 2–6F). At successively lower rates of interest the tendency is for investment demand to be correspondingly higher.

The rate of interest, in turn, is determined by the interaction of the supply of and demand for money. We take the supply of money as autonomously determined by the national monetary authorities.

The demand for money, or cash balances, may be separated into a *transactions demand*—cash balances required for transactions purposes—and an *asset demand,* which defines the desire of people to hold part of their assets in the form of money. Figure 2–6C represents the transactions demand for money (LP_y) as a direct function of income. As income rises, more money is required by the economy to finance exchange. The function LP_r in Figure 2–6B represents the asset demand for money (the *liquidity preference function*), an inverse function of the prevailing interest rate. At high interest rates, people for several reasons are willing to hold only relatively small cash balances. The reverse holds true at low interest rates when the asset demand for money is likely to be very high.

Figure 2–6D portrays the total demand for money ($LP_r + LP_y$) at different income levels Y_1, Y_2, and Y_3. The shape of the curves remains the same, but they shift to the right at higher income levels as successively larger quantities of money are demanded for transactions purposes. As noted above, the equilibrium interest rate prevailing in the economy is determined by the interaction of the total demand for money and the supply of money. Just as the interaction of supply and demand determines the price of any commodity, so supply and demand interaction determine the price of money—the interest rate.

In Figure 2–6E, the prevailing supply of money—which we said was autonomously determined by the national monetary authorities—is represented by the vertical line S_m. The total demand for money at a particular income level is given by $LP_y + LP_r$, of which only LP_r is important from the standpoint of the *shape* of the function. The equilibrium interest rate here is r_E.

At the equilibrium interest rate r_E, the investment demand stands at OI, which constitutes the I component of the $C + I + G$ aggregate demand function in Figure 2–6A. If for some reason the monetary authorities expand the money supply from S_m to S_m', this lowers interest rates fr m r_e to r_e', thereby increasing investment demand from OI to OI'. The increased investment demand raises the aggregate demand function from $C + I + G$ to $C + I' + G$, and, via the multiplier, income expands from Y_e to Y_e'. The reader can easily work out for himself the effect of restrictive monetary actions by simply reversing the process outlined here.

If the equilibrium level of the level of investment spending—via the multiplier—is a function of the rate of interest—via the investment demand schedule—then the equilibrium level of income must itself be a function of the rate of interest. This is represented in the form of the IS schedule in Figure 2–7. Successively lower rates of interest, causing correspondingly higher levels of investment spending, result in successively higher equilibrium income levels. At each point on the IS curve there is an equivalence of aggregate demand and earned income, with saving equal to investment— an equilibrium in the market for goods and services.

In a similar manner, we can relate all of the various rates of interest and levels of income that will yield equilibrium in the money market. Recall that the total demand for money is composed of the transactions de-

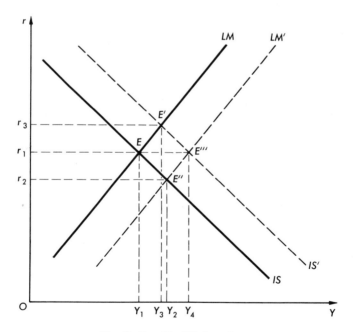

Fig. 2–7. Equilibrium income.

mand (a function of the level of income) and the asset demand (a function of the rate of interest). Since the total stock of money in existence must by definition be held by the people in some form, we have the relation

$$S_m = D_m = LP_y + LP_r.$$

At successively higher levels of income, assuming the supply of money remains constant and the velocity of money is unchanged, correspondingly larger amounts of money are demanded to meet transactions requirements (LP_y), thereby reducing the amounts left over for asset purposes (LP_r). According to the liquidity preference function in Figure 2–6B, a reduction of the amount of money available to fill the asset demand will cause the interest rate to rise. Hence, we can derive the LM function in Figure 2–7, which presents for each and every income level the equilibrium rate of interest in the money market associated with it. At each point along the LM curve, therefore, the money market is in equilibrium.

It will now be clear that the only possible general equilibrium that can exist is one that satisfies *both* equilibrium in the market for goods and services and in the market for money. There is only one combination of interest rate and income level where this can occur—at the intersection of the LM and IS curves, point E in Figure 2–7. At any other combination of interest rates and income levels, forces will be set in motion in one or both markets, eventually resulting in a return to the general equilibrium point.

The effects of government policy can also be demonstrated quite easily using LM and IS curves.

An increase in government spending, for example, will cause a rightward shift in the IS curve; any given interest rate will then correspond to a higher equilibrium income level due to the increased G component of the aggregate demand function. If the LM curve is unchanged, this will result in a new equilibrium (E' in Figure 2–7) at a higher income level and a higher rate of interest. Similarly, an increase in the national money supply will cause the LM curve to move to the right; at each rate of interest more money is available to finance transactions in the economy. Assuming the IS curve remains unchanged, a new equilibrium (E'') will result with a higher level of income and a lower rate of interest. Of course, the tools of monetary and fiscal policy can be used in combination to change the equilibrium level of income without simultaneously changing the rate of interest—a proportionate rightward shift of both the LM and IS curves.

Hopefully, this very simplified and brief review of the mechanics of microeconomics and income determination will be sufficient to indicate to the reader the level of analysis employed in this book. Those in need of further review are advised to consult one of the references cited in Section E-2.

I

Theory of
International Trade

3

WHY NATIONS TRADE

About 25 years ago, in 1948, world trade amounted to about $53 billion. By the mid-1970's it had reached almost $500 billion. Even allowing for inflation, this represents a phenomenal increase. The American share of this trade—based on export statistics—declined from about 24 per cent to 15 per cent, partly but not wholly due to inflated U.S. exports during the post-war reconstruction phase. Other losers were the developing countries (except the oil exporters), whose share declined from 25 per cent in 1948 to about 15 per cent in 1973. Meantime, Japan's share rose from 0.5 per cent to over 6 per cent, while that of the Western European nations expanded from 18 to about 40 per cent (see Figure 3-1).

What is the reason for this enormous volume of trade? In fact, why should nations trade with one another at all? What specific gains or benefits can be obtained by engaging in international trade? And how does international trade differ from interregional trade within a single nation, particularly with respect to the basic causal forces involved? Let us begin by trying to find some simple, common-sense explanations to questions such as these, before embarking on a more formal and rigorous analysis of the theory of international trade.

PRICES, COSTS, AND TRADE

There are profits to be made in international trade—profits that in a typical transaction result from the purchase of goods at lower prices in one country and their subsequent sale at higher prices in another country. An American buys a Japanese camera because he finds it to be considerably cheaper than a comparable item of U.S. manufacture. There is a basic difference in camera prices between the U.S. and Japan. A general, com-

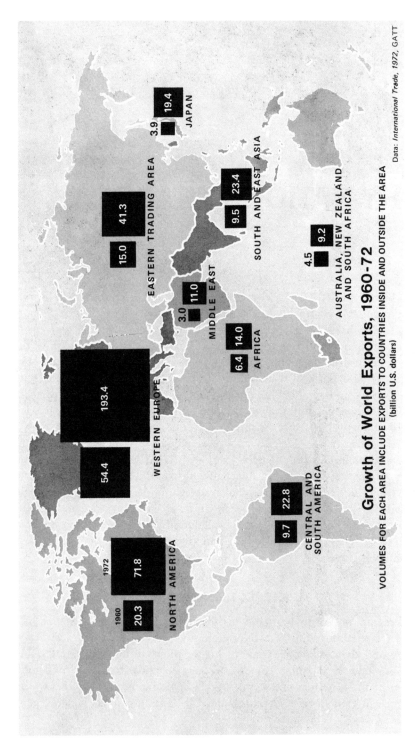

Fig. 3-1. Growth of world exports. Source: *International Trade, 1972*, GATT.

mon-sense explanation of international trade, then, would appear to be based on the differences in prices which are seen to prevail for various commodities among the nations of the world. It "pays" to trade.

But prices are really nothing more than an image of the costs of production with due allowance for the fact that market imperfections may distort somewhat the link between costs and prices. Production costs, in turn, are a reflection of the wages paid to labor, the cost of capital, the value of land, the cost of raw materials, and, certainly not least important, the degree of efficiency applied in the productive process. The cost of production is a composite of all of these elements, although any one may be powerful enough to constitute the determining factor with regard to international cost and price relationships.

It is often said that Taiwan exports great quantities of commodities which embody substantial amounts of labor in production—*labor-intensive* goods. Since Taiwanese wage levels are relatively low due to an abundance of workers in that country, one would expect its labor-intensive exports to compete effectively in countries where labor is relatively more scarce and wages are correspondingly higher. Similarly, a country such as Canada should logically export substantial quantities of wheat, a *land-intensive* good, given its greater abundance of land compared to most other countries of the world. By the same reasoning the U.S., a *capital-abundant* country, should be selling to other nations goods which require a great deal of capital in their manufacture. A simple explanation, then, is that each country merely *exports* goods using productive factors which it possesses in abundance and *imports* commodities requiring those factors of production which it finds to be relatively scarce at home.[1] But things are not quite that simple, even in a superficial examination of the subject.

Remember that the factors of production are not the sole influences on costs and prices. The efficiency with which they are used—productivity—is also of importance. Certainly Canada is land-abundant and should export grains, but so is Siberia. Canada does as we would predict, yet if Siberia were a sovereign country it is virtually certain that its grain exports would be negligible? Why? Because the *productivity* of land is much greater in Canada than in Siberia, even though both are equally land-abundant. In general, then, we ought to say also that climatic and geographical differences are important considerations in determining the productivity of land, and therefore in influencing the patterns of international trade.

---

[1] When we say that a particular factor is "abundant" in a given nation, we mean that it is abundant *in relation to* the supplies of other productive factors in that country, all compared with relative factor endowments as they exist in other countries. This is an important point to remember.

What has just been said about land is equally true of labor and capital. Not only are the wages of labor important, but also the productivity of labor. And capital itself is of little value without the technology to use it in an efficient manner. There are a great many considerations that effect the productivity of human, land, and capital resources in different ways throughout the world. Climate, which has already been mentioned, influences not only the productivity of land, but labor efficiency as well. The character of the people—their dexterity, ingenuity, organizational ability, entrepreneurial orientation, and acquisitive behavior—is of determining importance in the use of *all* resources in the productive process. No less significant is the economic, political, and social environment within which the productive process takes place. Finally technology—*useful knowledge*—is important in determining productivity both in its own right and in the embodiment in physical and human capital, as are the scale economies and diseconomies that are realized as output expands.

The immediate cause of international trade, then, seems to be the existence of differences in the price of goods between countries. Price differences are traceable to differences in production costs which, in turn, hinge on relative endowments of productive factors *as well as* the degree of efficiency with which these factors are employed. But there is one other important element yet to be discussed that is somewhat unique—the availability of natural resources.

The endowment of natural resources would appear to be highly important consideration in attempting to predict the direction of international trade. It is fairly safe to say that countries endowed with abundant natural resources of a certain kind would logically be expected to export quantities of that resource to other countries, and to export products requiring substantial amounts of that resource in the production process. But natural resource endowment alone is hardly foolproof as even a partial guide to trade patterns.

A large deposit of iron ore is virtually useless without massive infusions of capital in the form of mines and equipment for the extraction of the ore. Even then, further capital investment in transportation systems is needed to bring the ore to a point of shipment. A substantial force of workers is required to mine the ore and prepare it for shipment while technology—"know-how"—is necessary to enable the entire process to function effectively. Once all of these elements are present, the foundation has been built in a country for a trade pattern characterized by resource exports. This does not mean, however, that the country is yet ready for the export of *resource-intensive products,* since additional labor, capital, and knowledge are required before any such state is reached.

It is not true that countries *lacking* a certain natural resource will not be able to export commodities requiring that resource in manufacture. It merely means that such countries will have to import the needed raw material for conversion and final export as finished goods. This naturally becomes more complex when we begin to consider commodities which use large amounts of two or more resources in the production of, for instance, steel (iron ore, coal) and aluminum (bauxite, electricity).

The possession of natural resources, or the lack thereof, thus provides us with insufficient information for predicting with any degree of accuracy the commodity composition or direction of a nation's international trade. More information is required about the availability of capital, labor, and technology, as well as complementary natural resources, before a positive statement can be made. Trade in this area, as in all others, is founded on international price differences based on divergences in production costs which, in turn, are a reflection of variations in factor endowments and productivity. As such, natural resources can be treated as simply another factor of production.

Just as in the case of natural resources, the availability of any one of the agents of production may serve as a guide to the analysis of international trade flows. But availability, aside from being reflected in costs, may not always be a valid indicator of potential commodity movements internationally. As long as international trade flows are relatively free from restrictions, there is nothing to prevent the importation of goods containing considerable quantities of that productive agent which is lacking, and their subsequent re-export in more or less changed form to other countries.

DEMAND

In trying to find a common-sense explanation for trade between nations, we have considered a variety of factors operating on the *supply* side of the economic equation; i.e., endowments of the factors of production and levels of productive efficiency reflected in costs and prices, as well as the question of availability of particular agents of production. But what about *demand?* Is it not possible to visualize two countries producing given commodities at identical cost, yet having a substantial volume of trade between them? Differences in demand, again reflected in international price differentials, may be just as important as differences in the cost of production. Demand as a factor influencing international trade would seem to be largely a function of tastes and of incomes.

Tastes play an important and sometimes decisive role in affecting the demand for commodities across national boundaries. If the domestic availability of a certain good is limited, the excess demand may be satisfied by means of imports. Similarly, there are important, though often subtle, qualitative differences between seemingly uniform commodities, originating in different countries. The U.S. buys large quantities of French, German, and

Italian wines despite the domestic abundance of California and New York wines. Americans annually purchase large numbers of Japanese cameras, while Japanese simultaneously buy a surprising amount of U.S. cameras. Such commodities as beer, automobiles, tobacco, aircraft, and textiles are but a sampling of items for which tastes may predominate as the causal demand force in international trade. Demand responds to changing tastes, prices reflect the demand shifts, and trade in turn follows varying international differences in commodity prices.

Incomes are equally important. Demand for foreign *as well as* domestic goods is basically a function of the incomes available to consumers, businesses, and governments for expenditure on goods and services of all kinds. We would thus expect some sort of positive demand relationship between a country's national income and its purchases from abroad, or imports. A similar relation would appear to exist between that nation's exports and the respective national incomes of the foreign countries with which it trades. If our incomes rise, so does our demand for domestic and foreign goods and services, and so do our imports from abroad. At the same time, the rise in incomes may cause a rise in domestic prices, thus simultaneously rendering imported goods more competitive with domestic products. This itself would tend to result in a switching of purchases from domestic to foreign goods, and thus causes a secondary increase in imports, quite apart from that which was originally the result of the initial income growth.

Hence, both tastes and incomes, in their capacity to determine demand, would appear to be important further choices in our search for the factors affecting international trade. Together with factors operating on the supply side—availability and cost—they can tell us a great deal about the volume, commodity composition, and direction of trade.

So far, our discussion of the factors affecting international trade has been informal and hardly precise. Later, we shall look at each of these forces in greater detail. It is sufficient at this point, however, to have a general notion of the operation of trade between countries and the underlying causal relationships.

INTERNATIONAL AND INTERREGIONAL TRADE

The question quickly comes to mind whether all of the elements that seem to direct trade betwen nations do not apply equally well to commerce between different sections of a single country. Actually, there is no substantive difference between interregional and international flows of goods and services and the factors affecting them. The difference stems—as stated in Chapter 1—from the social, political, cultural, and economic boundaries that people have drawn around various geographical areas called *nations.*

International trade is based on differences in prices between countries.

Interregional trade is based on differences in prices between sections of the same country. In fact, all of the factors which affect prices internationally also affect prices interregionally. Endowments of the factors of production may vary substantially between different regions of a single nation, although in some countries such differences are more pronounced than in others. Productivity, or efficiency, behaves in the same way, being high in some regions and low in others. The availability of natural resources shows similar characteristics, varying markedly from region to region. All of the factors which are seen to influence costs, and therefore prices, are thus operative interregionally just as they are internationally. From a cost standpoint, therefore, there is ample justification for the large-scale interregional trade that we know exists in most countries.

This is no less true with regard to demand. If incomes grow in a certain part of a nation, it stimulates not only demand for locally manufactured goods, but commodities produced in other parts of the country as well. Certain products for which there is a demand are simply not available in some sections of a nation, and interregional trade is the only solution if this demand is to be satisfied. Tastes also vary between different sections of a country, just as they do between countries. The consumption patterns of the Sicilian, for instance, are hardly the same as those of his Milanese compatriot. But differences in tastes may well be perpetuated and intensified by the changing national character over extended periods of time, so that they may possibly play a larger role internationally than interregionally in determining the patterns of trade.

In spite of the fact that many of the *causative forces* bearing on trade operate in a similar manner both internationally and interregionally, there are numerous differences between the *operation* of trade among separate nation states, on the one hand, and among different regions of a single nation, on the other hand. These differences were discussed in Chapter 1 and should be kept in mind.

IMPORTANCE

We now have a rough idea of *why* nations trade with one another. But what is its importance to national economic well-being, defined perhaps as real income per capita and, more broadly, that of the world as a whole? The enormous volume of international trade that we perceive to exist, and its rapid growth, must be founded upon the tangible economic benefits it must hold for the world's community of nations. What, specifically, is the nature of these benefits?

For the answer we can go back to one of the earliest and most renowned contributors to the study of economics, Adam Smith. In his famous example of the pin-making factory, he proposed a notion that has long been a fundamental principle of economics, one that is almost second nature to today's students of the subject. If each individual producing-entity specializes in a certain more or less narrow aspect of the production process, total output will by far exceed that which would have been possible if each producing-entity carried through the entire production process from beginning to end. Maximization of output, and therefore optimization of economic well-being in terms of real income per capita, is based on interdependence and specialization, not independence and self-sufficiency. In short, every producing unit within a nation—individual, firm, region, and so forth—should specialize in those particular tasks which it can perform relatively better than others. Only in this way can output be maximized for the nation as a whole.

It is a simple task to carry Smith's idea one step further into the international arena. World output of goods and services can be maximized *only* if each nation concentrates on whatever tasks it can do relatively better than others. Here, too, the principles of specialization, division of labor, and interdependence apply. If Adam Smith was correct, then we would expect to observe an enormous volume of transactions between individuals, firms, and regions within a country—and we do. Internationally, we should likewise observe an enormous volume of trade in goods and services between the individual countries of the world—and we do.

Only the free movement of goods and services between the countries of the world will ensure that production is allocated to the most efficient of the world's suppliers, and that overall economic welfare, as we have defined it, is maximized. Trade plays a vital role in providing the highest possible level of living for the peoples of the world.

If this is true, it seems hardly sensible for nations to impose barriers to international trade. Yet everyone knows that myriad restrictions, ranging all the way from import tariffs to outright government control of international transactions, impede the flow of goods between countries. How can we explain such an apparently contradictory state of affairs? This is the task of the theory of commercial policy, with which we will concern ourselves later. At this point it is sufficient to acknowledge that while free trade is necessary for world output to be maximized with existing resources, national restrictions to trade can secure for a country or a group within a country a larger share of a somewhat diminished output at the expense of others.

TRADE AND FACTOR FLOWS

In addition to international trade in goods and services, a second major element in economic relations among nations is the flow of productive factors. The United States in the 1960's sent massive amounts of capital to

Western Europe and Canada; in the 1970's investment flows are beginning to turn increasingly to the developing countries and even Eastern Europe. During the past several decades, millions of workers from Spain, Portugal, North Africa, Turkey, Greece, and elsewhere have found employment in the industrial areas of Northern Europe. Clearly, international flows of these two mobile factors of production have assumed major proportions. Why?

The supply elements underlying the explanation are virtually identical to the basis of international trade. Factors of production move—when they are allowed to—from countries where they are abundant and/or their productivity is low to countries where they are scarce and/or their productivity is high. They move in response to differences in returns (yield on capital or wage rates) which are wide enough to more than offset the social cost of moving.

We conclude, therefore, that a country short of labor can either import labor-intensive goods or it can import labor itself, and will most probably end up doing both. Hence international trade and factor flows seem to be substitutes for each other, and there are real gains associated with both. This point is a very useful one to keep in mind, and we will return to it in more detail later.

We will now begin to formalize some of the ideas and concepts discussed. Try to remember four very basic questions which the theory of international trade must attempt to answer:

1. What countries will trade which commodities with whom? That is, what will be the direction, or *pattern* of trade, in goods and services among the nations of the world?
2. What are the specific *gains* from international trade, and how are they realized?
3. What impact does international trade have on the *economic structure* of a nation?
4. How does international trade affect the status of the various *productive factors* within an economy, especially with regard to the returns earned by each of them?

A SIMPLE MODEL

We shall proceed by working our way through a series of models—abstract representations of the real world with various simplifying assumptions—designed to be instructive about the way the real world operates. It is perhaps useful to illustrate how models can be applied to international trade by developing a simple partial equilibrium supply and demand analysis which illustrates some of the points we have made in this chapter.

Suppose we have a product that is produced and consumed in two coun-

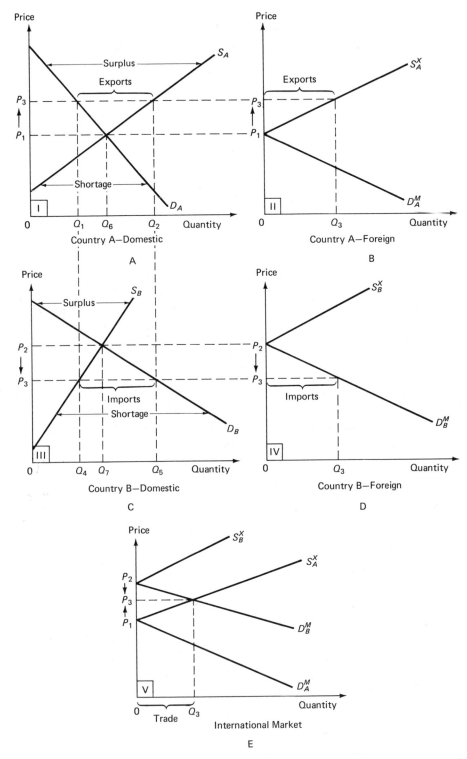

Fig. 3–2. International trade in partial equilibrium.

Variable	Without Trade	With Trade
Price in A	P_1	P_3
Price in B	P_2	P_3
Quantity supplied in A	OQ_6	OQ_2
Quantity demanded in A	OQ_6	OQ_1
Quantity supplied in B	OQ_7	OQ_4
Quantity demanded in B	OQ_7	OQ_5
Export supply in A	O	$OQ_3 = Q_1Q_2$
Export supply in B	O	O
Import demand in A	O	O
Import demand in B	O	$OQ_3 = Q_4Q_5$
Value of trade	O	$OQ_3 = Q_1Q_2 = Q_4Q_5$

tries, A and B, and there is no trade between these countries (*isolation*). Referring to Figure 3–2A, domestic demand equals domestic supply in Country A at a price P_1. At any price below P_1, quantity demanded exceeds quantity supplied by the horizontal distance between the two curves: this is the hypothetical *import demand* defined by curve D_A^M in Figure 3–2B. At any price above P_1 the reverse is true, and a hypothetical export supply is generated as domestic surpluses become available, defined by curve S_A^X. At any given price, $S_A^X = S_A - D_A$ and $D_A^M = D_A - S_A$, with $S_A = D_A$ (zero import demand and export supply) at a price of P_1. The same notation applies for Country B, whose domestic market for the product as well as the corresponding export supply and import demand functions are depicted in Figure 3–2C and D, with an equilibrium price P_2. The respective export supply and import demand functions are reproduced in Figure 3–2E.

Since $P_2 > P_1$ we know that when we open the system to trade, quantities of the product in question will flow from Country A to Country B. Prices in A will begin to rise, while prices in B will begin to fall, until they become equal at P_2 and there is no more money to be made by further expanding trade. At that price, A's export supply exactly equals B's import demand at quantity $OQ_3 = Q_1Q_2 = Q_4Q_5$. Once prices are equalized in the two countries, trade does not cease; it continues at that volume per unit time which serves to equalize prices.

The astute reader will quickly note we have assumed that transport costs will not affect the outcome, and that these are not considered in the model. He or she will also note that elasticities have a great deal to do with the volume of trade that develops. Think about these points for awhile. We shall return to them later.

4

INTRODUCTION TO THEORY

The discussion in Chapter 3 was intended to provide an intuitive feel for the factors underlying international trade flows. The simple partial-equilibrium model presented at the end of that chapter was included to provide a similar feel for the usefulness of abstract models in depicting real-world behavior, and will prove helpful as we proceed. That model considered trade between two countries in a single product. What happens when we add a second product?

ABSOLUTE ADVANTAGE

Suppose we look at a hypothetical world composed of only two countries, Canada and the U.S. Both countries produce significant quantities of wheat and oil for domestic consumption and there are absolutely no trade relations, factor movements, or other economic ties between them; i.e., each is taken to be operating in a state of isolation. Assume for the moment that the entire value of the two commodities is the amount of labor used in their production. Now suppose, further, that one man-hour of labor can produce the following quantities of wheat and oil in the two respective countries:

| | Output of One Man-Hour | |
Commodity	United States	Canada
Wheat (bu.)	2	5
Oil (bbl.)	20	10

In the time it takes a man to produce 1 bushel of wheat in the U.S. (½ hour), he can produce 10 barrels of oil. Hence a bushel of wheat in the U.S. is ten times as valuable as a barrel of oil. Things are a little different in Canada. There it takes a man only ⅕ hour to produce a bushel of wheat, yet he can turn out only 2 barrels of oil in that period of time.

Therefore, a bushel of wheat in Canada has only twice the value of a barrel of oil. The productivity of labor in wheat-growing is 2½ times as high in Canada as it is in the U.S. The reverse is true in oil production, where labor productivity in the U.S. is twice what it is in Canada. Apparently the U.S. has an absolute advantage in the production of oil, and Canada has an absolute advantage in the production of wheat.

Would it not pay, under such hypothesized conditions, for the two countries to trade with one another? The *direction* that trade would take can be immediately determined. Canada would export wheat to the U.S., in return for which the U.S. would export oil to Canada. For example, an enterprising American could take 20 barrels of U.S. oil to Canada, exchange them there for 10 bushels of Canadian wheat, and transport the wheat back to the United States. His 20 barrels of oil would have brought him only 2 bushels of wheat if he had exchanged them domestically in the U.S. His profit from trade, measured in wheat and assuming no transport costs: 8 bushels. If trade were opened up under these conditions, we would expect the volume of such transactions to reach rather large proportions, with both countries gaining in the process. Prices of the two commodities would be equalized in both countries. The U.S. would specialize increasingly in oil production, and Canada in the production of wheat (see Figure 4–1).

The simple model of absolute advantage just presented illustrates what such Classical economists as Adam Smith believed governed trade between

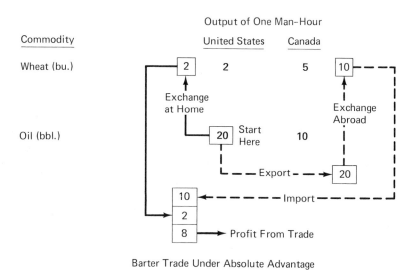

Barter Trade Under Absolute Advantage

Fig. 4–1.   Barter trade under absolute advantage.

the countries of the world. It was based on the labor theory of value and assumed, with some justification, that labor was completely free to move interregionally within a single country, yet was entirely immobile internationally. If labor were free to move between nations, then differences in wage rates—and hence commodity prices—could be equalized via labor migration, and there would be no need for international trade.

Aside from this assumption regarding labor mobility, it was also assumed that no transportation costs were involved in trade and that there existed no other barriers, such as tariffs and quotas, to trade between countries.

Under these assumptions, and believing in the labor theory of value, the absolute advantage theory of international trade might seem to be a fairly good representation of the forces governing commerce among nations. But what if one country has an absolute advantage in the production of *all* commodities? According to this theory there could be no trade, since the country of absolute advantage would have nothing to gain by engaging in commerce with other nations.

COMPARATIVE ADVANTAGE

It remained for David Ricardo and, later, John Stuart Mill to develop a *general theory* of international trade which could explain the apparent existence of inter-country trade deemed impossible by the theory of absolute advantage. In order to make explicit Ricardo's contribution—the theory of *comparative advantage*—let us change slightly the oil–wheat example, used earlier, as follows:

	Output of One Man-Hour	
Commodity	United States	Canada
Wheat (bu.)	10	8
Oil (bbl.)	20	12

Note the crucial difference. The U.S. now has an *absolute* advantage in the production of *both* wheat and oil, whereas in the earlier example it had an absolute advantage only in oil. Canada now has an absolute advantage in neither. Under these conditions will there be a basis for trade between the two countries? The theory of absolute advantage would certainly deny the possibility under such circumstances. The labor theory of value still applies, as do the other assumptions made earlier, but the theory of comparative advantage acknowledges the existence of grounds for international trade to occur.

Note that one man-hour of labor yields twice as much oil as wheat in the U.S. Hence, wheat will exchange for oil in the U.S. at a ratio of 1:2. In Canada, by way of contrast, a man-hour of labor yields only 1½ times as much oil as wheat. This gives us a Canadian domestic exchange ratio, wheat for oil, of $1:1\frac{1}{2}$. In the U.S., labor is twice as good at producing oil as it is at producing wheat, while Canada is only $1\frac{1}{2}$ times as good at it. Conclusion: the United States has an *absolute* advantage in producing both, but it has a *comparative* advantage in producing only oil, while Canada has an *absolute* advantage in producing neither, but it does possess a *comparative* advantage in the production of wheat.

An American trader wishing to exchange oil for wheat within the U.S. could get only 10 bushels for 20 barrels of oil. But if instead he were to take his 20 barrels of U.S. oil to Canada, he could exchange it there for $13\frac{1}{3}$ bushels of wheat (receiving 8 bushels for 12 barrels, plus $5\frac{1}{3}$ additional bushels of wheat for the remaining 8 barrels of oil) at the prevailing Canadian exchange ratio. Taking his $13\frac{1}{3}$ bushels of wheat back home, he finds that he has realized a profit, measured in wheat, of $3\frac{1}{3}$ bushels as a result of trade. A Canadian trader could profit similarly, by dealing in the opposite direction. Domestically he receives 12 barrels of oil for 8 bushels of wheat. But if he shipped the wheat to the U.S. he would receive 16 barrels of oil for it there. After returning the oil to Canada, he finds that he has realized a profit, in terms of oil, of 4 barrels as a result of international trade. (see Figure 4–2).

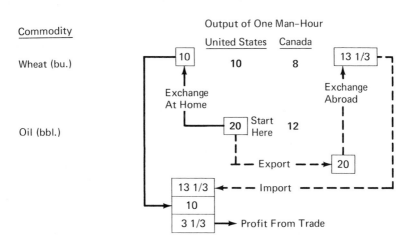

Barter Trade Under Comparative Advantage

Fig. 4–2.   Barter trade under comparative advantage.

The direction of trade in this simple model of comparative advantage is again easy to determine: Canada would export wheat to the U.S. in return for American exports of oil to Canada. Each country would begin to specialize in the production of that commodity in which it has a comparative advantage and import that good in the production of which it has a comparative disadvantage. Trade between the two countries would flourish, and apparently both would be better off as a result—both would realize gains from international trade attributable to the difference in the prevailing oil–wheat exchange ratios. The U.S. is anxious for trade with Canada even though it can produce both commodities more efficiently. In fact, the U.S. will be willing to trade oil for wheat and will gain by doing so, as long as the Canadian oil–wheat exchange ratio exceeds the 2:1 figure that prevails domestically within the U.S. Should the Canadian ratio drop to 2:1, oil for wheat, neither country would any longer possess even a comparative advantage. There would no longer be any reason for the U.S. to trade, since all potential for gain would have disappeared, and trade would cease.

COMPARATIVE ADVANTAGE USING MONEY

The principle of comparative advantage can be made a little clearer by repeating the example just presented in monetary terms. This enables us to show that relative cost differences became in fact the absolute price differences to which we originally attributed international trade.

Suppose the prevailing wage rate in Canada is 10 Canadian dollars (C$10.00) per hour, and that in the U.S. it is 10 U.S. dollars (US$10.00) per hour. Translating the above table into monetary terms, we would thus be left with the following:

	Cost of One Unit	
Commodity	United States	Canada
Wheat (bu.)	US$1.00	C$1.25
Oil (bbl.)	US$0.50	C$0.85

We assume total labor cost equals selling price in all cases. Since 1 man-hour of labor produces twice as much oil as wheat in the U.S., the price of a barrel of oil is half that of a bushel of wheat. In Canada, 1 man-hour produces only 1½ times as much oil as wheat, and hence the price of a barrel of oil is ⅔ that of a bushel of wheat. Clearly, *relative prices* of the two commodities differ between the two countries.

But what about *absolute* prices? The American trader knows little about the price of Canadian wheat or oil in terms of his own currency—U.S. dollars—until he knows the U.S. dollar value of one Canadian dollar, i.e., the *exchange rate*. Similarly, without knowing the exchange rate the Canadian trader has no information about the price of U.S. wheat and oil in his own currency.

Suppose the prevailing rate of exchange of the two currencies is C$1.00 = US$0.75 or, what is the same thing, US$1.00 = C$1.33. American oil exporters now realize about US$0.64 (C$0.85 × 0.75 = US$0.64) from every barrel of oil they sell to Canada, for a profit of US$0.14 per barrel. Canadian wheat exporters will receive C$1.33 (US$1.00 $\times$ 1.33 = C$1.33) for every bushel of wheat they sell in the U.S., yielding a profit of C$0.08 per bushel.

At that exchange rate, trade will occur in the same way as in the barter example given above. The price of oil will rise in the U.S. and fall in Canada, while the price of wheat will rise in Canada and fall in the U.S. Eventually, the prices of the two commodities, as well as the wage rates on which they are based, will be equalized in the two countries.

Suppose on the other hand, the exchange rate of the two currencies were C$1.00 = US$0.58, or US$1.00 = C$1.73. The U.S. oil exporter would not realize any profit in selling his product in Canada (C$0.85 $\times$ 0.58 = US$0.49), while Canadian wheat exporters would make enormous profits by selling in the U.S. (US$1.00 $\times$ 1.73 = C$1.73). Canadians would be more than willing to sell their wheat in the U.S. at that exchange rate, but Americans would not be willing to sell in Canada; hence there can be no trade at that rate of exchange between the two currencies. Conversely, the student can work out for himself or herself that at an exchange rate of C$1.00 = US$1.25 (which equals US$1.00 = C$0.80) the positions would be reversed. American oil exporters would receive large gains in exporting to Canada, but Canadians would gain nothing in exporting wheat to the U.S.—and again there could be no trade.

If we assume for the moment that economic relations between the U.S. and Canada are completely limited to trade in wheat and oil, then the U.S. dollar value of American oil exports *must* equal the U.S. dollar value of American wheat imports; i.e., trade must be balanced. This can only occur at some exchange rate, *between* the limits of C$1.00 = US$0.58 and C$1.00 = US$1.25, at which *both* countries find it profitable to trade. Whatever this exchange rate turns out to be, the money value of trade between the two countries must be balanced at that particular rate of exchange of Canadian dollars for U.S. dollars. If trade is not balanced, then the exchange rate will shift to a point at which the balance of trade is restored.

We shall have a great deal more to say about exchange rate determination at a later point. It only remains to be emphasized once again that the rate of exchange between two national currencies serves to convert relative price differences into absolute differences in price and hence may be essential to the outcomes—in terms of the direction and volume of trade—predicted by the law of comparative advantage.

The above examples should fix the concepts of absolute and comparative advantage in the mind of the reader. Of the two, the latter is clearly the less restrictive and represents a more general theory of international trade. The theory of comparative advantage is not limited to international transactions alone. Rather, it can be used to explain exchange between any two economic entities, even between individuals. The example of the manager and typist is often used to explain comparative advantage to beginning students of economics. The manager is both an excellent executive and a world-champion typist, while the typist cannot manage at all but can type reasonably well. Clearly, the manager has an *absolute* advantage in both managing and typing, while the typist has an *absolute* advantage in neither. Yet it obviously pays for the executive to hire the typist and concentrate his energies on managing, since this is where his *comparative* advantage lies, the secretary indeed possessing a *comparative* advantage in typing.

Let us now continue the search for a general theory of international exchange by extending somewhat the discussion of comparative advantage. We should try to make it more detailed, a little less restrictive, and more compatible as a general framework for the study of international trade.

SPECIALIZATION

As a first step in this direction, let us try to rid ourselves of the labor theory of value, which was assumed to apply in the discussion of absolute and comparative advantage up to this point. The production of goods and services involves the use of land and capital as well as labor—*all* of a nation's productive resources. Commodities are valued according to the amount of land, labor, and capital which they embody, not exclusively by the labor time used in the production process. In addition, the assumption—implicit in all of the above—that labor may validly be treated as a truly uniform factor of production clearly conflicts with reality. Labor varies widely in quality and enters the process of production in a variety of different ways, giving little credence to the idea that wages will automatically be equalized for all occupations within a country.

There is a way to circumvent the labor theory of value, and yet retain all of the salient characteristics of the theory of comparative advantage as a principle governing the behavior of international trade, if we use the production possibility curves, or transformation functions, reviewed in Chapter 2.

Referring to Figure 4–3, we can draw hypothetical transformation functions delineating the capacity to produce two commodities, wheat and cloth, by the U.S. and the United Kingdom. If the U.S. uses all of the factors of production at its disposal in the most efficient possible way, it can produce either 50 bushels of wheat or 30 yards of cloth, or any combination of the two along transformation curve *AB*. The U.K., on the other hand, is able to produce only 10 bushels of wheat or 20 yards of cloth, or any combination along transformation curve *CD*, if it also fully employs all of its resources in the most efficient manner possible.

Note that the transformation functions are linear, meaning that *constant opportunity costs* prevail. If it is decided to produce 1 additional bushel of wheat in the U.S., the economy must *always* sacrifice 0.6 yard of cloth to do so. This is true no matter whether a great deal of wheat and little cloth is produced or vice versa. Constant opportunity costs also prevail in the U.K., except that there the addition to output of 1 bushel of wheat

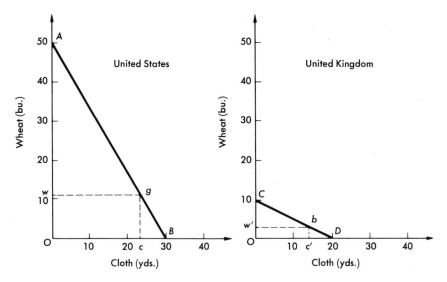

Fig. 4–3. Production and consumption in isolation: constant opportunity costs.

calls for the reduction in cloth output by 2 yards throughout. In short, the *marginal rate of transformation* of wheat for cloth is 1:0.6 in the U.S. and 1:2 in the U.K. These therefore also represent the ratios of the prices of oil and wheat, respectively, in the U.K. and the U.S.

In the hypothetical isolated state, the consumption alternatives of the two countries are entirely defined in terms of their respective production possibilities frontiers, or transformation functions. The U.S. can consume anywhere along curve *AB*, and the U.K. can consume anywhere along curve *CD*. The precise consumption point in each case will be determined by relative tastes and preferences that prevail in the two countries. The same is true of the U.K. These are the highest welfare levels the two countries can reach in isolation, given their respective production possibilities curves and consumption preferences (for example, points *g* and *b* in Figure 4-3).

The slope of the transformation function—the marginal rate of transformation—gives us the rate at which wheat exchanges for cloth in each country. This, we noted, is identical to the relative prices of wheat and cloth. In the U.S., 1 bushel of wheat "costs" 0.6 yard of cloth, and in the U.K. the same bushel of wheat "costs" 2 yards of cloth. It would appear that wheat is relatively cheaper in the U.S., and cloth is relatively cheaper in the U.K. The U.S. has an absolute advantage in the production of both, but it has a comparative advantage only in the production of wheat. The U.K. has an absolute disadvantage in both wheat and cloth, yet retains a comparative advantage in the production of cloth.

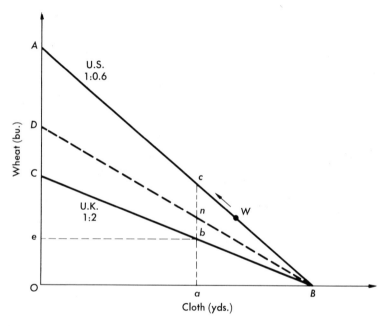

Fig. 4–4. Production and consumption with trade: constant opportunity costs.

According to the theory of comparative advantage the two nations would do well to trade, with the U.S. exporting wheat to the U.K. in return for cloth. Both should be able to enhance their economic well-being by so doing. In order to show this, it is convenient to simplify the analysis by expanding the British transformation curve so that it touches the corresponding U.S. curve at point B in Figure 4–4. Note that the British wheat –cloth exchange or price ratio, the slope of the line, has not been changed in the process.

GAINS FROM TRADE

Without trade, in our hypothetical situation, let us say that the U.K. is producing and consuming at point *b* on its transformation curve *CB: Oa* of cloth and *Oe* of wheat. Let us assume, further, that the U.S. is consuming and producing at point *W* on curve *AB*. Now trade opens, and the U.K. will tend to specialize completely in the production of cloth. It thus produces *OB* of cloth, decides to continue consuming only *Oa* of this, and exports the rest (*aB*) to the U.S. Trading at the U.S. wheat–cloth exchange ratio of 1 : 0.6, the British cloth exports of *aB* yield wheat imports of *ac*. Britain now consumes the same amount of cloth as before but a great deal more wheat (quantity *ac* versus *ab* before trade). Clearly, trade has enabled the U.K. to move from consumption point *b* to point *c,* which represents a much higher level of economic well-being, and which it could never have achieved in isolation. The U.S. is neither better nor worse off than without trade. The U.S. simply produces less cloth and more wheat than before; i.e., it moves *along* its transformation curve from *W* to *c*. It is the U.K. that receives all of the gains from trade—quantity *bc* of wheat.

The example could easily be reversed, with the U.S. specializing in wheat production and exporting its surplus wheat to the U.K. for exchange into cloth at Britain's prevailing 1 : 2 wheat–cloth exchange ratio. In this case, the U.S. would be able to attain a substantially higher welfare level than that permitted by its own transformation curve, and the U.K. would neither gain nor lose from trade.

But is it not possible, or even probable, that *both* countries will garner a portion of the gains from trade, rather than either one of the two countries taking all of them and the other none? This would be the case if the *international* wheat–cloth exchange ratio after trade came to rest somewhere between the two domestic exchange ratios, as represented by line *BD* in Figure 4–4. Here the U.K. is able to move from consumption point *b* before trade to point *n* after trade. Point *n* is clearly inferior to point *c*, which is attained if the U.K. received *all* of the gains from trade, but it is definitely superior to point *b*, which applied in isolation. Similarly, the U.S. will also be able to gain from trade by exchanging wheat for cloth at the international ratio *BD,* although its gain also will be less than if it had been able to trade at the British domestic wheat–cloth exchange ratio.

Where, precisely, will this new international wheat–cloth exchange ratio, *BD,* fall? The closer it lies to the British domestic ratio (*BC*), the greater will be the U.S. gain from trade relative to that of the U.K. We just noted that if the exchange ratio actually coincided with the U.K. domestic ratio, the U.S. would get all of the gains and the British none. Conversely, the closer the international exhange ratio *BD* falls to the U.S. domestic ratio (*BA*), the greater will be the U.K. gain relative to that attained by the U.S. Where will it ultimately fall? The answer lies in the strength of the demand for wheat and cloth in the two countries. The stronger the U.S. demand for cloth relative to the British demand for wheat, the closer the ratio will fall to the U.S. domestic one, and Britain will thus obtain most of the gains. The reverse is equally true. From the information given here, we cannot determine the position of the international terms of trade, *BD*, except to say that it will always lie somewhere between *BA* and *BC*.

BIG COUNTRIES AND LITTLE COUNTRIES

Referring once again to Figure 4–3, recall that the absolute productive capacity for wheat and cloth was much more limited in the U.K. than in the U.S. What does this mean for the conclusions just presented? Two points are important here.

First, the limited supply capability of the U.K. effectively limits the volume of trade that can develop between the two countries. With U.K. complete specialization in cloth, the difference between this level of output and domestic consumption is all that can be exported, then traded at the prevailing international exchange ratio for a certain amount of wheat that is imported. Hence the small country tends to determine the *upper bound* of realizable volume of trade.

Second, the chances are that the small country can achieve very favorable conditions of exchange for itself. A very small nation cannot significantly affect prices in a very big country no matter how much it buys or sells in the latter's market, simply because it is not a large enough factor in the market to matter very much. What does this mean? It means that the small country is likely to be able to trade at or near the *domestic* exchange ratio obtaining in the large country and hence—as we have seen—capture for itself the lion's share of the net gains from trade. This has been called "the significance of being insignificant." It is nothing new. The little guy often makes out surprisingly well in the real world.

SOURCE OF TRADE GAINS

Under conditions of constant opportunity costs that we have assumed in our simple comparative advantage model, each country will specialize in the production of that commodity in which it has the comparative advantage. The U.S. specializes in the production of wheat, importing all the cloth it needs from the U.K., while the U.K. does the opposite, specializing in cloth production. This specialization is *complete*. If both countries are indeed to gain from international trade, the total *combined* output of both commodities of the two countries, after trade is opened up, must exceed that prevailing before trade. These gains attributable to specialization are then divided among the two countries according to the final position of the international exchange ratio (*BD*) of the two commodities.

This can best be demonstrated by means of a diagram such as Figure 4–5. Again, we assume the wheat–cloth exchange ratios in isolation to be 1:0.6 (line *AB*) in the U.S. and 1:2 (line *CA'*) in the U.K. In the absence of trade, we will assume that the U.S. consumes and produces at point *R* (*Oa* of wheat and *Oc* of cloth), and that the U.K. produces and consumes at point *T* (*Od* of wheat and *Ob* of cloth). We can now

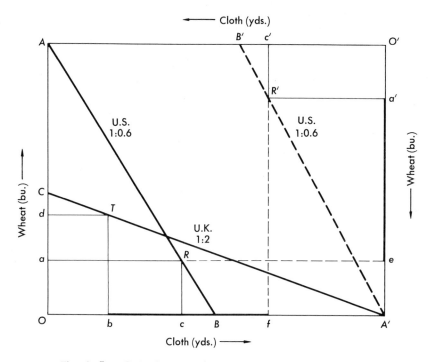

Fig. 4–5. Gain from trade: constant opportunity costs.

simply take the U.S. curve and, using *O'* as the origin, turn it upside down as *A'B'* but leave it otherwise unchanged; thus, U.S. production and consumption in isolation is at *R'* (*O'a'* of wheat and *O'c'* of cloth). In the absence of trade, total combined production of cloth is *Ob* (U.K.) plus *O'c'* (U.S.), while total combined production of wheat is *Od* (U.K.) plus *O'a'* (U.S.).

Now let us examine the same case *with* international trade. The U.K. specializes completely in cloth, producing a quantity *OA'*. The U.S. specializes completely in the production of wheat, turning out a quantity $O'A'$. As compared with output in the absence of international trade and specialization, total world production of wheat is larger by the amount $a'e$ and total output of cloth is larger by quantity bf.

Without trade:
    Total cloth production $= Ob$(U.K.) $+ O'c'$(U.S.)
    Total wheat production $= Od$(U.K.) $+ O'a'$(U.S.)
With trade:
    Total cloth production $= OA'$ (U.K. only)
    Total wheat production $= O'A'$ (U.S. only)
Production gains through trade:
    Expansion of total cloth production $= bf$
    Expansion of total wheat production $= a'e$

The gains in overall production of wheat and cloth resulting from international specialization, made possible by trade, are distributed between the two countries according to the international wheat–cloth exchange ratio that finally results.

Thus far, we have discussed the principle of comparative advantage as an explanation of trade between national economies by means of a simple two-country, two-commodity model. Trade is found to stem from differing production functions, or commodity-exchange ratios, between countries. Under constant opportunity cost conditions, trade results in the complete specialization of each country in the production of a single commodity, with total combined production of all commodities growing as a result. The gains from international trade may accrue to one or both countries involved, depending upon the relative strength of demand in the two countries as it ultimately affects the international exchange ratio.

TERMS OF TRADE

The international exchange ratio just mentioned is generally known as the *terms of trade* or, more accurately, the *commodity terms of trade*. If the ratio at which a country must exchange its export goods for import goods rises, we say that its commodity terms of trade improve or become more favorable. This is synonymous with saying that this country receives a greater *share* of the gains from international trade. It receives a greater quantity of imports for a given amount of its own exports.

Referring once more to Figure 4–4, the closer the commodity terms of trade (BD) settle to the U.S. domestic wheat–cloth exchange ratio, the more favorable they will be to the U.K., and the greater will be its relative gain from international trade. At the same time, this will mean a deterioration, or worsening, of the U.S. commodity terms of trade and signify a relative diminution of its gain from trade. In the examples discussed thus far, using a two-country, two-commodity model with constant opportunity costs, the *limits* to the commodity terms of trade are set by the domestic exchange ratios prevailing in the two countries, and the *actual, prevailing* commodity terms of trade are determined by the forces of international demand.

The commodity terms of trade, as we have used them here, are relatively easy to compute. If the U.S. exports 1 bushel of wheat and receives in return 2 yards of cloth, it would consider its commodity terms of trade substantially more favorable than if it received only 1 yard of cloth for its exported bushel of wheat. By way of contrast, the U.K. would consider its commodity terms of trade much more advantageous if it received 1 bushel of wheat for 1 yard of cloth than if it had to export 2 yards of cloth to get the 1 bushel of wheat. Commodity terms of trade which are relatively favorable for the U.S. signify relatively unfavorable commodity terms of trade for the U.K., and vice versa.

The commodity terms of trade can also be expressed in monetary terms. For example, suppose the prevailing price of cloth is $5.00 per yard, and the price of wheat is $2.50 per bushel, with free international trade between the U.S. and the U.K. The U.K. commodity terms of trade is thus $5.00/$2.50, which equals 2. Now suppose American demand for cloth suddenly expands, so that the price of cloth rises to $6.00. We thus find the British commodity terms of trade improving ($6.00/$2.50 = 2.4) as the price of its export-good (cloth) has risen and the price of its import-good (wheat) has remained the same. It will receive more wheat in return for each unit of cloth it exports than was true before the price of cloth rose. Simultaneously, the U.S. commodity terms of trade have deteriorated to the same degree. Terms of trade such as these can be applied not only to nations, but also to economic sectors (e.g., agriculture), firms, and even individuals.

5

SUPPLY-BASED ANALYSIS

The theory of international trade, as introduced in the previous chapter, evolved historically with an almost exclusive focus on *supply* elements: How much of what products and at what relative prices can individual nations produce and exchange among each other? Let us continue on this track for a while and identify as many supply-related factors as possible before introducing the *demand* side of the picture. We shall start with the same basic trade model and retain some of the assumptions implicit in that model, namely:

1. Free mobility of productive factors *within* a country
2. Complete factor immobility *between* countries
3. Tastes are given and do not change
4. No transportation costs
5. Technology and factor endowments are unchanging
6. No barriers to trade, such as tariffs and quotas
7. Pure competition prevails in all markets, with no government intervention in these markets
8. Full employment of productive resources

We will, however, relax the assumption of constant opportunity costs as a first step toward increased realism.

INCREASING OPPORTUNITY COSTS

The straight line *AB* in Figure 5–1 depicts a constant opportunity cost transformation curve representative of those with which we have been concerned so far. At each point along the linear transformation function *AB*, a fixed quantity of wheat must be sacrificed in order to produce one additional yard of cloth, even though a great deal of cloth and very little wheat is being produced, or vice versa. We say that the marginal rate of transformation of wheat for cloth is constant, i.e., constant opportunity costs.

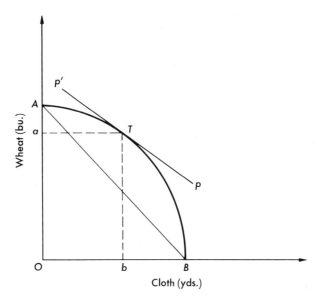

Fig. 5–1.   Increasing opportunity costs.

But is it not more realistic if, as more and more cloth is produced, successively greater amounts of wheat must be sacrificed in order to produce one additional yard of cloth? Common sense would suggest that a country undertaking increasing specialization in one particular good would find it more and more difficult to specialize even further. As the degree of specialization increases factor prices change as well, resulting in increasing opportunity costs—assuming constant returns to scale. Such a condition of *increasing opportunity costs* is represented by the curvilinear transformation function *AB* in Figure 5–1. No longer is the marginal rate of transformation, wheat for cloth, constant. Rather, the curve is characterized by a *diminishing* marginal rate of transformation of wheat for cloth throughout the length of the curve. Hence, it is drawn concave to the origin.

Under constant opportunity costs, with perfect competition prevailing in all markets, the cloth–wheat price ratio is constant. This is true no matter how much wheat or cloth is being produced. Under increasing opportunity costs, however, the relative prices of the two commodities change throughout the transformation function. If a great deal of wheat and little cloth is being produced, the price of wheat is high relative to the price of cloth. Conversely, the production of large amounts of cloth and little wheat signifies a high price of cloth relative to that of wheat. The relative prices, or exchange ratio, of the two commodities are given by the slope of a line drawn tangent to the transformation curve at the particular point at which the society chooses to produce and consume.

For instance, in Figure 5–1, suppose it is decided to produce and consume Oa of wheat and Ob of cloth at point T on the increasing opportunity cost transformation curve AB. At point T the ratio of the price of cloth to the price of wheat is given by the slope of the transformation curve at that point, and this is identical to the slope of a line pp' drawn tangent to the transformation curve at that point. In short, production and consumption of wheat, $Oa,$ and cloth, Ob, at point T means that the ratio of the prices of the two commodities will be pp'. Note that if it is decided to produce more cloth and less wheat (i.e., move from T toward B), the slope of pp' will increase, while a decision to increase wheat output (moving from T toward A) will mean a decline in the slope of pp'.

TRADE UNDER INCREASING OPPORTUNITY COSTS

Now let us apply the notion of increasing opportunity costs to the model of international trade that we discussed earlier under the assumption of constant costs. In so doing, we will be adding a substantial degree of realism to even such a simple model. All of the factors of production are *not* equally well suited to the production of wheat and cloth. Hence, increasing opportunity costs would seem to be a far better description of the character of a nation's production alternatives.

In Figure 5–2, suppose the U.K. is producing and consuming at point T (Oa of wheat and Ob of cloth) in isolation, i.e., in the absence of international trade. The prevailing domestic ratio of the price of cloth to the price of wheat is therefore given by the slope of line pp, tangent to the U.K. transformation curve AB at point T. Suppose further that in the U.S. the prevailing domestic cloth–wheat price ratio is much higher, with wheat being considerably less expensive relative to cloth than in the U.K. Would it not pay for the U.K. to export some of its cloth in exchange for wheat at the higher U.S. exchange ratio? The U.S. cloth–wheat exchange ratio is given by the slope of line $p'p'$. Britain could now move to point R on its transformation curve, specializing more in the production of cloth by increasing its output of that commodity and cutting back on wheat production—producing quantities Od of cloth and Oc of wheat. If it chose to continue to consume quantity Ob of cloth, it would have a quantity bd left to export to the U.S.; in return for this it would receive quantity eS of wheat at the U.S. domestic exchange ratio $p'p'$.

As a result of international trade, therefore, the U.K. is able to consume

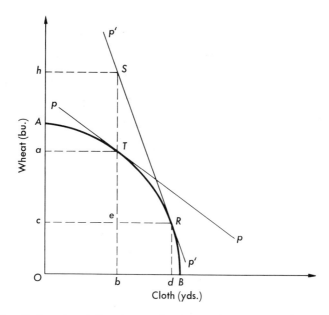

Fig. 5–2. Specialization under increasing opportunity costs.

Without Trade:	
Production	*Oa* of wheat and *Ob* of cloth
Consumption	*Oa* of wheat and *Ob* of cloth
Imports	None
Exports	None
Prices	Slope of *pp*
With Trade:	
Production	*Oc* of wheat and *Od* of cloth
Consumption	*Oh* of wheat and *Ob* of cloth
Imports	*ch* of wheat
Exports	*bd* of cloth
Prices	Slope of *p'p'*
Net Gain from Trade:	*ah* of wheat

a great deal more wheat, *without* consuming any less cloth. It is clearly better off at consumption point *S*, which lies well outside its own productive capabilities as defined by the transformation curve *AB*. Its gain from trade, measured in terms of wheat in Figure 5–2, is quantity *ST*. Of course, the U.K. could decide to consume more cloth *and* wheat, which would place the consumption point after trade somewhere between *S* and *R* on line *p'p'*. There would still be a gain from trade, since any such point would lie outside the U.K. transformation curve.

As a general proposition, as long as the *foreign* commodity-exchange ratio differs from the one prevailing at home, this model tells us that it pays for a country to trade internationally, and that it will gain in material well-being by doing so. The alert reader will recognize this immediately as nothing more than a restatement of the familiar principle of comparative advantage. As long as the foreign price ratio differs from that obtaining domestically, a country will benefit by engaging in international trade.

There is a fundamental difference between the basis for international trade under conditions of increasing and constant costs. In the latter, we found that the *complete* specialization of a country in the production of a single commodity was not out of the question in the simple model used. Under increasing opportunity costs, however, complete specialization is improbable. In Figure 5–2, the slope of line $p'p'$ would have to be great indeed in order to induce the U.K. to produce at, or close to, complete specialization, point B. In the U.S., wheat would have to be virtually worthless in terms of cloth in order for this condition to prevail—indeed unlikely. The increasing difficulty of drawing still more factors of production into the manufacture of cloth as the U.K. approaches specialization in cloth production is responsible, the principle of increasing opportunity costs.

As is true under constant opportunity costs, if the international exchange ratio of cloth for wheat (the commodity terms of trade), turns out to be near that prevailing domestically in the U.S. before trade, as in Figure 5–2, the U.K. will garner most of the gains from trade. The U.S. will stand to gain very little. The reverse holds if the post-trade cloth–wheat exchange ratio approximates the pre-existing U.K. ratio. Much more likely, of course, is that the commodity terms of trade will settle somewhere between these two extremes, thus dividing the gains from trade among the two countries. Again, the exact position of the terms of trade will hinge on the relative strength of demand for wheat and cloth prevailing in the U.S. and the U.K., respectively.

Figure 5–3 depicts such a case. In the absence of international trade, the U.K. is consuming and producing at point T (Oa of wheat and Ob of cloth), and the domestic cloth–wheat exchange ratio is given by the slope of line pp. Similarly, in isolation the U.S. is operating at point V on its transformation curve (Om of wheat and Ol of cloth); the slope of line $p'p'$ being the domestic exchange ratio of cloth to wheat. Now suppose, with international trade, the terms of trade—the *international* exchange ratio of the cloth for wheat—settles at p_ip_i, which is now common both to the U.K. and the U.S. Given the terms of trade p_ip_i, the U.S. moves from the no-trade production point V along its transformation curve CD to point W (Oj of cloth and Ok of wheat), thereby specializing more in the production of wheat. Assuming that it decides to hold constant the consumption of wheat, it can move to consumption point U, exporting quantity $mk(X')$ of wheat to the U.K. in return for quantity $jn(M')$ of cloth. It gains from international trade in the amount ln, measured in terms of cloth.

Meanwhile, the U.K. moves from its no-trade production and consumption point T, on its transformation curve AB, to production point R at the international cloth–wheat exchange ratio $p_i p_i$. It specializes more in the production of cloth. If we assume that the U.K. will hold constant its consumption of cloth, it will consume quantity Ob and export quantity bd (X). It return, it will receive quantity ch (M) of wheat from the

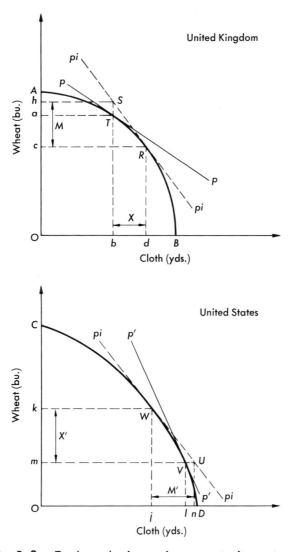

Fig. 5–3. Trade under increasing opportunity costs.

	United Kingdom		United States	
	Wheat	*Cloth*	*Wheat*	*Cloth*
Without Trade:				
Production	Oa	Ob	Om	Ol
Consumption	Oa	Ob	Om	Ol
Imports	none		none	
Exports	none		none	
Prices	Slope of pp		Slope of $p'p'$	
With Trade:				
Production	Oc	Od	Ok	Oj
Consumption	Oh	Ob	Om	On
Imports	ch	—		jn
Exports	—	bd	mk	
Prices	Slope of p_ip_i		Slope of p_ip_i	
Net Gain from Trade:	ah of wheat		ln of cloth	

U.S., which permits consumption at point S. The British gain from trade, measured in terms of wheat, is quantity ah.

The total volume of trade in this example is quantity jn (bd) of cloth, shipped from the U.K. to the U.S., and mk (ch) of wheat, shipped from the U.S. to the U.K. Each country specializes increasingly in the production of that commodity in which it has a comparative advantage, and both nations gain from international trade.

It is, of course, not necessary to assume that each country holds constant its consumption of the commodity in the production of which it has a comparative disadvantage. As long as each country is able to consume along the terms of trade line p_ip_i rather than along its own domestic transformation curve, the existence of gains in national material welfare, attributable to international trade and specialization, is clear. Again, it must be emphasized that the probability of complete specialization in the production of a single commodity under conditions of increasing opportunity costs is extremely slight, for reasons cited earlier.

Through all of the analysis presented here, the fundamental thought remains the theory of comparative advantage. The basic concept has been extended and modified, but nonetheless applies just as it did in the simplest model. It is a cohesive theory, predicting at once the direction of trade, the volume of trade, the source of gains from trade, and, certainly not least important, the changes in the economic structure of the participating countries brought about by international trade.

FACTOR ENDOWMENTS

The theory of trade we have just developed is based on international differences in "conditions of production." Certain things seem to be produced better in some countries than in others, and this fact can be exploited for everyone's benefit through trade. Technically, this has been expressed as differences between countries in transformation functions, or production-possibility curves. But what is behind these differences? The traditional theory of comparative advantage, as we have seen, suggests international variations of *factor-productivity*, or efficiency, as one very basic reason.

A second fundamental cause of international differences in the conditions of production are variations in the availability, or endowments, of the factors of production—land, labor, and capital. This concept was raised to prominence by Eli F. Heckscher and Bertil Ohlin, and is often called the Heckscher–Ohlin (H–O) theory.[1] They attributed international (and interregional) differences in comparative costs to (a) different prevailing endowments of productive factors, and (b) the fact that the production of various commodities requires that the factors of production be used with different degrees of intensity. The physical *productivity* of the factors themselves was deemed uniform throughout so that the quality, or efficiency, of one unit of a factor of production is the same in each country. Note the important difference between this approach and the earlier theory, which rested fundamentally on *differing* international production characteristics and factor productivities.

Even at first glance, the Heckscher-Ohlin thesis is appealing. It predicts that commodities requiring substantial amounts of labor should be produced in countries where labor is abundant relative to other factors of production, and where wage costs are therefore low relative to the cost of other productive factors. These countries then export labor-intensive commodities to other nations where labor is relatively scarce and wage rates relatively high. The same holds true for commodities using the other factors of production intensively in their manufacture. Offhand, then, it would seem that Japan should be specializing in labor-intensive goods and exporting them to western Europe and the U.S. Canada, Australia, and Argentina should be concentrating on the production of such land-intensive commodities as cereal grains, sheep, and cattle and be exporting them to Japan and western Europe. The U.S. should specialize in the production of various types of machinery and other mass-produced items requiring plentiful capital and export them to various capital-poor areas of the world.

Figure 5–4 is an illustration of the pattern of world trade that might be expected to ensue according to this approach if we add national resources as another distinct factor of production.[2]

---

[1] Eli F. Heckscher, "The Effect of Foreign Trade on the Distribution of Income," *Ekonomisk Tidskrift*, XXI, 1919, pp. 497–512. Bertil Ohlin, *Interregional and International Trade* (Cambridge: Harvard University Press, 1933).

[2] The conventional factor endowments theory does not consider natural resources as a distinct factor of production. We include it here in order to better illustrate the impact of factor endowments on the direction of trade.

Technical constraints, dictating which commodities are best produced using which predominant factors of production, would appear to control the nature of the goods entering the various trade flows. But this is only true as long as the factor proportions are technically fixed. If a certain good can be produced equally well by using *either* a lot of capital *or* a lot of labor, it would be difficult to characterize that particular commodity as being either capital-intensive or labor-intensive. Obviously, a multitude of goods fall into this category, and it is necessary to know a good deal more before a positive statement can be made integrating them into the overall scheme of international commercial flows.

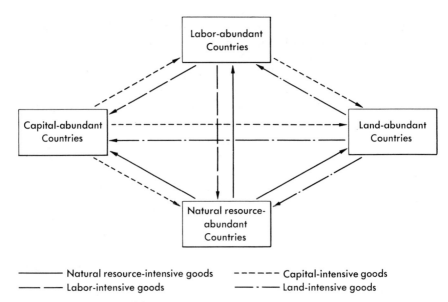

Natural resource-intensive goods ——————   Capital-intensive goods – – – – – –
Labor-intensive goods —— · ——   Land-intensive goods —— · ——

Fig. 5–4.   Factor endowments and the pattern of trade.

TRADE AND FACTOR PRICES

In the labor-abundant countries, wages are likely to be low relative to the cost of other factors of production. Cheap and abundant labor utilized in the production of labor-intensive goods would seem to justify export of labor-intensive commodities to other nations where this particular factor of production is scarce and relative wages are correspondingly higher. The same holds true for other factors of production.

What, then, are the effects of international trade? Suppose we take two countries, one (L) labor-abundant and the other (K) capital-abundant. *Labor-intensive* commodities begin to flow from Country L to Country K, while capital-intensive goods flow in the opposite direction. As more and more labor is absorbed in Country L for export production, labor begins to become relatively more scarce, and wages begin to rise. Simultaneously, Country L is importing *capital-intensive* goods from Country K. This displaces domestic production of capital-intensive commodities, causing capital to become relatively more abundant and thus lowering the cost of capital. In effect, the abundant factor (labor) becomes more scarce and its price rises, while the scarce factor (capital) becomes more abundant and its price falls, all as a result of international trade. Exactly the reverse happens in the capital-abundant Country K.

As labor becomes relatively scarcer in Country L and less scarce in Country K, and capital becomes relatively scarcer in Country K and less so in Country L, would there not be a tendency for wages and the cost of capital to equalize in the two countries? We have just seen that the answer to this question must be affirmative. Trade *tends to equalize* prices of the factors of production internationally. In fact, it may equalize factor prices just as effectively as if the productive factors themselves migrated from countries in which they are in relatively abundant supply to countries in which they are relatively scarce.

FACTOR-PRICE EQUALIZATION

It is easy to see how international trade leads to an equalization of *commodity* prices between countries. As long as price differences exist it pays to expand trade, and this will remain true until all price differences are eliminated. It is much more difficult to believe, however, that a complete equalization of relative *factor* prices will occur more or less automatically. Without barriers to international trade, and assuming factor productivity is everywhere the same, this would mean that U.S. wages, relative to the prices of other productive factors, would equal those prevailing in Japan, that the cost of capital in Germany would equal in relative terms that obtaining in Brazil, and so forth.

It is much more realistic to say, as did Heckscher and Ohlin, that international trade will tend to equalize the relative prices of factors of production. Only under certain very restrictive assumptions will factor–price equalization be complete.

It is much more realistic to say, as did Heckscher and Ohlin, that international trade will *tend to equalize* the relative prices of factors of production. Only under certain very restrictive assumptions will factor–price equalization be complete. These are as follows: 1. Two commodities are produced in the two countries both without and with trade. 2. Identical productive techniques prevail in both nations. 3. One product is always labor-intensive. 4. Both factors of production are qualitatively identical in all respects. 5. Both factors are used in the production of both goods. 6. No change occurs in the available supplies of productive factors. 7. There are no artificial restrictions to trade, and economic distances (transportation costs) are assumed to be zero. 8. Perfect competition prevails in all markets and productive factors cannot move internationally.[3]

It is at all realistic, for instance, to assume that the conditions under which production takes place are the same in each and every country? Identical production functions are necessary if the predictive value of the factor endowments theory is to be very substantial at all.

As economies grow, the techniques used in the productive process generally seem to reach some degree of uniformity among nations. Relative freedom of technological transfers promotes this. However, there is no certainty that productive techniques necessarily *will* be the same in every country. There is always a lag between invention and innovation on the one hand, and its general, world-wide application on the other hand. Also, simply because the advanced technology is *available* is no guarantee that it will be put to use in the most effective manner possible.

From a technological standpoint alone, then, nations may very well continue to differ, particularly, given the international leads and lags that we know exist. What about other aspects behind the production function—the character of the people, the climate, topographical conditions, the role of government, and so forth? All of these can be expected to differ in varying degrees among nations, and even though productive conditions may well be similar, they are certainly not homogeneous.

What about the productive factors themselves? Are they in fact "qualitatively identical"? Is an Indian worker as productive, given identical tools and techniques, as his American counterpart? Here again, differences in nutrition, education, discipline, and work habits might make one worker qualitatively quite different from his counterpart in another country, although such differences can easily be exaggerated.

Some of these assumptions are not always essential for factor-price equalization to occur in each and every circumstance. But, in the main, their restrictiveness is sufficient to render the notion of complete factor-price equalization non-operational for all practical purposes. But this hardly diminishes its significance; the indication of a *tendency* for trade to equalize factor prices internationally is of first-rate importance, and from a casual survey of real-world examples, the reader surely will find it appealing. But complete equalization of the prices of factors of production internationally hinges upon the free *mobility* of the factors themselves. Free trade is only a *partial* substitute for factor mobility.

[3] Paul A. Samuelson, "International Factor Price Equalization Once Again," *Economic Journal,* June, 1949.

TRADE AND THE DISTRIBUTION OF INCOME

The factor-endowments approach to international trade theory yields a number of important insights into the effects of trade on the various structural relationships prevailing internally in the various national economies. We know what happens to (a) commodity prices, (b) factor intensities, (c) the composition of output, and (d) the relative returns paid to the factors of production as a result of international trade. This last area would seem to require some further elaboration at this point.

As we know, trade increases the relative degree of scarcity of the productive factor in short supply. It thus brings about an increase in the relative returns paid to the abundant factor and lowers those paid to the scarce factor. Now suppose we look at a country where capital is abundant and labor is scarce. Will not international trade result in a dramatic reduction of wages relative to the cost of capital? If so, would it not be advisable from labor's standpoint to impede trade in some way and thereby keep relative wages at the existing high level and prevent their deterioration?

We have seen that international trade will bid up the prices of abundant factors of production and lower returns to scarce factors. If labor is indeed the scarce factor, it follows that wages will tend to decline relative to the earnings of capital and/or land, and that trade fundamentally shifts the distribution of income. That this is in fact true is shown in Section E-5A and the interested reader may want to refer to it at this point. In any case, it would seem to provide a ready-made argument for protection: If trade shifts income distribution one way, then surely trade barriers must shift it in the opposite direction. We shall explore this issue in much greater detail in later connection with commercial policy.

6

DEMAND AND GENERAL EQUILIBRIUM

A great deal has thus far been said about the factors affecting international trade. Yet, there is one significant gap in the analysis. Nothing has yet been mentioned about the role of *demand* in determining the direction, commodity composition, and terms of trade between nations. It would be inconceivable to make a general statement about "who trades what with whom and at what prices" while considering only the supply side of the economic equation and completely ignoring demand.

Every beginning student of economics knows that information about both supply and demand is necessary to arrive at an equilibrium price. So it is in international trade, where the prices at which commodities are exchanged for one another are called the *terms of trade*. Very early in our study of comparative costs we found that the terms of trade determine the proportions in which the gains derived from international specialization and division of labor are distributed among the various participating countries. At that point we set the terms of trade arbitrarily and went on from there. We no longer need do that once it is clear precisely how the terms of trade themselves are derived.

COMMUNITY INDIFFERENCE CURVES

To begin, let us introduce the role of demand by posing a small problem. Suppose two countries possess identical production functions—the proportions in which the different inputs must be combined to produce various quantities of output—as a result of identical prevailing production techniques, and identical endowments of productive factors. Therefore, they possess identical transformation functions. Comparative production costs of all commodities are the same in both countries. Is trade possible? According to the analysis presented in the preceding chapters, the answer would have to be decidedly in the negative. Trade is based on the existence of *differences* in comparative costs of production between nations, and without such differences there would appear to be no reason for international trade and no gains to be derived therefrom.

But once again let us turn to the real world. We find that trade does, in fact, flourish among countries which appear to have very similar factor endowments and technologies: Germany and Great Britain, Belgium and the Netherlands, France and Italy, and so on. Hence, there must be some other explanation for international trade besides the supply factors already enumerated. We must consider demand as well.

An individual's demand for goods and services is largely a function of two variables: (a) his personal tastes and preferences, and (b) his disposable income. His tastes, or relative preferences, for two commodities can be represented as an *indifference curve*. His income may be depicted in the form of a *consumption-possibilities line:* i.e., the maximum amounts of the two goods which he can buy with his limited income. Maximum satisfaction will be attained by consuming a combination of the two goods much that the consumption-possibilities line is tangent to one of the indifference curves. This represents the highest welfare level he can attain with his given income.

An individual presumably can determine, at least in a rough sort of way, which of two commodities he prefers under a variety of different circumstances and which are the best and the worst consumption combinations for him. Hence, there are few conceptual objections that can be raised against the construction of indifference curves for an individual. But what about the construction of indifference curves, *community indifference curves,* for an entire nation?

This proves to be much more difficult because of the impossibility of making interpersonal comparisons of consumer welfare levels. Suppose we assert that a nation would be just as well off by consuming 8 million cars and 100 million books as it is by consuming 4 million cars and 200 million books. Obviously, car lovers will be much better off under the former alternative, but book lovers will be far worse off. The two sets of individuals possess consumption indifference curves *of entirely different shapes,* and it is impossible to compare them. We thus cannot possibly state that community welfare would be unchanged by shifting the patterns of consumption from one combination of commodities to the other, and hence it is conceptually impossible to draw a single indifference curve for the entire community.

In view of such strenuous objections, it is all the more surprising that the community indifference curve has come to be the prime technique for expressing the influences of demand in international trade theory. Several of the early theorists used indifference curves to reflect community, or national, demand—without coming to grips with the problem of interpersonal comparisons—by simply assuming that they possessed the same characteristics as individual, consumer indifference curves. Later, it was determined that *if*, in a national shift in consumption patterns, the gainers were to compensate the losers in such a way that all would be equally well off, the construction of community indifference curves was indeed justified.[4]

Alternatively, it is simply assumed that all inhabitants of a nation possess fundamentally identical and unchanging tastes and factor endowments ". . . so that the indifference map, while it may differ as between a citizen of A and a citizen of B, is the same for all the citizens in either of the two countries."[5]

Despite these and other justifications and assumptions about the use of aggregative community indifference curves, it remains a tenuous concept at best. Yet, because of its value in portraying the impact of demand on the volume and direction of international trade, we cannot avoid employing the community indifference curve as a tool of analysis. However, it is necessary to always keep in mind its evident limitations and shortcomings.

Figure 6–1 portrays a nation in isolation, in the absence of international trade. It is endowed with factors of production and technology so that a transformation function, or production-possibilities curve, RS, results under conditions of increasing opportunity costs. With the community indifference map composed of the CIC curves, optimum consumption and production occurs at point T for maximum economic welfare. At this point, we recall that the marginal rate of substitution in consumption precisely equals the marginal rate of transformation in production, and that the prevailing domestic ratio of the price of radios to the price of TV sets is given by the slope of the common tangent pp. No other consumption or production point yields as high an economic welfare level. Only if the transformation function RS can somehow be expanded outward, by increasing endowments of productive factors or by enhancing productivity, can the national welfare level be raised to a higher community indifference curve.

[4] Tibor Scitovsky, "A Reconsideration of the Theory of Tariffs," *Review of Economic Studies,* Summer, 1942; reprinted in H. S. Ellis and L. A. Metzler (eds.), *Readings in the Theory of International Trade* (Homewood, Ill.: Richard D. Irwin, 1949).

[5] James E. Meade, *The Geometry of International Trade* (London: George Allen & Unwin, 1952), p. 9.

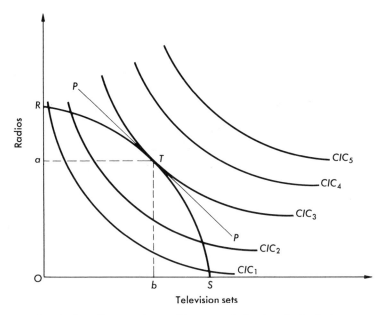

Fig. 6–1. Community welfare maximization in isolation.

DEMAND AND INTERNATIONAL TRADE

Suppose, now, that there are two countries possessing identical factor endowments and technologies but different tastes and preferences, i.e., differently shaped community indifference curves. As Figure 6–2 shows, trade will occur and both countries will be better off as a result.

Initially, in spite of equal comparative costs of production represented by the *identical* transformation curves, AB, the ratio of the price of the A-good to the price of the B-good differs in the two countries, represented by the slope of line pp in Country I and $p''p''$ in Country II. Country I prefers to consume larger quantities of the A-good at point S than does Country II at point S' in Figure 6–2. The obvious reason for this price variance is *not* different costs of production, but different tastes and preferences represented by the differently shaped community indifference curves.

The existence of the price difference attributable to demand variation creates the *basis* for trade. With international trade, the price of A- and B-goods will soon be equalized in the two countries, say at the ratio represented by the slope of line $p'p'$. At this price ratio, production in Country I moves from point S to point T, and consumption is enabled to advance to a higher indifference level (2) at point R. Quantity $b'b''$ of B is exported in return for $a'a''$ of A. Similarly, at the new price ratio $p'p'$, Country

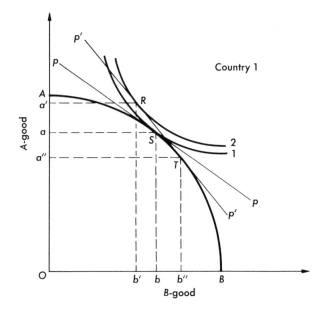

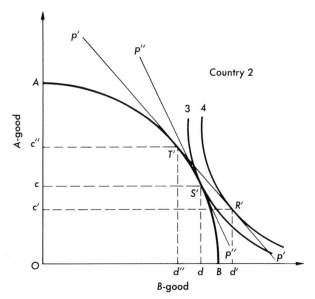

Fig. 6–2. Trade and production with identical supply and differing demand conditions.

II shifts production from S' to T', exporting quantity $c'c''$ of commodity *A* for $d'd''$ of imports of good *B,* and advances to a higher indifference level (*4*) by consuming at point R'. Both countries have gained in economic welfare as a result of international trade based solely on differences in national consumption preferences. Each has undergone a transformation in economic structure—in output combinations—with Country *I* specializing more in production of the *B*-good and Country *II* increasing its specialization in production of the *A*-good.

	Country I	*Country II*
Consumption:		
Without trade...........	$S(Oa$ of A and Ob of $B)$	$S'(Oc$ of A and Od of $B)$
With trade	$R(Oa'$ of A and Ob' of $B)$	$R'(Oc'$ of A and Od' of $B)$
Production:		
Without trade...........	$S(Oa$ of A and Ob of $B)$	$S'(Oc$ of A and Od of $B)$
With trade.............	$T(Oa''$ of A and Ob'' of $B)$	$T'(Oc''$ of A and Od'' of $B)$
Prices:		
Without trade	slope of pp	slope of $p''p''$
With trade.............	slope of $p'p'$	slope of $p'p'$
Direction of trade:		
Exports................	$b'b''$ of B	$c'c''$ of A
Imports................	$a'a''(=c'c'')$ of A	$d'd''(=b'b'')$ of B

What would have occurred if, instead of demand variation, the demand patterns and therefore the community indifference curves prevailing in the two countries had been identical, but with differing transformation functions due to differing factor endowments or technologies? Figure 5–3 provides the answer. Trade occurs and gains are realized along the lines of the by now familiar comparative cost model. In such a case, supply conditions *alone* are of determining importance. The addition of community indifference curves to that diagram would simply substantiate that the consumption point with free international trade lies on a higher indifference level than that attainable in isolation, and hence that there are welfare gains to be derived from international trade.

Finally, what happens, under constant or increasing opportunity cost conditions, when two countries possess identical technologies, identical factor endowments, and identical tastes? There will be no trade and no gains to be derived therefrom. Prices and costs, tastes and supply conditions are everywhere the same, so that no justification exists—either from the supply or from the demand side—for trade to occur. Only if there are significant realizable economies on scale, so that decreasing costs (increasing returns) prevail, will it pay to trade. Under such conditions each country will specialize in the production of one of the two commodities, and combined production of both will rise dramatically. This permits the attainment of higher community indifference curves by both countries.

Demand conditions are thus seen to play an important role in determining the volume and direction of international trade. Even if we question the validity of all analyses which lean heavily on community indifference curves, the significance of demand factors cannot be denied. They must be incorporated prominently into any general explanation of the agents governing commerce among the nations of the world.

RECIPROCAL DEMAND

At this point, the reader has acquired a fundamental, working knowledge of the respective roles played by supply and demand in international trade. But as yet we have failed to integrate the two into a cohesive, general model which at once helps us to predict the volume, direction, and terms of international trade. This is done in a general way by the *law of reciprocal demand,* and more rigorously, by the so-called *offer curves.*

Suppose that the domestic price ratios (determined by production costs) of two commodities, oil and wheat, are 1:2 in Country X and 1:3 in Country Y. If the international terms of trade of oil for wheat exceeded 1:2, Country X would be unwilling to trade; it could do better by exchanging oil for wheat at the prevailing domestic ratio. Similarly, if the international oil-wheat price ratio were lower than 1:3, Country Y would be unwilling to trade. Hence, the prevailing domestic commodity price ratios (here 1:2 and 1:3) set the limits within which the international price ratio—the terms of trade—must settle. Only within this range will *both* countries be willing to trade.

It was noted earlier that the closer to the domestic price ratio prevailing in Country X the terms of trade come to rest, the larger will be the proportion of the gains from trade garnered by Country Y, and vice-versa.

Precisely where, between these two domestic price ratios, will the terms of trade eventually settle? The answer is suggested by the *law of reciprocal demand,* first stated by John Stuart Mill, which says it is necessary to know the demand expressed by *both* countries for *both* commodities before the terms of trade can be precisely determined. In this case, if Country X, which has a comparative advantage in the production of oil, expresses an enormous demand for wheat—*both domestically produced and imported*—it is certain that the terms of trade will settle close to its own domestic oil–wheat price ratio and that its trading partner, Country Y, will derive most of the gains from international trade. In order to get all of the wheat Country X badly wants, it must offer its own export, oil, at progressively lower prices while the price of its import, wheat, becomes steadily higher. In the process, its terms of trade deteriorate until some equilibrium is reached close to its domestic, no-trade price ratio.

By way of contrast, Country Y finds the price of its export, wheat, rising while the price of its import, oil, falls. This represents a steady improvement in its terms of trade and an increase in its proportionate share of gains from trade at the expense of those of its trading partner.

Therefore, reciprocal demand determines the international price ratio, or terms of trade, at which all markets will be in equilibrium. Supply equals demand both in each country and between them. The law of reciprocal demand as a determinant of the terms of trade, however, is important only so long as demand in each of the countries is powerful enough to affect the prices of commodities in both of them. Consider trade in oil and wheat between the U.S. and Kuwait. No matter what the Kuwaiti demand for wheat and oil, it will be too weak to affect relative prices of the two commodities in the U.S. Hence, for all practical purposes, trade in oil and wheat between the U.S. and Kuwait will occur at the U.S. domestic price ratio. Kuwait will derive virtually all of the gains that result from such trade, assuming there are no monopoly or monopsony elements at work in the various markets.

Small and, from a demand standpoint, insignificant countries thus appear to be in a favorable position in the international economy. Of course, this is not an unmixed blessing, since it places their economies at the mercy of the vagaries of demand in the larger nations. A significant change in tastes, incomes, or technology in the large countries could easily wipe out highly specialized, export-oriented industries in the very same small countries previously reaping large gains from trade. This could damage their economies severely indeed.

OFFER ANALYSIS

There is another way to express the role of demand in international trade, one that is somewhat more amenable to use in our analysis later on. *Offer curves* were first developed by the British economists F. Y. Edgeworth, in the late nineteenth century, and Alfred Marshall some thirty years later. In terms of the construction of these curves, we shall follow the example of a modern British economist, James E. Meade.[6]

Referring to Figure 6–3, we have drawn in quadrant II of the coordinate plane, the familiar community indifference curve, C_1, and transformation curve, ab, equilibrium, under increasing opportunity cost conditions for a representative national economy producing two goods, A and B. Without trade, the economy can reach the welfare level represented by community

[6] James E. Meade, *A Geometry of International Trade* (London: George Allen and Unwin, 1952), chs. 2 and 3.

indifference curve C_1, with fixed production alternatives possible under set resource endowments and technology represented by transformation curve ab at point T. It produces and consumes quantities Om of good A and Ol of good B.

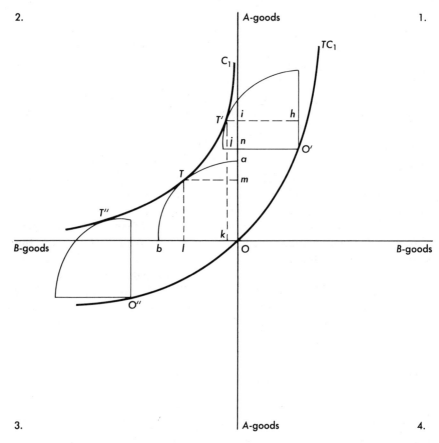

Fig. 6–3. Derivation of the trade indifference curve.

	Good A	Good B
Without trade (equilibrium at T):		
Production	Om	Ol
Consumption	Om	Ol
With trade (equilibrium at T'):		
Production	$O'h$	$O'j$
Consumption	Oi	Ok
Trade:		
Exports	—	$O'n$
Imports	kj	—

Suppose, now, that we simply take the nation's "production block" Oab and slide it up along community indifference curve C_1 to a new equilibrium point at T'. Consumption at T' is now Oi of good A and Ok of good B. Production at T' is $O'h$ of A and $O'j$ of good B. Quantity $O'n$ of good B is exported in return for imported quantity kj of good A.

Note that point T' is still on community indifference curve C_1 so that the country is *no better and no worse off* as a result of international trade; i.e., it is indifferent whether it trades or not. The same thing happens when we slide production block Oab *down* along the community indifference curve to some new equilibrium T''. Here again, although consumption and production patterns have changed drastically, the country is equally well off at T'' as it is at T' or, without any trade at all, at point T. All lie on the same community indifference curve.

As we slide the production bloc Oab up and down along community indifference curve C_1 to represent different production and consumption combinations at the same indifference level, the corner of the production bloc, O, traces out the curve TC_1. This is called the *trade indifference curve*. At any point along curve TC_1, the country is indifferent whether or not it engages in international trade. Why? Since curve TC_1 is directly derived from the community indifference curve, with constant supply conditions represented by the unchanging production block, it is as well off at *any* point along it as it is at the no-trade point O.

We can now derive a series of trade indifference curves corresponding to an equal number of community indifference curves, representing higher and lower levels of economic welfare (always leaving the size and shape of the production block completely unchanged). This is done in Figure 6–4. Trade indifference curves TC_1, TC_2, and TC_3 are derived from community indifference curves C_1, C_2, and C_3 respectively, traced by the corner of the production block Oab.

There is one trade indifference curve for each community indifference curve. The higher the trade indifference curve, the higher the level of welfare that has been attained. From the way in which they are constructed, it is clear that higher trade indifference curves must be related to correspondingly higher community indifference curves and, therefore, to advanced levels of economic well-being.

Keeping in mind the manner in which trade indifference curves are derived (i.e., *what is behind them*), we can now go ahead and use them to construct an *offer curve*. Suppose, in the absence of trade, that the relative domestic prices of the A- and B-goods are given by the slope of line OP_1 in Figure 6–5. Below this price ratio we, as a country, would certainly be unwilling to offer any of our B-goods in return for imports of A-goods—it is possible to get A-goods more cheaply at home. At the

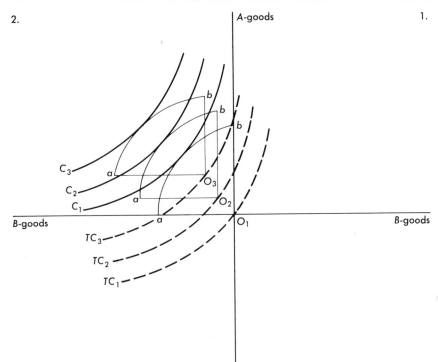

Fig. 6–4. Derivation of the trade indifference map from the consumption indifference map.

price ratio OP_1, however, we might just be willing to trade a small amount of B-goods for A-goods, rather than exchanging them at home since the price is the same, point V.

If the international price ratio rose to OP_2, however, we would be willing to offer a great deal more of our B-goods in return for imports of A-goods. The higher prices received for our exports, relative to those we have to pay for our imports—the improved terms of trade—permit us to move to a higher trade indifference curve and thus to a higher community welfare level as well. Hence, we are willing to offer substantially more of our B-goods for export at price OP_2 (point W) than at the domestic price ratio OP_1.

In fact, as our terms of trade continue to improve and we keep getting more A-goods per unit of the B-goods that we export, we are willing to offer more and more of our B-goods for sale abroad (for example, at

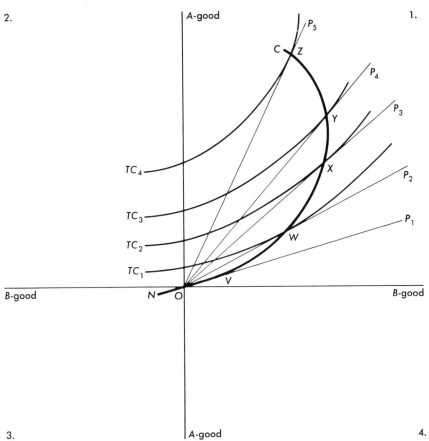

Fig. 6–5. Derivation of the offer curve.

terms of trade P_3 and P_4 and points X and Y, respectively). After a while however, we are exporting so much of our B-good that it becomes in short supply at home and therefore relatively more valuable. Similarly, we are importing so much of the A-good that our desire for even more of it is correspondingly diminished. At some point, we are willing to offer *no more* B-goods for A-goods. Beyond that point we are willing to take on more A-goods only if we have to give up less of the B-goods as a result (i.e., additional amounts of the B-good are a burden, or a nuisance, to us). Hence, at terms of trade such as P_5, our offer of B-goods in return for additional A-goods has become zero, and then negative (compare points Y and Z).

Curve NC, the tangency of all possible terms of trade lines with all possible trade indifference curves, is the *offer curve*. It shows how much of its exports a country is willing to offer in return for imports at each and every international price ratio, or terms of trade. The offer curve is a graphical representation of reciprocal demand, and subsumes domestic supply conditions and both domestic and foreign demand conditions.

In the same way that an offer curve was derived for one country, a second offer curve can be drawn for its trading partner. We simply construct the latter's transformation function and community indifference curves in the *fourth quadrant* of the coordinate plane, draw a second set of corresponding trade indifference curves, and construct an offer curve for the second country as well.

All of this is done in Figure 6–6 which presents the transformation curves and community indifference curves for two countries (X and

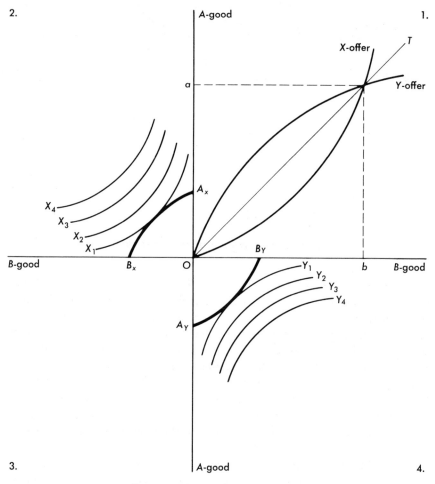

Fig. 6–6.   Trade equilibrium.

Y) and two commodities (*A* and *B*). The two countries' respective trade indifference curves (not drawn) are derived as in Figure 6–4 above, and their respective offer curves drawn from the tangencies of the trade indifference curves with the various terms of trade lines.

GENERAL EQUILIBRIUM

Figure 6–6 shows the two countries' respective offer curves crossing at point *R*, with the prevailing terms of trade given by the slope of the line *OT*. Only at this point does general equilibrium exist. The terms of trade *OT* exactly balance supply and demand for both commodities, *A* and *B*, in both countries, *X* and *Y*, and clear all markets, domestic and international. Let us see how this occurs.

At terms of trade *OT*, Country *X* is willing to offer quantity *Ob* of its *B*-goods in return for *Oa* of *A*-goods. Simultaneously, Country *Y* offers *Oa* of its exportable *A*-goods for quantity *Ob* of imports of the *B*-good. At those terms of trade, one country is willing to supply *precisely* what the other country demands.

	Import Demand	*Export Supply*
Country *X*	*Oa* of *A*	*Ob* of *B*
Country *Y*............	*Ob* of *B*	*Oa* of *A*

Quantity *Ob* of commodity *B* is thus exported by Country *X* and imported by Country *Y*, while *Oa* of good *A* is exported by Country *Y* and imported by Country *X*.

From the way we have derived the offer curves it is clear that, at the price ratio given by the terms of trade line *OT* which now prevails domestically in both countries *and* internationally, the supply of each commodity equals the demand. In Country *X*, domestic production of the *B*-good *minus* exports equals the domestic demand for it, while domestic production of the *A*-good *plus* imports equals the domestic demand for that commodity. The same is true, in an opposite manner, in Country *Y*. All markets are cleared, supply equals demand domestically and internationally, and prices have no further tendency to change. The system is in equilibrium.

Note that the *volume* of trade can readily be predicted from the information given by the offer analysis and general equilibrium. The *direction* of trade can be just as easily foretold, since the shape of a country's transformation function and community indifference map determine the shape of its trade indifference curves which, in turn, govern the shape of its offer curve. Once we have two intersecting offer curves derived in such a way, therefore, we are in a position to predict "who exports what to whom," i.e., the direction of trade, as well as the terms of trade.

Finally, by simply tracing the trade point, *R*, backwards through the same analysis, we arrive at a tangency of a country's production block (the corner of which rests at R) and one of its indifference curves. It is thus possible simultaneously to determine the impact of trade on production patterns, or economic structure, and consumption combinations as well.

This is done graphically in Figure 6–7. The two countries' respective offer curves intersect at point R, at terms of trade OT. Country X

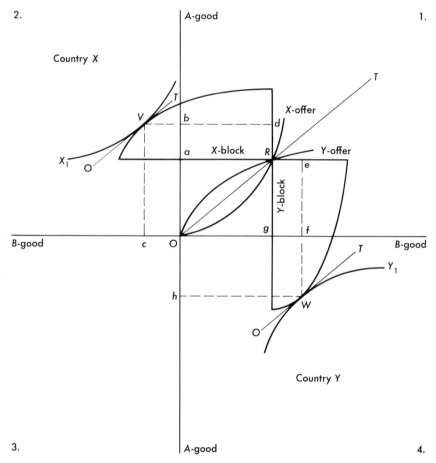

Fig. 6–7. General equilibrium: trade, production, and consumption.

exports quantity Og of commodity B to Country Y, which in return ships quantity Oa of commodity A to Country X. In Country X, production and consumption take place at point V. Quantity gc of the B-good is produced, of which Oc is consumed at home and Og is exported. Quantity Ob of the A-good is consumed, of which quantity ab is produced at home and quantity Oa is imported. In Country Y, on the other hand, production and consumption occur at point W. The B-good is consumed in the amount Of, quantity gf of which is produced domestically and the remainder, Og, imported. The A-good is produced in the amount ah, of which Oh is consumed at home and the rest, Oa, is exported.

The prices of the two commodities are the same in both countries, and they would be given by the slope of a common tangent to the relevant community indifference curves and the transformation curves at points V and W. The slopes of both of these common tangents must be the same as the slope of the terms of trade line, OT.

	Country X	Country Y
Trade:		
Exports....................	Og of B-good	Oa of A-good
Imports....................	Oa of A-good	Og of B-good
Production:		
Commodity A...............	ab	ah
Commodity B...............	gc	gf
Consumption:		
Commodity A...............	$Ob(ab + Oa)$	$Oh(ah - Oa)$
Commodity B...............	$Oc(gc - Og)$	$Of(gf + Og)$
Prices:		
Prevailing domestically........	OT	OT
Terms of trade...............	OT	OT

Thus a single, comprehensive analysis draws together all of the salient demand and supply forces and presents us with virtually all of the effects of international trade we are interested in.

1. The volume of trade,
2. The direction of trade,
3. The terms of trade,
4. The impact of international trade upon economic structure (the nation's production mix), and
5. Its effect on the patterns of consumption prevailing within each of the trading countries.

It incorporates both supply and demand factors, and, in a way, ties together everything we have said thus far.

How realistic is it? Is it possible to derive from a simple two-country, two-commodity model such as this, principles that possess significant predictive value in a world where there are many commodities and many countries, and in which supply and demand conditions are constantly undergoing change? What about the question, raised earlier, concerning the validity of using community indifference curves in this manner? How about transportation costs and other so-called *non-homogeneous* factors? These are some of the questions the sceptical and serious reader will immediately present to this discussion of general equilibrium. Nonetheless, the model does provide a starting point for analysis and organizes our thinking about international trade.

7

EXTENDING THE MODEL

The previous four chapters outlined the rudiments of the pure theory of international trade: supply, demand, and general equilibrium. Indeed, we concluded with a comprehensive analytical framework (Figure 6–7) which not only encompasses supply and demand elements that appear in the international economy, but also ties them back directly to corresponding elements at the national level. Using this model, we can trace through a shift in demand or supply conditions in one or both countries with respect to its impact on the terms of trade, the volume and composition of trade, and economic structure at home and abroad.

Up to now the presentation for the most part has been essentially *static* in nature. Very little has been said about the impact of changing factor supplies and technology upon the volume, direction, commodity composition, and terms of trade among nations—the *dynamics* of international trade. Yet this particular aspect is of first-order conceptual significance, if only because we do, after all, live in a world of constantly changing economic parameters. Demand shifts are a reality, as are continuing changes on the supply side of the economic equation.

Let us now try to find some ways in which our model of international trade may be useful for analytical purposes, and at the same time identify some of its evident limitations.

TERMS OF TRADE

It is important before continuing to define precisely what we mean by the *terms of trade*. Later on, especially when we discuss the role international trade plays in economic development, the terms of trade will be an important and useful concept.

So far, we have defined the terms of trade of a nation as representing

the prices of its export goods relative to the prices of the goods it imports—
the rate at which the two classes of commodities are exchanged for one
another in the international marketplace. Simply stated, the terms of trade,
TT, equal the index of export prices, Px, divided by the price index for
imports, Pm.

$$TT = \frac{Px}{Pm} \times 100$$

If we take 1976 as the base year ($= 100$), and we find that at the end
of 1977 a certain country's export prices had risen 10 per cent (to 110)
and its import prices had fallen 5 per cent (to 95), then its terms of
trade improved by about 15.8 per cent (110 divided by 95 and multiplied
by 100 = 115.8) during that time period.

If a country's terms of trade are seen to improve, either the prices
of exports must have risen or the prices of imports fallen, or both. Conversely, a deterioration of the terms of trade means an increase in import
prices, or a decline in export prices, or both.

An improvement in the terms of trade means that a smaller quantity
of export goods must be sold abroad to obtain a given quantity of imports. A deterioration in the terms of trade signifies that a greater sacrifice,
in terms of goods exported, is necessary to obtain a set quantum of imports. It is often said that maximum imports are the *objective* or *goal*
of international trade, and that exports are the *means* of obtaining that
objective. Hence, the origin of the terms "improvement" and "deterioration" in connection with the terms of trade.

When we are dealing with only two commodities, one imported and
the other exported, the terms of trade as defined here represent a precise
analytical tool and are properly referred to as the *commodity terms of
trade*. If the value of commodities is taken to equal the value of all of
the factors of production incorporated therein, then the terms under which
commodities are exchanged for one another internationally are really also
the terms under which productive factors are exchanged for each other.
Hence, the terms of trade as defined here could equally be called the
factoral terms of trade, referring either to a single factor of production
(such as labor) or to all productive factors in combination.

In practice, of course, the factoral terms of trade are extremely difficult
to calculate because factor inputs are constantly changing, both in composition and in productivity. Alfred Marshall, in his development of the theory
of reciprocal demand, treated imports and exports as containing uniform
"representative bales" of a nation's productive factors, with demand being
expressed internationally in terms of these "bales."[1] He based his theory
on the factoral terms of trade via the "representative bales" concept and

[1] Alfred Marshall, *Money, Credit, and Commerce* (London: Macmillan, 1923).

was severely criticized for overemphasizing demand and wrongly separating it from supply factors operating internationally.[2]

Suppose the prices of imports remain constant, and the prices of a country's exports rise by 20 per cent from 1976 to 1978. At the same time, however, productivity in the use of the factors of production at its disposal rises by 10 per cent. The *commodity terms of trade* obviously would show a 20 per cent improvement.

$$120 \div 100 = 1.2 \times 100 = 120$$

To find the *factoral terms of trade*, however, we have to take into account the increased productivity; i.e., each unit of exports now contains *smaller* amounts of the country's factors of production. Hence the factoral terms of trade show an improvement of 32 per cent:

$$120 \times 110 = 13,200 \div 100 = 132$$

The result: one unit of *exports* now buys 20 per cent more import goods, but one unit of the *factors of production* employed in the creation of these exports now buys 32 per cent more import commodities. The latter is called the *single factoral terms of trade.*

If instead we want to find out how many more foreign units of productive factors (e.g., labor hours) one exported unit of domestic productive factors will buy—the *double factoral terms of trade*—we must adjust the import price index by the amount of *foreign* productivity gain. Thus, if in this particular example foreign factor productivity has simultaneously risen by, say, 5 per cent, the gain in the double factoral terms of trade would be about 26 per cent.

$$(120 \times 110) \div (100 \times 105) \times 100 = 125.7$$

While there are clear conceptual advantages to using the factoral terms of trade, the difficulty in computing them in actual practice makes the commodity terms of trade the dominant concept. We shall return to the discussion of the terms of trade later on, in connection with both economic development and commercial policy.

SUPPLY AND DEMAND SHIFTS

Using the offer-curve analysis developed in the preceding chapter, it is now possible to portray the impact of shifts in supply and demand relationships upon the volume and on the terms of international trade. Basi-

---

[2] Frank D. Graham, *The Theory of International Values* (Princeton: Princeton University Press, 1948).

cally, what will be the effect of a change in factor endowments, or any change in supply conditions, upon the volume of trade and the terms of trade?

An increase in the endowment of the abundant factor or an increase in the level of factor productivity in the export sectors expands a nation's transformation curve accordingly; i.e., more of the export good can be produced. From the derivation of offer curves presented earlier, it is easy to see that if this is portrayed as an increase in the size of the *production block* of a country, demand patterns being constant, the result would be an *outward* shift of the offer curve. An increase in the quantity of the nation's exports tends to reduce the world price, forcing the country to export more, per unit of import, than before.

This is depicted in Figure 7–1. Beginning with the equilibrium trade point R, Country X is subject to an increase in productive capability of its export commodity B, as a result of an increase either in factor endowments or in factor productivity. Efforts to export more reduce the price of B in the international market, thus shifting its terms of trade from OT to OT' (Country Y's offer curve remaining unchanged), and its offer curve from OX to OX', resulting in a new equilibrium at R'. At the new terms of trade it must export a quantity bb' more than the initial exports of Ob, in order to get only slightly more imports (aa') in return. Its terms of trade have deteriorated, although the overall volume of trade has grown substantially (quantity bb' of commodity B plus aa' of commodity A).

If Country Y simultaneously underwent an expansion of its export supply, *both* countries' respective offer curves would shift outward, and some new equilibrium, such as R'', would result. Whether, under such circumstances, the resultant terms of trade, OT'', ultimately favor one country or the other as compared with the original terms of trade, OT, depends on the relative magnitude of the export supply changes occurring in each country. Assuming demand conditions to be unchanged, that country undergoing the greatest export supply expansion will find its terms of trade deteriorating.

Suppose, on the other hand, that the supply of *import-competing* goods expands instead. The reason for this might be an increase in the supply of the scarce productive factor or a rise in factor productivity in the import-competing sector. This would tend to result in a *backward* shift in the affected nation's offer curve and, everything else equal, an improvement in its terms of trade. The nation would then import only at the reduced prices obtaining for its own import-competing production, and the resultant fall in import prices would cause the terms of trade to improve.

Given two countries, X and Y, the net effect on the terms of trade of a rise in the supply of import-competing goods in *both* countries depends on the relative strength of the respective supply shifts. If the supply in-

crease attributable to changing factor supplies or factor productivity is
relatively greater in Country X, then its terms of trade will improve, and
those of Country Y will deteriorate. The reverse is equally true. The
reader can trace this out for himself by using intersection R'' in Figure
7–1 as a starting point and working back to the intersection at R. The
result in any case is a substantial decline in the *volume* of international
trade.

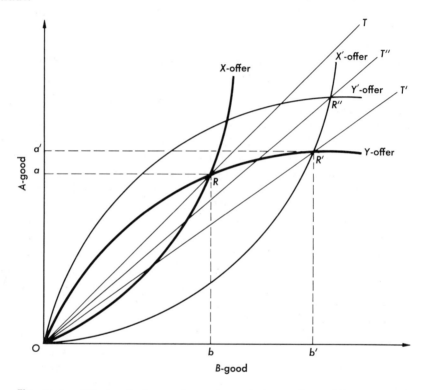

Fig. 7–1. Effects of changed supply and demand conditions upon the
volume and terms of trade.

Suppose, finally, that Country X undergoes a significant expansion of
output in the export sector, and Country Y simultaneously expands production in its import-competing sector, both due to shifts in factor supplies
or factor efficiency. Country X would find export prices falling for two
reasons—its own expanded export supply and its trading partner's increased
import-competing supply. Naturally, under *ceteris paribus* conditions, the
terms of trade of Country X will deteriorate as X's offer increases and
Y's offer is reduced.

Figure 7–1 can also be used to help explain the impact of changes in *demand* on the volume and terms of trade. Let us go back to the original case, where the two countries' respective offer curves intersect at point *R*, and the terms of trade are given by the slope of line *OT*. Now Country *X* for some reason undergoes a large increase in its demand for imports. In expanding its purchases of import good *A*, the price of imports rises and its terms of trade deteriorate from *OT* to *OT'*.

Again, there has been an outward shift in Country *X*'s offer curve, and a new equilibrium is reached at point *R'*. *X* finds that it must offer a great deal more of its export good (*bb'*) for only slightly more imports (*aa'*). If the increase in domestic demand is *general,* at once encompassing import goods *and* export goods, the deterioration of the terms of trade will not be as great. Although import prices still rise, export prices also increase due to the reduced supply available for sale abroad, and the deterioration of the terms of trade is kept in check.

Finally, if *both* countries undergo an increase in the demand for imports, *both* offer curves will expand outward and some new equilibrium such as *R''* will be reached. Assuming supply conditions to be constant, that country with the greatest expansion of demand for import goods will find that its terms of trade have deteriorated compared to what they were originally.

As a general proposition, any development which has as its result an increased national supply of export goods, a reduced national supply of import-competing goods, or an increased national demand for import goods—everything else being equal—will tend to lead to an increase in the volume of trade and a decline in the terms of trade of a nation. Conversely, developments leading to a reduced supply of export goods, a reduced demand for import goods, and an increased supply of import-competing goods tend to result in an improvement in a nation's terms of trade.

In actuality, the impact of a change in domestic or foreign supply or demand conditions on a given nation's terms of trade depends largely on the shape of the offer curve of its trading partner. From Figure 7–1, it is easy to see that no shift in Country *X*'s offer curve will result in a change in its terms of trade, if Country *Y*'s offer curve is a straight line (perfectly elastic). The more elastic the trading partner's offer curve, therefore, the less will be the impact of domestic supply or demand changes on a country's terms of trade.

The kind of supply and demand shifts, and their international consequences, discussed here may indeed occur in a *static* context—for example, as a result of crop failures or such government policy shifts as tariffs. They may also develop in a *dynamic* context in the process of economic growth, fundamentally affecting relative factor supplies and factor productivities and hence international comparative advantage and terms of trade. This dimension is explained in Section E-7.

TECHNOLOGY TRANSFERS

What happens when we impose changes in technology upon our model of international trade based on comparative costs? International differences in technology themselves constitute a prime reason for the existence of international trade, according to this model. These along with the other elements result in the intercountry differences in productive conditions, upon which the theory is founded. The U.S. is well-advanced in the technology of agriculture, and we thus find farm commodities to be prominent among America's exports. Japan has acquired the technology needed to mass-produce high quality, compact automobiles, and it is hardly surprising to find Japanese passenger cars gaining rapidly in the important automotive markets of the world. Such examples of international differences in technology giving rise to trade are not difficult to find, and they suggest ways in which technological change may affect the direction and volume of trade, as well as the respective economic structures of the participating nations.

As a more formal example, suppose we take two countries, the U.S. and the Philippines, producing two commodities, sugar and sewing machines. The relevant transformation functions, if these were the sole commodities produced, would appear roughly as we see them in Figure 7–2. The U.S. can produce substantial quantities of both goods, along CD, while the Philippines is able to produce a respectable quantity of sugar (OB), but no sewing machines. Its production-possibilities frontier is therefore really a single point B, the maximum quantity of sugar that can be produced, since lack of technology precludes any production of sewing machines. The two countries trade with one another at the terms of trade, P, and both are better off as a result. If both countries possess equivalent resource endowments, and other conditions of production are the same, trade in this instance may be entirely attributed to differences in technology.

Now imagine that the American know-how is somehow transferred to the Philippines. As soon as the new technology has fully entered the productive process, the Philippine production possibilities are altered from B to AB. Before the infusion of technology, the Philippines produced at point B, exported quantity bB of sugar to the U.S. in return for bS of sewing machines at the prevailing terms of trade, p, and consumed at point S. After the technological transfer, and assuming for simplicity that the terms of trade remain the same, Philippine production moves to point E on curve AB. It now exports hE of sewing machines in return for hS' of sugar and is thereby enabled to consume at point S'. Note that the direction of trade has changed, and that Philippine economic structure has been completely altered.

The U.S., origin of the technological transfer, continues to produce at

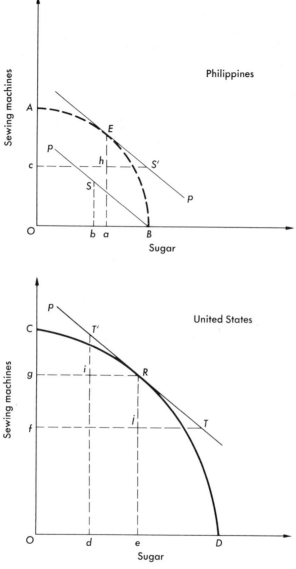

Fig. 7–2. Impact of technological transfers.

point R, assuming that the terms of trade are unchanged, undergoing no structural shift in its economy. Its consumption point, however, does change from T to T', and it converts from being a sewing-machine exporter and sugar importer to the role of sugar exporter and sewing-machine importer. The U.S. thus loses its comparative advantage in sewing-machine production to the Philippines and gains, in turn, a comparative advantage in the production of sugar. All of this is based on changing international differences in useful knowledge, or technology.

Technological transfers have enhanced economic well-being in one country without simultaneously reducing it in the other nation. This is in no way limited to transfers of knowledge from one country to another but applies equally to internally generated technological change which affects different industries in different nations at different times. The more a nation invests in "human capital" and basic research, or is able to adopt the knowledge developed in other nations, the more likely it is that technology will bring about a fundamental change in its economic structure and in its patterns of international trade.

Trade in innumerable commodities could be characterized as being profoundly affected by technological change. Aside from agricultural commodities and automobiles, already mentioned, there are all types of chemicals, aircraft, machine tools, textiles, earthmoving machinery, and communications equipment, to name just a few. The patterns of world trade are continually shifting, and differential change in technology is one of the most important underlying forces.

This points up the degree of subtlety involved in the analysis of the impact of technological change on the character of trade in the international economy. Technological progress most frequently occurs in the advanced, highly industrialized countries of the world, and a perpetual technological advantage on the part of these countries might even be considered *detrimental* to world trade. But technology is so easily transferable that such a case can be dismissed as generally unrealistic. Still, technology is not *perfectly* mobile. If it were—if each technical advance is immediately available to all supplies throughout the world—then technology would be eliminated as a cause of differing productive conditions internationally and, hence, as a cause of international trade. In point of fact, of course, there is a distinct lag in the dissemination of technological innovations, accented by patents and the institutional factors which effectively hinder their spread. Technological differences thus continue to play an important role in determining the patterns of international commerce.

TECHNOLOGY AND RELATIVE FACTOR SUPPLIES

Within the framework of the factor-endowments theory, technological change enters into the determination of trade flows in another way as well. Suppose a particular technological innovation results in a substantial saving of labor—that is, less labor is needed to produce a given quantum of output. Is not such labor-saving technological change analogous in its effects to an actual increase in labor supplies? Would the same thing not also be true of capital-saving technological change? In the first instance, the capital–labor ratio in production is raised and in the second case it is lowered. Finally, a technological innovation that influences the productivity of capital and labor in an identical manner (and is therefore neutral), leaves the capital–labor ratio unchanged but has an effect similar to an expansion of the supplies of both productive factors.

Referring to Figure 7–3, suppose a nation is producing quantity Ob of labor-intensive good X and Oe of capital-intensive good Y at point A on the (labor-abundant) transformation curve X_1Y_1. At the terms of

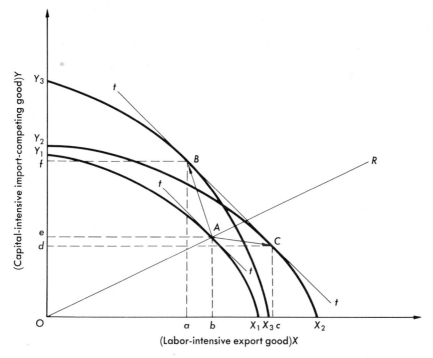

Fig. 7–3. Labor-saving and capital-saving technological change.

trade tt, the country exporting good X and importing good Y specializes in the production of the labor-intensive commodity in which it has a comparative advantage.

Now suppose a labor-saving innovation occurs. This permits a substantial expansion of output in the labor-intensive industry but only a moderate increase of production in the capital-intensive industry, as represented by the new transformation curve X_2Y_2. If the terms of trade remain the same, tt, production will shift from point A to point C. Output of the export good X is expanded by quantity bc while production of the import-competing good Y is reduced by quantity de. A labor-saving innovation equally applicable to all industries in a labor-abundant nation would thus appear to result in an expansion of both exports and imports.

Suppose, alternatively, that a capital-saving innovation occurs, which allows significant output expansion in the capital-intensive import-competing industry and much less of a production increase in the labor-intensive export industry. The corresponding transformation curve is X_3Y_3. Again assuming that the terms of trade remain unchanged at tt, production shifts from point A to point B. This time, output of the labor-intensive export good X is reduced by quantity ab, and production of the capital-intensive import-competing good Y is expanded by quantity ef. Clearly, this type of innovation would tend to reduce the overall volume of trade on both the export and the import sides.

In the case of technological change that affects all segments of an economy simultaneously, then, the following would seem to be true: Innovations that save the relatively abundant factors of production tend to expand the volume of both imports and exports (ultra-export-biased), while innovations that save the relatively scarce factors tend to reduce the volume of international trade on both the export and the import side (ultra-import-biased). The former strengthen the existing basis of comparative advantage, while the latter work in opposition to it. By the same reasoning, it should be evident that *neutral* technological innovations result in an expansion of output of *both* commodities, have no effect on the *shape* of the transformation curve, and cause an increase in exports of whatever goods the country specializes in producing that is somewhat larger than the resultant reduction in imports (export-biased).

It is next possible to drop the assumption that a given innovation affects both export and import-competing goods at once. Suppose we are again faced with a labor-abundant country specializing in the production of labor-intensive goods for export and importing capital-intensive commodities. Although it is beyond the scope of this book, it can be shown that a neutral innovation that occurs in the export industry will cause an expansion of both the volume of exports and the volume of imports (ultra-export-biased), while a neutral innovation occurring in the import-competing industry will prove to be ultra-import-biased. Labor-saving innovations will be ultra-export-biased if they occur in the export industry, and indeterminate in their effects if they occur in the import-competing industry. Finally, the effects of capital-saving innovations will be indeterminate if they occur in the export industry and ultra-import-biased if they occur in the import-competing industry.

To conclude, we should note that, according to the analysis presented at the beginning of this chapter, the assumption of constant relative commodity prices is unrealistic. Our conclusions concerning the impact of technological change must therefore be modified somewhat. Innovations that prove to be import-biased or ultra-import-biased will tend to raise the price of the export good relative to the import-competing good by improving the terms of trade. Export-biased or ultra-export-biased innovations will have the opposite effect, resulting in a deterioration of a nation's terms of trade—a reduction of the prices of export goods relative to import-competing goods. The resultant changes in relative commodity prices will cause the trade and production bias of any given innovation to be somewhat less pronounced than indicated above in the absence of terms of trade shifts.

FACTOR SUPPLIES AND TRADE

We have seen how changes in relative supplies of productive factors, as well as technological change, can affect the economic structure of a nation, as well as the volume and pattern of its international trade. Is it not also likely that international trade may itself influence the supplies of productive factors?

We know that trade tends to increase the relative scarcity of the abundant factor of production. In so doing, it tends to raise the relative price of the abundant factor. If productive factor supplies are presumed to be sensitive to prospective earnings, increases in factor returns will tend to result in a growth of the available supplies of that factor. For instance, in a labor-abundant country trade would tend to raise the relative wage rate, increase the labor force participation rate, and/or the average number of man hours worked per man, and thus effectively enhance the supply of labor.

The reverse happens in the case of the scarce factor of production. Trade tends to lower the relative returns paid to that factor by making it less scarce. By the above reasoning, this may lead to a partial withdrawal from the factor market and a commensurate reduction in available supplies.

In the absence of international movements of the factors of production themselves, we would be led to conclude that international trade tends to *increase* the differences in factor endowments that prevail between countries. It tends to raise the relative returns paid to abundant factors, and thereby induces further additions to the existing supplies of those factors. By reducing the relative scarcity of factors in short supply and thus lowering the relative returns paid to them, trade tends to result in additional reductions in available supplies of scarce factors. It tends to enhance the abundance of abundant factors as well as the scarcity of scarce factors. In this way, trade itself tends to enhance the comparative advantage basis for international trade based on differences in relative factor endowments.

REVERSAL IN FACTOR INTENSITIES

The fact that changes over time in relative factor supplies and efficiencies can influence—even reverse—the conditions of international trade is clear. This, for example, might result from a growth in factor supplies so that the scarce factor eventually becomes the abundant factor, and vice-versa. Applying the traditional factor-endowments analysis, the tendency would be for the commodity composition to shift with exportables becoming importables, and importables becoming exportables. The second way in which this reversal can occur involves changes in production functions; for example, a labor-intensive good becomes a capital-intensive good as a result of technological change. This would tend to reverse the commodity composition of trade in the absence of any change in relative factor supplies.

The factor-endowments theory requires that production functions be decidedly biased. Production of a given commodity is deemed to require that one particular factor of production be used intensively. For example, wheat is best produced land-intensively, consumer durables capital-intensively, and so forth, implying that a given commodity will always be characterized by either capital-, labor-, or land-intensity.

Suppose, however, that production functions need not be biased at all, or that their bias changes as technology advances. The first instance is demonstrated in Figure 7–4, with unbiased production functions represented by the symmetrical isoquants for goods X and Y. Both commodities can be equally well produced using either labor or capital.

If prevailing factor prices are as represented by isocosts lk and $l'k'$, it is easy to see that production of commodity X at point A is more labor-intensive than production of commodity Y at point B (employing Oh of labor and Oa of capital, and Og of labor and Ob of capital, respectively). By way of contrast, if factor prices happen to be as represented by isocosts l_2k_2 and $l_2'k_2'$, the production of commodity Y at point C will be more labor-intensive than production of commodity X at point D (using Of of labor and Oc of capital, and Oe of labor and Od of capital, respectively).

It can be shown that commodity X will indeed be more labor-intensive at factor price ratios that lead to production points to the left of point T, and that commodity Y will be the more labor-intensive at price ratios leading to factor combinations to the right of point T. Whenever we are faced with symmetrical production functions, therefore, we must expect factor reversal to occur. Therefore, under these conditions, factor endowments *do not necessarily determine* which commodities a nation will export and import. Hence, the factor-reversal hypothesis casts serious doubt on the validity of the factor-endowments theory in a static sense, at least in the case of certain commodities. Most probably labor-biased, capital-biased, and symmetrical production functions all exist across the range of interna-

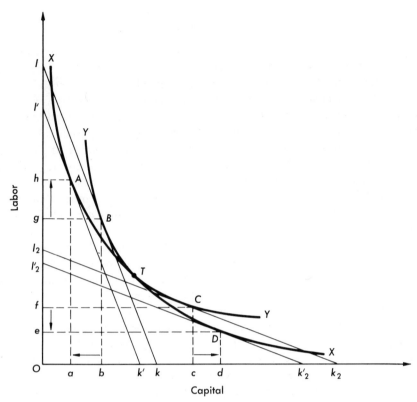

Fig. 7–4. Factor-intensity reversal.

	Price Ratio (L/K)	
	(slope of $lk = l'k'$)	(slope of $l_2k_2 = l_2'k_2'$)
Capital input X	Oa	Oe
Labor input X	Oh	Od
Capital input Y	Ob	Of
Labor input Y	Og	Oc
Labor-intensive good	X ⟶ Y	
Capital-intensive good	Y ⟶ X	

tionally traded commodities. For some commodities, therefore, the factor-endowments theory might be a reliable predictor, while for others it might not.

To this must be added the fact that production functions tend to be altered over time as a result of changing technology. Labor-biased production functions may become capital-biased, and vice-versa, causing a reversal of commodity flows. Or labor and capital-biased production functions may become symmetrical, with the opposite also possible.

DECREASING OPPORTUNITY COSTS

Up to now we have assumed that pure competition prevails in all markets, and that the cost structures, internal and external, of the producing units must adhere to those possible under this form of market structure. Only constant and increasing costs, or *increasing returns,* were ignored as a possibility since the definition of pure competition precludes the realization of internal economies of large-scale production. In the long run, all purely competitive firms are presumed to be operating at optimal plant size, and economies of large-scale production are not possible. Moreover, external economies, such as transport and communications facilities, are much more likely to play an important role under market structures other than pure competition, where the average size of producing entities normally is much larger.

Recall that the theory of international trade presented thus far attributes the existence of trade to differences in the conditions of production in different countries, which result in inter-country differences in relative costs and prices. What gives rise to these differences in production conditions? Variations in climate, soil conditions, and the character of the people were mentioned earlier as possible explanations, and obviously these contribute to international cost differences. But, when we talk about the highly complex industrial processes that characterize modern economic activity, production cost differentials between countries are likely to be attributable in large measure to international technological differences and to realized internal and external economies of scale in production. Trade in manufactured goods between such highly industrialized countries as Germany and the Netherlands, or the U.S. and Japan, would seem to be attributable, at least in part, to such factors.

Perhaps even more important to our understanding is the fact that pure competition simply does not present a realistic picture of market structures in today's developed economies, which contribute the lion's share to world trade. Few industries, if any, come close to the purely competitive model. Hence, the possibilities for decreasing opportunity costs are many and varied, and they may be just as characteristic of the real world as constant or increasing opportunity costs. There is ample justification for investigating the operation of international trade under such conditions. In this analysis, we shall once again ignore transport costs for the sake of simplicity.

Referring to Figure 7–5, instead of the conventional concave production possibilities frontier that prevails under conditions of increasing opportunity costs, *AB,* a nation's transformation curve approximates curve *AC.* Whereas wheat production is characterized by increasing opportunity costs, the manufacture of cloth is not. If cloth output is expanded beyond the flexion point N, where curve AC changes from concave to convex to the origin, the country will find that significant economies of scale may be realized in the cloth sector. These scale economies are assumed to be sufficiently powerful to outweigh elements which increase opportunity costs so that, on net, *decreasing opportunity costs* prevail in the cloth sector. While the realism of this assumption may be questioned, we shall retain it for the time being.

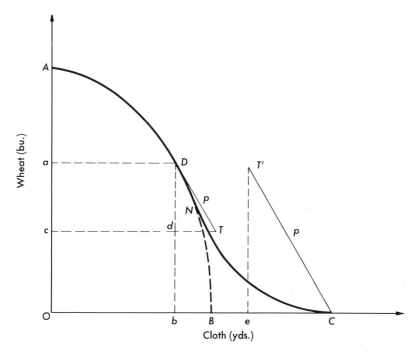

Fig. 7–5. Trade and production with decreasing opportunity costs prevailing for one commodity.

Suppose the country has been engaged in trade for some time, and that the cloth–wheat terms of trade have settled at p. The country produces Oa of wheat and Ob of cloth at point D, exports quantity dD of wheat in return for dT of cloth, and consumes at point T. It is specializing to a moderate degree in wheat production and realizes some gains from international trade, since point T lies outside its transformation curve. But what if output for some reason moves beyond N toward point C? Immediately it would be apparent that opportunity cost-reducing economies of large-scale production are realizeable through further increases in cloth production. Along the segment of the curve C, less and less wheat would have to be sacrificed for each additional yard of cloth produced. Conse-

quently, production would very quickly shift to point C—complete specialization in the production of cloth. If the terms of trade remained at p,
quantity eC of cloth could be exported in return for cT' of wheat, and
consumption could move to point T'. T' (or any point along the terms of
trade line going through point C) is apparently superior to T.

While the movement toward *complete* specialization may be out of the
question, the possibility nonetheless remains that a country can benefit substantially by specializing, at least partially, in those sectors for which
economies of scale are most significant.

The basic comparative cost theory of international trade thus may be
modified to encompass yet another economic phenomenon—economies of
scale as they affect opportunity costs. This serves to render the theoretical
framework still less narrow, and to enhance its usefulness as a predictor of
trade flows in the real world.

TRANSPORTATION COSTS AND ECONOMIC DISTANCE

We may now relax another of our earlier assumptions. We need no
longer stipulate the complete absence of transportation costs between countries by simply integrating this important consideration into the analysis.
What are transportation costs? Perhaps most clearly defined, they constitute the difference between the *value* of a commodity as it leaves the
production point and its *value* as it arrives at its destination. Defined
in this way, transport costs would include such items as freight charges,
insurance premiums, an interest provision for the time the goods are in
transit, as well as loading and unloading costs.

Suppose the price of wheat is $2.00 per bushel in Canada and $3.00
per bushel in the U.S. Ignoring transportation charges the Canadian price
is $1.00 less than the U.S. price. But this is hardly the relevant compari-
son. We need to know precisely how much *both* Canadian and U.S. wheat
sell for in a single, given market. By the time the Canadian wheat reaches
Houston, Texas, for instance, its price might actually be equal to that
of the competing U.S. commodity, thereby eliminating its former competitive edge. More generally, transportation costs cause international price
relationships to differ from what they would have been in the absence
of such charges. As such, they reduce the volume of trade, limit the gains
to be derived from trade, alter the trading nations' respective economic
structures, and may under certain conditions even change the direction
of international trade. In short, transportation charges importantly affect
comparative costs and everything connected with them.

Precisely how transport cost or, to use a better term, *economic distance*,
bears on international trade flows can easily be demonstrated in Figure 7–6,
which is nothing more than an elaboration of the diagram in Figure 5–3.

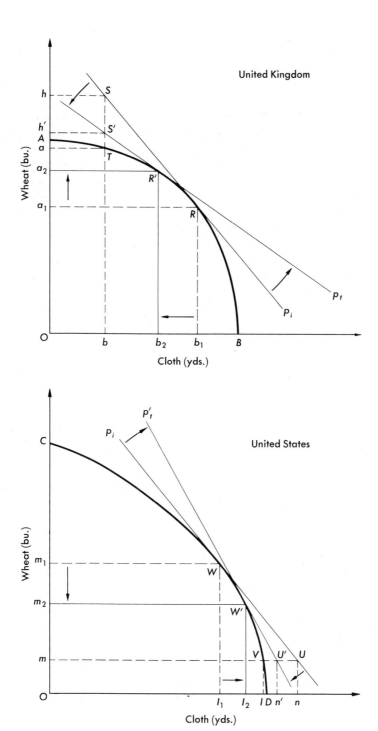

Fig. 7-6. Impact of transportation costs.

109

Suppose the international cloth–wheat exchange ratio—the commodity terms of trade—came to rest at p_i with trade between the U.S. and the U.K. under way for some time in the absence of all transportation costs. The U.K. is producing at point R and consuming at S, while the U.S. produces at point W and consumes at U. Both consumption points, of course, are located on the commodity terms of trade line.

Now let us introduce transport costs. Their incorporation results in both an increase in the price of imported cloth for the U.S. and an increase in the imported wheat price for the U.K., assuming all goods entering trade are sold on FOB terms.[3] Hence, the commodity terms of trade—the price of exports divided by the price of imports—move against *both* countries, from p_i to p_t for the U.K., and from p_i to p_t' for the U.S. The U.K. is now forced to consume along p_t, and the U.S. along line p_t'. The U.K. moves from consumption point S to S', and the U.S. shifts its consumption from point U to U'.

This assumes that domestic consumption of the *export* good remains constant in both countries. But since the relative price of the export product is lower in both countries with transport costs than without them, the likelihood is that more of the export good will be consumed in each nation. In the U.K., the actual consumption point is thus likely to fall to the right of S' on line p_t, while in the U.S. the consumption points will probably fall to the left of U' on p_t'. In any case the loss of consumption, as compared with the respective no-transport cost consumption points S and U, is clear.

Production shifts from point R and R' in the U.K., and from W to W' in the U.S. Both countries thus simultaneously reduce the degree of specialization in the production of that commodity in which they have a comparative advantage, and both are less well off as a result of the imposition of transportation costs. Transport charges, measured in terms of the two traded commodities, are hh' bushels of wheat for U.K. imports and nn' yards of cloth for U.S. imports.

The addition of the economic distance, or transportation cost, consideration thus represents an important modification of the theoretical structure of international trade relationships that we have constructed. It reduces the differences in comparative prices of delivered commodities internationally. By so doing, it cuts down the gains derived from trade as well as the overall volume of trade. In the absence of transport costs, the ratios of commodity prices are identical in all trading nations, but with transport costs they are not. If the international terms of trade in the absence of transport costs are close enough to the pre-trade domestic price ratio prevail-

---

[3] FOB stands for "free on board," meaning that the purchaser, and not the seller, pays all of the charges connected with transporting the goods beyond a specified point.

ing in one of the countries, transportation costs can cause trade to cease altogether. Finally, it should be noted that economic distance normally does not affect the *direction* of trade, but does influence the degree of national specialization in production, and therefore economic structure.

The impact of economic distance, as presented in Figure 7–6, can be summarized as follows, assuming once more that consumption of the export good is given:

	United Kingdom	United States
Production:		
In isolation..............................	T	V
With trade..............................	R	W
With trade and transport costs.............	R'	W'
Consumption:		
In isolation..............................	T	V
With trade..............................	S	U
With trade and transport costs.............	S'	U'
Terms of trade:		
Without transport costs....................	P_i	P_i
With transport costs......................	P_t	P'_t
Gains from trade:		
Without transport costs...................	ah(bu. of wheat)	l_n(yds. of cloth)
With transport costs......................	ah'(bu. of wheat)	l_n'(yds. of cloth)

A somewhat less comprehensive but nonetheless instructive presentation of the effect of transportation costs on international trade may be undertaken by means of a partial equilibrium, supply and demand analysis. Figure 7–7 depicts supply and demand curves for wheat and cloth in the U.S. and the U.K.

Without trade, we shall assume that the price (in terms of the currency of one of the two countries) of cloth is Oj in the U.K. and Oj' in the U.S., and that of wheat is Oi in the U.K. and Oi' in the U.S. With free and essentially costless trade between the two countries, the price of wheat and cloth will naturally equalize. In the U.S. the price of the import good, cloth, will fall, and the price of the export good, wheat, will rise. The reverse happens in the U.K.

Let us say that the common post-trade price of wheat is p' and that of cloth is p. At this price, the U.K. produces cloth at point c', consumes at d', and exports $c'd'$ to the U.S., which is thereby enabled to consume b' of cloth while only producing at point a'. Britain's excess cloth production is fully absorbed by U.S. imports, and the volume of trade in cloth is $a'b'$ (or $c'd'$) yards. Note that the price of cloth is higher than it would have been without trade in the exporting country, and lower than in the absence of trade in the importing country. The imposition of transport costs (t) lowers the price of cloth in the exporting country (U.K.) somewhat, and raises it in the importing country, thus simultaneously reducing the *volume* of trade from $a'b'$ (or $c'd'$) to ab (or cd) yards of cloth.

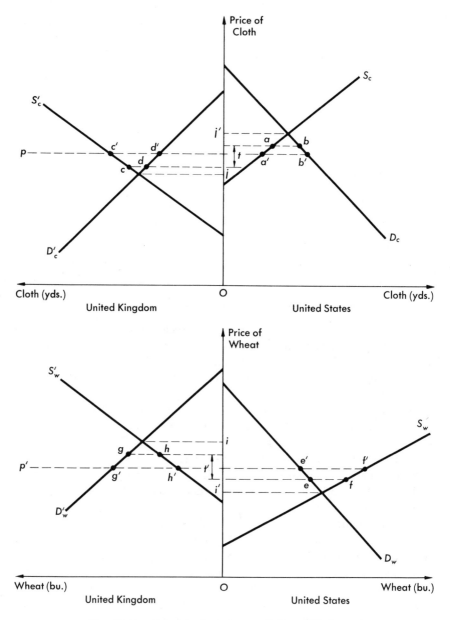

Fig. 7–7. Transport costs: partial equilibrium.

The reader may trace out in similar fashion the effect of transport costs for trade in wheat, in Figure 7–7. Even in such simple terms, the various effects of economic distance can be gauged. It reduces the volume of trade, causes prices of the same commodity to differ between the trading partners, and reduces the degree of specialization in production on the part of the countries concerned. In fact, if the cost of transportation exceeds the pre-trade, inter-country difference in the prices of a given commodity, there will be no scope for international trade at all. Again, this is the same conclusion reached in the earlier, more comprehensive *general equilibrium* analysis.

We mentioned that transport costs will generally not influence the *direction* of international trade. This is true only so long as transportation changes are nondiscriminatory with respect to the origin of the traded commodities. If transatlantic shipment of a barrel of beer costs $2.00 whether it is being transported from Germany to the U.S. or from the U.S. to Germany, transportation costs may cut down the volume of trade. But the determination of who exports to whom—the direction of trade—will remain comparatively unaffected. Yet if the shipping companies charge the American brewery $2.00 a barrel for shipment to Germany, but charge his German competitor only $1.00 to transport a barrel of beer to the U.S., transportation clearly will exert a distortive influence on trade *patterns* as well. While the U.S. might possess a comparative advantage in beer production and would therefore be expected to export beer to Germany, trade in this commodity under such discriminatory conditions may actually move in the opposite direction.

LOCATION AND TRANSPORTATION

The discussion of transportation costs should have made the reader aware of the importance of this factor in international trade, in spite of the fact that most of our trade models were constructed under the assumption of zero economic distance—the complete absence of transport costs. In reality, of course, we can scarcely ignore the role of economic distance. It is important not only from the standpoint of what it costs to transport goods from one geographical location to another, but also from point of the interest charges incurred during the time goods are in transit, as well as changes in market and supply conditions that may take place during the transport interval.

Think of a steel mill, an auto assembly plant, a machine tool factory, or any other industrial facility. Why is each located where it is? On the demand side, it clearly is desirable that the site be close to the major markets for its output. On the supply side it must have sufficient access to labor, raw materials, and other inputs. Hence, it should be close to the sources of supply. Both sets of considerations are intimately related to transportation costs, and some sort of optimal balance must be struck among demand elements, supply factors, *and* economic distance. This is the task of *location theory*, sometimes called *space economics* or the *economics of distance.*

Just as the economics of location operate within the confines of a nation's economic frontiers, they are also important in determining the location of economic activity internationally and, hence, in governing the patterns of international trade. There has been relatively little theoretical analysis of the interrelationships between trade and location, and what follows is little more than a delineation of some of the considerations that must be taken into account.

Transport costs affect different commodities in different ways. Frozen strawberries require an entirely different type of shipment than cement. It costs more to transport a small, private aircraft weighing 2,000 pounds than an automobile weighing 4,000 pounds. It is more expensive to ship some commodities a few hundred miles from Santos, Brazil, to a village in the interior than from Santos to Rotterdam, Holland. Such examples, multiplied a thousandfold in order to encompass all traded commodities, all possible directions of trade, plus the various alternative modes of transportation, convey an idea of the degree of complexity involved in attempting to apply transportation and location considerations to international trade. To this problem must be added the internal economics of the various transportation industries, which result in the added complexity of differing and often discriminatory shipping charges for similar, and sometimes identical, services provided.

COMMODITY ORIENTATION

It is possible to begin untangling the web of factors affecting location internationally by classifying commodities according to their orientation with regard to both supply and demand. If a commodity must be produced in close proximity to the source of supply of raw material and intermediate good inputs, we say it is *supply-oriented*. If, on the other hand, the cost of transporting inputs is a minor consideration relative to the benefits derived from having final production located close to the ultimate market, we say that a good is *demand-oriented*. Finally, if a good falls into neither category, it is called *neutral* with respect to its location orientation.

An important characteristic of *supply-oriented* goods is that the cost of transporting the inputs, including fuels, to the primary markets exceeds the cost of shipping the final product. Hence, we often find that such industries locate economically (but not necessarily geographically) near the sources of raw materials. In aluminum refining, for instance, we find the major plants near large-scale sources of electric power even when the major raw material, bauxite, is accessible only through proximate water transportation. Plants must be located close to the source of the electric power because the abundant power required to convert the bauxite to alumina has very high transmission costs.

Similarly, fruit and vegetable processing is generally located close to the sources of raw material supply in the farm areas. Many agricultural commodities lose weight in the manufacturing process and hence are cheaper to transport in the processed state; peas lose their pods, corn, its husks and cobs, coconut, its shell, and so forth. Forest products, fish, steel, and poultry, production also fall within the category of supply orientation.

For some commodities the cause-and-effect relationships between supply and transport costs for the various inputs are much more complex than for others. If production locates internationally according to supply characteristics (largely dictated by the cost of transportation), it follows logically that changes in transport conditions may well result in substantial shifts in the location of output and, hence, in the direction of international trade. The development of modern, large capacity cargo aircraft, for instance, has not only expanded the market of existing producers of goods ranging from orchids to transistors to cattle, but has affected the locus of production as well. Anyone visiting industrial sites such as the one adjacent to Shannon International Airport in Ireland, and other facilities constructed along similar lines throughout the world, will appreciate the future importance of changing modes of air transport. Developments in other means of transport also have brought about similar, sometimes even more spectacular, changes. Containerization of cargo, the Panama Canal, and the interstate highway system in the U.S. are but a few examples. Of course these, plus such basic innovations as the railroad, the automobile, the steamship, and transport aircraft give an idea of the magnitude of the changes wrought by transportation, both internationally and nationally.

Demand-oriented goods are less attracted to the sources of raw material supply than they are to the major origins of market demand. Sometimes, but not always, these may be characterized as size- or weight-gaining commodities. We can usually classify as weight-gaining those commodities for which water is a major component of the final weight, e.g., soft drinks.

Automobile assembly in large countries generally occurs close to the primary markets, with components shipped in from supplier plants all over the nation. The bulk of an automobile is substantially greater than all of its parts shipped individually. If the transport cost of the final commodity tends to exceed that of its raw material or component inputs, therefore, the locus of production tends to be near the market.

In some instances, the nature of a good or service requires the ultimate consumer or user to transport himself to it. Examples include dry cleaners, cinemas, auto laundries, and gasoline stations, all of which are of necessity located very close to the market. In other cases, industries require their customers to travel long distances despite the fact that they are primarily demand-oriented. Tourism is one, and specialized medical services fall into the same category. You cannot move the Alps, the Grand Canyon, or Paris to potential tourists any more than you can move the Mayo Clinic to its patients.

Perishable commodities are still strongly influenced by the market with respect to the locus of production, but this is changing with the evolution of transport systems. Pastry and other baked goods produced locally are running into heavy competition from national suppliers of frozen or pre-baked products. The consumption of strawberries, for instance, is neither restricted to those who live within a radius of 50 or 100 miles of the producer, nor limited in distribution to a few short weeks out of the year.

Neutral commodities are goods that are pulled neither to the sources of input supply nor to the origin of market demand in the location of their manufacture. If a commodity is extremely valuable, such as furs, diamonds, or scientific instruments, transportation costs may be of very little significance in relation to the cost of the good as a whole. Hence, it is of minor importance in determining the locus of production. Other commodities may be neither weight nor volume gaining or losing, thus making production at the supply or demand point equally logical.

In such instances, production tends to occur at either the supply or the demand point. It will generally not be in between unless a transfer from one *mode* of transportation to another is called for. In the petroleum industry, for example, it does not make much difference from a transport-cost standpoint whether the crude oil is refined before it is pumped aboard tankers in the oil-producing areas or after it is discharged at the destination. There is not much variation in weight or bulk between crude petroleum and its products. However, by the time it has been discharged from the low-cost (sea) mode of transportation and transferred to a high-cost (road or rail) transport for final distribution in the market centers, the refining process has generally been completed. Thus numerous ports of entry adjacent to major water routes have turned into refining centers. On the other hand, the tankship may discharge crude oil directly into a pipeline network, and then the refinery is likely to be located at the other end.

For most neutral commodities the location of the processing point, at one end of the transport route or the other, depends partly on the nature of the product itself and the character of demand in the market it serves. The more specialized the market demand, the more likely it is that the processing point will be close to the source of supply of raw materials, since it makes little sense to locate manufacturing near a market which absorbs only a fraction of the total output, the remainder having to be transshipped to other markets.

Since the point of manufacture of neutral commodities has little to do with transport costs, either because they are relatively unimportant as a component of final cost or because they are more or less identical for raw materials and finished products, we can apply the theory of international trade directly as it was developed earlier. These commodities are the ones for which trade is most likely to behave as we would expect, according to the theory of comparative costs, without significant modifications to account for transportation charges.

The classification of commodities into supply-oriented, demand-oriented, and neutral groupings is not meant to discount the manifold other factors that affect the location of production. A given commodity may be very supply- or demand-oriented but processing may still take place at some intermediate point because the required supply of skilled labor is not available elsewhere. Or location may be the result of tradition, entrepreneurship, the availability of external economies, benefits realized from concentration or agglomeration, or any of a host of factors, some of which may well outweigh transportation costs as a determinant of the locus of production. Transport considerations are important and may be a determining location factor in the case of certain commodities, but they clearly should not be taken in every case as *the* important factor.

8

APPLYING THE MODEL

We now have a reasonably coherent model of international trade, as developed in the preceding chapters. The basic model takes into consideration factor availability and efficiency on the supply side, and relative preferences for goods and services on the demand side. It permits the determination of the volume, direction, and product composition of commerce among nations, as well as the gains derived from it and the distribution of these gains. Moreover, it indicates the impact of trade on national economic structure, on product and factor prices, and hence on income distribution. It can easily be adapted to account for such dimensions as transportation costs and economic growth. All in all, a rather impressive conceptual apparatus.

Now comes the critical question: Is the model any good? Good for what? For forecasting the impact of shifts in important variables on national and international economic activity. In this chapter we shall attempt to answer this question, and to present recent advances and revisions in the basic model designed to improve its predictive performance in the real world. Like the real world, what we end up with will be rather heterogeneous. It is clear that a valid a priori predictor of international trade flows will be extremely complex, encompassing all of the elements operating on both the supply and demand sides. Should we attribute international comparative cost differences primarily to varying levels of productivity or to different factor endowments? Would it not be best, in a complex multi-commodity, multi-country world simply to adopt the eclectic, plausible view that in the real world both factors play an important role? Will we be satisfied with the imprecise generalizations and predictions that the latter approach invariably yields?

MANY GOODS AND MANY COUNTRIES

So far, all of the analytical tools developed in order to help explain the operation of the international trade mechanism have been built on an extremely simplified, two-country, two-commodity basis. This was done purely for the sake of simplicity and, although the reader may feel that much more needs to be said, the general principles that arise out of such simple models do govern trade relationships between countries in an infinitely more complex international economy.

In reality, of course, trade is carried on *multilaterally* among the countries of the world. Our simple models implied that, if the U.S. exported good X to the U.K., it would receive *in return* a certain quantity of good Y, this trade to be governed by the principle of comparative advantage. This is *bilateral* trade. In fact, the U.S. may ship good X to the U.K. and receive nothing directly in return. Rather, the U.K. may ship good Y to South Africa, which in turn sells good W to the U.S. America has exported good X, for which it has received good W in a very indirect way. The U.S. trades bilaterally with the rest of the world *as a whole,* but multilaterally with other countries. Nevertheless, the principle of comparative advantage holds equally well in this far more complex situation as it does under the simple formal models developed earlier. Although two countries might possess identical transformation functions, they can still trade profitably and in large volume in a multi-commodity, multi-country world by simply trading with third countries whose transformation functions are different.

Let us say there are 86 different countries in the world trading multilaterally with one another. We then have a maximum of 7,310 possible directions in which goods may flow internationally. Furthermore, suppose there are 3,500 distinct commodities which may enter international trade. This leaves us with a grand total of 25,585,000 possible commodity flows with which to contend. Imagine, under such circumstances, trying to predict the precise direction of world commodity trade on the basis of comparative costs! An impossible task, to be sure, especially since comparative costs are constantly undergoing change, as we have seen. The conditions which hold today may be quite different tomorrow as a result of a multitude of economic and non-economic factors, and yet we find that the tools which we have developed are extremely useful, in a very general way, in the analysis of direction, volume, commodity composition, and the gains from international trade.

To illustrate, let us take four representative countries—France, the U.K., Germany, and the U.S.—each of which produces two commodities, automobiles and corn. Suppose, in the absence of trade, the relative prices of the two commodities in the various countries (denominated in domestic units of account) might be as follows:

Country	Standard Automobile	Corn (bu.)
France	10,000	40
United Kingdom	500	5
Germany	2,000	10
United States	1,000	2

By comparing the domestic pre-trade price ratios of the two commodities for the various countries, a ranking of comparative advantage can be derived and some predictions made as to the general direction international trade will take. The U.S. has the greatest comparative advantage in corn production, while the U.K. holds the greatest comparative advantage in the manufacture of automobiles. The rankings, in order of greatest to least comparative advantage, would appear like this:

Country	Standard Automobile	Corn
France	3	2
United Kingdom	1	4
Germany	2	3
United States	4	1

Immediately, it is possible to state that in international trade, the U.K. will export automobiles for corn and that the U.S. will export corn in return for automobiles. Both can export these commodities to all of the other three nations since they possess a comparative advantage over all of them. But what about France and Germany? In automobile production, France has a comparative edge only over the U.S., while in corn production it has a comparative advantage over both Germany and the U.K. Most likely, it too will turn out to be a corn exporter and automobile importer. The reverse holds for Germany, which possesses a comparative advantage in corn only over the U.K. and in automobiles over both France and the U.S., and it should develop into an automobile exporter and corn importer.

All of this necessarily rests on the assumption that supply conditions, as governed by the principle of comparative advantage, are the sole factors of determining importance. In fact, of course, demand is equally significant as a factor affecting international trade flows, and the picture might be materially altered if this consideration were incorporated, as we shall do later on.

Just as a rough idea of the *pattern* of multi-country trade can be derived from an application of the principle of comparative costs, it is possible to gauge fairly readily the most likely *commodity composition* of a single country's trade with another country. It is only necessary once again to rank the various tradeable commodities in terms of comparative advantage. If we consider only two countries, Germany and Holland, the commodity in which Germany has the greatest comparative advantage must, by definition, be the one in which Holland has the greatest comparative disadvantage, and vice-versa. We could thus rank a series of tradeable goods in order of comparative advantage something like this:

Germany (rank)	Commodity	Holland (rank)
1	Machine tools	10
2	Automobiles	9
3	Chemicals	8
4	Pharmaceuticals	7
5	Optical equipment	6
6	Household appliances	5
7	Fluorescent lamps	4
8	Transport aircraft	3
9	Green vegetables	2
10	Tulip bulbs	1

With free international trade, it is fairly certain that the direction of trade in the first few commodities would be from Germany to Holland, and in the last several categories from Holland to Germany. But what about the others? The precise separation of imports and exports of the two countries is largely dependent upon the role of demand, as well as upon the rates of exchange of two national currencies. If the German demand for Dutch goods expands, relative to the demand for German goods on the part of Dutch buyers, the number of commodity categories Holland exports will grow. Here again, comparative advantage yields only a rough idea of the composition of trade. It must be amplified by demand considerations before any valid conclusions can be drawn.

By attempting to extend the theory of comparative advantage beyond the narrow limits of the two-country, two-commodity case, we thus find that a useful, if general, approximation can be made concerning the direction and commodity composition of trade among nations.

THE LEONTIEF PARADOX

Perhaps the most famous and controversial test of the Heckscher–Ohlin factor-endowments theory of comparative advantage was made by the Nobel Prizewinning economist Wassily W. Leontief and first published in 1953. According to the factor-endowments theory, a given country should be importing commodities requiring large amounts of productive factors which it finds to be in scarce supply domestically, and exporting those goods which intensively use factors in abundant supply at home. The U.S., which appears to have relatively abundant capital and scarce labor (i.e., a very high capital-labor ratio), would therefore clearly be exporting capital-intensive commodities and importing labor-intensive goods. Using data for the year 1947, Leontief came to the surprising conclusion that American exports actually appear to be labor-intensive and American imports capital-intensive—exactly the reverse of what the factor-endowments theory would lead us to believe.[1]

Does this finding—assuming the statistical methodology to be correct—disprove the Heckscher–Ohlin theory? A number of efforts have been made, by Leontief and others, to reconcile the contradictory statistical outcome with the theoretical indications:

1. If *human capital* as well as *physical capital* were included in the analysis, the results might have shown U.S. exports to be capital-intensive. That is, American labor may on the average be a good deal more efficient than foreign labor due to superior knowledge attributable to higher educational standards.
2. The American worker may be *physically* more effective than his foreign counterpart due to better health, working conditions, management, entrepreneurship, and so forth.
3. There are questions about the concept of capital employed in the analysis, especially the embodiment of capital in other productive factors.[2]
4. If natural resources are added as a third distinct productive factor, it is possible that the findings would show the U.S. to be both labor- and capital-abundant but short of natural resources. Testing this hypothesis might well result in a substantiation of the factor-endowments approach.[3]
5. Real-world conditions differ markedly from those presupposed to exist according to the factor-endowments theory. For example, there is no general full employment, production functions are not everywhere the same, there are many and varied barriers to trade, and most important of all, *demand* plays an important and often determining role in international commerce.

Two other economists, Irving B. Kravis and G. D. A. MacDougall, likewise discovered no empirical verification for the predictions of the fac-

[1] W. W. Leontief, "Domestic Production and Foreign Trade: The American Capital Position Re-examined," *Proceedings of the American Philosophical Society,* September, 1953; and "Factor Proportions and the Structure of American Trade: Further Theoretical and Empirical Analysis," *Review of Economics and Statistics,* November, 1956.

[2] Peter B. Kenen, "Nature, Capital and Trade," *Journal of Political Economy,* October, 1965.

[3] Janoslav Vanek, "The Natural Resource Content of Foreign Trade," *Review of Economic and Statistics,* September, 1959.

tor-endowments theory, although their respective methods were substantially less elaborate and comprehensive than that applied by Leontief.[4]

What about empirical test of the classical theory of comparative advantage based on differing production functions? Here the results are a bit more satisfactory. Bela Balassa finds that levels of productivity are a substantially better indicator of the direction of international trade than relative factor endowments.[5] Earlier, Irving Kravis had already indicated by comparing wage levels prevailing in the U.S. for industries concerned with production both for export and for the domestic market that labor productivity in export industries must be extraordinarily high. This lent credence to the classical notion of trade based on differing levels of factor productivity.

Finally, in the second part of his study on U.S.–British trade, MacDougall finds that there is a very high degree of correlation between labor productivity and export shares in trade between the two countries, again supporting the classical notion.[6]

What do we make of all this? The classical theory of comparative costs based on differences in productivity levels emerges as an important determinant of trade patterns, judging from the empirical studies surveyed. Experience with the factor-endowments model seems to show a somewhat more limited predictive value, although numerous and complex considerations are involved which, if taken into account, might change the picture quite materially.[7]

In recent years there has been a virtual epidemic of studies attempting to put some empirical clothes on the pure theory of international trade.[8] Most were triggered by the Leontief Paradox, which continued to disturb economists, with the intention of explaining why the results turned out the

[4] I. B. Kravis, "Availability and Other Influences on the Commodity Composition of Trade," *Journal of Political Economy,* April, 1956; and G. D. A. MacDougall, "British and American Exports: A Study Suggested by the Theory of Comparative Costs, Part I," *Economic Journal,* December, 1951.

[5] Bela Balassa, "An Empirical Demonstration of Classical Comparative Cost Theory," *Review of Economics and Statistics,* August, 1963.

[6] G. D. A. MacDougall, "British and American Exports: A Study Suggested by the Theory of Comparative Costs, Part II," *Economic Journal,* September, 1952.

[7] R. Robinson, "Factor Proportions and Comparative Advantage," *Quarterly Journal of Economics,* August, 1956; W. P. Travis, *The Theory of Trade and Protection* (Cambridge: Harvard University Press, 1964); and S. Valavanis-Vail, "Leontief's Scarce Factor Paradox," *Journal of Political Economy,* December, 1954.

[8] Two of the most useful are Robert E. Baldwin, "Determinants of the Commodity Structure of U.S. Trade," *American Economic Review,* March, 1971; and Gary C. Hufbauer, "The Impact of National Characteristics and Technology on the Commodity Composition of Trade in Manufactured Goods," in Raymond Vernon (ed.), *The Technology Factor in International Trade* (New York: National Bureau of Economic Research, 1970).

way they did. A few departed entirely from conventional theory with some rather original approaches.

HUMAN SKILLS

Already mentioned as a possible reason for the Leontief paradox is the idea that the quality of labor may not be everywhere the same, that labor in some countries may be more efficient than in others. Why would labor quality vary? One reason might be differences in the skill levels of workers, which, in turn, may be the product of major social investments in education and training—*human capital*. Clearly, the United States has a comparative advantage in electronic data processing equipment and commercial aircraft, the development and manufacture of which seems to be labor-intensive. More precisely, it is *skilled-labor-intensive,* with the skill inputs being largely the product of U.S. capital investment in human beings.

If this theory is correct, then skill-intensity ought to show up in employment patterns of various kinds of labor, and differences in these patterns ought to be related in some significant way to international trade flows. Wage differences among groups of varying skill levels might be used to indicate relative productivity, which in turn ought to determine in part a nation's comparative advantage. Studies that have focused on this issue show that U.S. exports are in fact more wage skill-intensive than U.S. imports— hence they are more human-capital-intensive—which is what one would expect.[9] Other studies have succeeded in generalizing the importance of this factor as a determinant of trade patterns in a variety of countries, indicating that the incorporation of human capital can indeed serve to reverse the Leontief Paradox, although a number of important methodological questions remain to be solved—such as imperfections in labor markets and the transferability of capital between embodiment in producer-goods and in human beings.

TECHNOLOGICAL GAPS

Another possible explanation for the real-world behavior of trade is that innovation (whether related to management knowhow, production processes, or products themselves) occurs in different countries at different rates of speed. A country which leads in innovation may enjoy an important comparative advantage in trade in technology-intensive products. A new product or process is developed. The technology does not yet exist abroad, so exports follow naturally. Then the technology becomes available abroad,

[9] Donald B. Keesing, "Labor Skills and Comparative Advantage," *American Economic Review,* May, 1966. Also Peter B. Kenen, "Nature, Capital and Trade," *Journal of Political Economy,* October, 1965.

and trade in the relevant products is put on an entirely different footing—
the technological gap is eliminated, and other factors take over as primary
determinants of comparative advantage. A persistent technological gap between one country and the rest of the world can, nonetheless, serve as an
important underpinning of its trade position, one which tends to be more
important the slower the international diffusion of technology.

One way to examine the importance of this factor in international trade
is to look at specific high-technology products, where they were first developed, and how their production spread internationally over time.[10] Using
the dates on which products were first traded as an indicator of the existence
of technological gaps, this measure is found to perform quite well as a predictor of trade flows, seeming to corroborate the importance of this factor
as a determinant of trade. The trouble is that the first trade dates are also
highly correlated with measures of capital abundance and measures of
human skills, so that it is not easy to tell just how important technological
gaps are relative to other explanations of trade.

Still, the presence of some kind of "gap-effect" is hard to deny, even
if its precise importance is difficult to pinpoint.[11] In the U.S., for example,
it turns out that industries making a strong research effort tend also to be
highly export-oriented.[12] And this fits well into conventional factor-endowments theory, since technological gaps are created by investment in research
and development—e.g., high-technology exports would be expected of capital-abundant countries. In any case, whatever gaps exist may well be narrowing as technology-diffusion becomes more efficient via international
licensing, consulting contacts, construction of "turnkey" plants and—probably most important—intra-firm transfers by multinational corporations.

PRODUCT CYCLE

A more elaborate version of the foregoing argument is the product-cycle
theory. A new product is developed, and starts out being produced in small
quantities by different firms, almost experimentally, with comparatively wide
differences in approach among firms. Markets develop and production becomes more homogeneous as national and international norms emerge and
less efficient techniques are shaken out. Those that remain become widely
accepted and standardized, and the products themselves change from marginal to basic manufacturing lines of the firms concerned. High-technology
firms in advanced countries tend to export goods which fall into the early

---

[10] Gary C. Hufbauer, *op. cit.*

[11] *Cf.* John Diebold, "Is the Gap Technological?" *Foreign Affairs,* January, 1968.

[12] W. Gruber, D. Mehta, and R. Veron, "The R&D Factor in International
Trade and International Investment of United States Industries," *Journal of Political
Economy,* February, 1967.

stages production diffuses internationally as standardization, mass-production, and mass-marketing occurs. The advanced nations gradually lose their competitive advantage as relative labor costs and other factors become determining.[13]

The product-cycle theory concentrates on the sequential transition from differentiation to standardization, which occurs according to different time-patterns for different products, to explain trade. How does it perform? Not too badly, it turns out. Using as a measure of product differentiation the relative variance of export values, there appears a high correlation between this factor and labor-skill inputs in U.S. trade, and a strong indicator that American exports tend to concentrate relatively heavily on the "front end" of the product cycle.[14]

The product-cycle theory, again, conforms quite well with the basic factor-endowments propositions via investment in human skills and research and development. It is also, however, demand-oriented to some extent, with major emphasis on the breadth and depth of the market and corresponding marketing characteristics.

SCALE ECONOMIES

Yet another possible explanation of trade patterns lies in the volume of production that can be attained either in large diversified firms or in long production runs in specialized firms. In either case, economies of large-scale production can be realized which reduce unit-costs and convey an international competitive advantage, embodying a high degree of product standardization. The large size of the internal U.S. market, for example, may permit American producers of tradeable products to operate at higher levels of efficiency than, say, British producers faced with a much smaller internal market. Production runs are larger and product differentiation is less. Hence scale economies may represent an important determinant of competitive advantage in certain sectors. The only way producers in small countries can achieve these same advantages is to have unrestricted access to—and a high degree of familiarity with—export markets. Even then, international differences in tastes and preferences will still serve to narrow the market—with the possible exception of internationally standardized products.[15]

A test of the scale-economies theory shows a rather high degree of associa-

---

[13] See R. Vernon, "International Investment and International Trade in the Product Cycle," *Quarterly Journal of Economics,* May, 1966.

[14] G. C. Hufbauer, *op. cit.;* see also Seev Hirsch, *Location of Industry and International Competitiveness* (London: Clarendon Press, 1967).

[15] Jacques Drèze, a Belgian economist, is particularly associated with this view. See Hufbauer, *op. cit.,* for a test of this theory.

tion between the large-scale production economies embodied in exports and the size of various national economies as measured by industrial output. The relationship is hardly perfect, since exports of large but poor countries such as India as well as small but rich countries such as Denmark and the Netherlands behave quite differently from what the theory predicts. Nevertheless for a significant range of product groups and trading countries the achievability of scale economies seems to be an important determinant of trade flows.

PREFERENCE SIMILARITY

Most of the explanations of trade flows discussed thus far have focused on supply factors, although some—such as the product-cycle and scale-economy theories—are strongly related to corresponding demand elements. Indeed, we have from the beginning emphasized the co-equal importance of supply and demand factors as determinants of international trade, particularly in the context of economic growth.

Suppose, for instance, that the demand for export commodities rises relatively faster than does the demand for imported goods, as a result of income growth. We would expect the nation's exports *and* imports to grow more slowly than if demand expansion affected both exportables and importables proportionately. Under such circumstances, it would not be unreasonable to expect the nation's terms of trade to improve. If, on the other hand, the demand for importables rises relatively faster than the demand for exportables, we would expect the volume of both exports and imports to rise, and the terms of trade to deteriorate somewhat.

Demand patterns naturally may also be altered in time, quite independently of income change—due perhaps to changes in tastes and preferences or income distribution. A shift in demand from importables to exportables would tend to reduce the volume of international trade of a nation and lead to an improvement in its terms of trade. A demand shift from exportables to importables would tend to have the opposite effects.

Comparative supply and demand conditions as co-equal determinants of international trade flows have been emphasized thus far in our study of commercial exchange between nations. The direction of trade—which countries specialize in the production of what commodities—is seen to depend upon international differences in factor endowments and productivity, on the supply side, in concert with international differences in demand for a wide variety of traded goods.

Many of these forces affecting international trade may well be "historical" in nature and closely connected with the process of economic growth. This would seem to hold for important elements both on the supply side, such as economies of large-scale production, and on the demand side—tastes and incomes. A most worthwhile argument much along these lines has been proposed by a Swedish economist, Staffan Burenstam Linder.[16]

Linder suggests that international differences in factor endowments may well govern trade in primary products, but this may not necessarily be true at all for manufactured goods. Here it would appear to be the similarity or dissimilarity of *demand patterns* between countries that governs the direction and volume of international trade. Since by far the greatest share of overall international trade is clearly composed of manufactures, it follows—if Linder is correct—that demand patterns must play an exceedingly important role as a determinant of trade flows in general.

To begin with, in order for a country to export a certain manufactured commodity, it must first possess an intensive *internal* demand for that good, thus permitting the potential export industry to grow to viable proportions and efficiency. "Among all non-primary products, a country has a range of potential exports. This range of exportable products is determined by *internal demand.*"[17] Active domestic demand thus enables an industry to reach a large enough production scale to allow it to become competitive in the international marketplace.

Moreover, a country usually discovers that the most promising foreign markets generally prove to be countries at stages of economic development similar to its own—where the demand for manufactured goods has grown to a point roughly equal to that prevailing in the home country. Trade thus should be most intense between countries with *similar* demand patterns and least intense between nations showing vastly different demand characteristics.

Figure 8–1 illustrates this relationship.[18] The vertical axis denotes the degree of sophistication that characterizes the national demand for manufactured goods, while the horizontal axis represents per capita income. Logically, one would expect growth in a nation's per capita income to call forth an ever increasing degree of quality, or sophistication, in the general run of goods demanded by its people. This is represented by the line *OP*.

Even in an affluent society there is a demand for both high- and low-quality goods. Hence, for every national level of per capita income there is a *range* of sophistication in the types of commodities demanded. Instead of the line *OP* to represent variations in the quality of demand with income, we can thus draw a *band,* which tends to increase in width as per capita income, or affluence, increases. This is represented by the shaded area, *Oxy,* in Figure 8–1.

[16] S. B. Linder, *An Essay on Trade and Transformation* (Stockholm: Almqvist & Wiksell, 1961).
[17] Linder, *ibid.,* p. 87.
[18] Adapted from Linder, *ibid.,* p. 100.

Now suppose we take two countries, *A* and *B*, that are characterized by per capita incomes of $1,500 and $2,500, respectively. Note the relevant demand patterns *AA'* and *BB'*. Country *A* demands goods in the quality range *fc*, while the demand patterns in the higher income Country *B* extends over quality range *be*. Level *g* is the average quality of goods consumed and invested in *A*, and the corresponding average demand sophistication in Country *B* is level *c*.

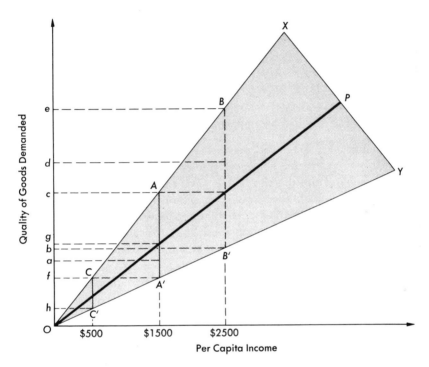

Fig. 8–1. Demand patterns as determinants of international trade.

In Country *A*, there is no demand for goods of a quality *higher* than *c*, and in Country *B* the demand for commodities of a quality *lower* than *b* is zero. Only the quality range *bc* is common to both countries. Since there is no demand in *A* for Country *B*'s goods of quality range *ce*, and no demand in *B* for Country *A*'s goods of a quality range *bf*, all trade between the two countries must fall in the range of goods *bc*. By the same reasoning, trade in *manufactured* goods between a highly developed country such as *A*, and a relatively poor country, such as *C*, should be very low and entirely determined by factor endowments, since there is no overlapping of demand patterns at all.

If we were to apply this theory to the real world, we would expect to see a large volume of trade in manufactures between such countries as Germany and the U.S., Great Britain and France, and Sweden and Japan. This would not be true, however, of trade between the U.S. and Nicaragua, Germany and Upper Volta, and Great Britain and Haiti. By carrying out an informal empirical test of his theory, Linder concludes that its predictive value could be substantial and that it should at least be subject to further testing.

Why is this particular idea so interesting? It seems diametrically opposed to the Heckscher–Ohlin factor-endowments theory of international trade. It says that trade in manufactures should be most intense between economically similar countries, whereas the factor-endowments approach implies that trade should be most pronounced between countries whose economic structures are fundamentally different. While it does not yet constitute a fully developed model, the Linder thesis does provide us with one more alternative for looking at the factors governing international trade relations. It is also related at least in part to the product-cycle and scale-economy theories, and tends to gain further in credibility when associated with so-called "gravity" models which combine GNP, population, economic distance, and historical trade ties as explanatory variables.[19]

PRODUCTION STAGES

A final line of reasoning concerning the causes of international trade relates the issue directly to the economic growth process. In the early stages of its growth, a country will produce many of its own consumer goods, such as textiles, and even export them in volume. Later on, having reached an advanced stage of development, it tends to export capital goods and sophisticated consumer goods and import simple manufactures. That is, economies as they grow tend to "integrate backward" from goods closer to the final consumer to goods successively less associated with direct consumption. This time–profile of production will of course influence trade patterns in terms of the product composition of traded manufactures.

Tests of this theory may focus on the relative importance of consumer goods in the production mix of various economies; and relating this variable to the pattern of trade. There are, however, severe statistical problems in defining and classifying product categories. Nevertheless, there is some evidence that backward integration is associated with emerging trade patterns, although the same sets of observations can be related to the predicted outcomes according to the traditional Heckscher–Ohlin and human-skills theories.[20]

[19] H. Linnemann, *An Econometric Study of International Trade Flows* (Amsterdam: North Holland, 1966).

[20] See Hufbauer, *op. cit.,* p. 184.

JOINING THE ISSUE: WHY DO NATIONS TRADE?

What do we end up with after all this? Quite clearly the traditional theory of trade is far from useless. Relative factor endowments and relative factor efficiency, as specified in traditional trade theory, are indeed important as determinants of trade in a broad range of products between economies. Perhaps its predictive power is greatest where trade with developing economies and trade in standardized products are involved.

At the same time, it is clear that the definition of "capital" must be broadened to include investment in knowledge (research and development) and human resources (labor skills) as well as physical production facilities. Such a broadening of the definition of capital is hardly at odds with the traditional theory and, if some of the measurement problems can be solved, promises to greatly enhance its predictive power—particularly with the incorporation of scale economies as an important determinant of costs. By closing the gap between abstract theoretical models and what goes on in the real world, we can thus combine supply-related determinants of trade which, even if complex, are operationally sound.

The same is true on the demand side, especially where supply and demand are clearly interactive—where internal demand begets an industry that eventually grows to be competitive in export markets. Without a carefully formulated handle on demand variables, as provided by the preference-similarity and product-cycle theories—there is a great deal we cannot explain. Why does the U.S. export *and* import cameras in large volume? Why does Germany do the same with automobiles? Particularly in trade among the developed countries, where a broad range of production capabilities exists in each of the trading partners, demand-oriented theories are proving to be most valuable.

We are left, then, with a somewhat eclectic formulation of the pure theory of international trade, but one that seems to get encouragingly close to the truth. How do we combine all of this into the kind of neat, conceptual, general model with which we began? Economists are still working on it. Reference to some of the important research in this field is provided in Section E-8.

II

Theory of Commercial Policy

9

THE POLITICAL
ECONOMY OF TRADE
POLICY

The theory of international trade teaches us that world output of goods and services can be maximized only under conditions of free trade and with international specialization completely unrestricted. The gains from trade are then distributed among the trading countries in accordance with the principle of reciprocal demand. Given imperfect international mobility of the factors of production, only essentially unrestricted trade between national economic systems can allocate productive resources in the most efficient possible manner, yielding output and income levels significantly higher than would obtain if international commerce were prohibited or subject to significant distortions by means of tariffs or other devices. The simple economic models employed earlier uncontestably show that this must be the case under certain fairly plausible assumptions. And yet the policy prescription following from this proposition—in favor of essentially free intercountry trade in goods and services—has never been fully implemented. Impressive movements toward trade liberalization have taken place from time to time, but they have often been followed by dramatic shifts in the opposite direction.

If economic theory is correct, why do the economic, social, and political interests that determine international trade policy fail to reflect such a basic proposition and serve to promote consistent and far-reaching liberalization on all fronts until essentially free trade is achieved? This is the topic of the present chapter, and it includes an examination of the political dimensions of the problem as well as the economic issues involved. We begin with a brief discussion of how trade policy affects the *national* perspective, and then go on to discover its impact on specific *groups* within a nation. We conclude by examining the behavior of these affected interest groups, and the political transformation of these interests at the national level—either into policy action undertaken unilaterally or into a policy position subject to subsequent international conciliation.

DEPARTURES FROM FREE TRADE AND THE NATIONAL INTEREST

An important rationale for departures from the free-trade position may be found in efforts to maximize the welfare of the *national* collectivity, given domestic and international social, political, and economic conditions as they evolve over time. These may be regarded as essentially *nonbiased* arguments for restriction of international commerce in the sense that they do not systematically favor or oppose freer trade and may weigh in one direction or the other in response to shifts in the underlying variables.

Terms of Trade

A nation may under certain conditions be able to improve its material well-being by imposing restrictions on its exports or imports *if* such action would result in a decline in the prices of products it buys from abroad and/or a rise in the prices of products it sells abroad. If foreign countries do not somehow retaliate, such policies would tend to improve the terms under which exports exchange for imports in the international marketplace, and hence improve the aggregate level of real income of the economy. Such gains can *only* be achieved at the expense of the economic welfare of trading partners; these in turn can attain corresponding gains at the expense of the home country. Hence—as will be demonstrated in Chapter 10—the terms of trade basis for barriers to free international commerce reduces to a matter of intercountry bargaining. It is well-known that the extent of barriers to access to the national market in part determines a country's strength in bargaining with trading partners, and hence such restrictions partially govern its ability to secure trade concessions in return for liberalization steps of its own.

Balance of Trade

International financial factors may exert an important influence on a nation's trade policy (see Chapter 24). Balance of payments deficits tend to bring political pressures for trade restrictions designed to cut expenditures on imports and for incentives to increase export earnings. Whether this rationale for trade distortions is invoked depends on the state and prevailing change of a country's balance of payments, the adequacy of its international reserves, the availability and political feasibility of alternative adjustment techniques, and rules of behavior imposed by international agreements, as well as probable reactions on the part of other nations.

Trade distortions, in that they affect prices inside the domestic economy in relation to those obtaining in the international marketplace, represent in a very real sense alterations in the value of a nation's currency. Conversely, changes in the value of the national currency may have significant implications for national commercial policy. Hence questions of *international trade policy* and *international monetary policy* are closely linked.

Clearly, a balance of payments deficit is more likely to move a country toward increased protectionism in its commercial policy and less likely to promote agreement on trade liberalization than balanced international payments or a payments surplus.

Competitive Distortions

Trade policy can be used to help counter distortions that may prevail within the national economy, e.g., to offset market control exercised by monopolistically organized industries or labor groups. To the extent that trade barriers serve to reallocate production from areas where such distortions are serious to areas where they are not so troublesome—and this reallocation is considered to yield greater benefits to the society than the economic cost of the barriers themselves—a net gain may be recorded by the nation as a whole. This issue is discussed more formally in terms of the "theory of second-best" in Chapter 15.

Unemployed Resources

A national economy operating at unacceptably low levels of capacity utilization may seek to alleviate unemployment of productive resources by means of trade-policy techniques. As we shall see in Chapter 20, restrictions on imports or export incentives tend to switch national expenditure patterns from goods and services produced abroad to those produced at home, thereby strengthening aggregate demand and helping to absorb idle resources in productive employment. Again, reductions in imports and/or artificial stimulation of exports by definition means that foreign economies must be selling fewer goods and services abroad and/or spending more on imports. If these economies are likewise subject to unused productive capacity and idle resources such developments will be adverse to their own interests and countermoves in the trade-policy field may be expected. The reverse is true in the case of a country undergoing inflationary pressures; the increased expenditures on imports reduce the effective demand for home-produced goods and subject domestic suppliers to a stiffening of foreign competition.

Growth

Under certain conditions a country may be willing to forego significant gains attributable to unhindered international exchanges of goods and services if this sacrifice promises even greater long-range benefits in terms of economic growth. The growth of important emerging industries or the economic survival of regional development zones may militate in favor of increased restriction of imports. A developing country, for instance, may justifiably wish to protect an emerging industry from low-cost foreign imports until such a time as that industry becomes internationally competitive, as explained in Chapter 28. Or it may decide to protect a group of such industries to promote diversification and growth through substitution of home-produced goods for imports. An assessment that the "gains from growth" outweigh the "gains from trade" in any given instance may underlie the application of appropriate obstacles to trade.

Revenue

Certain kinds of distortions of international trade produce substantial fiscal revenues. Tariffs, import levies and surcharges, license fees, and export taxes are some examples. National states, particularly those with unreliable or underdeveloped internal fiscal systems, frequently find it desirable to levy charges bearing on international exchanges of goods and services, thereby unavoidably distorting competitive conditions and intercountry trade flows.

Social Arguments

On occasion national social considerations are raised in defense of restrictions imposed on international trade—restrictions intended to insure the attainment of politically accepted goals relating to the quality of life. For example, heavy tariffs may be applied to imports of alcoholic beverages or tobacco products in order to reduce consumption levels. Export controls may be imposed on certain raw materials for ecological reasons or to conserve natural resources. Generally, trade policy is only one of many paths to the realization of such social goals, and it frequently represents a decidedly inferior alternative.

Politico-military Arguments

Trade policy is a major component of a nation's foreign economic policy, and hence is frequently employed in the pursuit of general foreign-policy goals. Trade concessions, in the form of reduced tariffs or other import restrictions, may be accorded to certain foreign countries for political reasons, and the withholding or withdrawal of such concessions may be similarly employed. On the export side as well, trade controls may be used to deny access to certain products to foreign countries. In spite of its frequent ineffectiveness in obtaining major political objectives, trade policy as a tool of economic warfare continues to be in widespread use.

Trade restrictions may also be employed to protect against import competition certain domestic industries whose output is ostensibly critical for the national defense. The importance of such industries in a national emergency is deemed sufficient to more than offset the annual costs incurred—in terms of the induced inefficiencies and the trade gains foregone—in insuring their survival. Such costs and foregone gains are considered in a very real sense an insurance premium that should be added to the cost of the national defense. National security considerations usually show up on the protectionist side of the ledger, although they may on occasion support freer trade.

All of the foregoing reasons for the existence of distortions of international trade have a single underlying theme: the pursuit of *national* economic, political, and social goals. The arguments presented do not necessarily favor specific groups *within* a nation. Whether such forces militate in favor of or against freer trade likewise depends on factors operating on a national and international level, and none of them is inherently biased for or against free trade. Their weight may shift in one direction or the other in accordance with shifts in the underlying economic, political, or social conditions.

TRADE AND INCOME DISTRIBUTION

In isolation, let us say that several groups of individuals are producing a number of commodities for domestic consumption, and their real incomes are determined by the laws of supply and demand operating freely both in the market for goods and in the market for productive factors.

Now let us assume free international trade. Production of those commodities in which the country has a comparative advantage expands to meet the export demand. Meanwhile, output of goods in which the country has a comparative disadvantage contracts under pressure from import competition. Real incomes of those engaged in the export industry will tend to rise, while real income of groups still engaged in import-competing employment will tend to fall. Income will be redistributed from one group to another, and some will be better off and some worse off as a result of international trade.

True, some of those employed in the import-competing industries will be released and absorbed by the export industries, thus shifting them from one group to the other. But it is still not possible to make valid generalizations about the impact of international trade on general social welfare. Who knows whether the loss of the losers is greater than the gain of the gainers, or vice versa? This would involve drawing interpersonal comparisons. And we have already said that it is impossible to make these comparisons in any really meaningful way.

Suppose, however, that some of the welfare gains of those engaged in the export industries are somehow taxed away in a nondistorting manner and given to those experiencing welfare losses. Income is redistributed in such a way that while some gain, at least others do not suffer a *reduction* in economic welfare as a result of trade. We can then say that overall welfare has indeed increased. No one would lose but some would gain, thus signifying an increase in welfare for the nation as a whole.

By assuming that income is equitably redistributed, we are in a position to make a positive statement about the welfare effects of free trade, even without being able to make interpersonal welfare comparisons. Unrestricted international trade will always *make possible* an increase in community welfare over and above that which prevails in isolation; i.e., free international trade is a *necessary, but not sufficient* condition for the maximization of social welfare when compared with no trade at all. Whether or not this overall welfare gain is actually realized depends entirely upon the degree to which real income is equitably redistributed from those who gain to those who lose as a result of international trade.

Carrying this over to an even broader scale, world production of goods and services *will* gain from the specialization and division of labor which free trade makes possible, while world economic welfare *may* gain as a result. This is again contingent upon the redistribution of real income that is undertaken.

It may be useful to consider the income-distributional aspects of commercial policy from the perspective of two basic interest groups.[1] The first of these—which might be called the *protection-biased sector*—advocates high levels of trade restriction in order to shield itself from foreign competition. The second group—the *trade-biased sector*—for equally compelling reasons of self-interest demands low trade-barrier levels. It strives to obtain for its own use low-cost imports, insure maximum access to foreign markets, or secure favorable policy actions on the part of foreign governments. The political process serves to resolve this conflict, and the existing national trade-policy position reflects this internal resolution, set against the essentially *nonbiased* considerations based on the national interest and outlined above. The final mix of commercial policies that results represents the bilateral and multilateral conciliation of differing national trade-policy positions on an international level. As the product of extended internal and external conflict resolution and constantly shifting economic and noneconomic condi-

[1] This discussion is based on "How Trade Policy is Made: A Politico-Economic Decision System" in Robert G. Hawkins and Ingo Walter, *The United States and International Markets* (Lexington, Mass.: D. C. Heath, 1972) and on Robert Loring Allen and Ingo Walter, *The Formation of United States Trade Policy: Retrospect and Prospect* (New York: New York University Institute of Finance, 1971).

tions, the resultant trade policy naturally cannot satisfy *both* the protection-biased and trade-biased groups at home (or abroad) and this gives rise to the observed, constant pressure for change in that policy.

Arguments for freer trade, when not blunted by considerations addressing themselves to the maximization of the national welfare, are based on static economic theory and assume effective competition in markets for goods, services, and productive factors, with commensurate flexibility in prices and costs. They do not take into account the pre-existence of relatively inefficient and internationally uncompetitive domestic producers and the continued survival of such suppliers as a result of barriers that would have to be dismantled in any move toward more liberal trade. The vital economic interests of such producers, their employees, managements, dependent municipalities and regions, suppliers, and other groups are affected. These forces will naturally resist freer trade as it affects their industry, and use whatever political power they have to prevent it. However, since international trade theory assures us that the benefits of freer trade will *on net* outweigh the damage it does to import-competing interests, obviously those groups in society which gain from liberalized trade could somehow compensate those groups suffering damage—and still be ahead.

Two problems arise, however. First, the damaged groups may be hurt to such a degree that the harm is irreparable. A firm may cease to exist. A job classification or skill may be eliminated. A town may lose all of its industry. As a result, those damaged may feel that no amount of adjustment assistance or compensation is sufficient to offset their losses. Whether or not just compensation would in fact be impossible, it is the *attitude* that is important and renders resistance to freer trade extremely vociferous in the political arena.

Second, even if it were possible to compensate the injured, there exists no effective economic or political mechanism to capture from those groups benefited just enough real income to effect equitable reparations. Both comprise highly diverse groups, with the benefits and costs attributable to freer trade distributed unevenly within these groups. In addition, the benefits of trade liberalization do not necessarily accrue to the economy during the same time period as the damages which must be absorbed. Finally, those benefited by freer trade would logically be expected to resist a removal of some of their gains for compensation purposes.

In short, the impossibility of intergroup and interpersonal comparisons of gains and losses in material welfare as a result of freer trade renders impossible not only effective compensation on a national scale but also a system of taxation and transfers which would make such a system feasible. In practice, therefore, the conflict between the gainers and losers from freer trade is inevitable in a system of commercial relations between politically sovereign national states.

COMPOSITION OF THE PROTECTION-BIASED
AND TRADE-BIASED SECTORS

Domestic business firms actually or potentially in competition with foreign firms for sales in the home market form the core of the protection-biased sector, and generally stand in opposition to a more liberal trade policy. They would prefer to see national tariffs and nontariff trade barriers become more restrictive as regards those products which they themselves supply. Around this core are grouped the labor unions and the owners of productive factors employed by these firms, other enterprises supplying the import-competing firms with raw materials and components, businesses producing complementary products, as well as the political representatives of the regions and communities affected. All tend to support increased trade restrictions. Only to the extent that any of the suppliers are dependent on imported raw materials or components would the pervasive interest in more restrictive trade policies be mitigated. If the various political representatives of this protection-biased sector acted in a manner *other* than to oppose trade liberalization, they would be neglecting their responsibilities to their respective constituencies. Hence those who support a more restrictive national trade policy constitute an important political power bloc, based on the logical expression of self-interest.

The opposing force—the trade-biased sector—is primarily concerned with access to foreign markets for exports, with the domestic availability and price of imported goods and services, and with foreign reactions to domestic trade-policy moves. Suppliers of exports realize that increased protectionism at home will tend to result in the imposition of more restrictive trade barriers abroad, and in a narrowing of their markets. At the same time, they are fully aware that they cannot widen their access to foreign markets—secured by reduced foreign trade restrictions—without simultaneously negotiated domestic concessions. This places the export suppliers squarely on the side of trade liberalization. Again, the owners of the factors of production used in the export-oriented industries, associated labor groups, firms supplying that industry with raw materials and intermediate inputs, and the representatives of export-dependent local and regional political jurisdictions join in opposing increased protection and in favoring generally freer trade. Export-oriented producers and linked interest groups are aided in their efforts by importers, distributors, retailers, and final consumers of imported goods and services, who likewise support trade liberalization from the standpoint of costs, prices, and sales volumes. Not least important are business firms, financial institutions, and individuals with substantial investments abroad, realizing full well that foreign retaliation against national trade-policy measures may manifest itself as investment controls detrimental to their interests. Multinational business firms are also concerned with free access to their foreign subsidiaries for raw materials, components, and capital goods. Together, these domestic interest groups combine to make up a respectable force diametrically opposed to the protectionist sector.

Of course, the alliance of forces for and against freer trade is not quite as simple as this, nor are the groupings as discrete. For example, most individuals are both consumers and producers; this would pose a conflict of interest for someone employed in an import-competing industry. Business firms, especially multi-product diversified enterprises, may have among their operating divisions some which are decidedly export-oriented and others falling into the import-competing group, while labor unions may have individual locals that identify their own interests fundamentally with one sector or the other. Such considerations and internal conflicts may render a company or union decision for or against freer trade extremely difficult, unless it can apply its influence in a discretionary manner according to the needs of its various interest sub-groups. Trade and industry associations, political representatives, and others may face no less severe internal decision problems in reaching a coherent and defensible position on the national commercial policy. Finally, foreign exporters concerned with access to the domestic market generally make themselves felt through vigorous lobbying efforts and occasional officially voiced concerns with regard to the direction of national developments in the trade sphere.

To summarize, it appears that the interests of the *nonbiased, protection-biased,* and *trade-biased* segments of the modern economy and of society, working through the political mechanism, determine the national trade-policy position. Their respective economic demands are mirrored, however imperfectly, in the national debate on commercial policy and in the final determination of the national trade-policy stance. Shifts in the salient variables—such as a change in the rate of inflation at home or abroad, a change in domestic or foreign technology or productive efficiency, or a shift in demand patterns—will produce corresponding changes in the positions of the various groups on the proper course of national commercial policy, and the political dynamics of trade-policy formation will tend to bring about ultimate changes in that policy itself.

BEHAVIOR OF THE PROTECTION-BIASED SECTOR

We have noted that domestic import-competing industries and the factors of production employed in these industries are the primary and most direct beneficiaries of trade barriers, as are the suppliers of inputs to these industries. Certain enterprises may be unable to enter a line of import-competing production because their costs are too high, so that they are merely *potential* producers, excluded from the market by the low import price of the product. Should increased trade restrictions be introduced, (a) the infra-marginal producers would suddenly find that they are earning substantially increased profits on larger volumes of output and higher prices; (b) the marginal producers would find that they are now operating at a profit and are in a position to expand; and (c) those producers who formerly had been excluded from the production of the import-competing lines find that the new price is sufficiently high that they can enter production and operate at viable profit levels. In the latter category, the firm hopes to be able to achieve economies of scale and to reduce its own costs through increased efficiency. Even after such infant industries outgrow the need for protection, there is a built-in tendency to push for continued protection, since it provides an element of security for high levels of output and profit which might not be possible in open competition.

At the other end of the scale, old and declining industries tend to be even more vigorous in their efforts to obtain protection. Dated management techniques, obsolete technology and capital facilities, labor restrictions, and many other factors may have reduced productivity to such an extent that the enterprise is no longer able to compete effectively against similar industries established more recently in other countries. These often tend to be relatively slow-growing sectors, tied to increases in population or similar long-term facets of the economy.

As national economies develop, the very new "front-edge" industries and those at the "back-edge" of the industrial spectrum will thus form the vanguard of protectionist interest. The former have not yet attained a competitive advantage in international trade, and the latter are gradually losing it. Major protectionist strength may be attained if the front-edge and back-edge industrial groups comprise a very major part of the national economic structure, powerful in relation to those highly efficient and export-oriented industries that have attained a technical or productive advantage in world markets.

In general, a liberal trade policy can be relied upon to "clean out" the lagging and increasingly noncompetitive producing units and sectors of the economy through import competition, thereby freeing productive factors for more efficient use in other parts of the economy. This "scavenging-effect" of international trade, if not impeded, may have a broad positive impact on economic growth. Economic development is always an uneven process, and one of the major symptoms of this unevenness is the continual emergence of front-edge and back-edge industries of the kind just described. Imports serve an important role in the growth process by efficiently cleaning out particularly the back-edge industries—supplanting their production with that of foreign suppliers possessing an international comparative advantage—and releasing the productive resources employed by these industries for use in other sectors of the economy, including the front-edge and exporting industries. In advanced countries, the emerging firms at the leading edge of national economic growth are generally able to fend for themselves or find other ways to insure their survival. The induced shift in resources from less efficient to more efficient employment is clearly beneficial from the standpoint of national economic growth, and represents an important and useful function performed by imports. To the extent that imports are impeded through tariffs or other trade restrictions, of course, their scavenging function is likewise impeded, with a corresponding deleterious implication for growth.

The economic health and well-being of many communities is closely linked to the prosperity of a domestic firm of industry engaged in import competition. This is particularly true of single-industry communities or in political jurisdictions where only a few enterprises dominate the area. Since national legislatures are normally elected on a local basis, their members are influenced by community pressures emanating from the economic position and the prospects of producers operating in their constituencies. Even in countries in which the national legislature does not specifically determine trade policy, it is often able to exercise great influence over the executive authority, or local pressures may be brought to bear in a variety of other ways.

Pressure for increased trade barriers may not, however, originate with the import-competing suppliers themselves. Recent years have seen the rapid expansion of multinational corporations—the operation of business enterprises on a global scale, allocating production, financing, and trade according to transnational logistical planning *within* the corporate entity. Faced with increased competition from imports, they frequently fail to follow the classic policy response outlined here. Rather, they may close down domestic plants and shift production to foreign affiliates or suppliers for subsequent captive-importation into the home market. The firm thus fails to seek commercial-policy relief; indeed, it adopts the values of the trade-biased sector. But the damaging effects on workers, suppliers, and localities are the same—if sometimes less obviously attributable to trade-related factors—and the battle for increased barriers to imports must be taken up directly by organized labor, regions, and localities, frequently against the interests of the producers themselves.

The protection-biased sector in general is in an inherently strong political position because the possibilities of gain or loss attributable to trade-policy shifts are *immediate* and *direct*. For them, increased trade barriers would seem to result in an obvious output expansion, increased employment and higher profits, regional prosperity, and a general gain in real income of all concerned. They need only point out that if imports were not present the domestic market would be served by the domestic producers, and this is often regarded by them as a "natural right." They can also argue that a reduction in trade barriers will result in a direct loss to them, a cut in their "fair share" of the market, a reduction in output and employment, idle capacity, and generally harmful effects upon their region of the country and the economy in general.

This is the kind of short-run pressure to which representatives in national governing bodies respond. It is their business in part to look after the economic interests of their constituents and, whenever possible, to mitigate any harmful behavior on the part of the government. However, political bodies sometimes take a considerable period of time in responding with concrete action. Furthermore, since trade policy is only one of many public-policy decisions before the national legislature, there may be offsetting coalitions of interests which can make it appear that trade policy has veered substantially from the causal economic forces and the political alliances that are based upon them.

BEHAVIOR OF THE TRADE-BIASED SECTOR

Consumer groups, insofar as they can organize for political action, tend to promote a more liberal national commercial policy. Trade barriers impose losses on consumers, who have less choice among competing products and pay a higher price for each unit purchased of protected items and products using protected inputs. Some, who would have purchased a given product at a lower price, are squeezed out of the market as a result of trade barriers. Those remaining in the market pay a higher price for the product, thus reducing their real incomes and their ability to purchase other products.

Consumers have tended to be the least effectual members of the trade-biased sector. This should not be taken to mean that the loss or gain in consumer satisfaction resulting from a trade-policy shift is not very substantial indeed. In many lines of production those consumers most heavily affected by trade barriers belong to low-income groups which depend heavily on low-cost imports to maximize their purchasing power, and this contributes to the frequent "regressive" nature of import restrictions. But consumers have in many cases been unable to translate even strong feelings into legislative action. They have not been well-organized, and tend to speak as individuals to government officials. Only in some rare instances has the consumer's fundamental interest in trade policy been articulated. Part of the difficulty derives from the fact, noted earlier, that consumers are normally producers as well. They are members of trade unions, employees of businesses, owners of capital, owners of land. They come from easily identified parts of the country where other interests may predominate, and their interests as producers may well be damaged by vigorous promotion of their interests as consumers.

In addition, the loss in consumer welfare resulting from increased trade barriers is difficult to identify in practice. With rare exceptions, they represent only a small portion of the price of the final imported product, and since imports themselves constitute a relatively small part of total consumption, per-capita consumer real income may be affected very little. The general state of the economy plays an important role as well. Under conditions of rapid economic growth and high employment, consumers simply refuse to get agitated about the marginal losses in real income attributed to trade barriers. During periods even of very gradual inflation, price increases due to higher trade barriers cannot be separated from the generally rising prices of goods and services in the economy, and therefore attract little notice.

Closely allied to the consumers in matters of trade policy are the importers, distributors, and retailers of foreign-made goods, whose welfare is very directly linked to the flow of these products into the national market. Large retail chains, discount houses, and small-order concerns tends to draw a major share of their low-priced consumer durables, textile products, footwear, toys, and various other items from foreign sources, and they are generally active in opposing trade restrictions and supporting liberalization. This sector tends to be particularly vociferous in its advocacy of liberal trade, and can usually be counted upon to represent the basic interests of consumers.

Consumers and importer-distributors are joined by exporters, anxious to promote minimum import barriers so that foreigners will be able to finance the purchase of their export goods and foreign reciprocal trade concessions can be secured. Moreover, they realize full well that trade-barrier increases may well trigger retaliatory increases in restrictions abroad. They tend to include some of the more vigorous and expanding industries in the economy, those in which new technology is being applied, new products are being introduced, and imaginative management techniques employed. Business firms investing in foreign production facilities also generally support freer trade. They may be interested in supplying foreign affiliates from the home country with raw materials, intermediates, or finished products, in serving the domestic market of other countries from the foreign base, or in maintaining a favorable investment climate abroad. Hence trade policy represents a factor influencing international investment patterns, while motivations centering around international direct investment flows simultaneously influence the formation of the national trade policy.

Support for a more liberal trade policy also may be expected from those domestic firms who find it advantageous to buy inputs from abroad, either raw materials or components. The interest of such firms is in buying inputs as cheaply as possible. For example, labor-intensive production by American firms in Mexico, Korea, Singapore, Hong Kong, Taiwan, and other countries is one of the reasons why such businesses are in the forefront of groups that frequently push for reduced U.S. trade barriers. Import-using firms may well be in the import-competing sector, which makes their stand on trade policy somewhat equivocal. If generally higher trade barriers are applied, their own output will be protected and prices are likely to rise. But at the same time prices of imported inputs will rise, which will have a negative impact on output and profits (see the discussion on "effective protection" in the following chapter).

Export interests often experience difficulty in translating their economic interests into effective political action. Since these interests generally represent vigorous, growing, and independent elements in the national economy, they are frequently tardy in demanding improved access to foreign markets, and often fail to see the relationship between the freedom of imports and the volume of their exports. They frequently suffer no direct damage as a result of increased domestic import restrictions; the damage constitutes a possible *foregone gain,* something that they might have had in the absence of import barriers, or if trade barriers were reduced—but an economic loss is not recorded or reflected in layoffs, cuts in output, or reduced profits.

In the absence of any apparent direct damage or visible social impact, it tends to be difficult for the export sector to generate very much interest or sympathy from labor, from its suppliers or customers, from the community at large, or from the relevant political forces. Political leadership would be quite concerned if exporters were able to show that their interests had indeed been harmed by the national trade policy, but they frequently cannot do this. They must argue simply that they are being harmed by the existence of domestic trade barriers, and that they would be in a better economic position if these were reduced. Only in areas where the government exercises controls over exports has this particular interest group been able to perceive a more direct link between trade restrictions and its own welfare.

Aside from purely domestic interest groups favoring liberal trade policies, foreign exporting interests—through their respective governments and through independent operations—are often found to be active in the formation of the national trade policy. Extensive public relations efforts directed toward opinion leaders and public policymakers are coupled with unmistakable official statements concerning the possible consequences of a more restrictive trade-policy position. This contributes credibility to foreign exporters' fears of market losses and serves to strengthen their arguments quite materially.

THE POLITICAL TRANSFORMATION

We have attempted to sort out the basic forces tending to determine the national trade-policy position: Two protagonists confront each other in the political arena, the trade-biased and the protection-biased sectors. A third set of essentially nonbiased forces may swing the balance in one direction or the other, and may be adopted by either side on behalf of its own position. It would not appear to be difficult, therefore, to forecast the impact on the national trade-policy position of any of a host of shifts in the underlying economic and noneconomic variables.

All such economic interests must operate within a domestic political structure that is essentially neutral with respect to trade policy. In this way a trade policy can be derived which presumably best promotes the interests of the collectivity. Unfortunately, the process of translating the economic interests into political influence is at best highly uncertain. Conflicting economic interests must be translated into conflicting political interests, and conflicting political interests must in turn be resolved in the light of prevailing nonbiased factors according to accepted procedures. Moreover, the political results may not necessarily reflect the economic balance of power, in part because of imperfections in the decision-making process, and in part because the national executive, responsible for *implementing* commercial policy, may in applying the techniques of trade policy generate results unlike those intended by the underlying political outcomes.

There are four major links in the process of trade-policy formation. They exist:

1. Between the underlying national and international economic and political developments and the attitude toward trade policy of domestic interest groups
2. Between the economic power of the interest groups and their political influence
3. Between the attitudes of individual political decision-makers and the resultant trade-policy actions
4. Between the enabling legislation or other political action and trade-policy implementation.

Because of uncertainty, error, and misinterpretation at each stage, it is therefore rather unlikely that the national trade-policy position in practice reflects accurately the underlying political and economic considerations.

Structural and competitive conditions at home and abroad undergo continuous change. When such change takes place, the economic groups affected by international trade must re-evaluate their positions. In some cases, a group which has favored a liberal trade policy in the past may find that under the new conditions a somewhat more restrictive commercial policy is better suited to its needs. When this is the case, the economic influence of that group may help to shift the political balance. The new political alignment may be successful in changing trade-policy legislation, and that legislation may lead to actual changes in the degree of protection. Thus, a change in the national commercial policy may result from a change in economic structure via the four linkages noted above. This pattern is clearly evident throughout the history of international trade-policy, and operates the linkages depicted in Figure 9–1.

Aside from changes in the underlying economic conditions national trade policy may also change because of a shift in any one of the linkages themselves, such as: (a) Increasing or decreasing political influence of a given interest group; (b) a different path of influence open to an interest group; (c) a revised interpretation of its best interests by such a group; (d) a new attitude as to what constitutes the national interest in the international economic and political arena; (e) new trade-policy techniques becoming available to certain groups, and so forth. These changes may arise even without a causal economic change, and often occur in an atmosphere of crisis.

Finally, it has already been pointed out that the political weight of opposing economic interests is hardly symmetrical as between the trade-biased and protection-biased interests. Because the beneficial effects of trade liberalization are often difficult to perceive, relatively long periods of time are generally required for the trade-biased sector to assert its full effort in behalf of lower restrictions to imports. Indeed, a marked swing of non-biased forces in the direction of freer trade, sometimes accompanied by crisis, has often been required to swing the balance in the direction of freer trade. By way of contrast, the protection-biased interests, actually or potentially facing damage from imports, have generally been able to assert themselves without much outside assistance on the basis of short-term economic exigencies.

Popular perceptions of the "national interest" may weigh in favor of or against liberal trade policies, and may be sufficient to swing the balance. The national interest of a country consists of a multitude of political, economic, strategic, diplomatic, and psychological considerations. Safeguarding and promoting the national interest is the chief function of government in the area of foreign policy. Although trade policy is a component of foreign economic policy, there can be no assurance that the commercial policy at a given point in time does in fact serve the national interest.

For instance, a given trade policy may protect certain domestic industries at the expense of foreign suppliers. The damage done foreign producers may in turn reflect negatively on the national interest abroad, while the support of private interests of specific domestic producing groups may simultaneously fail to elevate the national interest at home. Hence victory of the protection-biased sector on a given trade-policy issue does not necessarily serve the national interest in which strategic and political considerations may weigh heavily.

As a result of asymmetry in the influence of opposing groups and considerations related to the national interest, the observed national position on trade policy may not emerge from the political decision-making process in

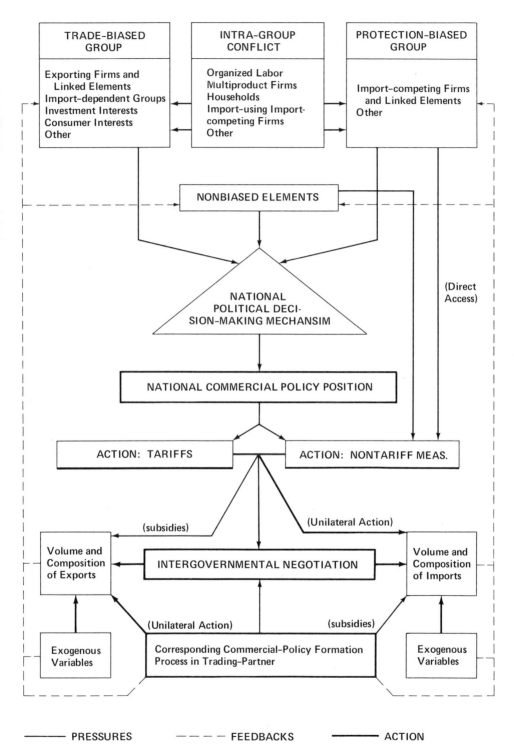

Fig. 9–1. Development of the national trade-policy position.

151

accordance with the balance of economic forces. Indeed, trade policy is only one of many related and unrelated issues in the national political arena at a given point in time. Consequently the resultant outcome with regard to the nature, magnitude, and even the direction of national commercial policy may be at odds with the expectations.

ACCESS TO THE INSTRUMENTS OF TRADE POLICY

Once a national trade-policy position has been established, along the lines indicated, it must be implemented. This involves the intensified application or liberalization of the techniques of international trade policy: *tariff* and *nontariff* obstacles to the free international mobility of goods and services, as discussed in the next two chapters. In part, the devices chosen depend on the pressures brought to bear during the course of the decision-making process just described. A particular protective device may be specified by elements in the protection-biased sector and be accepted in the course of the political transformation process. Or trade-policy devices other than those specified may be substituted in the bargaining process, either because they are less onerous than the former or because the danger of foreign repercussions is deemed to be less serious.

The output of the national decision-making process will be either to raise or to lower restrictions to trade, or to leave them unchanged. If the political balance weighs in favor of liberalization, a mandate is normally created for international negotiations designed to bring this about under the proviso that the bargaining outcome be as favorable as possible to the interests represented in the trade-biased sector and do as little damage as possible to the protection-biased sector. When the latter is quite obviously unavoidable, provision may be made for tax-financed adjustment assistance for injured industries and linked economic groups—a case of compensation by the gainers (the general public) to the losers from freer trade.

But suppose the political balance weighs in favor of increased trade restriction. The policy mix chosen will reflect the specific demands of the protection-biased sector as modified in the political decision-making process according to the influence of the opposition and nonbiased estimates of the least-cost course of action. Specific account must be taken of the likelihood of foreign trade-policy reactions and of damage to import-using groups, and the trade-policy techniques adopted will reflect these assessments. Once a course of action and mix of trade-policy devices is decided upon, application of the relevant measures is generally unilateral.

However, the availability of access to the instruments of trade policy, like the political weight of protection-biased and trade-biased arguments, may not be symmetrical as between the two interest groups. Whereas the trade-biased interests may have to expose themselves to the entire political decision-making mechanism, it is often possible for the protection-biased interests to short-circuit this process by resorting to certain nontariff barriers. Such restrictions are applied by a wide variety of governmental units, often with little apparent coordination, central direction or even awareness on the part of national decision-making units. Consequently, it is possible for individual protection-seeking forces to avail themselves of measures imposed under these conditions and thereby translate their interests into policy action without themselves being subject to public debate and scrutiny, as well as to the opposing forces in the political arena.

INTERNATIONAL CONCILIATION

Once a national trade-policy position has been established it must be exposed to corresponding forces operating in other national economies and emerging as foreign trade-policy positions.

The latter will often influence the domestic decision-making process and may be considered in this respect together with the nonbiased forces. If the foreign political outcome is such that an important trading partner applies or may be about to apply trade restrictions, this fact weighs in the domestic decision process in favor of the protection-biased sector. In some instances retaliation may be mandatory, as a result of pre-existing legal provisions designed to protect the trade-biased sector by discouraging unilateral restrictive action abroad. Conversely, tendencies abroad toward freer trade will be reflected in the national debate on the side of the trade-biased sector; a "climate" of trade liberalization may exist which adds momentum to any initiatives toward freer trade. Hence the national trade policy position is not formed in a vacuum. Rather, it is influenced by corresponding forces operating abroad, just as it affects the commercial policy stance of foreign countries. In general, therefore, it would appear that the interdependence factor would tend to produce mutual reinforcement of prevailing tendencies internationally.

The national trade-policy position, once established, emerges in the international arena to face corresponding positions formed abroad to be subjected to conciliation efforts bilaterally or under the auspices of established international institutions, particularly the General Agreement on Tariffs and Trade (GATT), as discussed in Chapter 12. A protection-biased trade policy position may be implemented "legally" or "illegally" under accepted international rules. In the former case the consultative process will tend to determine foreign policy responses, if any. In the latter case such responses are more likely to be unilateral with subsequent consultation. In either instance the general tendency will be toward a proliferation of trade barriers on an international scale.

On the other hand, a trade-biased policy position, if reflected abroad, will tend to produce international consultation leading to a general reduction of international trade barriers. The degree of this liberalization will depend upon the relative strength of the trade-biased forces in the participating countries, as reflected in the respective national commercial-policy positions and the negotiating mandates accorded representatives in the relevant international forums.

With this discussion of the politics of international commercial policy (additional readings may be found in Section E-9), let us turn to the economics of commercial policy.

10

THE THEORY OF TARIFFS

Certainly the most widely employed restriction to trade is the *tariff*. A tariff is a charge levied on goods as they enter a country by crossing the national customs frontier. Usually, their general purpose is to reduce the volume of imports.

There are two types of tariffs. *Ad valorem* tariffs are levied as a percentage of the total *value* of the commodity as it enters the country, including its cost and all transportation charges—its c.i.f. value.[1] *Specific* tariffs, on the other hand, constitute a fixed monetary duty per unit of the imported commodity (e.g., $20 per automobile, $5 per ton of a certain chemical, and so on). Of the two types of tariffs, the *ad valorem* duty is probably the more important.

While both of these levies apply to imports there also exist *export duties,* which are placed on goods leaving a country, and *transit duties,* which are placed on goods crossing a country on the way to a destination elsewhere. Neither of these levies is very important from a quantitative point of view. Export duties are unconstitutional in the United States, but they do raise some interesting questions, especially for commercial policy in developing countries, which we shall explore later on.[2]

In most cases, as we shall see, tariffs are applied with the sole intention of reducing the volume of imports. Naturally, they also raise government revenues, and sometimes tariffs are applied for this purpose alone. This final category of levies on international trade is called the *revenue tariff*.

---

[1] The term c.i.f. stands for cost, insurance, and freight, i.e., the value of the commodity as it arrives at its destination, the customs frontier of the importing country.

[2] *Constitution of the United States,* Article 1, Section 8, "No Tax or Duty shall be laid on Articles exported from any State."

How do tariffs impede imports? To take the simplest possible illustration, suppose we have two countries, A and B. Five pounds of sugar sells for \$0.60 in A and for \$0.40 in B without international trade. Naturally if free trade prevailed, manufacturers in B would export sugar to A, thus driving down the price of sugar in that country. In order to prevent this, all Country A has to do is levy a 50 per cent *ad valorem* tariff on imports of sugar from Country B. Assuming no transport costs, with the tariff the sugar produced in Country B would sell in Country A for exactly the same price as the domestic product (\$0.40 + 50 per cent *ad valorem* tariff = \$0.60). In the absence of quality differences there is no longer any reason for consumers in Country A to buy sugar from Country B, and imports would almost certainly cease.

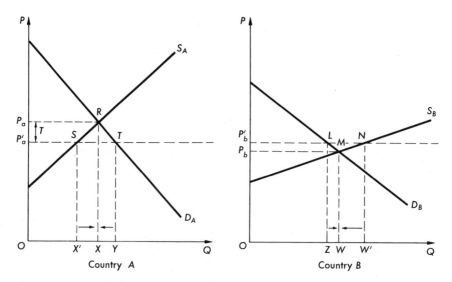

Fig. 10–1. Tariffs and the volume of trade.

This can be illustrated more generally by means of partial equilibrium supply and demand analysis as in Figure 10–1. Without international trade, equilibrium in Country A is at point R, with quantity OX of the commodity being produced and consumed at price P_a. Meanwhile, in Country B quantity OW is being produced and consumed at a price P_b. With international trade, an equilibrium price $P_a' = P_b'$ prevails in both countries. At that price, Country B produces a surplus ZW', which it exports to Country A where it exactly equals the shortage $X'Y$ prevailing there at the new price. The volume of trade thus is $X'Y$ or ZW'.

If Country A now wishes to prevent all imports, it need simply impose a tariff in the amount $P_a' - P_a$. This will raise the price of imports to P_a; domestic supply will expand from S to R; domestic quantity demanded will contract from T to R; and all imports will be shut out. In the exporting country the demand for its exports is eliminated, price falls, and supply contracts from N to M while domestic quantity demanded expands from L to M. Hence, in the absence of transport costs a tariff equal to the difference between the domestic pre-trade and post-trade price has the effect of eliminating trade between the two countries. With transport costs, a somewhat lower tariff will have the same effect. The reader can see for himself that a less restrictive tariff—less than $P_a' - P_a$—will reduce the volume of trade by a smaller amount, and thus will not eliminate it entirely.

TARIFFS, PRODUCTION, AND CONSUMPTION

Let us look next at the impact of a tariff on production and consumption. Figure 10–1 demonstrates that any tariff tends to raise the domestic price of a commodity above its free-trade level, and thereby stimulates domestic production and reduces domestic consumption of the commodity in question.

This is shown more clearly, again in terms of partial equilibrium analysis, in Figure 10–2. Curves Dd and Sd are the domestic demand and supply curves for the particular good under consideration. In isolation, production, consumption and commodity price are determined by their intersection at point E. Under free-trade conditions, however, the foreign supply—here assumed to be perfectly elastic—must be added to the domestic supply resulting in the overall supply curve $Sd + Sf$. Equilibrium is now at point F, with quantity OQ_2 being consumed at price P_1 of which OQ_1 is produced at home and the rest, Q_1Q_2, imported. Now an *ad valorem* tariff, T, is applied, which raises the free-trade supply curve (assuming foreign prices remain unchanged as a result), by the amount of the tariff to $Sd + Sf + T$.

Equilibrium now shifts to point G. As a result of the tariff, the domestic price has gone up to P_2, causing a reduction in consumption to OQ_4. At the same time, the higher prices have encouraged domestic suppliers to expand output to OQ_3, so that imports are reduced from Q_1Q_2 to Q_3Q_4.

Without the tariff, total consumer surplus is represented as the area NP_1F. With the tariff, it is reduced to NP_2G, for an overall consumer surplus loss of P_1P_2GF. This loss to consumers is absorbed in a number of ways.

The tariff makes it possible for the government to collect revenues from the import duty. Tariff revenues always equal the amount of the duty times the quantity of goods imported under it. Hence, here the revenue collected equals $P_1P_2 \times Q_3Q_4$, the area t in Figure 10–2. This represents that part of the loss in consumer surplus which is transferred to the government in the form of money—the *revenue effect* of a tariff.

A second part of the loss in consumer surplus (P_1P_2GF) is transferred, again in monetary terms, to domestic producers of the good in question. At the higher tariff-imposed price, producers receive additional economic rent in the amount r in Figure 10–2. Since this represents a reduction in con-

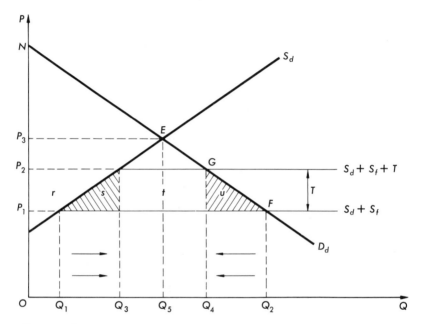

Fig. 10–2. Effect of a tariff on consumption, production, government revenues, and income distribution.

sumer surplus matched by an equivalent increase in producer surplus, it is tantamount to a redistribution of real income from consumers to producers—the *redistribution effect* of a tariff.

With areas r and t of the overall loss of consumer surplus P_1P_2GF thus accounted for, we need only explain the remaining areas s and u. By increasing output in the amount Q_1Q_3 as a result of the tariff, producers find that they must operate at successively higher unit-costs as they progress upward along their supply (marginal cost) curve. They must draw factors of production into the supply process at higher cost—factors which naturally are withdrawn from other sectors of the economy—in addition to possibly incurring diminishing returns. Hence, the area s of the consumer surplus loss is diverted into resources being drawn into the protected sector from other sectors and in a reduction in productive efficiency. It represents a real loss to the economy. This is usually called the *protective effect* of a tariff.

We have now accounted for almost all of the loss of consumer surplus P_1P_2GF attributed to the tariff; r is transferred to producers, t is transferred to the government, and s is a net loss to the economy resulting from the tariff-induced expansion of domestic output. The remainder, area u, is the residual loss of consumer satisfaction not accounted for in any of the above ways—the *consumption effect* of the tariff. It, too represents a real loss to the economy. The total net loss imposed by the tariff upon the economy is thus a sum of the *protective effect* and the *consumption effect*, areas $(s + u)$ in Figure 10–2.

We may summarize this *partial equilibrium* analysis of the effects of a tariff briefly as follows:

Without tariff:
    Consumption.................. OQ_2
    Production.................... OQ_1
    Imports...................... Q_1Q_2
    Price........................ P_1

With tariff:
    Consumption.................. OQ_4
    Production................... OQ_3
    Import....................... Q_3Q_4
    Price........................ P_2

Effects of the tariff:
    Consumption effect............ u
    Protective effect.............. s
    Revenue effect................ t
    Redistribution effect........... r
    Cost of tariff................. $s + u$

This analysis calls to mind some interesting questions. Suppose the tariff were raised to a level that blocked all imports. Imposition of such a *prohibitive tariff* would return equilibrium to that prevailing in isolation (point E in Figure 10–2). The "cost" of the tariff—the combined consumption and protective effects—would increase greatly, as would the redistribution effect. The revenues collected under the tariff would be zero, however, since no goods are imported to which a levy can be applied. The identical effects could be obtained by simply sealing the national frontiers to the particular good in question and thus banning all imports.

Note also that the more inelastic the domestic supply, the smaller will be the protective effect of a tariff, and the smaller the "cost" of the tariff to the economy. Fewer productive resources will be diverted, and reductions in productive efficiency involved with diminishing returns will be avoided. Similarly, the more inelastic the domestic demand for the commodity, the smaller will be the consumption effect and the associated "cost" of the tariff. In either case, the tariff will achieve a smaller reduction in imports, and its burden upon the economy will be correspondingly less.

THE THEORY OF EFFECTIVE PROTECTION

One of the basic questions that has arisen in connection with conventional tariff theory is whether tariff rates really measure what they are supposed to measure—namely protection of the domestic industry in competition with imports. In the foregoing discussion, the "protective effect" of a tariff was identified as the resultant increase in *output* by the import-competing industry that would not have been possible without increased protection. Instead of increased physical output, what really should be measured is the increased *value-added* (the value of final sales minus the value of all raw materials and intermediate inputs) that results from protection. Value-added measures the value of primary factor inputs—land, labor, and capital—used in a firm or an industry. The theory of effective protection points out that it is not only protection of final products that is important, but also the protection of all of the inputs into those final products.

To cite a very simple example, suppose Country *A* imposed a 20 per cent *ad valorem* duty on imports of poultry. Given some knowledge of domestic and foreign demand and supply conditions, we would feel qualified to make a statement concerning the degree of protection provided domestic poultry suppliers under the 20 per cent tariff. Suppose, now, that we were given the additional information that Country *A* has lowered its tariff on imports of feed grains from 20 per cent to zero. Clearly, domestic poultry producers' costs of production will fall, their competitive position will improve, and the volume of poultry imports will fall further if the existing duty is maintained.

The point is that a given duty on any finished product will have a substantially greater protective effect if it is combined with low tariffs on the inputs of the protected industry than if the tariffs on these inputs are high. Conversely, it will have a somewhat lesser protective effect if the national customs duties on the raw material and component inputs of that particular finished good are high rather than low. In short, a given protective tariff on a finished good may either overstate or understate the real or *effective* rate of protection accorded domestic suppliers, depending upon the level of the tariffs imposed on inputs. Under these conditions, the analysis of individual tariff *rates* is clearly insufficient and must be combined with an analysis of the national tariff *structure* in order to portray effectively the real protection involved.

This can be very simply illustrated with the help of a diagram such as

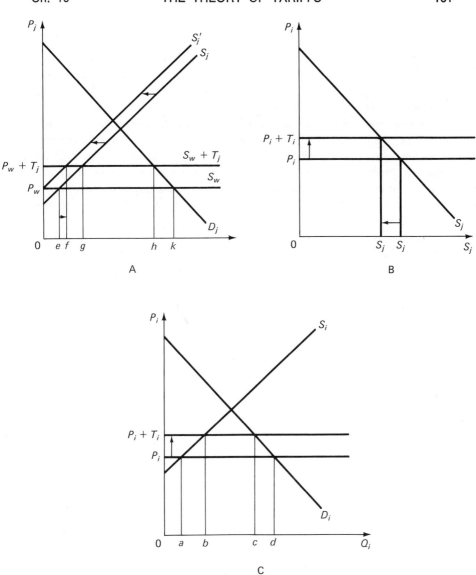

Fig. 10–3. Tariffs on imports to final products.

Figure 10–3. Part A of that diagram merely reproduces Figure 10–2 for a final good j. Using the nominal-protection concept, we would expect that a tariff of T_j and the resultant domestic price increase would raise domestic output along supply function S_j from quantity e to quantity g. This would be considered the protective effect of the tariff. Suppose, on the other hand, tariffs on other goods are increased at the same time, including good i which is an input into good j. Figure 10–3C shows that a tariff imposed on input i. This translates into a leftward shift in the S_j function in Figure 10–3A. will increase the marginal cost of producing final-good j. Figure 10–3B shows the supply of output j being an inverse function of the price of input i. This translates into a leftward shift in the S_j function in Figure 10–3A. At the new equilibrium quantity Of of j is produced. Hence the net protective effect of increased tariffs on both final-good j and input i on the industry producing good j is to raise output from e to f. This compares with the predicted protective effect of eg based on nominal protection of good j only. In other words, to the extent that tariffs are imposed on inputs as well, tariffs bearing on final goods only tend to *overstate* the degree of protection actually accorded.

What needs to be done to calculate the effective rate of protection (ERP) of value-added is to deduct from the nominal tariff on a given product the weighted average of the tariffs imposed on all inputs—the weights being the proportionate contribution of each input to the value of the final product—all relative to free-trade value-added.

It is not difficult to compute the effective rate of protection given suppliers of a particular finished commodity. The total value of any finished good reflects the value added by the manufacturer, *plus* the total value of all of the material inputs used. Per dollar of output, therefore, it is the value-added in that industry (v_j) plus the sum of the values of each input (i) contributed to a dollar's worth of output of that commodity (a_{ij}). This may be written as follows:

$$v_j + \sum_{i=1}^{n} a_{ij} = 1. \qquad (1)$$

If a tariff is placed on the competing imported commodity, the domestic selling price of good j will rise by the amount of the tariff, t_j. Assuming a perfectly elastic supply of inputs, all of this will be reflected in a higher value-added by the domestic suppliers (v_j'). With the tariff, the above equation thus becomes

$$v'_j + \sum_{i=1}^{n} a_{ij} = 1 + t_j. \qquad (2)$$

But tariffs may also be imposed on the inputs themselves, so that the value of each input becomes $1 + t_i$. Equation (2) then becomes

$$v'_j + \sum_{i=1}^{n} a_{ij}(1 + t_i) = 1 + t_j. \qquad (3)$$

The effective protective rate is defined as the total increase in the value-added domestically as a result of tariffs, i.e., the difference between v_j and v'_j, expressed as a percentage of the non-tariff value-added, or

$$\text{ERP}_j = \frac{v'_j - v_j}{v_j}. \tag{4}$$

Rewriting equations (1) and (3), we get

$$v_j = 1 - \sum_{i=1}^{n} a_{ij} \text{ (free-trade)}, \tag{5}$$

and

$$v'_j = 1 + t_j - \sum_{i=1}^{n} a_{ij}(1 + t_i) \text{ (with tariffs)}. \tag{6}$$

Substituting in the numerator of equation (4) gives us

$$\text{ERP}_j = \frac{[1 + t_j - \sum_{i=1}^{n} a_{ij}(1 + t_i)] - [1 - \sum_{i=1}^{n} a_{ij}]}{v_j}, \tag{7}$$

which simplifies to

$$\text{ERP}_j = \frac{t_j - \sum_{i=1}^{n} a_{ij}t_i}{v_j}. \tag{8}$$

It is clear that the effective protective rate of duty on a given finished good will be higher, the lower are the tariffs on raw material and component inputs, relative to the tariff on the commodity itself, i.e., the lower are the various values of t_i relative to the value of the tariff on the finished good itself (t_j).

Moreover, it is evident that only if (a) the weighted average of the tariffs on inputs precisely equals (b) the tariff on the output, will the stated tariff applying to the latter accurately reflect the effective degree of protection involved. If (a) exceeds (b), the tariff on the finished product will overstate the effective protective rate, and if (b) exceeds (a) the nominal tariff on the output will understate the effective protective rate.

Using effective protection to refer to both total value-added and that portion of value-added contributed by labor, one study concluded that U.S. nominal tariff rates greatly understate the rates of protection actually in effect. This understatement was much greater in the latter case than in the former.

Since all trade negotiations, designed to reduce international trade restrictions, involve estimates of the degree of protection embodied in each nation's tariffs, this recent addition to tariff theory is of substantial importance. It points out very clearly the limitations inherent in the use of nominal rates of duty in tariff bargaining, just as it is misleading to simply employ a mean tariff level to characterize the overall tariff barriers of a country. This should be kept in mind as we proceed.

TARIFFS AND THE TERMS OF TRADE

Aside from the various effects of a tariff just illustrated by the simple supply and demand analysis, customs duties also tend to improve the terms of trade of the country imposing them. Since the terms of trade determine the relative size of the gains from international trade accruing to each country, an improvement in a country's terms of trade represents an increase in its share of the gains from trade. If the terms of trade for one country improve, they must simultaneously deteriorate for one or more other countries. By thus increasing the size of its "slice of the pie"—the "pie" being the gains from trade—a country automatically reduces in size the gains attained by its trading partners, and it gains at their expense.

Perhaps the best and most complete way of illustrating the impact of tariffs on the terms of trade involves a return to the use of offer curves as an analytical tool. In Figure 10–4, offer curve OH is drawn for the

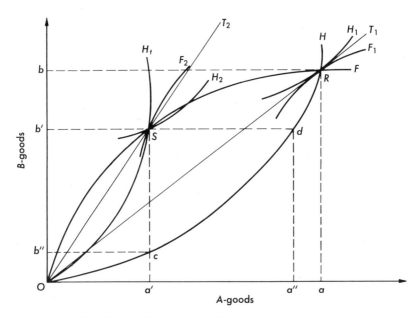

Fig. 10–4. Effect of a tariff on the terms of trade.

home country, exporting A-goods and importing B-goods, while offer curve OF is drawn for the foreign country (or the rest of the world), which exports B-goods and imports A-goods.

Under free trade conditions, intersection of the two countries' respective offer curves occurs at point R, with the prevailing terms of trade being given by the slope of the line OT_1. At the free-trade equilibrium point, the two countries' respective trade indifference curves (F_1 and H_1) are tangent, meaning that neither of the two countries can gain further from international trade without the other losing. A shift in the trade point to the left means a higher trade indifference level for Country H but a lower level for Country F, with the opposite being true if the trade point shifts to the right.

Now suppose the home country imposes a tariff on imports. In doing so, it in effect demands that the foreign nation give up a *larger* quantity of its export good in order to receive a given quantity of imports—the home country's export good. Or, putting it another way, the home country is willing to offer *less* of its export good in return for a certain quantity of imports from abroad. The result, of course, is a shift in the home country's offer curve to the left, say from OH to OH_t. We shall assume, for the moment, that the foreign country does not retaliate, so that the new equilibrium of the foreign offer curve OF and the domestic *tariff-distorted* offer curve OH_t occurs at point S.

Note that the new terms of trade (OT_2) are more favorable to the home country; it must now export fewer A-goods to get a given quantity of B-goods in return. Note also that the home country has reached a higher trade indifference level (H_2) by imposing the tariff, but that the foreign country's new trade indifference level (F_2) is substantially inferior to that prevailing under free-trade conditions.

The tariff itself can be measured in either of the two traded commodities. Without the tariff, Country H was willing to offer Oa'' of its A-goods in exchange for Ob' of the B-goods under its free trade offer curve OH. With the imposition of the tariff, the new tariff distorted offer curve shows that it is willing to offer only Oa' of A-goods in return for the same quantity Ob' of B-goods. Hence, the tariff, measured in terms of the home-country's exports, A-goods, is Sd (or $a'a''$), i.e., that amount of its exports which it was willing to offer in the absence of the tariff but which it is *not* willing to offer with the tariff, in return for an identical amount of imports.

Alternatively, the tariff can also be measured in terms of B-goods. Without the tariff, in return for quantity Oa' of its exports it was willing to accept $a'c$ (or Ob'') of imports, but now it wants $a'S$ (or Ob') of imports for the same amount of its exports. Hence the tariff, measured in terms of the imported B-good, is cS (or $b'b''$); i.e., the increase in the quantity of imports demanded in return for a set amount of exports. As a result of the tariff, the *volume* of trade declines from Oa exports plus Ob imports to Oa' exports plus Ob' imports. Once again, we can summarize all of this as follows:

Free trade:
Equilibrium..................... R
H-exports..................... Oa
F-exports..................... Ob
H-indifference level........... H_1
F-indifference level........... F_1
Terms of trade................ OT_1

With tariff:
Equilibrium.................. S
H-exports..................... Oa'
F-exports..................... Ob'
H-indifference level........... H_2
F-indifference level........... F_2
Terms of trade................ OT_2

The tariff:
Expressed in A-goods........... Sd
Expressed in B-goods........... Sc

Whereas the tariff *may* result in substantial improvement in terms of trade of the country imposing it, it *need* not do so. The other country may retaliate by imposing its own tariff. In addition, the extent of the improvement that one country can expect in (a) its terms of trade and (b) its trade-indifference level, by imposing a tariff, depends largely on the shape of the *other* country's offer curve. Let us examine these two conditions in turn.

Figure 10–5 illustrates the impact of retaliation, counter-retaliation, and tariff "wars" on the terms and volume of international trade. We begin once more with point R, where the two countries' respective offer curves cross under free-trade conditions. The terms of trade are given by the slope of line OT_1. Again, the home country imposes a tariff, shifting its offer curve OH_t, hoping thereby to attain a new equilibrium at S and improved terms of trade OT_2.

This time, however, the foreign country retaliates and imposes its own tariff on imports, thus shifting its offer curve to OF_t. Equilibrium of the two tariff-distorted offer curves is now V, where the terms of trade (slope of OT_3) may well be much below what the home country had originally intended by imposing its initial tariff, and which may actually be somewhat more favorable to the retaliating country than were the free-trade terms of trade. The result, of course, is that the initial intent of the tariff has back-fired.

The home country may now counter-retaliate by again raising the tariff on its imports of *B*-goods, and the foreign country may meet this new challenge with a higher tariff of its own. This cycle of retaliation and counter-retaliation may repeat itself over and over again until some point such as *W* is reached, where the ultimate, tariff-distorted offer curves of both countries $(H_t^*$ and $F_t^*)$ intersect in such a way that, from a terms-of-trade standpoint at least, nobody is the loser.

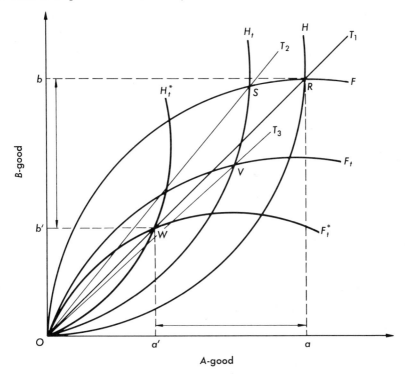

Fig. 10—5. Tariff retaliation and the terms of trade.

But look what has happened to the *volume* of trade. It has fallen from *Oa* of the *A*-good plus *Ob* of the *B*-good to *Oa'* of the *A*-good plus *Ob'* of the *B*-goods. The prices of import goods in both countries must have risen dramatically as a result of the successive increases in import duties, and consumption has been cut down commensurately. At the same time, combined production of both commodities is likely to have been substantially curtailed.

In short, if one country imposes a tariff which is not subject to retaliation it *may* gain at the expense of its trading partner. If the other country retaliates, and especially if this leads to counter-retaliation, *both* countries are likely to lose as a result.

The reader may recognize some interesting implications of this principle. For instance, the smaller and economically less significant a country, the less likely it is that other countries will retaliate against any changes in its tariffs. Hence, such countries may be much more easily able to improve their terms of trade via tariff changes than large countries whose every move calls forth instant response on the part of others. We shall return to this point a little later.

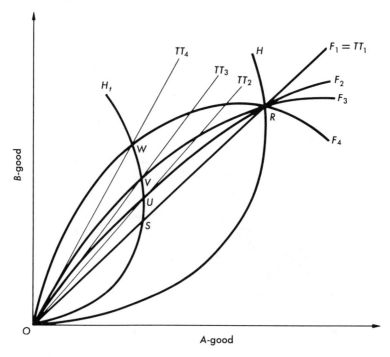

Fig. 10–6. Tariffs and the elasticity of offer curves.

The second point that needs to be mentioned here is that, aside from retaliation, the shape of the foreign country's offer curve will largely determine the degree to which a country will improve its terms of trade by imposing a tariff. In Figure 10–6 there are a number of foreign offer curves of different elasticities, OF_1, OF_2, OF_3, and OF_4. The home country imposes a tariff that shifts its offer curve from OH to OH_t. Note what happens to its terms of trade given the variously shaped foreign offer curves.

If the foreign offer curve is completely *elastic* (OF_1), it must be identical to the free-trade terms-of-trade line. A perfectly elastic offer curve means that a country is willing to offer its exports in return for imports at a certain fixed ratio of exchange, which never changes no matter how much it imports or exports. In this case, it is impossible for the home country to change its terms of trade no matter what it does to its tariffs. The terms of trade at S are the same as they were at R.

The *less* elastic the foreign country's offer curve, the more a given tariff change will improve the home country's terms of trade (again assuming no retaliation). Note that the same tariff-induced shift in the home country's offer curve (OH–OH_t) produces equilibria (S, U, V, W) which show increasingly favorable terms of trade (TT_1, TT_2, TT_3, TT_4), the less elastic the offer curve of the trading partner. Here again we can talk in terms of "small" versus "big" countries. For all intents and purposes, the offer curve of the rest of the world facing Guatemala, Upper Volta, and so on, are perfectly elastic, since these small countries are economically insignificant relative to their trading partner, the rest of the world. They possess no monopoly or monopsony power at all. Hence they are unable to affect their terms of trade by their own actions; the terms of trade are *dictated* to them. This again raises certain questions in connection with trade and economic development which will be of considerable interest later on.

THE OPTIMUM TARIFF?

From the analysis presented here it would seem that, in the absence of retaliation, a country should be able to levy a tariff on imports which yields some optimal terms of trade and, hence, an optimal level of community welfare. Beginning at the free-trade position (or any tariff-distorted trade position), as a country raises its tariffs unilaterally, the terms of trade improve and the volume of trade declines. The improvement in the terms of trade initially tends to more than offset the accompanying reduction in the volume of trade, hence a higher trade indifference curve is reached and community welfare is enhanced. Beyond some point, however, it is likely that the detrimental effect of the successive reductions in trade volume will begin to outweigh the positive effect of further improvements in the terms of trade so that community welfare begins to fall. Somewhere in between there must be a tariff which will optimize a country's welfare level under these conditions.

Figure 10–7 illustrates the existence of some optimum tariff level. Free-trade equilibrium again is at point R, where the home and foreign countries' respective offer curves intersect. At that point, the volume of trade is Og of the A-good and Oc of the B-good, and the terms of trade are given by the slope of line TT. The home country (H) now wishes to impose a tariff that will maximize its community welfare; i.e., place it on the highest possible trade-indifference curve *assuming no retaliation on the part of the foreign country*.

Under free trade conditions at R, Country H attains the trade indifference level h_1, which crosses the foreign offer curve (OF) at R and at

some other point T. *Any* tariff which distorts the home country's offer
curve in such a way that it crosses the foreign country's offer curve between
points T and R will lead to a higher trade indifference level. If the new
tariff-distorted trade point is at T, of course, the trade indifference level
will be unchanged.

The highest possible trade indifference curve that the home country
can reach is one that is *tangent* to the foreign offer curve. This is trade

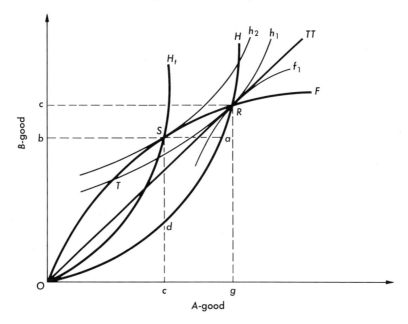

Fig. 10–7. Optimum tariff.

indifference curve h_2, tangent to foreign offer curve OF at point S. Hence,
if the home country can impose a tariff of such magnitude that the tariff-distorted offer curve (OH_t) touches the foreign offer curve (OF) at point
Sd. This is the *optimum tariff*. Given the foreign country's offer curve
terms of the A-good is quantity Sa or, in terms of the B-good, quantity
Sd. This is the *optimum tariff*. Given the foreign country's offer curve
OF, there is no tariff the home country can impose that will yield a higher
level of community welfare.

The magnitude of the optimum tariff depends upon the elasticity of
the foreign offer curve. We saw that if the foreign offer curve is perfectly
elastic, no tariff will yield the home country improved terms of trade.
Hence it cannot possibly advance to a higher trade indifference level. The
less elastic the foreign offer curve, the higher will be the optimum tariff.

Where the foreign offer curve has an elasticity of 1 and thus is horizontal, the optimum tariff will be infinity.

In actuality, the probability is that the foreign country will retaliate against the home country's imposition of an optimum tariff, since it is thereby placed on a lower trade-indifference curve. Hence, the foreign country may itself levy an optimum tariff that crosses the home-country's tariff-distorted offer curve at a point which yields the foreign nation a maximum trade-indifference level. Then the home country may counter-retaliate with another optimum tariff and the tariff-war process outlined in Figure 10–5 takes its usual course.

As indicated in Chapter 9, tariffs represent only one form of protection, albeit the most common one. Far more insidious barriers to the free international exchange of goods and services exist, as we shall see in the following chapter.

11

NONTARIFF
DISTORTIONS

Tariffs are by no means the only restrictions to the free movement of goods internationally. They are, however, the form of trade restriction that is the most widely used and the most easily regulated to provide the precise degree of protective shielding from imports that a given situation seems to require. Moreover, they can serve as a useful source of government revenues. Not least important, their effects on the domestic economy are in most cases relatively clear-cut. For all of these reasons, tariffs have become the most important tool of commercial policy in use today.

Still, we cannot afford to ignore other forms of trade barriers, especially the so-called *quantitative restrictions* to international commerce. The latter restrict imports of goods and services by permitting only a strictly limited amount, either in terms of value or physical quantity, to cross the national customs frontier. This type of trade barrier differs fundamentally from tariffs, which impose a certain monetary charge on imports but permit an unlimited quantity to enter the country as long as the import duty is paid. The effects of these two basically different types of trade impediments are, however, not at all dissimilar, as will soon be evident. From an examination of quantitative restrictions to trade, we shall go on to survey other types of trade impediments that fit neither of the two major categories, but which are by no means unimportant.

QUOTAS

The most important quantitative restriction to international trade is the *quota*. A quota constitutes an absolute limit on the physical quantity or value of goods or services that may be traded over a set period of time. Quotas may be applied to either imports or exports. For example,

Great Britain might rule that only 1 million tons of wheat are to be imported during 1976; this is an *import quota*. Or the Swedish government might declare that, in order to ensure the future health of the Swedish economy, it is necessary to limit exports of iron ore in 1976 to 20 million tons; this is an *export quota*. Quotas such as these are called *global,* or *non-discriminatory,* because they simply set a limit on the total trade in a certain good or service vis-à-vis the rest of the world as a whole. Once that limit is reached, all further trade is prohibited.

Global import quotas contrast with so-called *selective* or *discriminatory* quotas, which differentiate their treatment of imports according to the countries from which the goods originate. Country *A* might have a quota of 20 million oranges per year, of which 4 million must come from Country *B,* 3 million from Country *C,* 3 million from Country *D,* 6 million from Country *E,* and 4 million from Country *F.* This is a selective quota, and the import limits for each country are generally subject to bilateral negotiation. In many cases, selective quotas also may be traced to long-standing economic and political ties, economic warfare, and similar considerations.

A final type of quota is the *tariff quota,* which sets a limit on the amount or value of merchandise which may be imported under a given tariff rate, with any imports in excess of that limit subject to a higher duty. For instance, Mexico might place an *ad valorem* tariff of 20 per cent on the first 10,000 automobiles imported in 1976, 25 per cent on the next 5,000 cars, and so forth.

Here we are mainly concerned with global or non-discriminatory import quotas, the effects of which are very similar to those of tariffs. This is no less true of the reasons for their implementation.

Figure 11–1 is a partial equilibrium, supply-and-demand representation of quota effects for a single commodity and two countries. Under free trade, assuming zero transport costs and the absence of any other charges, in addition to perfectly elastic supply in the exporting country, the equilibrium price in both countries is *p*. At that price, Country *X*—which might represent the rest of the world—demands quantity *Oa*, produces *Oc*, and exports quantity *ac* to Country *M*. The imports of Country *M* (*eh*) make up the difference between domestic supply (*Oe*) and demand (*Oh*) at the equilibrium price *p*.

Now importing Country *M* decides to limit its imports of this particular commodity to a fixed quantity *fg* by imposing a quota in that amount. The reduction in imports from *eh* to *fg* raises the equilibrium price to *p'*, increases the domestic quantity supplied from *Oe* to *Of*, and reduces the quantity demanded from *Oh* to *Og*. In the exporting country, *X*, the import quota imposed by its trading partner automatically reduces its exports from quantity *ac* to *ab*. Equilibrium price stays the same due to

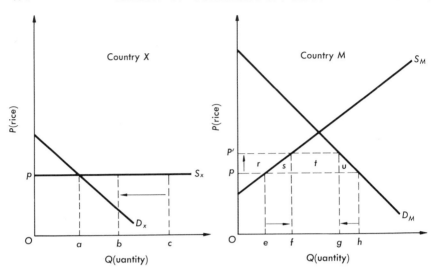

Fig. 11–1. Partial equilibrium analysis of the effects of import quotas.

the perfectly elastic supply, quantity demanded remains at Oa, but the quantity supplied falls from Oc to Ob.

In the importing country, the quota has had *protective* and *consumption* effects similar to those of a tariff. In fact either a tariff or a quota may be used with similar effect to increase domestic output and reduce domestic quantity demanded. Total loss of consumer surplus is represented as the area $r + s + t + u$. Of this total, the areas s and u in Figure 11–1 may again be considered the "cost" of the quota in terms of decreased productive efficiency and consumer satisfaction. Part of the lost consumer surplus is transferred to producers, the *income-redistribution* effect of a quota as represented by the area r, is also similar to that incurred under a tariff having the same impact on the volume of imports.

But what about the revenue effect of a quota? By imposing a quota, the government does not collect customs duties on imports, but the effects are very similar, and the lost consumer surplus represented by the area t must go to someone. If the foreign supply curve is perfectly elastic, as assumed here, and if the government does not interfere in the import procedure other than to impose the quota, these revenues will go to the importers. If, on the other hand, the government decides to sell permission (in the form of import licenses) to import under the quota to the highest bidder, then the government will collect revenues identical to those accruing to it under a tariff of equivalent import-restrictive effect. A third, perhaps less likely possibility is that these revenues will be collected by the foreign exporters—assuming the government does not sell import licenses, and if they are able to raise delivered prices sufficiently to be able to take away most or all of the revenues (t) otherwise accruing to the importers. The question of how such revenues would be divided hinges on the market structures prevailing among the exporters and importers concerned.

This analysis shows the primary effects of quotas to be very similar to those of tariffs. They (a) raise the prevailing domestic price of the commodity, (b) reduce the quantity of imports, (c) reduce the quantity demanded, (d) increase the domestic quantity supplied, (e) redistribute real income from consumers to producers, and (f) yield revenues which may go to the government or be divided among domestic importers and foreign exporters.

Note that once the import quota has been filled, the domestic price of the commodity under consideration will be entirely divorced from the foreign price. If there should be a rise in domestic demand, prices at home will increase but this will have no impact on prices or output abroad or on the volume of trade. The quota will permit no further imports. A similar rise in domestic demand under tariffs (except for prohibitive or confiscatory tariffs), however, would still raise imports and have an effect on prices and production at home and abroad. With tariffs, the connection between foreign and domestic prices and output is always maintained. Under quotas, once they are filled, this relationship is severed.

TERMS-OF-TRADE EFFECTS

Like tariffs, quotas may also be used by a country in an effort to improve its terms of trade vis-à-vis its trading partners, and for precisely the same reasons. The mechanisms and the results in this case, however, are quite different, as shown in Figure 11–2.

The free trade offer curves for the home and foreign countries are, respectively, OH and OF. The free-trade terms of trade are then given by the slope of line TT, and the home country exports quantity Oa of the A-good in return for quantity Ob of the B-good. Now the home country imposes a quota on imports of the B-good in the amount Ob'; the home country's offer of A-goods becomes zero once that quantity of imports has been reached. Hence, the home country's quota-distorted offer curve becomes OSb', and intersects the foreign country's offer curve OF at point T.

Its new terms of trade will be TT'. There is a substantial improvement over the free-trade terms of trade, as is true in the case of a tariff, and, depending on the shape of the home country's trade indifference curve, this may represent a corresponding improvement in economic welfare. The revenues attributable to the imposition of the quota may be represented, in terms of the A-good, as the quantity $a''a'$. If there is competitive bidding for import licenses, this revenue would go to the home country's government.

If there is collusion among exporters in the foreign country—i.e., domestic importers competing freely with one another—this revenue would go to the foreign exporters, and the nation's terms of trade may deteriorate, although this cannot be shown by means of offer curves which assume perfect competition. The reverse would be true if the exporters competed

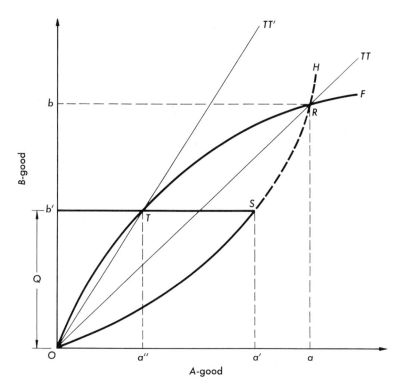

Fig. 11–2. Impact of a quota on the terms of trade.

freely and there was collusion among the importers; the importers would capture the revenues. Lastly, if there was collusion among both importers and exporters, the distribution of the quota-induced revenues is indeterminate unless the precise bargaining strengths of the two parties are known.

Again, the *potential* for improvement in the terms of trade as a result of the imposition of a quota—or any other import-limiting restriction—hinges upon the shape of the foreign country's offer curve and the retaliatory action, if any, that the latter decides to take. In this respect, the terms-of-trade effects of a quota are again similar to those induced by tariffs.

ARGUMENTS FOR QUOTAS

Most of the arguments for the imposition of tariffs, surveyed in the previous chapter, may be equally applied to quotas. Generally, these center around the protection of home industries. If domestic suppliers are able to produce 1 million units of good X at prevailing prices, and it looks like the demand for next year will be 1.2 million units, we may want to place a quota of 200,000 units on imports of good X. In this manner, we prevent a rise in prices brought about by shutting out all imports and permit domestic suppliers to market all of their output at current prices without fear of "ruinous" import competition.

This hints at one of the advantages of quotas over tariffs as an instrument of commercial policy. First of all, quotas are much more precise and, in their effect, much more certain. If an *ad valorem* tariff of 10 per cent is imposed on imports of wheat, no one knows how much wheat will be imported or at what prices it will be sold. This naturally depends on supply conditions prevailing abroad, over which we have no control. A bumper crop abroad and resultant falling world prices of wheat could lead to a surge of imports despite the 10 per cent tariff—and prove disastrous for domestic farmers. The quota avoids this difficulty. We simply set a price for wheat that will yield our farmers a "fair" return, estimate the demand at that price and how much of that demand domestic farmers will be able to satisfy, and set an import quota for the remainder. Uncertainty with regard to foreign supply conditions thus constitutes a strong reason for the use of quotas as opposed to tariffs as an instrument of protection.

Second, if domestic demand for a particular imported commodity is particularly *inelastic,* a strong case may also be made for quotas. For instance, suppose a large quantity of automobiles is imported even after a tariff has been successively raised. If we still desire to reduce automobile imports, a quota offers an effective alternative to raising the tariff still further. Imports of cars are limited to a set number, and buyers and sellers then bid for them, with the market price being established in the usual way. Similarly, a highly inelastic foreign supply may give rise to the use of quotas, as opposed to tariffs, by the home country. If foreign producers must sell the goods they have on hand at virtually any price, they can and will hurdle just about any tariff in order to compete on the domestic market. Here again, if we decide to protect domestic producers, the tariff will not do the job and import quotas provide a ready and effective alternative.

Third, and perhaps equally important, is the fact that quotas tend to be more flexible, more easily imposed, and more easily removed instruments of commercial policy than tariffs. Tariffs are often regarded as relatively permanent measures and rapidly build powerful vested interests which make them all the more difficult to remove. Quotas have many characteristics of a more temporary measure, are designed to deal only with a current problem, and are removable as soon as circumstances warrant. By the same token, they may be more easily implemented as emergency measures. They are usually unencumbered by reciprocal trade agreements and other institutional forces making for rigidity. Other countries may be less apt to view quotas as permanent trade barriers and as threats to their exports, and thus are perhaps less likely to retaliate swiftly with new trade impediments of their own.

Finally, quotas may also be useful as a measure to prevent the international transmissions of severe recessions in economic activity. A country undergoing a recession may attempt to alleviate it by stimulating exports in a variety of ways, and if the recession is accompanied by price reductions in the form of deflation, the export stimulus will indeed be automatic. Such increased exports will appear as rising imports in other countries. If the latter nations are already under some recessionary pressure, the increased imports will make matters worse and may do lasting damage if the mobility of productive resources is severely limited. Hence, in order to avoid aggravating the domestic situation and partly to insulate itself from the economic misfortunes of other countries, a nation may invoke quotas as the most administratively feasible way of cutting back the potentially damaging wave of imports. In any case, such temporary maladjustments in economic activity may be no reflection of the underlying comparative cost relationships. The gain in achieving relative economic stability may well outweigh the costs associated with the quotas under these circumstances.

All of this is designed to show that, just as in the case of tariffs, there are some conditions under which quotas may be useful and, indeed, beneficial, as well as instances where the quota may be superior to the tariff as an instrument of commercial policy. Now let us examine the other side of the coin.

First, quotas tend to be far more arbitrary than tariffs. They do much to damage the international trade mechanism by *removing* it from the operation of the price system and market forces. There is great danger of a variety of problems arising as a result of errors made by trade administrators, operating without the guidance of relatively freely determined prices. This danger is multiplied in importance if quotas are granted on a selective, or discriminatory basis, with political, military, social, and other considerations interfering in the operation of trade between nations.

Second, we have seen that quotas tend to support concentration among importers and exporters. The administrative allocation of quotas to importers reduces competition and fosters the development of import monopolies. Similarly, among the foreign exporters, quotas tend to promote concentration which must be sufficiently powerful to bargain effectively with the home country's importers. If we agree that import and export monopolies constitute a decided liability, as we shall see in the next chapter, then quotas definitely appear to be an inferior instrument of commercial policy on this account alone.

Third, in a period of inflationary pressure, quotas tend to feed the flames of inflation by keeping out import competition—just as they help control further downward pressure on the economy in times of recession by reducing domestic expenditures on imports. This is a characteristic common to both quotas and tariffs.

QUOTAS VERSUS TARIFFS

Given a decision to protect a particular industry, a country must reach a decision on the type of trade barriers to use. Apart from obligations under international agreements which may *fix* the level of tariffs or commit countries to abstinence from quotas, there are considerable differences in the economic effects of the two types of trade restrictions which influence their relative social costs.

Consider, for example, Figure 11-3. Diagram A shows a nominal protective effect of ac being secured by import-competing production via a tariff

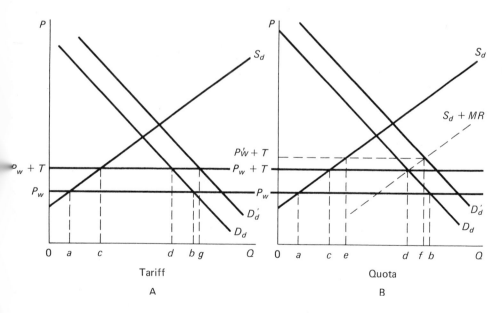

Fig. 11–3. Tariffs versus quotas in partial equilibrium.

which raises price from P_w to $P_w + T$. Diagram B shows the same nominal protection (ac) resulting from a *static-equivalent* quota of ed, raising domestic price by the same amount. Apparently, tariff and quota have the same impact, except for possible differences in the revenue-effects, already discussed.

But suppose domestic demand for the product expands. With the tariff, price remains at $P_w + T$ and imports expand from cd to cg. With the quota, quantity imported remains constant at $cd = ef$, and price rises to $P_w' + T$. In effect, the quota results in a new supply function $S_d + MR$, as opposed to the perfectly elastic world supply at $P_w + T$ in the case of the tariff. Hence expanding domestic demands (or contracting domestic supply) means a relatively greater degree of trade restriction and negative welfare implications in the case of quotas as opposed to static-equivalent tariffs. The reader can work out for himself what happens when domestic demand *declines* relative to domestic supply, when quotas turn out to be superior to tariffs in terms of welfare shifts.

There are a variety of additional welfare differences between tariffs and quotas, which have been explored extensively in the literature, and the interested reader is referred to the studies cited in Section E-12.

ANALYSIS OF NONTARIFF DISTORTIONS

There are a variety of nontariff barriers (NTB's) to international trade, other than explicit quotas.

Import-directed NTB's tend to result in higher prices of imports and import-competing goods for domestic purchasers, or to reduce the supply of goods available by: (a) imposing significant extra costs on foreign exporters or domestic importers; (b) limiting the volume of imports permitted; (c) imposing conditions of high uncertainty and risk on domestic importers or foreign exporters, to which they respond by limiting the volume of trade; or (d) a combination of the above.

Export-directed NTB's may artificially stimulate foreign sales by lowering or removing costs that would otherwise have to be borne by exporters. This permits lower export prices and enhances domestic suppliers' competitiveness in world markets relative to their foreign counterparts. For foreign consumers or users, such measures will—if successful—bring about lower prices and increased supplies of the commodities in question. Export-directed nontariff barriers may also be aimed at *impeding* sales abroad, particularly of primary commodities, when it is desired to increase value-added at home or to avoid resource depletion.

Unlike tariffs, nontariff barriers are subject to substantial uncertainty, which imposes an increased risk on exporters and importers alike. They may be varied substantially from one period of time to the next—even when import-destined goods are already in transit—and are often subject to wide administrative discretion. To the extent that importers and foreign exporters are risk-averters, the impact of NTB's on the volume of trade may in fact be many times that implied by the associated costs themselves. Foreign exporters may shift sales to domestic markets or export markets in countries that do not impose NTB's, even in the face of lower prices. Wholesalers and retailers may shift their purchases to domestic suppliers—in spite of their higher prices—rather than face substantial uncertainty about the final prices or availability of imports.

Nontariff barriers, then, tend to operate primarily through: (a) subsidies to import-competing suppliers, (b) costs imposed on imports, (c) quantitative restrictions on imports, (d) cost-reducing subsidies to export suppliers, and (e) quantitative restrictions on exports. There are a wide variety of NTB's which may be identified, all of which work in one or more of these ways. There are also a large number of distortions to trade which are generally considered NTB's, but which are applied without the specific purpose of impeding imports or artificially stimulating exports. This has important implications for their impact on trade as well as for attempts at their liberalization. The following typology is useful for analytical purposes:

Type I. Measures designed primarily to protect domestic industry from import competition, to restrict exports, or to strengthen domestic industry in competing with imports or competing for export markets. These are subclassified into import-directed and export-directed groups.

Type II. Trade-distorting policies and practices which are imposed primarily with the intent of dealing with nontrade-related problems, but which are periodically and purposely employed for trade-restrictive reasons.

Type III. Policies and practices applied exclusively for nontrade-related reasons, but which unavoidably serve to distort international competitive conditions and hence affect trade.

TYPE I RESTRICTIONS: IMPORT-DIRECTED

There are about a dozen NTB's that can be distinguished as belonging to the Type I classification. They are implemented with the specific intent of impeding imports or stimulating exports in a manner distortive of trade. This category also includes measures designed to restrict the exports of *trading partners* for the purpose of protecting domestic industry.

Quantitative Restrictions

Quotas, as discussed above, and discretionary licensing imposed on imports are included in this category. Also, quotas and licensing designed to restrict exports, including "voluntary export restrictions" to which a nation may submit either under pressure from trading partners desiring to reduce their own imports of the commodity in question, or as part of a multinational agreement.

Variable Levies

These encompass essentially *ad valorem* import surcharges which may be varied according to conditions prevailing on the domestic market, including tariff quotas. Variable levies are applied most often to imports of agricultural commodities, in order to insure that the domestic price of farm produce remains within a range specified under national agricultural policies. A twofold protective effect may be felt, as a result of the levy itself *and* increased uncertainty among foreign suppliers and traders as to their ability to compete in the protected market. It may be argued that any administrative prerogative to raise tariffs in an *ad hoc* manner for whatever reason represents a form of variable levy. Escape-clause and "national security" provisions for increased tariff protection are two examples of this. In the case of the U.S., two additional examples are provisions under the Tariff Act of 1930 which permit tariff increases in order to "equalize costs of production" and offset "unfair acts" on the part of foreign exporters.

Supplementary Charges

These charges include lump-sum, specific charges on imports, as opposed to the *ad valorem* charges usually associated with variable levies. The impact on costs and uncertainty is essentially the same as under variable levies.

Minimum Import Prices

Such prices are often applied, in connection with variable levies or supplementary charges, to imports of agricultural commodities. A minimum import price is fixed which will not disrupt the domestic market. Foreign suppliers must offer their commodities for import at or above this price. Otherwise, a supplementary charge or variable levy will be applied so that the c.i.f. import price equals the established minimum and domestic suppliers are safeguarded. Minimum import prices may also be applied in conjunction with state-trading practices—outlined below—and quantitative import controls.

Conditional Imports

This involves application of a system similar to that employed under minimum import prices to quantitative import restrictions. Quantitative barriers are set according to the state of the domestic market, with imports freely permitted under certain conditions and severely restricted under other circumstances. Generally, conditional imports are characteristic of trade in agricultural commodities, with the size of the domestic harvest acting as the determining variable. Once more, there is a twofold restrictive effect operating through a quantitative limitation of imports and increased uncertainty.

Import Calendars

These are usually implemented in connection with quantitative restrictions—and sometimes with supplementary charges and variable levies—on imports of agricultural commodities. Typically, imports are restricted from the time a domestic crop is harvested until all of it has been consumed. They are relatively free from restriction during the remainder of the year.

Mixing, Milling, and Domestic-content Regulations

These restrict trade by specifying the domestically produced content of all products of a certain type permitted to be offered for sale in the importing countries. Such regulations may serve as a trade barrier in terms of both reducing the imported content allowed and raising the cost of the product due to the necessity of further processing within the importing country.

Discriminatory Government Purchasing

This involves discrimination in purchases for government account of goods and services in favor of domestic suppliers. Whereas there may at times be sound reasons—with regard to quality and service—for domestic purchases by national and state–local government and quasi-governmental units, restricted bidding and other "buy domestic" practices and legislation—as well as domestic-content regulations imposed on government contractors and subcontractors—clearly represent intentional import restrictions. This includes "tying" foreign-aid credits and grants to purchases in the donor country.

Buy-domestic Extensions

Such a category entails government action designed to coerce the general public or nationalized, government-regulated, or government-influenced industries or business firms to purchase import-competing goods or services in preference to imports. This distortion may apply both to goods already in existence as well as goods to be produced in the future—such as aircraft—which require long production lead-times and a major public or private capital commitment.

Subsidies

Direct government subsidization of import-competing suppliers through tax rebates, credits, and so forth, is involved.

Antidumping Measures

These measures include practices and attendant legislation designed to impede "dumped" imports, except when used against predatory dumping by foreign suppliers—see the discussion of dumping in Chapter 15. These are generally implemented in the form of quantitative import restrictions or import surcharges, but may also involve government subsidization of import-competing suppliers.

State Trading

These are practices associated with trading by government monopolies insofar as they are distortive of competition and designed to protect import-competing suppliers.

TYPE I RESTRICTIONS: EXPORT-DIRECTED

Certain Type I nontariff restrictions are specifically aimed at promoting or restraining *exports*. These are probably of substantially less overall significance in terms of their distortive impact on trade than are nontariff barriers intended to protect domestic suppliers from import competition.

Subsidies

Direct government subsidization of exports by means of rebates, resale arrangements, and so forth, are included in this category.

Export-credit-insurance Subsidization

This involves actuarily unsound export credit insurance schemes—to protect exporters against commercial and political risk—that have historically operated with deficits covered by the government.

Dumping

Dumping entails pricing practices of a predatory or disruptive nature specifically designed to disrupt foreign markets, whether or not engaged in with overt or covert government support (see Chapter 15).

State Trading

This category includes subsidization of exports under the guise of state trading, as practices by government export monopolies.

Quantitative Export Restrictions

These are designed to impede exports of certain products in order to increase domestic value-added, preserve domestic resources, avoid disruption of foreign markets, prevent the export of defense-related technology, or for related reasons. Restriction may take the form of quotas or discretionary licensing of exports.

Export Charges

Their purpose is similar to that of quantitative export restrictions. They are normally applied to exports of primary commodities only.

TYPE II RESTRICTIONS

More numerous than those policies and practices specifically aimed at affecting imports or exports are trade-distortive measures employed as trade barriers collaterally with their primary intent of dealing with other economic, social, or political problems. Such measures can operate either on the import or export side; often they affect both imports and exports simultaneously.

Customs Valuation

These are discriminatory or arbitrary procedures designed to raise the dutiable value of imported commodities in order to increase the real tariff burden borne by the product. Valuation procedures may or may not be intentionally protective.

Customs Classification

Such a measure entails discrimination by customs authorities in classifying imports in terms of low-tariff and high-tariff categories. This factor may be especially important when significant discretion is allowed the individual customs agents in the classification process.

Border Tax Adjustments

These are applied in connection with national indirect tax systems. Tax-rebates on exports granted by a country may be overcompensated or under-compensated by countervailing duties levied by the importing nation. Border tax adjustments may be turned into implicit export subsidies by means of increased rebates, or into implicit import surcharges by means of increased countervailing duties.

Mark-of-origin Regulations

These may be imposed in a discriminatory manner on imports, thereby increasing costs. Variability in such regulations may additionally serve to increase uncertainty on the part of importers and hence retard trade. Mark-of-origin regulations may be used as a protectionist device if they require that the country of origin be noted on the imported commodity in a particularly striking or obtrusive manner. Under certain conditions, the importer, wholesaler, or retailer may simply find the goods unsaleable and will terminate his purchases. Obviously, there are differences among those involved as to what is "obtrusive" and hence trade-retarding, and what is not.

Marketing Standards

Advertising and marketing regulations are used to discriminate against imports. For example, a product may not be advertised and sold as "beer" in certain countries unless it is of a stipulated composition of ingredients, and a number of countries forbid the inclusion of corn oil in food products sold under commonly accepted generic names.

Safety Requirements

This measure involves application of legitimate safety requirements in such a way as to be discriminatory against imports. Especially vulnerable to such restrictions are imports of transportation services on public carriers, automotive vehicles, gas cylinders and other pressure vessels, and industrial machinery. Safety regulations may require inspection and approval by agencies which only operate within the importing country, so that an import may not be approved even after the transportation costs have been incurred, thereby raising the risk so high as to in effect exclude foreign-made products.

Health Requirements

These regulations concern the sanitary and health characteristics of imports of food and nonfood items when applied in a manner clearly discriminatory against imports. Such restrictions impose costs on importers through service fees, additional processing required before sale, or long inspection delays.

Internal Transport Charges

Discriminatory charges on transportation commodities within countries, with preferences granted to selected export or import-competing industries by nationalized, government-regulated, or government-influenced common carriers are involved here.

Customs Procedures

Cost-imposing border-clearance procedures are included, especially those applied at the customs frontier itself such as appraisal and duty-determination. This includes customs-clearance practices aimed at imposing costs and increasing uncertainty through harassment and undue delay.

Use Taxes

These are imposed on imported commodities in a discriminatory manner. This restriction may be important when applied to automotive motor vehicles based on horsepower, weight, or piston-displacement. Generally, such taxes are levied on a highly progressive basis, with most import-competing products falling at the low end and imported goods falling at the high end of the tax-rate scale.

Advance Deposits

This category entails cash deposits required in advance of importation for duties, variable levies, or other import charges anticipated to be incurred by the imported product. Advance deposits may also be based on the value of the imports themselves. Such restrictions impose an interest cost which falls on the importer. They are especially significant when the required deposits exceed substantially the amount of the charges payable or are fixed at a high percentage of the value of imports.

Media Restrictions

These include limitations on advertisement of imported products and on the amount of foreign content permitted in imported and locally published newspapers, books, and magazines, or in motion picture films and television and radio programs.

Government Entrepreneurship

This involves production of import-competing and export goods that would not be supplied without government initiative. This may hold special significance if it involves the formation of government-sponsored consortia and is applied in connection with "buy domestic" programs in procurement by the government or government-influenced business firms.

Government Financing

Low-cost financing provided or guaranteed by the government of investments in physical plant and equipment or research and development, to be employed in the production of import-competing or export goods is included here.

Trade Agreements

These are bilateral or multilateral in nature, which operate to the complete or partial exclusion of competitive suppliers in certain countries. They include long-term delivery contracts, bulk-purchase agreements, buffer stocks, and bilateral or multilateral commodity agreements.

Monetary Restrictions

These include exchange controls, multiple exchange rates, and other devices, applied for balance of payments reasons, which affect imports and protect import-competing suppliers or serve to stimulate or retard exports. (See Chapter 24). Such restrictions may be applied with specific protective intent, apart from their primary purpose on the monetary side.

TYPE III RESTRICTIONS

Most of the NTB's falling under the third classification may be considered ancillary side-effects of policies and measures applied substantially without regard to their probable impact on imports or exports. Nevertheless, some of these may have an important bearing on trade flows, even if the protective intent is absent.

Variation in Tariff Classification and Valuation

The existence of different tariff classification systems or valuation systems may have an effect on costs by reducing efficiency in trade below what it would be in the event of uniform practices. There may also be some trade-retarding effect attributable to increased uncertainty.

Variation in Indirect Tax Systems

If not fully compensated by border tax adjustments—compensation which may under certain conditions be extremely difficult—such variations may serve to distort trade without intent to do so on the part of the responsible authorities.

Variation in Direct Tax Systems

If it can be shown that variations of direct taxes imposed on business firms bear on their ability to reinvest earnings, and that this in turn affects price and quality of tradeable goods, such variations may affect trade to some degree. This may be especially true if differences in direct tax structures have an impact on *future* international competitiveness, via their effect on current business investment in physical plant and in research and development.

Variation in Depreciation Methods

There are significant intercountry differences in permissible methods of depreciation for tax purposes. These affect the cash-flow of business firms and may influence the quality and productivity of capital equipment employed in production. In this way, there may be some connection between this and the long-term price and quality competitiveness of export and import-competing suppliers.

Variation in Weights and Measures

International differences in electrical standards, measuring systems, driving practices, and so forth, affect production costs, product quality, and international competitiveness. Such differences may not be maintained for restrictive purposes, but increased standardization would serve to facilitate both imports and exports of most industrial countries.

Variation in National Consumption Patterns and Related Governmental Policies

As influenced by government policies and practices, differences in national cultural social and dietary patterns affect tastes and the composition of consumer purchases. This category may include a broad range of actions including income-distribution policies, anti-smoking campaigns, and so on. Especially important may be sumptuary laws and regulations designed to affect consumption of certain products, particularly alcoholic beverages, for social, moral, religious, or other reasons.

Variation in Social Charges

Differences in social security systems and health-insurance schemes in terms of their burden on producers, coverage, and method of application are involved here.

Government-sponsored R&D

This includes government-financed, subsidized, or otherwise materially supported research and development programs affecting export or import-competing goods. This includes spillovers from R&D expenditures not necessarily related to production of tradeable commodities, particularly with regard to the defense and aerospace areas.

Government-induced Scale-effects

Impact of massive government procurement of military or other goods and services on the cost and quality of export and import-competing commodities will make itself felt via economies of scale achieved by the affected industries.

Direct Defense Spillovers

Closely related to the two preceding categories—but included here as a separate entity—is the cost-reducing impact of government defense-related development contracts and subsequent production of nondefense versions of the same or similar products by export- or import-competing industries. Also included is the use of government-owned plant and equipment for other than government-purchased production of tradeable goods and services.

Transfer Costs

These include docking and port delays and congestion, pilferage and other security lapses, longshoremen's strikes, dockside bribery, inadequate port and warehousing facilities for imports, high dock charges, and so forth, as well as "smuggling duties" for the procurement of licenses. All of these affect costs, either directly or indirectly, as in the case of increased insurance changes. They may also affect delivery times, merchandise quality, and other factors influencing competitiveness. All are subject to government regulation to some degree.

International Cartels

Cartels involve international, government-sanctioned private market-sharing or price-fixing agreements, with respect to trade in goods and services supplied by the participating firms (see also Chapter 15). There may also be important secondary effects, as in the case of the International Air Transport Association (IATA) and the various shipping conferences. Such service cartels, with or without government participation, may grant discriminatory shipping rates in the process of maximizing collective profits. Such discrimination may be applied randomly, but may nevertheless bear disproportionately on the exports of certain countries.

This brief survey of nontariff trade barriers, summarized in Table 11–1, should impress the reader with the extent of such measures in the real world—and with the number of opportunities for overt and covert protection that are available. Very frequently tariffs represent the least of the worries of those concerned with free access to international markets. The trouble with NTB's is that they are extremely difficult to analyze and even to identify. But this hardly makes them any less important.

ACCESS TO SUPPLY: EXPORT CONTROLS

Events in the early 1970's have added a new dimension to international commercial policy, traditionally concerned almost exclusively with *import* barriers and access to markets—that is, assured access to sources of supply, particularly fuels, industrial raw materials and food products. The energy crisis of 1973–1974 and U.S. restrictions on exports of soybeans and other commodities particularly highlighted the importance of stable import supplies. The problems of supply and market access, of course, are not independent, and liberal policies in the latter area will generally serve to reduce periodic problems in the former area. Two types of export controls may be analyzed: (a) those imposed on the home country's own exports and (b) those imposed on the exports of its trading partners.

The second of the two categories is perhaps most easily disposed of. The effects of export quotas, imposed by foreign countries, are to some extent similar to the effects of equally restrictive import quotas imposed by the home country itself. Prices in the home country rise, domestic output (if any) increases, and consumption is reduced. The terms of trade of the home country tend to deteriorate as import prices rise relative to export prices—in terms of Figure 11–2, the foreign country's offer curve becomes vertical once the quota has been filled. Whatever additional revenues arise out of the foreign export quota are virtually certain to be garnered by the foreign exporters, who would appear to possess all of the monopoly power.

These conclusions do not hold, of course, whenever the export-quota-imposing nation is in competition with other countries exporting the same commodity. They do bear up, however, whenever there is collusion among all such exporters. The result in the home country may well be generally inflationary, especially if the restricted commodity is a raw material used as an input in a broad spectrum of manufactured goods. The competitiveness, in turn, of the home country's exports of these manufacturers will not normally be impaired, since the raw material export quotas will—if they are applied on a non-discriminatory basis—raise the costs of rivals in foreign countries as well.

In some cases, the imposition of export quotas by foreign countries may be a direct extension of the commercial policy of the home country. An example of this is the imposition of textile export quotas by Japan at the behest of the U.S. during the mid-1960's. The U.S. was able to force Japan to impose these quotas on its own exports largely as a result of a very strong bargaining position. Thus, it was able to protect its own textile suppliers without itself bearing the onus of imposing protective mea-

Table 11–1

Classification of Non-Tariff Measures According to Intent and Manner of Operation (*)

Type I Measures
(Primary Distortive Intent)

A. Import-Directed Measures
1. Quantitatively-operating
   a. Import quotas, globally administered.
   b. Import quotas, selectively administered.
   c. Licensing, discretionary/restrictive.
   d. Liberal licensing.
   e. "Voluntary" export restrictions.
   f. Embargoes.
   g. Domestic-procurement practices by national governments or other public units.
   h. State-trading practices.
   i. Domestic-content and mixing regulations.
2. Operating through costs and prices
   a. Variable levies and supplementary import charges.
   b. Advance-deposit requirements.
   c. Antidumping and countervailing charges.
   d. Direct subsidies to import-competitors.
   e. Credit restrictions on importers.
   f. Tax benefits and other indirect subsidies to import-competitors, including credit concessions.
   g. Discriminatory internal transport charges.

Type II Measures
(Secondary Restrictive Intent)

1. Quantitatively-operating
   a. Communications-media restrictions.
   b. Quantitative advertising and marketing restrictions.
2. Operating through costs and prices
   a. Packaging & labeling regulations.
   b. Health, sanitary and quality standards.
   c. Safety and industrial standards and regulations.
   d. Border-tax adjustments.
   e. Use taxes and excises.
   f. Customs clearance procedures, consular formalities and related practices.
   g. Customs classification procedures and related practices.
   h. Customs valuation procedures and related practices.
   i. Exchange restrictions.
   j. Disclosure regulations and "administrative guidance."
   k. Government-provided entrepreneurship, research and development financing and related aids for the import-competing and export sectors.

Type III Measures
(No Apparent Trade-Distortive Intent)

a. Government manufacturing, sales, and distribution monopolies covering individual products or groups of products.
b. Government structural and regional development policies affecting trade.
c. *Ad hoc* government balance of payments policy measures.
d. Variations in national tax systems.
e. Variations in national social insurance systems and related programs.
f. Variations in allowable capital-depreciation methods.
g. Spillovers from government-financed defense, aerospace, and non-military procurement.
h. Scale-effects induced by government procurement.
i. Variations in national standards regulations and practices.
j. External transport charges and government-sanctioned international transport agreements.
k. Port transfer costs.

    h. International commodity agreements and other orderly-marketing arrangements.

B. Export-Directed Measures
    1. Quantitatively-operating
       a. State trading practices.
       b. Export quotas and licensing.
    2. Operating through costs and prices
       a. Direct subsidies to exporters.
       b. Indirect subsidies to exporters, including tax and credit measures.
       c. Government-supported dumping practices.
       d. Export charges.
       e. International commodity agreements and other orderly-marketing arrangements.

Source: Ingo Walter, "Non-Tariff Obstacles to Trade Among Industrial Countries: Some Preliminary Evidence", *Economia Internazionale*, May, 1971.

sures. Such cases however are rare and, due to the possibility of adverse terms of trade effects, may indeed be inferior to domestic import-restricting programs.

The first category, the imposition of export quotas by the home country, deserves some additional analysis. Figure 11–4 is a partial equilibrium representation of the impact of export quotas. (Figure 11–2 above can be used to draw very similar conclusions from a general equilibrium point of view.)

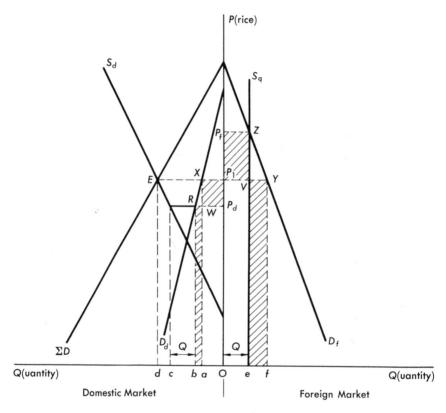

Fig. 11–4. Effect of export quotas: partial equilibrium.

In Figure 11–4, D_d represents domestic demand for the commodity in question, D_f is the foreign demand, ΣD is the sum of the domestic and foreign demand, and S_d is the domestic supply. Under free-trade conditions, price P_1 prevails, with equilibrium at E. Quantity Od is produced, of which Oa is used at home (point X) and ad (Of) is exported. Total export receipts are represented by the area OP_1Yf, and domestic receipts by the area OP_1Xa.

Now suppose the country imposes an export quota in the amount

bc (Oe). The quantity sold domestically rises to Ob with a fall in the domestic price to P_d. Quantity exported is reduced by the quota to bc (Oe) represented by perfectly inelastic supply Sq, with a rise in the export price to P_f. Total export receipts are now represented by the area OP_fZe. As a result of the quota, the net change in export receipts is $OP_1Yf + P_1P_fZV - eVYf$. This reflects the effect of higher export prices combined with lower export volume. The net change in domestic sales is $OP_1Xa + aWRb - P_dP_1WX$, the combined effect of lower domestic prices and higher sales volume.

It is not difficult to see that the effect on total commodity sales (domestic and foreign) of a given export quota will be more favorable: (a) the less elastic the foreign demand for the commodity, (b) the more elastic the domestic demand for the commodity, and (c) the less elastic the domestic supply of the commodity. Each of these will tend to increase those shaded areas in Figure 11-4 that represent higher sales revenues relative to those areas representing a reduction in receipts. The more inelastic is the foreign demand also, the more likely it is that export quotas will result in improved terms of trade, since this will ensure a substantial rise in export prices. It will also ensure that export receipts rise; i.e., that the fall in quantity exported has a lesser bearing on foreign sales than the rise in export prices.

In this particular example, exports alone are restricted. The result, from the standpoint of domestic consumers, is a reduction in price. But the same *international* effect can be brought about with quite different ramifications for domestic consumers. Suppose the country simply limits total production of the export commodity or simply destroys some of its output. Under appropriate elasticity conditions, producers will still benefit due to increased receipts. Domestic consumers will now lose as prices at home are forced to rise *along with* export prices (the domestic supply curve in Figure 11-4 shifts to the left).

We shall return to export-restriction schemes in greater detail at a later point, in connection with the economic problems of the primary-commodity producing areas of the world. Suffice it here to say that a variety of factors make such programs unworkable in most instances—they suffer from internal tensions of the kind that generally beset all supply-restricting arrangements. Only under very limited conditions do they represent viable alternatives to other instruments of commercial policy.

12

TRADE LIBERALIZATION

Thus far, our discussion of commercial policy has focused almost exclusively on *departures* from the free international exchange of goods and services. We have found that there are many reasons—all having to do with national or group interests and welfare—why distortions of international competitive conditions exist in spite of the evident gains associated with freer trade. In this chapter we will *start* from a position where trade and specialization are widely distorted and suppressed by tariff and nontariff barriers, and examine the conditions under which it may make economic and political sense to move toward freer international exchange on a *nondiscriminatory* basis. The following chapter will examine the same issue on a *regional* basis: the formation of free-trade zones among more or less cohesive groups of countries.

TRADE LIBERALIZATION IN THEORY

Suppose myriad restrictions have reduced a nation's trade substantially below what it would have been in the absence of such restraints. Will we be better or worse off by *unilaterally* removing part or all of our national import and export barriers, thereby stimulating the volume of trade and once again expanding the potential for international specialization and gains from trade? Or is it advisable to remove our own restrictions only if our trading partners *reciprocate* by removing their barriers to our exports? Let us pursue some answers to these questions by using the analytical tools developed in connection with the theory of tariffs in the preceding chapter.

Figure 12–1 presents a case where only one country has imposed a tariff; for example, a small country imposes an import duty without incurring retaliatory tariffs on the part of its trading partners. Offer curves OH and OF represent the home and foreign countries, respectively, with the free trade point being R. Under free trade, the home country reaches a welfare level represented by the trade indifference curve h_1, which may cross the foreign offer curve a second time at some point S.

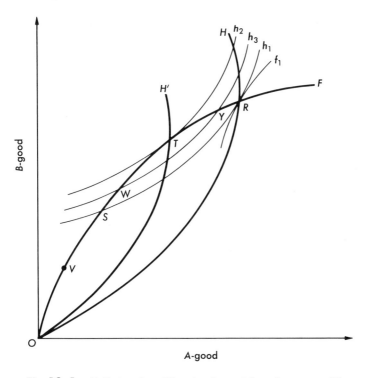

Fig. 12–1. Unilateral tariff reduction with only one tariff.

If the home country has imposed the *optimum* tariff or lower, so that its tariff-distorted offer curve OH' intersects the foreign offer curve OF at or to the right of the point of tangency (T) with one of its own trade indifference curves (h_2), there is no way by which it can reduce its tariff and thereby improve its welfare level. Any reduction in the optimum tariff (or in a tariff lower than the optimum), including the elimination of the tariff entirely, will cause the gain in trade volume to be more than offset by the deterioration in the terms of trade, leading to a lower trade-indifference level.

If, on the other hand, the levy imposed is higher than the optimum tariff, so that the trade point lies between S and T (e.g., point W), a unilateral reduction in the import duty *closer* to the optimum tariff (between W and T, or Y and T) will result in a welfare gain. A tariff reduction leading to a trade point between Y and R will leave the country worse off. Finally, if the trade point with the tariff falls to the left of S on the foreign offer curve (for example, V), then *complete* elimination of the tariff will also lead to a higher trade-indifference curve and welfare level. But in this case the gain in welfare attending complete tariff elimination will be less than if the tariff is only *partially* reduced, and the new tariff level is set closer to the optimum tariff so that the trade point falls between R and S.

Taking a more realistic situation, suppose both countries maintain import duties. This means that the trade point, where the two countries' respective tariff-distorted offer curves intersect, must lie *within* the area bounded by the two free-trade offer curves. Referring again to Figure 12–1, the trade point will fall somewhere inside the boundaries OH and OF. The precise location of the trade point, of course, depends upon the levels of the two countries respective import duties.

Under such conditions, it would pay for a country to reduce its tariffs unilaterally *only* if the resultant shift of the trade point along the foreign country's tariff-distorted offer curve leads to a higher trade-indifference level. Hence the same statement made above with regard to the geometry of unilateral tariff reduction also applies here, except that everything will be related to a *foreign* offer curve that is distorted by a tariff.

Instead of unilateral tariff reduction, *bilateral* reduction of trade restrictions through negotiation promises a substantially higher probability of success in raising the national welfare level. Let us take two cases. In one it is agreed to remove completely all tariffs between the two countries, and in the other the agreement states merely that the tariff barriers of both nations should be reduced. We shall look at both situations from the point of view of the home country.

In Figure 12–2 we again have the two free-trade offer curves OH and OF characterizing the home and foreign country, respectively, intersecting at point T, and placing the home country on the trade-indifference curve h_1. If both countries levy a tariff the new trade point, where the two tariff-distorted offer curves intersect, must lie somewhere within the area bounded by OH and OF. In order to be beneficial for the home country, the movement from the tariff-distorted trade point back to the free-trade point R must involve a movement to a higher trade-indifference level. Should the tariff distorted offer curves be OH' and OF' in Figure 12–2, for example—with the trade point falling at S—it is clear that the removal of all tariffs by both countries and a return to the free-trade point R represents a higher trade-indifference level for the home country and is therefore desirable.

What if, however, the trade point with tariffs falls somewhere in the area M? Bilateral removal of all import duties and a return to the free-trade point R will then represent a *decline* in welfare and a lower trade-indifference level for the home country, and therefore would be undesirable from its point of view. As a general statement, then, we can say that if the tariff-distorted trade point falls within the area bounded by the foreign free-trade offer curve (OF) and the trade-indifference curve apply-ing to the home country under free trade (h_1) (the area M in Figure 12–2) it is not advisable for the home country to engage in negotiated tariff removal. It will be better off leaving both its own and the foreign country's respective tariffs as they are. If, on the other hand, the tariff-dis-torted trade point falls anywhere else in the area bounded by OH and OF—that is, anywhere *except* the area M—the home country will gain from a return to free trade conditions and a removal of all tariffs by both nations.

It is much more likely that both countries will agree not to remove tariffs between themselves completely, but to simply lower them some-

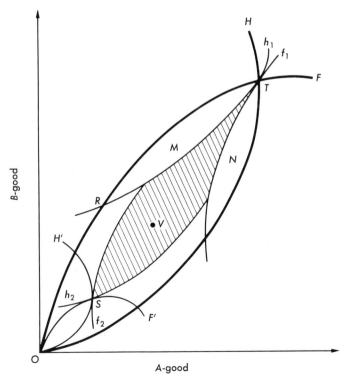

Fig. 12–2. Tariff reduction by negotiation.

what—to *liberalize* trade but not free it entirely. In geometric terms, this means a shift from the tariff-distorted trade point, *not* to the free-trade point but to some *other* point within the area bounded by OF and OH. Under what conditions will it then pay for the home country to engage in a bilateral negotiated reduction, but not removal, of tariffs?

In Figure 12–2, suppose that the tariff-distorted offer curves OH' and OF' intersect at point S. The home country attains the trade indifference level h_2, while the foreign country reaches f_2 under these conditions. *Both* countries will gain from negotiated tariff reduction only if the new trade point lies inside these two curves—within the shaded area—such as at point V. Since neither country is likely to accept a tariff settlement which renders it worse off than before, only trade points which represent higher welfare levels for both countries can be considered as possible outcomes.

Once a new trade point such as V is reached (which represents reduced tariffs on the part of both countries), negotiations for further tariff reductions can begin anew. This time point V would be the corner of a second "shaded area," within which the new trade point would lie. Successive tariff negotiations such as this could ultimately reduce all tariffs to zero and herald a return to free trade at point T. In the process, all of the adverse effects of the tariff would have been destroyed and neither country would have undergone a decline in welfare in the process. As was noted above in connection with tariff removal, only if the trade point fell in the areas marked M and N in Figure 12–2 would it not be in the interest of one or the other two countries to pursue tariff negotiations to their ultimate conclusion in free trade.

All of the analysis presented here rests on the assumption built into offer curves and community indifference curves, the weaknesses of which we recognized long ago. Hence, we can talk only in terms of "tendencies" and "likelihoods" when we discuss the impact of trade liberalization upon the economic well-being of the countries involved. Nonetheless, such theoretical models do help us to understand what goes on in the real world and to render reasonably sound judgments on the probable effects of actual or proposed measures affecting the freedom of trade among nations.

CONSTRAINED OPTIMA: THE THEORY OF SECOND BEST

What is the "best" trade policy that a country can follow to optimize the material well-being of its people? As we discussed at the beginning of Chapter 9, maximum efficiency is not necessarily the same thing as optimum welfare, if we accept the fact that we cannot make interpersonal welfare comparisons, and that changes in trade do indeed affect income distribution. But what if we did discover a theoretically optimal commercial policy, do conditions existing in the real world approximate those contained in whatever theoretical formulations we use to arrive at this policy? Suppose they do not, or suppose the optimal trade policy is otherwise blocked as a realistic alternative. What would be the next best solution?

For a partial answer, let us go back for a moment to the beginning of our discussion of the theory of commercial policy. What determines social welfare? How do we know whether a given trade policy measure will benefit or harm overall economic welfare if we cannot make interpersonal comparisons—the gains of the gainers against the losses of the losers? In Chapter 9, we simply stated that social welfare increased if some gained but no one lost. If this condition is not automatically fulfilled, perhaps income could be redistributed in such a way that it is.

It is much simpler to define changes in social welfare as follows: the economic welfare of each individual is determined by what he buys and what he sells during a given time interval. If the *value* of what he buys exceeds the value sacrificed, or *cost,* of what he sells (including his services) during this time period, he is better off afterward than before. His personal economic welfare has increased.

Social welfare—the welfare of the nation as a whole—is simply the sum of the respective personal economic welfares of all of the individuals that make up a nation, to which weights may be attached if it is decided by common consent of the people that some members of society possess a greater marginal utility of income than others. If this summation of personal economic welfare increases as a result of some development in the economy, we may then say that social welfare—which is really the same thing as national economic efficiency—is similarly enhanced. Social welfare is maximized only when marginal social value equals marginal social cost throughout. If any transaction involves a marginal value to the buyer which is greater than the marginal cost to the seller, overall social welfare improves.

In general, we may say that if all of the conditions for social welfare optimization are satisfied, and marginal cost equals marginal value in each transaction, then free international trade is the only "best" trade policy for the *world* as a whole. Moreover, barring retaliation, there exists some optimum degree of import restriction that will maximize *national* welfare.

In reality marginal cost to the seller does indeed often diverge from marginal value to the buyer. This is because the above conditions necessary for the optimization of social welfare do not hold true. (a) There rarely exists perfect competition, either in the markets for goods and services or in the markets for the factors of production, (b) governments intervene with all sorts of subsidies and taxes, and (c) there do exist external economies and diseconomies in production. Under such conditions it is *not* a foregone conclusion that trade liberalization, for instance, improves social welfare and economic efficiency, while increased trade restrictions are harmful. In fact, the welfare impact of *any* commercial policy measure under such conditions is uncertain.

All we can say is that any commercial policy that reduces the divergence between social value and social cost in the economy—whether it involves increased or decreased trade restrictions—will improve economic efficiency and social welfare. For example, suppose the U.S. lowers its tariffs on imports of automobiles. The divergence between the marginal social cost and marginal social value of cars in the U.S. may thus be narrowed, and social welfare gains as a result. But the resultant rise in American automobile purchases will simultaneously cause a rise in U.S. sales of tires, gasoline, oil, and so forth in which the divergence between marginal social value and marginal social cost may very well be large. The result of the latter is a social welfare loss. Moreover, the rise in U.S. automobile purchases thus induced may additionally result in a decline in purchases of television sets, in the production and sale of which there may be very little or no divergence at all between marginal social value and marginal social cost. Hence if (a) the resulting *increased* divergences attending rising sales of automotive supplies as well as the transfers in spending from television sets to automobiles outweighs (b) the *reduced* divergence in automobile production, social welfare will indeed decline as a result of the tariff reduction.

Such arguments can be used to justify the existence of trade restrictions in, for instance, cases where a franchised import-competing monopoly exists, in the case of agricultural support programs, and in the case of heavy existing taxes on domestic import-competing production.

Many other examples of this nature could be cited here which would include not only the impact of a given commercial policy action upon social welfare in the importing country, but also in the exporting country and other countries as well. The conclusion—in a highly imperfect world, free trade probably is still the "best" solution. But if universal free trade is unattainable and a "second-best" solution has to be found, it is not at all certain whether increased or decreased trade restrictions will ensure the attainment of this goal. In each instance, the impact of the specific commercial policy upon all affected divergences between social value and social cost must be considered. Only if the *net result* is a decreased overall divergence can the policy be judged beneficial from the standpoint of social welfare.

This high degree of uncertainty and imperfection that exists in a complex world is what makes the impact of any trade policy on world and national welfare so difficult to foresee. Even completely unrestricted international trade may not be the best policy under such conditions. On the other hand, it would be absurd to justify the arbitrary erection of trade barriers simply on account of the apparent fact that their full impact is, at best, uncertain.

TRADE LIBERALIZATION IN PRACTICE

Although we have attempted to limit ourselves in this book as much as possible to the conceptual and analytical questions of international economics, a working knowledge of the institutions that have been created to achieve certain goals is at times indispensable. Hence, we shall devote a brief section here to a description of how the nations of the world—and the U.S. in particular—have attempted to implement the liberalization of international trade in recent times. Our main emphasis is on the re-structuring of the domestic economy in response to import liberalization.

The great depression of the 1930's was a time of international economic disintegration and fragmentation. Impediments to trade attained levels that virtually precluded meaningful international specialization as nations strove to bolster national economic independence and self-sufficiency. Each nation fought to insulate itself from the world-wide economic collapse that was occurring and, in so doing, ensured that the international depression reached the depths that it did. For the U.S., the famed Hawley–Smoot tariff of 1930 marked the high point of protection. Some 25,000 commodities, about 53 per cent of all imports, were subject to a tariff at that time. Mainly politically motivated, the Hawley–Smoot tariff did much to accelerate the upward movement of tariffs on the part of other countries as well, and sabotaged efforts by the League of Nations to reverse the dangerous trend of economic disintegration.

Not long thereafter, however, an era of trade liberalization took hold that has continued until today. Marked by repeated successes and failures, as well as a world war, this period has succeeded in instilling a widely held feeling that increases in impediments to trade constitute setbacks to world economic progress. This has created at least the psychological basis for a possible eventual implementation of world-wide free trade.

Only a few years after the Hawley–Smoot tariff, the U.S. instituted the Reciprocal Trade Agreement Act. This Act allowed the President to negotiate tariff reductions (or increases) with other countries without the permission of the Senate by up to 50 per cent, contingent upon full reciprocity on the part of the other country concerned. (Previously tariff reductions were accomplished by treaty, requiring Senate approval.) This greatly increased American flexibility in trade negotiations, but it was still premised on commodity-by-commodity haggling and applied only to bilateral discussions between the U.S. and its individual foreign trading partners.

The Reciprocal Trade Agreement Act, which originally was to apply for three years, was subsequently extended periodically with some variations until 1962. It embodied as part of U.S. trade policy the *unconditional most-favored-nation* (*mfn*) treatment, under which any tariff concessions granted to a single foreign country would automatically be extended to all other countries as well—in return for which the foreign country had to agree to grant similar most-favored-nation treatment to the U.S. This effort to render multilateral what were essentially bilateral trade agreements was offset by a *chief supplier clause,* which permitted tariff reductions to be applied exclusively to imports from a country which was or had the potential of becoming the principal supplier of U.S. imports of the particular commodity in question—thereby circumventing *mfn* treatment.

After the end of World War II, the movement toward trade liberalization gained momentum, although implementation continued to be slow, partially due to the problems faced by a Europe undergoing reconstruction of its war-torn economies. Nonetheless, 1948 saw the drafting of the Havana Charter, designed to create the International Trade Organization (ITO). It was to be the task of this institution to effect a broad, world-wide reduction of the barriers to trade and to promote economic growth and stability. Finally, there was hope of establishing a central, multi-national coordinating agency which promised to help implement trade liberalization on a broad scale.

This hope dimmed when strong political opposition caused the U.S. to fail to ratify the Havana Charter. Since the U.S. at that time remained the single most important nation, from a trade point of view, ITO was doomed to failure.

Not all was lost, however. While the ITO Charter was being drafted, the General Agreement on Tariffs and Trade (GATT) was established as a temporary measure to effect mutual tariff reductions while the ITO was being set up.

The GATT, which still exists today as the single most effective mechanism for world-wide trade liberalization, constitutes a basic set of rules under which trade negotiations take place. Unconditional most-favored-nation treatment, for instance, is incorporated as a clause in the GATT, as are other provisions for non-discrimination. The uniform *escape clause* arrangements permits signatories to modify trade agreements if excessive injury occurs to domestic producers. The record of the GATT is an enviable one, encompassing seven separate rounds of tariff conferences since its inception.

The U.S. Trade Expansion Act of 1962 granted the President subtially greater authority than the previous trade legislation. It allowed him to make far more significant tariff concessions and then to help structure the domestic economy to the new import competition by promoting the necessary readjustments with federal assistance.

This latter provision represented a new departure in U.S. trade legislation. It clearly recognized that trade liberalization is indeed costly in terms of the movement of labor and capital out of affected import-competing industries and into other more viable pursuits.

In the course of normal economic activity on the national level, such dislocation costs are an accepted fact of life: a firm scores a technological, cost-reducing, or product-differentiating breakthrough, and drives competitors out of business or captures a larger share of the market. Factors employed by the lagging firms must make the often costly move to new pursuits. Yet such costs are rarely considered for what they are, and are generally recognized as being a necessary part of the economic growth process. They are repaid many times over in terms of increased real incomes.

In trade liberalization, this dislocation process and the costs involved are no different. Yet the very fact that institutionalized restraints to foreign competition have prevented them from occurring renders them more noticeable—and often more severe—than those occurring in the normal course of national economic growth. Since the economy as a whole will benefit from trade liberalization in terms of accelerated real income growth, why should not the economy as a whole bear some of the costs involved in relocating the productive factors displaced by the reduction of long-standing trade barriers?

This is the rationale employed in the adjustment assistance provisions of the Trade Expansion Act. It strives to increase the *mobility* of productive resources by providing firms with technical assistance, tax relief, and financial aid to facilitate any necessary changes in the operations of affected firms. Similarly, it proposes to cover the cost of labor retraining and relocation, as well as income assistance to displaced workers during the adjustment period.

The Trade Expansion Act of 1962 served as the basis for the "Kennedy Round" of trade negotiations under the auspices of the GATT—a reciprocal bargaining process that extended from 1963 to 1967. Major tariff reductions were agreed upon which averaged almost 40 per cent, spread over a wide variety of manufactured and semi-manufactured products. These reductions were implemented according to a pre-determined schedule, and concluded in 1972. The Kennedy Round is probably the most successful exercise in broad-gauge trade liberalization ever undertaken.

As tariff rates were negotiated downward on a reciprocal product-by-product basis, the relative importance of nontariff barriers grew. An initial attempt was made to reduce certain NTB's under the Kennedy Round; it failed because the U.S. had no prior negotiating authority in this area under the Trade Expansion Act, and agreements reached in Geneva failed subsequently to be ratified by the Congress. Consequently, the early 1970's saw feverish activity aimed at identifying, classifying, and examining the possible impact of nontariff distortions, both in the GATT and in other organizations such as the United Nations Conference on Trade and Development (UNCTAD) and the Organization for Economic Cooperation and Development (OECD). Apart from the relative growth of importance of NTB's, there was the fear that such devices would be used to offset the desirable trade expansion due to tariff reductions. Very little progress was made, however, not least due to the extreme difficulty of developing viable negotiating strategies applicable to the complex of NTB's.

Meantime, new proposals began to develop for further tariff liberalization, in part motivated by a feeling that a policy vacuum following the highly successful Kennedy Round would inevitably favor backsliding into protectionism. Again the U.S. took the initiative by advocating essentially free trade in industrial products, coupled with broad-scale agricultural trade liberalization but also tied to more ready access to safeguard arrangements which would make it easier to apply import charges or quantitative restrictions in the event severe competitive pressure leads to politically unacceptable adjustment costs. The proposals were contained in the Trade Act of 1974, upon which a new round of *Multilateral Trade Negotiations* (MTN) got underway in Geneva in 1975. At the same time, the developing countries pressed for *favored* access to the markets of the industrial nations via the so-called Generalized System of Preferences (GSP). Negotiated under the auspices of OECD and UNCTAD, the GSP is designed to give the developing nations a head start on freer trade by reducing or eliminating industrial countries' tariffs on their exports *without* requiring reciprocity. We shall discuss the GSP in greater detail in Chapter 28.

All of the moves toward freer trade mentioned here involve essentially *global* liberalization, reaching out to substantially all countries that generally subscribe to the set of trading rules embodied in the GATT. These have been paralleled by a corresponding move toward freer trade on a regional basis among countries tied by common economic interests.

In practice, then, trade liberalization has made a great deal of progress since the days of the Great Depression. But some contend, and with a good deal of justification, that any progress that was made falls far short of what could have been done. The very existence of regional trade blocs attests to this. How much greater would world production of goods and services be today if the law of comparative advantage had been completely free to govern international trade flows for the past twenty years? No one knows. We can only add that a great many other considerations—social, political, and military among them—enter into the abolition or retention of barriers to international commerce. Any judgment of the successes and failures of the international trade mechanism must take all of these considerations into account as well. The objectivity with which we can often gauge policy measures in the economic sphere alone may indeed not be fully applicable in this instance.

13

CUSTOMS UNION THEORY: THE STATICS OF ECONOMIC INTEGRATION

Since the mid-1950's, the term *economic integration* has become standard in the vocabulary of economists, government representatives and politicians, journalists and businessmen throughout the world. While economic integration is an extremely old concept, having been implemented in various forms and at various times for centuries, only since the end of the reconstruction era following World War II has it become a more general phenomenon in the international economy. During this period, regional integration has variously influenced economic relations between nations, and has taken hold of the imagination of the public in many of the world's advanced and developing nations. Today, it represents a significant force in the economic life of countries involved in integration programs of various kinds, and in influencing the international economic policies of countries that are not participating in such projects.

THE CHARACTER OF ECONOMIC INTEGRATION

Perhaps it is best to begin by attempting to define precisely what economic integration is all about. Carried through to the ultimate degree, integration is the fusion of two or more national economies into a single, multinational regional economic entity. Using the United States as an example of an economically integrated region, imagine five or six countries in Europe,

Africa, or anywhere else combining to create a single, unified regional economy. International economic relations as we know them disappear within such a union. They become simply *interregional*.

While few attempts at economic union have succeeded in implementing the degree of integration just described, there are a wide variety of lesser forms of integration, many of which have been applied quite effectively over the years. All possess one or more of the following characteristics:

1. Freedom of trade in goods and services among participating countries
2. Freedom of movement of labor and capital among member nations
3. Free mobility of business enterprise, including the right to establish subsidiaries or affiliates in any member country
4. A unified legal environment for business within the integrated area
5. Harmonization of national policies affecting the intercountry flow of goods, service, labor, and capital
6. A uniform set of policies governing economic relations of member countries with nonmember nations
7. Harmonization of monetary and fiscal policies, including substantial equalization of indirect taxes
8. Coordination of other economic and social policies, including regional development programs, social security measures, agricultural policies, and so forth.

Total integration of the type just described presupposes all of the eight points listed. Yet in the strictest sense, *all* developments that tend to facilitate trade, payments, or the mobility of productive factors between individual national economies may be described as movements toward economic integration, particularly when they are applied on a regional basis among a relatively cohesive group of countries. There are a number of different "stages" of economic integration, ranging from simple trade liberalization on a multinational basis to complete unification of national economies.

The Free-Trade Area

This is perhaps the most elementary form of integration, and is concerned almost exclusively with the elimination of restrictions to trade among participating countries. Each nation abolishes its tariffs on imports from member countries, generally on a gradual basis over a five or ten year adjustment period. This permits the industries in each country, faced with reduced protection and heightened competition from imports, to adopt progressively to the new competitive environment. Adjustment assistance to import-competing industries and their employees may also be provided by the national governments involved.

While the internal removal of tariffs is assured under a free-trade area, each participating country remains free to set its own tariffs on imports from nonmember countries. Consequently, there is the danger that goods originating in nonmember nations may be imported into a member country maintaining a high external tariff via a fellow member state imposing a low external duty. This is called *trade deflection,* and must be prevented by means of relatively complex administrative procedures and "rules of origin." Moreover, the establishment of *tariff factories* in member countries imposing low external duties, which use imported raw materials and components in manufacture for subsequent export to high-external-tariff partner countries, must be similarly prevented.

In addition to eliminating internal tariffs—while maintaining individual national external tariffs—the free-trade area often works to reduce or eliminate certain internal nontariff restrictions to trade, including quantitative limits on imports and a variety of more or less subtle administrative distortions. Due to its very nature the free-trade area must maintain customs frontiers between members, which provides an opportunity for the application of various nontariff barriers to trade by individual member states and compounds the difficulties attending their removal.

There are a number of possible modifications of the free-trade area concept which provide for special conditions obtaining in the countries undergoing integration. For example, certain member countries may be permitted to retain restrictions on imports from periods longer than others, in order to take account of special economic or social conditions. These exemptions, particularly when applied to trade in agricultural commodities, may remain in force for very extended periods of time.

The Customs Union

This arrangement represents a somewhat higher level of economic integration. As in the free-trade area, barriers to trade among the member countries are removed, but each nation is no longer free to determine its own tariffs with respect to the outside world. Rather, a common external system of tariffs and perhaps other trade restrictions is established that embraces the entire customs union. Ultimately, each nation maintains identical restrictions on imports from nonmember countries. Solely from the standpoint of free movement of goods, then, the customs union attains a full measure of integration, and intraunion trade conditions approximate those which tend to prevail interregionally within any single nation. On this point the customs union differs from the free-trade area, where differing external restrictions among members force the retention of at least some internal barriers to trade.

The elimination of internal tariffs and nontariff trade barriers, and the harmonization of external restrictions, proves to be just as difficult under a customs union as under a free-trade area. Again, a more or less extended "adjustment period" often is called for, especially in view of the creation of a uniform set of external trade restrictions to which each member economy must adapt. Exemptions from the common external import restrictions may remain for extended periods of time, depending in part upon differences and similarities in economic structure among participating states. Especially difficult is the harmonization of nontariff barriers to imports from nonmember countries. In general, the customs union tends to be more cohesive than the free-trade area, and the more ambitious scope of this form of integration may accelerate the pace at which regional free trade is attained.

The Common Market

Beyond the creation of the single, unified market for goods and services provided by the customs union the next logical step toward full integration is the establishment of free mobility of productive factors: labor and capital.

Workers and professionals of all kinds are free to move anywhere within the integrated area in response to differences in prevailing wages and salaries as well as employment opportunities. Similarly, capital is free to seek out the highest obtainable yields anywhere within the area. The intent, of course, is to extend the unified market for output of goods and services to productive factor inputs as well. Common markets usually include the abolition of restrictions to the free mobility of proprietorships, partnerships, and corporate business enterprises to insure that entrepreneurship may also be responsive to changing markets and the economic conditions.

The inclusion of free factor mobility in common market arrangements raises problems substantially more serious than those related to the implementation of regional free trade. For example, the mobility of labor may not be very great even within a single country, as the experience of many nations has shown. Numerous institutional changes on the national as well as international level also may have to be implemented before free capital mobility will come about. That is, the renewal of international restrictions to factor mobility alone will not guarantee that labor and capital will indeed move according to changes in employment and investment opportunities within the common market.

The Economic Union

The formation of a common market creates a number of difficulties in the area of economic policy. Suppose the intraunion movement of goods, services, labor, capital, and entrepreneurship were completely free, and most of the rigidities impeding factor mobility were overcome. If there remained substantial differences between the member countries in terms of governmental economic and social policies, significant distortion of intraunion trade and factor flows could result. Particularly important in this respect are monetary and fiscal policies implemented by the member states for purpose of domestic economic control, as well as national direct and indirect taxations systems, agricultural support programs, social security programs, transport policies, regional planning, government subsidies to selected industries, and so forth.

The economic union purports to alleviate difficulties arising out of such differences in national policies by bringing about their coordination of harmonization within the framework of the union as a whole. This clearly represents an advanced form of integration, and will tend to incur political and economic problems substantially more serious than those associated with the implementation of regional free trade alone. On the other hand, the difficulties involved in the application of free intracommunity trade in agricultural products and other goods and services—the production of which is profoundly influenced by government policy—may render policy harmonization a prerequisite to the successful application of a common market for such products.

Monetary Union

Once integration approaches the economic union stage, with free internal trade and factor mobility supported by substantial economic policy harmonization, the next logical step in the integration process is the creation of a monetary union. This requires the eventual replacement of the individual members' national currencies by a single currency encompassing the entire integrated area.

The implications of monetary union are clear. The power to create and destroy money must be vested in a supranational agency. Such an agency acquires complete control of monetary policy for the region as a whole, and thus is able to influence credit conditions, investment activity, as well as income and employment levels in each of the member countries. Balance of payments and exchange rate considerations within the union disappear, since international payments in effect become interregional with only a single currency involved.

The Unified Regional Economy

At this stage, very little remains to be done in order for complete economic union to be attained. Regional free trade has been created and a set of common external trade restrictions established. National policies tending to distort intercountry trade within the union have been coordinated or harmonized, while free internal factor mobility has been implemented.

Once monetary union has been achieved, it is clear that the member countries are willing and able to transfer a substantial degree of national sovereignty to a supranational agency in the area of economic control. To complete the integration process, member states must give up their autonomy of action in virtually every other aspect of economic policy as well, and the relationship of the central authority and the individual member nations assumes a form not unlike the federal–state economic relations in the United States. By this time, regional economic integration has run its full course, and several national economies have been welded into a larger, multinational economy that may truly be considered a unified whole.

It may well be that a substantial degree of *political* integration is required before a total unification of national economies, as described here, will be possible. At least it is evident that all totally integrated economic areas existing today embody a certain measure of political integration.

STATICS AND DYNAMICS

It is convenient to discuss the effects of regional free mobility of goods, services, and productive factors in terms of their *static* and *dynamic* effects upon the national economies involved. In disscussing the statics of integration we refer to induced, once-and-for-all shifts in productive efficiency and consumer welfare. Presumably in any viable integration scheme these will be positive, resulting in a significant increase in potential real income per capita—i.e., attainable real income per capita under full-employment conditions—*for all member countries combined* over a relatively short period of time. As we shall see, however, the statics of integration need not work themselves out positively, and indeed may under certain conditions exert a net negative influence on economic well-being in the participating nations.

The dynamics of integration, on the other hand, relate to the impact of economic union on the rate of growth of the member economies. The creation of a single regional market composed of several national economies will hopefully increase the rate of capital formation and perhaps labor-force growth, technological innovation and human-resource development, and the realization of economies of large-scale production and similar economic variables in the union; hence, the collective rate of economic advance in the member countries should accelerate. Unlike the static effects, it is most unlikely that the dynamic elements of integration would make themselves felt in a negative manner, although the extent of their beneficial impact may vary widely from one integration project to the next.

We can very simply differentiate between the static and dynamic effects of economic integration in terms of hypothetical time–series such as those depicted in Figure 13–1. Using the vertical axis to measure real income per capita under full-employment conditions (Y^*/N), assume that the combined, historical rate of growth of the member economies is represented by time series M which, in the absence of integration at time I, would continue more or less as before. Positive static benefits in the amount X—allowing five years for them to make themselves felt—would result in a new growth path *S* that is at a substantially higher *level* than *M* but does not represent an increase in the rate of growth. Alternatively, if we assume an absence of static benefits but considerable dynamic gains, series *D* would apply. Note that the enhanced rate of economic growth insures that the level of Y^*/N eventually exceeds that attained earlier by static gains alone, which is one reason why some economists consider the dynamic effects of integration to be of generally greater significance than the static effects. The relative importance of the two effects depends on their respective magnitudes and how rapidly they can be absorbed by the economies of the integrating countries. Optimally, of course, both static and dynamic effects would make themselves felt in a positive manner, as in the case of growth path $S + D$ in Figure 13–1.

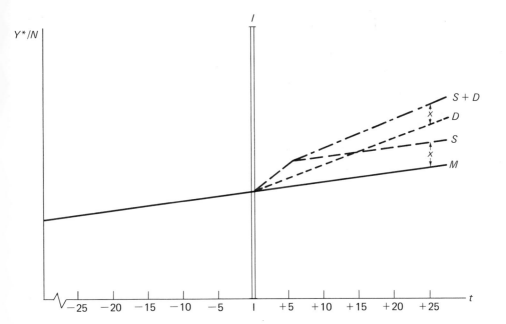

Fig. 13–1. Static and dynamic effects of integration.

Having distinguished between the static and dynamic influences of integration on a central measure of economic advance, the per-capita real income-generating capability of participating economies, we may now examine the sources of these effects and the factors tending to promote or retard them.

CONSUMPTION AND PRODUCTION EFFECTS OF REGIONAL FREE TRADE

The creation of a customs union or free-trade area signals a departure from the protected market in favor of a condition of *limited* free trade—i.e., trade limited to the participating nations. Tariff walls, quotas, and other restrictions among all partner countries are abolished, and discrimination between domestically produced goods and those supplied by manufacturers in partner countries is ended, at least in principle. The entire market of the customs union is open to the lowest cost, most efficient suppliers within that union. At the same time, the range of choice of consumers in each member country is broadened and, if they can now buy at lower prices, their effective incomes are raised. Whereas tariff and quota discrimination no longer exists inside the union, it still applies to suppliers located in non-member countries, which now must hurdle common external trade restrictions in the case of a customs union or, in the case of a free-trade area, the national external trade barriers, in order to compete in the new and larger protected market created by the union.

Within the union itself, consumers will tend to shift their purchases from high cost, relatively inefficient domestic producers which have long enjoyed a protected national market, to low cost suppliers located in partner countries. Indeed, production of each commodity will tend to shift from less efficient suppliers to the lowest cost, most efficient producers within the customs union. This is called the *positive production effect* of regional free trade, and is of course beneficial to overall productive efficiency.

If national suppliers cannot adjust their cost levels to meet the new competition, they will suffer heavy losses in their respective market shares. Should these producers prove to be marginal, they may ultimately be driven from the market. Within the framework of the union, the production of each and every good theoretically will shift toward the lowest cost supplier, and ultimately approach some hypothetical least cost optimum. Simultaneously, the volume of trade among member countries will increase rapidly as the intraunion reallocation of production proceeds.

Consumers, too, benefit in the process. They are no longer restricted to high priced domestic products, but are free to search out the lowest prices obtainable within the entire union. Consequently, since prices of the things they buy fall, their real incomes are increased. The range of consumer choice also is broadened and this, whether or not associated with price declines, tends to increase consumer welfare. Such decidedly beneficial influences of regional free trade on the economic status of consumers fall under the heading of *positive consumption effects,* and likewise tend to result in substantial increases in the volume of trade between member countries.

The positive production and consumption effects thus involve a basic reallocation of production and consumption patterns within the free-trade zone, and stimulate trade and specialization among the member economies. The overall process is called *trade creation*.

Without regional free trade, the domestic market of each one of the prospective member nations is—for those commodities subject to very low trade restrictions, or none at all—open to the lowest cost producer anywhere in the world. If a foreign supplier is efficient enough, and if transport costs do not prove to be an insurmountable barrier, he is free to compete for a share of the national market. With the creation of regional free trade, · however, producers in nonmember countries are faced with a set of trade barriers that do not apply to competing suppliers in member nations. It is entirely possible that in many cases production will be shifted from low cost producers in nonmember nations to high cost suppliers in partner countries. To the extent that this occurs, production will clearly have been reallocated from low cost to high cost suppliers, and productive efficiency from a world standpoint will suffer. The diversion of trade from nonmember countries to member countries is termed the *negative production effect* of regional free trade.

Such developments also make themselves felt directly in the area of consumer welfare. In the absence of regional free trade, consumers are able to purchase commodities that are not subject to import restrictions—or are imported after incurring the restrictions—at world-market prices. These tend to approximate the selling prices of the most efficient of world suppliers. After integration however, the elimination of intraunion tariffs and nontariff trade barriers in the face of existing or newly imposed restrictions on imports from the rest of the world force the consumer to shift his purchases from the low-price suppliers in nonmember countries to high price suppliers in partner countries. The higher outlays that he incurs result in a decline in his effective income, and his range of choice among competitive suppliers is directly reduced. We refer to this as the *negative consumption effect* and, like the negative production effect, it also serves to divert trade from nonmember to member countries.

Negative consumption and production effects of regional free trade thus tend to depress the volume of trade of participating nations with nonmember countries by diverting it to other member nations. This process is termed *trade diversion*. The overall volume of trade will not necessarily change, although it may well decline somewhat. Trade changes in *direction* and becomes increasingly inward-oriented. That is, it becomes more "regionalized" within the confines of the free-trade zone.

A few qualifications must be added to this brief survey of the positive and negative consumption and production effects of customs unions. If, in the case of any one commodity, the union turns out to include the lowest cost world producer, then it can only have a beneficial, or trade-creating effect with regard to that particular good. There can be no negative production or consumption effects in a static sense and therefore no trade diversion. If, on the other hand, *none* of the member countries has produced a particular commodity before formation of the union, and all imported it from nonmember countries, they will continue to do so after integration and the union have no impact on trade patterns at all—no positive or negative consumption or production effects, and therefore no trade creation or trade diversion will result.

Finally, suppose all member countries produce a particular good before integration. In this instance the net effect of the union will in all probability be trade-creating, since the low cost producers will displace high cost suppliers in their previously protected markets. Depending on the relative costs of the most efficient suppliers inside and outside the union, little of this displacement may be at the expense of external producers.

CUSTOMS UNION VERSUS TRADE LIBERALIZATION

The *production effects* accompanying the formation of customs unions give us some basis for evaluating the latter's impact on economic welfare. The shift in production from high-cost domestic producers to low-cost suppliers in partner countries clearly tends to enhance economic efficiency. On the other hand, negative production effects resulting from the discriminatory elimination of trade barriers exclusively on imports from partner countries, thereby causing supply shifts from low-cost world producers to high-cost firms in member nations, are harmful to economic efficiency. Regarding the problem only from the supply side, then, gives us some insight into the net impact of a customs union on economic welfare, but it is necessarily an incomplete picture.

It was shown that the *consumption effects* must also be taken into account in order to achieve a more complete basis for evaluating the net contribution of customs unions. If the formation of a customs union broadens the range of choice of consumers and enables them to buy at reduced prices by shifting their purchases from domestic suppliers to those of partner-countries, their effective income and material well-being will be enhanced. If, however, it actually *narrows* their range of choice and forces them to buy high-priced goods produced within the customs union, instead of low-priced items produced by suppliers in non-member nations, they will suffer a reduction in real income and welfare. Again, the net consumption effect of customs unions will constitute some kind of balance between these two opposing forces.

If we can establish in this way the net production and consumption effects of a customs union on the economic welfare of a single member country, it will then be possible to determine—at least in a general way—the overall impact of the customs union on that economy. This may be done by striking a balance between the net consumption effect and the net production effect.

Suppose for a given country the conclusion is that, from a static point of view, its membership in a customs union has been largely beneficial. Nonetheless, the thoughtful observer will soon raise a very important point. Granted, the country is better off as a member of the customs union than it was before. But is customs union the best possible solution? That is, could the country not have done *even better* by taking an alternative course in its commercial policy, thereby actually rendering customs unions sub-optimal or second-best from its own point of view?

A PARTIAL EQUILIBRIUM VIEW

One alternative to customs union involves simply reducing trade barriers unilaterally, on a non-discriminatory basis; i.e., lowering or eliminating tariffs and quotas on imports from *all* other countries, regardless of origin. It is possible to show that such a step would, under certain conditions, actually lead to greater welfare gain than would membership in a customs union. This may be true even if other countries do not reciprocally lower their own import barriers.

In Figure 13–2, curves Dd and Sd denote a certain nation's domestic demand and supply curves for a given commodity, produced under conditions of increasing costs. In isolation—without international trade—equilibrium would be attained at point L, with quantity OQ_2 produced and consumed at price P_2. Domestic output at that price exactly equals the quantity demanded by the nation's consumers.

Curve Sw represents supply conditions on the world market as faced by this particular country. It is assumed that the country is not an important force in world market demand, and that therefore it cannot affect the world price of the good by its purchases (i.e., it cannot influence its own *terms of trade* by varying its imports). Hence, the curve Sw is horizontal. With completely free trade, therefore, equilibrium of supply and demand would be reached at point Y, with quantity OQ_4 demanded at world price T, entirely satisfied by imports, with domestic production being nonexistent.

Suppose now that the country does import this commodity but imposes a tariff of TP_1 on each unit imported. Consumers now demand an amount OQ_3 and are paying a price P_1 for each unit. The demand is satisfied in the amount OQ_1 by domestic suppliers, and the rest Q_1Q_3, is imported from the cheapest available source at the world market supply price T. If the country decides to enter into a customs union with one or more other nations, we will define the customs union supply function as S_u comprising domestic supply plus that of the partner countries. The price to consumers will remain at P_1 and, although the consumers' range of choice will be somewhat narrowed, there seem to be no significant negative consumption effects. Quantity Q_3 will still be demanded, but it will be supplied exclusively by producers within the customs union. The original imports, Q_1Q_3, from the rest of the world will be eliminated, as will the tariff revenues previously collected.

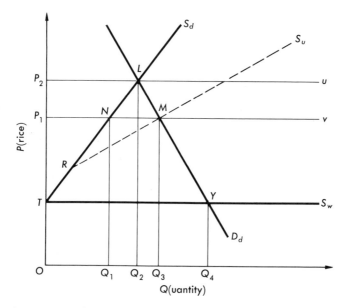

Fig. 13–2. Customs union versus unilateral tariff reduction.

Whereas customs union in this case involves no detrimental consumption effects, the production effects tell quite a different story. Clearly, the elimination of Q_1Q_3 of imports at world market price T, and their replacement by the output of producers in partner countries at price P_1 constitutes a shift from a lower to a higher cost supplier and is therefore harmful to overall productive efficiency—trade diversion through negative production effects.

The same conclusions with regard to consumption and production effects will be equally true if the initial tariff was anywhere below TP_1. With zero consumption effects and negative production effects, the net effect of customs union in either case is, therefore, detrimental.

If, on the other hand, the initial tariff was at or above TP_2, then total consumption before customs union was satisfied by domestic production at price P_2, or above. There were no imports from the rest of the world. Formation of a customs union under such circumstances results in the partial displacement of high cost domestic production by the output of other member countries. At the same time, the cost to the consumer is reduced from P_2, or above, to P_1 and his range of choice is broadened. We thus have positive production effects—shifts in production from high cost domestic to low cost union suppliers—plus positive consumption effects. Customs union in this instance is trade-creating and entirely beneficial from the standpoint of both consumption and production.

The effect of entry into a customs union is fairly clear cut, then, if the pre-union tariff level was above TP_2 or below TP_1. But what if the initial tariff rested between TP_1 and TP_2? Customs union benefits the consumers by lowering the price to P_1, but at the same time somewhat narrows their range of choice. On balance, there would probably be a positive consumption effect. Without customs union, demand was satisfied partly by domestic suppliers and partly by imports from the lowest cost world source of supply. After union, domestic output is reduced to OQ_1, but the low-cost suppliers, S_w, are displaced by producers in partner countries, S_u, thus raising the real cost of supply to the economy. The net production effect in this case is therefore partly positive and partly negative.

From the three cases discussed here, it appears that customs union will always be detrimental if the nation's initial tariff in Figure 13–2 was below TP_1 (negative production and consumption effects), but beneficial if the initial tariff equalled or exceeded TP_2 (positive consumption and production effects). If the initial tariff rested between TP_1 and TP_2 or exceeded TP_2, however, could the nation not have benefited *more* if, instead of joining a customs union, it simply lowered its tariffs unilaterally and on a nondiscriminatory basis to TP_1? The positive consumption effect in either instance would be the same as in customs union, yet the higher cost suppliers in partner countries, S_u, would be displaced in each instance by low cost nonmember suppliers, S_w. At the same time, the nation would be collecting customs revenues equal to $TP_1 \times Q_1Q_3$.

We are left, then, with a choice between customs union and unilateral tariff reduction. Of the two, the second course seems preferable. Yet by joining a customs union, other nations simultaneously reduce their own barriers to the exports of the home country. There occurs a general shift in the direction of optimum allocation of production and consumption within the framework of the entire union—a beneficial consequence that does not apply to unilateral tariff reduction. The gains attainable through unilateral tariff reduction thus might not exceed those entailed by customs union. Moreover, the customs-union approach, even if it does appear to be second best from the viewpoint of productive efficiency and consumer welfare, may well be by far the more feasible and practical solution from a policy standpoint.

A GENERAL EQUILIBRIUM VIEW

Another way of arriving at a similar conclusion is to use a general equilibrium analysis, which with similar limitations, concerns itself with the impact of customs unions upon the economic welfare of one of its members.

Referring to Figure 13–3, two goods, X and Y can be produced by a country along a linear transformation function, but it chooses to specialize in the production of Y at N, exporting part of its Y in return for imports of X. The lowest cost foreign supplier of good X is country A, and the exchange of Y for X at the terms of trade NA enables the home country to reach a welfare level represented by the community indifference curve I. This is the free-trade solution at the consumption point V.

Now suppose it is decided to place an *ad valorem* tariff on all imports of good X. The tariff changes the internal price ratio of X to Y from NA to DD. The highest possible community indifference curve that can now be reached is II with consumption at point Z—the tangency solution of the post-tariff price line and indifference curve II. Since the community indifference curve II is substantially lower than curve I, the imposition

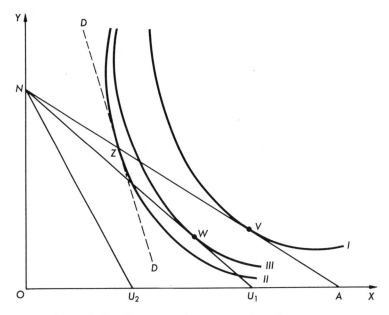

Fig. 13–3. Customs union as a policy alternative.

of a tariff has resulted in a community-welfare level clearly inferior to that prevailing under free trade.

It is then decided to enter into a customs union with another country. If the other member of the union harbors the lowest cost foreign supplier (Country A), the consumption point returns from point Z to point V, and the welfare losses caused by the tariff will have been recovered. In fact, no matter how many countries the customs union eventually encompasses, as long as Country A is included welfare will return to its free-trade level. If, however, Country A is excluded and a higher cost country U_1 is included instead, the home country's community indifference curve will rise from II to III, and consumption will be at point W. The community welfare level is now higher than that existing before customs union, but is definitely lower than with free trade.

The lowest cost supplier (A) has been excluded. Customs union has increased overall economic welfare, but not by as much as a return to free trade would have done. By looking at Figure 13–3, the reader can easily see that as long as the price ratios of X and Y, connected with any country entering the union, *intersect* the community indifference curve (II) associated with the tariff, which is true of NU_1, the country will be better off after customs union than before, but worse off than if it simply removed all tariffs and returned to free trade with Country A at point V.

If, on the other hand, the nation finally included in the customs union produces good X at extremely high cost, such as country U_2 with attendant X/Y price ratio NU_2, the home country will be worse off after customs union than with the tariff, if it does not itself produce the imported commodity. This conclusion will be reached whenever the X/Y price ratio, connected with a prospective member country, does not intersect community indifference curve II, prevailing under the tariff.

This analysis demonstrates that a country considering customs union may or may not be better off by doing so from a consumption standpoint, depending upon the production costs of the partner countries. Only if the union embraces the lowest cost world supplier, however, will community welfare reach the maximum attainable through tariff elimination. Here again the choice must be made between customs union and trade liberalization.

Having delineated the sources of the static production and consumption effects of regional free trade, we should now examine the major factors governing the anticipated size and direction of these effects in any given integration project. That is, what determines whether the combined net static effects of a customs union or free-trade area will indeed be positive and, if they are, how substantial they will be? Four of the more important determinants may be readily identified, and will be discussed in turn: (1) economic size, (2) economic distance, (3) economic structure, and (4) the level of pre-existing trade restrictions. Each will also have a bearing on the dynamic effects of integration.

THE ECONOMIC SIZE OF FREE-TRADE ZONES

The greater the economic size of the area undergoing integration the more likely will be the kinds of production and consumption reallocations identified with static gains. The probability that the low cost suppliers of tradeable goods will be included in a given union is naturally higher, the larger the absolute size of that union and the more producing units it encompasses.

To illustrate, suppose Countries X and Y both produce radios for their limited domestic markets and impose high protective tariffs to keep out imports. Country Z also produces radios but at a much lower cost than either X or Y. It applies a negligible or zero tariff on imports of radios and competes actively on world markets for the product. Suppose, further, that integration is contemplated between X and Y. Since both national radio industries produce at high cost relative to Z, and if the existing cost differences between the two countries are presumed to be slight, we would expect very little increase in the radio trade between them after all barriers have been removed (assuming no trade is induced by differences in quality or tastes). Hence the potential static benefits of such a union, both in production and consumption, of this particular commodity, is slight.

If, on the other hand, the union is extended to include Country Z, internal trade in radios would develop rapidly, and production shifts from the high cost suppliers in X and Y to the more efficient producers in Z. Indeed, if most producers in X and Y turn out to be marginal, radio production in these two countries will be sharply curtailed. Alternatively, they will be forced to step up efficiency in production to the point where they are competitive with suppliers in Z. Total combined production of radios by all three countries in all probability would rise. Increases in the size of integration projects are thus likely to raise both total output and productive efficiency by embracing more and more low cost suppliers. But if the growth in size of the union necessitates pervasive changes in economic structures, these conclusions may not necessarily hold, and may even be reversed.

The measurement of economic size is of substantial interest as an ancillary problem. In order to develop a reasonably valid gauge of the economic size of regional free-trade zones, each increase in the market size should bring with it a high probability that more and more competing firms and industries will be included in the extension of the economic area. Population as a measure of economic size may be rejected on the grounds that it fails to indicate the scope for intraunion specialization and division of labor that is being sought. Gross domestic product would seem to be a more suitable indicator of economic size. However, even GDP may not be sufficient for purposes of estimating the possibilities for increased competition and trade creation.

Substantial existing differences in national tastes and preferences would tend to limit the market for many commodities, and the extension of the size of a union would do little to increase the size of the market facing the suppliers of the affected goods. But this limiting factor may be overcome or mitigated in time, partly as a result of the integration process itself. Moreover, differences in measurement standards, specifications, and business practices also may to some extent limit the economic area facing producers in a customs union or free-trade area, despite the absence of explicit trade barriers. These may create problems for the rapid expansion of intraarea trade and, although such difficulties probably tend to resolve themselves fairly quickly, they do involve costs of various kinds.

ECONOMIC DISTANCE

A second factor tending to govern the size and direction of the static production and consumption effects of regional free trade is the economic distance between member countries. Even if all of the other factors involved seem to indicate that a given integration project would lead to substantial static gains for the participating economies, there is little scope for trade creation if the passage of goods between member countries is obstructed by inefficient or otherwise high cost transport systems. It is possible to state, as a general proposition, that increased trade and specialization within a customs union will be greater, the smaller the economic distance between member nations.

Economic distance, as a concept, is probably most useful when it is defined in terms of transport costs. The spatial element is a force affecting the potential shifts in trade flows and production patterns as a result of economic integration. In regional free trade, the higher the transport costs within the union, the less will be its potential benefits. Natural obstacles, such as mountain ranges, jungles, and swamps, as well as the prevailing modes of transportation clearly influence economic distance. And, although geographical distances may be small, economic distances may be large.

Another entirely different application of the idea of economic distance to economic integration, already implied in connection with economic size, centers around differences in tastes and preferences, national character, and customs. If two countries contemplating customs union are characterized by vastly different tastes, levels of living, and the character of their respective peoples, one might expect the degree of trade between them to grow relatively less rapidly then between two nations demonstrating greater affinity.

However, it is possible—if not probable—that the greater the degree of industrialization of the participating countries, the less will be the importance of such factors. Industrialization and the growth of personal disposable income appear to foster the development of similar demand patterns on the part of consumers, no matter what their social or cultural background may be. In addition, all industrialized countries require substantially the same broad types of capital equipment which vary little whether imported or manufactured domestically. On the other hand, in the case of agricultural commodities, trade may indeed be impeded by differences in national tastes and preferences, at least in the beginning of an integration program.

ECONOMIC STRUCTURE

The degree of overlapping, or rivalry, which exists between the respective economic structures of two or more national economies before the creation of a regional free trade zone is another important factor that is likely to affect the potential benefits of such a union. *Competitiveness* and *complementarity* in economic structure are perhaps best defined in terms of the existing range of tradeable goods being produced in countries contemplating integration.

Two economies are said to be *competitive* if there exists considerable overlapping in the range of goods produced in the two by industries sheltered from import competition by protective tariffs. This holds whether or not the goods are exported and actually do compete in international markets. Conversely, *complementarity* would characterize two economies with a great deal of differentiation in their respective economic structures. For example, the German and Canadian economies would be considered complementary—Canada to a large degree specializes in the production of agricultural commodities while German output is characterized predominantly by industrial goods. In contrast, the German and Japanese economies might be described as being primarily competitive in nature. Both are highly industrialized and produce a very similar range of goods.

Generalizing on this definition of competitiveness and complementarity, the more complementary are the economies facing integration (i.e., the less the degree of overlapping of their respective outputs), the less will be the potential static benefits of regional free trade. Hence, integration between a highly industrialized country and a predominantly agricultural one may yield relatively few benefits for either economy. It would probably tend toward discrimination against third countries and toward increased inward-orientation and economic self-sufficiency. Any increase in trade between complementary economies due to integration will tend to occur primarily at the expense of imports from nonmember countries.

Conversely, the greater the structural competitiveness, or rivalry, between two such economies prior to integration, the greater will be the potential static benefits. Initial tariffs between such economies are likely to be relatively high and their removal may easily lead to a shift from high cost to low cost producers within the union. All else equal, marginal firms will be eliminated and production will increasingly be concentrated on the most efficient firms in the union. Moreover, the larger the pre-union differences in production costs, the greater will be the consequent increase in efficiency. Intraunion trade will increase rapidly, and discrimination against outside suppliers in the form of decreased imports may well turn out to be relatively minor. Even when cost differences are unimportant, integration of competitive economies will tend to increase the range of choice of consumers and thereby presumably enhance their economic well-being.

PRE-UNION TARIFF LEVELS

One final consideration in estimating the potential impact of a given customs union is the nature of restrictions to trade which the member countries maintained prior to the formation of the union. In general, the more restrictive the pre-union tariffs and quotas, the greater the anticipated benefit of a customs union. This is likely to be true for two reasons.

First, from an internal point of view, very restrictive pre-union tariffs imply the existence of highly protected national markets, and their removal in all probability will lead to a rapid growth of intraunion trade. Reallocation of production will proceed in favor of low cost union suppliers, and consumers will benefit substantially from the resultant price reductions. Positive production and consumption effects—trade creation—is therefore likely to be quite substantial with the danger of trade diversion commensurately reduced.

Second, and perhaps of equal importance, is the fact that the existence of high pre-union national tariffs suggests that the volume of trade with *nonmember* countries before the union was small. To be sure, such trade may not grow very much as a result of the union, since suppliers in third countries must now hurdle the common external tariff, but neither will it be diverted in large volume from nonmember to member countries. High pre-union tariffs therefore imply few negative production and consumption effects as a result of the union—little trade diversion.

On balance, then, it may be said that the more restrictive the pre-union barriers to trade, the greater is the likelihood that trade creation will outweigh trade diversion, and the greater the potential benefit of the customs union. Where tariffs of potential member-nations have been confiscatory, or where the same effect has been achieved by quotas (and specialization and trade has been prevented altogether), the potential benefits brought about by a customs union and the total abolition of internal tariffs will be at a maximum. At the other extreme, where the imports of prospective member nations were already essentially free from tariffs and quantitative trade restrictions, the benefits derived by the participating countries from an economic union, all other things being equal, should be minimal.

Another aspect of the tariff question is whether or not the *expectation,* on the part of businessmen and others, of a gradual elimination of internal trade restrictions in a customs union causes trade within the union to increase substantially more than that which would be expected to result solely from individual reductions of trade barriers. Precisely this assertion has been made in connection with the European Common Market: that internal tariff reductions in fact had little to do with the rapid increase in intra-EEC trade during the first several years of its existence, and that expectations caused trade growth to *lead* tariff reductions by a considerable extent. The evidence supporting this notion appears to be substantial. It may as a general phenomenon bear on the *timing* of the static production and consumption effects in response to the formation of a customs union.

There are other factors which may well militate against free competition on a union-wide scale, even if the reduction of tariffs and quotas are indeed sufficient to substantially remove all internal trade barriers. To the extent that such explicit or implicit nontariff barriers to trade are effective in preventing the free interplay of competitive forces, the increase in the volume of intraunion trade—and, more basically, the redistribution of production and consumption patterns—will be correspondingly less.

Wide differences in the protective power of national indirect taxation systems, national fiscal levies imposed exclusively on imports, protective technical and procedural import regulations and extensive government-sponsored "buy domestic" programs are examples in this category. Finally, subsidies of various types accorded domestic producers also may prevent desirable competitive shifts in the patterns of trade and production in a customs union. Such subsidies are difficult to pinpoint, both because they are usually well disguised and because of the widespread government ownership of, or participation in, various industries.

OTHER GAINS

Two other sources of static gains from the formation of customs unions are deserving of mention here: administrative economies resulting from the elimination of internal trade barriers, and induced shifts of the member-nations' collective terms of trade.

The existence of restrictions to trade between nations obviously means that an extensive and costly administrative apparatus must be maintained in order to enforce the prevailing tariffs and quotas. Border-crossing points must be manned, customs offices staffed, boundaries patrolled to prevent smuggling, and so forth. Each nation must maintain its own tariff commission to set import restrictions and classify commodity groups for tariff purposes, hear appeals from domestic manufacturers, and change tariffs and quotas when necessary. In addition, administrative agencies dealing with health, product quality, advertising, and other standards also have a hand in controlling the flow of imports.

With all internal tariffs eliminated, the cost saving to the national member-governments resulting from the total or partial liquidations of such agencies would be substantial in itself. Moreover, the creation of a common external tariff and the combination and centralization of all such tasks with regard to imports from nonmembers also can result in substantial further economies.

But this is not the entire saving resulting from the implementation of a customs union. It may not even be the major one. A great deal of time and effort is involved in crossing international customs frontiers, and if all the connected explicit and implicit costs were added, their magnitude would undoubtedly be surprising. This is in addition to other activities involved in export-import trade, which are not required in domestic transactions and which would be eliminated by the abolition of internal trade restrictions.

In sum, the administrative economies which may be expected to result from a customs union are of substantial significance. They apply, however, only to a true customs union and will not occur, for example, in a free-trade area. In the last, there is no provision for a common external tariff, and internal customs frontiers must either be maintained or replaced by a complex system of *certificates of origin*. Certificates of origin are designed to prevent the importation of goods from a nonmember country to a high tariff member country via a low tariff member country. This is usually called *trade deflection*. Failure to harmonize external trade restrictions in a free-trade area results in this and certain other difficulties, in addition to causing the integration project to be far less cohesive than a customs union.

Aside from yielding important administrative economies, a customs union may also improve the collective *terms of trade* of its members. This is especially true if the union tends to be trade-diverting. If the elimination of internal trade restrictions and the imposition of common external trade barriers diverts imports from nonmember to member countries, it will tend to depress the union's import prices and, with export prices remaining constant, the collective terms of trade of the members will improve. If the elasticity of demand for the union's imports is high, and if it is an important force in the world market, the terms of trade improvement may be quite substantial.

In terms of offer-curve analysis, the combined offer curve of the members may shift backward, thereby inducing an improvement in their terms of trade, just as effectively as if they had all raised their tariffs simultaneously against the outside world. The larger the economic size of a customs union, and the greater its trade-diverting impact, the more will the terms of trade of its members be likely to improve vis-à-vis the rest of the world.

On the export side, too, customs unions may improve their members' terms of trade. A customs union acting in international trade negotiations, especially if it is large, has a great deal more bargaining power than any of its individual members. It can exact tariff concessions on the part of nonmember countries that would otherwise be unthinkable.

The prospect of declining import prices relative to export prices, then, makes improving terms of trade an important ancillary effect of customs unions, which is not to be overlooked.

This chapter has examined the short-term, *static* effects of one of the most important aspects of regional, international economic integration: the formation of a customs union. It has shown that member nations may expect gains in various forms from membership in a customs union and from the regional free trade it entails.

But these effects of integration constitute only part of the story, perhaps even the less important part. It is the impact of economic integration on the rate of economic growth in participating countries which will concern us in the next chapter, not only with regard to free internal trade, but also as it relates to the free mobility of entrepreneurship and the factors of production. These are the *dynamics* of economic integration, which many economists feel are of overriding importance in any project involving economic union.

14

DYNAMIC GAINS FROM INTERNATIONAL ECONOMIC INTEGRATION

With a reasonably clear idea of the statics of economic integration, as surveyed in the foregoing chapter, we may now proceed to examine the second major source of gains from regional free trade and factor mobility: its impact upon the member nations' collective and individual rates of economic growth. We shall find that all of the elements governing the magnitude and direction of the static allocation effects of economic union simultaneously affect the dynamics of economic integration, but in ways quite different from those outlined earlier. The dynamic gains discussed here are associated with large markets—markets which may be achieved *either* in a regional context via integration or in a broader context via trade liberalization. We shall thus use the term "international economic integration" to describe the process of freeing trade and productive-factor movements among nations.

SCALE ECONOMIES AND COMPETITION

Economists generally consider the impact of freer trade on productive efficiency to be one of the most important growth benefits to be derived from the attendant creation of a larger market out of several smaller national markets. This is certainly true for economic integration among industrial economies. The effective size of the market governs the volume of output possible in various industries. This, in turn, determines the realization of scale economies in those industries.

Economies of scale are attributable to a variety of factors, each of which is influenced by effective market size. Certain types of capital equipment may only be used effectively whenever the volume of production is sufficiently large. Likewise the most advanced production methods, which are almost synonymous with the application of sophisticated capital equipment, are only feasible when they are applied to similar large output quantities. Economies of scale attributable to mass production know-how and capital equipment may be found in the manufacture of virtually every kind of good subject to large volume consumption, from processed food to consumer durables.

High volume production and consumption also yield per-unit cost savings as a result of relatively smaller required inventory stocks and by permitting the performance of purchasing, handling, shipping, and sales functions in bulk. Labor, too, can be used more effectively in large-scale operations. Highly trained, specialized personnel are justified in the production process only under such circumstances, and this is also true for staff employed in the design, sales, and research and development capacities. Few such functions could be justified in small firms producing for a severely limited market. Finally, and certainly not least important, is the quality of management. This tends to be substantially higher in large firms than in small ones, and itself may be the source of noteworthy gains in operating efficiency.

All of this is not to say that these always exists a perfect correspondence between output volume, or firm size, and per-unit cost of production. But there is a high probability that the functional relationships tend in this direction. For this reason alone it is likely that the institution of freer trade resulting in high output volumes of firms competing for a new, larger market will in fact yield significant scale economies. This will thereby benefit the economic growth of the participating nations. Even without resorting to the argument resting on increased plant size, freer trade may force existing plants to specialize in considerably fewer products, thereby realizing similar possibilities for economies of scale in their operations.

Aside from inducing increases in economic efficiency attributable to economies of large-scale production, the creation of a relatively free market for goods and services among a number of national economies can benefit long-run efficiency in other ways as well. The increase in competition among business firms forces individual enterprises consistently to be as efficient as possible in order to retain a viable share of the more extensive market for their particular output. To the extent that firms are willing or are forced to compete intensively with one another, preexisting oligopolistic or near-monopoly markets will be destroyed by integration. Inefficiency attributable to restricted market structures will be eliminated and, as a result, the economic growth of the member economies stands to benefit over the long term.

The stimulative effect of regional or broad-based trade liberalization on interfirm competition will only materialize if firms are not able or permitted to create monopolies or cartels on a broader, union-wide scale. Presumably government policy—either through cooperation between the various participating nations or via the creation of a supranational anti-monopoly organization—will prevent such regional international monopoly formation, if it is fully realized that economic growth will suffer therefrom. We discuss this problem more fully in the following chapter.

Immediately after the formation of a free-trade zone, for example, the number of firms producing a certain product may be relatively large. With the passage of time it is likely that the number of firms competing for a given market will diminish, and that firms will merge into larger, more competitive units. This in itself is certainly no indication of a diminution of competition. It is a natural course of events attributable to the new competitive environment in a larger market. One should not assume, therefore, that the reduction in the *number* of suppliers of a given commodity in an economic union signifies that competition is being stifled or that its contribution to economic growth will suffer. Rather, the reverse may actually be the case.

PHYSICAL CAPITAL: SAVINGS, INVESTMENT, AND RISK

The physical capital stock of an economy, however measured, constitutes a major determinant of the capacity to produce. In terms of labor productivity, the higher the capital–labor ratio, the higher will be output per man-hour. In the past, physical capital formation was thought to be the dominant component of economic growth. A nation's economic advance was considered to depend primarily upon the rate of growth in the capital stock that it was able to muster. Today, economists are not nearly so certain of this. Investment in human capital and technological change have grown markedly in importance as acknowledged agents of growth, particularly in economically advanced regions. This is not meant to diminish the importance of physical capital formation. Quite to the contrary. A nation cannot develop beyond a very low level without a substantial stock of physical capital, although the relative importance of this growth element will vary as the nation proceeds upward along its development path.

The physical capital endowment of a nation is a stock concept. Net additions to this stock comprise total investment less replacement investment, *net capital formation*, which is a flow concept. This is based upon: (a) the savings rate, (b) the investment rate, and (c) the flow of investment funds from one economy to another. Government policy will effect capital formation by influencing all three determinants. The prevailing tax system, the level of the tax, and the treatment of investment are an important considera-tion, as are government measures related to competition and business–labor relations. Whereas these forces bearing on savings and investment might be classed as *objective* in nature, there are a number of important *subjective* factors to be considered as well. These center around the role of expecta-tions and uncertainty in investment decisions. It is hardly necessary, for instance, to dwell on the devastating effect on the demand for investment capital that a shock to business confidence may have. Its effect may far exceed that which would be expected on the basis of the objective situation that caused it. A basically market-oriented, capitalistic economy can easily be subjected to such shocks, resulting in an undermining of the confidence of both entrepreneurial groups and savers.

Besides considering the factors affecting the stock of tangible capital, we ought to look also at changes in the *quality of capital*. Suppose, for exam-ple, a machine wears out and is replaced by another, so that the national stock of physical capital is unchanged. It is likely that the new machine is more productive than the old one because it is of higher technological quality, so that national output will rise as a result, even though no net capital formation has occurred. Technology is embodied in capital, at least to some degree, so that *replacement* investment will also tend to contribute to growth.

How does trade liberalization influence physical capital formation in the participating economies—in terms of its effect on savings, investment, and the quality of the capital stock? First, it is not at all certain that freer trade or regional economic integration by itself stimulates the rate of savings. In-deed, there is little immediate evidence, for example, that internally gen-erated capital formation has accelerated as a result of regional economic integration projects presently underway. Yet experience has shown that integration does indeed tend to attract substantial investment capital from nonmember countries. This has been particularly true with regard to U.S. investment flows into the EEC, which reached enormous proportions during the first half of the 1960's. This may be termed the *new-investment benefit* of economic union. Firms and individuals may be reluctant to invest heavily in production facilities for small, fragmented national markets. Yet they may consider a large, integrated market as an opportunity to send substantial volumes of capital into the area. In addition, the stimulus that freer trade is expected to exert on productive efficiency and on economic growth tends to enhance the attractiveness investment projects from the standpoint of long-term profit potential.

The integration of national markets may also reduce the degree of risk associated with investment. A large market decreases the likelihood that a specific investment undertaking will fail. And the elimination of trade barriers helps to insure that investment is channeled only into the most productive, or competitive, enterprises which will be able to survive in an integrated market.

The ramifications of reduced uncertainty or risk are not limited to investment activity alone, particularly within regional economic integration projects. Intraunion trade is itself subject to far less uncertainty under conditions of regional free trade, thereby aiding the development of that sector of the economy engaged in foreign transactions. No longer is there the possibility of administrative variation of tariffs and other trade restrictions within the union, and the eventuality of explicit or implicit costs involved in foreign trade is eliminated. Firms are more willing to enter into extensive intraunion international transactions—transactions which they would have been reluctant to engage in if the chances of adverse administrative measures still existed. The reduction of uncertainty of any kind represents a boon to economic growth. It makes provision for "risk premiums" unnecessary—costs which may or may not be incurred due to unforeseen events.

INTERNATIONAL LABOR MOBILITY

Regarding labor as a source of economic growth involves looking at it in two ways: (a) the growth of the labor force and changes in the average amount of labor time devoted to productive tasks per man per year, and (b) change in the quality of the labor force in terms of training and skills. Labor force growth depends on (a) the growth of the population and (b) changes in the labor force participation rate. Population growth, in turn, hinges on the direction and volume of migration, the birth rate, and the death rate.

The labor force participation rate tends to be a fairly constant fraction of the population, although a variety of factors may cause gradual changes in it. For example, shifts in the age composition of the population may increase the proportion grouped in the very old and the very young segments. Neither of these will participate in productive employment, and hence the labor force participation rate will fall. Also, changes in educational patterns, demanding that young people stay in school longer, lowers the labor force participation rate, as do changes in retirement programs that pull people out of the labor force sooner. Offsetting these, however, may be an increase in the labor force participation by women, a phenomenon that has characterized many industrial economies since World War II.

Once we have applied changes in the labor force participation rate to population growth, we know the development of the labor force in terms of the number of people actively engaged in it. In order to finally determine the labor component of a nation's total productive resources, we need simply apply the number of hours worked per man to the labor force. Historically, hours of work have tended to decline over the past two decades in most industrial countries.

The factors affecting population growth, labor force participation rates, and hours of work determine the growth of the available *quantity* of labor as a productive resource. Still, an accurate estimate of labor's total contribution to economic growth can be gained only by determining concurrent changes in the *quality* of labor. Clearly, one hour's labor on the part of a highly skilled individual is likely to be substantially more productive on the average than that of an unskilled laborer. To some extent, skills are inherent. To a far greater extent, however, they are acquired through a conscious educational experience. Providing this educational experience calls for sacrifices on the part of the national economy, both with regard to the explicit costs of education and in terms of the productive services of the individual that must be foregone for a certain period of time. In part, these sacrifices must of course be borne by the individual himself. In any case, they constitute an investment—an investment in *human capital*.

In recent years it has come to be recognized that education—that type of training which increases the productivity and hence the quality of labor—plays a far more important role in economic growth than was previously thought. Partly, this can be seen in the surprisingly high rate of return, both private and social, that seems to inhere in educational investment. The role of education appears especially important when on-the-job-training, adult education, the cost of labor market information, and the cost of migration are included, as properly they should be. Finally, education is not the only factor determining the quality of labor. Health is of major importance, and the provision of all kinds of health services, both physical and mental, also constitutes an investment by the society in human capital and represents an improvement in the labor force.

Economic integration may influence the labor component of economic growth in three ways:

1. By instituting free labor mobility and permitting countries with scarce labor to expend output without detracting from production in labor-surplus countries
2. By attracting labor into the union from nonmember countries
3. By fostering broad-based improvement of labor quality within the integrated area

It is often alleged that workers are not really very responsive to changing geographical supply and demand conditions prevailing in the labor markets. Wages may be higher and job opportunities greater in some parts of a country than in others. Yet workers seem reluctant to move in order to take advantage of changing labor conditions. They seem to possess deep roots in their home location and would rather muddle through what they regard as temporary crises than pull up and move away. Such inertia is generally held responsible for the prolonged structural unemployment which besets various regions of virtually all industrial countries from time to time. Still, within a nation the labor is free to move if it so desires. If the inertia can be overcome, the affected workers and the economy as a whole will benefit markedly as a result of the allocation of labor in favor of the most productive tasks.

This is generally not the case between countries, however. Individual national states maintain prohibitive restrictions on immigration in order to "protect" the domestic work force, although such barriers have historically been subject to modification or elimination whenever it was deemed to be in the country's own self-interest to do so. Policies of this sort govern the international movement of labor regardless of whether it is permanent or migratory in nature.

As economic integration proceeds from a unified market for goods and services to a unified market for the factors of production, the barriers to international labor movements within the economic union are eliminated. Labor is free to move anywhere within the integrated area, exactly as it is within a single nation.

The benefits derived from free international labor mobility will be greater, the more extensive is the disparity between the participating labor-surplus and labor-deficit countries. Suppose one or more countries possess substantial labor surpluses, and others suffer from a measure of labor scarcity. Combined output and the overall material welfare of the nations involved will benefit greatly from the temporary or permanent migration of labor from the surplus to the deficit areas. If labor does in fact move in response to wage differentials, which are assumed to reliably reflect relative productivity, then the transfer of workers from low to high productivity employment will benefit all concerned. Maximum gain is attained when unemployed (zero productivity) or underemployed workers are able to find highly productive jobs elsewhere in the union.

Labor migration benefits the recipient countries by permitting them to expand output, which was not possible before the infusion of new workers. The country of origin may benefit by return flows of wage and salary remittances, increased exports of home products to the expatriate labor force, and a reduction in the number of unproductive individuals domestically.

The overall effects of free labor mobility brought about by international economic integration are by no means all beneficial. For instance, if the movement of labor results in a depletion of the labor supply of the heretofore labor-surplus areas, then the possibilities of future economic development in such areas will be limited indeed. At the same time, if it is predominantly the skilled workers who migrate, the labor-surplus area may well be worse off than before. The level of living of the people remaining behind may well decline absolutely as well as relatively.

We noted earlier that numerous impediments present themselves with respect to labor movements within a country. Such impediments are likely to be considerably more powerful internationally, even within a closely knit economic union. Social and religious factors, as well as climate, are not to be overlooked in impeding labor movements from one country to another, even though all government-imposed restrictions are removed. We have not even considered the question of language, which may well constitute the single most important barrier to international labor mobility among countries.

It seems fairly safe to say that the beneficial aspects of free labor mobility at least under integration schemes outweigh the possible drawbacks in most instances. This is especially true if there results an eventual return flow of labor into the home areas—labor that has become more highly skilled than it was initially. The European experience has shown that the labor mobility effects of integration need not be limited to the integrated area alone, and that it may draw substantial numbers of skilled and semi-skilled workers, as well as managerial-technical talent, from nonmember countries. At the same time, integration-induced training and retraining programs as part of an adjustment-assistance program may help to upgrade the quality of labor. Finally, induced institutional change in educational and training facilities attributable to integration may exert a positive impact on growth through the labor component.

NATURAL RESOURCES

The third resource feeding into the growth process is the availability of natural resources. These are composed of various kinds of natural endowments that promise to be useful in the productive process. Included are fuel and mineral deposits of various types—coal, iron ore, oil, natural gas, bauxite, as well as timber stands, high-yield fishing areas, and so on. But are such sources really "natural?" Is the mere presence of such a resource really a boon to economic growth? Natural resources such as these are useless unless they can be exploited, and their exploitation hinges upon the application of labor, capital, and technology. Even if all the resources in the world were equally distributed among nations, there would still be vast differences in their effects on economic growth, since only some countries would have the technology to discover them and the technology, labor, and capital needed to exploit them. Over and above this, the contribution of natural resources to development is also a function of the effort, character, and resourcefulness of the people. A natural resource is "created" initially by applying other productive factors and by resourcefulness on the part of those discovering and exploiting it. By the same token it can be "recreated" through new applications even after it has apparently lost its value.

The contributions of natural resources to growth vary enormously from one stage of economic advance to the next, and from one nation to another. There is little question that differences in natural resource endowments play an important part in charting the course of economic growth for countries at specific stages of the growth process. Yet they are not of determining importance. If a nation is able to trade internationally, and if its other sources of growth are conducive to rapid development, it is safe to say that a lack of this or that natural resource, or even of many natural resources, need ever be an insurmountable obstacle to economic advance.

Economic integration serves to reduce further the importance of natural resources to the economic growth of the participating nations. By assuring access to raw materials supplies, it permits a country to import freely any lacking raw materials produced by other countries and at the same time assures it of a permanent market for exports with which to pay for them. The absence of natural resources, for example, is no more a barrier to the growth of an economy participating in an effective economic union than it is to a region of a single national economy. At the same time, if integration includes the freedom of business firms to establish themselves anywhere within the union, the absence of resources such as land for industrial expansion, clean air and water, or inland waterways need not hinder the growth of industries requiring them.

TECHNOLOGY, INNOVATION, AND EXTERNAL ECONOMIES

The major factor determining how efficiently the three types of resources discussed above are used in the productive process of technology. Consequently technological change, whether or not embodied in labor and capital, is one of the most important elements contributing to economic growth. Technology may be considered quite simply as *useful knowledge*—knowledge that by its very nature helps an economy to use its productive resources to greater advantage. It refers not only to scientific and technical know-how, although these are often considered of overriding importance, but also to nontechnical innovations, business improvements, and so forth. Technological change, then, is best defined rather broadly to include not only the development of new and different products and processes, but also the adaptation of existing ones to new and different uses, which in itself adds something to the productive process.

What determines the rate of technological change achieved by an economy? First, and most apparent, internally generated technology is a function of the amount of investment of productive resources that a nation devotes to it. This, in turn, is dependent upon the expected rate of return on investments in technology (research and development) which at any one time may or may not exceed the rate of return obtainable on alternative investments in physical or human capital. Second, the rate of technological change is notably influenced by the adoption of innovations originating in other nations and their adaptation to local conditions. This process is far less costly, and hence requires a much lower rate of return to make it worthwhile. Technological imitation is perhaps most applicable to nations that are technologically backward or "catching up" than it is to the technological leaders. But even the leaders sooner or later profit from international technological transfers.

International economic integration may represent an important force in support of economic growth by fostering technological change. For example, experience tells us that large firms can afford to engage in extensive research and development programs, while small firms are decidedly limited in this regard. If freer trade does, in fact, result in increased firm size because of the extension of the market, these larger firms may then initiate ambitious research programs that they alone have the financial capabilities to undertake. This is especially pertinent as general technological advance makes research increasingly costly, requiring extensive facilities and large, permanent staffs and development of high cost, high quality, specialized talent.

Moreover, economies of scale may also characterize research and development activities, just as they are known to apply in the direct productive process as indicated earlier. As a firm extends the size and scope of its research activities, it tends to become increasingly efficient at performing these functions. Productivity in research is thus enhanced. All of this implies that by stimulating the *quantity* of research done, as well as the *efficiency* with which it is performed, economic integration will add to the rate of technological change and thereby contribute notably to economic growth itself.

Such advances in useful knowledge need not, of course, be limited to the technical field. Changes in managerial practices, including streamlined business organizations and the application of advanced data processing systems, may result from increased firm size and heightened competition attributable to integration. Moreover, the "new investment benefit" mentioned earlier may lead to infusions of a managerial as well as a technical sort from outside the integrated area. There is ample evidence, for example, that the much publicized managerial revolution sweeping the EEC countries in the 1960's was in large measure triggered by U.S. firms enticed into the field by prospects of an integrated and rapidly growing market.

A related dynamic effect of international economic integration on growth concerns the realization of *external* economies by firms not possible before economic union. Industries producing for a large and geographically diverse market tend to locate in areas best suited to optimum productive efficiency from all points of view. This leads to the development of regions of rather intense industrial concentration. Interactions among firms located in such industrial centers—in terms of the flows of physical goods, labor, capital, entrepreneurship, and technology—greatly benefit efficiency in overall production. This also calls forth the development of effective transportation systems, communications facilities, and other elements in the so-called economic *infrastructure*. These in themselves support economic growth.

Nonetheless, anyone familiar with congested, urban areas of heavy industrialization will be quick to object that, after a certain point, the incurred external diseconomies may begin to outweight any further gains in the external economies just cited. Hence, it may well be true that the impact of economic integration on economic growth, through external economies, is substantially greater if it involves less developed, relatively backward countries than if it is undertaken among highly developed, industrial nations.

NATIONAL CHARACTER

A second factor tending to govern the effectiveness of resource-use in the achievement of rapid growth is national character. Economists generally try to avoid placing a great deal of emphasis upon this element, in part because national character is a nebulous concept, at best—one inexorably interwoven with the respective contributions to growth of labor, capital, and natural resource development. It is nebulous in part because, while we are sure that the character of the people influences growth, we are also certain that economic growth affects the character of the people. Sociological and religious factors help determine the rate of population growth, and hence the rate of labor force growth. The nature of the family as a social unit can influence a large number of growth variables such as the attitude toward saving and investment, the attitude toward work and hence the labor force participation rate and, certainly not least important, the mobility of labor both geographically and structurally to meet the ever-changing needs that invariably characterize the growth process. Such factors also typically influence the degree of entrepreneurship that exists, and the role of women as contributors to economic advance.

The structure of the typical community itself, as well as its size, is important in many respects, as are interpersonal relations and changes in these elements attributable to the process of urbanization. Class and race relations have impeded economic growth in various countries at various times. Rapid growth demands efficient use of labor resources and this efficiency is impeded to the extent that economic mobility is restricted by social, class, racial, and religious barriers, or by any other means.

The very complexity of this particular element in the growth process makes it impossible to talk about the impact of international economic integration in anything but the most general items. Some have argued that integration will induce a "growth mentality" on the part of individuals both in the household and business sector, and thus positively affect economic advance by stimulating savings, investment, and the rate of innovation. While such an assertion would be difficult indeed to substantiate, it is quite reasonable that integration and the competition and productive factor movements it engenders would work in this direction.

ESTABLISHMENT OF ENTERPRISES AND MULTINATIONAL CORPORATE OPERATIONS

Perhaps more concrete is the effect of international economic integration on entrepreneurial behavior in participating economies, both in terms of changes occurring from within as well as new patterns of entrepreneurship accompanying investments from nonmember countries. This falls largely under the heading of freedom of establishment.

There generally are few restrictions to the establishment and operation of business firms or other enterprises anywhere within nations characterized by market-oriented economies. A variety of differences in regulations may exist between regional or local governmental units—e.g., rules governing the chartering of corporations—but these normally will not constitute serious obstructions to the ability of businessmen to establish wherever they desire. All areas of a country are usually open to those willing and able to assume business risks and supply venture capital.

Again, this is not nearly as true internationally. The establishment of foreign-owned business firms is governed by rules and regulations which vary markedly from one host country to the next. But this is not the most serious problem. Regulations that exist today may be changed tomorrow, and since they are completely an internal concern of the host country, they are outside the scope of the foreign firm's direct influence. This lends an aura of uncertainty, over and above normal business risk, to all international business ventures which involve the establishment of foreign affiliates. The direct investment of foreign productive capital and the establishment of foreign-owned firms may be actively encouraged by the host country at one time, only to be subject to restrictive and punitive measures at a future date.

Freedom of entrepreneurial mobility is important for two basic reasons. First, we know that an economy must possess individuals or organization willing and able to assume risks—i.e., willing to move in new and different directions—in order to grow. For this reason alone, the mobility of entrepreneurship from one geographical area to another may be of determining importance from the standpoint of the recipient region's economic development.

Second, direct investment in productive physical capital requires the existence of someone willing to take on substantial risks. Without the free mobility of entrepreneurship, there would be relatively more limited room for direct-investment capital flows between countries.

All of this is not to say that international movements of capital and entrepreneurship have not assumed large proportions. But it is entirely possible that these flows would have been even more extensive and beneficial had there been fewer restrictions, and that the economic gains derived by both the recipient and donor countries could have been all the greater.

Presumably, the elimination of restrictions to free establishment will be part of any significant movement toward regional economic union. Firms located in one member country which are interested in organizing wholly or partly-owned subsidiaries or affiliates in another may do so freely. The same is true of individual entrepreneurs. Not only is the willingness to bear risk thus more evenly distributed among the cooperating countries, but also the movement of capital in the form of direct investment is encouraged. In addition, the probability that capital will be channeled into the most productive uses on a union-wide scale is enhanced. The risks involved in international investments and business operations are reduced, and the managerial skills that generally accompany entrepreneurial movements are more easily disseminated. The combined economic welfare of the member nations is enhanced, with benefits accruing to both the recipient countries and the countries of origin.

Undesirable or harmful movements of entrepreneurship are certainly not excluded as a possible side-effect of the institution of free entrepreneurial mobility. For instance, favorable treatment of business profits or capital gains in one country may attract entrepreneurs, even though this may be entirely unjustified on purely economic grounds. Other differences in national policies, as they affect the climate of business operations, may similarly lead to unsound movements of entrepreneurial activities. But such problems can to a great extent be avoided through the harmonization or coordination of national economic and other policies.

In recent years the role of the multinational corporation (MNC) in the international economy has been hotly debated. An MNC is any enterprise which has production units in two or more countries and which attempts to optimize its competitive position by implementing a marketing, sourcing, and financing plan which transcends national political boundaries. The typical MNC undertakes both international trade and international factor transfers. Much of what it does would take place anyway, as international differences in production and demand conditions along the lines of comparative advantage discussed in the first few chapters of this book. The MNC serves to bring about these changes much more rapidly and perhaps much more efficiently. Consequently, the multinational enterprise is of crucial importance in the modern international economy and particularly in determining the size and direction of the dynamic effects of freer trade and factor movements—whether on a regional or global basis. We shall discuss the role of the MNC in greater detail in Chapter 29.

15

TRADE AND MARKET STRUCTURE

In discussing the theory of commercial policy, we have surveyed in some detail a variety of elements which determine whether producers *can* compete in international markets. The present chapter focuses on the elements which determine whether producers *do* compete, and whether the competitive environment within which firms operate internationally is conducive to the maximization of gains from international trade and specialization.

The theory of commercial policy concerns itself with the impact of restrictions to free international commerce upon the volume and direction of international trade, national economic structure, income distribution, and world and national economic welfare. It attempts to reconcile the obvious existence of barriers to trade with the powerful arguments that can be invoked in favor of freer trade.

Even the arguments for free trade have one basic weakness—they generally rest on a price system that is free to operate perfectly in response to changes in supply and demand conditions, both in the markets for goods and services and in the markets for productive factors. This condition, of course, does not normally hold in the real world. Whether all of the distinctive factors that bear on the efficiency of the price system are sufficient to upset seriously the case for freedom of trade in general is uncertain, as we have seen in connection with second-best analysis above.

We shall be satisfied here with an examination of a variety of forces that may distort competition internationally and their probable effects on international trade patterns.

ELEMENTS OF PERFECT COMPETITION

The theory of international trade and commercial policy is based largely upon the existence of perfect competition in the markets for both goods and services and the factors of production. Occasionally, an exception is made, as in the discussion of economies of scale and in our survey of second-best analysis. In the main, however, the theme centers around the optimal allocation of productive resources both domestically and internationally via free trade and perfect competition, and the disturbance of this allocation caused by impediments to trade.

Every student of economics eventually learns that market structure in the real world seldom corresponds to the purely competitive model. This is true of both the markets for goods and the markets for productive factors. Under pure competition the seller cannot have control over the price of his product. This price is determined in the market by the forces of supply and demand and is dictated to him. At that market price he can sell all he can produce, but at a higher price he can sell nothing. Perfect competition can prevail only if (a) the product of the various competing suppliers is homogeneous with respect to quality, (b) there are a large number of competing firms, each one of which holds only a small share of the market, (c) there is free entry and exit, (d) there is perfect knowledge, and so forth.

Whereas the perfect competitor finds that his selling price is dictated to him, he can still freely vary the quantity he produces. He will, therefore, continue to increase output as long as one extra unit sold yields additional revenues which exceed the additional costs involved in producing that one extra unit. That is, as long as *marginal revenue* exceeds *marginal cost,* it pays him to expand output. His profits will attain a maximum when marginal cost equals marginal revenue. Since for the perfect competitor the price of the extra unit sold is the same regardless of how many units he sells, marginal revenue and price are identical. He will therefore produce a quantity sufficient to insure that the marginal cost of the last unit sold just equals the selling price.

This is presented diagrammatically in Figure 15–1. The price of the commodity, $P,$ is determined by the interaction of supply and demand in the market and dictated to the firm. Since the firm can sell all it can produce at that price, its demand curve, $D_F,$ is horizontal. At the same time, each additional unit sold yields the additional revenue of $P,$ so the marginal revenue curve, $MR,$ is identical with the demand curve. The perfectly competitive firm produces quantity $OQ_F,$ where marginal cost (MC) equals marginal revenue (MR). With free entry and exit, there can be no long-run monopoly profits under pure competition, so that the average total cost curve (ATC) is tangent to the demand or average revenue curve. Since the average total cost curve is always intersected by the marginal cost curve at its minimum point, this tangency $(MC = MR = ATC)$ must occur at minimum average total cost.

If perfect competition prevails both in the markets for productive factors and in the markets for goods and services, resource allocation and output are highly responsive to demand patterns. Since production always occurs at minimum average total cost, these resources are employed in the productive process with optium efficiency. Because there can be no long-run profits, total commodity price always equals the sum of the individual resource costs. Finally, if perfect competition prevails in the market for pro-

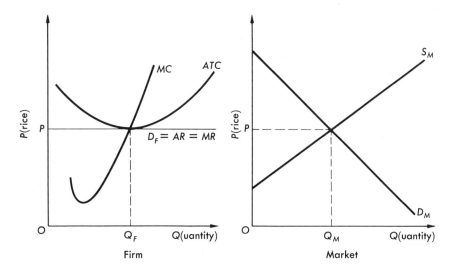

Fig. 15–1. Price and output determination under perfect competition.

ductive resources as well, the factor costs must be identical with what they could earn in alternative employment in any industry, i.e., equal to its *marginal revenue product*. All of this tends to occur *automatically* via the price mechanism.

This is the market structure assumed to exist in the theory of international trade. It may not be an entirely unrealistic assumption. Before the Industrial Revolution it may well have been true that international trade involved goods produced under highly competitive conditions—basically, primary commodities. Hence, monopolistic elements in the markets for goods and productive factors could possibly be discounted as bearing heavily on the factors affecting international trade at that time. This is certainly not true today. Most traded goods are produced and distributed under decidedly monopolistic conditions.

ELEMENTS OF MONOPOLY

A vast majority of the goods entering international trade today are not homogeneous to any significant degree. They are differentiated from one another in a variety of ways. Entry into industries today is rarely free—with patents, technological know-how, heavy capital requirements, and other obstacles that must be overcome. Knowledge is not perfect; with very few exceptions it is impossible to know what is going on in all parts of the market for a given good simultaneously. Firms are not small relative to the total market size, nor should they be, with significant economies of scale to be realized. Meanwhile, in the market for productive factors similar departures from perfect competition may be observed, with monopolistic elements often characterizing factor supply and monopsonistic influences operating on the factor demand side.

A firm operating in an industry characterized by a monopolistic market structure has at least some control over price. Since its product is more or less differentiated from that of its competitors, it may raise its price without losing all of its customers. Increased sales are possible only at lower prices. Hence, the demand curve facing the imperfectly-competitive firm is downward-sloping. Its marginal revenue curve falls below the demand curve, since it must lower the price of *all* units to sell one additional unit, marginal revenue is always less than average revenue.

Referring to Figure 15–2, we note how imperfect competition differs from perfect competition. The demand (average revenue) curve is downward-sloping and the marginal revenue curve falls somewhere below it. With cost curves similar to those presented above in connection with perfect competition, the firm under monopolistic competition will again maximize profits or minimize losses where marginal cost equals marginal revenue, at point S. It will, therefore, sell quantity OQ at price P. Its average total cost is Oa and, with an average revenue of OP, its profit per unit is aP. Hence, total revenues are represented by the area $OPTQ$, total costs are $OaRQ$, and total economic profits are $aPTR$.

Note that the firm operates at a cost level (R) which is higher than the minimum attainable with a given plant size (V). This means that resources are being employed in production with less than optimum efficiency. Note also that the output level at which $MR = MC$ is less than that at which $MC = ATC$. Since the perfectly competitive firm in the long run always produces where $MR = MC = ATC$, it follows that output levels under imperfect competition tend to be less than corresponding, perfectly competitive output levels. Finally, pure or economic profits are possible under this form of competition due to the absence of completely free entry into the industry.

We have designated here as operating under imperfect competition all

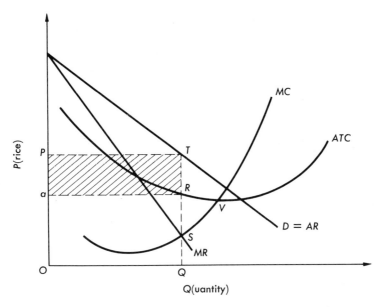

Fig. 15–2. Price and output determination of an imperfectly competitive firm.

firms facing a downward-sloping demand curve. Taken in the broadest sense, this would include both pure monopoly (one supplier) and oligopoly (few suppliers), and monopolistic competition. Economists usually claim that under such conditions output will be lower, prices higher, and resources utilized less efficiently than under perfect competition. Imperfect competition in the productive factor markets has a similar effect. The economy is not nearly as free to adjust to changing competitiveness, either domestic or international, and this rigidity can influence the reliability of comparative advantage as a predictor of international trade relationships. On the other hand, we have seen that economies of scale—which are possible only under imperfect competition—can be an important force in influencing comparative costs internationally.

The specific impact of imperfect competition on international trade is extremely difficult to assess. The output of suppliers located in various parts of the world indeed are *not* perfect substitutes for one another. This would tend to result in a reduction in the volume of trade below what it would be if they were perfectly substitutable. Yet the demand forces operating internationally thrive on international product differentiation. The cross-trading of commodities is enormous: automobiles from Germany to France and France to Germany, machine tools from Belgium to Great Britain and vice-versa, and so on *ad infinitum*. The stimulus that product differentiation brings to international trade through demand variation may well outweigh its possibly negative effects on the supply side. In addition, the role of economies of scale also helps to reduce the potential negative impact of imperfect competition on international trade. It does, however, demand that we employ the classical analytical tools of international trade with some caution and consider seriously such techniques as second-best analysis.

In what follows, we shall concentrate on the impact of several more clearly defined manifestations of imperfect competition on international competitiveness and international trade.

INTERNATIONAL CARTELS AND PRICE DISCRIMINATION

Suppose only two firms in the world produce a certain type of chemical; one located in the U.S. and the other in Germany. The demand for this chemical is presumed to be widespread throughout the world, and both concerns compete actively for each and every market. The German firm even competes for a share of the U.S. market, and vice-versa. Given this particular situation, would it not be profitable for the two firms to *agree not to compete,* either explicitly or implicitly, as follows: the world market for this type of chemical would be divided by agreement between the two firms, with neither invading the territory of the other. Each would have a monopoly position in its own market, setting prices at whatever level maximizes its own profits—a level presumably above the competitive price. Such an agreement would be called an *international cartel.*

Any formal agreement between firms to share the market or otherwise restrict competition may be classified as a cartel. When such agreements across international frontiers, they become of direct concern to us in our study of the behavior of international trade. The purpose of cartels is simple: to secure profits for each participating firm in excess of what it could have earned under conditions of unrestricted competition. We shall see a little later that the problem of mutual distrust in cartels is such that virtually every such organization is faced with internal tensions that constantly threaten to break it up. For this reason, an international cartel will often be very formally structured by some sort of association that has the power to hold it together.

International cartels probably had their heyday between the two world wars. Pharmaceuticals, chemicals, electrical machinery, and machine tools head a long list of goods in which international trade was subject to the influence or control of cartels. Of the total volume of world trade during the interwar period, it appears that around one-third came under the direct influence of cartels. This certainly takes us far from the perfectly competitive ideal. As late as 1964 in Europe, there was considerable discussion of a grand cartel in the production of automobiles between Volkswagen, Fiat, and Renault that would divide the European market either geographically or by type of vehicle for the collective benefit of the three giant manufacturers.

The general goal of a cartel is to maximize profits of its members by' suppressing competition among them. In effect, a cartel creates a monopoly in a market where at least some degree of competition, most probably oligopoly, existed beforehand. One method is to split up the overall market geographically, or by product, so that each member firm has an effective monopoly in its own particular segment of the market. Resale from one market to another is prevented. Each firm sets prices to maximize profits given demand conditions in its particular designated market.

Alternatively, the cartel may supply the entire market by allocating output quotas to its members and jointly marketing the product. Or, the cartel may simply fix the price of the good or service in question, and the members compete for the market on the basis of quality considerations alone. These are only a few of the forms a cartel may take.

Only a monopoly or a cartel has the ability to discriminate between markets in terms of prices charged for a relatively uniform good or service. Hence, if resale is prevented in some way, one price could be charged for a certain commodity in Germany, another in France, and still another in Italy, according to the demand conditions prevailing in the three markets.

Total profits of the cartel as a whole are maximized if *each individual buyer* of a good or service can be induced to pay the maximum amount he is willing to pay rather than go without it. This form of price discrimination is clearly impossible to realize fully in practice. Much more likely is the division of the market into *broad segments* according to uniform demand criteria, and then charging each *segment* a different price. The criterion for price discrimination in two or more markets is the elasticity of demand prevailing in each.

Suppose we take an international wine cartel, selling in France and England. Frenchmen, it is well known, are habitual wine-drinkers and hence their price elasticity of demand is likely to be low; i.e., an increase in the price of wine is likely to cause a relatively small reduction in consumption. The British, on the other hand, adopt more of a "take it or leave it" attitude, using beer and ale as good substitutes for wine. Hence, they are likely to possess a substantially higher price elasticity of demand for wine. The cartel would be wise, therefore, to charge higher prices for a given type of wine in France than in England, thereby maximizing overall revenues and profits.

This can be shown graphically in Figure 15–3, which presents the average and marginal revenue curves for two national markets, characterized by different price elasticities of demand—AR_1, MR_1, and AR_2, MR_2, respectively. By simply adding the marginal revenue curves for the two markets, the combined marginal revenue (ΣMR) curve facing the cartel is derived. The marginal cost curve (MC) and the average total cost curve (ATC) for the cartel are also drawn.

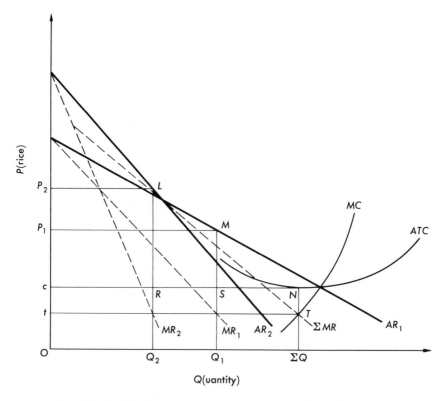

Fig. 15–3. Market segmentation and price discrimination.

In order to maximize profits, the cartel will operate where marginal cost equals the combined marginal revenue at point T, producing a total quantity $O\Sigma Q$. Of this total, it sells quantity OQ_1 in the first market (where $MC = MR_1$) and OQ_2 in the second (where $MC = MR_2$). The first market is willing to take quantity OQ_1 at price P_1 while the second market is willing to absorb quantity OQ_2, at price P_2. Marginal cost has thus been equated with marginal revenue in each of the two markets. Total costs are represented by the area $O\Sigma QNc$, and total revenue is $OQ_1MP_1 + OQ_2LP_2$, leaving economic profits of $cSMP_1 + cRLP_2$. Maximum profits are attained for each market, the total of which substantially exceeds the profits that would have been attained if a uniform price had been set for *both* markets. By preventing the establishment of a uniform price through free competition, therefore, the international cartel assures that the profits of each of its members are enhanced.

All cartels possess a basic inner tension which can easily lead to their demise. A cartel member, allocated a certain market area, may be unable to resist invading his neighbor's territory whenever it appears safe to do so. Even if he is forced to sell below average total cost, any additional sales over and above those possible in his own market may help to cover fixed costs and thus serve to raise profits. Hence, unless it is well-organized and tightly controlled, its own internal forces may cause a cartel to degenerate into some form of noncollusive oligopoly—which may indeed benefit the consumer but which is certainly detrimental to the profits of the producers.

How are international cartels controlled and prevented from reassuming the importance they enjoyed during the interwar period? Many countries, led by the U.S. and Great Britain, have adopted legal and other types of restrictions that hinder or totally prevent the operation of cartels. Where cartels are thought to be unavoidable, government control and participation in cartel negotiations have been imposed. Even Germany, traditionally a hotbed of cartel activity, has become decidedly cool to this form of collusion. Not least important, we shall see later, is that the European Common Market has adopted a position that discourages and attempts to control international agreements which restrict competition.

DUMPING

A special case of international price discrimination relates to the practice of *dumping,* with which we dealt briefly in Chapter 7 as a possible justification for tariffs or other forms of restriction. Dumping, it will be recalled, is merely the practice of selling goods abroad at prices lower than those charged domestic buyers.

A monopolist who finds that the elasticity of demand for his output abroad is greater than at home is operating in a perfectly rational way if he charges higher prices at home than he does in the export market. He is simply maximizing his total profits by practicing price discrimination of the type analyzed above. This is true as long as the export price still exceeds his average variable costs so that it contributes something to his fixed charges. If he is operating in the area of increasing marginal costs, it is likely that the practice of dumping will raise the monopolist's domestic selling price, thus further increasing the spread between the home and export price.

In fact, if the monopolist is in a position to sell in several foreign markets characterized by varying degrees of price elasticity of demand, each of which is greater than that prevailing at home, it pays for him to dump in each of these markets at different prices. It would seem, then, that the possibilities for dumping are virtually unlimited in international trade, but this is not true. Remember that price discrimination is possible only if *resale* from one market to another is somehow prevented. Such a condition is not often fulfilled in the international economy; thus a strict limit is placed on the scope that dumping may assume.

Suppose, for instance, that a firm is selling matches at home for 20 cents a pack and dumping them abroad for 10 cents a pack. If there are no restrictions to trade and if transport costs are minimal, what is to prevent enterprising individuals from buying matches abroad at 10 cents and re-importing them for sale at home for something less than 20 cents, and earning a tidy profit in the process? Under such conditions international commodity arbitrage such as this will, in fact, see to it that the domestic and foreign price of matches is quickly equalized and that the dumping practice ceases.

While this example may be somewhat extreme, it is nonetheless true that the *maximum* difference between the home price and the dumping price abroad is always determined by the possibility and cost of resale in the domestic market. For some commodities, arbitrage may be very effective and virtually costless so that the scope for dumping may be narrow indeed. For others, the reverse may be the case, with substantial possibilities for dumping.

If transport costs are important, and if the home country levies an import duty on the commodity in question, then at least some scope for dumping is assured. Going back to the above example, suppose it costs 1 cent to ship a pack of matches from one country to another, and the home country levies a 50 per cent *ad valorem* duty on the c.i.f. import value of matches. The least that the dumped and re-imported matches could be sold for at home is 16½ cents (10 cents dumping price plus 1 cent transport cost plus 5½ cents import duty on c.i.f. value equals 16½ cents). Hence the *minimum* spread between the home and foreign prices available to the dumping firm is 3½ cents. This spread will widen the more limited are the possibilities for international arbitrage in this particular commodity.

At first glance, the practice of dumping would seem to bring about a volume of trade that tends to be somewhat higher than if this practice did not occur. In addition it would appear to result in expanded production on the part of the dumping firm. In reality, of course, the foreign country is likely to possess its own import-competing suppliers whose output will be reduced commensurately as a result of increased volume of dumped imports. It does not take long under such conditions for the importing country to levy its own tariff or to otherwise restrict imports, thereby wholly or partially eliminating the practice of dumping.

We have dealt here with dumping as merely a specific case of international price discrimination via market segmentation. As such, the word "dumping" is really a misnomer, since it connotes the elimination of some sort of *surplus* of commodities which is being alleviated by "dumping" it in the foreign market. This is not necessarily true. The practice of selling abroad at prices lower than those prevailing at home is, as we have seen, perfectly rational behavior on the part of any firm in a position to practice international price discrimination. As such, it is hardly a temporary or sporadic measure connected with passing supply conditions but a behavioral characteristic of a certain type of market structure.

There are, however, some forms of dumping that more closely fit the connotations of the word itself. *Sporadic* dumping may be engaged in temporarily by firms with excess inventories. A firm manufacturing dresses may find that the domestic demand for a certain style is rapidly fading, and it feels that it is advisable to sell its inventory on foreign markets for anything it can get. Or the domestic demand for a given good may be slack during a period of economic recession, resulting in layoffs and extensive unused capacity. Under such circumstances, the temporary condition of the domestic market also may call for sales abroad at prices which cover all variable costs and in addition make some contribution toward the ongoing fixed costs—thereby enabling the producer to minimize his losses.

Both of these latter reasons for dumping abroad also are not necessarily to be condemned out of hand. They really constitute little more than normal behavior on the part of businessmen faced with passing adverse market conditions.

Predatory dumping, however, can be condemned on the same grounds as predatory pricing policies are challenged domestically. A firm may be said to pursue a predatory pricing policy if it reduces the price of a given commodity to such an extent that its competitors are driven out of business. It then raises prices again in accordance with its new monopoly position. Predatory dumping is the same thing but on an international scale. Once its foreign competitors are ruined, the firm again raises prices in accordance with demand conditions prevailing in the foreign market. In fact, if foreign demand is sufficiently inelastic, the subsequent price abroad may actually be *higher* than the domestic price. Predatory dumping in this form is probably the only type that can be condemned, and, as we noted in Chapter 7, it constitutes a powerful argument for protection.

Temporary dumping as a means of *establishing* a product in a foreign market, by way of contrast, is nothing more than an extension of a practice fully tolerated domestically, and hardly varies from other forms of sales promotion.

COMMODITY AGREEMENTS

For many commodities—basically, agricultural produce and raw materials—the elasticity of demand and the elasticity of supply are very low. Hence, small variations in demand or supply can cause very large fluctuations in price in the short run. In addition, developing nations contend that the prices of these commodities are gradually falling. Since the prices of the manufactured goods that such primary-commodity-producing countries buy are relatively stable and are rising secularly, their terms of trade and economic well-being may be subject to severe instability and uncertainty in the short run, combined with an asserted gradual deterioration in the long run.[1] This is nothing more than the old "parity" problem in agriculture in a more general form. In order to prevent such instability and the gradual erosion of terms of trade, the only solution is to control supply. This is the task of commodity agreements.

Figure 15-4 presents short-run demand-and-supply functions for a certain commodity—say coffee—facing the individual supplier and prevailing in the market. If we assume that the market for coffee is perfectly competitive, then the demand curve facing a producer who is largely or entirely specialized in this commodity is horizontal. In the first case, A, a decline in foreign incomes or a change in tastes abroad causes the market demand curve for coffee to shift slightly to the left, resulting in a substantial drop in market price.

The producer is made to feel this as a fall in his horizontal demand curve and, with supply unchanged, a reduction in his sales revenues represented by the shaded area a . Since the prices of the goods he must buy are assumed to remain stable, he is that much worse off.

In the second case, B, particularly fortunate climatic conditions cause a rightward shift in the market supply curve, which, with demand constant, similarly results in a substantial price decline. For the individual producer this again means a drop in his horizontal demand curve and a loss in sales receipts (shaded area a). This time, however, his loss is not as great, since he partakes of the general supply increase with a rightward shift in his short-run supply curve. The loss induced by the price decline (a) may or may not outweigh the gain due to the increase in quantity sold (b).

There is only one way that commodity producers falling under this sort of market structure can protect themselves from price reductions—by restricting supply. In Figure 15-4, the original price could have been maintained and the producers' losses minimized if all suppliers had simply agreed

---

[1] The notion of unstable and secularly declining terms of trade of developing countries will be examined more fully—and more severely questioned—in Chapter 28.

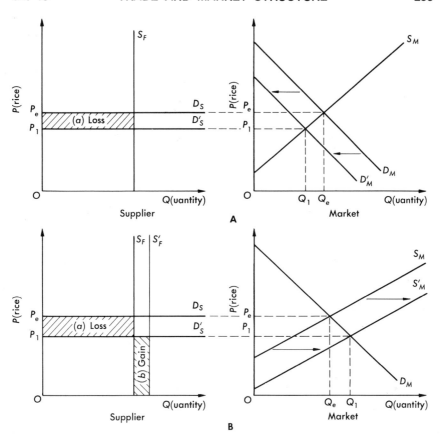

Fig. 15–4. Changing market conditions and commodity price. A. Demand shift. B. Supply shift.

to reduce the amount of coffee coming to market. This is the task of commodity agreements, which can benefit suppliers whether the market structure is perfectly competitive, as above, or monopolistic in nature.

Agreements controlling the world-wide supply of commodities subject to supply and demand characteristics of the type described here may be either private or intergovernmental.

Private commodity agreements are essentially cartels and involve the creation of a central association that allocates production quotas to each supplier. This is done in such a way that the world price is maintained at the desired level. Excess supplies, if they occur, must either be stored or destroyed. This is the weakness inherent in private commodity agreements, since each individual supplier is understandably anxious to dispose of his surplus in a way that still yields at least some revenues, however minimal they may be. Any significant undercutting of the private commodity agreements in this manner invariably leads to its demise. The tendency for circumvention of the agreement is so great in the case of many primary commodities—largely because of the low short-run supply elasticities involved—that supply-controlling organizations of this sort are virtually unworkable.

The result is the evolution of intergovernmental commodity agreements, which elevate the question of controlling supply to a level of national importance. The representatives of countries that are important suppliers of a given commodity may get together and agree that a certain overall supply of the commodity will maintain its world price at some mutually agreeable level. This total supply quota is then divided into export quotas, one for each country, according to a prearranged formula. Each country may sell no more than its quota on world markets during the time period covered by the agreement. Each country, in turn, divides its export quota among its own suppliers. In this way the chance that the supply-limiting pact will succeed is substantially enhanced, since the only way the agreement can be destroyed is if an entire nation—not just a single producer—breaks its supply quota. This is presumably somewhat less likely.

There are many variations of this sort of commodity agreement. For instance, the nations representing important markets for the commodity in question may be parties to the agreement as well. They may agree to import a certain quantity regardless of domestic demand conditions and thereby help to stabilize prices. Or the supplier countries may accumulate huge stocks of the commodity in times of excess supply. These stocks are then sold on the world markets at firm prices during periods of strong demand or "lean" years when supply is unable to keep up with the demand.

The critical reader will be quick to question the justification for commodity agreements, since periods of high prices (supply reductions or demand spurts) are just as likely as periods of low prices (supply gluts or sluggish demand). But this is not the point. The primary *economic* justification for commodity agreements is the *stability* they contribute. Individual suppliers and even entire countries are so specialized in the production of certain commodities that their economic well-being can be equated with the price of those commodities on the world market. Prolonged periods of low prices can ruin suppliers and do lasting damage to a nation's economy if the factors of production thus employed cannot be effectively utilized elsewhere. Such structural rigidities and the increased stability they require constitute a valid justification for the existence of commodity agreements. At the same time, there may be some benefits to be derived by consumers and manufacturers from stable as opposed to continually fluctuating commodity prices.

The advantages of commodity agreements must be weighed against their disadvantages. They may be easily abused to insure not only price stability, but prices that persistently exceed unregulated market prices. By so doing, commodity agreements in effect protect high cost suppliers and adversely influence the allocation of resources and productive efficiency. On the other hand, the continued artificial maintenance of high prices in this manner may encourage the use of substitute commodities and eventually backfire on the affected countries themselves. Moreover, by providing price stability, they may discourage individual suppliers and entire nations from diversifying their output mix, thus prolonging their dependence upon the commodity agreement as the sole source of stability, and in other ways impeding economic growth.

The beneficial effects of individual commodity agreements, then, must be weighed against their deleterious influences before passing judgment. It is indeed possible that supply agreements of this sort are much more necessary and beneficial in the case of some commodities than in others. Each instance must be considered in its turn and on its own merits. We shall have more to say about commodity agreements later on, particularly with regard to their long-range ramifications.

EXPORT CONTROL

The control of exports on the part of a single country has a great deal in common with intergovernmental commodity agreements. As we noted in connection with export quotas in the previous chapter, the objective is to limit the supply of the commodity on the world market, increase its price, and thus improve the nation's terms of trade. What a commodity agreement attempts to do multilaterally, export control seeks to achieve unilaterally. The basic prerequisite for the success of export control in improving a nation's terms of trade is that the nation be a supplier of some importance of the commodity in question. Whether an improvement in the terms of trade actually comes about as a result of export control schemes depends on the nature of the demand for the export and how important, relative to others, the country is as a supplier of the commodity in question.

We have already noted that if the demand for an exported commodity facing a country is less than perfectly elastic, unilateral restriction of that export will increase its price. Import prices remaining constant, its terms of trade will improve. The question is whether or not the improvement in the terms of trade will be more than offset by the necessary decline in the volume of exports. This depends upon the elasticity of foreign demand. The lower the elasticity, the more likely it is that the country will benefit from restricting exports unilaterally. Similarly, the lower the domestic elasticity of supply, the more appropriate will be the restriction of exports since there is little likelihood of reductions in output at lower home prices.

Suppose, for example, Chile were the sole producer of copper in the world. The demand for copper is relatively inelastic (since there are few good substitutes), and so is the supply. By simply reducing its exports Chile would be able to drive the world price of copper upward. The consequent improvement in its terms of trade, import prices remaining unchanged, would more than offset the relatively small reductions in volume of exports required to achieve it. Chile would simply be acting rationally, as any good monopolist, supplying copper to the rest of the world up to a point where its marginal receipts equal its marginal cost per unit of exports.

There are two ways in which exports can be restricted: by limiting the exports themselves and by effecting a reduction in output. The first interferes only with the supplies reaching buyers abroad, while the second limits quantities available to both domestic and foreign consumers.

The *export quota* merely limits the amount of goods that can be sold abroad. Domestic prices may fall drastically while export prices rise or remain stable. The glut on the domestic market under such conditions may be eliminated by means of stockpiling or destruction. Domestic consumers and producers both benefit in real terms at the expense of foreign consumers.

Alternatively, an *export duty* may be imposed. This causes suppliers' receipts from exports to be lower than those from domestic sales at identical prices, and hence the duty discourages exports. This will have an effect similar to that of export quotas. In order to be successful, both export quotas and export duties demand accurate knowledge of the foreign elasticity of demand, which is not always readily available.

The same terms-of-trade effects provided by interference with exports themselves can be achieved by limiting production, although the impact on the domestic economy will be quite different. A country may (a) dictate that suppliers limit output by executive decree, (b) purchase part of the output and destroy it, and (c) purchase all of the output, destroy or stockpile part of it, and sell the rest. All of these measures will have the effect of limiting supplies available to *both* foreign and domestic purchasers, and increase the prices paid by both.

The terms-of-trade effects of the latter set of measures, everything else being equal, will be the same as in the case of pure export restriction. But the price to domestic consumers will rise, and there is likely to be a redistribution of real income from consumers to producers. In this case, domestic producers will tend to benefit at the expense of both foreign and domestic consumers.

Export restriction, in any event, depends for its success in improving the terms of trade upon the partial or complete absence of good substitutes and competing suppliers in other countries. Like commodity agreements, it can be justified in terms of reductions in severe price fluctuations. In addition, it may serve to achieve a permanent improvement in a country's terms of trade. The latter effect will be limited, however, if substitute commodities are likely to be developed insofar as they do not already exist. Steel, silver, and aluminum can be made to substitute for copper, for example, just as atomic energy, hydroelectric and solar power, natural gas and coal can be made to substitute for virtually all uses of oil. Considering such possibilities, export restrictions may well backfire and cause such damage to an economy that it may not soon recover. In the long run, there is always the likelihood of substitution as technological change meets the new market conditions.

STATE TRADING

Up to now, we have assumed that international trade is carried out by profit-maximizing private agents, responding solely to real or potential international price differences. The government interferes only by imposing sanctions and controls of various types which bear on all firms engaged in international trade. It does not directly assume control of trade itself by replacing the importer and the exporter by its own governmental agencies. This condition, where *all* international transactions are handled privately, is almost never met today.

In some countries, notably the Soviet Union, Communist China, and the various other centrally planned economies, the state handles *all* international transactions. In others, such as India and the U.K., international trade is conducted partly by the state and partly by private firms. Still other countries, such as the U.S., West Germany, and Switzerland conduct their international trade predominantly on a private-enterprise basis, although the government does enter directly into international transactions in a relatively few instances.

Whenever the national government or any of its agencies directly engages in imports or exports of goods and services it is said to be involved in *state trading*. There is no apparent reason why state trading need differ from private control of international commerce. In fact, if the government agencies simply limit themselves to buying in the cheapest market and selling in the dearest market, with the objective of maximizing profits, there is no difference—but they do not. In actuality, the pattern of state-controlled foreign trade differs markedly from that which exists under private trade. State trading very rarely conforms to the patterns of comparative advantage, because it is influenced by a large number of considerations other than relative prices and costs.

Political considerations play an important role in state trading. Why should Czechoslovakia, which traded predominantly with the countries of western Europe during the period between World War I and World War II, suddenly shift its trade almost exclusively toward the Soviet Union in the late 1940's and 1950's? The answer is obvious, and has nothing at all to do with comparative advantage. The directions of trade under systems of government-controlled imports and exports tend to be arbitrary, motivated more by political expediency than by international differences in supply and demand conditions.

This is no different in times of hot or cold war, when even those countries normally not characterized by state trading of necessity move further in that direction. Exports must at times be strictly controlled so that strategic materials reach friendly nations on favorable terms and fail to reach real or potential adversaries.

Imports may be manipulated so that they bolster the economies of friendly countries, harm the economies of unfriendly nations, or keep strategic goods away from the enemy. Sanctions of this type have variously been employed in recent times against Cuba, China, Albania, and to a lesser extent other eastern countries, as well as South Africa and Rhodesia, for entirely political reasons. The Soviet Union uses its system of state trading as a weapon in the Cold War by dumping various commodities in the world markets to depress prices when the occasion is called for, and it meets its import requirements whenever possible by purchases from politically favored suppliers.

Complete state trading imposes both an import and an export monopoly on the foreign trade of a country. Hence, it suffers from many of the ills connected with trade monopolies outlined earlier. By controlling all imports and exports state trading can, however, be used as a tool to improve the national terms of trade, thereby increasing a country's share of the gains from international trade. Similarly, it can be employed to protect certain segments of the domestic economy from import competition, or to support other industries artificially by directly or indirectly subsidizing the sale of their products on world markets.

State trading typically operates through *bilateral trade agreements,* which may be expressed in physical (barter) or monetary terms. In most instances, the bilateral trade agreement will specify the rates of exchange at which the goods will be traded. For example, the Soviet Union agrees to sell Cuba a certain X number of tractors in return for Y tons of sugar. Or, the price may be set in monetary terms, using some generally acceptable currency. Sometimes price may be left open, subject to negotiation at the time the goods are actually traded.

Bulk-purchase is another favorite state-trading device, which is used periodically in noncentrally planned economies. The importing government agrees to buy annually a certain quantity of a commodity from a chosen supplier country, or it may even agree to purchase all of a country's exportable surpluses for a set number of years. This enhances the degree of certainty on the part of consumers in the importing country and producers in the exporting nation. Indeed, it is sometimes argued that bulk-purchase agreements contribute to economic efficiency by making future available commodity supplies and prices less uncertain for domestic consumers and users, and future market possibilities and prices less uncertain for the foreign suppliers. This must, however, be weighed against the costs connected with foregoing the principles of comparative advantage. Bulk-purchase agreements tie the buyer to the seller and vice versa over an extended period of time, regardless of what happens to relative world supply and demand conditions in the interim.

Because the centrally planned Communist economies combine state trading with a system of internal pricing more or less removed from market forces, it is extremely difficult to analyze Communist-bloc trade in really meaningful terms. Until very recently, the combination of centrally directed internal and external economic activity made international cost comparison virtually impossible. Like domestic production, international trade was determined by administrative fiat.

Today, the Communist nations of the world still indulge exclusively in state trading, but internally there seems to be a growing appreciation of market forces as a guide to production. Hence, it may not be long before trade among Communist countries can be subject to valid analysis based on its conformity, or lack thereof, to meaningful international cost and price differences. State trading, then, is not inherently inferior to privately operated international trade, but in practice it almost always is. If the forces of international supply and demand were free to work themselves out, reflected in international price disparities, there would be no difference between the two. The state export and import monopolies would act exclusively as agents or intermediaries. They might even be able to perform this function as efficiently as private exporters and importers. But the influences of so many noneconomic forces in state trading renders it an inferior alternative. Nonetheless, it is hardly inappropriate to argue that state trading indeed may not be a totally inferior alternative in a world in which international trade is already characterized by myriad restrictions and distortions.

III

International Payments and Foreign Exchange

16

BALANCE OF PAYMENTS

Throughout the previous chapters of this book we wound our way through the intricacies of international trade and commercial policy, and virtually nothing was said about money. Everything was put in real terms: the physical flows of goods and services, both domestically and internationally. We were concerned with the pure theory of trade and commercial policy. Most economists differentiate this from the monetary theory of international trade, which focuses on money flows—on the payment for goods and services rather than on the flows of goods and services themselves. Both, as we shall soon discover, are important and the distinction is made for good reason.

In this and in the following chapter we begin our survey of international monetary relations with an analysis of monetary flows between nations as recorded in an accounting statement called the balance of payments. From there we shall proceed to discuss the *foreign exchange market,* which makes possible the efficient conversion of national currencies into each other, and its relationship to the balance of payments. Before beginning, the reader is referred to Section E-16 which presents a useful glossary of terms commonly used in balance of payments analysis. Familiarity with these terms will make the reading easier.

We shall attempt to present balance of payments accounting in as simple and straightforward a manner as possible. Nevertheless, some of the finer and more subtle points must also be understood if we are to use the balance of payments as an effective analytical tool.

To begin, the balance of payments ideally provides a careful and complete record of all monetary transactions between one nation and the rest of the world. It may perhaps best be defined as a *systematic and complete record of a country's monetary payments to foreigners and its receipts from foreigners.* More precisely, it is a statement of all monetary transfers between the *residents* of one country and the *residents* of all other countries over a given period of time. Included are payments for goods and services, gifts, investments, loans, and all other transactions that call for international money flows.

We define as *residents* any individuals, business firms, government agencies, or other institutions and organizations legally domiciled in the country in question. Hence, a *subsidiary* of a foreign firm legally established in the U.S. would be treated as any other U.S. enterprise for balance of payments purposes. In contrast, international organizations or *agencies* of foreign firms not legally established in the home country are not considered residents. Any dealings with them enter into the balance of payments accounts as external transactions.

When we say that the balance of payments records "all" monetary transactions between the home country and the rest of the world, this constitutes the ideal state of affairs and is virtually never attained in practice. As we shall see later on, there are manifold statistical problems connected with measuring and recording international payments and receipts. These render a complete record of international monetary transactions virtually unattainable. The degree of accuracy that can be attained, however, is sufficiently high for practical and analytical purposes. Nonetheless, efforts are continually under way to improve the data.

The balance of payments consists of a series of debit and credit entries. Any transaction that gives rise to a foreign monetary claim on the home country is a *debit,* or *minus,* entry. Any transaction giving rise to a monetary claim by residents of the home country on foreign countries is a *credit,* or *plus,* entry. As with any double-entry accounting statement, each credit entry must be accompanied by an equal and opposite debit entry. This results in the familiar statement to the effect that "the balance of payment always balances." If it always balances, why worry about it? We are concerned not with *whether* the balance of payment balances, but *how* it balances—with the interrelationships among the various accounts that go to make up this statement of international monetary transactions.

The balance of payments may be conveniently divided into four separate accounts: (a) current transactions, (b) international capital flows, (c) unilateral transfers, and (d) official reserves. For accounting purposes the first three may be considered *active* accounts, and the latter a *passive* or *balancing* account. We shall look at each of these in turn.

CURRENT ACCOUNT

The current account of the balance of payments records all monetary transactions arising out of imports and exports of goods and services, in addition to international flows of income from investments.

Suppose a U.S. importer decides to buy 100 tons of coffee from a Brazilian exporter. The goods arrive in New York and he pays for them by writing a check on his bank in favor of the Brazilian. Brazil now has a dollar claim on the U.S., and the coffee import is recorded as a debit (minus) item in the current account of the U.S. balance of payments.

Suppose a Frenchman buys a ticket from Paris to New York on a U.S. airline. He pays for it in French francs, and, from a balance of payments standpoint, the U.S. now has a franc claim against France—a credit (a plus) on the U.S. current account.

Finally, suppose a German firm remits an interest payment on a loan that it has received from an American bank. This again presents the U.S. with a monetary claim on a foreign country, in the form of a *deutsche Mark* claim on Germany, and is recorded as a credit (a plus) item in the U.S. current account.

These are just a few examples of typical current transactions. *Merchandise* (or visible) trade includes all physical goods exchanged between the home country and the rest of the world. *Invisible* trade encompasses all types of services. When a U.S. tourist pays his traveling expenses, hotel bills, admissions to museums, and similar charges, these are included as invisible imports in the U.S. current account—payments for tourist services rendered by foreigners. Transportation charges on merchandise trade also are classified as services in the current account of the balance of payments insofar as they involve foreign-owned ships or other transport vehicles. Freight charges for domestic goods shipped on domestic carriers do not enter into the balance of payments of the home country. Transportation charges are excluded from the valuation of the goods themselves, and thus are classified separately.

Other types of services may also result in significant current account entries. Insurance premiums, royalties, consulting fees, certain military expenditures, and construction fees are some of these. A final type of service entering into current account transactions is the payment of interest and dividends on foreign investments. When a loan or investment is made abroad, foreigners have the use of the capital, and their interest or dividend payments are classified as a return for services rendered.

Table 16–1 presents the full current account of the balance of payments. All debit (minus) entries are recorded on the right side of the *pro forma* statement, and all credit (plus) entries on the left side. Credits and debits are then added and the difference between the two is termed the *balance on current account*. If the balance on current account for a given year is a credit (plus) balance, it means that the home country earned more on current transactions than it paid out. A

Table 16-1
Current Account of the Balance of Payments

Transactions giving rise to money claims on foreigners (credits):	Transactions giving rise to foreign money claims on home country (debits):
1. Merchandise exports (sale of goods)	1. Merchandise imports (purchase of goods)
2. Invisible exports (sale of services)	2. Invisible imports (purchase of services)
a. Transport services sold abroad	a. Transport services purchased from abroad
b. Insurance services sold abroad	b. Insurance services purchased from abroad
c. Foreign tourist expenditures in home country	c. Tourist expenditures abroad
d. Other services sold abroad	d. Other services purchased from abroad
e. Income received on loans and investments abroad	e. Income paid on foreign loans and investments in home country
3. Total receipts on current account	3. Total payments on current account

Balance on Current Account

debit (minus) balance shows that its payments on current transactions exceeded its receipts. The question that is answered by the balance on current account is, "As a result of all our current international transactions during the year do we, *on net*, owe foreigners something or do they owe us?"

In practice, the current account is often divided into several subsidiary "balances" for analytical purposes. We can determine, for instance, whether the value of U.S. sales of goods abroad for any given year exceeds its purchases of goods from foreigners, by simply subtracting U.S. merchandise imports from merchandise exports, i.e., the *balance of merchandise trade*. In a similar way we can easily develop a *balance of invisible trade*. By simply adding the two balances, or by subtracting total imports of goods and services from total exports of goods and services, we can return to the familiar *balance on current account*. Schematically, these various balances can be presented as follows:

Merchandise exports *minus* merchandise imports = balance of visible trade.

Services exports *minus* services imports = balance of invisible trade.

Balance of visible trade *plus* balance of invisible trade = balance on current account.

A variety of other balances also exists and are used for numerous illustrative purposes: a balance of tourist expenditures, a balance of investment income, a balance of transport expenditures, and so forth. Each may be useful under certain conditions. However, as we shall presently see, the presentation of a single such balance without reference to all of the other balance of payments accounts can lead to unwarranted and misleading conclusions. Tourist expenditures are especially vulnerable in this regard.

UNILATERAL TRANSFERS ACCOUNT

The second balance of payments account with which we are concerned involves *unilateral transfers*. This is really nothing more than another term for *gifts*. As Table 16–2 shows, unilateral transfers include remittances of private individuals to friends and relatives living abroad, as well as government grants to foreign countries for development assistance, reparations, disaster relief, and so forth.

Unilateral transfers are handled no differently than other balance of payments accounts. Suppose an Italian immigrant to the U.S. sends a check for $1,000 to his father in Bologna. From a U.S. balance of payments standpoint, Italy receives a claim on U.S. dollars in that amount; hence, it must be recorded as a debit (minus) for the U.S. Similarly, American aid

Table 16–2
Unilateral Transfers Account of the Balance of Payments

Transactions giving rise to monetary claims on foreigners (credits):	Transactions giving rise to foreign monetary claims on home country (debits):
1. Private remittances received from abroad	1. Private remittances abroad
2. Pension payments received from abroad	2. Pension payments abroad
3. Government grants received from abroad	3. Government grants abroad
4. Receipts of unilateral transfers.	4. Total unilateral transfers abroad.

Balance on Unilateral Transfers Account

grants to foreign governments likewise constitute a debit entry in the unilateral transfers account of the U.S. balance of payments.

In the case of many advanced countries, including the U.S., receipts of gifts and foreign government grants are of virtually no significance. Hence, the balance on unilateral transfers is *expected* to be a negative one. But even a large debit balance on the unilateral transfers account by itself says virtually nothing about the role of such transfers in the balance of payments as a whole.

The unilateral transfers account is sometimes incorporated into the current account on the grounds that such remissions are really current transactions in nature, instead of being stated separately.

CAPITAL ACCOUNT

A third major balance of payments account records all short-term and long-term international movements of capital. The criterion for deciding whether a given transaction should be recorded as a credit (plus) or a debit (minus) item in the balance of payments is the same as that used in connection with the current account. Any transaction that gives the home country a monetary claim on a foreign country is a credit, and any transaction giving foreigners a monetary claim on the home country is a debit.

To illustrate, an American firm invests $1 million in Japan by buying 20 per cent of the outstanding shares of a Japanese sewing-machine manufacturer. This transaction is represented as a debit (minus) in the U.S. balance payments; it is a *long-term private direct capital outflow*.

A wealthy American decides to deposit $100,000 in a Swiss bank. Again, even though the American retains ownership of the deposit, this gives foreigners a monetary claim on the U.S., and represents a debit (minus) in the American balance of payments—a *short-term private capital outflow*. Similarly, government loans to foreigners are recorded as debit items in the home country's balance of payments.

Table 16–3 presents the capital account of the balance of payments.

Table 16–3
Capital Account of the Balance of Payments

Transactions giving rise to monetary claims on foreigners (credits):	*Transactions giving rise to foreign monetary claims on home country (debits):*
1. Foreign long-term investments in home country (less redemptions and repayments)	1. Long-term investment abroad (less redemptions and repayments)
a. Direct investments in home country	a. Direct investments abroad
b. Foreign investments in domestic securities	b. Investments in foreign securities
c. Other investments of foreigners in home country	c. Other investments abroad
d. Foreign government loans to home country	d. Government loans to foreign countries
2. Short-term capital (net inflow), including bank deposits: increase in short-term liabilities to foreigners	2. Short-term capital (net outflow), including bank deposits: increase in short-term liabilities of foreigners to residents of the home country
3. Total capital inflow	3. Total capital outflow

Balance on Capital Account

Note that a pronounced division is made between long-term and short-term items. The importance of this division will become clear as we continue.

Direct investments abroad relate only to actual flows of capital into foreign business ventures in which residents of the home country are deemed to have an important voice in management. The same holds true for direct investments of foreigners in the home country. Portfolio investments, on the other hand, include purchases of stocks and bonds as well as other long-term evidences of debt which do not fall under the heading of direct investment. The government loans category encompasses all lending activities of national governments and their various agencies, but does not include grants and other formally nonrepayable capital transfers.

All long-term capital flows are recorded in the balance of payments *net* of repayments and redemptions. That is, if the U.S. records a total capital outflow of $1 billion during a given year, with repayments and redemptions of $300 million, the net long-term capital outflow recorded in the balance of payments for that year would be $700 million. Note also that there is no provision in the capital account for interest and dividend payments. These are recorded in the current account as noted earlier, since they are really payments for the services of capital.

Short-term capital flows include purchases and sales of all types of financial assets with a maturity of less than one year. Everything else falls under the heading of long-term capital. Hence, international flows of funds into demand deposits (i.e., into foreign currency bank balances), time deposits, certificates of deposit, treasury bills, bankers' acceptances, and a host of similar relatively liquid assets—including long-term obligations with less than a year to maturity—are all considered short-term capital flows.

As in the current account, it may be instructive to strike various balances *within* the capital account. The balance on private direct investment, the balance on portfolio investment and the balance on short-term capital all prove to be instructive in and of themselves. Here again, as we shall see, the extraction of a single balance and its analysis out of context can be highly misleading. Such statements as "in 1964 the United States had a negative (debit) balance on private direct investment of $2.3 billion" say very little by themselves about the total impact of these individual flows on the overall balance of payments. This is particularly true when we are considering the balance of payments of a country over a number of years.

OFFICIAL RESERVES ACCOUNT

Suppose we take stock of the balance of payments accounts reviewed thus far and find that the following figures apply for a certain country in a given year: (a) the current account has a debit (negative) balance of $100 million, (b) the unilateral transfer account shows a negative (debit) balance of $20 million, and (c) the capital account has a credit (positive) balance of $50 million. Adding the three balances, we find that during this particular year, the country has spent a total of $70 million more abroad than it has earned. It has a deficit in its balance of payments in the amount of $70 million.

How is this deficit settled? Somehow the country in question must pay its foreign creditors the $70 million that it owes them. It must make up the deficit in its balance of payments by paying the foreigners off in gold or by other generally acceptable means of international payment. These are classified as *official reserves* and constitute the holdings, by official government agencies, of gold and other means of payment that are readily available to meet balance of payments deficits. In our example, the active items in the balance of payments (the current, capital, and unilateral transfers accounts) showed the combined deficit, or negative balance, of $70 million which is paid out of official reserves—the passive, compensating, or balancing item in the balance of payments. The balance of payments always balances. The official reserves account is the balancing element.

The complete *pro forma* balance of payments for a country looks much like that shown in Table 16–4. In order for the official reserves account to balance the balance of payments, it must always compensate exactly for the overall, combined positive or negative balance of the other three accounts. Transactions in the official reserves account are handled in precisely the same way as the others.

If the other three accounts have a combined negative (debit) balance at $3 billion, then the official reserve account must show a $3 billion positive (credit) balance, which can be achieved only by selling (exporting) gold and generally acceptable foreign currencies—the currencies of countries that virtually all nations are willing to accept in settlement of payments deficits—or some other means of international payment. Alternatively, if the three active accounts show a combined surplus (credit balance) of $3 billion, the official reserves account will show a debit balance of $3 billion via purchases (imports) of gold, foreign currencies, etc., which then go to increase official reserve holdings.

In Table 16–4, we added all debit and credit payments entries in lines 1–7 and took the difference as the deficit or surplus in the balance of payments. This then had to be made up by official reserve transactions. We can achieve the same result by simply adding the various individual account balances developed earlier. We know that the sum of the balances of all *four* accounts must equal zero, since total debits always equal total credits. If we let

C = balance on current account,
U = balance on unilateral transfers account,
K = balance on capital account, and
R = balance on official reserves account,

we know that

$$C + U + K + R = 0.$$

This means that if the three active accounts show a positive or negative balance, the compensating official reserves account will show a balance which is identical but has the opposite sign. That is,

$$C + U + K = -R.$$

For example, a balance of payment surplus (credit balance) of $2 billion signifies official reserve transactions resulting in the purchase of gold and foreign currencies (debit) in the same amount.

Table 16–4
Combined Balance of Payments Accounts

Transactions giving rise to money claims on foreigners (credits):	*Transactions giving rise to foreign money claims on the home country (debits):*
Current Account:	Current Account:
1. Merchandise exports (sale of goods)	1. Merchandise imports (purchase of goods)
2. Invisible exports (sale of services)	2. Invisible imports (purchase of services)
a. Transport services sold abroad	a. Transport services purchased from abroad
b. Insurance services sold abroad	b. Insurance services purchased from abroad
c. Foreign tourist expenditures in home country	c. Tourist expenditures abroad
d. Other services sold abroad	d. Other services purchased from abroad
e. Incomes received on loans and investments abroad	e. Income paid on loans and investments in home country
Unilateral Transfers Account:	Unilateral Transfers Account:
3. Private remittances received from abroad	3. Private remittances abroad
4. Pension payments received from abroad	4. Pension payments abroad
5. Government grants received from abroad	5. Government grants abroad
Capital Account:	Capital Account:
6. Foreign long-term investments in home country (less redemptions and repayments)	6. Long-term investments abroad (less redemptions and repayments)
a. Direct investments in home country	a. Direct investments abroad
b. Foreign investments in domestic securities	b. Investments in foreign securities
c. Other investments of foreigners in home country	c. Other investments abroad
d. Foreign governments loans to home country	d. Government loans to foreign countries
7. Foreign short-term investments in home country	7. Short-term investments abroad.
Official Reserves Account:	Official Reserves Account:
8. Official sales of gold abroad	8. Official purchases of gold from abroad
9. Official sales of foreign currencies abroad	9. Official purchases of foreign currencies
Total Credits	= Total Debits

MECHANICS OF BALANCE OF PAYMENTS ACCOUNTING

We now know that the balance of payments must always balance and that this balance comes about via the official reserves account. Let us look a little more closely and see how this occurs *automatically*. We shall do this by means of several examples, which should enable us to see a little more clearly exactly how the double-entry balance of payments accounting works.

Example 1. An American importer buys $100,000 worth of cameras from a German manufacturer. The cameras arrive, and he pays for them by writing a check on his New York bank. The German manufacturer now owns the $100,000 which is still deposited in New York. Balance of payments entry:

	Credit	Debit
Merchandise Imports............................		$100,000
Short-Term Capital Inflow..................	$100,000	

Naturally, the German wants his money in *deutsche Mark,* and he goes to his bank and exchanges it for his home currency at the prevailing exchange rate. Now the German bank owns the $100,000 deposit in New York, having given the camera manufacturer the D.M. equivalent. This changes nothing in the U.S. balance of payments. It is merely a transfer of ownership.

Sooner or later, however, the German commercial bank may also demand *deutsche Mark* and goes to the *Bundesbank,* the German central bank, to make the exchange. Now the German central bank, a foreign official financial institution, has ownership of the $100,000 deposit in New York and adds it to its international monetary reserves. The corresponding U.S. balance of payments entry is:

	Credits	Debits
Short-Term Capital Outflow.......................		$100,000
U.S. Dollar Liabilities to Foreign Official Financial Institutions...........................	$100,000	

The original import has been paid for by a buildup of dollar balances on the part of a foreign central bank. If, now, the *Bundesbank* decides that it would prefer to have gold rather than dollars in its international reserves, it can go to the U.S. Treasury and make the conversion, which is entered in the American balance of payments as:

	Credits	Debits
U.S. Dollar Liabilities to Foreign Official Financial Institutions.......................		$100,000
Gold Exports............................	$100,000	

This latter transaction has no effect on the overall balance of payments. It is merely an exchange of one reserve item for another.

In this particular example, the imports bear directly on the U.S. balance of payments position since they are ultimately paid for in a reserve transaction. Suppose the German exporter or commercial bank had decided to keep the funds received as a result of the transaction in dollars in New York for investment purposes. The import debit would then have been precisely offset by the credit on short-term capital account with no net effect on the U.S. balance of payments.

Example 2. An American firm decides to invest $1 million in a Belgian subsidiary:

	Credits	Debits
Private Long-Term Capital Outflow...............		$1 million
Short-Term Capital Inflow.................	$1 million	

The short-term capital inflow offsets the long-term capital outflow since the Belgian subsidiary keeps the funds in a U.S. bank until it needs it.

Suppose the Belgian affiliate uses $500,000 to build a plant addition, which it must pay for in Belgian francs. It exchanges the dollars for francs at a Belgian commercial bank, which then does likewise at the Belgian central bank:

	Credits	Debits
Short-Term Capital Outflow.......................		$500,000
U.S. Dollar Liabilities to Foreign Official Financial Institutions...........................	$500,000	

Suppose, further, that the subsidiary uses the other $500,000 to import machinery from the U.S. which it needs to equip the expanded plant:

	Credits	Debits
Merchandise Exports.............................	$500,000	
Short-Term Capital Outflow..................		$500,000

In summary, only half of the initial $1 million U.S. outflow of long-term capital is finally reflected in the U.S. balance of payments position—only that part which is ultimately settled by means of official reserve transactions.

Example 3. The U.S. gives the government of Nigeria $20 million with which to buy machinery under the U.S. foreign aid program.

	Credits	Debits
Unilateral Transfers (Government Grants)........		$20 million
Short-Term Capital Inflow...............	$20 million	

However, the American aid agreement stipulates that at least 80 per cent of the funds must be spent in the U.S. The Nigerian government complies with this regulation.

	Credits	Debits
Merchandise Exports..........................	$16 million	
Short-Term Capital Outflow..............		$16 million

The remaining $4 million is spent in the purchase of some Japanese machinery. This changes the ownership of the remaining foreign-held dollar balances, but it has no effect on the U.S. balance of payments. The Japanese machinery exporter trades the dollars for *yen* at his bank in Japan, and the $4 million eventually find their way into the reserves of the Japanese central bank. For the U.S. balance of payments this means:

	Credits	Debits
Short-Term Capital Outflow		$4 million
Foreign Official Dollar Balances	$4 million	

Of the original $20 million gift to Nigeria, the net adverse impact on the U.S. balance of payments comes to only $4 million.

The student can work out for himself innumerable other examples of this sort. The important thing to remember is that a given international transaction has no net impact on the balance of payments position of a country *unless* it is eventually reflected in an official reserve transaction. Here, then, is the crux of the problem. When we say that a country has a balance of payments *deficit* or *surplus,* we are talking about the difference between total payments and total receipts on all transactions *except* official reserve transactions. This difference will then be compensated for in the official reserves account, thus restoring balance to the balance of payments.

We say that the active balance of payments accounts are *above the line,* and that the compensating official reserve accounts are *below the line.* A deficit above the line means that gold is exported and/or generally acceptable reserve currencies or other international reserves are transferred to the creditor countries. A surplus above the line means that the home country will accumulate gold and acceptable foreign currencies in that amount in its own official reserves account.

WHY A BALANCE OF PAYMENTS?

It is not very difficult to see that the national balance of payments, as described here, differs little from all sorts of other balances of payments that may be drawn for individuals, business firms, government agencies, state and local governments, regions of a single country, and so forth. Each of these economic entities has its own balance of payments, operating in a manner very similar to that of the national balance of payments.

Take an individual. It would be a simple matter indeed to draw up a statement of personal monetary receipts and expenditures (credits and debits) over a given time period such as a year. On the receipts side would be such items as personal income (personal exports of goods or services), borrowing (personal short-term or long-term capital inflow), and gifts received (personal unilateral transfer receipts).

On the expenditure side we would expect to find entries recording such transactions as purchases of food, household items, consumer durables, services (personal imports of goods and services), bank savings deposits (personal short-term capital outflow), perhaps a few stocks (personal long-term capital outflow), and some gifts to charity and relatives (personal unilateral transfer payments). If we were to add all of the items on the expenditure side and compare them with the sum of the receipts, we would find out whether the individual has had a surplus or deficit in his personal balance of payments during that year.

If his expenditures exceeded his receipts (deficit), he would find that his personal monetary *reserves,* cash and demand deposits, were less at the end of the year than at the beginning. Conversely, a personal balance of payments surplus, with receipts exceeding expenditures, would result in an increase in the individual's personal monetary reserves. Just as in the national balance of payments, an individual's payment surplus or deficit is settled by compensating reserve transactions, which restore balance to his personal balance of payments.

Similarly, a balance of payments statement could be drawn up for a business firm or a governmental unit. More instructive however, would be a balance of payments of a given region of a country. Suppose, for instance, we were to draw up a statement of monetary receipts and expenditures for the New York metropolitan area. We could easily incorporate exports, imports, capital inflows and outflows, as well as unilateral transfers disbursed and received. Any deficit of surplus would automatically be settled by a transfer of bank balances—a reserve transaction—between the New York area and the remainder of the U.S.

Why is it, given the foregoing, that the balance of payments of a nation attracts so much attention while the balances of payments of all kinds of other economic entities—although clearly appropriate—are either not recognized for what they are or are completely ignored? The answer is inherent in the fact that a uniform means of payment—the *national currency*—prevails domestically. Internationally, each nation-state possesses its own national currency which cannot be used as a means of payment outside its national political boundaries.

Domestically, a buyer pays a seller in a nationally acceptable monetary unit and both are perfectly agreeable to do their business in this way. In international transactions, by way of contrast, the buyer wants to pay in his home currency while the seller wants to be paid in the national currency in use where he resides. Any international transaction—whether between buyer and seller, borrower and lender, donor and recipient—involves the exchange of one national currency for another in the *foreign-exchange market,* as detailed in Chapter 18.

If one country finds that it has a deficit in its balance of payments, it generally cannot settle this deficit in its home currency, which is naturally worthless in the creditor countries. Rather, deficits must be settled by some means of payment acceptable to *both* the creditor and the debtor countries. This *international* means of payment comprises gold and other assets which nations are willing to accept in settlement of payments surpluses. The total such assets that a country has at its disposal for making such payments comprise its *international reserves.* Hence, a deficit in a country's balance of payments will normally result in a reduction in its international reserves. A balance of payments surplus causes a buildup in a nation's international reserves.

Now there is no longer any question as to why so much importance is attached to the national balance of payments vis-à-vis the rest of the world, while other balances of payments which concern only a single currency go largely unnoticed. Diminishing international reserves as a result of chronic balance of payments deficits year after year can endanger a country's ability to deal internationally. For many nations this could spell economic disaster, and a sharp eye is always kept on the status of the national balance of payments. Moreover, as we shall discover later on, the balance of payments of an economic entity operating within a geographic area characterized by one currency and a relatively homogeneous set of economic policies has a tendency to come into balance automatically. This is not true internationally, however. Specific actions may have to be taken on the part of a country to force the balance of payments back into balance, and thereby to avoid an unacceptable further reduction in its international reserves.

VARIOUS BALANCES

There are a variety of alternative measures of balance of payments surpluses and deficits. The concept utilized up to now is only one of these—albeit perhaps the most logical one. It is called the *official settlements* concept of the balance of payments.

What is the most useful general measure of a balance of payments deficit or surplus? Granted, we are interested primarily in determining how present and prospective future payments conditions will affect a nation's international reserves and the soundness of its currency. But how can we best go about this?

Short-term capital flows into and out of a country, for instance, are the result of a variety of economic and noneconomic forces which are not necessarily connected with the underlying conditions of the national economy. Should we not therefore exclude such short-term monetary transactions in our concept of the balance of payments, since they are not always indicative of basic economic forces?

There are three primary concepts of "balance" in the international balance of payments; (a) the *basic balance,* (b) the *liquidity balance,* and (c) the *official settlements balance.* They differ fundamentally in terms of where the "line" is drawn—i.e., which items are considered active international payments and which are considered merely compensating or passive ones.

BASIC BALANCE

The basic balance concept may be computed as shown in Table 16–5. Note that only transactions in goods and services, long-term capital flows, and unilateral transfers are considered "active" elements in the balance of payments, with short-term capital flows being placed below the line as a compensating item. Errors and omissions, which may constitute

Table 16–5
Basic Transactions Concept of the Balance of Payments

1. Balance on current account
   plus
2. Balance on unilateral transfers account
   plus
3. Balance on long-term capital account
   equals
   _____
4. Balance on basic transactions
   _____
   which is settled by
5. Balance on short-term capital account
   plus
6. Balance on official reserves account
   plus
7. Net errors and omissions

an important balance of payments element, are generally considered to result largely from unrecorded short-term capital flows and are thus also placed below the line.

The basic balance in this form does not pretend to show directly all of the forces affecting international reserves. It attempts to incorporate only those transactions which are indicative of the basic, long-term trends in the economy. Volatile, short-term capital movements and their attendant errors and omissions are separated and placed below the line. Hence, erratic flows of short-term capital, which may affect international reserves currently but which are of little long-range significance, are eliminated as active balance of payments elements.

The basic balance concept is open to criticism on several counts. Short-term capital movements often serve to finance current transactions in goods and services and thus respond to the same fundamental forces. Conversely, changing credit conditions which result in short-term international capital flows may affect transactions in goods and services as well. Short-term credits subject to successive renewals may not, in fact, be short term in nature. At the same time, direct investments themselves give rise to large-scale international short-term capital flows. Errors and omissions are not entirely connected with short-term capital flows, but are characteristic of most other types of transactions as well. Hence, there is little justification for placing it below the line.

LIQUIDITY BALANCE

The liquidity balance differs from the basic balance in several ways. It considers both errors and omissions and *some* short-term capital flows as active elements in the balance of payments and thus places them above the line. The liquidity balance is computed as in Table 16–6.

Table 16–6
Liquidity Balance Concept of the Balance of Payments

1. Balance on current account
   plus
2. Balance on unilateral transfers account
   plus
3. Balance on long-term capital account
   plus
4. Balance on short-term capital of domestic residents
   plus
5. Net errors and omissions
   plus
6. Foreign commercial credits
   equals

---

7. Liquidity balance

---

   which is settled by
8. Balance on short-term capital (except commercial credits) of foreign residents
   plus
9. Balance on official reserves account

Note that all international short-term capital transactions of domestic residents are placed above the line, while similar short-term capital transactions of foreign residents are located below the line. If a domestic resident invests $1 million abroad, it is registered as a *minus* balance of payments item in that amount. But if a foreign resident invests $1 million in short-term assets in the home country it is treated as a *compensating* or balancing item.

There is a good reason for this apparently asymmetrical treatment.

Short-term investments abroad by domestic residents may at any time become a drain on official reserves if they fall into the hands of foreign official monetary institutions. Hence, they should properly be counted as *minus* items. Short-term investments by foreign residents in the home country should not, however, be counted as *plus* items by the same reasoning.

Since any such investments still belong to foreigners, they can be withdrawn at any time as a drain of official reserves. Only foreign commercial credits received are treated above the line. Using these procedures, the liquidity balance concept is purposely pessimistic and conservative, and comes up with as large a deficit—or as small a surplus—as possible.

Again, there are powerful arguments that can be invoked against this particular balance of payments concept, which has been preferred by the U.S. Department of Commerce. True, foreign short-term investments *may* be withdrawn at any time and result in a drain of official reserves, but is the assumption that they *will* be withdrawn justified? If American short-term investments abroad are treated as a minus item in the U.S. balance of payments, then certainly foreign short-term investments in the U.S. should be treated as plus items. Moreover, asymmetrical treatment of short-term international investments by foreigners and domestic residents is used only by the U.S., making offhand balance of payments comparisons virtually meaningless.

As we shall see later, however, the peculiar situation of the U.S. in the world of international finance to some extent justifies, and is largely responsible for, the existence of the liquidity balance concept.

OFFICIAL SETTLEMENTS BALANCE

Perhaps the most logical formulation of the balance of payments is the *official settlements* concept, which is computed as in Table 16–7. Short-term capital transactions of foreigners are treated in the same manner as those of domestic residents. Both are considered active elements in the balance of payments and are placed above the line. The sole exception are changes in short-term holdings of foreign official monetary institutions.

The latter represent the only type of foreign holding that can be directly withdrawn in the form of a drain on official reserves.

All compensating items below the line can now be classified as *reserve transactions,* since any change in short term balances of foreign official monetary institutions is regarded as a change in their official reserves. A deficit computed according to this balance of payments concept would show only the net drain on official reserves plus the *potential* reserve drain contained in a buildup of short-term assets of foreign official monetary institutions.

This particular concept of balance has a number of advantages. It

Table 16–7
Official Settlements Concept of the Balance of Payments

1. Balance on current account
   plus
2. Balance on unilateral transfers account
   plus
3. Balance on long-term capital account
   plus
4. Balance on short-term capital account, except foreign short-term capital of official monetary institutions
   plus
5. Net errors and omissions
   equals

6. Official settlements balance

   which is settled by
7. Balance on official reserves account
   plus
8. Foreign short-term capital of official monetary institutions

avoids the asymmetry, which in the liquidity balance concept is caused by differential treatment of private foreign and domestic short-term capital flows, by placing both above the line as active balance of payments elements. It further avoids the problems caused in the placement of net errors and omissions below the line by moving them above the line along with all private short-term capital flows. Improved comparability with the balance of payments accounting concepts used by other countries is a further advantage.

Most important, however, is the idea that the motivations determining international short-term capital flows are very similar for domestic and foreign residents alike, while they differ fundamentally in the case of official monetary institutions. A tight case can therefore be made for separating official monetary institutions from all others dealing in international short-term capital flows for analytical purposes, as opposed to merely distinguishing between foreign and domestic residents for balance of payments reasons.

BALANCE OF PAYMENTS PRESENTATION

Table 16–8 presents the U.S. balance of payments as it appears in official publications. Note that this differs somewhat from the *pro forma* formats we have used in this chapter, and that it combines the basic balance, liquidity, and official settlements concepts just discussed.

In current international transactions military sales are separated, while income on U.S. investments abroad is separated as to whether or not it results from direct investments. There is no unilateral transfers account as such. Instead, private and governmental transfers (lines 12 and 14) are

integrated into the current account. Long-term capital transfers are classified into governmental and private flows and added to the current account
balance (line 15) to produce the "balance on current account and long-term
capital" (line 26), essentially our basic balance. U.S. short-term investments abroad are added, separated into bank and nonbank transactions,
together with additions to U.S. reserves of IMF "Special Drawing Rights"
(see Glossary in Section E-16 and Chapter 25) and net errors and omissions,
to generate the "net liquidity balance" (line 33). When foreign short-term
investments in the U.S. are included, the "official reserve transactions balance" is produced (line 42), which in 1973 was a deficit of $5.3 billion.
This was financed in 1973 by increased liabilities to foreign official agencies
of $5.5 billion, a reduction of U.S. reserve assets of $207 million, adjusted
for redemptions of $475 million in U.S. nonliquid liabilities to foreign official
agencies.

Several other balance of payments formats are also commonly used. Perhaps the most common is the so-called "standard presentation" used by the
International Monetary Fund, which is as follows:

A. *Goods, Services, and Unrequited Transfers*
Goods and services
  1. Merchandise
  2. Nonmonetary gold
  3. Freight and insurance on merchandise
  4. Other transportation
  5. Travel
  6. Investment income
  7. Other government
  8. Other private unrequited transfers
  9. Private grants
  10. Government grants
B. *Capital* (excluding reserves and related items)
Nonmonetary sectors
  11. Direct investment
  12. Other private long-term
  13. Private short-term
  14. Local government
  15. Central government
Monetary sectors
  16. Private institutions
  17. Central institutions
C. 18. *Allocation of SDRs*
D. *Reserves and Related Items*
  19. Liabilities
  20. Assets

Table 16–8
United States Balance of Payments Summary, 1972–1973

Line	(Credits +; Debits −)	1972	1973	Change: 1972–73
1	Merchandise trade balance	−6,912	688	7,600
2	Exports	48,769	70,255	21,486
3	Imports	−55,681	−69,567	−13,886
4	Military transactions, net	−3,558	−2,171	1,387
5	Travel and transportation, net	−2,853	−2,312	541
6	Investment income, net	7,863	9,723	1,860
7	U.S. direct investments abroad	10,433	13,974	3,541
8	Other U.S. investments abroad	3,492	4,576	1,084
9	Foreign investments in the United States	−6,062	−8,827	−2,765
10	Other services, net	851	972	121
11	**Balance on goods and services**	**−4,610**	**6,900**	**11,510**
12	Remittances, pensions and other transfers	−1,570	−1,913	−343
13	**Balance on goods, services and remittances**	**−6,180**	**4,987**	**11,167**
14	U.S. Government grants (excluding military)	−2,174	−1,947	227
15	**Balance on current account**	**−8,353**	**3,041**	**11,394**
16	U.S. Government capital flows excluding nonscheduled repayments, net.	−1,714	−2,894	−1,180
17	Nonscheduled repayments of U.S. Government assets	137	289	152
18	U.S. Government nonliquid liabilities to other than foreign official reserve agencies	238	1,136	898
19	Long-term private capital flows, net	−152	−357	−205
20	U.S. direct investments abroad	−3,404	−4,855	−1,451
21	Foreign direct investments in the United States	160	2,068	1,908
22	Foreign securities	−614	−791	−177
23	U.S. securities other than Treasury issues	4,335	4,093	−242
24	Other, reported by U.S. banks	−1,120	−596	524
25	Other, reported by U.S. nonbanking concerns	492	−276	−768
26	**Balance on current account and long-term capital**	**−9,843**	**1,214**	**11,057**
27	Nonliquid short-term private capital flows, net	−1,637	−4,210	−2,573
28	Claims reported by U.S. banks	−1,495	−3,953	−2,458
29	Claims reported by U.S. nonbanking concerns	−315	−735	−420
30	Liabilities reported by U.S. nonbanking concerns	173	478	305
31	Allocations of special drawing rights (SDR)	710	. . .	−710
32	Errors and omissions, net	−3,112	−4,793	−1,681

Table 16–8 (Continued)

Line	(Credits +; Debits −)	1972	1973	Change: 1972–73
33	**Net liquidity balance**	−13,882	−7,789	6,093
34	Liquid private capital flows, net	3,542	2,503	−1,039
35	Liquid claims	−1,234	−1,933	−699
36	Reported by U.S. banks	−742	−1,100	−358
37	Reported by U.S. nonbanking concerns	−492	−833	−341
38	Liquid liabilities	4,776	4,436	−340
39	To foreign commercial banks	3,862	2,863	−999
40	To international and regional organizations	104	373	269
41	To other foreigners	810	1,200	390
42	**Official reserve transactions balance**	−10,340	−5,286	5,054
	Financed by changes in:			
43	Liquid liabilities to foreign official agencies	9,720	4,434	−5,286
44	Other readily marketable liabilities to foreign official agencies	399	1,118	719
45	Nonliquid liabilities to foreign official reserve agencies reported by U.S. Government	189	−475	−664
46	U.S. official reserve assets, net	32	209	177

Source: Survey of Current Business, March, 1974.

BALANCE OF PAYMENTS DATA

It is perhaps useful to survey at this point some of the problems involved in obtaining the data employed in computing the balance of payments of a nation. There is never a question about the payments deficit or surplus as a whole, simply because the balancing or settlement items—the reserve transactions—are known. Hence, when we say "the U.S. had a balance of payments deficit in 1973 of $5.286 billion," this figure is accurate.

What we are really interested in, however, is how this deficit came about. Was it the result of a weakness in the current account, or was it due to a large-scale, long-term capital outflow? Could it be attributed at least in part to unilateral transfers, and how much of the deficit did short-term capital outflows contribute? Questions such as these form the essence of balance of payments analysis and raise the most significant problems of data accuracy.

Beginning with merchandise trade statistics, the balance of payments data on imports are sometimes lacking in accuracy due to valuation problems. Balance of payments accounting requires that merchandise imports be valued at the actual price paid by the importer. But the available data, which are collected largely for customs purposes, can easily depart from this standard. Similarly, in the case of merchandise exports, where balance of payments accounting also requires the actual selling price, noncommercial transactions can be especially bothersome.

For both imports and exports it is sometimes extremely difficult to solicit accurate data from those directly involved—the importers and the exporters—for the simple reason that they may not have the required data readily at hand and are reluctant to spend a great deal of time and effort to get them. In both imports and exports, too, the cost of shipment must be excluded in the valuation of the goods, since this comes under services and may or may not enter into the balance of payments.

Services present similar, thorny data problems. For instance, it is often impossible to determine accurately the expenditures of tourists abroad and the expenditures of foreign tourists in the home country. Equally necessary is information on the nationality of the common carriers used in travel, and the currency employed in buying passage. Data on freight charges also present problems of accuracy. Conceptually, the transport cost between two ports comprises the difference between the f.a.s. (free alongside ship)· valuation of the goods at the point of export and the c.i.f. (costs, insurance, and freight) valuation at the point of import. This amount must then be separated into freight and insurance components, and the nationalities of the firms involved must be known. With U.S. ocean transport transactions coming to around $5 billion annually, it is easy to see how important accurate data are in this area. In addition, there are a large number of service transactions—advertising, consulting, royalties, commissions, and so forth—on which practically no data exist. The data on income from foreign investments, on the other hand, tend to be fairly reliable.

The current account of the balance of payments constitutes an important contributor to the "errors and omissions" item because of a lack of accuracy in the data. In general, the services component of the current account seems to present substantially more serious problems than the merchandise trade component.

Data problems with regard to international capital movements are somewhat more serious. These vary widely in their contribution to balance of payments errors and omissions over a period of time because the capital movements are themselves subject to wide variation. Some firms do not report international direct investment data, which sometimes are difficult to develop accurately. More serious are portfolio investments. In the U.S. only international portfolio transactions exceeding $100,000 are required to be reported. All others are not recorded in international capital flows and come to be reflected in errors and omissions. Double-counting, determination of ownership of investments in the U.S., deliberate concealment, and a variety of other factors play an important role in rendering the capital account the prime contributor to the errors and omissions term in the balance of payments.

Less significant as a source of error are unilateral transfers. Private transfers usually are a relatively small balance of payments component. Hence, although most private remittances tend to go undetected, their contribution to errors and omissions is not great. Government transfers are relatively accurate as far as balance of payments data go, although there may be some double-counting when they are tied to merchandise exports.

It must be remembered that the positive and negative errors in the various balance of payments accounts are largely mutually offsetting so that the "errors and omissions" item will be much smaller than the sum of all the errors made. Hence, it is very difficult to attribute the errors and omissions to specific accounts. Only when a significant change in errors and omissions occurs simultaneously with a pronounced change in one of the accounts—all others being relatively stable—is there room for arguing that one particular account is responsible in one particular instance. On these grounds, the assertion is that recent errors and omissions in the U.S. balance of payments arose largely out of private short-term capital flows, but this, too, is open to doubt.

Because of the size of the errors and omissions term, it is important that every effort be made to improve balance of payments data. Net errors in the neighborhood of $1 billion in the U.S. balance of payments and the much larger connected gross errors, for instance, are of a size sufficient to raise substantial difficulties in the analysis of the data. This is especially true if the error term varies markedly from one period to the next.

THE INTERNATIONAL INVESTMENT POSITION

An accounting statement closely connected with the balance of payments, though not to be confused with it, is the balance of international indebtedness, also called the "international investment position." We know that the balance of payments is a *flow* concept, recording monetary receipts and payments between one country and the rest of the world over a given period of time. The balance of international indebtedness, however, is a *stock* concept. It presents the holdings of foreign capital assets by residents of the home country, relative to the holdings of domestic capital assets by foreigners, at a given point in time. In 1972, for example, total U.S. investment claims on the rest of the world came to about $181 billion, while foreign investment claims on the U.S. amounted to around $123 billion. Hence, the U.S. in 1963 was a net creditor country to the extent of about $57 billion, vis-à-vis the rest of the world (see Table 16-9).

Table 16–9
The International Investment Position of
the United States
(millions of dollars)

Type of investment	1960	1970	1971	1972
Net international investment position of the United States	**44,658**	**69,077**	**57,615**	**50,635**
U.S. assets abroad	**85,577**	**166,764**	**180,714**	**199,285**
Nonliquid assets	66,158	149,865	164,586	180,932
U.S. Government	16,854	32,079	34,097	36,146
Long-term credits:				
Repayable in dollars	} 13,956	23,445	25,529	28,407
Other		6,185	6,178	5,745
Foreign currencies and other short-term assets	2,892	2,449	2,390	1,994
Private, long-term	44,497	104,960	115,867	128,360
Direct investments abroad	31,865	78,178	86,198	94,031
Foreign securities:				
Foreign bonds	5,574	13,160	14,654	15,844
Foreign corporate stocks	3,984	6,437	7,050	9,049
Other claims, reported by U.S. banks	1,698	3,035	3,647	4,916
Other claims, reported by U.S. nonbanking concerns	1,376	4,150	4,318	4,520
Private, short-term nonliquid	4,813	12,826	14,622	16,426
Claims, reported by U.S. banks	3,594	9,592	10,872	12,367
Claims reported by U.S. nonbanking concerns	1,219	3,234	3,750	4,059
Liquid assets	19,359	16,899	16,128	18,353
Private	n.a.	2,412	3,961	5,202
Claims reported by U.S. banks	n.a.	1,210	2,400	3,142
Claims reported by U.S. nonbanking concerns	n.a.	1,202	1,561	2,060
U.S. monetary reserve assets	19,359	14,487	12,167	13,151
Gold	17,804	11,072	10,206	10,487
SDR		851	1,100	1,958
Convertible currencies		629	276	241
Gold tranche position in IMF	1,555	1,935	585	465
U.S. liabilities to foreigners	**40,859**	**97,687**	**123,099**	**148,650**
Nonliquid, liabilities to other than foreign official agencies	19,830	50,681	55,252	65,719
U.S. Government	793	2,005	1,558	1,796
Private, long term	18,418	44,785	49,761	59,817
Direct investments in the United States	6,910	13,270	13,655	14,363
U.S. securities:				
Corporate and other bonds	649	6,878	8,626	10,911
Corporate stocks	9,302	18,689	21,429	27,649
Other liabilities, reported by U.S. banks	7	1,008	758	907
Other liabilities, reported by U.S. nonbanking concerns	1,550	4,940	5,293	5,987

Table 16-9 (Continued)

Type of investment	1960	1970	1971	1972
Private, short-term nonliquid, reported by U.S. nonbanking concerns	619	3,891	3,933	4,106
Liquid liabilities to private foreigners and liquid, other readily marketable, and nonliquid liabilities to foreign official agencies	21,029	47,006	67,847	82,931
To private foreigners	9,139	22,619	16,613	21,389
To foreign commercial banks	4,818	17,169	10,949	14,810
To international and regional organizations	1,541	846	1,523	1,627
To other foreigners	2,780	4,604	4,141	4,952
To foreign official agencies	11,890	24,387	51,234	61,542
Liquid	11,888	20,623	47,610	57,330
Other readily marketable		695	144	543
Nonliquid, reported by U.S. Government	2	3,069	3,480	3,669

Source: Survey of Current Business, October, 1973.

The connection between the balance of payments and the balance of international indebtedness resides in the capital account and in the claims of official monetary institutions. A $2 billion debit balance on the U.S. long-term capital account, for instance, means that the American net creditor position improves by that amount. The same thing can be said about the balance on short-term capital account.

Whenever a country registers a net capital outflow (private or government), its balance of international indebtedness improves. That is, its net creditor position is enhanced or its net debtor position is reduced. This is not true, of course, in the case of government grants which carry no repayment stipulation, although there is sometimes a blurred line between loans and grants.

Aside from those elements appearing in the capital account of the balance of payments, certain reserve transactions will also affect the balance of international indebtedness. If, for example, a country has a deficit in its balance of payments that is settled by a buildup of local short-term balances owned by foreign official monetary institutions, this increases the creditor position (or decreases the debtor position) of the foreign nations concerned and has the opposite effect on the domestic creditor-debtor position internationally. The reverse is true, of course, in the case of a balance of payments surplus that is settled by a reduction of short-term liabilities to foreign official monetary institutions.

Finally, a country may hold as part of its international monetary reserves—in addition to gold—the currencies of other countries and IMF Special Drawing Rights (SDR's). A deficit in its balance of payments will, in this manner, also reduce its net creditor position or increase its debtor position, while a balance of payments surplus will have the opposite effect.

It is thus possible for a country to have a net capital outflow of, say, but which does not change the balance of international indebtedness at all! To illustrate, suppose the country has a deficit on capital account of $1 billion, and, everything else equal, this results in a balance of payments deficit of $1 billion settled by gold exports. The balance of international indebtedness thus shifts in its favor by $1 billion. But if its $1 billion balance of payments deficit were settled by an equal buildup of short-term balances of foreign official monetary institutions, or by a loss of foreign currencies in the official reserves account, the balance of international indebtedness would be unchanged. Only if the payments deficit is settled wholly or in part by an export of gold or SDR's will the balance of international indebtedness be changed in its favor.

This leads us to a generalization. Only if a net capital outflow is accompanied by an equal, combined positive balance on current, unilateral transfer and gold–SDR accounts will it serve to improve a country's balance of international indebtedness.

The balance of international indebtedness is a useful analytical device only if it includes a breakdown of international capital holdings by type. The short-term investment position gives some indication of the potential that exists for capital withdrawal (outflow). Hence, it indicates the potential pressure on a country's balance of payments should circumstances cause such an outflow to take place. However, it is not the balance of the short-term investment position that is important in the first instance, but rather the amount of short-term liabilities outstanding to foreigners only, since these represent the potential danger of withdrawal.

In addition to the short-term capital position in the balance of international indebtedness, the balance of official monetary holdings is also important. If the domestic short-term liabilities to foreign official monetary institutions are far in excess of foreign-currency holdings of domestic official monetary institutions, there is a potential danger not only to the country's balance of payments, but to the stability of its currency. A decision of foreign official monetary institutions to withdraw their short-term balances, which have served to settle past payments deficits and exceed domestic reserve holdings of foreign currencies, means conversion into gold or SDR's. Table 16–10 emphasizes this point by presenting a series of "liquidity-ratios," derived from the data contained in the previous table, for the period 1960–1972. The stability of the domestic currency then hinges upon the adequacy of the country's gold and SDR stock, which may or may not be able to satisfy the foreign claims.

Table 16–10

Liquidity Ratios: Outstanding U.S. Assets Abroad to Liabilities to Foreigners, by Degree of Liquidity

Ratios	1960	1961	1962	1963	1964	1965	1966	1967	1968	1969	1970	1971	1972
Monetary combinations													
Reserves / Liabilities to foreign official agencies	1.63	1.48	1.26	1.11	1.00	0.93	0.93	0.77	0.85	1.00	0.59	0.24	0.21
Liquid assets / Liquid liabilities to private foreigners and liquid and nonliquid liabilities to foreign official agencies	.92	.82	.71	.70	.66	.58	.54	.47	.48	.43	.36	.24	.22
Other combinations													
Liquid and nonliquid short-term assets / Liquid and nonliquid short-term liabilities and nonliquid liabilities to foreign official agencies	1.12	1.06	.98	.92	.91	.84	.79	.71	.70	.64	.58	.43	.40
Long-term assets / Long-term liabilities to other than foreign official reserve agencies	3.20	3.00	3.38	3.25	3.27	3.36	3.56	3.37	2.94	3.03	2.93	2.93	2.67
Total U.S. assets abroad / Total U.S. liabilities to foreigners	2.09	2.00	2.08	2.02	2.02	2.05	2.08	1.94	1.81	1.74	1.71	1.47	1.34

Source: Table 16-9.

In the first instance, then, it is the balance of international indebtedness on short-term claims held by official monetary institutions that is important. The short-term investment position can also be of use analytically in deciding upon the potential pressure which short-term investment outflows may exert on a country's balance of payments, and, via official monetary claims, on the stability of its currency.

The long-term investment position is of less immediate importance. Long-term investments are unlikely to be withdrawn on short notice and tend to respond more to long-range, basic economic considerations. However, as we shall see in the following chapter, the long-term investment position is of significance in determining the international flows of interest and dividend payments, which appear in the current account of the balance of payments.

The balance of international indebtedness is sometimes also considered limited in its analytical usefulness because of the problems of data collection. The fact that there are gaps in tracing all international investment flows for balance of payments purposes, as we saw earlier, also means that there must be substantial gaps in the data on the international investment position. In addition, some international investments possess an uncertain legal status, due perhaps to political upheaval, while others for various reasons remain clandestine in nature. Since there is no need for "balance" in the balance of international indebtedness, there is no automatic indicator of how accurate the estimates really are. Finally, there is the problem of valuation in a world in which historical cost often differs enormously from market value.

But all of these deficiencies of the balance of international indebtedness do not succeed in completely negating its value as an analytical tool. We can still learn a great deal from a breakdown of the international investment position of a country.

17

BALANCE OF PAYMENTS ANALYSIS

In the previous chapter we discussed balance of payments accounting in substantial detail. Analysis of international payments flows involves a great many subtleties, some of which we shall try to clarify here. We already know that it is extremely important to know precisely what is meant when statements are made about "the balance of payments," in order to correctly interpret them. Even more important, we need to understand the relationships that exist among various types of international transactions—a dimension that is not always fully understood by politicians and others who typically make public pronouncements on the state of the national balance of payments. Even more important, competent analysis of the balance of payments is a prerequisite for the formulation of the sound policy decisions necessary to bring about desired balance of payments conditions.

THE PROBLEM

We know that a balance of payments deficit, settled by means of international reserve losses, is untenable in the long run. It is limited, apparently, by the stock of international reserves—however denominated—that a country has at its disposal for the settlement of international payments deficits.

It is this particular point that ties the problem of balance of payments adjustment directly to the prevailing monetary standard—the existing system of exchange-rate determination—as we shall see in the following chapters. We shall learn that the need to administratively avoid chronic balance of payments deficits exists only under a system of pegged exchange rates.

Under flexible exchange rates, a deficit will tend to cure itself by causing the domestic currency to depreciate relative to other national currencies. Under the gold standard—or any other system under which the ratio between a country's money supply and its stock of international reserves remains fixed—a balance of payments deficit tends to cure itself by causing certain internal adjustments in the economies of the home country and of foreign countries.

With pegged exchange rates and monetary authorities free to influence the national money supplies in any desired manner, independent of each other and their respective stocks of international reserves, this is not true. The exchange rate is *not* free to adjust to changing balance of payments conditions, *nor* is the level of national economic activity necessarily affected by the status of the balance of payments and its effects on the money supply. Hence, our concern over the depletion of international reserves as a result of payments deficits stems directly from the peculiarities of the balance of payments adjustment process under a pegged exchange rate system as it governs international monetary standards. All of this will become clear in the following several chapters, but needs to be borne in mind at this point as well.

Once a nation's international reserves are exhausted, and unless it has the ability to borrow from other nations, its ability to engage freely in international trade and capital transactions is severely curtailed. Its international credit standing becomes impaired, and, as we shall see later, long before this happens its currency will come under powerful pressures that will endanger its stability.

What if, on the other hand, other nations are willing to hold a given country's currency as part of their own international reserves? A deficit in its balance of payments settled by reserve transactions does not then necessarily mean a reduction in its own international reserves. Since other nations are willing to hold its currency, its deficit may be wholly or partly settled by a buildup of short-term liabilities to foreign official monetary institutions.

Does this signify that such "reserve currency" countries can go on running balance of payments deficits *ad infinitum?* The answer is emphatically in the negative. The willingness of other nations to hold any single country's currency as part of their own international reserves is governed by the soundness of that currency. Continued buildup of a nation's short-term liabilities to foreign central banks, accompanied by a dwindling stock of owned international reserves, impinge upon that soundness and eventually may lead to a downfall of the nation's currency.

Continued deficits in the balance of payments of *any* country over a very extended period of time, therefore, are untenable. Something must be done to bring the balance of payments back into balance. Continued balance of payments surpluses are equally, though not as immediately, undesirable. These surpluses lead to nothing more than a buildup of gold and foreign currencies in the coffers of a nation's central bank. Such inordinately large international reserve stocks may represent sacrifices of goods and services by the national economy without corresponding goods and services being made available to it (an excess of exports over imports). Large reserves may also have arisen out of long- and short-term capital inflows, on which substantial interest and dividend payments must be made, while the yield on a country's gold reserves is nil, and the return on its officially held foreign currency reserves is relatively modest. Finally, since by definition one country's balance of payments *surplus* must represent an equal balance of payments *deficit* on the part of the rest of the world—one or more other countries—a nation may come under additional pressure from the outside to correct a chronic surplus.

A country is faced, then, with the problem of maintaining a balance in its balance of payments over the long term. It may run a payments deficit or surplus for one, two, even five years, but in the long run balance must prevail with very few exceptions.[1] In order to generate some idea about how the balance may be restored in the event this should become necessary, a fundamental knowledge of the cause-and-effect relationships among balance of payments accounts is essential.

Suppose a country's balance of payments shows a substantial long-run deficit which it feels must be eliminated. Assuming balance will not in fact be restored automatically, its policy decisions may be one or more of the following: (a) reduce imports of goods and services and/or expand exports; (b) reduce capital outflows and/or promote capital inflows; and (c) reduce unilateral transfers to foreigners or secure increased aid in the form of grants from foreign countries. Whichever decision is made involves the assigning of *responsibility* for the deficit to one or more of the balance of payments accounts.

For instance, the current account may show a sizeable surplus and the unilateral transfers account a negligible deficit, with a large-scale capital outflow apparently responsible for the balance of payments deficit. Should we now move to curtail capital outflows and, if we do, will it indeed have the desired effect? In order to find answers to such questions—many of which are quite subtle—we need a precise idea of the interrelationships that exist among the various balance of payments accounts—the so-called *feedback effects*.

---

[1] We will note later that the U.S., which has seen balance of payments deficits for well over ten years at a time, is one of these exceptions.

PRIVATE LONG-TERM CAPITAL

Let us take a country whose balance of payments appears as in Table 17–1. The data for three years seem to indicate that direct investments in foreign countries are responsible for much of the balance of payments deficits shown. Whereas other long-term investments seem to have remained relatively stable, direct investments show a marked upward trend.

Offhand, the problem seems to be that a substantial and growing surplus earned on current account was wiped out by deficits in the other accounts for which direct investments were primarily responsible. Hence, perhaps placing some controls on direct investments abroad by domestic residents would reduce the outflow. However, would such a step achieve the intended reduction in the balance of payments deficit?

For an answer, we must first look at the connection between direct investments and exports, recognized long ago by an Austrian economist named Eugen von Böhm-Bawerk. Direct capital investments abroad give rise to a *primary feedback* in the form of increased exports. For instance, an American manufacturer of automobiles, who decides to set up an as-

Table 17–1
The Balance of Payments of Country X, 1975, 1976, and 1977
(millions of currency units)

Account Balance	1975	1976	1977
Current:			
Merchandise trade.................	+3,500	+3,600	+4,200
Services.........................	+ 500	+ 400	+ 400
Interest and dividends..............	+ 400	+ 450	+ 500
Capital:			
Direct investments.................	−2,500	−3,000	−4,000
Other long-term investments.........	−1,000	− 800	−1,000
Short-term capital.................	− 600	− 600	− 200
Transfers:			
Unilateral transfers................	− 500	− 400	− 200
Balance...........................	− 200	− 250	− 300
settled by:			
Official reserves....................	+ 200	+ 250	+ 300
Gold.............................	(50)	(100)	(200)
Foreign currencies.................	(150)	(150)	(100)

sembly operation in Australia, needs to equip his Australian plant with special equipment suited to his customary mass-production techniques. Since his domestic operation is largely equipped with U.S. machinery, he would logically prefer to set up his Australian facility in a similar manner. The result is an export of capital equipment from the U.S. *as a direct consequence* of the capital outflow—i.e., primary feedback.

Moreover, since this particular example involves only an assembly operation, we also can talk in terms of a *secondary feedback* in the form of
large and continued U.S. exports of components and parts to Australia.
Whereas the original direct investment may appear as a large negative
item in the U.S. balance of payments for that year, the feedback effects
via the merchandise trade account almost certainly will more than make
up for this in a relatively short period of years.

Even if the overseas direct investment does not involve an important
secondary feedback in terms of continued induced exports of raw materials
and components, technical fees, patent rights, and so forth, the primary
feedback in the form of capital equipment exports may well be large enough
to offset much of the initial capital outflow. The immediate, short-term
"balance of payments cost" of direct investments abroad is, therefore, the
direct investment outflow *less any* increased exports induced thereby. If
the primary feedback is significant, policy measures designed to reduce
direct investments abroad will simultaneously reduce exports and the current
account balance, and fall short of their goal. Whether the *net* impact
of such a policy on the balance of payments will be positive or negative
depends, of course, directly on the magnitude of the primary feedback
effects.

We need to look at a second important connection between direct investment and the current account, i.e., the remission of profits. Every investor, an individual or a business firm, expects a given capital investment
to bear a yield equal to or higher than any known alternative employment
of the capital having roughly the same degree of risk. He also expects
that the cumulative receipt of profits or dividends, plus any residual, will
eventually exceed the initial investment. More precisely, he would normally
expect the present value of future earnings to be greater than the original
investment cost, employing an appropriate discount factor.

For the balance of payments, this is extremely important. If international investments are no different from any other kinds of investments,
the ultimate inflows of profits and dividends from direct investments abroad
will eventually exceed the initial capital outflow. Hence, even though a
current capital outflow via direct investments may be detrimental, the balance of payments will certainly benefit from the feedback via the interest
and dividend portion of the current account. These inflows will finally
come to exceed the initial capital outflow, and thus the *net* balance of
payments effect will be beneficial.

On the basis of this connection between direct foreign investments and
the current account of the balance of payments, we must also conclude
that any policy designed to reduce direct investment outflows today will
similarly reduce earnings inflows tomorrow. If we take a country's balance
of payments over, say, a twenty-year period, it is certainly not unlikely

that the net effect of a reduction of direct investment abroad would indeed be detrimental to the balance of payments.

Additional feedback might well be found in increases in exports of goods and services by the home country complementary to those being provided by the foreign facility. For example, a U.S. computer manufacturer may set up a manufacturing plant abroad to supply the foreign market, and yet continue to export the required satellite equipment from his plants in the U.S.

Of course, not all of the balance of payments feedbacks of private direct investment abroad are positive. Some are negative, particularly when the foreign facilities are being set up to supplant exports from the home country. There are two possibilities here. The direct investment abroad might be in response to diminishing competitiveness of exports from the home country, or it may be in response to restrictive commercial policies against the home country's exports on the part of the foreign nations involved. In either case, however, it is likely that export volume will eventually be reduced, whether or not direct foreign investment takes place. (Foreign investment may cause it to occur somewhat more rapidly.)

It may also be argued that direct investments in foreign industries whose output the home country *imports* can also have beneficial balance of payments effects to the extent that they are cost-reducing and cut down import expenditures.

Looking at the combined feedback effects of direct foreign investments via the current account—exports, imports, and profit remissions—it may turn out to be deleterious to institute policies designed to reduce direct investment capital outflows. Table 17-2 presents a calculation which comes to such a conclusion in the case of U.S. direct investments in Europe. And yet such policies are often implemented. Why?

The answer is twofold. First, it is not always certain that the earnings will be repatriated. This is of less importance to countries such as the U.S. than it is to countries with a less certain political and economic climate. Second, it is a question of *timing*. Within the context of certain balance of payments situations it may well be advisable to impede direct investment outflows *now* and pay the price in terms perhaps of reduced exports and earnings inflows *later*. We shall return to this problem later on.

In the case of other types of long-term private investment, primarily bank loans and portfolio investments, the primary feedback takes the form of receipts of interest and dividend incomes. There is no direct connection between these types of long-term capital outflows and exports. Hence, it is somewhat easier to justify an interruption of this type of capital outflow for balance of payments reasons, simply because the overall feedback effect is not as strong. Here too, however, the receipts of interest and dividends,

Table 17-2

Estimated Balance-of-Payments Effects of $1,000 of Direct Investment in Manufacturing Facilities in Europe*

Item	Year 0	Year 1	Year 2	Year 3	Year 4	Year 5	Year 6	Year 7	Year 8	Year 9	Year 10
1. New direct investment[a]	$1,000	$ 0	$ 0	$ 0	$ 0	$ 0	$ 0	$ 0	$ 0	$ 0	$ 0
2. Cumulative direct investment end of year	1,000	1,081	1,169	1,264	1,366	1,477	1,596	1,725	1,865	2,016	3,179
3. Export stimulus	0	106	115	124	134	145	157	169	183	198	214
4. Royalties and fees	0	23	25	27	29	31	34	37	40	43	46
5. Repatriation earnings	0	87	94	102	110	119	128	139	150	162	175
6. Import stimulus	0	−65	−70	−76	−82	−89	−96	−104	−112	−121	−131
Balance of payments:[b]											
7. Annual net effect	−1,000	151	164	177	191	206	223	241	261	282	304
8. Cumulative effect	−1,000	−849	−685	−508	−317	−111	112	353	614	896	1,200

Line 2 = Line 2 for preceding year plus 8.0 per cent (retained earnings of current year).

Line 3 = 10.6 per cent of investment (Line 2 of preceding year).

Line 4 = 2.3 per cent of investment (Line 2 of preceding year).

Line 5 = 51.8 per cent of total earnings, which are assumed to be 16.8 per cent of investment, making retained earnings 8.7 per cent of investment (Line 2 of preceding year).

Line 6 = 6.5 per cent of investment (Line 2 of preceding year).

Line 7 = Lines 1 + 3 + 4 + 5 + 6.

[a] It is assumed that the investment was made at the end of year 0.

[b] Excluding (1) related export stimulation; (2) American import replacement of foreign owned production by American-owned production; and (3) displacement of U.S. exports by American-owned foreign production.

* Walter S. Salant, et al., The United States Balance of Payments in 1968 (Washington, D.C.: Brookings Institution, 1963), p. 144.

plus redemptions and repayments, normally will always exceed the original outflow ultimately. Only in extraordinary situations where this is not likely to be true, or where the question of timing is important, can a strong argument be made for policies designed to reduce portfolio investments and loans abroad.

One final summary feedback effect concerns all types of long-term capital investments abroad. A capital outflow will have an immediate detrimental effect on the balance of payments only if part of it eventually comes to rest in the coffers of some reserve-accumulating country. However, most countries of the world immediately spend abroad all of the foreign exchange they receive. Only if part of a given capital investment finally lands in a country which demands payment in gold or acceptable foreign currencies will there be an immediate detrimental impact on the home country's balance of payments. Hence, there is substantial likelihood that most or all of any U.S. long-term capital outflow to underdeveloped countries will be directly or indirectly fed back to the U.S., with little net effect on the balance of payments. But this probability is much lower in the case of investment flows to countries such as Germany, France, or the Netherlands.

PRIVATE SHORT-TERM CAPITAL

The analysis of the overall effects of short-term capital flows on the balance of payments is somewhat less complex than that connected with long-term capital investments.

Like direct investments abroad, short-term capital outflows are often connected with merchandise exports but for entirely different reasons. In the former instance, the direct investments in foreign countries *caused* an increase in exports. With short-term capital outflows, the exports themselves are the motivating factor.

Let us take an example. A German toy manufacturer is anxious to sell $250,000 worth of assorted toys to a Brazilian retail chain. The Brazilians, however, demand 180-day terms: 20 per cent payable within 30 days and the remainder at the end of 180 days at 6 per cent interest. With prevailing interest rates extremely high in Brazil, the 180-day credit is very important to the importer and weighs heavily in his buying decisions. Looking at this situation from a national point of view, if Germany is not willing to endure a short-term capital outflow—$50,000 for 30 days and $200,000 for 180 days—it most probably will lose $250,000 worth of exports.

Short-term capital outflows which go to finance international commercial transactions, then, are always beneficial for a nation's balance of payments. The immediate impact is virtually zero, as increased exports equal the short-term capital outflow, but the net impact is, of course, positive as the short-term loan plus any accrued interest is repaid. It would indeed be foolish, therefore, for a nation to impede capital outflows representing commercial credits, especially inasmuch as financing terms in some markets of the world often outweigh price and quality considerations as a criterion for purchase.

To a lesser extent, long-term and intermediate-term capital outflows also take on the role of directly financing exports and should be mentioned briefly in this connection. In the highly competitive export markets of the world, the importing countries at times demand up to seven years' terms for purchases of such goods as wheat, chemicals, and capital equipment. If an exporting nation is not willing to endure an intermediate-term capital outflow, even equal in amount to the value of the connected exports, a country may well be excluded from the market. By the time the export credit has matured, of course, the balance of payments of such a nation has benefited substantially, although the question of timing can play an important role in such a case. By way of caution, however, it should be noted that intermediate- and long-term export credits can easily lead to pleas for extensions and sometimes to default.

Short-term capital outflows not connected with the financing of exports are beneficial to a country's balance of payments only to the extent of the interest earned. An American $1 million, 90-day loan abroad in the form of purchases by American residents of some short-term foreign debt obligations at 8 per cent, which is repatriated within the calendar year, constitutes a credit in the current account in the amount of $20,000 (8 per cent per annum for 90 days), with no net effect on the capital account. Even short-term capital outflows extending from one year to the next can be deemed beneficial; the negative impact on the balance of payments during the year of outflow is more than made up when the principal and interest are returned.

Sometimes, however, a short-term capital outflow in reality may represent a long-term exodus of capital: the short-term assets are simply rolled over at maturity for new obligations. In such an instance, the balance of payments justification for capital outflows must rest entirely on the interest earnings repatriated via the current account over the long haul, as in the case of portfolio capital outflows. Government restrictions on such outflows can be justified on the basis of timing, within the context of certain short-run balance of payments difficulties. A practical problem nonetheless is inherent in separating this type of short-term capital investments abroad from others which are truly short-term in nature.

We should also consider short-term capital outflows which find their way into foreign currency holdings in the form of demand deposits. Here the capital outflow may involve a question of political stability, economic uncertainty, or perhaps a lack of faith in the value of the home currency. The net effect of such outflows, insofar as they are eventually repatriated, is close to zero. Any interest earned on this type of asset is negligible—in fact, a country such as Switzerland might even demand payment of a fee *for* the service of holding foreign deposits. In times of a balance of payments emergency, therefore, a strong case can be made for restricting this type of capital outflow into foreign demand deposits. Again, it may be difficult to separate such capital flows from others which go to finance exports, or which are in reality a manifestation of interest-bearing short-term or long-term investments.

Finally, it should be noted that the balance of both long- and short-term capital flows is comprised of transactions by domestic residents *and* foreigners. When foreign residents invest in the home country, all of the effects portrayed here are reversed. Direct-investment inflows are accompanied by increased imports and earnings remissions abroad. Portfolio investments and all types of short-term capital inflows result in payments of interest and dividends to foreigners and, eventually, in repayment or redemption. In addition, trade credit extended by foreigners to domestic residents generally accompanies imports. While foreign-capital inflows are generally regarded as favorable influences on the domestic balance of payments, it is clear that the total payments must ultimately exceed the receipts, just as the reverse is true of domestic capital outflows.

Table 17–3 summarizes the various balance of payments effects of capital outflows, which can easily be reversed in the analysis of foreign-owned capital inflows. It also notes the impact of government loans abroad, to which we shall turn our attention next.

GOVERNMENT CAPITAL

The impact of government capital flows on the balance of payments differs significantly from that of private loans and investments. For this reason we shall treat it separately here. We asserted earlier that private international capital transactions are fundamentally motivated by the expectation of profit. This insures that, from a balance of payments standpoint, insofar as the expectations of the investors are fulfilled, the return flow of earnings and principal will always exceed the initial capital outflow. In the case of government loans, however, the motivation is quite different and so may be the effects.

A government loan may be made in order to enable a foreign nation to purchase the home country's exports—e.g., the U.S. Export-Import Bank operations. Such credits may be long-term or short-term, and often are extended when private financing is unavailable or excessively costly for

Table 17-3

Balance-of-Payments Effects of Various Types of Capital Outflows, in Summary Form

Capital Outflow	Primary Impact	Feedback #1	Feedback #2	Feedback #3	Feedback #4
1. Direct investment	Long-term capital (−)	Exports (+)	Dividend and other remissions (+)	Possible further exports of goods and services (+)	Possible reduction of supplanted exports (−)
2. Portfolio investment	Long-term capital (−)	Interest and dividend income (+)	Redemption (+)		
3. Other long-term capital	Long-term capital (−)	Interest and dividend income (+)	Repayment and redemption (+)		
4. Trade credit	Short-term capital (−)	Exports (+)	Interest income (+)	Repayment (+)	
5. Investments in foreign short-term liabilities	Short-term capital (−)	Interest income (+)	Redemption and repayment (+)		
6. Investments in foreign demand deposits and currency	Short-term capital (−)	Repatriation (+)			
7. Government export credits	Long-term capital (−)	Exports (+)	Interest income and repayments (+)	Possible opportunity cost in terms of private borrowing foregone at higher interest rates (−)	
8. Government development loans	Long-term capital (−)	Exports (+)	Interest income and repayments (+)	Possible upward pressure on domestic incomes and prices, if tied; hence possible expansion of imports and contraction of exports (−)	

the purchasing country. The obvious balance of payments offset to the government capital outflow is a corresponding, equal increase in exports. As in the case of private export credits, the eventual repayment of the loan, plus interest, yield an eventual net beneficial balance of payments impact in that amount. But there is a subtler aspect to this apparently straightforward reasoning.

What if the government had refused to extend the export credit? One possibility is that the export sales might have gone to a competitor country. On the other hand, the importing nation might have been forced to finance the imports by private borrowing at higher rates of interest in the home country. In such an instance, the net beneficial impact on the exporting country's balance of payments under higher interest private financing would have exceeded that incurred under the lower interest government loan. Also, the importing nation might have purchased the commodities for cash, or it might have financed the transaction by borrowing in some third country. These two alternatives might appear preferable to government export credits from a short-run balance of payments standpoint, but they are certainly inferior in the longer run, when the interest receipts over the life of the loan are considered.

Sometimes government export credits are made on a "soft" basis. For instance, they may be repayable over long periods of time at extremely low interest rates, or they may be repayable in the importing country's currency which is not convertible into the currency of the lender. In such cases the question is, would the importing nation have borrowed privately, paid cash, or borrowed in third countries had the government loan not been available, or would it have foregone the imports? If the answer is the former, then the balance of payments "opportunity cost" of the government's liberal export credit will be relatively high.

Government loans to foreign countries are often an integral part of a nation's foreign-aid program. As such, they may be made for specific purposes in the economic development scheme of the recipient country, or they may be general-purpose balance of payments loans. Often they are "tied" to purchases of goods and services in the home country—i.e., it is stipulated that a certain percentage of the loan must be spent on exports of the donor country. But even if they are not restricted in this manner, it is probable than the export feedback of such government development loans will be relatively large. To this must be added the interest payments and repayments of principal, with the result that government development or balance of payments loans may eventually benefit the lender's own balance of payments substantially.

The question of government loans and grants that are tied to purchases in the home country becomes somewhat more complex when we consider what happens as a result to the economy of the donor country. Tied foreign aid, when compared with nontied aid, has a stimulating effect on the domestic economy—quite similar in nature to increased government spending—via the increased exports that result. At full employment, this tends to cause prices to rise at home, which in turn stimulates imports and reduces exports, and therefore cuts down the net balance of payments benefits derived from tying foreign aid. Even at times of less than full employment at home, the increased exports resulting from tied aid (as opposed to nontied aid) tends to stimulate the domestic economy. The resulting rise in national income then tends to cause spending on imports to rise, thereby again reducing the net benefit of tied aid from a balance of payments standpoint.

Comparing this type of government capital outflow to private long-term investment abroad, it seems that the export feedback is somewhat more certain in the former instance due to the high probability or certainty that the loan will be restricted to home purchases. On the other hand, the feedback from payments of interest is likely to be less in the case of government loans because of the more favorable terms granted in intergovernmental lending. In both of these respects, the balance of payments impact of government loans abroad may be compared to private direct investments in foreign countries. While the latter are generally undertaken for an indefinite period of time, however, government loans do normally involve a repayment of principal.

The net impact of government loans on the lender's balance of payments will be less favorable, of course, the "softer" are the terms on which the loans are extended. Finally, it is normally impossible to talk in terms of an "opportunity" cost of development loan, due to higher cost-private loans and investments foregone, since such alternatives may not be open to the borrowing country. The one significant exception would be development loans extended by the International Bank for Reconstruction and Development (IBRD), or World Bank, which, in turn, sells its obligations to private investors in the world's capital markets.

UNILATERAL TRANSFERS

The net balance of payments effect of private remittance and pension payments is fairly straightforward although, as was brought out in the previous chapter, they are often difficult to estimate in practice. With the exception of gift parcels, which today probably represent an insignificant part of the total, private unilateral transfers are rarely fed *directly* back to the donor country in the form of exports of goods and services.

Pension payments are typically utilized by the recipient to meet his local costs of living. Other private remittances also fall into the same category of helping to maintain the standard of living of friends and relatives abroad. Unless the recipient country accumulates international reserves by running balance of payments surpluses, however, such private transfers may eventually return indirectly to the donor country, either in the form of exports or via capital inflows.

Private remittances and pensions play a relatively minor role in the balance of payments position of most countries. Notable exceptions are (a) nations that employ large numbers of foreign workers, many of whom remit significant portions of their earnings to relatives at home, and (b) the nations from which such workers emigrate. Thus outflows of private remittances have been important balance of payments elements in Germany, the Netherlands, Switzerland, and France with receipts bolstering the balances of payments of Spain, Italy, Greece, and Turkey during the past decade or so.

By far the major portion of the unilateral transfers account is devoted to government grants, which generally are for purposes of reconstruction and development assistance but also can be for military purposes. Judging by the net outflow of government grants of countries such as the U.S., it would be easy to conclude—mistakenly—that a balance of payments deficit might be alleviated by merely reducing foreign aid. But such grants are generally explicitly or implicitly tied to purchases of goods and services in the home country, and any reduction in government grants simultaneously reduces exports and the net balance of payments benefit may be small indeed. It is estimated, for example, that 80 per cent of U.S. foreign aid is tied to U.S. purchases. Hence, a reduction in such aid would hardly be the answer to any American balance of payments deficit.

Serious and informed advocates of aid reduction for balance of payments purposes counter with the following argument: Suppose we were to reduce our foreign aid payments in some areas. Would the recipient country not find it possible somehow to import the commodity or groups of commodities from us after all, with attendant benefits to our balance of payments? This is, indeed, an intriguing question. American soft-currency sales or gifts of wheat to developing countries under Public Law 480, for instance, may enable those nations to use their scarce foreign exchange to import other, less essential commodities. A halt in U.S. wheat shipments would force the recipient countries to shift their imports to wheat and, insofar as this wheat is purchased from the U.S., would benefit the American balance of payments commensurately. This assumes, of course, that the recipient nations continue to import the wheat from the U.S., and that the foreign exchange originally liberated by the wheat grants was not used to buy other U.S. exports in the first place. In the latter instance, the halting of aid shipments of wheat or other commodities would merely result in the reduction of other U.S. exports. In any case, the volume of such aid always depends upon the national farm policies that are being pursued.

At best, the argument for a reduction in tied foreign-aid grants in order to improve the balance of payments is useful only under highly restrictive conditions. Even then, the modest balance of payments gain might well be outweighed by political losses which would accompany such a policy.

As we shall see later on in connection with trade, aid, and economic development, there are important arguments favoring nontied aid—aid which may be used by the recipient country for purchases from the best possible supplier, no matter where he is located. Suppose U.S. foreign aid were not restricted largely to purchases in the U.S. How harmful would this be for the American balance of payments? In the first place, there would no longer be an explicit export-feedback effect of government grants on the balance of payments. In point of fact, however, the export feedback would probably continue to be important, since whatever is not spent in the U.S. would be expended in third countries which, to the extent that these nations are not reserve-accumulators, would in turn import from the U.S. Nontied intergovernmental grants constitute a drain on the country's balance of payments only to the extent that a portion of these grants eventually find their way into foreign official monetary reserves and must therefore be settled by means of reserve transactions.

MILITARY EXPENDITURES

Some countries, such as the U.S. and the U.K., have been deeply involved in overseas military ventures that carry substantial balance of payments costs. It has been regularly asserted, for instance, that the maintenance of U.S. and British troops in West Germany represented a substantial balance of payments burden for these countries that should somehow be lessened.

Overseas defense expenditures enter the balance of payments accounts only to the extent that they involve currency conversion. For example, the construction and maintenance of overseas bases involving the use of indigenous labor and contractual services clearly enters the balance of payments as a negative item. But keeping the base supplied with military equipment originating from the home country does not.

The maintenance of troops and other personnel, and their dependents abroad involves a balance of payments cost to the extent that wages and subsistence payments are converted to local currencies for household expenses, entertainment, travel, and similar purposes. This cost can be reduced in various ways—by stocking the post exchanges largely with home-produced commodities, providing on-base living quarters, restricting travel to military or domestically owned forms of transportation, and so forth. Although such measures may reduce the balance of payments cost of maintaining overseas bases, they may very well raise the real cost to the government by a significant margin.

Overseas procurement of materials and supplies, as well as equipment of various types, naturally also enter into the balance of payments as a negative item.

In the area of military assistance, offshore procurement and cost-sharing programs within military alliances, as well as local costs of construction, involve balance of payments costs in the first instance. Military aid in the form of equipment grants do not, and sales of equipment to foreign countries may represent a positive balance of payments item.

The balance of payments costs of military activities abroad can be alleviated by reducing the foreign-currency share of overseas expenditures. Alternatively, the foreign countries themselves may be induced to pay a larger share of the foreign-exchange cost, or to offset it in some way by increasing their own procurement in the home country.

It is sometimes argued that military assistance substitutes for development assistance, since the recipient countries may then use their scarce foreign exchange to import nonmilitary goods. This may well be a significant positive feedback from military-aid programs.

It is extremely difficult to implement programs designed to reduce the balance of payments cost of military programs abroad. This involves not only an analysis of all of the connected economic variables, but also such imponderables as its impact on the national security, international political relations, and other elements which render an accurate weighing of the alternatives an extremely hazardous proposition.

INCOME EFFECTS

We have sought here to establish some of the various interrelationships that appear to exist among balance of payments accounts—how a development in one account affects one or more others, either immediately or over an extended period of time, so that the net effect upon the balance of payments is by no means as certain as it would appear at first glance. International flows of long-term and short-term private and government capital, as well as unilateral transfers, all involve a variety of more or less direct feedback effects which, in turn, influence the balance of payments, usually in the opposite direction. These effects are exerted over varying time periods. A competent balance of payments analyst will take as many of them as possible into account and make his policy recommendations accordingly, with a view toward the time context within which they make themselves felt and the particular balance of payments problems involved.

There is one further, indirect feedback effect that needs to be considered, even if it does not lend itself readily to accurate prediction. This is the *income effect,* about which we shall subsequently have much more to say in connection with the economics of balance of payments adjustment. Any monetary outflow—whether in the form of direct or portfolio investments, loans, short-term capital, private remittances, or government loans and grants—presumably is put to productive use abroad, either directly or indirectly. They thus serve to increase foreign incomes. Even military grants, it can be argued, serve to liberate foreign resources for other more productive purposes and thereby enhance incomes abroad.

In Chaper 13 it will be formally demonstrated that there exists a direct connection between national income and imports. Any factor which serves to stimulate national income thus also acts indirectly to enhance a country's imports of goods and services. To the extent that these *induced* imports are drawn from the home country in the form of exports, therefore, monetary balance of payments outflows trigger a further feedback in eventual increased exports.

This is not limited to outflows of grants and capital alone. As we shall see in the following chapter, an autonomous or induced increase in imports exerting a negative force on the balance of payments eventually brings with it an induced increase in exports.

In summary, balance of payments analysis is not as straightforward as it would at first appear. We began this chapter by posing a problem: How do you apportion the responsibility for a balance of payments deficit among the various payments accounts? We now conclude that the answer to this question involves a subtle and complex analysis of the manifold direct and indirect interaccount relationships that exist within the balance of payments. Moreover, we are not surprised when policies formulated on the basis of sometimes unavoidably incomplete information fail to achieve their intended objectives and at times appear self-defeating, especially when viewed over an extended period of time.

Finally, we should note once again that the problem of balance of payments analysis in surplus countries involves relationships that work in the reverse direction. Capital inflows mean increased imports, payments of interest, and dividends abroad, and eventual repayments and redemptions, and so forth. The restoration of balance in the balance of payments of surplus countries therefore involves analysis and the formulation of policies designed to cope with problems diametrically opposed to those outlined here. However, the problems of surplus countries are by no means as acute, and can be more easily rectified than those of deficit countries. Hence, the concentration upon the problems of the latter. In either case, however, it is necessary to gain a sound appreciation for the complexities involved.

18

FOREIGN EXCHANGE

Each of the international transactions enumerated in the balance of payments normally represents two separate exchanges: (a) the commercial, financial, or unrequited exchange itself, *and* (b) the transfer of one national currency into another required to effect payment. A U.S. exporter selling in France naturally wants to be paid in dollars. His French business partner, therefore, must somehow trade his francs for dollars in order to accommodate the American and successfully conclude the transaction. An American wishing to invest in a German business must find a way to exchange his dollars for marks in order to complete his investment. In each instance, there is an exchange of one national currency for another: the Frenchman in the first example buys U.S. dollars with his francs, and the American in the second example buys German marks with his dollars. These are called foreign-exchange transactions and take place on the foreign-exchange market. Broadly defined, the foreign-exchange market is a vehicle that makes possible the exchange of different national currencies.

THE FOREIGN EXCHANGE MARKET

The foreign-exchange market today derives its importance largely from the existence of different national monetary standards. At a time when international payments could be effected in gold anywhere in the world, and all currencies were fully backed by gold, there was no need for a foreign-exchange market in its present form. International transactions could universally be settled in gold. All that was needed was a free market for gold in each country or the use of gold itself as the medium of exchange. Today, as everyone knows, these conditions are no longer fulfilled. The *value* of national currencies, both in terms of gold and in terms of each other, is regulated by government fiat. Thus a U.S. dollar does not have the same value, in terms of the goods and services it will buy as a German mark, a Dutch guilder, a Swiss franc, or even a Canadian dollar. Hence, there is clearly a need for a market in which national currencies can be exchanged for one another in accordance with their respective values. The latter are reflected in the *exchange rate*, the price of a unit of one national currency in terms of a unit of another national currency.

The foreign-exchange market itself is a broad, somewhat nebulous institutional arrangement. Most banks dealing internationally maintain balances in a number of foreign currencies with correspondent banks or affiliates abroad. American banks hold mark deposits in German banks, kronor deposits in Swedish banks, and so forth. At the same time, foreign banks hold dollar deposits in American banks. A U.S. bank may not have a deposit in each and every foreign currency, but it normally will hold deposits in currencies which are from its own point of view the most important ones. The same holds true for foreign banks.

Foreign-exchange transactions are merely accounting debits and credits relating to the foreign-currency balances of banks. To take a very simple illustrative example: suppose an American wants $1,000 worth of Swiss francs. He transfers his dollars to his bank in New York, which cables its Swiss correspondent in Zurich: "Credit my Swiss franc account with you and I'll credit your dollar account here by an equivalent amount." The American's dollars now belong to the Swiss bank, in return for which he now has claim to the Swiss francs credited to the New York bank's account in Zurich—a very simple, straightforward transaction.

Naturally a given bank may not have a deposit in Burmese currency but it can find a bank, domestic or foreign, that does. In such a case, the foreign-exchange transaction is handled in the same way, except that a third bank becomes a party to the exchange. As a result of such overlapping foreign-currency holdings by banks, it is possible to exchange any two currencies for one another quickly and efficiently.

In practice, foreign-exchange transactions are generally made by means of a *cable transfer,* which effects the necessary change in the ownership of a foreign-currency deposit. The actual accounting entries on the books of the foreign and domestic bank are made two days after the cable is sent, and confirmed by mail. The costs of the transfer are billed to the buyer of the foreign exchange. Other types of transfers, particularly air mail, are also used, although less extensively.

The foreign-exchange market, then, consists of an unorganized group of banks throughout the world that simply maintain foreign-currency balances with one another. If a bank finds itself with excess foreign-currency balances, it can sell these balances to other banks, foreign-currency brokers, and sometimes official foreign monetary institutions. Similarly, these same institutions serve as sources of foreign currency supply should a bank find that its foreign-currency balances are deficient.

THE EXCHANGE RATE

When an international monetary transaction is made, there obviously has to be some exchange rate for the currencies involved. An American in the market for German marks is certainly better off if he receives D.M. 2.30 per dollar than if he only gets DM 2.20 for his dollar. For the German buying dollars the reverse is true. He has to pay less in his home currency for one dollar at DM 2.20 = U.S. $1.00 than at DM 2.30 = U.S. $1.00.

The *exchange rate* is nothing more than the *price* of one currency in terms of another. If one dollar costs four marks, one mark must cost twenty-five cents. This is really no different from the price of goods and services, except that here the items involved are currencies. In buying bananas, we say that 10 bananas cost $1.00. We do not say that $1.00 costs 10 bananas. In foreign exchange transactions we do. The *exchange rate* expresses currency *A* in terms of currency *B*, and vice versa.

The price of bananas is settled largely by the forces of supply and demand. If demand increases and supply is not perfectly elastic, the price of bananas rises. If supply increases, and demand is not perfectly elastic, the price of bananas falls. This is conceptually no different in the foreign-exchange market. If the dollar–mark rate is 1.00 : 2.20 and the demand for German marks increases, the price of marks in terms of dollars will tend to rise. We say that the German mark *appreciates* in terms of U.S. dollars. Conversely, we can also say in this instance that the U.S. dollar *depreciates* in terms of German marks. All of this assumes, of course, that neither the supply of nor the demand for dollars is perfectly elastic.

Both the demand for, and the supply of, foreign exchange are *derived* from the underlying demand for domestic and foreign goods, services, and investment opportunities.

Assuming for the moment that international transactions are limited to trade in goods and services and again using U.S. dollars and German marks, at each successively lower exchange rate (the price of one mark in terms of dollars), German goods and services become progressively cheaper for U.S. buyers in terms of their home currency.

In order to purchase German goods and services, of course, Americans must convert dollars into marks. Hence, as the exchange rate falls—as the dollar price of each German mark is reduced—the quantity of marks demanded rises. The demand for marks is *derived* from the U.S. demand for German goods and services. The more elastic this demand, the more elastic will be the demand for marks, i.e., the demand for foreign exchange.

What about the *supply* of marks? It, too, is derived. If Germans want to purchase American goods and services, they must first convert their marks to dollars. Hence, the German *supply* of marks is entirely contingent upon the German *demand* for dollars. At successively lower exchange rates (the dollar price of one German mark), the corresponding mark price of one dollar is raised, and U.S. goods and services become progressively less attractive to Germans. Hence, at lower exchange rates the quantity of marks supplied (quantity of dollars demanded) falls. Again, the more elastic the German demand for U.S. goods and services, the more elastic the German demand for dollars and, hence, the supply of marks.

This can be illustrated in terms such as Table 18–1. A series of dol-

Table 18–1
Derivation of the Supply of Foreign Exchange from the Foreign Demand for the Home Currency*

(in millions of currency units)

(1) Dollar Price per Mark	(2) Quantity of Marks Demanded	(3) Quantity of Marks Supplied	(4) Quantity of Dollars Demanded	(5) Mark Price per Dollar
$0.50	100.00	900.00	450.000	DM 2.00
0.45	200.00	800.00	360.36	2.22
0.40	300.00	700.00	280.00	2.50
0.35	400.00	600.00	209.79	2.86
0.30	500.00	500.00	150.15	3.33
0.25	600.00	400.00	100.00	4.00
0.20	700.00	300.00	60.00	5.00
0.15	800.00	200.00	29.99	6.67
0.10	900.00	100.00	10.00	10.00

* Column 1 figures are the reciprocals of the corresponding Column 5 figures, and vice-versa. Columns 2 and 4 are given. Column 3, the supply of marks, is derived by multiplying the given figures in Column 4 by the corresponding exchange rate in Column 5.

lar–mark exchange rates is given in Column 1, along with the quantity of marks demanded at each. Notice that as the exchange rate—the *dollar price per mark*—falls, the quantity of foreign exchange demanded rises. The identical series of exchange rates, this time expressed as the *mark price per dollar* is given in Column 5. As the exchange rate falls from the U.S. vantage point—i.e., as the mark price of dollars *rises* from the German point of view—the quantity of dollars demanded by Germans falls (Column 4). Since the quantity of marks supplied at each exchange rate is nothing more than the quantity of dollars demanded multiplied by that exchange rate, the quantity of marks supplied falls at successively lower dollar–mark exchange rates (successively higher mark–dollar rates). Column 2 thus represents the demand for foreign exchange and Column 3 the supply of foreign exchange. It is evident that an exchange rate of DM 1.00 = $0.30 ($1.00 = DM 3.33) is the equilibrium rate of exchange in this example.

Figure 18–1 presents the foreign-exchange demand and supply, and the equilibrium exchange rate of U.S. dollars for German marks in graphical form. The curves depicting the demand for marks (D_m) and the supply of marks (S_m) intersect at point E. The equilibrium exchange rate is R_1, with quantity OM_1 of foreign-exchange transactions taking place.

At any higher exchange rate, say R_3, the quantity of marks supplied would exceed the quantity demanded in the amount M_5M_3. At that rate Americans find German goods and services too costly in terms of dollars and cut back their purchases of marks. At that rate also, Germans find

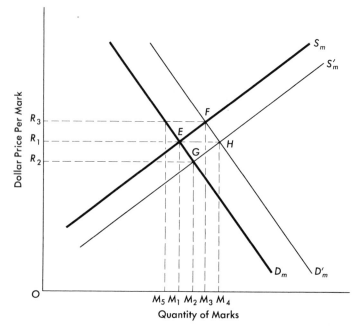

Fig. 18–1. Determination of the equilibrium exchange rate.

American goods and services pleasantly inexpensive in terms of marks and are eager to offer marks for exchange into dollars. With quantity supplied in excess of quantity demanded, the dollar–mark rate is depressed until equilibrium is reached at R_1.

Conversely, at any exchange rate below equilibrium, such as R_2, the American quantity of marks demanded in order to purchase German goods and services exceeds the German offer of marks in return for dollars. Marks are "cheap" in terms of dollars and dollars are "costly" in terms of marks. The quantity of foreign exchange demanded at that exchange rate exceeds quantity supplied by the amount M_5M_2 and the exchange rate is forced back up to R_1, where supply and demand are once again in equilibrium.

Now suppose for some reason—a change in tastes, incomes, and so forth—the U.S. demand for German goods and services rises. The demand for marks shifts from D_m to D_m' and the new equilibrium (F) yields the exchange rate R_3, a higher exchange rate. Americans must now pay more for a German mark, while Germans pay less for a U.S. dollar and are thus willing to offer an increased quantity M_1M_3 of marks. The mark has appreciated in terms of dollars while the dollar has depreciated in terms of marks.

The reverse is the case if the German supply of marks on the foreign exchange market—their demand for dollars—suddenly increases. The supply curve for marks shifts from S_m to S_m' and a new equilibrium exchange rate R_2 is set at point G. At that rate, marks are cheaper in terms of dollars, and Americans are willing to demand quantity M_1M_2 more marks, i.e., *supply* more dollars. The mark depreciates in terms of dollars, and the dollar appreciates in terms of marks.

If, as a result of increased trade in *both* directions, the supply *and* demand for marks rise equally, the exchange rate indeed may not be altered (equilibrium H at R_1) but the dollar–mark foreign-exchange transactions will grow substantially, from OM_1 to OM_4.

From this simple two-country, two-currency model of exchange rate determination, considering only trade in goods and services, it is easy to proceed to a more realistic situation, where dollars are traded not only for marks, but for French francs, Dutch guilders, Danish kroners, and many other currencies. Since virtually every national currency is traded for every other national currency, there must be an exchange rate in each instance: dollar–mark, mark–kroner, kroner–guilder, guilder–dollar, and so on.

These exchange rates will *always* be consistent with each other. It is not likely, for example, for the dollar–mark to be $1.00 = DM 2.50, while the dollar–guilder rate is $1.00 = Hfl. 2.40, if the mark–guilder rate is DM 1.00 Hfl. 1.00. It would be a simple matter then for someone to buy 2.50 marks for 1 dollar, exchange them for 2.50 Dutch guilders, and in turn exchange them for $1.04. Large-scale transactions of this sort would immediately see to it that the mark appreciates in terms of the dollar, the guilder appreciates in terms of the mark, and the dollar appreciates in terms of the guilder. Such inter-currency transfers, which keep all exchange rates consistent with one another, come under the heading of *arbitrage*.

ARBITRAGE

Most banks dealing in foreign exchange maintain well-paid staffs of very quick-witted specialists who do nothing but keep an eye on exchange rates throughout the world. They immediately spring into action upon spotting an exchange rate that is out of line. These are the foreign-exchange *arbitrageurs* who see to it that a consistent constellation of exchange rates prevails at all times throughout the international economy—besides, of course, making a tidy profit for their employers.

To take the simplest case, suppose the dollar–pound sterling exchange rate is £1.00 = $2.499606 in New York but in London it is £1.00 = $2.499894. Immediately, foreign-exchange traders would go into action and buy sterling for dollars in New York and resell it in London or, what amounts to the same thing, buy dollars in London for sterling and sell them again in New York. All of this for a price difference of $0.000188 per pound sterling? On a transaction of $5 million, the profit at this difference is $1,440! Not bad for five minutes' work. As the demand for dollars increases in London and the demand for sterling increases in New York, the pound depreciates in London and appreciates in New York until the two rates are equal at, say £1.00 = $2.499755, and all potential for profitable arbitrage is eliminated. This is called *two-point arbitrage,* and equalizes the exchange rate of one currency for another between two geographic locations.

More intricate, and therefore in fact offering greater potential for profit, is *three-point arbitrage.* Suppose prevailing exchange rates are as follows:

U.S $1.00 = DM 2.49746 in New York
DM 1.00 = Bfrs 1.21343 in Frankfurt
U.S. $1.00 = Bfrs 3.01267 in Brussels

Arbitrageurs would immediately buy marks for dollars in New York, sell these marks for Belgian francs in Frankfurt, and resell the francs for dollars in Brussels. In New York $1,000,000 exchanges for DM 2,497,460. These marks then exchange for Bfrs. 3,030,493 in Frankfurt and the Belgian francs can then be exchanged in Brussels for $1,005,916—a profit of $5,916 on the transaction. Of course, the rates do not stay that way for long. As the volume of arbitrage transactions grows, the mark appreciates in New York in terms of dollars, the Belgian franc appreciates in Frankfurt in terms of marks, and the U.S. dollar appreciates in Brussels in terms of Belgian francs. All rates are soon equalized and the profit opportunity disappears.

The simple rule to remember regarding three-point arbitrage, as well as the even more complex versions of arbitrage, is to *buy* undervalued currencies and *sell* overvalued ones. The art, of course, lies in keeping constant track of a large number of exchange rates in a large number of geographical locations, and in taking advantage of a lack of knowledge on the part of other foreign-exchange traders in the foreign-exchange markets of the world. This is in part where the foreign-exchange traders of the large international banks earn their keep.

Arbitrage is the element that unifies the foreign-exchange market. We stated earlier that the market for foreign-exchange is a very loose one, with many currencies being traded in many different locations. Because of arbitrage, however, the market can be regarded as a unified whole. The essentially costless nature of arbitrage permits it to bring about a consistent set of exchange rates which reflect underlying supply and demand conditions. This will not necessarily occur, as we shall see, whenever restrictions are placed on the purchase or sale of foreign currencies, or when a lack of knowledge causes foreign-exchange traders to act irrationally.

ELEMENTS OF DEMAND AND SUPPLY IN EXCHANGE RATE DETERMINATION

We said earlier that the exchange rate—any exchange rate—is determined by the demand for foreign currencies on the part of domestic residents, and the supply of foreign currencies (demand for the domestic currency) by foreigners. This is true only as long as the exchange rate is free to respond to changes in supply and demand, as we shall see later on. Under the conditions of a free-exchange market, then, let us take a more detailed look at what is *behind* the demand for the supply of foreign currencies, taking into account as well international transactions other than trade in goods and services.

Any export of goods and services involves, as a sale to foreigners, a payment of foreign currency. On the foreign-exchange market this foreign currency is then converted to the domestic currency which is paid to the domestic exporter. Exports of goods and services thus constitute an important element in the supply of foreign exchange—but not the *only* element. Whenever foreigners invest or lend in the home country, or domestic residents repatriate capital previously sent abroad, they must convert foreign currencies into the domestic currency on the foreign-exchange market. Capital inflows, both long- and short-term, thus constitute a further, important source of supply of foreign exchange. Gifts *received* from abroad are a final supply element in the determination of the exchange rate—one which may or may not be important, depending on the country involved. In short, the supply of foreign exchange is contingent upon the value of exports, the volume of capital inflows, and the magnitude of gift and grant receipts.

On the demand side, imports of goods and services give rise to *one* demand for foreign exchange, as residents strive to convert the domestic currency into foreign currencies in order to effect payment. Capital outflows as a result of domestic residents investing or lending abroad, or foreign residents repatriating their funds previously invested in the home country, give rise to an additional demand for foreign exchange. Finally, gifts *to* foreign countries form another element of demand in the foreign-exchange market.

The supply of foreign exchange would appear to be determined by the *total* of exports, capital inflows, and transfers received; while the demand for foreign exchange would appear to depend on the total of imports, capital outflows, and transfers abroad. This is not necessarily true. Only those transactions actually involving the conversion of one national currency into another enter into the supply of and demand for foreign exchange. Foreign-aid grants that are "tied" to the exports of the donor country, for example, do not represent foreign-exchange transactions, and hence they do not enter into the determination of the exchange rate. The same is true of capital outflows that are immediately connected with exports, without ever being converted to a foreign currency.

We have seen that the supply of and demand for foreign exchange, *arising out of import and export transactions,* are clearly functions of the exchange rate. The higher the exchange rate (e.g., the more dollars it takes to buy one unit of the foreign currency), the more expensive are foreign goods and services for domestic buyers and the smaller is the volume of their purchases—the lower the quantity of foreign currencies demanded. The higher the exchange rate—the more dollars a foreigner receives per unit of his own currency—the cheaper domestic goods and services appear to foreigners, and the higher is the latter's quantity of foreign exchange supplied.

As Figure 18–2 shows, the import demand for foreign exchange is an

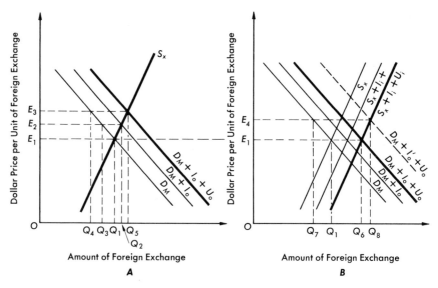

Fig. 18–2. Demand, supply, and exchange-rate determination.

inverse function of the exchange rate, while the export supply of foreign exchange is a *direct* function of the exchange rate, curves D_m and S_x, respectively.

But the supply of foreign exchange arising out of capital inflows is not necessarily a function of the exchange rate. This is naturally also true of the demand for foreign exchange attributable to capital outflows. Whether an investment or loan is undertaken abroad depends largely upon its projected yield and other considerations not associated with the prevailing exchange rate. Only if investors *expect* the exchange rate to change in the future will international capital flows respond to the exchange rate. With given investment yields and the higher the *anticipated* future exchange rate relative to that prevailing today, the larger will be the capital outflow and the smaller the capital inflow. For purposes of analysis, however, we can simply add the *investment demand* for and supply of foreign exchange to that arising out of commercial transactions.

Finally, the demand for and supply of foreign exchange attributable to grants, pensions, and other unilateral transfers are also not likely to vary with the exchange rate. Many of these transfers are contractually fixed in the home currency of the donor and, hence, are not subject to variation. On the other hand, it can be argued with some validity that the recipient countries often require a certain amount of additional aid in terms of the domestic currency to complete agreed-upon projects, and any weakness in the donor's currency will increase the demand for foreign exchange for these purposes. But, in general, the unilateral transfers demand for and supply of foreign exchange also may be added to that originating in the commercial and capital sectors.

Referring to Figure 18–2A, suppose the foreign exchange demand and supply functions facing the home country—derived from the home demand for imports and the foreign demand for domestic goods and services—are given by curves D_m and S_x, respectively. Assume for the moment that S_x represents the sole supply of foreign exchange and remains constant. If we then add to this the demand for foreign exchange arising from capital outflows $(D_m + I_o)$, we find that the equilibrium exchange rate rises from E_1 to E_2, and quantity traded rises from Q_1 to Q_2. Note, however, that by adding the investment demand for foreign exchange and thus inducing a higher exchange rate, the amount of foreign exchange demanded for imports shrinks from Q_1 to Q_3. In fact, if we also add unilateral transfers abroad and thus derive the *total* demand for foreign exchange $(D_m + I_o + U_o)$, the exchange rate becomes higher still (E_3), and the quantity of foreign exchange demanded for imports shrinks still further, to Q_4.

Of course, the total supply of foreign exchange does not arise out of the foreign demand for the home country's exports alone (S_x), but includes also capital inflows (I_i) and receipts of unilateral transfers (U_i), thus yielding the total supply curve $S_x + I_i + U_i$ in Figure 18–2B. The equilibrium exchange rate at the intersection of the total demand and total supply functions may well be equivalent to that arising out of commercial transactions alone (E_1), but this is not *necessarily* true. The greater (a) the sum of capital outflows and unilateral transfers abroad $(I_o + U_o)$, relative to (b) the sum of capital inflows and unilateral transfer receipts $(I_i + U_i)$, the higher will be the final equilibrium exchange rate compared to that prevailing with commercial transactions alone. The greater (b) relative to (a), the lower will be the final exchange rate relative to that applying only to imports and exports.

Note that increased investment outflows, represented by the curve $D_m + I_o' + U_o$, will tend to drive the exchange rate upward (to E_4 with Q_8 traded), thus leading to a reduction in the import demand for foreign exchange from Q_1 to Q_7. If the supply of foreign exchange remains constant, *any* increase in the term $(I_o + U_o)$ will have this effect, and *any* decrease in that term will cause the quantity of foreign exchange demanded for imports to rise. Alternatively, if the demand for foreign exchange remains constant, any increase in the term $(S_x + I_i + U_i)$ will cause the exchange rate to fall and the quantity of foreign exchange demanded for imports to rise, and any decrease in that term will have the opposite effect.

Each determinant of the supply and demand of foreign exchange can of course be broken down still further. A change in any one of these elements has a tendency to alter the exchange rate and render the value of the domestic currency higher or lower relative to that of the other currencies of the world.

EXCHANGE RATE AND THE BALANCE OF PAYMENTS

There is a close connection between the balance of payments and foreign-exchange rates. A deficit in the balance of payments, with the value of imports, capital outflows, and unilateral transfers abroad exceeding total receipts from abroad, means that the supply of the home currency on the foreign-exchange market is large relative to the demand for it. The equilibrium exchange rate, therefore, would tend to fall under such conditions. That is, a balance of payments *deficit* tends to reduce the value of the domestic currency relative to other national currencies. The reverse is true of a balance of payment surplus, when the demand for the home currency exceeds the supply, and the equilibrium exchange rate tends to rise. The relationship between the balance of payments and the exchange rate is by no means perfect, because not all balance of payments items involve the foreign-exchange market. It is sufficiently close, however, so that we can make a general statement: If the exchange rate is permitted to respond freely to changing supply and demand conditions, the status of the balance

of payments of a country *tends to determine* the value of its currency relative
to the currencies of other nations.

This is generally known as the *balance of payments theory* of exchange-
rate determination. It has important implications for international cost
and price comparisons. Assume that it costs $1.00 to produce a ballpoint
pen in the U.S. and DM 2.50 to produce the same item in Germany,
with the dollar–mark exchange rate at $1.00 = DM 2.50. Obviously, costs
are identical between the two countries. Now suppose there occurs a large-
scale flow of capital from the U.S. to Germany, and as a consequence
the exchange rate shifts to $1.00 = DM 2.00. The ballpoint pen now costs
$1.00 for the U.S. item and $1.25 for its German counterpart at the new
exchange rate. On the world market for ballpoint pens, the U.S. suppliers
have gained a distinct price advantage over their German competitors,
even through the underlying cost conditions in that industry are unchanged.

With the balance of payments—virtually the *entire* balance of payments—influencing the determination of the exchange rate, it necessarily
need not constitute a direct link between costs and prices in one country
and those prevailing in other countries at any given point in time. This
is especially true in the short run, when short-term capital flows in large
volume may assume a strong position in the foreign-exchange market and
may temporarily distort the exchange rate far out of line from what it
would have been in their absence. Under such conditions, too, the exchange
rate can be somewhat unstable, and this in itself may evolve as an important
force in international trade.

PURCHASING POWER PARITY

An attempt to avoid such difficulties and to develop a consistent means
of comparing costs and prices internationally, called the *purchasing power
parity (PPP)* theory of exchange rates, evolved during the period between
the two wars.

This theory concludes that the equilibrium rate of exchange between
two national currencies must equalize the "purchasing power" of the two
currencies. If the purchasing power of the U.S. dollar is twice that of the
German mark, then the equilibrium-exchange rate should be $1.00 = DM
2.00. In relative terms, if the purchasing power of one currency declines
compared to that of another, this decline should be reflected in the exchange
rate. For two consecutive time periods, this can be formulated as

$$\frac{R_0}{R_1} = \frac{P_o{}^x}{P_o{}^y} \div \frac{P_1{}^x}{P_1{}^y}$$

where R_0 and R_1 represent the exchange rates prevailing, respectively, in
the base year and the year under consideration.

The term $P_0{}^x/P_1{}^y$ represents the same relationship for the terminal year. It is easy to see that if the price level in one country doubles from the base to the terminal period while that of the other remains the same, the exchange rate should also be doubled.

As an example, assume the original dollar–mark exchange rate was 1:2 in 1975. However, by 1980 the relevant price index in Germany had risen to 250 (1975 = 100), while the corresponding price index in the U.S. advanced only to 180 (1975 = 100). That is, the purchasing power of the mark in 1980 is substantially less than half what is was in 1975, while that of the dollar has been reduced to a level somewhat greater than half that prevailing in the base period. What should be the new equilibrium exchange rate according to the purchasing power parity theory?

It is easy to calculate:

$$\frac{2.00}{R_1} = \frac{100}{100} \div \frac{250}{180}$$
$$R_1 = 2.78$$

That is, the new exchange rate should be $1.00 = DM 2.78 as a result of the decline in the purchasing power of the mark relative to that of the dollar.

The strict purchasing power parity doctrine not only stated that the exchange rate *should* reflect relative currency values; it also stated that it *would* do so if no interferences prevented it. But there are a number of weighty factors that militate against the PPP theory of exchange-rate determination as an analytical tool—despite the obvious appeal to common sense that is inherent in this theory.

First, the exchange rate according to this doctrine should reflect the prices of all goods and services in an economy. Yet only *some* (in some economies, a minority) of these goods and services ever enter international trade in terms of export or import competition. Construction, the majority of services, as well as a host of commodities typically exert an important effect on the domestic price level, yet have no bearing at all on international trade or the market for foreign exchange. Changes in prices of all such goods and services should be reflected in the PPP exchange rate only insofar as they affect the costs and prices of traded goods and services, which is necessarily only partially.

Second, transport costs also will result in price differences of commodities traded internationally. All goods entering international trade will be more expensive in the importing country than in the exporting country by the amount of the freight charges, insurance premiums, and other costs associated with transport.

Third, incomes, tastes, and other factors serve as determinants of international-trade flows in addition to simple price differences. Even if the purchasing power of one currency deteriorates, the balance of trade of that country may actually improve and the exchange rate shift in its favor as a result of factors other than price changes. Moreover, we can assume that price changes correspond to income changes only during periods of full employment and even then only in an upward direction. Only at such times is a rise in monetary incomes likely to be reflected rather fully in the form of a general rise in prices and an equivalent decline in the purchasing power of the national currency.

Fourth, whereas a case can be made for the PPP doctrine as a way of avoiding exchange-rate disturbances of a temporary nature, attributable to short-term capital flows, long-term international capital movements clearly need to be reflected in the exchange rate. For instance, a long-term capital outflow that lasts for a period of years may indeed have to be accompanied by a currency depreciation so that exports will be stimulated sufficiently to bring the balance of payments back into balance.

Fifth, what shall we use as a measure of the national price level? We have a choice of export prices, the gross national product deflator, wholesale prices, retail prices, cost of living indexes, and so forth. None of these precisely fulfill the desired purpose. But even if an acceptable index of prices were discovered, can we be sure that we can find a comparable index for foreign countries? Consumption patterns differ markedly between nations, and entail weighting problems that would make such an index difficult to use.

Sixth, in the real world, myriad restrictions to international trade variously separate the price structure prevailing in one country from those obtaining in others. Hence, the purchasing power parity theory in practice is even further limited as a guide to equilibrium-exchange rates.

Even given these limitations, the PPP theory might be considered a rough indicator of long-term, secular shifts in the equilibrium-exchange rate. Yet, in an age of large-scale, long-term capital flows in varying directions, variable unilateral transfers of large magnitude, and military commitments involving substantial, rigid flows of international payments, even this use of the PPP theory may be lost. In fact, the theory may even prove to be highly misleading about the equilibrium rate of exchange under such conditions.

FORWARD MARKET

Everything we have said about the foreign-exchange market thus far has implied that all transactions in international currencies are consummated immediately; i.e., currencies are sold for immediate delivery at rates of exchange prevailing at the time the transaction is made. But it is also possible to purchase foreign exchange at a certain time for delivery at some *future* date. The market for foreign exchange for immediate delivery—as discussed up to now—is called the *spot market*. The market for foreign exchange for future delivery is termed the *forward market*.

Why would anyone be interested in buying foreign exchange for delivery at some specified future date?

The forces of supply and demand cause the exchange rate, the *spot* rate, to fluctuate in any period of time. During one period the foreign demand for dollars may be strong, or the U.S. demand for foreign currencies weak, and the spot dollar rate advances. During a subsequent time period the reverse may be the case, and the spot dollar rate falls. This variation in spot rates spells one thing for individuals, business firms, and public institutions which must make use of the foreign-exchange market—*uncertainty*.

Suppose an American is due to be paid 1 million German marks in three months' time for exports, as income on loans or investments, or for any other reason. How many dollars will he receive? If the dollar–mark spot rate in three months' time is $1.00 = DM 2.50 he will get $400,000, but if it is $1.00 = DM 2.60 he will receive only $384,615. On the other hand, if the spot dollar–mark exchange rate in three months is $1.00 = DM 2.40, he will receive $416,667, more than he had expected. The normal businessman, or anyone else dealing in foreign-exchange transactions, is usually not willing to take this chance. He has numerous financial commitments, and these make it imperative for him to be able to count on receiving a fixed amount of dollars with certainty.

He may eliminate the uncertainty by making use of the forward market. He simply sells DM 1 million forward. That is, he makes a contract with a foreign-exchange trader to exchange DM 1 million for dollars in three months' time at a specified exchange rate, called the *forward rate*. He "sells" marks forward or, what is the same thing, "buys" forward dollars. If the contract calls for a three-month forward rate of $1.00 = DM 2.55, the American will deliver his million marks at that time and receive in return $392,157. He can now make his financial plans with the certainty that he will receive precisely that amount of dollars. He has hedged his exchange risk—he has secured *forward cover* for his transaction.

What about the foreign-exchange trader? In three months he must deliver the $392,157 and will receive a million marks. If he decides to take on the foreign-exchange risk himself, he must see to it that he is able to exchange a million marks for dollars on the spot market in the meantime at a more favorable rate than that he has given the businessman in the forward contract. Thus, if the spot rate at that time is $1.00 = DM 2.50, the speculator will be able to exchange his million marks for $400,000 spot, deliver $392,157 to the businessman as per the agreement, and earn a profit of $7,843 for himself. If, however, he is faced with a less favorable spot rate, say $1.00 = DM 2.60, he will receive only $384,615 for his million marks, and since he has to deliver $392,157 to the businessman, the trader will make a loss of $7,542 on the transaction. In either case the foreign-exchange trader has assumed the role of speculator.

In reality, the sellers of forward contracts most often are really not speculators at all. They are primarily large international banks which make forward contracts in many currencies, in many directions. Hence, on a given date a large New York bank that may have outstanding 90-day forward contracts to buy 20 million German marks for dollars simultaneously may have an equivalent amount of forward contracts to buy dollars for German marks. It is really not taking any risk. To the extent that a bank covers each forward contract with equivalent forward contracts in the opposite direction, it eliminates uncertainty due to exchange-rate variation. Only if it established a forward *position* in one or more foreign currencies (i.e., its contracts to buy exceed its contracts to sell) does it take a chance and assume the role of exchange-rate speculator. Otherwise, its profits come primarily from fees and spreads between its buying and selling rates.

In short, the forward market permits businessmen and others to hedge, or cover, the foreign-exchange risk in the transfer of anticipated future receipts or payments out of or into foreign currencies. The exchange risk is *transferred* to the dealer in foreign exchange via the forward contract. The dealer may assume the exchange risk himself or he may cover himself. If he assumes the risk, he may or may not make a profit on the transaction, depending upon the relationship of the rate stipulated in the forward contract to the spot rate at which he must ultimately make the exchange.

The foreign-exchange speculators who actually do take a position in foreign currencies (also usually large international banks) attempt to forecast future exchange rates and set the terms of their forward contracts accordingly. In this way, they attempt to minimize the risk of loss and maximize the chance of gain on such transactions. If the speculator feels that a given exchange rate is going to rise, he will sell the affected foreign currency at a *premium,* and if he feels it will fall, he will sell it at a *discount.* If the spot German mark rate is 2.49164 marks per dollar and 90-day forward contracts are being quoted at 2.49092 we say that there exists a premium on 90-day forward marks or, what amounts to the same thing, a discount on 90-day forward dollars.

The forward exchange rate is set in the same way as the spot rate, i.e., via supply and demand. An increase in demand for relative to the supply of forward contracts to buy a given currency will raise the forward rate, while increased forward sales of a currency relative to purchases will lower the forward rate. Only those transactions making use of the forward market, of course, enter into the setting of the forward rate of exchange.

The forward exchange market serves the international economy in several very important ways. As we have already mentioned, it provides business firms and others with a way to hedge against the uncertainty of future exchange rates and thus is of immediate value to them in their day-to-day transactions. But since forward contracts are normally for 30, 60, 90, or 180 days, they do not provide a complete answer because many transactions are of longer duration. It is possible, however, to renew a forward contract and thus extend the time period covered, but the terms of renewal may well be less favorable than those of the original agreement.

The forward market also provides a way for *investors* to avoid the possibility that exchange-rate fluctuations will wipe out part or all of their gains. For instance, an American investing in British debt obligations at £1.00 = $2.40 would suffer substantial loss if he had to convert back to dollars at maturity at a rate of £1.00 = $2.39. A fall in the relative value of the home currency, as in this instance, will always simultaneously reduce home-currency value of assets denominated in foreign currencies. However, the investor can protect himself against this risk via the forward-exchange market. If he decides to buy 90-day British Treasury securities, he need simply sell sterling forward under a 90-day contract. If the effective yield—after deducting the cost of hedging—is still acceptable to him, he can go ahead and make his investment without fear of loss due to exchange-rate variation.

All types of short-term investments can be protected against foreign-exchange losses in this manner, as long as forward contracts are available for the desired period of time. If a currency is likely to be extremely unstable, it may be advisable to bear the probable increased hedging cost of successive renewals of forward contracts even on long term investments abroad.

As we have seen, the forward exchange market provides an opportunity for speculators to profit from dealings in foreign currencies. This is also possible, of course, on the spot market. For instance, a British resident may buy 1 million pounds worth of Dutch guilders at today's exchange rate and take a position in that currency, hoping that the rate will fall and the pound sterling depreciate in terms of the guilder. If this happens, he sells his guilders for pounds sterling on the spot market at an appropriate future date and clears a tidy profit. He holds foreign currencies, or more probably assets denominated in foreign currencies, with the sole hope that the spot exchange rate will turn in his favor.

Forward exchange speculation naturally differs from speculation on the spot market. If a speculator believes, for example, that the value of Swiss francs will rise in the near future in terms of dollars, he would do well to buy Swiss francs forward for dollars, and take a position in that currency. If the franc rate indeed does go up, he sells the francs he receives at maturity of the forward contract on the spot market at the new, higher exchange rate, settles his contract in dollars at the old forward rate, and realizes a profit. Speculators thus establish forward positions in foreign exchange which are really no different from the spot positions held by banks and others in foreign currencies.

Non-bank speculators in forward exchange often find it difficult to secure the speculative forward contracts they desire. The reason is simple. They must deal with another type of speculator, the banks, who have access to exactly the same information on the relative strength of foreign currencies as they do. Hence, the banks are understandably reluctant to enter into a forward contract for purely speculative purposes and possibly take a loss in the bargain, if they find it impossible to secure forward cover. However, business firms and others who regularly make use of the forward market for legitimate *defensive* reasons are often tempted to use it for purely speculative purposes as well.

COVERED INTEREST ARBITRAGE

The relationship between exchange rates prevailing on the spot and forward markets is largely determined by what is known as *interest arbitrage*. Short-term capital movements are highly sensitive to international differences in yields on short-term securities. Suppose the U.S. Treasury bill rate is 8½ per cent and the rate on U.K. Treasury bills is 10 per cent. Given a choice between these two obligations of substantially equal quality, the investor in U.S. Treasuries would immediately desire to sell them, buy the U.K. Treasuries, and claim the 1½ per cent higher yield. But things are not quite that simple.

In order to buy U.K. Treasury bills, the investor must first buy British pounds sterling on the spot market. Moreover, in order to cover himself against the risk of exchange-rate variations he should sell sterling forward, so that he is certain of the number of dollars he will receive when the U.K. Treasuries mature. The *effective* yield differential is thus the apparent differential of 1½ per cent *minus* the cost of hedging. The higher the cost of hedging, the lower the effective yield differential, and the smaller the incentive for the investor to switch from U.S. to U.K. Treasury bills.

Suppose we let R_s represent the spot rate of exchange and R_f stand for the forward rate of exchange. If an investor buys spot and sells 90-day forward exchange his gain or loss expressed as a percentage on an annual basis[1] will be

$$F = \frac{R_s - R_f}{R_s} \times 4.$$

This must be taken into account when the investor computes the net yield on 90-day foreign securities. The yield *differential* between domestic and foreign securities will thus be

$$I = i_f - i_d - F$$

where I is the yield *incentive* to invest abroad i_f is the foreign yield, i_d is the comparable domestic yield, and F is the hedging differential computed above.

Let us follow an example through and see what happens. Assume initially the prevailing spot *and* forward sterling–dollar rates are

£1.00 = $2.40

and U.S. Treasuries go for a yield of 8½ per cent and U.K. Treasuries for 10 per cent. The effective, fully hedged yield differential is thus 1½ per cent (in terms of the above equation),

$$I = i_f - i_d - F = .10 - .085 - 0 = .015$$

Immediately, investors would sell their U.S. Treasury bills, buy spot sterling, sell sterling forward, and buy U.K. Treasury bills.

The large-scale selling of U.S. Treasuries would tend to drive their price down and thereby raise U.S. yields. Large-scale purchases of spot sterling drives up the spot rate, while simultaneous equivalent sales of forward sterling drive down the forward rate. In short, the spread between the spot and the forward rate widens and the cost of hedging rises. Meanwhile, the large-scale purchases of U.K. Treasuries has driven up their price and lowered the U.K. yield.

What has happened? The yield on U.S. Treasury bills has risen and the yield on U.K. Treasury has fallen, while the cost of forward cover has increased. The *effective yields* (I) on the two securities have been equalized. The term i_f has fallen, i_d has risen, and F has taken on a value equal to $i_f - i_d$, the spread between the spot and forward exchange rates has widened sufficiently to offset any remaining yield differential.

---

[1] For 60-day contracts, it would thus be $F = \dfrac{R_s - R_f}{R_s} \times 6$, for 30-day contracts $F = \dfrac{R_s - R_f}{R_s} \times 12$, and so forth, always converting the spot-forward differential to an annual percentage rate. A more precise statement of the mathematics of covered interest arbitrage can be found in Leland B. Yeager, *International Monetary Relations* (New York: Harper & Row, 1966).

This can be very nicely demonstrated in general terms in a diagram, such as Figure 18–3, using short-term money rates. Initially, supply and demand are in equilibrium on both the spot and the forward foreign-exchange markets at £1.00 = $2.40. In the U.S. the supply of short-term, 90-day loanable funds equals the demand at a yield of 8.5 per cent; the prevailing yield for the U.K. is 10 per cent. Since there is no cost of hedg-

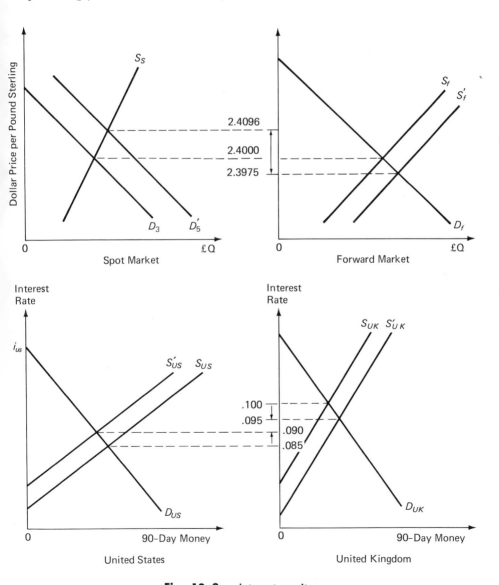

Fig. 18–3.   **Interest parity.**

ing, the initial effective yield differential on 90-day money is 1.5 per cent. The voluminous sales of U.S. short-term assets are reflected as a shift in the loanable funds supply curve S_{us} to the left (S'_{us}). The price of short-term financial assets falls and the yield rises to 9.0 per cent. Simultaneously, the increased demand for U.K. short-term assets is represented as a shift in the loanable funds supply curve S_{uk} to the right (S'_{uk}), a rise in the price of the British securities, and a decline in their yield to 9.5 per cent.

On the foreign-exchange market, the increased demand for spot sterling raises the spot rate to 2.6751, while the simultaneously increased supply of forward sterling lowers the forward rate to 2.3407. The effective, fully hedged yield differential has changed from 1½ per cent to zero.[2]

Interest arbitrage, then, provides a tying link between the forward and spot exchange rates. The wider the short-term yield differential on comparable securities between two countries, the wider is likely to be the spread between the forward and spot rates of exchange. If yields on domestic short-term securities exceed those available abroad, the domestic currency is likely to sell forward at a premium relative to spot rate; conversely, short-term yields abroad in excess of prevailing domestic yields will tend to cause the home currency to sell at a discount on the forward market.

This can be illustrated even more clearly with the help of Figure 18-4. The vertical axis measures the apparent interest-rate differential for comparable securities between the domestic financial market and a given foreign money center. This differential may be positive ($i_d < i_f$) or negative ($i_f < i_d$). The horizontal axis measures the discount or premium on forward sales of the currency of the relevant foreign money center. If there is a discount ($-$), obtaining forward cover involves a cost (capital loss); if there is a premium ($+$), obtaining forward cover involves a capital gain. The diagonal, the *interest-parity line*, depicts all possible combinations of interest-rate differentials and comparable hedging losses/gains where the one exactly balances out the other and interest-parity is achieved.

Our earlier example assumed a 1½ per cent interest differential in favor of the U.K. and the same spot and forward dollar–sterling exchange rate—i.e., zero cost of hedging—represented by point A in Figure 18-4. We thus have an incentive to move funds out of the U.S. and into the U.K., the nominal interest differential narrows and the cost of hedging becomes positive; that is, point **A** moves toward the interest-parity line, and eventually falls on it. Indeed, any point to the right of the interest-parity line will trigger a *capital outflow,* and set in motion forces that will tend to restore interest parity.

[2] Computed as follows:

$$F = \frac{R_s - R_f}{R_s} \times 4 = \frac{2.6751 - 2.3407}{2.6751} \times 4 = 0.5,$$

and $I = i_f - i_d - F = .095 - .090 - .005 = 0.$

At point B in Figure 18–4, we have the opposite example. There is a 2 per cent nominal interest differential in favor of the home country, to which is added a 1 per cent gain from hedging (viewed from abroad). Hence a net capital inflow will develop, domestic interest rates will rise, foreign interest rates fall, and the net cost of hedging will grow until point B falls on the interest-parity line. Any point to the left of the interest-parity line will trigger a *capital inflow* into the home country.

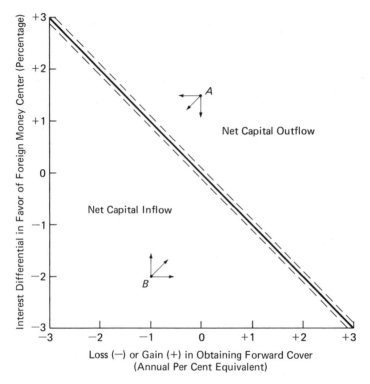

Fig. 18–4.   Covered interest arbitrage.

Two further points. First, note that restoration of interest parity may involve *only* changes in domestic and foreign interest rate (vertical movement of points A/B), or *only* changes in the net cost of hedging (horizontal movement of points A/B), or some combination. A glance at Figure 18–3 will confirm that the degree of adjustment that occurs in the capital markets, relative to that taken up by the foreign-exchange markets, depends on the relevant demand and supply elasticities in the four markets. Second, selling and buying securities and national currencies involves costs, and so the interest-arbitrage "line" in Figure 18–4 is actually a band, whose width indicates *market efficiency,* or transaction costs.

The discount, or premium, on forward exchange will not necessarily always equal the difference in short-term yields. In the first place, some investors will buy short-term securities abroad on an unhedged basis. They will buy spot foreign currency and use it to purchase foreign bills without, at the same time, selling the foreign currency forward to cover the transaction. Such investors are speculating in the foreign-exchange market *while* they are taking advantage of international yield differentials. They gamble that when the securities mature the foreign currency will sell *spot* at a higher rate than it sells *forward* when they purchase these securities. Unhedged transactions such as these, in terms of Figure 18–3, raise domestic yields, lower foreign yields, and raise the cost of spot foreign exchange. But they fail to lower the forward rate, since they do not involve forward cover, and hence the link between spot and forward rates is partially broken.

There is no single rate in each country that can be singled out as the applicable "short-term yield" in the interest arbitrage relation specified here. Interest rates vary for a host of different types of short-term obligations, such as commercial paper, certificates of deposit, treasury bills, and so on. Hence, interest parity may not always be maintained, and some minimum deviation from it may be necessary before arbitrage transactions take place.

Some investors might simply find it more convenient to maintain their funds in a given money market even at the clear opportunity cost of not investing at higher short-term yields elsewhere. If this is true, then such investors add to present and obtained yields some subjective "convenience" yield which in their minds equalizes returns between two money markets. Hence, they have no incentive to engage in interest arbitrage, even though an objective incentive in terms of the existence of a covered yield differential actually exists.

Moreover, monetary authorities may in some manner prohibit interest arbitrage. They may partially or entirely forbid the purchase of foreign securities by domestic residents for balance of payments reasons—to stem a short-term capital outflow, for example. Then, forward transactions will arise largely or completely out of regular commercial dealings. It is hardly likely that supply and demand for forward exchange arising out of such transactions will result in interest parity. Moreover, the hedging function of the foreign-exchange market may be impaired by such investment restrictions.

We must assume that the flows of funds out of the securities and currency of one country and into the short-term securities and currency of another will be strong enough to affect both the spot and forward exchange rates. This assumption may not always hold true because, for political and other reasons, investors in one country may not be willing to place their funds abroad no matter what the yield differential. They may even be unaware of the investment opportunities available abroad, or frightened off by the prospect of various legal formalities, and the reporting of funds outflows to the government. Or, sufficient funds to take advantage of interest arbitrage opportunities simply may not be available for credit rationing or other reasons. In such cases the international short-term capital flows may be insufficient to affect interest parity rates of exchange on the spot and forward markets.

Finally, we should consider speculation. If one currency is considered weak, large-scale short-term capital outflows will occur, and *both* the spot and the forward exchange rates will depreciate. Interest arbitrage no longer is the force establishing the relation between the spot and forward rates. Rather, the forward discount on the weak currency becomes little more than an indication of the strength of that currency; i.e., the greater the forward discount, the weaker the currency.

By way of summary, interest arbitrage under a system of flexible exchange rates closely links the forward and spot foreign-exchange markets, though not always perfectly. Unless somehow impeded or otherwise rendered ineffective, interest arbitrage will ensure that the fully hedged yield on foreign short-term securities will approximately equal that available on domestic securities. Spot or forward exchange transactions originating from some other source, which disturb the interest parity relationship between domestic and foreign yields and spot and forward exchange rates, will tend to set in motion capital flows which restore that relationship. Nonetheless, there are a variety of factors that impede interest arbitrage so that the relationship between forward and spot foreign exchange rates and international yield differentials is by no means perfect.

THE EURODOLLAR MARKET

A peculiar development that has arisen in recent years is the creation of substantial foreign markets for U.S. dollars and other currencies. Foreign banks—typically in Continental Europe, Great Britain, Japan, and Canada—will accept deposits denominated in U.S. dollars, thereby incurring dollar liabilities to the depositors. The depositors may be Americans, but often they are foreigners holding dollars that they may have acquired in the normal course of business in the U.S. The foreign banks receiving these short-term dollar deposits then make dollar loans to various types of borrowers. These loans are also generally short-term in nature. Interestingly enough, the Eurodollar market seems to have had its beginning as a result of some Eastern European banks rather than with U.S. banks. Stimulated by the restoration of full nonresident currency convertibility in 1958, and the imposition of several selective restrictions on international capital transactions by European governments and the U.S., the Eurodollar market grew rapidly. At the end of 1964, about $9 billion in Eurodollar deposits were estimated to exist. By 1969 this had grown to an estimated $37.5 billion. Offshore markets for other national currency-denominated deposits also emerged, and by the end of 1972 total *Eurocurrency* deposits were estimated to have reached $91 billion! How, exactly, does the Eurodollar market work?

Suppose a European bank has $10 million in dollar deposits at a given point in time. In reality, these represent $10 million in deposits in American banks, the ownership of which has been transfered to the European bank by the Eurodollar depositors. The bank may retain $1 million of this as reserves and extend $9 million, the remainder, as short-term dollar loans. The borrowers now have claim to the $9 million of deposits in American banks. What has happened? The initial Eurodollar depositors have claim to $10 million in deposits, and the Eurodollar borrowers have claim to another $9 million, for a total of $19 million in claims. If the Eurodollar borrowings, in turn, end up as Eurodollar deposits, the total dollar claims based on the initial deposit will expand still further. The result may be a "pyramiding" of Eurodollars that may render the whole system somewhat vulnerable because of the possibility of leakages out of the European banks, since there is no guarantee that Eurodollars will continue to be held in U.S. banks.

Yields on Eurodollar deposits frequently exceed those available on deposits in the U.S. itself. Also, by paying interest on very short-term deposits, European banks have attracted funds that otherwise would have gone into noninterest-bearing demand deposits. By operating on very small margins, Eurodollar lending rates have been relatively attractive, and much of the lending has actually been done in the U.S. or has involved U.S. firms operating abroad. In fact, American firms have been active in the Eurodollar on both the lending and borrowing side. They may be able to lend Eurodollars at higher rates and borrow them at lower rates than are available at home. In a very real sense, the Eurodollar market thus competes directly with U.S. domestic financial markets on both the deposit and loan sides of the financial picture.

Eurodollars, of course, may be converted into foreign currencies in the normal manner and used for interest-arbitrage purposes or to pay off other dollar or foreign-currency debts, to finance trade, and so forth. The result has been a distinct increase in the degree of money-market competition internationally, a notable convergence of domestic and foreign yields, and a heightened degree of international monetary–policy interdependence.

Eurodollars may reduce the need for international liquidity, since a large volume of international transactions can be financed by a set amount of dollar deposits with a lessened need for official reserve financing. Moreover, their use may result in a bolstering of the existing international monetary system by making it relatively less attractive for foreigners to convert their dollar balances into other currencies, and thus eventually resting in the hordes of foreign central banks with the potential for conversion to gold.

On the debit side, the pyramiding effect and the added vulnerability Eurodollars contribute may partly offset these possibly beneficial aspects. As another possibly deleterious effect, the existence of Eurodollars opens up a highly effective means to circumvent national interest rate limits and capital-transfer restrictions on international transactions. If the U.S. government decided to limit capital outflows, there is nothing to prevent dollar deposits abroad, since the deposits are never actually withdrawn from American banks.

Whatever the effects of the Eurodollar market, and the foreign markets in other currencies as well, there seems to be little doubt that they will be a lasting fixture of the international monetary scene—with implications for the balance of payments, international liquidity, and monetary policy.

CREDIT AND THE FOREIGN-EXCHANGE MARKET

The foreign-exchange market acts as a vehicle for the financing of exports and imports, in addition to its contribution as a way of hedging against exchange risks. As in any type of commercial exchange involving the movement of goods from the seller to the purchaser, international trade requires that financing be available during this interim period. Often, the purchaser is not the ultimate buyer at all, and he may demand that he be granted payment terms which allow him to resell the goods and be paid first himself. The goods must be financed in the meantime, regardless of who does the financing.

In international trade, credit transactions can take on a variety of forms. The exporter may give the importer 30-, 60-, or 90-day terms—or even longer—during which time the importer sells the goods, is paid for them, and pays off the exporter on the due date. Of course, the exporter himself may be financed in such a transaction, either by a bank or by one or more of his own suppliers. On the other hand, it is not at all uncommon for the importer to finance the exporter by making an advance payment on the transaction. Even if the transaction is for "cash" someone finances it; the exporter if it is shipped cash on delivery, and the importer if payment is made as the goods leave the exporter's premises.

Normally such financing is done by banks either on the exporter or the importer's side, or even by banks located in third countries. Who does the financing is determined largely by relative interest rates prevailing in the different countries for the time period over which a trade credit is desired. In many countries this is done by means of the *bankers' acceptance*. An acceptance is nothing more than a promise to pay which is guaranteed by a bank. Even if the importer defaults, the bank must pay. By "accepting" this promise to pay, the bank renders it a negotiable instrument which can then be sold to any lender at prevailing money market rates.

Suppose an American firm has signed a contract to deliver 50,000 airplane models to a Swedish importer on ninety-day terms. He has no desire or ability to finance the transaction himself. He merely requests the Swedish importer to have his bank issue a *letter of credit* in his favor, which authorizes the exporter to draw one or more bills on that bank for the amount stipulated in the contract. Once he receives the letter of credit, the exporter ships the goods and draws up a bill on the importer. This bill, along with shipping, insurance, and other documents, is sent to the Swedish bank which accepts it and thereby guarantees payment in 90 days. The exporter may now sell the acceptance to the Swedish bank, a U.S. bank, or any other money-market investor at a discount reflecting the prevailing short-term interest rate. The exporter receives his money, and the transaction is financed by some third party—the ultimate buyer of the bankers' acceptance. The accepting bank receives a fee for its payment guarantee which is generally paid by the importer.

Necessarily, there are many variations on this type of bankers' acceptance financing. The accepting bank and the ultimate lender may be in the country of the exporter or of the importer, or in a third country. Moreover, acceptance financing is also employed—with some differences—in capital transactions. The precise pattern of the financing itself is generally dependent, as noted above, upon relative short-term interest rates. In each case, the importer must see to it that he sells foreign currency in which payment is specified forward to hedge against the exchange risk. Or, if payment is stipulated in the currency of the importer, it is the acceptance holder who must take this step.

Besides bankers' acceptance financing of foreign transactions, any time a bill of exchange is drawn on the importer—whether or not it is accepted by a bank—it involves an extension of credit. The importer may accept it himself, and if there is a market for *commercial acceptances,* it may be discounted in the money market just as in the case of the bankers' acceptance. Or the exporter's bank may hold the bill of exchange to maturity, or as yet another alternative, the exporter may have to hold it himself and finance the transaction.

Finally, *open book accounts* may be used to finance foreign trade between businesses extremely well known to each other, and where the importer is considered highly credit-worthy. The exporter simply ships the goods on 30-, 60-, or perhaps 90-day terms and sends an invoice to the importer. He then adds to his "accounts receivable" the amount of the invoice and waits for payment. The exporter grants the credit, although he himself may be financed on a working capital basis by a bank.

In contrast, *sight bills* and drafts involve no extension of credit over and above the time it takes for the bill to reach the importer and for payment to be received by the exporter. Normally the goods will be shipped by the exporter, and as evidence of this the shipping company will give a *bill of lading* and connected documents to the exporter. The latter will then send this bill of lading, via his bank and its correspondent in the importing country, to the importer along with a sight bill for payment of the agreed-upon amount. Upon paying this bill the importer receives the bill of lading and can claim his goods when they arrive. Who finances, or owns, the goods while they are in transit? This depends upon the point in time that the sight bill is presented to the importer for payment. If this occurs right after the goods are shipped, the importer finances them in transit. If the bill is presented for payment just before the goods arrive, the exporter finances them during this time interval. All sight transactions naturally do not involve an exchange risk, as do time transactions, and hence do not require any dealings in forward exchange. Because payment is generally accomplished via air mail, the applicable exchange rate is close to the spot, or "cable" rate.

19

INTERNATIONAL MONETARY STANDARDS

EXCHANGE STANDARDS

Having studied the foreign-exchange market with regard to its hedging and credit functions, as well as the establishment of spot and forward exchange rates and how they may or may not reflect prices, costs, and interest rates internationally, it remains for us now to survey briefly the various different systems under which the exchange rate is determined. This is in preparation for our subsequent discussion of balance of payments adjustment for which the prevailing exchange standard is of determining importance.

FLEXIBLE RATES

Our discussion thus far has implicitly assumed the existence of *flexible exchange rates*.[1] The rate of exchange of one currency for another has been considered to be determined solely by supply and demand arising out of a variety of commercial and financial transactions.

Under these conditions, the exchange rate is free to move up and down, reflecting changes in supply and demand, just as the price of any commodity

---

[1] We shall define flexible exchange rates—along with most other writers—to mean that the rate of exchange is completely unrestricted in responding freely to shifts in the supply of and demand for foreign exchange. This is assumed to hold true for both the spot and forward markets. All government intervention in the foreign-exchange markets is absent. Some writers variously term flexible exchange rates "freely fluctuating," "free," or "freely flexible." This terminological divergence is too often a source of confusion for students and experts alike.

in a free market mirrors demand and supply shifts. The relative elasticities of foreign-exchange supply and demand determine the sensitivity of the exchange rate to any such shifts. The less elastic the supply of foreign exchange, the greater will be the change in the rate as a result of a given shift in the demand for foreign exchange. Similarly, the less elastic the demand for foreign exchange, the more pronounced the response of the exchange rate to a given shift in supply.

Since any change in the demand for and supply of foreign exchange is free to affect the exchange rate unchecked, it may be that flexible exchange rates are prey to instability. Suppose, under flexible exchange rates, speculators feel that the dollar will in the near future depreciate relative to the Dutch guilder. They will thus want to convert dollars into guilders as soon as possible. Dutch speculators bring their dollar balances home, while U.S. and foreign speculators "take a position" in the guilder, uncovered of course. The resulting spot sale of dollars for guilders may indeed cause the dollar to depreciate relative to the guilder, and the expectations of the speculators may have been verified thereby.

Yet the basic economic forces—trade in goods and services and non-speculative capital flows—may not have warranted such a depreciation of the dollar in terms of the *equilibrium* exchange rate. The speculators may eventually realize their error, and the flow of speculative short-term capital may then be reversed. The dollar once again appreciates relative to the guilder.

This is called *destabilizing speculation*. Speculators' *expectations* in the above example at first caused a depreciation of the dollar, and then reversed themselves with a similar appreciation of the dollar. The danger that this will repeat itself must be considered. In the process, the exchange rate may be subject to substantial fluctuations around a hypothetical equilibrium rate. To the extent that flexible exchange rates are subject to some measure of instability due to such speculative flows—*which is by no means certain*—a number of undesirable effects may be incurred.

International trade may be impeded by increasing the uncertainty involved in credit transactions. Widespread speculation against the dollar, for example, may under flexible exchange rates cause the forward market for dollars to dry up fairly quickly. Few will want to buy forward dollars at a time when a marked depreciation is in the offing, yet everyone wants to sell dollars forward. The resulting discount on forward dollars may become sufficiently large so that an effective forward market may no longer exist. The reverse may hold true when speculation turns in the opposite direction. On the other hand, monetary authorities may be able to offset this by promoting the forward markets.

In either case, international trade may be impeded. If indeed forward facilities do shrink, so does the possibility for traders to hedge against the exchange risk. Alternatively, the forward market may become so narrow and the cost of hedging so high that international commercial transactions are similarly impeded.

Exchange rate instability may also impede international capital flows, although this is much less certain. The possibility of obtaining forward cover for short-term capital transactions may, under certain conditions, be eliminated or made much more costly. The opportunity for interest arbitrage may thus be narrowed, and hence the connecting link between foreign and domestic money markets may be broken. Long-term investments may become somewhat sporadic under these conditions. Capital outflows, as well as repayments and redemptions, may then occur primarily at times when the exchange rate is favorable.

Speculation in this form may prove to be harmful to international trade and capital flows, if it can be shown to be destabilizing in nature. Speculation can also, however, be stabilizing. To the extent that speculators' expectations of shifts in the equilibrium exchange rate correctly anticipate such shifts, their actions will serve to stabilize the exchange rate.

Let us take an example of *stabilizing speculation*. Suppose at the existing exchange rate Dutch exports are relatively cheap in the U.S., while American goods are relatively expensive in Holland so that the guilder is temporarily *undervalued* with respect to the dollar. Sooner or later increases in the U.S. quantity of Dutch goods demanded and a reduction in the amount of American goods demanded in Holland will bring about a depreciation of the dollar relative to the guilder. If speculators expect this to happen, they will quickly shift funds from the U.S. to Holland and accelerate the dollar depreciation that would have occurred somewhat later anyway.

On the other hand, if a given exchange rate appreciation or depreciation is only temporary, as a result of extraordinary factors—particularly noneconomic forces—a reverse flow of speculative capital will return the exchange rate to its original level and thereby serve as a stabilizing agent.

Stabilizing speculation under flexible exchange rates serves a positive purpose. It decreases exchange rate fluctuations and hence diminishes the foreign-exchange risk involved in international trade and capital transactions. To the extent that speculators' expectations of the equilibrium exchange rate are correct, speculation will be stabilizing and constructive.

The question of whether, under a flexible exchange rate system, speculation will indeed be stabilizing or destabilizing will concern us in more detail later on, in connection with flexible exchange rates as an alternative international monetary standard.

GOVERNMENT STABILIZATION

Suppose it is decided that flexible exchange rates will contribute excessive instability to the international economy—whether this concern is justified or not is of no importance for the moment—and yet the inherent advantages of having the exchange rate respond to underlying demand and supply forces is clearly recognized. Is there a way to retain the advantages of flexible rates without incurring their real or imagined disadvantages? Exchange-rate stabilization via minimal government intervention in the foreign exchange markets provides one answer.

An agency may be delegated in each country—the central bank, treasury, or an exchange stabilization fund especially set up for the purpose—to prevent "excessive" exchange rate fluctuations. This agency may hold large amounts of gold, foreign currencies, and the domestic currency. If an undesired depreciation of the domestic currency is in the offing, the agency simply buys large amounts of the home currency in the foreign-exchange markets for an equivalent amount of foreign currencies. It may operate on both the spot and forward markets. In the process, it bolsters the exchange rate and prevents the undesired depreciation from occurring. Later it may replenish its stock of foreign currencies by very gradually selling the domestic currency on the foreign-exchange markets, in order not to disturb the exchange rate. If an unwanted appreciation of the domestic currency is in the offing, the exchange stabilization agency simply acts in reverse, selling the home currency for foreign currencies and depressing the exchange rate, eliminating its excess foreign currency holdings later on by gradual conversion on the exchange markets.

In this way, if the exchange stabilization agency does its work well, the responsiveness of flexible exchange rates to basic supply and demand forces is unimpeded, while the potentially harmful effects of destabilizing speculation are avoided.

There is a danger, nonetheless, that the exchange rate maintained via government intervention may be artificially high or low. However, the ability of the exchange stabilization agency to maintain rates that are inconsistent with market supply and demand forces is presumably limited by its own stocks of foreign currencies and other reserve assets, and by its ability to borrow these from other countries. A currency under heavy downward pressure thus can only be bolstered by government action as long as it does not run out of reserves. Similarly, there is presumably a limit to the amount of reserves that such an agency would be willing to accumulate in the process of attempting to restrain the exchange rate of a currency under upward pressure.

Speculative capital flows still exist as before, except that now speculators must try to guess what the exchange stabilization agency will do. If they expect the stabilizing agency to let the exchange rate slide, based on a presumed belief on its part that a depreciation is warranted, their actions will hasten the exchange-rate shift. If they are not correct, either because a depreciation is unwarranted or because the stabilization agency feels that it is, their actions will place the exchange stabilization agency under heavy pressure. For this reason, exchange stabilizing action would be undertaken in complete secrecy, avoiding any hint of official exchange-rate policy.

Official stabilization of the exchange rate can be shown graphically, as in Figure 19–1. Suppose the initial equilibrium exchange rate is R_1 at point E. The government decides that the exchange rate should not exceed R_3 or go below R_2, as a result of speculative capital flows and as long as equilibrium rate R_1 holds. When the rate reaches R_3, due to speculative capital outflows and speculative decline in capital inflows,

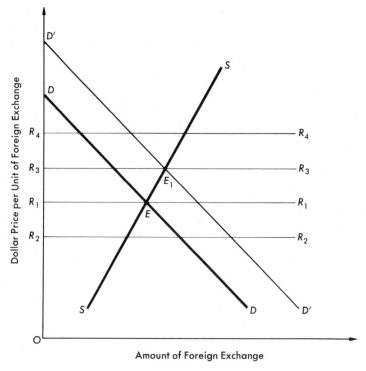

Fig. 19–1. Exchange-rate stabilization.

the exchange stabilizing agency enters the foreign-exchange market and buys all amounts of the domestic currency offered to it at that rate, thus preventing the home currency from depreciating any further. The supply curve of foreign exchange therefore becomes horizontal at that point—R_3 instead of SS. No matter how large the speculative capital outflows are, once that rate is reached, the exchange rate will not exceed R_3. Similarly, if speculation causes the domestic currency to appreciate and the exchange rate falls, the government will intervene at exchange rate R_2, with unlimited purchases of foreign currency for foreign currencies. Hence the demand for foreign currencies becomes horizontal at that point (R_2 instead of DD)—speculative capital inflows and reductions in capital outflows will not be able to depress the exchange rate below R_2.

Suppose that the demand for foreign goods and services increases, so that the demand for foreign exchange shifts from DD to $D'D'$. The new equilibrium rate of exchange is now R_4 at point E_1. Presumably the government will now establish new maximum and minimum rates of exchange, R_1 (minimum) and R_4 (maximum), at which it will intervene in the foreign-exchange market. If this is done, exchange stabilization does not impede the basic adaptability of flexible exchange rates to changing economic conditions. The question is, of course, whether the government will permit this depreciation of the home currency, and even if it does, whether it will be able to distinguish between speculative and nonspeculative financial flows.

THE GOLD STANDARD

In contrast to flexible exchange rates, the value of each national currency under the gold standard is fixed in terms of gold. Each currency is defined as so many fine ounces of gold of standard purity. Whether the currency itself is gold, or whether it is merely fully or partially backed by gold is immaterial. What is important is that the government be willing to buy and sell gold for the national currency freely to everyone and in unlimited quantities. If the U.S. government buys and sells unlimited quantities of gold for dollars at $35.00 per fine ounce, while the German government does the same at DM 70.00 per fine ounce, obviously the exchange rate can only be $1.00 = DM 2.00—provided, that is, gold can be freely transported internationally.

The exchange rate under the gold standard—*the mint rate*—is equivalent to the gold content of one currency relative to that of another. Suppose, returning to the above example, the dollar–mark rate in New York is $1.00 = DM 2.05. An enterprising individual could take $1,000,000, convert it to 2,050,000 marks in New York, ship them to Germany, and buy gold at DM 70 per ounce which he could then resell in New York for $1,012,500 (at $35 per ounce) for a profit of $12,500. Of course, we must qualify this to the extent that there are certain shipping and insurance charges involved in transporting the gold. In point of fact, under the gold standard the exchange rate between two currencies cannot vary above or below the mint rate by more than the cost of shipping gold from one country to the other. Any variation in excess of this shipping cost will be met by large-scale gold flows, which will effectively maintain the exchange rate within these limits.

This can be easily demonstrated with the aid of Figure 19–2. Curve

DD' defines the U.S. demand for pounds sterling, and *SS'* represents the British supply of pounds sterling (the British demand for dollars). The mint rate is £1.00 = $2.40, and it costs $0.02 to ship £1.00 worth of gold from the U.S. to Britain, and vice versa. Hence, any exchange rate that differs from the mint rate by more than the cost of transferring gold ($2.40 ± $0.02) is untenable.

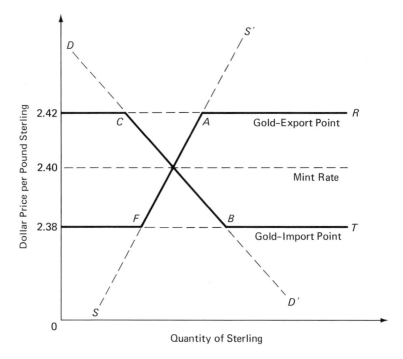

Fig. 19–2. Gold-standard variation in exchange rates.

Suppose an increase in the U.S. demand for pounds sterling or a reduction in the British demand for American dollars (reduced supply of sterling) were to drive the rate up in New York. The exchange rate would reach $2.42, the *gold export point,* at which it becomes profitable to ship gold to England in exchange for pounds-sterling at the mint rate there. The exchange rate would therefore never exceed this figure. Similarly, a reduced American demand for sterling or an increased British demand for dollars (supply of sterling) could never drive the exchange rate below £1.00 = $2.38. At that exchange rate—the *gold import point*—it becomes profitable to buy gold in London with pounds and ship it to New York for sale in dollars at the U.S. mint rate. Hence the demand curve for sterling becomes $VCBT$, and the supply curve for sterling becomes $WFAR$, instead of DD' and SS', respectively. The cost of shipping defines the limits beyond which the exchange rate cannot move.

Because the limits to exchange-rate variation under the gold standard are so narrow, we can talk in terms of a *fixed* exchange rate. As opposed to flexible rates, even after considering government stabilization programs, the gold standard provides international payments with an atmosphere of *certainty*. There is no such thing as destabilizing speculation because, as everyone knows including the speculators, the exchange rate cannot possibly vary above or below the gold export and import points. Moreover, because under the gold standard international gold flows tend to have a direct bearing on the domestic money supply, short-term capital flows will tend to move in the opposite direction from prevailing gold flows. But we shall return to this point in the following chapter.

PEGGED EXCHANGE RATES

Most students of economics and history are well aware of the fate of the gold standard during the depression years of the 1930's. We will have the opportunity of discovering a little later why its basic strength—stability—proved to be its fatal weakness as a viable basis for the international monetary system. Today, the supply of most national currencies is no longer tied to the national stock of gold. National monetary authorities control the domestic money supply and regulate its value more or less at will, consistent with national economic policy. National monetary stocks are today essentially composed of fiat money.

Internationally, there would appear to be no problem in applying flexible exchange rates to this system and permitting the forces of supply and demand to regulate the relative value of national currencies, with perhaps some minimal stabilization by the government to prevent abrupt, short-term variations in the exchange rate which might prove deleterious. But, it can be argued, the degree of stability provided by this sort of arrangement may well be insufficient. What may be needed is the stability of the gold standard without its rigidity. One answer is provided by *pegged* exchange rates.

Under such a system, the value of the national currency is set in terms of gold or the currency of one or more other countries—whatever the individual country considers to comprise its means of international payment. Hence, even though gold has little relation to today's dollar, the U.S. Treasury still offers—with some reluctance—to trade unlimited quantities of gold with foreign official monetary institutions at a fixed price $35.00 per fine ounce. Other countries also set the value of their currencies in terms of gold, or in terms of one of the currencies that it uses to finance international transactions—generally one which is tied to gold.

Exchange rates are thus officially pegged by monetary authorities. Although they are permitted to fluctuate within prescribed limits with supply and demand, any potential variation outside these limits is met by official stabilization action and, if it becomes evident that the current exchange rate peg is untenable, by *devaluation* or *upward revaluation* of the currency to a new peg.

Pegged exchange rates thus combine some of the rigid stability of the gold standard with the possibility of variation with market forces that lies at the heart of flexible rates. As we shall see in substantial detail later on, pegged exchange rates are by their very nature a compromise and constitute the source of a great deal of difficulty in international monetary relations. We bring them up here only by way of introduction.

FLOATING EXCHANGE RATES

In the early 1970's the term "floating" came into widespread use. Floating really is nothing more than exchange-rate flexibility. Hence, given our previous discussion which covered everything from absolutely fixed to completely flexible and market-determined rates of exchange, all we need do here is fit the terminology to the concepts.

Clean floating refers to essentially flexible exchange rates with no government intervention in foreign-exchange markets.

Dirty floating, also called "managed floating," is the same as government stabilization of exchange rates, discussed above. The degree of "dirtiness" depends on the amount of intervention that is undertaken to maintain disequilibrium rates, either as a stabilization measure or—more particularly—to maintain an artificially low exchange rate designed to encourage exports and discourage imports. Benchmark exchange rates from which "true" stabilization activity is undertaken are often called *central rates.*

Interim floating refers to an agreed system of pegged exchange rates under which, instead of undertaking discrete administrative currency revaluations or devaluations when needed, the currency is simply cut loose to find its own level in the market. When that level has been found, the currency is repegged.

Bloc-floating relates to an agreement among a select group of countries to peg exchange rates *within* the bloc to relatively narrow limits, but to let the bloc-currencies *as a group* float relatively cleanly against nonmember currencies. This is often called the "snake-in-a-tunnel," with the member currencies (the snake) undulating modestly within the winding "tunnel"— the bloc against third currencies. The technique was attempted most notably in the 1970's by the EEC countries as a stepping-stone toward Common Market monetary unification, albeit with limited success.

EXCHANGE CONTROL

All of the alternative exchange systems discussed thus far are based largely on the operation of market supply and demand, combined with greater or lesser degrees of government interference. In each case, however, this interference was designed largely to neutralize disorderly aspects of the foreign-exchange market and thereby to help facilitate the operation of more basic demand and supply aspects of international economic and financial relations. Each system permitted price to allocate foreign exchange. As a final system of exchange rates, we need to introduce at this point one which is diametrically opposed to all of the others. The reader will recall that, in connection with commercial policy, we mentioned *exchange control* as a possible protective device. Actually, exchange control is much broader in its impact than is mere protection.

Complete exchange control can perhaps best be defined as government domination of the foreign-exchange market. Each international transaction requiring payment in foreign currencies must be sanctioned by the government, and necessary foreign exchange secured from the government. Similarly, all foreign-exchange receipts from international transactions must immediately be surrendered to the government. There is no foreign-exchange market. The *government* rations out the available foreign exchange according to its own order of priorities. The exchange rate is arbitrarily set by the government, or *multiple exchange rates* may be established under which the most favorable rates are granted the most favored types of payments.

For example, under exchange control all imports must normally first be officially sanctioned by means of an import license or foreign-exchange permit. Imports deemed to be of national importance receive such permits without difficulty, while luxuries and other nondesirables may not and are thereby effectively kept out. Payments of interest and dividends abroad require similar permits and are usually severely restricted. Investment outflows are often banned.

Meanwhile, all foreign-exchange receipts, whether from exports, capital inflows, or any other source are collected by the government and exchanged for the domestic currency at the applicable official rate. Here, too, multiple exchange rates may be used to stimulate certain types of exports for which the demand is found to be relatively elastic, with unfavorable rates given on exports for which an inelastic foreign demand is felt to prevail.

Exchange control need not necessarily be complete and may apply only to certain types of international transactions, such as investments. Nevertheless, because the market mechanism is short-circuited the temptation to circumvent any type of exchange control often proves irresistible. To the extent that the domestic currency can be smuggled out, or foreign currencies smuggled in, lively black markets develop in which the prevailing exchange rate may be several times the official rate. Illegal markets in foreign currencies necessarily undermine the government effort at exchange control, and those profiteers caught are subjected to severe penalties.

There are other ways to avoid exchange controls, such as "under-invoicing." The exporter bills the foreign importer an amount less than what the importer actually pays. The officially invoiced amount is duly surrendered to the exchange-control authorities, and the balance is placed in a foreign bank account in the exporter's name. Similarly domestic importers can arrange to be "over-invoiced" by foreign sellers, and a part of the licensed foreign exchange granted by the government then placed in a foreign bank account by the exporter in the importer's name.

Although completely different *in kind* from other international monetary standards, and totally removed from the market mechanism, exchange control is extremely important. It is used in essentially all socialist countries of Eastern Europe and Asia, in most developing countries, and from time to time in advanced market-oriented economies as well. We shall return to this question in greater detail later on.

IV

International
Monetary Theory

20

INTERNATIONAL TRANSMISSION OF ECONOMIC CONDITIONS

In this section we shall begin to delve into the heart of international monetary relations—the theory of balance of payments adjustment. Precisely what is the link between the prevailing international monetary standard and the balance of payments adjustment mechanism? To what extent does payments balance tend to be restored automatically under different exchange standards? To what extent is it a matter of manipulation of the tools of national economic and commercial policy? We recognize the need for payments balance and therefore must analyze the cause-and-effect relationships which work to eliminate payments imbalances that do occur. Preliminary to this discussion—and as a prerequisite to an understanding of it—we need to acquire a working knowledge of the connections between a nation's international trade and the level of economic activity.

Two broad statements will suffice to introduce the present topic. (a) Changes in the level of national income have a distinct bearing on the volume of a nation's foreign trade; and (b) international trade may play a major role in determining the level of a nation's economic activity and, therefore, the material well-being of its people.

If these statements are true, it is hardly surprising that in nations that are very much dependent on foreign trade for the maintenance of a high level of living (such as Denmark, New Zealand, and Holland), a great deal of attention is focused on the foreign sector in teaching students the elements of national income determination. In the U.S., by way of contrast, the foreign sector contributes relatively less to aggregate economic activity. Hence, it is usually assumed that we live in a *closed economy* without any foreign transactions, which makes teaching the theory of income determination to American students somewhat easier and still not too far removed from reality.

Precisely how changes in domestic economic activity influence the volume of international trade and, equally important, the relation between trade and the level of national economic activity are the questions to which we want to address ourselves at this point.

PROPENSITY TO IMPORT

There exists a direct relation between national income, or output, and the volume of goods imported by a country. Most students find it logical that when national income rises, the demand for imported goods and services will tend to rise as well. When the U.S. or U.K. enters a boom period, it finds that it is buying more foreign-made automobiles, cameras, and transister radios, to say nothing of the legions of prosperous tourists it sends abroad. This coincides with the increased demand for domestically produced goods and services that is characteristic of an economic expansion. During a recession in economic activity, on the other hand, imports of goods and services tend to drop off, just as purchases of domestically produced goods and services slow down during such a period.

The relation of imports to national income over a given time period is called the *average propensity to import.* If the U.S. national income for a certain year is \$900 billion, and the value of imports comes to \$70 billion, the U.S. average propensity to import for that year is 0.08. Hence, the average propensity to import is written as follows:

$$APM = \frac{M}{Y}$$

APM stands for the average propensity to import, M represents the value of imports, and Y the level of national income.

The average propensity to import tends to differ in individual countries, according to both the absolute size of the national economy and the degree of specialization that characterizes national production. Large and diverse economies like the U.S. and the Soviet Union tend to have relatively low average propensities to import. Small and specialized economies dependent on foreign trade, such as Denmark, Belgium, and the Netherlands, will show high average propensities to import. Of course, there is not always a direct relation between economic size and the degree of economic specialization; hence, a large but comparatively specialized economy such as the U.K. possesses a relatively high propensity to import.

From the average propensity to import it is an easy step to another analytically more useful concept—the *marginal propensity to import.* If U.S.

national income grows from $900 billion to $950 billion during the course of a year, while imports concurrently grow from $70 billion to $72 billion, the marginal propensity to import is 0.04. The marginal propensity to import is defined as the proportion of any increase in national income that is spent on imports. Thus,

$$MPM = \frac{\Delta M}{\Delta Y}$$

MPM represents the marginal propensity to import, ΔM is the change in imports, and ΔY is the causative change in national income.

Note that, in the example given above, the *average* propensity to import was 0.08, but the *marginal* propensity to import was 0.04. This is not unusual. In fact, the value of the marginal propensity may differ quite markedly from the average propensity to import for any given economy.

Import propensities are not constant, but tend to vary over time. During a given year, for instance, Germany's marginal propensity to import may be high, while the following year may show a notable decline. This variation depends largely on which sectors of the economy contribute most to economic expansion or contraction. If an increase in national income is in significant measure attributable to the expansion of economic sectors dependent upon imported raw materials or components, naturally the marginal propensity to import will be high.

IMPORT ELASTICITIES

Whereas the marginal and average propensities to import are based on data in absolute terms—import and national income figures—it is often necessary to talk in relative terms. That is, if national income grows by 10 per cent this year, by what percentage will imports tend to rise? This necessitates a third concept, the *income elasticity of demand for imports,* which is a measure of the relative response of imports to relative changes in national income. This concept is very similar to the elasticity concepts discussed in Chapter 2.

Simply stated, the income elasticity of demand for imports is

$$e_{ym} = \frac{\dfrac{\Delta M}{M}}{\dfrac{\Delta Y}{Y}}$$

where M represents the value of imports and Y the national income. This is nothing more than the percentage change in imports divided by the corresponding percentage change in national income. If income grows by 10 per cent and the value of imports rises by 4 per cent, then the income elasticity of imports is 4; i.e., imports are relatively *income elastic.* A coefficient of income elasticity of imports that is less than unity means that a

1 per cent increase in income calls forth less than 1 per cent increase in imports, and that imports are relatively *income inelastic.* Unitary income elasticity of imports, of course, indicates that a given percentage change in income will be accompanied by an identical percentage change in the value of imports.

The income elasticity concept was introduced here primarily because of its very close relationship to the average and marginal propensities to import. We will have occasion to use it as an analytical tool later on.

We now have some idea of the kind of relationships that exist between national income and international trade. An increase in U.S. national income tends to increase American imports and, therefore, the exports of foreign countries. Increase in national income abroad raises the level of their imports and hence expands U.S. exports. But it is equally true that changes in exports and imports have a substantial impact on the level of national income, resulting in the existence of a two-way cause-and-effect relationship between international trade and domestic economic activity.

FOREIGN-TRADE MULTIPLIER, CASE I

As soon as we remove the assumption of a closed economy, we must add imports and exports to the basic national income relationships. Exports constitute domestic output that is not consumed at home, while imports represent the product of foreign suppliers available for domestic consumption. Hence, we must add exports as a fourth element of demand, and imports as a second element of supply. Instead of the basic identity,

$$Y = C + I + G,$$

we now have

$$Y + M = C + I + G + X,$$

or

$$Y = C + I + G + (X - M).$$

The term $(X - M)$, the balance of trade, is often called *net foreign investment* and may be either positive or negative, depending on the relative magnitude of imports and exports.

To begin with, let us assume there is no government expenditure, no investment, and no savings. In this case, I and G are zero, and all income is consumed $(Y = C)$. Hence, at equilibrium

$$Y + M = C + X,$$

and

$$M = X.$$

At any equilibrium level of income, in the absence of savings and investment, imports must equal exports in order for earned income to equal total desired spending. If there is an autonomous increase in exports, income will grow, again by a series of respending steps as in the multiplier process developed earlier. This time, however, we have assumed that no income is saved. Hence, the only income leakage is into imports—goods consumed but not produced at home. The amount of this import-leakage is given by the marginal propensity to import as defined above. We can thus write the *foreign trade multiplier* as follows:

$$k_f = \frac{1}{\dfrac{\Delta M}{\Delta Y}} = \frac{1}{MPM}.$$

The effect on income of an autonomous increase in exports under these conditions would be

$$\Delta Y = \Delta X \left[\frac{1}{MPM} \right].$$

Any autonomous increase in exports (or decrease in imports) will result in a multiple respending cycle which is diminished gradually each time by the marginal propensity to import. The reverse holds true for autonomous reductions in exports or increases in imports. Once the new equilibrium income is reached, the sum of the income leakages into imports will equal the initial change in the trade balance, and once again exports will equal imports.

This is presented graphically in Figure 20–1. Since there is no saving and no investment, the consumption function is identical with the 45° line; i.e., every increase in income is fully spent in consumption. But the slope of the aggregate demand function, comprised of consumption plus exports minus imports $(C + X - M)$ is slightly less than the 45° line. This is due to the marginal propensity to import which has a value of less than unity. For every increase in income, domestic spending rises but not by as much as the income change, since a portion of the increased income is spent on imports and thus is removed from the income stream.

An autonomous increase in exports from X to X' now raises the aggregate demand function, and via the multiple respending process, a new equilibrium at $Y'e$ is attained where once again exports equal imports. An autonomous decline inexports or increase in imports, both of which constitute a reduction in the $(X - M)$ component of the aggregate demand function, will result in a new, lower equilibrium income, again via the foreign-trade multiplier.

FOREIGN-TRADE MULTIPLIER, CASE II

We can now go ahead and apply the foreign-trade multiplier, as developed above in the absence of savings, to the general income determination model by simply dropping the assumption of zero savings, investment,

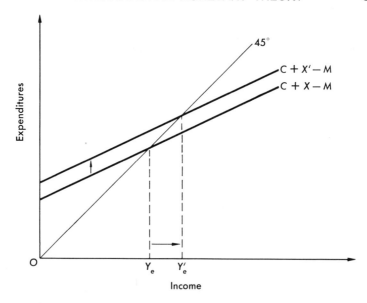

Fig. 20–1. Effect of export expansion on equilibrium income: no savings, investment, or government spending.

and government spending. This enables us to return to our original identity

$$Y = C + I + G + X - M.$$

However, it is first necessary to develop a composite multiplier that takes into account the leakages from the domestic income stream attributable *both* to savings and to imports. This can be done by simply summing the marginal propensity to save and the marginal propensity to import,

$$k_{fd} = \frac{1}{MPS + MPM} = \frac{1}{\dfrac{\Delta S}{\Delta Y} + \dfrac{\Delta M}{\Delta Y}}.$$

If we now wish to predict the effect of *any* change in aggregate demand upon equilibrium income, we simply use the familiar procedure as applied to a closed economy, with the exception that we also take into account the leakages from the income stream into imports.

$$\Delta Y = \Delta Spending \left[\frac{1}{MPS + MPM} \right]$$

It may be helpful to work through a numerical example of the operation of the multiplier in an open economy. Suppose equilibrium income initially is $100 billion, the marginal propensity to consume is $\frac{3}{4}$, and the marginal propensity to import is $\frac{1}{8}$. Aggregate demand now rises by $5 billion due to, say, and increase in investment. Equilibrium income will rise as follows:

$$\Delta Y = \Delta I \left[\frac{1}{MPS + MPM} \right],$$

which equals

$$\Delta Y = \Delta I \left[\frac{1}{1 - MPC + MPM} \right],$$

and, numerically,

$$\Delta Y = \$5 \text{ billion} \left[\frac{1}{1 - \frac{3}{4} + \frac{1}{8}} \right].$$

Working it out, we find that equilibrium income increases by $13.3 billion to a new level of $113.3 billion. Note, by way of contrast, that in a closed economy the increased investment would have raised equilibrium income as follows:

$$\Delta Y = \Delta I \left[\frac{1}{MPS} \right].$$

If the reader works this out using the given marginal propensity to save of ¼, he will find that income would have risen by $20 billion instead of by the $13.3 billion for the open economy. This demonstrates that the foreign-trade multiplier is actually *less powerful* than the multiplier which operates in a closed economy. The reason for this is simply that the total leakages from the domestic income stream are greater when spending on imports is included.

All of this is represented diagramatically in Figure 20–2. The aggregate demand function for the open economy is $C + I + G + X - M$. Its slope incorporates both the marginal propensity to save and the marginal propensity to import. The initial equilibrium income is at Ye. An increase in investment spending raises this aggregate demand function to $C + I' + G + X - M$ and, via the composite foreign-trade multiplier, causes a shift to a new equilibrium at Ye'. Note that the aggregate demand function for the closed economy $(C + I + G)$ has a greater slope than that representing the open economy, since it does not incorporate the marginal propensity to import. Hence, the same increase in investment (ΔI) raises equilibrium income from Ye to Ye'', and results in a substantially larger rise in income in the closed economy (ΔY_d) than in the open economy (ΔY_f). This illustrates the earlier statement that the multiplier is more powerful in the closed economy than in the open economy which incorporates the addition of one more leakage from the domestic income stream.

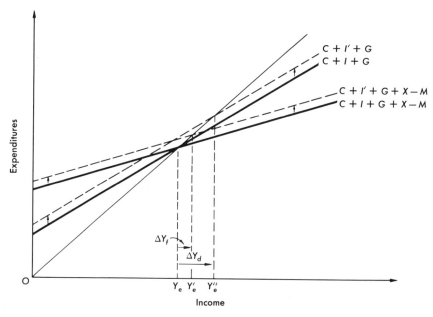

Fig. 20–2. Foreign trade multiplier, with savings, investment, and government spending, compared with the closed economy multiplier.

ASSUMPTIONS AND IMPLICATIONS

Our presentation of multiplier analysis, in the Keynesian *comparative statistics* manner, was necessarily extremely simple. It was intended to show the implications of shifting from a closed economy model to an open one and the impact of a change in exports or imports on the level of national economic activity. The effect of the latter, it turns out, is not very different from a shift in any of the other components of spending—consumption, investment, or government expenditures. An autonomous increase in exports or decline in imports will raise the level of national income via the foreign-trade multiplier, while a decline in exports or an increase in imports will have the opposite effect. The former constitutes an increase in *net foreign investment*—exports minus imports—while the latter represents a decrease in it.

All changes in national income were taken to represent *real* changes, thus eliminating problems introduced by changing prices, and the propensities to consume and import also were expressed in real terms. Nothing was said about the factors affecting the level of investment, which was assumed to be autonomously determined, or about the degree of capacity utilization in the economy—the attainment of full employment of productive resources naturally puts a stop to any further gains in *real* income.

All of this was done for the sake of simplicity, in order to isolate the effect of removing the assumption of a closed economy.

It was also assumed that imports and consumption are purely a function of incomes, which is not entirely true since such factors as interest rates also play an important role, but this does not materially reduce the validity of our analysis. A relaxation of this and some of the other assumptions is not difficult. All of these considerations plus the effect of such variables as taxes and government transfer payments can be built into the basic income-determination model. But these questions lie outside the main theme of this text, and hence should not be considered further here.

There is one assumption, however, which does need to be relaxed at this point. Up to now, it was assumed that the level of exports was autonomously determined. Imports were said to be primarily a function of real income. But what determines exports? Each item that the home country exports must be imported by some other country—our exports are the imports of other nations. Since the foreign countries' imports themselves depend primarily upon their respective real incomes, it follows that the home country's exports must hinge at least partly on the real incomes of the nations with which it trades. Conversely, the home country's real income governs the volume of its imports and, hence, the exports of its trading partners. This begins to get at the so-called *foreign repercussions effect*.

TRADE, INCOME, AND FOREIGN REPERCUSSIONS

Suppose there are only two countries, Germany and France, which trade freely with each other but with no one else. Real incomes of both countries are in equilibrium and trade between them is balanced; i.e., the value of imports exactly equals that of exports. Now consumers' tastes in France change in such a way that there occurs a substantial increase in French imports from Germany. This naturally represents an increase in Germany's exports. Via the multiplier effect, it simultaneously causes a decline in French national income and a rise in Germany's national income. As Germany's real income rises and that of France falls, Germany's imports rise (so French exports rise) and French imports fall (so German exports fall). This process is repeated over and over, as illustrated in Figure 20–3.

Germany's net export increase is ultimately reduced in magnitude by the successive impacts of those exports on its own and on France's economic activity. Germany's new, higher equilibrium income thus falls substantially short of what would have been expected on the basis of the initial export rise and the foreign-trade multiplier alone.

On the other hand, the detrimental impact of the French import rise on its own domestic economic activity is also reduced by the repercussions of the increase in its imports on the German economy. French imports (German exports) rise, but as the German economy is stimulated, German imports (French exports) also rise and the net change in French imports is reduced. These repercussions echo back and forth, and ultimately they cause the net negative income change in France to be considerably smaller than we would have expected only on the basis of its initial import rise and the foreign-trade multiplier.

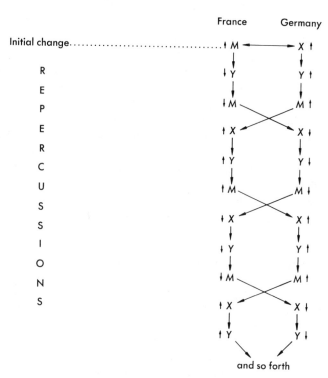

Fig. 20–3.   Foreign-repercussions effect.

The foreign-repercussions effect is by no means limited to initial, autonomous changes in imports and exports as will be shown below. *Any* change in the aggregate demand function in one of the two countries will set off the chain reaction of foreign repercussions. An increase in government spending in Germany will raise German national income and, therefore, its imports. Hence French exports rise, French national income increases and its imports rise, which means that German exports rise, and so forth. In a sense, then, the real national income of one country is partly a function of the real national income of its trading partners, via the foreign-repercussions effect. National changes in aggregate demand—business cycle developments in general—are thus easily transmitted from one nation to another whenever there are no barriers to trade between them.

FOREIGN-TRADE MULTIPLIER, CASE III

A numerical example of the foreign-repercussions effect is provided in Table 20–1. Two countries, A and B, are involved, both of which are characterized by identical marginal propensities to save and import. Initially, income in both countries is in equilibrium, but this is disturbed by an autonomous, sustained increase in A's exports and B's imports in the amount of $100. This causes income, consumption, and savings to rise in Country A and to fall in Country B.

The rise in A's income, in turn, results in an induced increase in its imports and, hence, in B's exports. Simultaneously, the fall in B's income is reflected in a reduction in its imports and, therefore, in a fall in A's exports. These induced changes in the balance of trade $(X - M)$ have further effects on incomes, which again effect imports and exports, and so forth. Ultimately, the resultant rise in A's income is $125, which equals the fall in B's income.

Suppose, instead of marginal propensities to save and import of 0.2 and 0.3, respectively, Country A is assumed to be a closed economy possessing a marginal propensity to save of 0.5. An equivalent injection of $100 into the domestic income stream would then have brought about an increase in equilibrium income of $200.[1] The same would be true if we retained the above values for the marginal propensity to save and import in an open economy, but assumed that there were no foreign repercussions.[2] This illustrates the potential importance of the foreign-repercussions effect and shows how it lowers the value of the foreign-trade multiplier. It also indicates that the foreign-repercussions effect may act as an "automatic stabilizer" with respect to changes in domestic economic activity by dampening the ultimate response of income to variations in aggregate demand.

As a result of the foreign-repercussions effect, it is necessary for us to revise our formula for the multiplier one more time. Income changes in one country trigger income changes in other countries. The latter, in turn, feed back to the home country, and this means, as we have said earlier,

[1] $100 \times \dfrac{1}{MPS} = 100 \times \dfrac{1}{0.5} = 100 \times 2 = 200.$

[2] $100 \times \dfrac{1}{MPS + MPM} = 100 \times \dfrac{1}{0.2 + 0.3} = 100 \times 2 = 200.$

Table

The Foreign-Repercussions Effect Illustrated: Autonomous

				Country A: MPS = 0.2, MPM = 0.3				
Period	Past ΔY	ΔC	ΔS	Induced ΔM	Induced ΔX	Initial ΔX	Net X − M	Current ΔY
1						100.00	+100.00	100.00
2	100.00	50.00	20.00	30.00	−30.00	100.00	+40.00	120.00
3	120.00	60.00	24.00	36.00	−36.00	100.00	+28.00	124.00
4	124.00	62.00	24.80	37.20	−37.20	100.00	+25.60	124.80
5	124.80	62.40	24.96	37.44	−37.44	100.00	+25.12	124.96
6	124.96	62.48	24.99	37.49	−37.49	100.00	+25.02	124.99
n	125.00	62.50	25.00	37.50	−37.50	100.00	25.00	125.00
Columns	A	B	C	D	E	F	G	H
Derivations	= Col. H_{t-1}	ΔY(1 − MPS)	ΔY(MPS)	ΔY(MPM)	= Col. L	= Col. N	Col. F + E − D	Col. B + E + F

*Adapted from: Fritz Machlup, *International Trade and the National Income Multiplier* (Philadelphia: Blakiston,

that the multiplier for any one nation will be less powerful than without foreign repercussion.

The leakages from the domestic income stream are greater due to the reduction of exports resulting from the decline in foreign demand for imports. The value of this additional leakage is the foreign marginal propensity to import corrected for induced changes in the rate of saving in both countries.

If we have two countries, A and B, the new multiplier for a change in imports or exports, including the foreign repercussion, for the two countries are, respectively,

$$k_A = \frac{1}{MPS_A + MPM_A + MPM_B \left[\dfrac{MPS_A}{MPS_B} \right]}$$

$$k_B = \frac{1}{MPS_B + MPM_B + MPM_A \left[\dfrac{MPS_B}{MPS_A} \right]}.$$

The terms (MPS_A/MPS_B) and (MPS_B/MPS_A) are included to allow for the fact that as the home country's income rises, its savings also rise, thus

20–1

Sustained Exports from Country A to Country B*

					Country B: MPS = 0.2, MPM = 0.3		
Past ΔY	ΔC	ΔS	Induced ΔM	Induced ΔX	Initial ΔM	Net X − M	Current ΔY
					100.00	−100.00	−100.00
−100.00	−50.00	−20.00	−30.00	+30.00	100.00	−40.00	−120.00
−120.00	−60.00	−24.00	−36.00	+36.00	100.00	−28.00	−124.00
−124.00	−62.00	−24.80	−37.20	+37.20	100.00	−25.60	−124.80
−124.80	−62.40	−24.96	−37.44	+37.44	100.00	−25.12	−124.96
−124.96	−62.48	−24.99	−37.49	+37.49	100.00	−25.02	−124.99
～～～	～～～	～～～	～～～	～～～	～～～	～～～	～～～
−125.00	−62.50	−25.00	−37.50	+37.50	100.00	−25.00	−125.00
I	J	K	L	M	N	O	P
= Col. P_{t-1}	$\Delta Y(1 - MPS)$	$\Delta Y(MPS)$	$\Delta Y(MPM)$	= Col. D	= Col. F	Col. N + M − L	Col. J + L + M

1943), p. 68, Table IV-b.

cutting down its consumption and also its imports from the foreign country. Simultaneously, the decline in savings in the foreign country tends to offset the decline in its imports and hence, also in the home country's exports.

The formulas presented here clearly imply a number of things. The smaller the *domestic* marginal propensity to import and the *foreign* marginal propensity to import, the smaller will be the leakages out of the domestic income stream, and the larger will therefore be the value of the multiplier. Moreover, the value of the multiplier will be larger, the smaller the domestic marginal propensity to save and the larger the foreign marginal propensity to save, since they again signify reduced leakages out of domestic income.

So far, we have always assumed that the initial injection or leakage with respect to the domestic income stream resulted from an autonomous change in exports or imports, and that the various multipliers were derived accordingly. If, however, the initial increase or reduction in aggregate demand is attributable to a change in *domestic* consumption (ΔC), investment (ΔI), or government spending (ΔG), after allowing for the effect of transfer payments, the value of the multiplier will be somewhat larger than that derived above. Its value is then given for two countries, A and B, by the formulas

$$k_A^* = \frac{1 + \left[\dfrac{MPM_B}{MPS_B}\right]}{MPS_A + MPM_A + MPM_B \left[\dfrac{MPS_A}{MPS_B}\right]}$$

$$k_B^* = \frac{1 + \left[\dfrac{MPM_A}{MPS_A}\right]}{MPS_B + MPM_B + MPM_A \left[\dfrac{MPS_B}{MSP_A}\right]}.$$

Instead of a decline in domestic exports because of falling national incomes abroad, as was true in the earlier case where the initial injection was a rise in the home country's exports (foreign imports), in this case we actually see induced *increases* in exports. Expanded domestic consumption, investment, or government spending in Country A increases its own imports, the exports of Country B, and the increasing incomes abroad are fed back to Country A as further increases in exports. The extent of this feedback is determined by the marginal propensities to save and to import prevailing abroad. In short, the ratio of the foreign nation's marginal propensity to import to its marginal propensity to save, expressed in the numerator of the above equations, represents a foreign repercussion *supporting* the prevailing change in domestic incomes, rather than *counteracting* it.

This can perhaps more easily be illustrated in terms of Figure 20–4. The vertical and horizontal axes indicate the level of income in two countries A and B (or in one country and the rest of the world). If functions $Y_A = Y_A$ and $Y_B = Y_B$ prevail, income in each is entirely independent of the other. Foreign repercussions would give the curves a positive slope, such as $Y_B = f(Y_A)$. Suppose curves $Y_B = f(Y_A)$ and $Y_A = f(Y_B)$ obtain. Suppose, further, that an upward shift in domestic spending in B causes a $Y_B - Y_B'$ shift. With no foreign repercussions, income in B rises by an amount $Y_1 - Y_3$ while income in A is unaffected. With foreign repercussions, income in B rises by an amount $(Y_3 - Y_6) > (Y_1 - Y_3)$, while a rise of $Y_8 - Y_9$ is induced in country A. If the disturbance originates in the foreign sector as an increase in B's exports to A, the $Y_B - Y_B'$ shift faces $Y_A - Y_A'$ shift in the importing country. As a result, income in B rises by an amount $(Y_3 - Y_5) < (Y_1 - Y_3)$, while a decline of $Y_8 - Y_{10}$ is induced in B. For country B, again, foreign repercussions *reinforce* aggregate spending shifts if they are domestic in origin, and *offset* them if they arise in the foreign sector.

FOREIGN-TRADE MULTIPLIERS IN USE

How dependable are the foreign-trade multipliers, developed here, as analytical tools? In order to predict the effects on domestic income, in

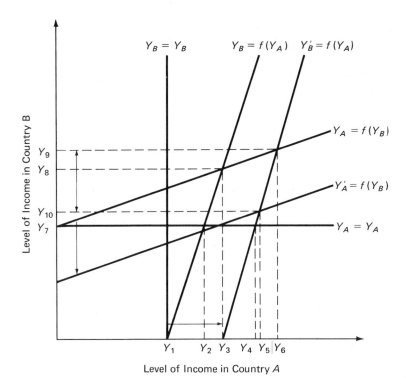

Fig. 20–4.   Foreign repercussion effect.

an open economy, of autonomous changes in exports or domestic spending, we must have a reasonably good idea of the marginal propensities to save (or consume) and import, on which the entire analysis depends. Furthermore, we must have some assurance that these propensities will remain *stable* throughout the period during which the various primary and foreign repercussions effects are played out.

Both the marginal propensity to consume (and, hence, the marginal propensity to save) and the marginal propensity to import are relatively easy to compute for any country which collects the relevant data accurately and systematically. Since most of the world's developed countries fall into this category, and since they are the most important from a trade point of view, there are comparatively few problems on this score.

There are some difficulties, however, regarding the stability of these propensities. The marginal propensity to consume seems to vary according to prevailing business conditions. It tends to take on a higher value in times of boom and a lower value during depressions and marked recessions. Similarly, when the economy is in a boom period and operating close to its own productive capacity, the marginal propensity to import tends to be relatively high, since large-scale increases in the availability of commodities for consumption or investment can only come from abroad. During recessions, when excess capacity is a dominant characteristic of the prevailing state of the economy, such increases are much more likely to come out of domestic production and the value of the marginal propensity to import will be low.

The marginal propensity to import also depends on the economic structure of the nation involved. If a country's imports are largely composed of consumption goods, and the source of an economic expansion is a rise in consumer spending, naturally the marginal propensity to import will be high. Similarly, if the country imports primarily raw materials and other bulk goods, the marginal propensity to import will rise dramatically during an economic expansion induced by a buildup of inventories.

All of this is intended to caution the reader that we are not dealing with a set of precise analytical tools which will unerringly yield accurate results in each and every application. The foreign-trade multiplier, when applied to real world situations, is valid only as long as the marginal propensities to consume and import are accurate and relatively stable. Hence, it is not surprising that forecasts based on this concept can fall substantially short of the desired degree of accuracy.

It is also important to note that for small countries, with limited economic significance in relation to the rest of the world as a whole, the foreign-repercussions effect will be virtually nil. This is true simply because any change in such a country's imports or exports will have little or no effect on the national income of its trading partner—all other countries combined. Moreover, any change in the national income of one of the larger and economically more important nations may have little effect on exports and income in the small country because a large nation's marginal propensity to import from the small country is likely to be very low. The latter would not apply, of course, to small countries which are highly specialized in the production of a single commodity, the market for which is concentrated in a small group of large, industrialized nations.

Since the above analysis of the foreign-trade multiplier is entirely couched in *real terms,* it applies only to changes in incomes below the full employment level. An injection into the income stream of an economy already operating at full employment raises *money* incomes without expanding the production of real, or *physical,* goods and services.

We should conclude by saying that we cannot ignore the fact that all of these income and trade interactions operate with lags of varying magnitudes, which in itself makes forecasting difficult. Moreover, since income changes may also result in induced changes in investment (the *accelerator*) at home and abroad, this factor should also be taken into account in any attempt to develop a valid predictor.

21

EQUILIBRIUM ADJUSTMENT SYSTEMS: FIXED EXCHANGE RATES

In our study of the balance of payments and the foreign-exchange markets, we noted how international monetary transactions were recorded, the interrelationships that exist between various types of international transactions, and the manner in which international payments are effected. We shall now embark on the basic core of international monetary theory: adjustment of the balance of payments. If outflows exceed inflows, or vice versa, what forces are set into motion—and under what conditions—that will eventually lead to a restoration of payments balance. We shall begin our discussion by describing this adjustment process under two "equilibrium" systems, where restoration of balance takes place essentially automatically: under fixed and flexible exchange-rate regimes. In each case the "rules of the game" will be carefully outlined. What happens when these rules are broken, as they almost invariably are in the real world, will be considered in our discussion of "disequilibrium" systems, where balance of payments adjustment is primarily a matter of government policy.

Suppose, under fixed exchange rates, a country is plagued by a balance of payments deficit year after year. We know that each successive deficit normally diminishes its stock of international reserves in which these deficits are settled, unless, of course, the country's currency is being held as international reserves by other nations. We also know, therefore, that such deficits cannot go on forever. Sooner or later the country will normally run out

of international reserves and it will be, in effect, internationally bankrupt. The need for adjustment exists even if foreign governments are willing to hold the currency of the deficit country as part of their own international reserves. The continued buildup of short-term liabilities to foreign official financial institutions, relative to the stock of owned reserves, gradually erodes the willingness of foreigners to hold such balances. It therefore subjects the deficit nation to the same ultimate constraint, necessitating eventual balance of payments adjustment.
payments adjustment.

Looking at the other side of the problem, assume that a country is subjected to chronic balance of payments surplus. Year after year its stock of gold and foreign currencies build up. Its exports may continually exceed its enjoyment of those produced by others. Investment inflows may outstrip investment outflows. This subjects the country to high interest and dividend payments in the future. The loss is insured as the country merely converts part of these into low-yield official reserve balances abroad and into gold, which yields nothing at all. Chronic surpluses are just as unhealthy as chronic deficits, although the need for a restoration of balance of payments balance is not as immediately obvious and often is not clearly recognized.

But the point has been made before. If a country is subjected to either balance of payments deficits or surpluses, at some point these imbalances must be eliminated.

INCOME-SPECIE FLOW MECHANISM

In order for payments balance to be restored automatically under fixed exchange rates, the balance of payments must be directly and unalterably tied to the determination of the national money supply. This condition is, of course, met under the classical gold standard where balance of payments surpluses and deficits produce gold inflows and outflows, which, in turn, directly affect the money supply—either because (a) the money supply is comprised of gold, or (b) the money supply is fully backed by gold. It also applies to the gold standard modifications under which the money supply (demand deposits and currency) is fractionally backed by gold in a specific and *constant* ratio. Finally, it applies to the conventional fixed exchange rate system, under which payments imbalances are settled in gold or other acceptable assets just as long as the ratio between a nation's international reserves and its money supply remains constant.

For convenience, we shall assume that gold represents the only international medium of exchange, although we just noted that this is not a *necessary* condition for the automatic fixed exchange rate adjustment mechanism to function effectively. We shall also assume that there are no restrictions to international gold flows, capital movements, or trade and that the price of gold in terms of all affected currencies remains unchanged. Under these conditions, adjustment of the balance of payments occurs via what we shall call the *income-specie flow mechanism*.

Suppose a country finds itself with a balance of payments deficit attributable to, say, a large-scale capital outflow. Its international payments exceed its receipts, and at the prevailing exchange rate the demand for foreign exchange exceeds the supply. Under the gold standard, as we noted in Chapter 19, the exchange rate rises slightly to the gold export point, and gold flows out of the country. In effect, the country has settled its balance of payments deficit by exporting gold.

The balance of payments deficit of this particular country thus involves an outflow of gold and a commensurate reduction in the domestic money supply. At the same time, since world payments and receipts are equal by definition, one or more other countries must simultaneously be incurring balance of payments surpluses—gold inflows—and an expansion of their respective national stocks of money.

Both in the home country and abroad, these specie flows will affect interest rates, prices, and incomes in such a way that the balance of payments sooner or later automatically tends to return to equilibrium. It therefore represents an *equilibrium system* of balance of payments adjustment.

INTEREST EFFECT

We shall call the deficit nation Country A and the surplus nation (or the rest of the world) Country B. The balance of payments deficits of A automatically reduce its money supply as a result of the outflow of gold. At the same time, the inflow of gold into B similarly raises its money supply. We will assume that prices of goods and services are *not* perfectly flexible.

In Figure 21–1, the money supply in the two countries is represented by the vertical lines S_A and S_B, respectively. Since the money supply in each instance is entirely dependent upon the national gold stock, its position is determined by increases or decreases of monetary gold supplies—new production, changes in nonmonetary holdings, and international payments. The demand curve for money (LP_A and LP_B) takes its usual downward-sloping shape, the demand for money being a function of the interest rate and the level of income. It is nothing more than the Keynesian liquidity-preference schedule, combining the asset demand and the transactions demand for money, as outlined in Chapter 2. The equilibrium interest rate is given by the intersection of the demand and supply curves for money.

As a result of its balance of payments deficit induced by a capital outflow, Country A exports gold and its money supply is thereby reduced from, say, S_A to S_A'. The prevailing interest rate, as a consequence, rises from R_1 to R_2, with the demand for money remaining constant. Meanwhile Country B enjoys a gold inflow equivalent to the gold outflow of Country A. Its money supply expands accordingly, from S_B to S_B', and the equilibrium interest rate falls from R_3 to R_4. What has happened? The prevailing rate of interest has fallen in the deficit country and risen in the surplus country due to the impact of the international gold flows on the two countries' respective money supplies.

Naturally, a rise in A's interest rate discourages further capital outflows, since domestic yields have improved. Moreover, the fall in B's interest

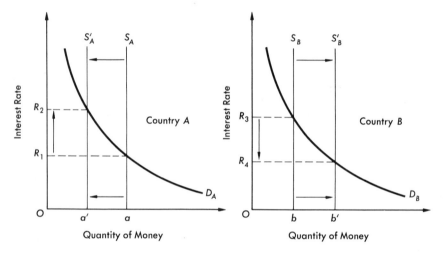

Fig. 21–1.   Response of interest rates to changes in the money supply.

rates discourages lenders and investors in A from sending additional investment funds abroad. In fact, both developments tend to make it worthwhile for them to bring their money home. At the same time, lenders and investors in Country B find foreign interest rates improving while domestic yields are falling and are thus encouraged to send their funds abroad.

Hence, we have a first movement toward restoration of payments balance. Changes in relative interest rates due to the automatic impact of international specie flows on national money supplies and interest rates tend to cause an inflow of capital into the deficit country and a capital outflow from the surplus country. Country A's deficit is reduced, and so is Country B's balance of payments surplus. All of this tends to occur automatically.

INCOME EFFECT

But this is not the only tendency for restoration of payments balance in this instance. We know that interest rates will tend to rise in the deficit country and to fall in the surplus country. According to modern national-income analysis, as reviewed in Chapter 2, we also know that investment is generally considered to be a function of the interest rate; i.e., the lower the interest rate, the higher the investment level in the economy tends to be. Moreover, since investment is an important component of the open-economy aggregate demand function (consumption, investment, government spending, and net exports), any changes in investment will, via the multiplier, be reflected in incomes. Finally, because imports are a function of national income, via the propensity to import, any changes in incomes will be reflected in international trade. With the aid of Figures 21–2 and 21–3, we can now trace through a second way in which gold standard specie flows may promote automatic balance of payments adjustment.

Referring to Figure 21–2, the rise in interest rates in the deficit country from R_1 to R_2, due to gold outflows and a consequent reduction in the money supply, causes investment to decline from I_a to I_a'. This investment reduction lowers Country A's aggregate demand function by the same amount, from $C + I_a + G + X - M$ to $C + I_a' + G + X - M$ and, via the multiplier, reduces national income from Y_a to Y_a'. The reverse happens in surplus Country B. Gold inflows expand the money supply and reduce interest rates. These, in turn, result in an increase of investment demand which raises the aggregate demand function and, through the multiplier effect, national income as well. In short, incomes fall in the deficit country and rise in the surplus country.

The extent of these income changes in response to the initial gold flows depend upon (a) the interest elasticity of the demand for money, (b) the interest elasticity of investment demand, and (c) the value of the national income multiplier, including any foreign-repercussions effects. The *lower* the interest elasticity of demand for money, the larger will be the impact of a given change in the money supply (or gold stock) on interest rates. The *larger* the interest elasticity of investment demand, the greater will be the response of investment to a given change in the interest rate. Finally, the *larger* the value of the multiplier, the greater will be the effect of a given change in investments upon national income.

In Figure 21–3, we can see how this income effect of specie flows tends to promote balance of payments adjustment. We know that imports (M) are a function of national income (Y), and that the marginal propensity to import is included in computing the value of the multiplier. Hence, the reduction of income in the deficit country A from Y_a to Y_a', determined above, simultaneously causes its imports to be reduced from M_a to M_a', and therefore reduces the exports of the surplus country B by the same amount. Meanwhile, the income expansion in the surplus country $(Y_b - Y_b')$ raises its imports (and Country A's exports) in the amount $M_b - M_b'$. The *balance of trade* of the deficit country thus improves,

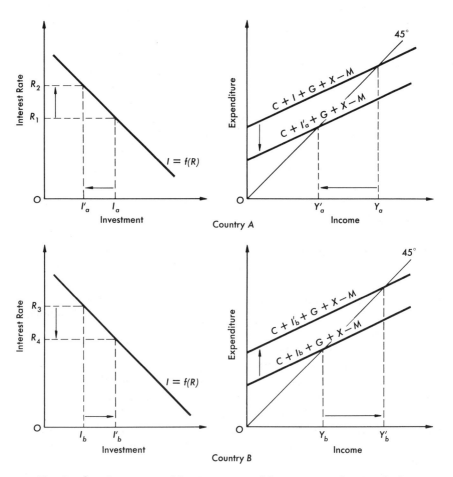

Fig. 21–2. Response of investment and incomes to changes in interest rates.

while that of the surplus country deteriorates. The magnitude of these income-induced changes in imports depends, of course, on the marginal propensity to import; the larger the marginal propensity to import in both countries, the greater will be the response of trade to income changes.

Here we have, then, a second force tending to adjust the balance of payments under the gold standard. The initial gold flows from the deficit to the surplus country set in motion forces which, via interest rates, investment demand, and incomes, shift trade flows in favor of the deficit country. Exports of that country grow while its imports decline. At the same time imports of the surplus nation increase while its exports are reduced. The strength of this income effect of balance of payments adjustment under the specie-flow mechanism hinges on the interest elasticity of investment demand and of the demand for money, as well as on the marginal propensities to save and to import. Adjustment in this way will be "automatic" only if the money supply is fully tied to gold, if nothing prevents interest rates from responding freely and affecting incomes, and if there are no restrictions to international trade and payments.

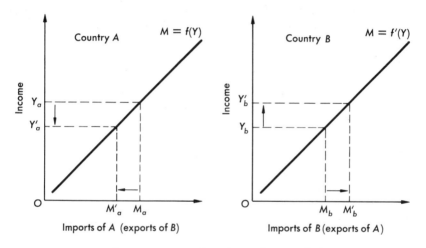

Fig. 21–3. Response of trade to changes in income.

PRICE EFFECT

There is yet a third way in which automatic balance of payments adjustment may come about under the gold standard in this case. Declining incomes in the deficit country tend to reduce its demand for both imports and domestically produced goods, while rising incomes in the surplus country have precisely the opposite effect of tending to raise demand for both home and import goods.

The extent of the rise in Country B's demand for Country A's exports is, of course, determined by the former's marginal propensity to import; the larger it is, the more pronounced will be the effect of its income expansion on import demand. By the same token, how much Country A's demand for imports (Country B's exports) falls as a result of its income decline depends upon the magnitude of its own marginal propensity to import.

The net change in the *total* demand for A's goods (reduced domestic demand versus increased export demand) and B's goods (increased domestic demand versus reduced export demand) will determine the tendency of any movement in the relative prices of their goods and services. It appears that if the sum of the marginal propensities to import of A and B is *less than unity*, the result will be a net overall decline in the demand for A's products and a net overall increase in the demand for B's products.[1] Under such conditions, A's prices may decline relative to B's prices, and the *terms of trade* may thus shift against the deficit country; i.e., A's goods and services may become cheaper relative to those of B on world markets. This is the same thing as saying that—to the extent that prices are indeed flexible to some degree—the prices of the exports of the surplus country, B, may increase relative to those of its imports (the exports of deficit country A), and its terms of trade improve.

With the possibility of the terms of trade shifting against the deficit country, A, and in favor of the surplus country, B, it is to be expected that there will occur a change in demand patterns in favor of the deficit country. Since the imports of the former become relatively more expensive, its purchases from abroad will tend to decline. At the same time, the surplus country finds its imports becoming relatively cheaper and tends to expand its purchases from abroad accordingly. The result is a tendency for further decline in Country A's imports and an expansion of its exports, while Country B tends to expand its imports and undergo a reduction in its exports. The balance of trade of the deficit country thus tends to improve once more, while that of the surplus country deteriorates, thereby promoting the third and final balance of payments adjustment—the price effect.

GENERAL EQUILIBRIUM ANALYSIS

It may be helpful to illustrate the income-specie flow mechanism of balance of payments adjustment in another way, utilizing a geometric technique that employs the *LM* and *IS* functions reviewed in Chapter 2.

Recall that the *LM* function represents all possible pairs of interest rates and income levels consistent with the existence of an equilibrium in the money market. The *IS* function, in turn, defines all possible pairs of interest rates and income levels consistent with equilibrium in the market for goods and services. Only one combination of interest rates and income

[1] This reasoning is traced through in greater detail in James E. Meade, *The Balance of Payments* (London: Oxford University Press, 1951), chs. vii, xiv, and xv. It can be shown that if the sum of the marginal propensities to import equals unity, the demand increase will exactly equal the demand decline for *both* A's and B's products, so that the terms of trade will not change. Meade contends, however, that a value of less than unity is "the normal case" (p. 193).

level satisfies both and occurs where the two curves intersect, point E in Figure 21–4.

To this conventional diagram we can add an external balance function FF. The preceding discussion of the interest and income effects of payments adjustment indicated that there is (a) a positive relation between the rate of interest and the degree of payments surplus, and (b) a negative relation between the level of national income and the degree of payments surplus. Hence, payment *balance* can be maintained *either* with low income levels and interest rates *or* with high income levels and interest rates. Curve FF in Figure 21–4 represents all possible pairs of interest rates and income levels consistent with balance in the balance of payments. Any interest rate and income combination represented by a point to the left of FF, therefore, must denote a payments surplus, and any point to the right of FF must denote a payments deficit.

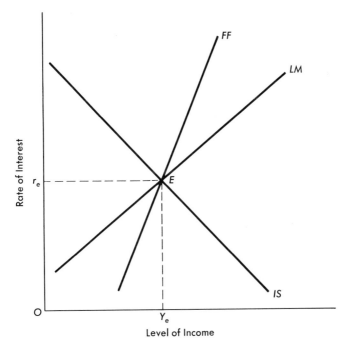

Fig. 21–4. General equilibrium.

Again, only one combination of interest rates and income levels will simultaneously produce equilibrium in (a) the market for goods and services, (b) the money market, and (c) the balance of payments. This unique *general equilibrium* occurs at point E in the figure, with the prevailing interest rate and level of income being R_e and Y_e, respectively.

Referring now to Figure 21-5, suppose as in our earlier example we have an autonomously induced capital transfer and corresponding specie flow from Country A to Country B. The result is a leftward shift of the FF_A function in the deficit country; i.e., a higher interest rate and/or lower income level than prevail at E_A are necessary in order to restore payments

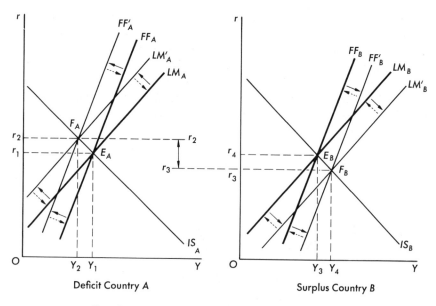

Deficit Country A   Surplus Country B

Fig. 21-5.   Restoration of general equilibrium.

balance. This, of course, comes about automatically under the income-specie flow mechanism. The outflow of specie automatically causes a contraction of the money supply, causing a leftward shift of the LM_A function. The rising interest rate and falling income levels eventually re-establish equilibrium at F_A.

The reverse happens in the surplus country, with a rightward shift in the FF_B curve due to the capital inflow, and an induced increase in the money supply shifting the LM_B curve to the right as well, re-establishing equilibrium at F_B. Note, however, that the interest rate (r_2) in Country A is now substantially higher than in Country B (r_3). We, therefore, expect an induced return flow of capital from B to A with a commensurate reversal in specie flows. The FF_A and LM_A' curves thus shift once more to the right—and the FF_B and LM_B curves to the left—toward the initial respective equilibria at E_A and E_B. Once again a general equilibrium, satisfying both internal and external balance requirements, is restored via shifts in interest rates and income levels.

Note that developments *within* the two national economies, in terms of prevailing interest rates and income levels, serve to bring about all of the necessary adjustments. To be sure, the initial conditions ultimately tend to be restored, but during the adjustment period substantial changes in national economies and in money market conditions do occur, and without them there could be no restoration of equilibrium. Transitory economic recessions and tight money are a *necessary* part of the adjustment process for the deficit countries, just as economic expansions and easy money are *required* in surplus countries.

SUMMARY OF EFFECTS

We can summarize balance of payments adjustments to an imbalance caused by capital flows under the income-specie flow mechanism, then, in terms of the three ways in which adjustment takes place (see Figure 21-6). Specie flows from the deficit to the surplus country, raising interest rates in the former and lowering them in the latter as a result of changes in their respective money supplies. This change in relative yields dampens the flow of capital from the deficit to the surplus country and stimulates capital flows in the opposite direction, thereby helping to bring the payments back into balance.

The rise in interest rates in the deficit country dampens investment demand which, via the multiplier, depresses national income and, hence, imports. The reverse occurs in the surplus country, with investment demand, national income, and imports rising. The consequent income-induced shift in trade flows in favor of the deficit country thus serves as another balancing force.

Finally, the reduction of national income in the deficit country, and its rise in the surplus country lowers domestic demand for home products in the former nation and raises it in the latter. To the extent that the sum of the marginal propensities to import of the two countries is less than unity, the opposite changes in export demand will not offset the prevailing changes in domestic demand, and the *overall* demand for the deficit country's products will fall. It will rise in the case of the surplus country's products. If prices are at least partly responsive to changing supply and demand, these changes in overall demand for home goods will tend to raise prices in the surplus country and lower them in the deficit country. Internationally, the terms of trade shift against the deficit country, and they provide a third and final contribution to balance of payments adjustment by improving the balance of trade of the deficit country and reducing that of the surplus country.[2]

---

[2] As will be shown below, in connection with our discussion of balance of payments adjustment under flexible exchange rates, this will occur only if the sum of the two countries' respective price elasticities of demand for imports exceeds unity (the Marshall–Lerner condition discussed in Chapter 22).

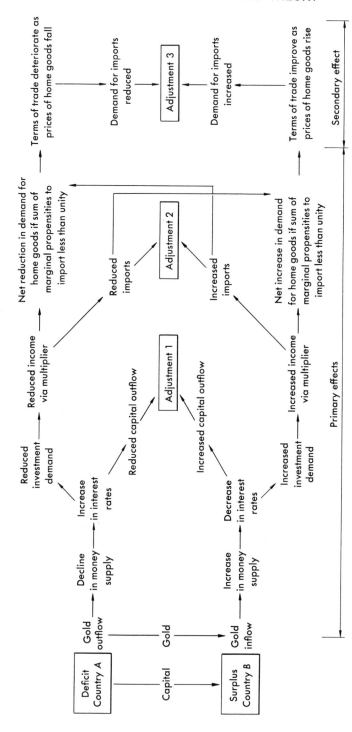

Fig. 21–6. Balance of payments adjustment under the income-specie flow mechanism in response to an autonomous flow of capital. (Adapted from James E. Meade, *The Balance of Payments.* London: Oxford University Press, 1951, p. 192.)

The income-specie flow adjustment process outlined here applies equally well to *unilateral transfers* that cause a balance of payments deficit, i.e., if they are not tied to purchases in the donor country. If on the other hand, the deficit is caused by *surplus of imports over exports* (due to, say, a demand shift) as a second possibility, the adjustment mechanism is slightly different. First, internationally, the demand for the surplus country's goods clearly exceeds the demand for the deficit country's products, and, hence, the prices of the latter—to the extent that they are flexible—will tend to fall and those of the former will tend to rise. This price effect will help to restore balance. Second, since the deficit country's imports exceed its exports, its national income will tend to fall, and so will its imports. The reverse happens in the surplus country, and both aid in the restoration of payments balance (income effect.) Third, even though the flow of specie out of the deficit country reduces its money supply, the simultaneous import-induced reduction in incomes lower the transactions demand for money, and, as a result, interest rates may not rise very significantly. For the same reason, the rate of interest may not fall by very much in the surplus country, so that the *interest-effect* on adjustment may be relatively minor.

Finally, a payments imbalance may be caused by an *economic expansion* in Country *A* and/or recession in Country *B*, as reflected in imports and exports and capital flows. This will tend to (a) cause Country *A* to run a *deficit* in its trade of goods and services with Country *B*, as a result of the effects of income on imports in both countries; (b) cause Country *A* to run a *surplus* on capital account as its rising interest rates relative to those in *B* cause a net capital inflow; and (c) cause *A* to run a deficit in its trade of goods and services with *B* if its prices rise relative to those in *B* as a result of the differential movement in aggregate demand. If (a) and (c) above outweigh point (b), Country *A* will have a balance of payments deficit and a gold loss; but if point (b) outweighs the combination of (a) and (c), it will undergo a gold inflow and balance of payments surplus. In either case, balance will tend to be restored along the lines noted earlier.

THE PRICE-SPECIE FLOW MECHANISM

The elements tending to bring about adjustment of the balance of payments under fixed exchange rates, as discussed above, are founded in modern Keynesian national income theory applied to specie-flow conditions. Thus the burden of adjustment is borne by changes in interest rates and incomes resulting from international gold flows. Whether the price effect is of importance at all hinges upon the flexibility of costs and prices with changes in aggregate demand. In times of relative full employment, there is no question but that additional demand tends to raise prices. But this is not necessarily true when there is excess productive capacity available in the economy, and today's students of economics would certainly voice doubts about the *downward* flexibility of prices under any circumstances.

Before the advent of Keynesian theory, the price effect was considered the most important element in the balance of payments adjustment mechanism under the gold standard. This is easy to explain. Economists by and large adhered to the famous *quantity theory of money*, under which the price level varied directly with the money supply.

Irving Fisher's equation of exchange,

$$MV = PT$$

should be familiar to the reader. With the velocity of money (V) and the physical production of goods and services (T) remaining relatively constant, any change in the money supply (M) would immediately be reflected in the price level (P). Gold flows into the surplus country and raises the money supply. Instead of purchasing financial assets and driving interest rates down as in the case of Keynesian analysis above, people use the additional money to buy goods and services. Since prices are assumed to be flexible and real output will not respond to the increase in aggregate spending, prices will rise. In the deficit country, with gold out-flows and monetary contraction, the reverse will happen and prices will decline. Hence, the international flow of gold through its effect on the money supply has an immediate impact on prices, which fall in the deficit country and rise in the surplus country, setting the adjustment process into motion. This is the so-called *price-specie flow mechanism*.

This traditional link between the money supply and the price level is neither simply assumed to be true, nor simply assumed to be completely false. Some faith can still be placed in the price effect, if prices and wages are thought to be flexible at least to some extent. An outflow of gold tends to raise interest rates; investment projects are postponed or cancelled and inventories are run off. Employment is reduced in the affected industries, disposable income declines, and we note a further decline in the demand for consumer goods. Prices may then become depressed as inventories are disposed of, and even wages may decline as the unemployed seek to offer their services to employers at lower rates. Thus, domestic products of the deficit country become relatively cheaper, while the reverse occurs in the surplus country undergoing a gold inflow.

But even this formulation of the link between prices and gold flows is probably too direct. With the rigidities that we know to exist in prices and wages, particularly the resistance to change in the downward direction, we can express legitimate doubts about whether the price effect can today be an important adjustment element under the specie flow mechanism—if, indeed, it ever was.

This lack of faith in the price-specie flow mechanism and its successors caused us to place a greater burden of adjustment under the gold standard upon the income effects of trade, and the effect of changing interest rates on capital flows.

But to return to our main point: under the income-specie flow mechanism, if all of the necessary conditions hold true—no restrictions to trade and payments, the money supply firmly tied to specie flows or changes in international reserves, and so forth—balance of payments adjustment will be virtually automatic. The individual *national economies* do the adjusting in terms of interest rates, output, employment, and, perhaps to some extent, prices. A country possessing a payments deficit *must* submit itself to the "rules of the game" and allow the automatic income-specie flow adjustment to run its course, despite the painful internal adjustments it may entail.

That the countries of the world are no longer willing to play by these rules—that, in fact, balance of payments adjustment under the gold standard perhaps never was really automatic—is little wonder. What happens when these rules are violated will occupy our attention a little later.

THE GOLD STANDARD BEFORE AND AFTER 1914

When discussing the "balance of payments problem," many people hark back to the good old gold standard when payments adjustment was indeed "automatic," and payments crises were "nonexistent." ·Everyone played the game according to the rules and thereby insured the smooth operation of the gold-standard adjustment mechanism. Was it ever like this? The answer would have to be negative. Modern economic historians tend to agree that the gold-standard adjustment mechanism was never really "automatic," even before World War I.

A deficit country undergoing a gold outflow must permit its money supply to contract, and a surplus country must permit an expansion of its money supply when it incurs a gold inflow. Their monetary authorities must follow this basic rule, otherwise *none* of the adjustment effects can work themselves out. The evidence is, however, that governments did not obey this rule. Rather, gold inflows and outflows were often countered by open-market operations and other measures of monetary control that wiped out their impact on the money supply and, hence, their effects on interest rates, incomes, and prices.

In spite of this, there were relatively few serious balance of payments disturbances under the gold standard. The reason appears to lie in the equilibrating role of productive factor movements, especially international capital flows. Interregionally there are no balance of payments problems because disequilibria and maladjustments are immediately met by capital movements and, in the long run, by movements of both labor and capital. With close relations existing between important international financial centers and few restrictions to trade or capital flows, there is no reason why the equilibrating role of capital movements cannot also make itself felt internationally. Before 1914, this indeed seems to have occurred with compensatory capital flows making large-scale gold movements unnecessary and providing time for more basic, underlying structural readjustments. Even these were widely achieved by means of international flows of capital and—since there existed few restrictions to immigration—labor as well. Hence, the fact that the rules of the game were not followed precisely may have had relatively little impact.

Much of this freedom was lacking during the post-World War I operation of the gold standard, 1925–1931. Again the gold standard rules were not followed, but the restrictions to trade, capital flows, and immigration, as well as the loose ties among the world's banking and financial centers, made this failure much less pardonable. Adjustment now did have to occur according to the rules of the gold standard, since international capital and labor movements could not exert their cushioning influence. To the extent that these rules were violated, with interest rates, incomes, and prices not permitted to adjust in order to restore payments balance, the gold standard was doomed. The depression of the 1930's served to put an end to it.

To summarize, balance of payments adjustment under an equilibrium system of fixed exchange rates depends on shifts in interest rates and income levels, which set in motion international trade and capital flows that serve to restore payments balance. Under such a system the ratio of international reserves to the domestic money stock must remain fixed (i.e., active monetary policy is out of the question), and each country must willingly undergo recessions or inflations when balance of payments adjustment demands it. That no modern national state is willing to play by these rules is no great secret, and explains why automatic balance of payments adjustment as discussed here is politically out of the question. But elements of this adjustment process do play a vital role in the real world.

22

EQUILIBRIUM ADJUSTMENT SYSTEMS: FLEXIBLE EXCHANGE RATES

At the beginning of the last chapter we noted that we would commence our study of balance of payments adjustment by examining various types of equilibrium systems, i.e., those which foster virtually automatic restoration of payments balance. The first of these was the income– and price–specie flow mechanism, and variants thereof, under which balance of payments adjustment results from induced changes in incomes, interest rates, and prices obtained within the national economies under consideration. The balance of payments adjustment mechanism under flexible exchange rates, although also representing an equilibrium system, is quite different. It is not primarily based on internal adjustments of the individual national economies involved, but rather upon shifts in the exchange rate in response to changing supply and demand conditions on the foreign-exchange market. Again, however, adjustment is essentially automatic barring interferences with the operation of the mechanism.

Once more, we can identify three elements tending to bring about adjustment under flexible exchange rates: changing relative prices of goods and services internationally and their bearing on trade, the effect of variations in interest rates on international capital flows, and the effect on imports of changing incomes. Of the three, the price effect is by far the most important under flexible exchange rates, in contrast to the various forms of fixed-exchange rate adjustment mechanism, under which the interest and income effects appear to assume the leading role.

PRICE EFFECT AND STABILITY CONDITIONS

If a country has a balance of payments deficit under a system of flexible-exchange rates, the supply of its currency will by definition exceed the demand for it on the foreign-exchange markets. Or, what is the same thing, its demand for foreign exchange exceeds the supply of foreign exchange available to it. In any case, the result is a depreciation of the deficit country's currency relative to those of other nations. If we again assume a two-country world, and an initial disturbance caused by a capital flow from *A* to *B,* we can say that the currency of the deficit country (*A*) depreciates, while that of the surplus country (*B*) appreciates.

A depreciation of Country *A*'s currency means that imports become relatively more expensive to domestic consumers in terms of the home currency, and it is to be expected that their purchases of goods from abroad will be reduced. At the same time, businesses and individuals in Country *B* find that imports are becoming relatively cheaper in their home currency and tend to expand their foreign purchases. The depreciation of the deficit country's currency, relative to that of the surplus country, will thus tend to cause an increase in its exports and a decline in its imports, thereby helping to restore payments balance. We speak of a *tendency* here because we cannot be certain that the depreciation of the deficit nation's currency will improve its balance of trade until the relevant *import elasticities* are known.

The depreciation of the deficit country's currency in terms of foreign exchange constitutes a *de facto* rise in its import prices in terms of the domestic currency, and a decline in its export prices in terms of the currency of Country *B*; i.e., the terms of trade shift in its disfavor. The decline in export prices of the deficit country in terms of foreign currency will increase its receipts from exports *only* if the elasticity of demand for its exports (the foreign import elasticity) is greater than zero. The rise in domestic currency import prices will bring about a decline in expenditures on imports only if its own elasticity of import demand is greater than unity. This much should be quite evident.

If Country *A*'s import elasticity and Country *B*'s import elasticity are *both* less than unity, the general rule is that the decline in the foreign-exchange prices of goods produced by the deficit country, relative to the domestic-currency prices of the deficit country's imports, will contribute to balance of payments adjustment only on condition that *the sum of the two countries' respective elasticities of demand for import exceeds unity.* This is the so-called *Marshall-Lerner condition.* It is not difficult to understand why this relation must hold if the price effect is to make itself felt as an element in the adjustment process.

If the deficit country's elasticity of demand for imports is indeed greater than unity, the depreciation-induced shift in the terms of trade in its disfavor *must* improve its balance of trade no matter what the foreign elasticity of demand for its exports—the surplus country's demand for imports. Under such conditions the reduction of its expenditures on imports, in response to rising domestic-currency import prices, will insure that its balance of trade improves, even if its domestic-currency export receipts remain the same in the face of a perfectly inelastic foreign import demand. On the other hand, if the *surplus* country's elasticity of demand for imports exceeds unity, the exports of the deficit country will expand to such an extent that its balance of trade will improve, even if its expenditures on imports rise in proportion to the depreciation with the rising domestic-currency import prices under an inelastic domestic demand for imports. In both cases, the sum of the two countries' elasticities of import demand naturally exceeds unity.

If, however, both nations' elasticities of import demand are less than unity, but the *sum* of the elasticities of demand for imports of both the deficit and the surplus countries exceeds unity, the balance of payments of the deficit country will improve. With a sum of less than unity, it will deteriorate. If the sum of the elasticities of demand for imports of the two countries is greater than one, for the deficit country the increase in domestic-currency expenditures on imports as a result of the adverse terms of trade shift will be more than offset by an increase in domestic-currency export receipts, and the balance of trade will improve, thus aiding in balance of payments adjustment. With a sum of less than unity, however, the deficit country's domestic-currency increase in expenditures on imports due to rising import prices will outweigh the rise in domestic-currency export receipts, and the balance of trade and, hence, the balance of payments will deteriorate further.

All of this is represented schematically in Table 22–1, showing the reaction of the balance of trade of the deficit country (A), as expressed in its own currency, to a shift in the terms of trade in its disfavor under varying elasticity conditions. It is not difficult to see that the sum of the import-demand elasticities must indeed exceed unity if the balance of trade of the country undergoing an adverse shift in the terms of trade is to improve; i.e., the Marshall–Lerner condition must hold.

We should, however, bring up one important qualification at this juncture. The relationships expressed here depend in part upon the relevant elasticities of supply. The above discussion implicitly assumes infinite elasticities of supply. But, if, for example, the elasticity of export supply is relatively low, export prices of the deficit country will not fall very far, and the balance of trade may improve even if the sum of the two countries' respective import-demand elasticities is less than unity. This can occur

Table 22–1

The Effect of a Shift in the Terms of Trade Against Country A upon its
Balance of Trade Under Different Import Elasticities

(in terms of the currency of Country A)

Elasticity of import demand— Country A	Elasticity of import demand— Country B	Sum of the elastici- ties	A's expendi- ture on imports will	A's receipts from exports will	A's *balance of trade will*
$e_m \geq 1$	$e_m \geq 1$	>1	Fall	Rise	Improve: Expenditures on imports fall and export receipts rise
$e_m > 1$	0	>1	Fall	Remain unchanged	Improve: Fall in expenditures on imports with no change in export receipts
0	$e_m > 1$	>1	Rise	Rise	Improve: Rise in expenditure on imports more than offset by rise in export receipts
$0 < e_m < 1$	$0 < e_m < 1$	<1	Rise	Rise	Deteriorate: Import payments rise and export expansion insufficient to offset it
$0 < e_m < 1$	$0 < e_m < 1$	>1	Rise	Rise	Improve: Import payments rise but export expansion more than offsets it
$0 < e_m < 1$	$0 < e_m < 1$	=1	Rise	Rise	Unchanged: Import payments rise and export expansion exactly offsets it

under certain conditions, and especially if export capacity is virtually exhausted and the potential for increased exports is strictly limited. Similarly, if the elasticity of import supply (foreign export supply) is low, import expenditures for the deficit country may not rise very high, and the Marshall-Lerner condition need not necessarily hold true in order for the balance of trade to improve.

We have introduced the Marshall-Lerner condition here, in connection with our discussion of balance of payments adjustment under flexible exchange rates, precisely because it assumes a major role in the adjustment process.

This brings up a very important application of the Marshall-Lerner condition to the foreign-exchange market under flexible exchange rates. If a country has a balance of payments deficit, its currency depreciates. If, moreover, the sum of the elasticities of demand for imports is *less* than unity, the depreciation will result in a *worsening* of its deficit, since an increase in import expenditures outweighs the simultaneous rise in export receipts. This leads to further depreciation, an even larger deficit, and so forth. In short, if the Marshall-Lerner *stability conditions* are not met, everything else being equal, the balance of payments under flexible-exchange rates is inherently unstable and—because it is determined entirely by supply and demand—so is the exchange rate.

This is shown graphically in Figure 22–1. In part A of Figure 22–1 the usual supply and demand curves for foreign exchange are drawn. If the home country's currency depreciates, and the exchange rate rises as a result of a payments deficit induced by a capital outflow, its import demand for foreign currencies falls since imports become relatively more expensive. The demand curve for foreign exchange and, if we are only

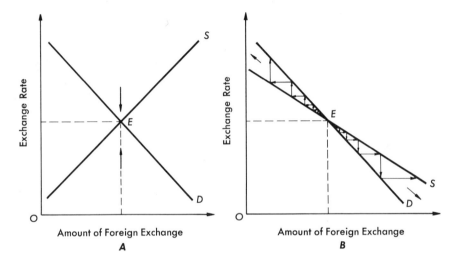

Fig. 22–1. Stable and unstable exchange rates.

talking about merchandise trade, the demand curve for imports, is negatively sloped and has an elasticity coefficient of between zero and infinity. The supply curve of foreign exchange—the foreign demand for the home country's exports—is positively sloped. As the home currency depreciates, and its exports become relatively cheaper for foreigners, the home country's exports (foreign imports) rise. Under such conditions, with the sum of the elasticities greater than unity, the balance of payments and the exchange rates tend toward stability. Any exchange rate above or below equilibrium (E) sets into motion forces which drive the rate back toward the equilibrium position.

Not so, however, in Figure 22–1B. Here the demand curve for foreign exchange assumes its usual shape, but the supply of foreign exchange is negatively sloped. A balance of payments deficit will immediately cause a depreciation of the exchange rate. This causes a decline in export receipts in excess of the decline in import payments, if the sum of the two import elasticities is less than one, and this results in a further deficit, a further depreciation, and so forth. The reverse occurs in the case of a country with a balance of payments surplus. In any case, it is easy to see that if the stability conditions are not met, and the sum of the elasticities of demand for imports is less than unity, neither the balance of payments nor the exchange rate will tend toward equilibrium and the adjustment mechanism falls apart. If the relevant supply elasticities are less than infinite, as noted above, the stability conditions can be violated slightly without resulting in instability.

Measurements of price elasticities in international trade have been partly aimed at providing a definitive answer to the question whether the Marshall–Lerner conditions actually hold in the real world. Most recent estimates—as well as actual experience with floating exchange rates since August 1971—seem to indicate that they do. One problem is that the lag between an exchange-rate shift and its impact on trade flows may be somewhat extended. One study indicated that, for a variety of manufactured goods, the reaction time is 4 to 5 years or longer, with only half the ultimate effect occurring over the first 3 years and 90 per cent over the first 5 years. This is thought to differ from the traditional 18 to 24 month estimates, based mainly on intuition, for the following reasons:

1. *Managerial* recognition lags in perceiving changed competitive conditions
2. *Decision* lags in forming new business connections
3. *Delivery* lags between the time orders are placed and the time they are reflected in trade and payments flows
4. *Replacement* lags for using up existing inventories
5. *Production* lags related to suppliers' response to new and presumably permanent market opportunities.[1]

Lags in the adjustment process are thus an important consideration under flexible exchange rates even if adjustment ultimately comes about.

In summary we have, then, the primary balance of payments adjustment under flexible exchange rates; i.e., if the sum of the elasticities of demand for imports exceeds unity, the shift in the terms of trade against the deficit country caused by the depreciation of its currency will bring about an improvement in its balance of trade and, hence, in its balance of payments. In fact, the effect of the depreciation on trade flows by itself may be sufficient to completely restore balance, thereby requiring no adjustment at all on the part of the national economies involved. If the Marshall-Lerner condition does not hold, a nation's balance of payments,

[1] See Helen Junz and Rudolf R. Rhomberg, "Price Competitiveness in Export Trade Among Industrial Countries", *American Economic Review*, May, 1973.

as well as the exchange rate itself, will be unstable and there evidently can be no adjustment under flexible exchange rates.

INTEREST EFFECT

Assuming that the price effect of balance of payments adjustment under flexible exchange rates does indeed occur, the overall demand—both foreign and domestic—for the products of the deficit country will tend to rise. The exchange-rate depreciation causes a substitution of domestic for imported goods at home and increases the export demand from abroad. The reverse will tend to occur in the surplus country, with increased imports and reduced exports leading to an overall reduction in the demand for its products. In order to maintain internal balance—i.e., to avoid any export-led inflation—monetary authorities may restrict the money supply and force interest rates upward in the deficit country. In the surplus country, on the other hand, in order to avoid recessionary pressure due to the excess of imports over exports resulting from the exchange-rate adjustment, monetary authorities may expand the monetary supply and bring about lower interest rates. This movement in interest rates may occur even without any policy response on the part of the two countries. In the deficit country, the overall increase in the demand for its products causes the transactions demand for money to rise and, the money supply remaining constant, the interest rates to increase. The reverse may happen in the surplus country.

The rise of interest rates in the deficit country and their fall in the surplus country makes the former relatively more attractive for loans and investments. Hence the tendency is for capital flows to be reduced from deficit Country A to surplus Country B, but increased from Country B to Country A.

A second balance of payments adjustment may then occur. The interest effect making for balance of payments adjustment under flexible exchange rates is likely to be substantially weaker than the price effect resulting from the exchange-rate depreciation. In fact, it *depends* upon the latter. Only to the extent that the price effect of the deficit nation's currency depreciation is substantial will there be any marked tendency for changes in interest rates in both countries.

INCOME EFFECT

With the possibility of increasing interest rates in the deficit country, the same reasoning used in connection with the income effect under the income-specie flow mechanism would lead us to believe that national income in the deficit country should tend to be reduced. Increased interest rates tend to result in a reduction in investment expenditure (via the investment-demand function), and this, via the multiplier, tends to depress national income. In the surplus country the reduced interest rates presumably stimulate expenditures and income by the same token.

As long as the marginal propensity to import lies above zero, the resulting decline in national income in the deficit country—if any—will tend to cause a further reduction of imports. Similarly, any rise in national income induced by lower interest rates in the surplus country tends to result in a further reduction of imports. Similarly, any rise in national income induced by lower interest rates in the surplus country tends to result in a further expansion of imports. Hence, with a possible tendency for the deficit country's imports to decline and its exports to rise as a consequence of income changes at home and abroad, and the reverse occurring in the surplus country, a third tendency for balance of payments adjustment may be achieved.

GENERAL EQUILIBRIUM ANALYSIS

Balance of payments adjustment under flexible exchange rates can also be illustrated using the general equilibrium internal–external balance diagram introduced in the previous chapter. In Figure 22–2, a capital outflow

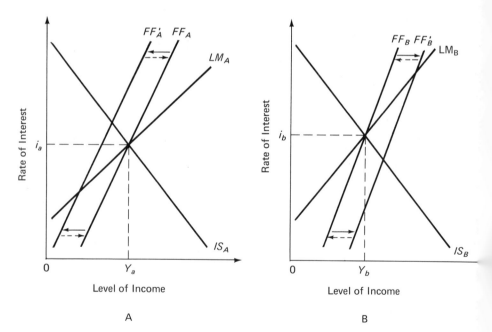

Fig. 22–2. Balance of payments adjustment under flexible rates.

shifts the foreign-balance function in Country A to the left, indicating a payments deficit at interest rate i_a and income level Y_a. At the same time it shifts Country B's foreign balance function to the right, yielding a balance of payments surplus at prevailing interest rate i_b and income level Y_b. However, the excess of foreign-exchange demand over supply in A causes its currency to depreciate, while the reverse causes B's currency to appreciate. As a result, A's trade balance improves while B's trade balance deteriorates, and the two FF curves drift back toward their original positions. Lags in the system may, however, produce interim interest-rate and income effects, as noted above. Flexible exchange rates thus partially insulate the domestic economies from international disturbances.

SUMMARY OF EFFECTS

The entire process of balance of payments adjustment under flexible exchange rates in response to a capital flow is presented in Figure 22–3. The price effect is the primary adjusting vehicle, with the interest effect and the income effect (internal adjustments) largely depending upon it because of shifts in relative currency values caused by the price effect.

In the case of a *unilateral transfer* that affects the exchange rate, the adjustment process under flexible exchange rates is similar to that outlined here. If, on the other hand, the initial imbalance results from an *autonomous increase in imports* on the part of one of the countries, the resulting exchange-rate shift will simply tend to reverse the trade flow until balance has been restored. Under these conditions, no internal effects at all are likely.

Suppose, finally, that the imbalance is caused by the impact of an *economic expansion* in A and/or recession in B. Balance will again tend to be restored as a result of the induced increase in A's import demand, relative to that of Country B, and its effect on the exchange rate. The depreciation on A's currency will tend to reverse the trade flows and to restore balance. If monetary authorities decide to offset the economic expansion in A by restrictive monetary policies, or authorities in B decide to adopt expansionary monetary measures, interest rates will rise in A relative to those in B, and the resulting capital flows from B to A may restore balance even without a change in the exchange rate.

Note the differences in adjustment under the income-specie flow mechanism and flexible exchange rates by comparing Figures 21–6 and 22–3. Unlike adjustment of the balance of payments under fixed exchange rates, the economy itself needs to do very little adjusting under flexible exchange rates. Most of the burden is carried by the shift in the exchange rate. This, via the price effect, immediately exerts a powerful force in the direction of payments adjustment. Even if the ancillary effects on in-

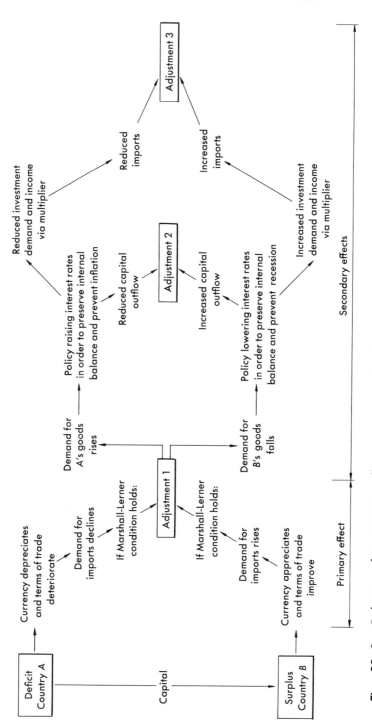

Fig. 22-3. Balance of payments adjustment under flexible exchange rates in response to an autonomous flow of capital. (Adapted from Meade, op. cit., p. 192.)

comes and interest rates were neutralized by national monetary authorities this adjustment would still tend to come about. Thus the internal operation of the economy can to a large extent be shielded from external forces. Domestic economic policy measures can be implemented with little regard to their impact on the balance of payments, since the exchange rate will automatically make the necessary adjustment.

It would seem that flexible exchange rates—if the elasticity conditions promote stability—are much more suitable to the present economic environment than the gold standard. Today, national governments pursue the generally accepted economic policy goals of reasonably full employment, price-level stability, and a viable rate of economic growth by means of a wide variety of monetary and fiscal instruments. They do this more or less independently of one another, and any impact of such measures on the balance of payments often assumes a secondary role in the formulation of economic policy. How can this be reconciled with the requirements of balance of payments adjustment under fixed-exchange rates, where international considerations play a determining role in domestic economic activity? It cannot. Yet adoption of entirely flexible exchange rates, thus severing the tie between international reserves and the national money supply completely, also may have some disadvantages related to the stability of the exchange rate itself and the impact unstable rates can have on international trade and payments.

1. Flexible exchange rates will serve the cause of balance of payments adjustment only if the Marshall-Lerner condition holds true, with suitable adjustments made for less than perfectly elastic supply functions. It is conceivable that under some circumstances the demand for imports may indeed be highly inelastic, especially in the short run, and that flexible exchange rates could thus be subject to some degree of instability.

2. We noted in Chapter 19 that flexible exchange rates may possibly have certain detrimental effects on international trade and investment. While their impact on international long-term capital flows can be debated, considering the potential role of speculative capital flows, the increased uncertainty they may engender could adversely affect international commerce to some degree.

3. Exchange flexibility may eliminate one important constraint to the formulation of economic policy. Under flexible exchange rates, the objective of full employment can be pursued through government deficit spending and other policy tools without the fear that any inflationary pressures thus brought about could have adverse external effects. The exchange rate simply shifts and absorbs any change in the domestic price level and eliminates any potential for external imbalance. However, the assumption that the adoption of a system of flexible exchange rates and the removal of the external constraint

would lead to reckless economic policy constitutes a pretty dim view of the capacity of economic policy makers.

The fact is, of course, that *neither* of the two equilibrium systems of balance of payments adjustment has been operative in the postwar international economy. Until August 1971, we had a system of stable exchange rates under which the respective values of national currencies were fixed in terms of one another and/or gold. Changes in these "pegged" exchange rates were made administratively, by government action. At the same time, governments were free to vary the national money supply and affect national economic activity by assorted monetary and fiscal measures, which were largely independent of one another and of the status of the balance of international payments. Under these conditions, the matter of balance of payments adjustment was largely one of administrative policy decisions; governments *decided* to vary the exchange rates, the money supply and interest rates, the level of economic activity, and so forth in the interest of restoring payments balance. Since 1971 we have had a system of floating exchange rates, embodying a considerable amount of flexibility but also a good deal of government intervention. The real world is thus characterized by a *disequilibrium* balance of payment adjustment system, which embodies elements of *both* of the equilibrium systems we have discussed but which incorporates the full automaticity of *neither* one. The analysis of such systems will be the subject of the following chapters.

23

DISEQUILIBRIUM
SYSTEMS: ADJUSTMENT
VIA INCOMES

We have stressed in the previous two chapters how imbalances in international payments tend to alleviate themselves under fixed and flexible exchange rates, so long as certain basic ground rules are obeyed and the adjustment mechanisms are free to operate without restrictions. It was stressed, however, that neither self-equilibrating system conforms to reality; and that today's international monetary system combines several of the characteristics of each and, hence, some of the advantages and disadvantages of both. One thing is certain: there is relatively little automaticity in balance of payments adjustment in the real world. Adjustment under *pegged* exchange rates will occur automatically only so long as the money supply, interest rates, income, employment, and/or prices are allowed to respond freely to changes in international reserves. Balance of payments adjustment under *flexible* exchange rates can take place automatically only if exchange rates are permitted to vary freely with shifts in the supply of and demand for foreign exchange. Neither of these conditions is, in fact, entirely satisfied today. Rather, balance of payments adjustments has become largely a matter of *policy*.

As will soon become evident, a wide variety of instruments stand available to national governments for the restoration of payments balance. These include, of course, changes in interest rates and income, as in the adjustment mechanism under fixed exchange rates, and exchange-rate shifts through currency *revaluation*, as under flexible rates. If floating exchange rates obtain, decisions have to be made as to when and to what extent authorities should intervene in foreign-exchange markets for stabilization purposes—i.e., the "cleanness" of the float. Moreover, the consequences of exchange-rate depreciation or appreciation are not always economically or politically desirable, inducing governments to engage in prolonged market intervention to maintain disequilibrium exchange rates.

CHARACTERISTICS OF A DISEQUILIBRIUM SYSTEM

We know that a disequilibrium system of balance of payments adjustment differs from the equilibrium systems surveyed in the preceding chapters essentially in that there exists no neutral, self-governing mechanism guaranteeing an eventual return to general equilibrium—one encompassing both internal and external economic conditions. The commitment of national governments to the maintenance of high employment, stable prices, and viable rates of economic growth by means of independently implemented monetary and fiscal measures certainly precludes the required impact of balance of payments surplus or deficit on the national economy that is necessary for a restoration of equilibrium under fixed exchange rates.

We can once again employ general equilibrium analysis to show that an automatic return to equilibrium is at best unlikely under the conditions that exist today. Recall the necessary conditions for the maintenance of internal and external balance. Only one combination of interest rates and income levels can at any one time simultaneously insures payments balance (FF), money market balance (LM), and balance in the market for goods and services (IS). Under an equilibrium system of fixed exchange rates (see Figure 21–5) or flexible exchange rates (see Figure 22–2), displacement of the FF curve automatically sets into motion forces which tend to restore general equilibrium.

The original, general equilibrium situation is reproduced in Figure 23–1. The common intersection of the FF, IS, and LM functions occurs at E_A in Country A and at E_B in Country B, with the prevailing interest rates and income levels being r_A, and Y_A, and r_B and Y_B, respectively. We shall assume that points E_A and E_B represent conditions of internal balance, i.e., full employment, noninflationary equilibria. Let us again impose an autonomously induced flow of capital from A to B, causing a balance of payments deficit and loss of international reserves for Country A, and a surplus and reserve gain in Country B. The external balance function (FF) in A shifts to the left, and in B it shifts to the right, say, to $FF_A{}'$ and $FF_B{}'$, respectively. If the changes in international reserves were free to affect the national money supply, under fixed exchange rates curves LM_A and LM_B would shift toward the new equilibrium points at F_A and F_B. This would herald a transitory economic recession and higher interest rates in A and an economic expansion and lower interest rates in B, and from there adjustment would proceed by the familiar income–specie flow route. The movement would again proceed in the direction of the initial equilibria at E_A and E_B.

But economic policymakers are not willing to let this internal adjustment process occur, because both countries are in internal, full-employment, noninflationary equilibrium at Y_A and Y_B to begin with. In A, the authorities use quantitative monetary techniques to *neutralize* the inherent contractionary effects of the loss of international reserves, thereby leaving the LM_A function where it is. In B, authorities similarly neutralize the expansionary effects of the reserves inflow. E_A and E_B remain as *partial* equilibria, with a deficit and reserve loss in A, and a surplus and reserve gain in B. As long as the capital flow continues, the transfer of reserves from A to B similarly prevails—as long as A has the international gold and/or foreign-currency reserves to service the drain.

In Country A, contractionary fiscal policy could be used to shift the IS_A curve leftward to restore external and internal balance at G_A. Similarly, Country B could accomplish the same thing via expansionary fiscal measures, causing a shift in the IS_B function to G_B. But the unwillingness to sacrifice internal balance, even temporarily, for the sake of payments balance is evident here as well. Note that the movement away from internal balance at E_A and E_B would be substantially greater as a result of shifts in the IS functions than as a result of movements in the LM curves.

Alternatively, suppose floating exchange rates prevail. The equilibrating adjustment process would involve depreciation of A's currency and appreciation of B's currency, resulting in an improvement in A's balance of trade with B and a gradual drift of the two FF functions back toward their original positions. However, if government intervention in foreign exchange markets prevents the shift in relative currency values, adjustment along these lines cannot occur and the disequilibrium persists.

The problem of payments disequilibrium is quite a bit more complex than we have indicated here. It is therefore worthwhile to categorize the various types of disequilibria, according to the nature of their origin, at this point.

CYCLICAL DISEQUILIBRIUM

Much earlier in this study, it became evident that there exists a positive relationship between national income and imports, just as a positive relationship prevails between national income and consumption. The connection between income and imports is given by the average propensity to import and the marginal propensity to import. The former establishes the proportion of total income spent on imports, while the latter defines the proportion of any increase in income that will be spent on imports. It is very likely, under the reasonable assumption that the marginal propensity to import is greater than zero, that a rise in the level of domestic economic activity— and, hence, national income—will shortly be reflected in a country's balance of payments as an increase in imports. Assuming that the balance of payments was in equilibrium before, and exchange rates are pegged, it will be in disequilibrium now by the amount of increased imports. After the foreign repercussions effect has worked itself out, there is still likely to be a balance of payments deficit despite the secondary export expansion.

A similar balance of payments deficit might be caused by reductions in incomes abroad. Economic recessions in foreign countries result in domestic export reductions. Even if the resultant decline in domestic incomes offsets part of this with decreased imports, the balance of payments deficit is likely to remain. Either domestic-income expansion, via increased imports, or foreign-income decline, via decreased exports, can thus be the source of balance of payments deficits. Conversely, a decline in domestic incomes or an increase in foreign incomes tends to result in a balance of payments surplus via reduced imports and increased exports, respectively. Because balance of payments deficits and surpluses arising in this manner are so closely tied to the prevailing level of economic activity at home and abroad, they are often grouped under the heading of *cyclical disequilibrium*.

It is easy to visualize that balance of payments disequilibria arising from this source will be greater, the *less* are business cycle developments in different countries synchronized with one another. If domestic and foreign incomes always rise and fall together, changes in imports will tend to be largely offset by correspondingly changed exports, and the balance of payment effect may well be minor. If, on the other hand, domestic incomes are high when foreign incomes are low, and vice versa, imports will rise at the very time exports fall, and the impact on the balance of payments will be great indeed—alternating deficits and surpluses. Even after foreign repercussions are considered, we can still say that the more nearly synchronous is the timing of business cycle developments at home and abroad, the smaller will be the cyclical disequilibria in the balance of payments arising as a result.

Even under the assumption that the timing of business cycles coincides perfectly in one nation and another, balance of payments disequilibria can still result from changing levels of economic activity, if the marginal propensity to import varies between nations. If income rises at the same rate both at home and abroad, yet the home country possesses a high marginal propensity to import while that prevailing abroad is low, a balance of payments deficit will still result on the part of the home country; imports simply rise faster than exports. In times of recession the reverse is true; imports fall faster than exports, resulting in a balance of payments surplus. We can thus make a further statement: the more divergent are the marginal propensities to import for the various trading countries, the greater is the likelihood of cyclical balance of payments disequilibria.

The *composition* of imports must be considered as well. The trade of some countries is concentrated in commodities highly susceptible to cyclical fluctations, while the trade of other nations is not. Raw materials, for example, comprise an important segment of the imports of industrialized countries, and virtually all of the exports of developing countries. When a recession hits industrialized nations, therefore, they tend first to draw down their raw materials inventories, cutting back sharply on imports. In times of economic expansion, an equally pronounced raw-materials buildup leads to a sharp import rise. This behavior tends to give such nations a high marginal propensity to import, much to the distress of the developing countries, whose balances of payments are almost entirely at the mercy of business conditions prevailing abroad. When the industrialized economies expand, so do their exports; an economic slump abroad signifies a substantial export reduction. We shall return to the problem of balance of payments vulnerability on the part of developing countries later, in connection with a discussion of economic development.

Cyclical disequilibrium of the balance of payments, then, is an important element to be considered. Its importance varies with the magnitude of business cycles, the coincidence of timing, the relationship of the various countries' respective marginal propensities to import, and trade composition.

It also poses a problem with floating exchange rates. If these rates were free to reflect shifts in economic conditions, domestic expansion (foreign contraction) would cause a depreciation of the domestic currency and alter the flow of trade—only to have this flow shift back again when economic conditions reverse themselves. Such two-way shifts in international competitiveness are not at all costless, and may provide ample justification for at least partly neutralizing cyclical exchange-rate swings.

STRUCTURAL DISEQUILIBRIUM: TRADE

Another source of balance of payments disequilibrium, which is reflected primarily in imports and exports, has to do with changes in the structure of demand and supply patterns, both at home and abroad.

Suppose, for instance, domestic tastes change in such a way that an increase in imports results. The change in tastes may not necessarily involve a type of commodity that can only be supplied from abroad. It may simply be a general shift in consumer preferences. But if domestic producers are unwilling or unable to restructure their own output accordingly, this can easily be reflected in expanded imports and result in a balance of payments deficit.

More generally, the process of economic growth itself involves continual changes in demand patterns. Economic growth, after all, involves not merely "more and more of the same," but an ever changing composition of demand and output which tends in the direction of increasing sophistication as the economy develops. Necessarily, supply and demand do not coincide perfectly throughout the growth process, and it is to be expected that demand patterns will diverge from prevailing supply patterns from time to time. This divergence will vary in magnitude and is often reflected in the changing composition and volume of imports and exports and in periodic balance of payments disequilibria.

Changes in *demand* patterns, whether attributed simply to changes in tastes or considered as part of the overall process of economic growth, will influence the balance of payments to the extent that resources are not perfectly mobile. If resources were perfectly mobile, a shift in demand in favor of imported goods would immediately give rise to an import-competing industry which could, in turn, render the balance of payments impact of the demand shift relatively minor. But resources are not perfectly mobile, and even if it is possible to reallocate resources in a manner consistent with the new demand patterns, this reallocation will be gradual and involves a time lag of varying duration. In either case, there will be an impact on the balance of payments of greater or lesser magnitude.

No less importantly, shifts in *supply* conditions may contribute to structural balance of payments disequilibrium. A nation's endowments of the factors of production, as well as the efficiency with which these factors are employed in the productive process, undergo continual change. Hence, we expect the comparative advantage basis of international trade—whether founded in differences in relative factor endowments or in productivity—to change over time. With it will change international specialization in the production of goods and services. Any such changes of considerable magnitude are likely to result in structural balance of payments disequilibria.

For example, a country undergoing rapid industrialization may develop efficient import-competing industries that gradually reduce the demand for imports. Eventually, these same industries may turn into export suppliers and compete with the former suppliers of imports. At the same time, previous exports of primary products may be reduced due to increased home demand for raw materials and the volume of primary commodities imported may grow. All such changes are likely to contribute to balance of payments disequilibrium in one way or another. This is simply because we cannot expect the supply shifts to be mutually offsetting and perfectly timed to render the balance of payments impact minor.

As comparative advantage and demand patterns shift, with imperfect resource mobility, we thus come to expect balance of payments surpluses in some countries and deficits in others—arising out of structural disequilibria attributable to varying flows of trade in goods and services. Presumably, equilibrium will sooner or later be restored. The question is, of course, whether the restoration of balance of payments equilibrium will come soon enough. Hopefully, it will come before the depletion of the deficit countries' international reserves causes them to take action to force the balance of payments back into line—action that may well be harmful to international trade and capital flows.

Structural balance of payments disequilibria may also arise from changing *terms of trade*. A country which finds its terms of trade to be deteriorating, with the prices of its imports rising and/or exports prices falling significantly, may find its balance of payments deteriorating. Although the *volume* of exports may rise, the *value* of (receipts from) these exports may decline due to falling prices. On the other hand, *expenditures* on imports may rise because the prices of imported commodities are rising even though the volume of imports stays the same or declines somewhat. Or, the two effects may occur simultaneously.

We saw earlier in some detail how, in a real sense, deteriorating terms of trade reduce a nation's share of the gains from international trade. We now see that in a *monetary* sense, deteriorating terms of trade can result in a structural balance of payments deficit. The opposite holds true, of course, for countries undergoing improvements in their respective international terms of trade.

An excellent example was provided by the oil crisis of 1973–1974, when the price of internationally traded crude petroleum increased fourfold in a relatively short period of time, resulting in a serious deterioration of the terms of trade of all but the oil-exporting countries. The problem was that the structural current-account deficits among the oil-importing countries did not match the pattern of oil-money reflows in the form of import and investment spending by the oil exporters. Even floating exchange rates, which absorbed the initial shock of the oil crisis, did not contribute much to alleviating the disequilibrium for the oil-importers *as a group*—since currency appreciations and depreciations impacted primarily trade flows *within* the group.

STRUCTURAL DISEQUILIBRIUM: CAPITAL FLOWS

Structural balance of payments disequilibria may also result from changes in international flows of long-term capital. An example might be applied to the enormous flow of U.S. investments into western Europe during the late 1950's and the 1960's. Assume that at some point this flow suddenly came to a halt. What would happen?

The respective balances of payments and exchange rates of many European nations embodied large-scale capital inflows. For some countries, the importation of machinery and other capital equipment financed by the massive capital inflows may have permitted the increased allocation of domestic productive resources to consumer goods industries. For other countries, the capital inflows may have in fact financed imports of raw materials and consumer goods, while domestic resources were employed in capital formation. A sudden cessation of the flow of capital from the U.S. to western Europe would certainly have put a severe strain on the balances of payments of those countries. The necessary shifts in resource allocation to meet the new conditions would have taken time, and in the interim balance of payments disequilibria would almost certainly have been the result.

Structural balance of payments disequilibrium can also be attributed to the international capital flows themselves, rather than to the impact of *changes* in capital movements upon trade flows as in the above example. Investment outflows, of course, constitute domestic savings that make possible productive capital formation abroad, not at home. As such, they effectively serve to expand productive capacity in foreign countries at the expense of productive capacity at home. This can fundamentally alter the basis of international specialization and lead to shifts in trade patterns that may later result in structural balance of payments disequilibrium. Reduced domestic productive capacity in some sectors, relative to that of other countries, may lead to an expansion of imports and a contraction of exports, which will be offset to some extent by remissions of interest and profits.

Disequilibrium of the balance of payments attributed to long-term capital flows is rightfully termed *structural*. Such flows fundamentally alter the structures of the domestic and foreign economies and affect comparative advantage and the international flows of goods and services. Such disequilibria are not likely to be "permanent," however—structural balance of payments disequilibria, such as the "dollar shortage" of the early post-World War II years, have eventually been rectified without exception.

DISEQUILIBRIUM AND THE PRICE LEVEL

We have considered balance of payments disequilibria attributable to changing levels of economic activity, shifting supply and demand patterns, and capital flows (the latter two causal elements being closely connected with the economic structures of the trading countries).

Is it not also possible, however, that the exchange rate of one currency for another may fail to reflect relative costs and prices, and that such overvaluation or undervaluation can cause a balance of payments disequilibrium? Under flexible exchange rates and the classical gold standard, of course, such a condition would be impossible. With *flexible rates*, it is not possible for the exchange rate to be out of line with the underlying forces of supply and demand—and, hence, with relative prices and costs—over extended periods of time. Under the *gold standard*, with gold freely transferable from one country to another and national economic conditions freely responsive to international gold flows, the relative values of all currencies are absolutely fixed in terms of gold. What if, however, a system of *pegged* exchange rates is used, with the value of one currency in terms of others in effect set by government fiat?

If the exchange rate is pegged too low (i.e., if the domestic-currency price per unit of foreign currency is low), so that imports are relatively cheap for domestic buyers while exports are relatively expensive for foreign customers, exports will tend to be depressed and imports expand. The result is that an *overvaluation* of the home currency causes a so-called *exchange-rate disequilibrium* in that country's balance of payments. The reverse tends to be true when the home currency is *undervalued* with respect to other currencies, and the peg is set too high. The result will then tend to be a chronic balance of payments surplus.

Exchange-rate disequilibria are not necessarily always attributable to relative overvaluation or undervaluation of the *home* currency as a result of actions by the domestic government. They may also occur if *foreign* currencies are valued inconsistently with relative costs and prices. An overvaluation of a foreign currency tends to cause a balance of payments surplus in the home country, while foreign undervaluation tends to have an opposite, deficit-inducing effect. All of these effects work through changes in international price-competitiveness and flows of goods and services.

However, exchange-rate disequilibrium may bear on the balance of payments in other ways as well. If it is known that the exchange rate is out of line—either overvalued or undervalued—with respect to relative costs and prices, large-scale capital movements may add to the balance of payments disequilibrium. An overvalued currency is always a potential candidate for future devaluation, and it encourages speculative capital outflows, while an undervalued currency tends to attract speculative capital in large measure.

Balance of payments surpluses attending undervalued currencies may tend to be inflationary as a result of combined exports in excess of imports. This inflation may then reduce the degree of undervaluation and eventually—unless offset by restrictive monetary and fiscal measures—cause the balance of payments disequilibrium to turn from surplus to deficit.

This leads us to a final type of balance of payments disequilibrium, one associated with the price level. If exchange rates are fixed, a rise in the price level in one country, relative to that in other countries, tends to cause a reduction in its exports and an increase in its imports. It exports simply become relatively less competitive in world markets, while the exports of other countries become relatively more competitive at home. Hence, a relative rise in prices in one country can lead to a balance of payments deficit, while relative price increases abroad may result in a balance of payments surplus. In both instances, we can talk about a *monetary disequilibrium* of the balance of payments.

Monetary disequilibrium should not be confused with the cyclical disequilibrium discussed earlier, although they are closely related. Cyclical disequilibrium is associated with changes in *real incomes,* which exert an impact upon trade via the marginal propensity to import at home and abroad. Monetary disequilibrium is related to changes in relative *price levels,* which affect trade through changes in international price competitiveness. They are related because income and price changes tend to occur together. During a business expansion real incomes rise and so do imports. As full employment of productive resources is approached, however, the price level tends to rise as well and, again, so do imports. We have, then, an income and a price effect upon the balance of payments associated with changes in economic activity. If the income effect predominates, we can identify any resulting balance of payments disequilibrium as being primarily *cyclical* in nature, and if the price effect predominates, we can consider it to be primarily *monetary.*

We noted earlier that the timing of business cycles varies from country to country and, for this reason, cyclical balance of payments disequilibrium is hardly uncommon. The same holds true for monetary disequilibrium. Economic policies pursued by national governments are largely autonomous. Hence, we would expect that the rate of price level change will vary internationally, and that consequently monetary disequilibrium will periodically characterize the balance of payments of various countries.

It should be clear that floating exchange rates, to the extent that they are free to reflect the impact of changing price levels on international competitiveness, go far to alleviate balance of payments disequilibria attributable to differential rates of inflation.

DEFLATION—THE CLASSICAL MEDICINE

In the previous section, we surveyed briefly the various sources of balance of payments disequilibrium: changes in demand patterns, shifts in supply conditions and the terms of trade, differential movements in economic activity capital flows, price-level changes, and inconsistencies in pegged exchange rates. Given the existing disequilibrium system, and given the partial adjustment provided by floating exchange rates, what measures can be implemented in order to restore payments balance without resorting to restrictions to international trade and payments?

Balance of payments adjustment via changes in interest rates, incomes, and prices at home is a matter of economic policy on the part of the deficit country. The opposite developments in surplus countries are completely out of its hands. Adjustment will occur via the classical route only if the government desires it to occur, and then only through domestic developments. Under a fixed exchange-rate system one solution to a balance of payments deficit is thus the deliberate restriction of domestic economic activity by national monetary and fiscal authorities—deflation. As is true under the familiar income–specie flow mechanism, if exchange rates are to remain unchanged it is the economy that must do the adjusting. Let us see how this may occur by tracing through a hypothetical case.

Suppose a country comes up with a severe balance of payments deficit for several consecutive years. Its international reserves of gold and foreign currencies are gradually being eroded, as is its ability to borrow from the other countries and from the International Monetary Fund. The country decides to attempt a restoration of external balance by means of domestic adjustments.

It may first employ the tools of monetary policy to contract the domestic supply of money and tighten credit—it will move to point F_A in Figure 23–1. The central bank may perhaps raise its discount rate, sell securities

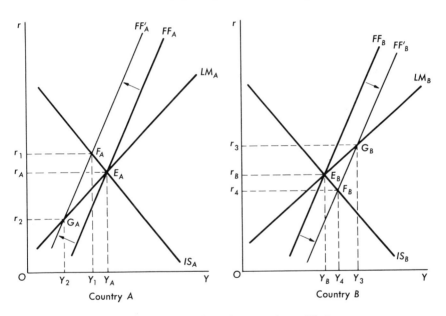

Fig. 23–1. Partial and general equilibrium.

on the open market to soak up bank reserves, raise statutory bank-reserve requirements, or employ a combination of the three quantitative weapons of monetary control. The tightening of general credit conditions will cause domestic interest rates to rise relative to those prevailing abroad. Investors and lenders at home will have less incentive to place their funds abroad, while foreigners are faced with increasing incentives to take advantage of the new, higher yields in the home country and to shift their funds accordingly. The home country's balance of payments thus would tend to improve via the capital account.

So far, the direction of adjustment is the same as under the automatic mechanism; the crucial difference is that the tightening of domestic credit conditions is the result of conscious policy measures, rather than the automatic consequence of deficit-induced reserve losses.

It should be noted again that losses of international reserves on the part of the home country would result in a reduction in the domestic money supply in any event, insofar as they are not deliberately countered by "defensive" monetary expansion on the part of the central bank. Similarly, surplus countries would have to undergo a monetary expansion as their international reserves accumulate. But again, foreign countries might be unwilling to subject themselves to inflationary pressures by allowing the balance of payments surplus to lead to expansion of the domestic money supply. Rather, they might decide to neutralize the effect of the accumulation of international reserves by simply following "defensive" restrictive monetary policies.

Without automatic money-supply expansion abroad, any automatic contractionary effect at home—insofar as it is permitted—might well be too weak to contribute significantly to balance of payments adjustment. Hence, the contraction of the domestic money supply must be made a matter of deliberate policy action.

With a rise in domestic interest rates (and little certainty about what is happening abroad), the likelihood is that aggregate home demand will be reduced as the cost of investment capital rises. At the same time consumer borrowing, and perhaps state and local government borrowing, also will be restricted. The multiplier effect will see to it that income declines along with, in all probability, employment. Via the marginal propensity to import, the value of imports will then be reduced, and the balance of payments improve by way of the current account.

Even without a significant price effect, the interest and income effects may well be sufficient to restore payments balance. If all countries find themselves in a state of gradual price-level increase, the restriction of domestic economic activity may cause the home prices to rise *more slowly* than those abroad, and thus renew the possibility of a significant price effect without the necessity of any actual downward movement.

Monetary policy is certainly not the only technique that can be used to bring about domestic deflation. Fiscal policy—reduced government spending and/or increased taxes—may be used with effectiveness under certain conditions (movement to point G_A in Figure 23–1), in which case it will be the income and price effects which will have to bring about the main restoration of payments balance. One notable qualification is that, if the money supply remains unchanged, restrictive fiscal measures will tend to be reflected in reduced interest rates and, hence, cause negative capital flows that may offset any positive income and price effects. The adjustment characteristics, whether monetary or fiscal techniques are used, are the same; and the level of domestic economic activity is directed to meet the needs of external balance.

Finally, we should also consider the possibility that the brunt of the adjustment burden may well be borne by the interest effect alone, and that under such circumstances very little reduction may be required of incomes, employment, and prices. Suppose there are no restrictions to international capital movements, and the international flow of investment funds is highly sensitive to differentials in yields as a result of well-developed capital markets. The improvement in the capital account of the balance of payments, resulting from a rise in domestic yields relative to those prevailing abroad, may well be sufficient to restore balance, at least temporarily. Such a situation can be consciously brought about if it is possible for monetary authorities to raise those yields which primarily affect international capital movements, while preventing a substantial rise in those interest rates affecting primarily domestic economic activity.

We have assumed here that the economy striving to eliminate its balance of payments deficit has no control over what goes on in other economies and, hence, must effect all of the necessary adjustments itself. In a strict sense, this is true. Each nation, as an autonomous political entity, is nominally the sole determinant of its own economic policies. Simply because the gold-standard rules indicate that deficit countries should deflate and surplus countries inflate their respective economies is no guarantee that the latter will abide by these rules. On the contrary, the typical surplus country already operating near full capacity may strive to maintain price-level stability via restrictive monetary and fiscal measures and thereby prevent an "imported inflation." The deficit country is then left on its own, to restore balance as best it can under conditions that have foreign countries pursuing economic policies which might even promote *increased* payments imbalances.

International cooperation can, however, serve to modify this somewhat pessimistic conclusion on balance of payments adjustment under essentially fixed-exchange rates. Foreign governments may agree to combat inflation by means of restrictive fiscal rather than monetary policies, for instance, and thus avoid forcing the deficit country to raise its interest rates even higher to prevent adverse capital flows. Or, a number of governments may be able to agree—under favorable political and economic circumstances—to coordinate national monetary and fiscal policies in such a way that balance of payments disturbances are minimized for the benefit of all concerned. We shall have more to say about international monetary cooperation later on.

Every national government subscribes to some common set of goals with respect to the state of the national economy. The maintenance of reasonably full employment, price level stability, a viable balance of payments, and a satisfactory rate of economic growth perhaps broadly define these goals. The relative importance of the individual objectives may vary widely from one country to the next. In order to attain these objectives, governments generally have a variety of tools at their disposal. The variation of government tax receipts, expenditures, trade and payments controls, and interest rates, either selectively or on an overall basis, are probably most important in market-oriented economies. Physical "planning" controls, direct government participation in business activity, as well as moral suasion are also used to a greater or lesser extent, depending upon the nature of the economy in question as well as the circumstances involved.

ACHIEVING INTERNAL BALANCE

In a static sense, the primary task of economic policy is the maintenance of *internal balance,* i.e., a fully employed economy characterized by stable prices. In a dynamic context, this means insuring that economic activity grows along with the *capacity* of the economy to produce in roughly parallel fashion. *Actual* output should approximate *potential* output, so that there are as few unemployed resources as possible. If possible, aggregate demand also should not outstrip productive capacity, with inflation as the result.

Students of economics soon learn that internal balance is rarely, if ever, achieved in practice. There are always some idle resources, and efforts to bring them into productive use tend to result in rising prices. We can, however, draw up a working definition of internal balance by simply stipulating the achievement of *acceptable* capacity utilization combined with *acceptable* price level stability. Some economists would agree that an economy with 2½ per cent of the labor force unemployed and an annual price level rise of 4 per cent per year is acceptable. Others would not, maintaining that 4 per cent unemployment and 2 per cent inflation is decidedly preferable. The precise definition of internal balance is thus an elusive one, and is largely a matter of value judgement on the part of those responsible for the formulation of economic policy. Ultimately, it is a political question. Still, internal balance is an extremely useful concept for analytical purposes.

Imbalances in the national economy may be either inflationary or recessionary. The former involves aggregate demand—originating in consumer, government, and investment spending—that outstrips the capacity of the economy to produce and thereby results in an inflationary rise in the price level. In Keynesian terms, the equilibrium income level exceeds full-employment equilibrium. A recessionary imbalance is quite the opposite. Equilibrium income falls short of full-employment equilibrium, with significant unemployment of productive resources the result. For simplicity, we will simply call these two internal imbalances *inflation* and *recession*.

Each of these calls for a different policy response on the part of the government. Inflation requires some combination of tax increase, reduced government spending, and monetary restraint—in short, restrictive monetary, fiscal, and tax policies—for the restoration of internal balance. Recession, on the other hand, demands expansionary monetary, fiscal, and tax measures. How do these policy requirements of internal balance relate to the policy requisites for *external* balance?

ACHIEVING EXTERNAL BALANCE

Assume for the moment that it is impossible or undesirable to employ restrictions to international trade and payments in order to achieve external balance—balance in the balance of payments. Neither is it desirable to adopt a system of flexible rates. Adjustment of a balance of payments deficit thus calls for restrictive economic policies that will reduce domestic incomes, and perhaps prices, and raise domestic interest rates. Imports would then be reduced, and it is possible that exports will rise while capital flows shift in favor of the home country, and the balance of payments will improve. Whether restrictive *monetary* or *fiscal* policies are used to restore external balance would seem at first glance to depend upon such factors as (a) the value of the marginal propensity to import, (b) the responsiveness of prices to decreasing aggregate demand, (c) the domestic- and foreign-price elasticity of demand for imports, and (d) the responsiveness of capital flows to changes in domestic interest rates.

A balance of payments surplus under the same circumstances would, by the same reasoning, appear to call for the opposite policy responses, with credit ease and expansionary fiscal measures resulting in a restoration of balance through increased imports, reduced exports, and a capital outflow.

POLICY CONFLICTS

Will a given monetary or fiscal policy measure, designed to redress either an external or an internal imbalance, simultaneously serve to alleviate the other? Or will the correct policy response to external imbalances prove to be precisely the wrong "medicine" for the purpose of restoring internal balance, and vice versa? An idea of the possible areas of conflict is conveyed in Table 23–1.

Case 1, domestic inflation accompanied by a balance of payments deficit,

Table 23–1

Policy Requirements Under Varying Conditions of Internal and External Balance

Case	Internal Condition	Policy Requirement	External Condition	Policy Requirement
1	Inflation	Restraint	Deficit	Restraint
2	Recession	Expansion	Surplus	Expansion
3	Inflation	Restraint	Surplus	Expansion
4	Recession	Expansion	Deficit	Restraint
5	Balance	None	Deficit	Restraint
6	Balance	None	Surplus	Expansion
7	Inflation	Restraint	Balance	None
8	Recession	Expansion	Balance	None
9	Balance	None	Balance	None

presents no problem. Monetary policies designed to raise domestic interest rates and thereby depress aggregate home demand will simultaneously attract foreign capital and reduce the outflow of domestic capital. This will help to restore payments balance. To the extent that restrictive monetary measures are indeed successful in depressing aggregate domestic demand and incomes, they will also benefit the balance of payments in terms of reduced imports. Restrictive fiscal policies would have a similar effect on incomes and imports, and, to the extent that prices are flexible in a downward direction, the balance of payments would benefit additionally through increased price competitiveness of home products. Restrictive monetary and fiscal policies in Case 1 thus help to restore *both* internal and external balance under these conditions. Any policy which helps to cure the payments deficit automatically serves to aid in the restoration of internal balance as well. The payments deficit itself acts as a brake on domestic inflation in that the import surplus helps to satisfy rampant home demand and acts as a depressing influence on domestic incomes, while any net capital outflow tends to tighten domestic credit. Both of these are desirable from the standpoint of internal balance, and if left alone, they might in and of themselves lead to a restoration of both internal and external balance.

Case 2, domestic recession coupled with a balance of payments surplus, tells a similar story. Again the payments surplus itself—in the form of an excess of exports over imports or a net capital inflow—acts as a stimulus to the domestic economy, and if economic policy remained neutral might eventually restore balance in both sectors. While it is doubtful that monetary or fiscal measures would be applied *specifically* in order to wipe out the payments surplus, any techniques intended to restore internal balance by stimulating domestic economic activity would automatically tend to have this effect. Expansionary monetary policies and the concomitant lower domestic interest rates will tend to alleviate any net capital inflow and, with or without expansionary government expenditure and tax measures, will result in a rise in domestic incomes and perhaps prices, thus easing any trade surplus.

In both cases—inflation-deficit and recession-surplus—the goals of economic policy are consistent with one another. Policy moves to restore internal balance automatically help to restore external balance as well, and vice versa.

But what about Case 3 in Table 23–1, domestic inflation accompanied by a balance of payments surplus? Any effort to combat the inflation at home will simultaneously aggravate the balance of payments surplus. Monetary restraint at home will result in higher domestic interest rates and net capital inflows which, besides increasing the payments surplus, partly serve to offset the efforts to achieve domestic credit restriction. Restrictive tax and government-expenditure policies, by reducing imports and perhaps increasing exports, also will tend to increase the size of the surplus which, in turn, aggravates the inflationary pressure at home. Any attempt to restore internal balance under these circumstances thus aggravates the external imbalance. Even though a country might be able to live with a chronic payments surplus for a time, it eventually will come under pressure to correct it so that the conflict is a real one of long-range importance. However, the nation is almost certain to place the restoration of internal balance ahead of external balance as a policy goal.

Even more serious a problem is an economic slump at home combined with a balance of payments deficit (Case 4). Unlike the case of external imbalance characterized by a payments surplus, a nation *must* eliminate its deficit before it exhausts its international reserves, the ability to borrow, or the willingness of foreigners to hold its currency. Similarly, it will be under powerful pressure to stimulate the domestic economy and return to reasonably full employment. An important conflict exists. Monetary restraint and restrictive fiscal and tax policies may benefit the balance of payments, but they will almost surely drive the domestic economy deeper into recession. Conversely, the monetary and fiscal ease prescribed as a cure for the domestic recessionary situation will only result in a worsening of the payments deficit.

The solution to this dilemma lies in manipulating the tools of economic policy in such a way that the positive response to a given policy measure in one area exceeds the negative response in the other. To illustrate: suppose international capital flows appear to be highly sensitive to changes in interest rates in the home country. Restrictive monetary policies resulting in higher interest rates would thus cause a significant improvement in the capital account of the balance of payments. The negative impact of this development on aggregate domestic demand could be offset by expansionary expenditure or tax measures, and result in a net improvement in the balance of payments without an accompanying deterioration in the domestic situation. In fact, if the marginal propensity to import is sufficiently low, the expansionary expenditures and tax measures could more than offset the monetary restraint, thereby leading to an improvement both in domestic economic activity and in the balance of payments. The induced imports would not offset the favorable capital flows.

POLICY MIX

One suggestion much along these lines—involving a separation of policy goals and tools—has been raised by Robert A. Mundell.[1] In order to be consistent with his "principle of effective market classification," each policy weapon ought to be aimed at those variables upon which it has the greatest relative influence. Hence, if monetary policy affects external balance more than it does internal balance, then it should be used to promote payments balance and be neutralized with respect to national economic activity by opposite fiscal policies. Mundell contends that the use of any other policy mix will actually promote external and internal imbalances.

This is very neatly demonstrated in Figure 23–2. There are only two policy variables: the interest rate and the state of the government budget. Both external and internal balance can be maintained by using different combinations of budgetary and monetary policies. Curve FF' shows all possible combinations of interest rates and states of the budget which will maintain *external* balance; payment balance can be assured by using large budgetary surpluses combined with low interest rates (a strong current account balance offsets a weak capital account balance), or budgetary deficits combined with high interest rates (strong capital account balance and weak current account balance). Any combinations of interest rates and budgetary conditions along FF' will thus insure external balance.

Similarly, curve XX' presents the combinations of budgetary and monetary conditions that will ensure *internal* balance. Noninflationary full employment can be maintained by monetary restraint combined with budgetary ease, or restrictive budgetary measures accompanying monetary ease. Note that there is only one combination of monetary and budgetary policies—state of the budget *b*, and interest rate *r*—that will assure *both* internal and external balance.

Any combination of budgetary and monetary measures represented by a point to the right of line FF' represents a balance of payments surplus, while any point to the left of FF' signifies a payments deficit. Similarly, any point to the right of line XX' represents a domestic recession, while any combination of interest rates and states of the budget represented by

[1] "The Appropriate Use of Monetary and Fiscal Policy for Internal and External Stability," *IMF Staff Papers*, March, 1962.

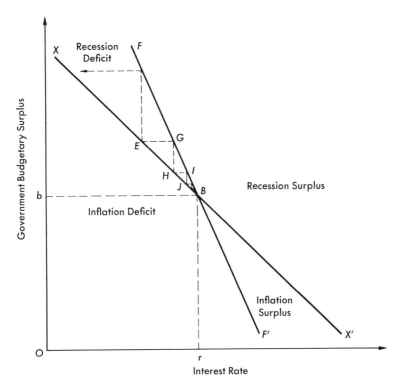

Fig. 23–2. Selecting policies for internal and external balance.

a point to the left of XX' signifies a domestic inflation. Hence any point in the area to the right of $X'BF$ represents a recession–surplus, and any point to the left of XBF' represents an inflation–deficit combination. Points in between—below $F'BX'$ and above FBX—represent inflation–surplus and recession–deficit combinations, respectively.

As we stated earlier, there is no problem with inflation–deficit and recession–surplus combinations, since the restoration of both internal and external balance calls for the same policy responses. Any measure designed to promote balance in one area will automatically promote balance in the other, and drive the point closer to equilibrium at B. Rather, it is under conditions of inflation–surplus and recession–deficit that the policy conflict arises. Each measure designed to promote balance in one area will work *against* balances in the other.

Suppose we begin at some point H in Figure 23–2. The domestic economy is in balance but there is a balance of payments deficit. We attempt to restore external balance by increasing the budgetary surplus, and moving to point G. External balance has been attained, but a recession has been created in the domestic economy. Internal balance can be restored by simply lowering the interest rate and moving to point *E*, but this results in a renewal of the payments deficit. By applying fiscal policy for external balance and monetary policy for internal balance, we find ourselves moving even further from overall equilibrium via a series of alternating external and internal imbalances.

What if we reverse the policy mix and employ *monetary* policy for external balance and *fiscal* policy for internal balance? Returning to the initial point, *H*, combining internal balance with a payments deficit, we raise interest rates until external balance is secured at point *I*. This represents a domestic recession, but it is offset by expansionary fiscal policy and a restoration of internal balance occurs at point *J*; each is *closer* to the overall equilibrium at *B* than the one preceding it. Hence, the use of a policy mix stipulating monetary policy for external balance and fiscal policy for internal balance will eventually lead to equilibrium in both areas.

Why is it that this particular policy mix works, while the other does not? The answer lies in the way the *XX'* and *FF'* functions are drawn. Note that the foreign balance line is steeper than that representing the domestic balance. Since capital is assumed to be free to move internationally, monetary policy is presumed to have a relatively stronger effect upon the balance of payments than upon the level of national income. Even if international capital flows are left out of the picture entirely, it may still be reasonable to expect that a change in domestic (investment) expenditure resulting from a change in interest rates has a greater bearing upon imports than an identical expenditure change induced by means of fiscal policy.

More broadly, internal and external balance, in cases where the policy effects conflict, can be maintained by means of *any* two policy tools as long as they do not have exactly the same impact upon the two objectives. The sole requirement is to mate a given policy weapon to that particular objective upon which it has the greatest impact.

Mundell's approach to the choice of policy designed to maintain internal and external balance is useful one, and it shows that it may be possible to obtain both objectives without resorting to flexibility in the currency values or *ad hoc* restrictions on international trade and payments.

PROBLEM OF CHOICE

Besides internal and external balance, there are other objectives that an economy sets for itself, such as a viable rate of economic growth, a politically acceptable role of government in the economy, perhaps stable exchange rates internationally, and a general reduction of barriers to international trade and payments. All of these goals *cannot* be pursued simultaneously. Jan Tinbergen, a Dutch economist, once stated that to pursue a given number of conflicting policy goals, it is necessary to have an equal number of policy tools.[2] This is broadly correct, although the number of available tools depends largely on their definition; e.g., does *fiscal* policy constitute one or two tools, as when it is divided into government expenditures and tax policy?

We have seen that the maintenance of noninflationary full employment may be possible concurrently with payments balance by using only monetary and fiscal policies—two goals and two tools. Changes in the value of the home currency and trade and payments restrictions may not be necessary. Now let us add a third goal, rapid economic growth, which would seem to demand relatively low long-term interest rates. If external balance responds primarily to short-term interest rates, it may be possible to use high short-term rate changes for external balance, low long-term rates for economic growth, and fiscal policy for internal balance—three goals and three tools.

But suppose it is not possible to vary short-term and long-term interest rates independently of one another. We then have three policy goals and only two tools. The only solution is to add another tool, such as *ad hoc* restrictions on trade or payments—or a variation in the relative value of the home currency. By employing such methods, it is naturally impossible to retain free trade and payments (or, alternatively, pegged exchange rates) as policy goals and they must be sacrificed.

In this chapter we have attempted to outline problems of balance of payments adjustment in the absence of exchange-rate flexibility. Once this constraint is removed, it is easy to see that adjustment becomes less difficult. Depending on the degree of exchange-rate flexibility, the foreign-balance functions in Figures 23–1 and 23–2 became "manageable." They will either drift back toward general equilibrium on their own, as trade flows respond to shifts in relative currency values, or they can be made to do so via active exchange-rate policies. This issue will be explored in the following chapter.

[2] Jan Tinbergen, *The Theory of Economic Policy* (Amsterdam: North Holland Publishing Co., 1956), ch. 4.

24

DISEQUILIBRIUM SYSTEMS: ADJUSTMENT VIA PRICES AND DIRECT CONTROLS

Attempts to control the balance of payments by manipulating real output and incomes—and the rate of interest—are not easy, as we have seen in the previous chapter. Things would be much easier if exchange rates were indeed flexible enough to absorb most balance of payments shocks, permitting national macroeconomic policy to be focused largely on national objectives. Flexible (or floating) exchange rates essentially serve to switch expenditures between domestic and foreign buyers and sellers, responding to shifts in relative prices, in such a way that external balance is fostered. In this chapter we shall consider the economics of expenditure switching, both via flexibility in exchange rates and via the imposition of barriers to international trade and capital flows.

DEPRECIATION/DEVALUATION

Certainly the most elegant solution to the external-balance problem for a country with a balance of payments deficit under existing exchange rates is simply to let the relative value of its currency fall. With flexible exchange rates or a relatively "clean" float, this variation in relative currency values occurs automatically on a day-to-day basis as a result of the interplay of the forces of supply and demand. If, for instance, the deficit country's demand for foreign exchange exceeds the available supply engendered by the foreign demand for its own currency, its currency will depreciate. Under a system of pegged-exchange rates or heavy government intervention in foreign exchange markets, this automatic depreciation will not occur. Rather, any change in the value of a national currency is a matter, again, of policy decisions.

Suppose a nation is plagued by a prolonged balance of payments disequilibrium of a "monetary" sort. Its price level has risen more rapidly than those of other countries with the result that its exports are overpriced in world markets, while its imports appear extremely inexpensive to domestic purchasers. Exports have lagged and imports have grown substantially as a result, bringing with them a serious balance of payments deficit. If it is generally recognized that prices and wages are not flexible in a downward direction, deflation and balance of payments adjustment according to the gold-standard rules—via internal adjustments—would create a great deal of hardship without really solving the problem of bringing costs and prices back into line. Capital flows in response to increased domestic interest rates would ease the situation only temporarily. The home currency is simply *overvalued* relative to those of other countries, and this is the source of the balance of payments pressure.

The solution—if the exchange rate is pegged—lies in devaluation. It may be decided to undertake a sharp, once-and-for-all reduction in the value of the home currency. This is done by simply moving the currency peg—its tie to gold, SDR's or to other national currencies. The par value of the home currency is thus reduced, and the prices of exports to foreign buyers are lowered while the prices of imports to domestic purchasers are raised. If the foreign demand for the exports of the devaluing country is relatively price elastic, and if the same is true of home demand for imports, the balance of trade will undergo marked improvement. Applying once again the familiar Marshall–Lerner condition, if the sum of the price elasticities of demand for the home country's imports and exports exceeds unity (assuming infinite supply elasticities), devaluation will improve the balance of trade and hence the balance of payments of a country. If this condition is not met, devaluation will be harmful from a balance of payments standpoint. All of this assumes, of course, that there are no competitive devaluations on the part of other countries. Alternatively, the currency may simply be allowed to float to a new equilibrium level.

The resulting expansion of economic activity originating in the export- and import-competing industries may in addition lead to a rise in interest rates. If this is not offset by expansionary monetary policy, there may be an additional beneficial effect on the balance of payments by way of increased capital inflows and reduced capital outflows. Finally, if the induced increase in domestic interest rates causes a reduction in incomes and employment, another balance of payments improvement may be felt, via the marginal propensity to import.

By far the major adjustment burden, however, rests on the price effect of the currency devaluation or controlled depreciation. There is no certainty that restrictive effects will be felt by the national economy as a result of inaction on the part of monetary authorities, or even by monetary contraction, and indeed none is necessary. To the extent that the devaluation/depreciation is of sufficient magnitude, with favorable import and export elasticities, the price effect alone will restore payments balance.

By its very nature, the devaluation or depreciation is best suited to cure balance of payments disequilibria of a very specific sort. If the disequilibrium is the result of structural factors or capital flows, it may indeed be of very little use. The desire to avoid internal adjustments for the sake of external balance "at all costs," however, may drive a country to devaluation or depreciation, no matter what the cause of the balance of payments disequilibrium. There may be some improvement in the balance of payments under any conditions but the crux of the matter may not have been reached by the devaluation or the depreciation, and it may only be a relatively short time before the disequilibrium reappears.

Similarly, even with a balance of payments disequilibrium, such as that in the above example, which truly justifies devaluation or depreciation, such a move unaccompanied by monetary and fiscal restraint will only be a temporary solution. If the rise in the domestic price level is allowed to proceed unchecked, it will not be very long before another currency value change is called for.

THE ABSORPTION APPROACH

Balance of payments adjustment resulting from a depreciation, such as that depicted here, would seem to be dependent very largely upon the relevant elasticities of demand for imports—i.e., upon the applicability of the Marshall–Lerner condition to the case in question, with appropriate adjustments for less than infinite supply elasticities. Depreciation causes a shift in relative prices internationally, and the adjustment results from a change in demand patterns and response to this shift.

But we have also seen that a currency depreciation may have effects upon domestic and foreign incomes and prices, and that the resultant income and price changes could have offsetting, adverse effects upon the balance of trade, thereby nullifying at least part of the improvement attributable to the price effect.

The reasoning involved is simple. Under appropriate elasticity conditions, the depreciation will result in an improvement of the balance of trade. The consequent reduction in imports and expansion of exports serves to stimulate economic activity and incomes in the home country, via the multiplier, while causing a contracting of incomes abroad. If the home economy is operating at or near full employment, domestic prices also are likely to rise.

As domestic incomes rises, imports also tend to rise, via the marginal propensity to import. Meanwhile, the reduction in incomes abroad tends to result in a decline in those nations' imports, the home country's exports. The resultant negative income effect of the depreciation upon the balance of payments thus tends to work against the initial positive price effect; and the stronger the price effect, the more powerful will be the income effect. A systematic approach to the income effects of a depreciation is called the absorption approach to balance of payments adjustment.[1]

We start with the simple identity that the balance of trade, the net imports or exports of a nation (B), must equal total national output of goods and services (Y) minus total national absorption, in terms of consumption and investment, of goods and services (A). If absorption exceeds output, the balance of trade must be negative; if output exceeds absorption, the trade balance will be positive. We thus have the expression,

$$B = Y - A.$$

If a currency depreciation is to bring about an improvement in the balance of trade and, hence, in the balance of payments, absorption (A) must decline in relation to output (Y).

The depreciation initially renders domestic goods cheaper relative to foreign goods. Domestic residents are encouraged to switch their purchases from imports to home-produced goods, while foreigners .find it advisable to shift their buying patterns in favor of imports. The balance of trade of the deficit country thus improves along the lines outlined earlier.

The rise in exports and/or decline in imports resulting in the improved balance of trade, as we know, acts as a stimulus to domestic economic activity in the deficit country. It induces the rise in income via the multiplier. This, in turn, causes a rise in imports, the magnitude of which is determined by the marginal propensity to import. The extent of the negative income effects of a depreciation on the balance of trade depends upon (a) the marginal propensity to consume and, (b) the marginal propensity to import. If the economy is operating at less than full employment, these propensities are likely to be such that the income effects do not outweigh the initial improvement in the balance of trade. Output (Y) will rise relative to absorption (A), with a net improvement in the trade balance (B) taking place.

If, on the other hand, the economy is operating at or very close to full

---

[1] Sidney S. Alexander, "Effects of a Devaluation on a Trade Balance," *IMF Staff Papers*, Vol. 2, April, 1952; and his "Effects of a Devaluation: A Simplified Synthesis of Elasticities and Absorption Approaches," *American Economic Review*, Vol. 49, March, 1959.

employment levels, output is already at a ceiling. The stimulus provided by the depreciation will result only in a rise in money incomes, not real incomes, and the prices of home-produced goods will therefore tend to increase. Much of the induced-demand increase will thus spill over onto imports, thereby tending to reverse the initial improvement in the balance of trade. In fact, if the result is a rise in absorption (A), with little or no possibility of increasing output (Y), the depreciation can only result in a deterioration in the balance of trade (B). Only to the extent that a rise in *hoarding* occurs may absorption actually fall relative to output, and thus permit an ultimate improvement in the balance of trade under such conditions.

The question thus focuses on the extent to which a currency depreciation will indeed lead to a rise in hoarding, thereby resulting in an increase in the $(Y - A)$ term in the above equation. Alexander points up several reasons why this might be the case.

1. If the money supply is inflexible and money holders wish to maintain given real cash balances, they will be forced to hoard as prices rise and thus reduce real expenditures.
2. Since wages tend to lag behind prices, profits will rise faster than wages, thereby redistributing income from groups with a high propensity to absorb to those inclined to hoard.
3. The "money illusion" effect may lead people to consume less at higher prices, even though their money incomes are also higher.
4. *Expectations* may play a role resulting in either an increase or a decline in absorption relative to output.

But even given these possibilities, the probability that a shift in currency value can improve the balance of trade under full employment conditions is nonetheless slight. Hence, Alexander recommends other policies under full-employment conditions. For example, a decrease in absorption may be brought about by restrictive credit policies, or even direct controls, designed to discourage consumption and investment. Increased taxes may also be used to limit consumption. This combined with depreciation would seem to have a much better chance of improving the balance of trade under full employment by shifting domestic output from domestic to foreign purchasers.

The elasticities approach to the balance of payments effects of a devaluation or depreciation concerns itself only with the initial effects of its induced switch from foreign to home-produced goods. It assumed incomes and prices to be constant. The absorption approach concentrates on the income effects and its impact on trade flows. Each tells part of the story and must be carefully weighed in any analysis of balance of payments adjustment through changes in relative currency values.

SHIFTING CURRENCY VALUES AND INTERNATIONAL CAPITAL FLOWS

Depreciation of a national currency, designed to aid the balance of payments, may also have certain implications with regard to the international flow of capital. Anyone holding monetary assets in the country in question immediately incurs a paper loss, in terms of other currencies, as a result of the devaluation. A German owner of 1 million marks worth of bank deposits in the U.S. would immediately realize a loss of DM 200,000 in the event of a 20 per cent depreciation of the dollar. An American, under the same circumstances, would lose nothing in terms of his home currency, but he would have done well to move his money out of the U.S. before the depreciation and buy dollars back afterward, thus realizing a 20 per cent gain. Depreciation thus imposes a real cost on foreigners and an opportunity cost on domestic residents to the extent that both are holders of monetary assets in the devaluing country.

No country ever hints at an impending devaluation or controlled depreciation beforehand. They are undertaken suddenly, without warning, and are preceded by categorical denials so that no one will be able to cut losses or realize profits as a result. Once a currency value shift has been completed, it is understood that the new value is to be "permanent." But government pronouncements on impending depreciation usually are hardly needed to convey what is to come. The overvaluation of a national currency, resulting in a balance of payments disequilibrium, reduces the confidence of investors in that currency. They well realize that depreciation may be the answer to that country's payments difficulties, and that in the absence of domestic contractionary policies it will come sooner or later.

The result of any such heavy capital outflow in anticipation of a devaluation or controlled depreciation severely limits the affected country's ability to maintain the existing exchange rate. Its remaining reserves may rapidly diminish, and it may be forced to devalue under circumstances not of its own choosing. Besides, there is the clearly undesirable effect of imposing windfall gains on some and catastrophic losses on others, which really serve no useful purpose, especially since the speculators cannot lose. In shifting currency values administratively, care should be taken to prevent any large-scale anticipatory capital flows.

In international investment, the investor is really buying two separate assets: the foreign physical or financial asset he is interested in *and* foreign currency. How he makes out depends on the relative yield on the investment—including anticipated capital gains—*and* the change in relative currency values which will determine the value of the earnings stream and additional capital gains or losses. Hence investors' *expectations* of future currency values will influence their behavior. The more freely currency val-

ues are determined by market forces, the less international capital flows distort the balance of payments adjustment process.

TARIFFS AND QUOTAS

The commercial-policy tools of tariffs and quantitative restrictions to
trade may also be used to help alleviate a balance of payments deficit. To
the extent that tariffs and quotas succeed in cutting down expenditures
on imports—without at the same time materially reducing export receipts
—they will improve the balance of trade and thus benefit the balance
of payments. This can be easily shown by simply reproducing the partial-
equilibrium diagram used for the analysis of the effects of tariffs in Chapter
10, in Figure 24–1. Curve S_d represents the home supply of the commodity,
D_d the home demand, and S_w the foreign (world) supply, which is assumed
to be perfectly elastic.

In the absence of the tariff, quantity OQ_1 is supplied domestically, and
with total quantity demanded being OQ_4, quantity Q_1Q_4 is imported. The
total *value* of imports is thus represented by the rectangle Q_1BAQ_4; i.e.,
quantity Q_1Q_4 times import price P_f. The imposition of the tariff increases
domestic production in the amount Q_1Q_2 and reduces consumption by

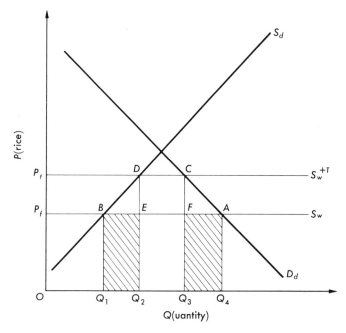

Fig. 24–1. Impact of tariffs and quotas on the balance of payments.

Q_4Q_3; both changes are a result of the tariff-induced increase in price to P_t. It thus reduces the quantity of imports to Q_2Q_3. The total value of imports is now only Q_2EFQ_3. Hence, the imposition of a tariff has resulted in a reduction in expenditures on imports of $Q_1BEQ_2 + Q_3FAQ_4$, the shaded area in Figure 24–1. If there is no foreign retaliation as a result of the imposition of this particular import charge, the balance of trade has been improved by that amount.

The impact of quotas on the balance of trade can be analyzed in precisely the same way, except that imports are administratively limited to quantity Q_2Q_3. Expenditures on imports will be reduced by approximately the same amount as under a tariff of equal restrictive force, unless foreign exporters are able to raise prices in the face of the quota.

Of course, this partial-equilibrium analysis applies only to a single commodity, for which the domestic-demand curve and the domestic and foreign supply curves are drawn. But, if all goods which makes up a nation's imports behaved in more or less the same way, it appears certain that an increase in the general level of tariffs and quantitative restrictions to trade will improve the balance of trade and, hence, the balance of payments. But is this so certain?

1. Increases in tariffs, particularly on the part of large, economically significant countries, are very likely to result in retaliation on the part of other countries. The reduction in import expenditures resulting from the home tariff must then be weighed against the possible consequent reductions in export receipts resulting from the foreign retaliatory tariff measures, in order for the net impact upon the balance of trade to be determined.

2. The amount of reduction in import expenditures as a result of increased tariff barriers depends upon the home elasticities of demand and supply applicable to the affected commodities. The higher these elasticities, the greater will be the reduction of expenditures on imports in response to increased tariffs. Also to be considered in this connection are the relevant foreign supply elasticities. If these are less than infinite a rise in tariffs of the home country or an increase in the restrictiveness of its quotas will tend to raise import prices, which to some extent will offset the reduction in import quantities. Moreover, suppose there is foreign retaliation. If an increase in domestic tariffs is met with equal retaliatory increases in tariffs abroad, and combined foreign supply and demand elasticities exceed those prevailing at home, the result can easily be a worsening of the balance of trade, rather than an improvement in it.

3. Even assuming no retaliation and perfectly elastic foreign supply, the effects of tariffs on the balance of trade are by no means certain. Decreased spending on imports as a result of heightened trade barriers means that domestic demand is raised. With an increase

in aggregate home demand, domestic income will be increased via the foreign-trade multiplier. Increased income means increased imports, which go to offset the initial decline in imports brought about by the raised trade restrictions. The result may be a far smaller improvement in the balance of trade than originally evisioned.

4. Suppose we also consider the foreign repercussion effect. Decreased home imports mean decreased foreign exports. These serve to depress foreign incomes, which in turn reduces imports (the home country's exports). The net improvement in the domestic balance of trade will then be even smaller.

5. Finally, if we consider the impact of increased domestic demand on investment (the *accelerator*) and the effect of this induced investment on incomes and imports, there is a further question whether the improvement in the balance of trade will be at all significant.

Quotas would appear to have somewhat the same impact as tariffs on the level of national economic activity. By effectively reducing the volume of imports, they cut down the amount of import-leakage out of the domestic income stream, raise the "net foreign investment" $(X - M)$ component of the aggregate demand function, and thus stimulate national income via the foreign trade multiplier. But if quotas are applied to *all* imports, they not only result in the equivalent of an autonomous injection into the domestic income stream, but also in the complete elimination of imports as an income leakage, once all of the quotas are filled. By thus forcing the marginal propensity to import to become zero, the value of the multiplier is increased.

The use of tariffs and quotas to improve the balance of trade and, therefore, the balance of payments is generally decried—and with ample justification. One country's employment of this technique to improve its own payments situation automatically means that the balance of payments of one or more other countries will be worsened. Since trade restrictions as a policy tool are available to every nation, the threat of retaliation and counter-retaliation is to be considered. The real loss in such a case is the reduced world trade, production, and efficiency in the allocation of resources that results. Such beggar-thy-neighbor techniques are costly in real terms for all concerned. Even in the home country, the undesirable side effects of increased tariffs and quotas upon the economic structure and productive efficiency make these tools a poor choice for balance of payments adjustment.

Conversely, there is some question about whether the best way to restore balance for countries with chronic payments surpluses is to lower their trade restrictions unilaterally. Depending upon their own supply and demand elasticities and those prevailing abroad, as well as the effect of increased imports on incomes (and imports) at home and abroad, the net impact of reduced trade barriers upon the balance of payments is by no means certain. In this case, the real gains from increased trade and efficiency make such reductions desirable in and of themselves, apart from any balance of payments effect. Nonetheless, the loss of bargaining power accompanying unilateral trade liberalization may be another argument against this method of surplus adjustment.

OTHER RESTRICTIONS

There are a variety of other *ad hoc* measures that can be employed to help restore payments balance in addition to those noted above. None of them is as harsh as exchange control, multiple rates, and explicit trade restrictions, such as tariffs and quotas, but most of them in one way or another involve some distortion of competitive conditions.

One device, already mentioned in connection with commercial policy, consists of "buy at home" appeals, which are often based on balance of payments considerations. In the minds of the uninitiated, the purchase of imported goods is somehow associated with an outflow of national gold into foreign coffers. If the appeal is successful, a feeling of guilt—no matter how subtle—will be connected with the purchase of imports. It hardly takes much of a price or quality difference to overcome this guilt feeling, however, and it is primarily in more or less identical goods and services that such measures can make themselves felt.

In government purchases abroad, especially for the military, and in government-financed projects at home, it is possible to enforce policies aimed at redirecting expenditures from foreign to domestic suppliers. Similarly, the foreign-exchange cost of aid to other countries can be reduced by tying the aid to domestic purchases.

Government influence on the balance of payments can also be exerted on international capital flows by the use of techniques that fall far short of outright exchange control. The U.S. Interest Equalization Tax (IET), proposed in 1963 and implemented in 1964, was a good example. Levies were placed on purchases of foreign stocks and bonds (with some exceptions) by U.S. residents, in order to equalize the yields available at home and abroad. The threat of such a tax during the interval between its proposal in the summer of 1963 and its implementation early in 1964 caused outflows of capital in the form of affected investments to come to a virtual halt. Once the tax was implemented and the uncertainty removed, the capital outflow was revived, although in reduced measure.

Similarly, measures to stem U.S. direct investments abroad were also employed for a time during the 1960's and early 1970's. Business firms exceeding a certain size were requested not to expand their direct investments abroad by more than a certain percentage over that of the preceding time period ". . . in the interest of the balance of payments." This policy, extending the then prevailing domestic guidelines for wage- and price-level stability to the balance of payments sphere, constituted a simple appeal for cooperation between government and business for the solution of the U.S. balance of payments deficit. In addition, businesses were required to report their own international expenditures and receipts periodically to the Secretary of Commerce, which introduced a further incentive to economize on purchases of goods and services and on investments abroad. Stronger controls over loans and investments abroad were subsequently made mandatory under the Office of Foreign Direct Investments (OFDI). Both the IET and OFDI controls were removed early in 1974.

In all of the measures designed to help restore payments balance, great care must be taken that the net, or overall (not merely the initial), impact on the balance of payments is beneficial. This involves a careful analysis of all the possible feedback effects of such techniques, which were surveyed in some detail in Chapter 17. Moreover, it must be considered that these measures, like all restrictions to international trade and payments, are distortive in their effects and therefore are associated with a cost in terms of possible reduced productive efficiency and consumer welfare.

EXCHANGE CONTROL

Perhaps the most drastic means of balance of payments adjustment available to a nation—and perhaps the most undesirable from an economic standpoint—is exchange control. We have dealt with this form of payments restriction twice before in connection both with commercial policy and with the foreign-exchange market. From a balance of payments standpoint, the sole purpose of exchange controls is to ration out the available supply of international reserves according to some predetermined set of priorities. With complete exchange control a balance of payments deficit is impossible, simply because foreign-exchange receipts from exports, foreign aid, and capital inflows are administratively allocated to payments for imports, capital outflows, and transfers abroad of precisely equal or lesser magnitude.

There are also a variety of "milder" versions of exchange control which merely limit certain sources of demand for foreign exchange and thus eliminate them or reduce their importance as contributors to a balance of payments deficit. For example, tourist expenditures and capital transfers abroad by domestic residents are two payments outflows particularly susceptible to restriction. Partial exchange control such as this tends to be temporary in nature and often is scrapped after a more basic improvement in the balance of payments has occurred.

From the start of World War II until 1951, partial or complete exchange control characterized the international payments of virtually all of the world's nations. This was largely the result of the War itself and its aftermath, the so-called "dollar-shortage" era. The European economies, with their production capacity largely in shambles, sought to pursue reconstruction as rapidly as possible. Their desire to import from the U.S., the only industrial country practically unscathed by the War, was enormous, but their capacity to earn the foreign exchange needed to pay for these imports with their own exports was severely limited. The result was a worldwide shortage of U.S. dollars, and this made it necessary for most countries to control international payment flows very strictly. Foreign currencies acquired could only be sold to official institutions, which, in turn, rationed them out for purposes deemed absolutely essential for reconstruction.

Exchange controls were gradually removed during the middle 1950's, and by 1959 full convertibility had been restored to most of the important currencies of the nonCommunist countries. Students of international economics often find it surprising indeed how recent the return to relatively free international payments really is. Yet there are numerous important countries, including all of the Communist bloc, that continue to maintain strict exchange control so that this form of administrative payments adjustment is still a fact of life and will be for years to come.

Complete exchange control, as detailed earlier in the book, gives the government a monopoly over foreign-exchange transactions. Foreign currencies can only be acquired by licenses from the government at the official exchange rate, while all foreign exchange earned must be surrendered to the government, again at the official rate of exchange. By setting its receipts of foreign exchange exactly equal to its disbursements, the government can easily maintain payments balance.

A wide variety of arguments has been used to justify exchange control. Severe structural balance of payments disequilibrium, like that resulting from the impairment of productive capacity in the European countries after World War II, is obviously an important consideration. When an important national goal (e.g., reconstruction) can only be achieved by careful rationing of international payments, exchange controls may well be justified. Similarly, during wartime, the freedom of international payments obviously has to be subordinated to other considerations.

Exchange controls permit national economic policy-makers broad freedom of action, not only in times of national emergency, but in more normal times as well. Exchange controls "insulate" the national economy. No matter what happens internally, the balance of payments will be unaffected. Hence, the national money supply can be expanded without limit, and government spending can be as liberal as the political considerations will allow, without even an instance of trepidation about the possible balance of payments effect of such measures. With exchange control, the goals of rapid national economic growth and full employment can be pursued without restriction, as long as the measures used remain politically acceptable. It is difficult to separate the situations in which exchange control may be warranted from those in which they are not. The benefits exchange control yields for the national economy, if any, must be weighed against its costs both to the nation itself and to other countries.

Another justification of exchange control is that it can be very useful in preventing "destructive" international capital flows. Adverse political or military developments may cause large-scale capital outflows, a regular *flight* of capital from one country to another. Understandably, the affected nation is vitally interested in halting this flow, and exchange control limited to capital transactions is the most effective way of doing this. Because over- and under-invoicing of goods in trade, tourist travel, and other non-capital transactions can easily be used to circumvent such restrictions, it may well be necessary to make the control of foreign exchange complete. Once the incentive for capital flight is removed, the exchange controls can be eliminated. The danger is, of course, that they will remain in force even after they are no longer justified, and that the damage they cause to trade, production, and the allocation of resources will go far to offset their potential benefits.

By insulating the national economy from balance of payments disequilibria and thus providing greatly increased freedom of domestic economic policy, exchange controls may leave the way open for a serious inflation of costs and prices. As domestic prices rise relative to those prevailing abroad, the official exchange rate becomes even further removed from the "equilibrium" exchange rate that would prevail in the absence of exchange controls; i.e., the official exchange rate represents an *overvaluation* of the home currency. If exchange controls were suddenly removed and the currency peg remained the same, serious balance of payments disequilibrium would result. Hence, the greater the overvaluation resulting from inflation at home, the less is the likelihood that exchange controls will be removed. Meanwhile, the retention of exchange controls may add further upward pressure to cost and prices, due both to the possibility of continued imprudent economic policies and to pricing measures on the part of producers and owners of productive factors essentially freed from import-competition.

BILATERAL AND MULTILATERAL CLEARING ARRANGEMENTS

The logical extension of exchange control is a system of international trade and payments based on barter. Country *A* agrees to buy 500 million barrels of oil from Country *B*, and pays for them at an agreed upon exchange rate in its own currency which is, of course, inconvertible. Country *B* then uses this currency to purchase goods from *A*. This form of *bilateral clearing* was used extensively by Germany before World War II, and it is still employed in trade involving many of the Communist countries.

Bilateral clearing may be relatively liberal or it may be highly restrictive. Liberal clearing arrangements may merely set the exchange rate and leave pricing and purchasing decisions entirely in the hands of privately owned or state-controlled business firms. If it so happens that payments during a given year equal receipts and that all accounts are cleared, there is little noticeable trade restriction except, of course, that the source of supply of imports and the market for exports are strictly prescribed. When one country's exports exceed its imports, however, the surplus country's account in the deficit country builds up. This can occur only as long as both countries are willing to permit it. It may, however, set in motion certain forces which can bring about eventual adjustment.

In the creditor country, with an export surplus, the exporters may have to wait for payment until additional amounts of the local currency are paid into the clearing account for imports as a result of additional purchases from the deficit country. Or, the central bank must extend credit to them. If the exporters are paid in this way—via an expansion of the domestic money supply—money incomes will rise in the surplus country, imports will grow, and the country's creditor position will be reduced. On the other hand, if exporters are forced to wait until imports make available sufficient funds, they themselves finance the exports and their costs rise as a result. Eventually this in itself presumably will tend to reduce the volume of exports and help to restore balance.

The debtor country, on the other hand, is simultaneously being subjected to deflationary pressures as a result of its imports exceeding exports. The money supply tends to shrink as increasing amounts of its currency are paid into the account of the creditor nation, although this may be easily offset by means of appropriate monetary measures.

In both cases, the tendency for restoration of balance is clear. Under normal circumstances, of course, there presumably will not be an infinite extension of this debtor-creditor relationship, and balance will be restored administratively.

One of the disadvantages of bilateral clearing arrangements of all types is that they are strictly limited to commodity trade. Other kinds of payments, particularly capital flows, are excluded. This problem can be partly overcome by *payments agreements;* i.e., the clearing arrangement that may already be applied to trade is merely extended to include other types of payments as well, particularly outstanding debts. In this way, the creditor country can gradually reduce its "frozen" balances, if the debtor country agrees to reduce its imports in order to make this possible. Similarly, payments agreements can also include payments for shipping services, interest charges, tourism, and so forth.

A clear disadvantage of bilateral payments agreements, whether or not they are strictly limited to merchandise trade, is that they channel trade

tterns substantially removed from those which would prevail in the
e of exchange control. Trade cannot conform to the dictates of
arative advantage, which requires full multilateralism. A partial solu-
to this problem may be found in *multilateral payments agreements,*
ayments unions.

As we saw earlier, after World War II the international payments of
ost countries were characterized by strict exchange control. This resulted
ı myriad bilateral payments agreements. The only real exception was
he *Sterling Area,* composed of the U.K. and most of the Commonwealth,
within which relatively free multilateral payments were permitted. In essence, the Sterling Area functioned as a multilateral payments agreement.
Transfers with nonmembers were still severely limited. It was not until
1954 that this system was broadened to include a total of fifty-one countries.
Current transactions could then be cleared multilaterally among all of
these nations possessing "transferable accounts" in London.

Perhaps even more illustrative of multilateral payments agreements is
the European Payments Union (EPU), which existed from 1950 to 1958,
when it was superseded by the European Monetary Agreement (EMA).
With the exception of international monetary relations within the sterling
bloc, the exigencies of reconstruction forced all western European countries
to impose strict payments controls. Since these controls were ultimately
concerned primarily with rationing available supplies of U.S. dollars, it
proved to be easier to restore relatively free payments among the affected
countries themselves while at the same time retaining controls on dollar
payments.

By 1947, it had become apparent that bilateral clearing was hindering
the reconstruction process and restricting the growth of trade. Consequently, the Organization for European Economic Cooperation (OEEC) recommended that a multilateral clearing system be devised as quickly as
possible. Late in 1947, the First Agreement on Multilateral Compensation
was signed. This provided that each participating country report to the
Bank for International Settlements (BIS) its debtor or creditor position
vis-à-vis every other country on a monthly basis. The payments debts would
then be offset against each other and a net debtor or creditor position
worked out for each country. The Agreement proved to be an outright
failure and was superseded in 1948 by the Intra-European Payments Agreement, after considerable pressure from the U.S. This agreement linked
Marshall Plan aid payments to intra-European multilateral clearing and,
on balance, proved to be successful in expanding trade rapidly and econo-
mizing on dollar expenditures.

Several versions of the Intra-European Payments Agreement were finally
replaced, in 1950, by the European Payments Union, a truly multilateral
payments arrangement which finally eliminated all vestiges of internal bi-

lateralism. Each member simply struck a payments balance with respect to *all* the other members of the union and thus arrived at a net debtor or creditor position. A net creditor country would extend credit to the Union, while a debtor country would receive an interim credit from the Union. This was made possible by an initial U.S. grant of $350 million. Settlement was increasingly stipulated to be in gold and U.S. dollars, thus gradually increasing the degree of stringency involved.[2]

No longer was it necessary for any one country to discriminate against imports from any other country with which it had a bilateral payments deficit, since this deficit could be offset by a bilateral payments credit with some third country. It was only required to adjust total debits and credits with regard to the Union as a whole. The EPU thus made possible a very rapid expansion of intra-European trade, and, eventually, the full restoration of convertibility in 1958.

MULTIPLE EXCHANGE RATES

Another method of administratively insuring payments balance, closely allied with exchange controls, is the practice of *multiple exchange rates.* Like bilateral-trade agreements, multiple exchange rates were widely used by Germany during the 1930's, and adopted by numerous other countries after the war.

The principle involved is disarmingly simple. A high exchange rate is granted for undesirable imports, such as luxuries, and for exports facing a high foreign-demand elasticity—reducing imports expensive to domestic buyers and exports inexpensive to foreign buyers. A low exchange rate is granted for desirable imports, such as raw materials, and exports for which the foreign-price elasticity of demand is low. The number of different exchange rates involved might be two, three, or even more. In this manner, all international monetary transactions can be influenced so that payments balance is insured, and the goals of the national economic planners are attained.

The simplest form of multiple exchange rate is the *dual rate,* involving an official rate and a free rate. All exports of the commodity for which the country is an important supplier and for which the foreign-demand elasticity is low must be sold at the official *overvalued* rate of exchange. This enables the country to obtain more foreign exchange per unit of exports. All other exports go at the free-exchange rate. All import transactions, with the possible exception of some necessities granted the official rate, also are made at the free rate. The supply and demand for foreign

[1] Members of the EPU were Austria, Belgium-Luxembourg, Denmark, France, Germany, Greece, Iceland, Italy, Netherlands, Norway, Portugal, Sweden, Switzerland, Turkey, and the Sterling Area.

exchange will tend to set a free-exchange rate which clears the imports and exports falling under it. Thus, combined with government regulation of trade under the official rate, payments balance or surplus is virtually assured. If it is not, the transfer of certain commodities from the official to the free rate can bring it about quite easily.

More complex are multiple fixed-exchange rates, under which no single rate is set by the forces of supply and demand, and all are fixed administratively. Each broad category of international transactions—tourist expenditures, capital transfers, imports of luxuries, necessities, and so forth—receives its own administratively allocated exchange rate. The number of such categories may, of course, vary along with the transactions grouped under them. The principle involved is the same as under the dual rate system, except that *all* rates are fixed and enforced by means of exchange control. The desired balance of payments conditions are then achieved by simply juggling the various exchange rates by trial and error.

A clear danger of multiple fixed rates, as well as of dual exchange rates where certain "desirable" imports fall under the overvalued official rate, is the formation of black markets and the consequent undermining of the government foreign-exchange policy.

Multiple exchange rates of all types distort competitive conditions. Hence, they also distort the economic structure of trading nations. Favored industries—both export- and import-competing—are artificially supported by exchange rates which serve to undervalue the home currency, while others are penalized as a result of exchange rates which overvalue the domestic currency. The former encourage exports and discourage imports, while the latter have precisely the opposite effect. The economic structure of the home country tends to become substantially different from what it would be in the absence of multiple exchange rates, with similar effects on resource allocation. In favored export- and import-competing industries, resources may be used inefficiently. Meanwhile, the employment of resources is hindered in other industries, even though they might well be able to hold their own in both foreign and domestic markets. Multiple exchange rates thus involve a real "cost" to the economy, the magnitude of which is difficult to gauge.

While the effects of multiple exchange rates on the home economy are of primary concern, it is also necessary to look at their impact on other countries. Overvaluation of the home currency, by making imports relatively cheaper for domestic buyers, supports foreign-export industries. Overvaluation simultaneously hinders domestic exports and thus supports import-competing industries abroad. Undervaluation, on the other hand, artificially reduces the price competitiveness of both foreign import-competing industries and foreign-export industries. Multiple exchange rate practices applied by one country thus have a distinct bearing on trade, economic structure, and productive efficiency in foreign nations as well. Such effects will be greater, the more important the home country is as a market for exports and as a source of supply of imports with regard to its trading partners, foreign nations. If the effects of multiple exchange rate practices are severe, certain counter measures may be applied by foreign countries which may then serve to offset partially the more harmful effects on their respective economies.

One advantage of multiple exchange rates, as opposed to strict exchange control, is that the manifold complexities entailed by the strict control are largely circumvented. It is not necessary to ration foreign exchange to prospective importers arbitrarily, and large administrative staffs, potential improprieties, and a host of other problems are avoided. Any import can be obtained, but only under the applicable exchange rate. The rationing of foreign exchange occurs through administered prices, rather than through administered quantities of foreign exchange, and the complexities involved may be much less serious. Still, the distortive effects of multiple exchange rates with respect to trade, competitive conditions, and economic structure render it an instrument of desperation in balance of payments adjustment.

PRIVATE COMPENSATION

Exchange control and multiple exchange rates sometimes give rise to a variety of ingenious private and quasi-official transactions, designed to circumvent the official exchange policies and yet remain within the framework of their intended objectives. Suppose, for example, a U.S. firm in the late 1940's desired to sell $1 million worth of machinery to a Belgian company. It could ship the machines to Belgium and be paid in Belgian francs. But Belgian exchange control would prevent conversion of the francs into dollars. What to do? The U.S. firm could use its francs to buy goods in Belgium or in countries to which Belgian exchange control did not apply. It could then ship these goods to the U.S. and sell them in order to obtain its money. The exporter thus becomes an importer. It would be expected, however, that limits would be placed on such private compensation transactions, so that no exports are employed in the private-compensation dealings that could have been sold outside the exchange-control area anyway.

Alternatively, the U.S. firm might be able to use its blocked balances to meet local currency needs, such as executive travel, employment of local nationals, or even—though rarely permitted by local government authorities—investments in local firms.

Private compensation may be subject to stringent restrictions on the types of transactions that can be used to liquidate blocked balances, or such trade may be relatively easy to pursue. If blocked balances can only be used for certain very limited purposes, and if the loss to the firm thus engendered is quite substantial, the firm will be bent upon exhausting these balances in one way or another and will take care thereafter not to accumulate any more. Its imports from a country with strict controls will rise in the short-run as efforts are made to liquidate blocked balances, but its exports to that country will tend to decline. In some cases, of course, the accumulation of blocked balances cannot be prevented, as in the payment of royalties, interest, and dividends. Under multiple exchange rates, on the other hand, the repatriation of interest and dividends could conceivably be affected by purchases of local goods for export at favorable exchange rates and their subsequent resale abroad.

Private compensation arises out of situations involving exchange controls, and while it partly succeeds in circumventing the manifold restrictions they entail, it does not go very far in this direction. Besides, it involves even more government control, with regulations and stipulations regarding the permissible employment of blocked balances. The rule of thumb is as follows: blocked balances may not be used for any purpose which in their absence would have led to foreign-exchange receipts from outside the area of exchange control. In order to implement this rule, a complex apparatus is required which, in turn, is superimposed upon the already existing complex and costly exchange-control administration.

Moreover, like exchange controls under which it operates, private compensation severely distorts international competitive conditions. Trade subject to these arrangements does not follow the dictates of comparative cost—either in composition or in direction—but rather, it pursues the exigencies of the location of the blocked balances and their repatriation. Indeed, goods may be purchased at prices well above those prevailing elsewhere and resold at a loss. Even so, the end result may be superior to the indefinite retention of blocked balances, at least from the standpoint of the firm or the individual most directly involved.

STRUCTURAL CHANGE

Payments imbalances, as we have seen, can be alleviated in a variety of ways. The policy response, given that the automatic adjustment process is not permitted to run its course under existing political and institutional conditions, must be tailored to the cause of the imbalance. No single technique provides a universal answer, and each in its own way involves a cost, either to the home economy or to foreign economies, or to both. Suppose a country suffers from a *structural* balance of payments deficit. None of the methods designed to restore payments balance surveyed above constitutes a permanent solution, if only because they do not attack the root of the problem.

It will be recalled that structural balance of payments disequilibrium can take on many forms. It may be the result of changes in supply or demand conditions at home or abroad which affect the volume and direction of international trade. Or, broader economic forces, such as differential rates of economic growth, may give rise to important flows of long-term capital between nations. Devaluation would not alleviate such disequilibria. At best, it would probably constitute only a temporary palliative.

The answer, of course, lies in effecting basic, structural changes in the domestic economy in order to adapt it to the changed conditions in the world economy as a whole. This is much more easily said than done.

Changed domestic demand conditions may be met partly through stimulating import-competing industries by increasing the mobility of productive resources by means of *temporary* protection, subsidies, tax incentives, and so forth. Altered foreign demand conditions call for a different set of remedies designed to channel output from one set of export industries to another. Again, the government can do a great deal in the way of retraining programs, temporary financial assistance to the firms involved, and so forth. This is far easier, of course, in the case of diversified economies where a re-direction of productive resources is at least possible. But what does Colombia do in the face of a precipitous decline in the world demand for coffee?

Perhaps even more difficult is the solution of structural disequilibria resulting from economic-growth considerations. Domestic capital formation or productivity growth may lag significantly behind other countries, and far-reaching changes in the economic structure of the nation may be called for. Fundamental changes in the educational and social system, consumption and savings patterns, and the very character of the people are extremely difficult to achieve and take a great deal of time. Temporarily, restrictions to trade or payments, or devaluation may be used to provide that time. But the ultimate structural shifts, however painful, cannot be avoided if such a country is to assume a viable role in the world economy.

THE COST OF ADJUSTMENT

In our discussion of balance of payments adjustment, with its many facets, we have implied time and again that it is by no means a costless process.

The costs to the national economy associated with expenditure-switching measures designed to restore payments balance are clear. Restrictions to international trade and payments result in a reallocation of productive resources which in and of itself is costly and which, in addition, may lead to significantly reduced efficiency in production—and hence in reduced real incomes. Therefore, the real cost of such measures is the consequent real income foregone, solely for the sake of payments balance. This burden may be borne largely by the deficit country imposing the *ad hoc* restrictions, or by the rest of the world alone, but most probably it will be shared by both.

For example, let us say that a deficit country raises its tariff levels in order to eliminate the payments imbalance. Domestically, we would expect a reallocation of productive resources into import-competing industries and away from more efficient employments elsewhere in the economy. As exports to the deficit nation decline, we would furthermore expect resources in other countries to be shifted from export industries into less productive uses in other sectors. All of the affected economies share in the cost of balance of payments adjustment via expenditure-switching measures such as tariffs. Moreover, the cost is a continuing one—one which will prevail as long as the restrictive measures are in effect. Because resource mobility is never perfect, and therefore never costless, this shifting of resources represents an added real sacrifice to the various economies, one which will recur once the restrictions are removed.

In a similar manner, it can be shown that restrictions on capital flows call forth a cost to all economies involved. Exchange controls are no different in this regard, and they are perhaps even more severe in terms of the magnitude of the burden placed on the individual national economies. Again, the costs associated with all restrictive adjustment techniques are continuous in nature, since an optimization of resource allocation cannot occur until they are modified.

Balance of payments adjustment is always a *mutual* process; by definition, for every deficit country there exist one or more surplus countries. Each time a deficit country acts to restore balance in a multi-country world, one or a combination of the following must occur: (a) a reduction in the payments surplus of one or more nations, (b) a movement from payments balance into payments deficit on the part of one or more countries, and (c) an increase in the pre-existing payments deficit of one or more countries. If a deficit country uses the above restrictive techniques to restore payments balance, and external adjustment is accomplished by countries falling into group (a), the adjustment costs may well be limited to those already enumerated. But if countries in groups (b) and (c) are forced to incur additional deficits as a result of the restrictive techniques used by the deficit nation, their own efforts to return to payments balance may substantially increase the costs of adjustment.

Suppose a nation employs the "classical medicine" of deflation in order to cure its payments deficit. Again, there is a cost involved. Restrictive economic policies depress aggregate demand at home, which results in a reduction of national income and, most probably, a significant unemployment of productive resources. The cost, in terms of total output foregone, continues to mount until payments balance has been restored and all re-sources are re-absorbed in the productive process. As deflation in the deficit country reduces its imports, the exports of other countries decline in like amount, thus raising the possibility of unemployed and adversely reallocated resources in those economies as well. Again, the cost of adjustment is shared by the deflating country and its trading partners—a temporary cost associated with the restoration of payments balance, and one which disappears once both internal and external balance has been restored.

Finally, what if payments imbalances are alleviated through currency depreciation? A depreciation by the deficit country tends to stimulate activity in export industries and in import-competing industries, thereby causing a cost-inducing transfer of resources from other sectors of the economy into these possibly less efficient areas. Furthermore a failure to cure the roots of the disequilibrium through depreciation could eventually result in a costly reversal of resource flows. But the trading partners of the depreciating country are subject to potentially even greater costs, both in terms of temporarily unemployed and in misallocated resources. A surplus country undertaking an appreciation of its currency subjects itself to similar costs resulting from transitional unemployment of productive factors and reallocation costs.

Since the traditional means of alleviating payments imbalances all involve costs of one sort or another, the really interesting problem lies in the discovery of that particular technique which will minimize the costs to the adjusting country. Assuming that a given payments deficit must be resolved, and that the usual variety of measures are available for use, what technique or combination of techniques will minimize adjustment costs?

One obvious possibility is to *transfer* as large a portion of the adjustment costs as possible to other countries. Depreciation as well as trade and payments restrictions may well permit the deficit country to refrain from imposing a deflation upon itself. Since it is likely that the real costs associated with the former are substantially less than those attending the latter, it is in its own interest to employ such techniques of adjustment. But these same techniques tend to result in unemployed resources abroad. When we consider the total costs of adjustment, therefore, the deficit country in this way has succeeded in reducing its share of the burden and increasing its trading partners' share.

One author has analyzed the international sharing of adjustment costs in a most interesting manner in terms of the interplay of international *power*—the capacity to avoid the adjustment burdens—in the international economy.[3] According to Cohen, the factors assuring a dominant role in determining the proportion of the adjustment costs borne by the various

[3] Benjamin J. Cohen, *Adjustment Costs and the Distribution of New Reserves,* Studies in International Finance No. 18 (Princeton, N.J.: International Finance Section, Princeton University, 1966).

countries involved are (a) diversification of production, with the most diversified economies in the most favorable position, (b) the degree of industrialization, with the primary producing countries at a decided disadvantage, (c) the international investment status, with capital-exporting countries generally in a favored position compared with capital importers, and (d) the rate of economic growth, with the rapidly growing countries able to escape with a relatively lighter adjustment burden than slow-growth economies.

Moreover, the actual techniques used by individual countries to bring about payments balance, Cohen asserts, represent much more than the straightforward application of the most effective measures by economic policymakers. Rather, they reflect the relative economic—and political—strengths and weaknesses of the countries concerned. In the context of this international power play, each nation tends to adopt those techniques that will minimize its share of the adjustment burden, given the degree of leverage at its disposal.

It is quite reasonable to contend that in the adjustment of monetary balance of payments disequilibria—e.g., where one country undertakes imprudent economic policies ending in substantial inflation—the cost of adjustment should be borne by country in which the disturbance originates. No less reasonable is the idea that the cost of adjustment to structural disequilibrium should be shared by all countries involved. But these "equitable" notions hardly seem to conform to a reality in which each nation considers a fair distribution of the adjustment burden to be one which minimizes its own contribution to the overall costs involved. Viewed in this particular light, adjustment measures such as the German-Dutch upward revaluation of 1961, the U.S. interest-equalization tax of 1964, and the British deflation of 1965–1966 and devaluation of 1967 take on quite a different complexion.

V

The International Monetary System

25

INTERNATIONAL LIQUIDITY

Up to this point we have studied the concept of the balance of payments, the factors affecting it, and its adjustment. Under the classical gold standard the flexible exchange rates, with neutral government economic policies and appropriate elasticity conditions, we found that balance of payments adjustment tends to occur virtually automatically. Otherwise, it is a matter of policy, either of deliberate income adjustments, or *ad hoc* restrictions of international trade and payments, or changes in the relative value of the national currency. Such adjustments require time—time that can be provided only by a cushion of international reserves.

The international monetary system requires that a nation incurring a balance of payments deficit settle that deficit by transferring some generally accepted means of international payment of its creditors. This normally reduces its own stock of international reserves and increases that of the surplus countries.

INTERNATIONAL AND PERSONAL RESERVES

International reserves are really not very different from personal reserves. Presumably, every individual is involved in monetary receipts and payments and enters into a wide variety of transactions that yield monetary inflows, i.e., salaries and wages, gifts, dividends, and so forth. Simultaneously, he also incurs a broad range of monetary expenditures for goods, housing, entertainment, donations, and so on.

If, during a given month or any other accounting period, his expenditures exceed his receipts, he is forced to draw on his monetary balances and he then finds that he has less money in cash or demand deposits at the end of the period than he had at the beginning. Using our terminology, he ran a deficit in his personal *balance of payments* and therefore has had to draw down his personal *reserves* to settle it.

Conversely, if someone's receipts exceed his expenditures over a period of time, his personal balance of payments will show a surplus, resulting in a buildup of his personal reserves, i.e., his bank deposits, which are subject to immediate withdrawal and currency holdings. Personal reserves are composed of the generally accepted means of payment for settling transactions among individuals—the local currency.

It is not very difficult to see that if personal income and expenditures somehow coincided precisely in time, there would be very little need for personal reserves—perhaps none at all. If an individual's monthly expenditures, including savings, could always be settled at the moment his paycheck arrives, thus using up all monetary receipts, there would be no need for reserves. But this is rarely the case. One month receipts may exceed expenditures and the next month they may fall short. Furthermore, money received at one point in time is gradually spent until the next payment arrives. Future expenditures and receipts always involve a degree of uncertainty; the precautionary motive explains in part why individuals hold money. In short, there are *imbalances* in individuals' monetary receipts and payments which require the maintenance of personal reserves.

The greater these imbalances are, the greater will be the need for reserves. For instance, the author, whose royalty checks arrive only once a year, has greater need for personal reserve than the executive of substantially the same income who is paid by the month. It is apparent, moreover, that the greater is the absolute *volume* of monetary receipts and payments, the greater will be the need for reserves, if the relative imbalances are held constant.

Just as an individual requires monetary reserves in order to pursue his day-to-day activities, so also does a business firm, a unit of government, or any other economic entity involved in monetary receipts and disbursements. In all of these cases, reserves are defined in terms of the generally accepted means of payment—the national currency. A nation has a similar need for reserves, this time defined in terms of generally accepted *international* means of payment—gold and acceptable foreign currencies. Its need for reserves, like that of the individual, hinges upon the imbalances in its balance of payments and the overall volume of its international commercial and capital transactions. To the extent that individuals, firms, governments, or nations can borrow to finance their payments deficits, their need for reserves will be commensurately reduced. In any case, whether payments, or nations can borrow to finance their payments deficits, their need for balance of payments adjustment is undiminished.

OWNED AND BORROWED RESERVES

In a strict sense, the international reserves of a country, as defined here, encompass only the gold and acceptable foreign currencies actually in its possession. These are the so-called *owned* reserves. But suppose a nation incurs successive balance of payments deficits that result in a depletion of its owned reserves. True, it will have to struggle for a restoration of payments balance. But what if balance cannot be restored, without having to resort to devaluation or *ad hoc* restrictions, before its international reserves are threatened with exhaustion? A way must be open to the country to replenish its reserves, thereby providing the sorely needed time for adjustment to be accomplished.

The nation may be able to *borrow* international reserves in order to bridge the gap. The lenders may be one or more foreign countries that have reserves in excess of what they feel are immediately needed, or they may be foreign financial institutions, or perhaps an international agency expressly created for this purpose. Suppose it happens that the ability of a country to borrow international reserves from one or more such sources is virtually guaranteed. That nation may then legitimately add those reserves which it has the capacity to borrow, if needed, to its owned reserves in order to compute its *total* international reserve position.

Total international reserves—owned and borrowed—define the amount of cushioning available to a country in times of balance of payments deficit. If the approximate size of such deficits can be foreseen, the total reserve position simultaneously defines the amount of time available for completion of the necessary balance of payments adjustment.

Once again, this can be compared usefully with the personal situation of the fortunate student who, in addition to owned reserves of cash and demand deposit balances, finds it possible to borrow additional cash from his father in times of need. To the extent that such borrowing rights are virtually a foregone conclusion, the student may take them into consideration when calculating his overall personal reserve position. This then gives him an idea of the size of the deficits in his personal balance of payments that he can afford and of how long he can incur them before making the inevitable adjustment in his expenditure and income patterns.

INTERNATIONAL LIQUIDITY

The sum total of the international reserves of all nations participating in the world monetary system, as we know it, is called *international liquidity*—i.e., the world supply of international reserves. As in the case of an individual country's need for international reserves, the world's need for international liquidity is contingent upon (a) the *volume* of international commercial and financial transactions, and (b) the *imbalances* that characterize these transactions. With a given volume of world trade and payments, the greater are the collective payments imbalances of the participating nations, and the more pronounced will be the overall need for international liquidity.

The need for liquidity is also related to the degree of flexibility of exchange rates. At the limit, if exchange rates are completely determined by market forces, there would be no need for reserves. As soon as the authorities begin to intervene in foreign-exchange markets, the need becomes evident for reserves which can be exchanged for foreign currencies for use in exchange-stabilization operations. The greater the official involvement in exchange stabilization, the greater the need for reserves. If exchange rates are pegged for extended periods of time, reserves play a critical role in financing imbalances attributable to the prevailing disequilibrium exchange rates. Virtually any monetary standard, therefore, requires the existence of international reserves, with the aggregate need for liquidity varying inversely with the degree of flexibility in exchange rates.

What happens if the *supply* of international liquidity—under whatever exchange-rate regime exists—does not match the *need* for it? Suppose, for example, there exists a world liquidity *shortage*. The deficit nations of the world may find that they do not have sufficient cushioning international reserves to allow them time to restore payments balance without resorting to ad hoc trade and payments restrictions. They may be forced to cut back on imports, to promote exports in every conceivable way, and to limit international capital flows. Retaliatory action on the part of other nations, feeling themselves injured by these measures, would certainly not be out of the question.

If the consequences of such restrictions reverberate throughout the international economy, the inevitable result is a marked reduction in world trade and capital flows. This, as we know, tends to have depressing effects on world output of goods and services, and, hence, on real incomes. The result may be a broad-based recession in economic activity—one largely attributable to a shortage of international liquidity.

Now what about a liquidity *surplus?* Suppose there is a surfeit of international liquidity, and virtually all countries find themselves with more than ample international reserves. It is not unreasonable to expect that under such conditions deficit countries will refrain as long as possible from the sometimes painful economic policies needed to restore payments balance. They have sufficient international reserves, after all, to sustain extended periods of successive balance of payments deficits. The danger of severe inflationary pressures is especially noteworthy in such instances. The external balance constraint that normally calls forth anti-inflationary actions is, for all practical purposes, absent.

As we noted earlier, inflation in one or more countries tends to be transmitted to others. The inflation-plagued countries develop an import surplus. This represents an export surplus for their trading partners which, if they are already operating at or near full employment, adds to the pressures of inflation in these nations. Capital flows that may be induced by excess international liquidity can have a supporting effect. As a general proposition, a surplus of international liquidity tends to have a broad, inflationary impact upon the international economy.

Given the institutional arrangement and goals of the international monetary system as they exist today, the problem essentially comes down to an attempt to insure that there exists neither a liquidity surplus nor a liquidity shortage. The supply of, and demand for, international liquidity must be balanced so that it exerts as few as possible expansionary or contractionary forces of its own upon the international economy. In an ideal sense, international liquidity should be substantially *neutral*. It should lubricate the international trade and payments mechanism without exerting undue and potentially destructive forces of its own.

We thus need to consider, in turn, the sources of supply of and demand for international liquidity and the problems involved in reconciling the two.

THE SUPPLY OF LIQUIDITY: GOLD

Of the generally accepted means of international payment that comprise international liquidity, gold has historically played by far the most important role. Although, from a quantitative standpoint, it still plays a significant part in international dealings, we shall see that the world economy will have to look elsewhere in the future for a source of international liquidity. Economists are sometimes tempted to underrate the role of gold in the international payments mechanism, but gold still contributes a significant proportion of the total world stock of international liquidity.

Let us assume for the moment that international liquidity must grow substantially over the next decade or two. How much of this additional liquidity can be supplied by gold? It is evident that the supply hinges upon the total quantity of gold (a) produced and (b) released into international monetary reserves from other sources, less (c) the amount absorbed for nonmonetary uses.

As is true for any ore deposit, gold mining at a given site involves rising costs as incremental amounts become increasingly difficult to extract. In addition to the cost-increasing effect of resource depletion, labor and other money costs of production also have had a tendency to rise, and these factors have been only partially offset by enhanced productivity. Hence gold output is largely dependent upon price. Apart from the traditional major gold exporters—the Soviet Union and South Africa—the gold price in the postwar period was too low to encourage increased production. United States production dwindled to insignificance and Canada had to resort to subsidies to encourage gold mining, for example. Even in the richest gold-mining areas, the extraction of gold often is only a by-product of some other line of activity such as uranium mining. In the absence of important new gold strikes or revolutionary technological advances—such as the extraction of gold from sea water as a by-product of water purification—future additions to the world's gold stock from new production seemed limited indeed. The replacement of a controlled market for gold with a free market in 1968 caused substantial price increases in the early 1970's, leading to increased profitability in gold mining.

What sources of gold are there besides new production? Perhaps most important is the possibility of releases of gold from gold hoards in various parts of the world. For example, during the 1931–1936 period, about 42 million fine ounces reached the world gold markets from Chinese and Indian hoards alone. It is impossible to estimate the total quantity of gold that today rests in private hoards. There is little question that those hoards are enormous, all things considered. The release of gold from hoards into monetary uses can hardly be counted upon as a reliable source of future monetary gold. Except in wartime or national revolution, the conversion of gold jewelry and other articles to monetary use is equally unlikely.

A substantial quantity of gold is used annually for artistic purposes; and a reduction in the use of gold in jewelry, for instance, seems particularly remote. In addition, there is a rapidly growing demand for gold as a metal for scientific and manufacturing applications. A second nonmonetary source of demand for gold is hoarding. This is particularly important in certain developing nations where the absence or backwardness of financial institutions, coupled with political and economic instability, makes gold the most reliable store of value. In Europe, the flow of gold into hoards is less pronounced, although sporadic hoarding has at times reached large proportions. However, evident opportunity cost incurred in holding gold is quite high, and keeps a lid on frivolous hoarding as was demonstrated when it became legal for Americans to own gold at the beginning of 1975.

Finally, we also should consider the domestic monetary systems of the nations of the world. The more countries move away from gold as a basis for the domestic money supply, the more gold becomes available. The U.S. has been moving in this direction. Other countries, especially in the Middle East, have taken the opposite tack, progressing toward an internal gold-coin standard.

We have, then, a set of sources of gold (new production, dishoarding, and exports of Communist countries) and a set of uses (hoarding, industrial and artistic applications, and as a domestic monetary base).

Supply and demand are cleared on the free gold market at the daily equilibrium price, as in any commodity market. Government gold holdings have largely been separated from the free market on both the buying and selling sides. Governments may agree to charge the price of their own gold holdings for intergovernmental transactions purposes, but there is at present no organic connection between the free market for gold and its role in international liquidity. The free gold market does, however, serve as a very sensitive barometer of confidence in national currencies, as investors buy and sell gold for speculative reasons. As a source of international liquidity, however, the role of gold promises to be increasingly limited.

THE SUPPLY OF LIQUIDITY: FOREIGN CURRENCIES

International liquidity, as we have stressed, has historically been composed of gold and acceptable foreign currencies available for settlement of payments imbalances among nations. We have already considered the supply of gold. What about the supply of foreign currencies as a future source of additional liquidity?

Under the international monetary system that prevailed for almost 30 years since World War II, two national currencies were considered generally acceptable for international payments purposes—the British pound sterling and the U.S. dollar. These were the so-called *reserve currencies,* or *key currencies,* deriving their status from the fact that nations have usually been willing to hold them along with, or in place of, gold in their international reserves.

The British pound sterling derives its reserve currency characteristics largely as a result of historical circumstances. For centuries, London was the commercial and financial capital of the world, probably reaching its zenith during 1870–1914. The gold standard at that time was universal, and many countries maintained their reserves in London. Since the pound was freely convertible into gold, international payments and international reserves were often denominated entirely in sterling. In fact, the pre-eminence and stability of the London financial system itself probably contributed a great deal to the smooth functioning of the pre-World War I gold standard.

By 1928, London had substantially recovered from the war-induced dislocations, and the international gold standard once again emerged as the international monetary mechanism. Since gold-standard countries freely converted their home currencies into gold, and Great Britain was pre-eminent among them, many nations again maintained their international reserves in sterling, mostly in the form of short-term assets in London. Not only were these short-term sterling balances freely convertible to gold but, unlike gold, they earned a return as well.

For Great Britain, the massive accumulation of foreign-owned short-term balances, always subject to at least some volatility, contributed serious vulnerability and ultimately forced her to go off gold during the international banking panic of 1931. A number of countries subsequently chose to retain their monetary reserves in sterling balances, thereby fixing the value of their own currencies in terms of the British pound sterling rather than gold. Sterling thus retained the status of a reserve currency for most of the British Empire and the Scandinavian countries—the *Sterling Area*. The importance of Britain in the trade of the Sterling Area countries rendered this a logical solution.

After World War II, sterling retained its status as a reserve currency, although the composition and character of the Sterling Area changed somewhat. The scarcity of gold and U.S. dollars during the postwar reconstruction period, accompanied by the inevitable patchwork of exchange controls, lent ample justification for the retention of a block of countries carrying on relatively free trade and payments among themselves, yet conserving gold and dollars in transactions with other countries. When sterling once again became fully convertible into gold and all other currencies in 1958, the British pound retained the status of reserve currency for most of the nations previously involved in the Sterling Bloc.

The U.S. dollar as a reserve currency, and hence as a component of international liquidity, has a somewhat different background. Not until after World War I did New York become a significant financial center geared to foreign trade, yet its stature as an international money market grew very rapidly. It never attained the prominence of London in the inter-war period, however, and the dislocations of the depression and World War II precluded the accession of the dollar to the role of a significant reserve currency.

Both the U.S. and the dollar emerged from World War II in extremely sound shape. The productive capability of much of the rest of the developed world had been decimated by the hostilities. In contrast, the productive capacity of the U.S. was not only unimpaired by the war but even strengthened, and the European reconstruction efforts resulted in an acute shortage of the dollars with which foreign countries could buy sorely needed American exports of capital and consumer goods. This was the so-called *dollar-shortage* era, and the seemingly insatiable foreign demand for dollars resulted in a massive U.S. inflow of gold amounting to $5.2 billion between 1946 and 1949.

By the time the Korean conflict began, bringing with it a decline in the U.S. trade surplus, the dollar was firmly established as a reserve currency. Foreign countries were only too happy to maintain their reserves in interest-bearing short-term dollar assets, especially since the dollar remained fully convertible into gold.

From 1950 to 1960, recurring U.S. balance of payment deficits resulted in the sale of $6.3 billion in gold to foreign countries, plus a buildup of foreign official holdings of dollars in the amount of $9.7 billion. The sale of U.S. gold abroad represented merely a transfer of international reserves from the U.S. to other countries. The total supply of world liquidity stays the same. But the buildup of foreign official dollars assets constitutes a net addition to world liquidity in the amount of $9.7 billion, since these dollars have become international reserves of foreign countries. The substantial U.S. deficits after 1960 also were settled largely by increases in foreign dollar reserve holdings. The U.S. balance of payments deficits during most of the postwar period, constituted the most important single source of international liquidity growth.

The reserve currency status of both sterling and the dollar underwent considerable change in the late 1960's and early 1970's. Sterling's role was placed into question late in 1967, when a devaluation of the pound visited losses of 14.3 per cent on countries holding their reserves in London. Chronic balance of payments difficulties since that time have left sterling as a dubious reserve asset and compromised its role as a key currency.

The dollar's role as a reserve currency, strengthened throughout the 1950's and early 1960's, was increasingly called into question in the late 1960's as liabilities to foreign official financial institutions greatly exceeded U.S. reserves. In August 1971 the dollar was declared inconvertible into gold, and was subsequently devalued as part of the Smithsonian Agreement in December of that year (see below). Since then, both the dollar and sterling have floated more or less freely in international currency markets, determining the purchasing power of reserves held in those currencies. Both are, however, continuing to play a major role as reserve currencies.

Other strong currencies, such as the German mark, the French franc, and the Japanese yen have not played a principal role as reserve currencies because they have not maintained the kinds of sustained payments deficits that have induced foreign governments to build up reserve balances. With the increase in raw-materials prices, especially oil, the importance of these currencies for reserve purposes may be strengthened.

SPECIAL DRAWING RIGHTS

Because of the inherent weaknesses of gold and national currencies as reliable, controllable elements in matching the supply of and need for international reserves, a new reserve asset was created in the early 1970's. Called International Monetary Fund Special Drawing Rights (SDRs), the idea was to create an asset which could be transferred among countries in settlement of payments imbalances, and which could be regulated in supply by mutual agreement in order to guarantee reserve adequacy.

The concept behind the creation of SDRs is as follows: When countries having 85 per cent of the IMF voting rights concur that the growth of international liquidity has been inadequate and that additional liquidity is needed, a permanent special drawing facility of an agreed-upon amount would be created. Each IMF member nation would have unconditional access to this facility in proportion to its regular IMF quota, and would be able to draw all or part of its allocation as it sees fit. The supply of international liquidity would thus be permanently augmented by the amount of the SDRs thus created. In addition to settling payments imbalances in gold and reserve currencies, nations would then be able to transfer SDR balances in settlement of payments deficits. A surplus country would not be required to accept SDRs once its SDR balance reached 300 per cent of its initial allocation, although it could choose to continue building up SDR balances if it so desired. In the case of a deficit country, its SDR balance could be drawn to zero, if necessary, but should normally average at least 30 per cent of its allocation over the long run.

With respect to operations on the foreign exchange market, a country would be able to transfer some of its SDRs to other nations in return for the latter's currencies, using these to sell off against its own currency in the foreign exchange market.

Countries that draw down their SDR allocation must pay interest on them, while countries that build up SDR balances receive interest.

The initial allocation of SDRs amounted to $9.5 billion during the 1970–72 period, or about 4 per cent of the total stock of international reserves. Subsequent allocations followed, and the SDR took on increased importance with the initiation of floating exchange rates in 1971. Because currencies were floating against each other, the SDR—valued according to a "bundle" of national currencies—assumed the role of a *numéraire,* or unit of account, for international official transactions. This is an important function, which the SDR has effectively taken over from the dollar, at least for official accounting purposes.

The SDRs represent the first major step in improving the flexibility of the international financial system and its responsiveness to growth and changes in the volume and patterns of international transactions. Furthermore, they constitute a mechanism whereby international liquidity may be expanded on a permanent basis by mutual consent of the majority of trading nations. Safeguards are retained in the 85 per cent voting majority provision—giving both the U.S. and the European Common Market countries effective veto power in each instance of prospective SDR expansion.

BORROWED RESERVES: THE INTERNATIONAL MONETARY FUND

We have just discussed the sources of *owned* international reserves—gold, reserve currencies, and SDRs. It is also possible for countries to *borrow* reserves they may need to finance payments deficits at existing exchange rates. A principal source of such borrowings is the IMF.

In essence, the Fund is simply a pool of gold and the national currencies of the member countries. Each participating country is required to deposit with the Fund a specified amount of gold and its own currency. This deposit is called a *quota*. The size of a nation's quota depends on a variety of factors, such as its holdings of international reserves, its national income, and its volume of foreign trade. IMF decisions are made by a system of weighted voting, under which the size of a nation's quota determines its voice. The amount of gold a country is required to deposit equals 10 per cent of its international gold and dollar reserves or 25 per cent of its total quota, whichever is less.

Now suppose a country incurs a balance of payments deficit that it finds impossible or unfeasible to settle by drawing down its owned reserves of SDRs, foreign currencies, and gold. It can then go to the IMF and "purchase" the foreign currency or currencies it needs by depositing with the IMF an equivalent amount of its own currency. In effect, it is borrowing foreign exchange from the IMF, using its own currency as security.

Naturally, there are limits placed on such borrowings. Any member country may *automatically* borrow, in the form of foreign currencies, an amount equal to 25 per cent of its quota by depositing an equivalent amount of its own currency at the Fund. Since this is normally equivalent to that part of its quota which the country originally deposited in gold, it is called the *gold tranche*. When countries calculate their *owned* international reserve positions, they usually include their IMF gold tranche, since these drawing rights are automatic.

Once a country draws its entire gold tranche, the IMF is holding 100 per cent of its quota in that nation's own currency. At that point, its gold tranche has gone to zero. Meanwhile, the countries whose currencies are being borrowed undergo an equivalent *increase* in their respective gold-tranche positions. The gold tranche of any single country could conceivably increase to 100 per cent of its quota if sufficient amounts of its currency are being borrowed by other nations.

Through borrowings from the IMF world liquidity increases. The borrowing country deducts the amounts drawn from the gold-tranche component of its international reserves, and adds an equal amount in acceptable foreign currencies. Its own international reserves thus do not change, but the country whose currency is being borrowed receives an increase in its gold tranche and, hence, in its international reserves. International liquidity thus grows by the amount of the original borrowing. Once the IMF gold-tranche drawing is repaid—which may occur in *any* convertible currency—world liquidity reverts to its previous level.

In short, any foreign-currency borrowings by a member country from the IMF reduce the gold component of its quota and increase the currency share. Borrowings by other nations of a nation's currency, on the other hand, increase the proportion of its quota in gold and reduce the currency share. Repayments have the opposite effect.

As we have seen, by drawing under its IMF gold tranche, a nation is not increasing its own international reserve position. However, it may borrow foreign currencies from the IMF *in excess* of the 25 per cent of its quota that normally comprises its gold tranche. Such borrowings are carried out under a *credit tranche*. The upper limit of such borrowings is reached when the Fund's holdings of the borrowing country's currency reach 200 per cent of its quota.

This can be easily illustrated by a simple arithmetic example. Suppose Germany's IMF quota were SDR 750 million in *deutsche Mark* and SDR 250 million in gold.

It could then draw from the IMF SDR 250 million under its gold tranche and SDR 1 billion under its credit tranche. Only after it had exhausted both its gold and its credit tranches, thereby selling SDR 1.25 billion of its own currency to the IMF, plus its original SDR 750 million *deutsche Mark* currency deposit, would the Fund's holdings of *deutsche Mark* reach 200 per cent of Germany's quota. This would normally be considered the limit of its borrowing rights.

In practice, a nation's IMF drawings in excess of the gold tranche required special permission, granted only after the Fund has satisfied itself that the country has taken reasonable measures to correct its payments imbalances. The IMF has the right to refuse credit-tranche drawings to any country that in its opinion is not taking appropriate remedial balance of payments actions, or that is using the drawings as a quasi-permanent addition to its international reserves. Borrowings from the IMF *in excess* of the credit tranche require a special waiver from IMF authorities.

Whereas gold-tranche IMF drawings do not increase a nation's international reserves of both the borrower *and* the country whose currency credit-tranche drawings do expand the reserves of a country taking advantage of them. Because credit-tranche drawings at once increase the international reserves of both the borrower *and* the country whose currency is being borrowed (by increasing the latter's gold tranche), they have a powerful expansionary effect upon international liquidity as a whole. Even more important, liquidity expansion via IMF credit-tranche drawings involves some discretion on the part of IMF authorities, which is not true of automatic borrowings under the gold tranche. Any international liquidity expansion resulting from credit-tranche drawings, however, is also liquidated as soon as the borrowings are repaid.

In order to further encourage balance of payments adjustment, the IMF puts its members under pressure to repay their gold- and credit-tranche drawings by charging a considerable "service charge." There is a charge of ½ or 1 per cent on all drawings. Over and above this, the charge varies with (a) the amount of the drawing, relative to the borrowing country's quota and (b) the length of time the loan has been outstanding.

IMF borrowings do not represent consistent sources of additional international liquidity, as do increases in international monetary gold or SDR stocks or acceptable foreign currency holdings. It adds to supply of international liquidity when it lends under the gold tranche, and more particularly under the credit tranche, but these are merely temporary liquidity increases that are rescinded when the borrowings are repaid. The Fund, however, does add significant flexibility to the international monetary system by making the supply of international liquidity substantially more responsive to the changing need for it. It increases the time available for a nation to restore payments balance by adding to its *owned* international reserves—gold, acceptable foreign currencies, and IMF gold-tranche position—*conditional* reserves which are accessible in time of need. In addition, it adds an element of control over the supply of international liquidity, albeit a limited one, since the IMF has some discretion in the granting of drawing privileges.

It was noted earlier that the IMF drawings of member countries are subject to a specified set of conditions designed to prevent abuse of borrowing privileges, as well as insuring effective and timely action aimed at the source of the payments imbalances. For this reason alone, a nation cannot categorically assume that its credit-tranche drawing rights will be available to it under any circumstances, and hence assume that they are part of its international-reserve position. In practice, however, the IMF treats drawings in the amount of 25 per cent of national quotas in excess of the gold tranche very liberally. Permission for such "first credit-tranche" drawings is usually regarded as a foregone conclusion.

Moreover, in 1952, the Fund initiated its system of *standby arrangements*. Instead of immediately drawing on IMF resources whenever it needs additional reserves, a country can obtain Fund assurances that permission to borrow will be granted in the event that this should become necessary. The nation thus has the assurance of additional reserves and can take them into account when formulating its balance of payments adjustment programs. Great Britain took advantage of standby arrangements during the Suez crisis in 1956, for example, and a number of other countries have done the same. Again, the purpose is added resiliency, since the mere assurance of supplementary reserves may be sufficient to alleviate balance of payments pressures, particularly those stemming from speculative capital flows.

BORROWED RESERVES: INTERNATIONAL MONETARY COOPERATION

Complementing the efforts of the IMF to instill some additional resiliency in the international monetary system—and flexibility to the supply of international liquidity—have been reciprocal borrowing arrangements, either bilateral or multilateral, among individual countries. These will not be supplanted by the SDRs just mentioned. Significantly, these reciprocal borrowing arrangements have involved close cooperation among national monetary authorities and have prevented severe payments crises in instances where even the resources of the IMF seemed insufficient.

Perhaps the most important such arrangement is the *General Agreements to Borrow,* established in 1962 among the IMF and ten major industrial countries—Belgium, Canada, France, Germany, Italy, Japan, the Netherlands, Sweden, the U.K., and the U.S.—the so-called *Group of Ten.* If a country becomes involved in payments difficulties beyond the scope of IMF assistance, the ten countries agree to go to the assistance of the beleaguered nation with massive doses of their own currencies.

Originally, the Group of Ten agreed to lend up to $6 billion to the IMF for just such purposes. Both in 1964 and 1965, the IMF took advantage of these resources to come to the aid of the British pound sterling, at that time under heavy attack. Again in 1967, after the 14.3 per cent devaluation of the British pound, a $3 billion credit facility was made available to the U.K. in order to help dampen further speculation against sterling. By lending to the IMF, which in turn lends to the country in difficulty, such actions effectively increase the world supply of liquidity. Again, as soon as such borrowings are repaid, reserves once more revert to their original standing; hence, the General Agreements to Borrow do not constitute a means of permanently expanding the supply of international liquidity. They merely expand the resources of the IMF, as an intermediary, in order to provide temporary additional reserves.

The activities of the Group of Ten might be classified as multilateral international monetary cooperation designed to shore up the monetary system in cooperation with the IMF. Other programs with a similar purpose have also been developed without the direct participation, but generally with the approbation, of the International Monetary Fund.

One such program, bilateral in nature, is the so-called *currency swaps* which have played an important role in international monetary affairs since 1962. A swap agreement, otherwise known as a *reciprocal credit facility,* consists of a pact between two central banks to exchange their currencies, up to a stipulated maximum amount and at a specified exchange rate, over a limited period of time. For instance, the Federal Reserve and the Bank of England might negotiate a swap facility for $50 million at £1.00 = $2.40 for six months. If the facility were used, about £21 million would be credited to the U.S. Federal Reserve account in return for $50 million credited to the Bank of England. At the end of six months, the transaction would be reversed at the same exchange rate. In the meantime, each country has a substantial amount of the other's currency at its disposal and, for a limited time, international liquidity has been increased.

Precisely what is the use of the foreign currencies obtained under currency swaps? The country initiating the swap normally will use the foreign currency so acquired to buy its own currency on the spot market, or to cover itself on forward purchases of its own currency, thereby supporting its exchange rate. This tends to reduce speculation against that nation's currency by inducing an added element of risk for speculators. For example, speculators selling dollars forward in the hope that the spot dollar rate will fall run the risk of heavy losses if the spot rate is supported by Federal Reserve dollar purchases in the spot foreign-exchange market. Often the *threat* of such intervention, and the ready availability of foreign currencies under swap arrangements, will be sufficient to forestall adverse currency speculation, at least temporarily.

After engaging in such currency operations on the foreign-exchange market, the central bank will gradually buy back the foreign currency it has sold. It will then reverse the swap at the end of the agreed upon period, although swaps are usually renewable upon agreement of both parties.

While swaps do not serve to finance balance of payments deficits, they do help to ease payments deficits by discouraging speculative funds outflows. Perhaps the most dramatic use of swaps was the support of the dollar against panic speculative capital outflows immediately after President Kennedy's assassination in 1963. This single operation (and the New York Federal Reserve officials who organized it) is generally recognized as a masterpiece in international finance.

Swaps may help to reduce payments deficits in another way as well. We saw earlier that international short-term capital flows tend to respond to *covered* yield differentials—differences in yields on short-term investments after account has been taken of foreign-exchange risk via forward purchases of the home currency. If monetary authorities can bolster the forward rate to increase the cost of hedging, the covered yield differential will narrow, hopefully sufficiently to reduce capital outflows. In this way, the impact of abrupt changes in foreign monetary conditions upon the domestic balance of payment may be softened.

Swaps have taken on increasing importance since the advent of floating exchange rates in 1971, largely in order to maintain orderly conditions on foreign exchange markets. Table 25–1 illustrates swap commitments outstanding to the Federal Reserve System in July 1973 and changes therein during the following three months.

Swaps and other forms of international monetary cooperation, such as the operations of the Group of Ten, serve to supply a degree of flexibility not possible any other way under the existing monetary arrangements. They do not, however, serve the longer-range purpose of insuring an increase in the supply of international liquidity that will be adequate to meet the prospects of a growing need for it.

Table 25–1
Federal Reserve System Drawings and Repayments
under Reciprocal Currency Arrangements
(million U.S. dollar equivalents)

Transactions with	System swap commitments, July 31, 1973	Drawings (+) or repayments (−) August 1 through October 31	System swap commitments, October 31, 1973
National Bank of Belgium	396.0	−123.8	272.2
Bank of France	47.0	− 47.0	—0—
German Federal Bank	220.5	{ +236.1 / −456.6	—0—
Netherlands Bank	—0—	± 2.9	—0—
Swiss National Bank	565.0	—0—	565.0
Bank for International Settlements (Swiss francs)	600.0	—0—	600.0
Total[1]	1,828.4	{ +238.9 / −630.2	1,437.2

[1] Figures may not add because of rounding.

Source: Federal Reserve Bank of New York

REDUCING THE NEED FOR LIQUIDITY

Earlier, we found that the demand for international liquidity is largely a function of (a) the overall volume of international payments, (b) the opportunity costs of holding reserves and the liquidity preference of central banks, and (c) the imbalances in the international receipts and expenditures, both in size and distribution, of the nations of the world.

The first of these two variables cannot (or should not) be the subject of policies designed to modify liquidity needs. International liquidity should be adequate to promote maximum possible international trade and capital flows, not the other way around. The third set of variables, the imbalances, may indeed be subject to modification by (a) increasing the flexibility of exchange rates, and (b) by programs designed to synchronize economic activity, interest rates, and other elements affecting international payments among the countries of the world. Using either technique, it may be possible to economize on the existing supply of international liquidity and thereby help to forestall a liquidity shortage and its detrimental effects. Both are discussed in greater detail in Chapter 26. A few words will suffice to review the interconnection between the need for reserves and economic policy.

The greater are the discrepancies in the timing of movements in economic activity between countries, the greater will be the need for international liquidity. We know that a nation in recession tends to run a balance of payments surplus, due largely to reduced imports and expanded exports resulting from the attendant price and income effects, if other countries are simultaneously enjoying buoyant demand. The latter, in turn, tend to be subjected to balance of payments deficits, again via the trade account, as high real incomes foster expanded imports and sagging exports. If real incomes in different countries could be made to move in concert, on the other hand, payment imbalances would be substantially reduced and, hence, so would the need for international liquidity.

But how can movements in real incomes be synchronized internationally? It would be absurd to ask countries undergoing economic expansion to apply fiscal and monetary brakes merely to economize on international liquidity—especially if their own reserve positions are still adequate. Such suggestions often give rise to charges of advocating policies leading to "the tail wagging the dog," especially in the larger countries with relatively limited foreign sectors. More appropriate would be cooperative programs designed to permit the recessionary economies to recover as rapidly as possible.

Of course, there is also the question of inflation and the soundness of monetary and fiscal management. A nation undergoing a more rapid rate of inflation than its trading partners is eventually likely to run a balance of payments deficit which, if uncorrected, will threaten the soundness of its currency. Today such a threat to international monetary stability normally will call forth multi-national consultations designed to help solve the problem. This is particularly true among the members of regional economic blocs, such as the European Common Market and the nations in the IMF. Again, such "free advice" is often resented by politicians and economic policymakers, who charge that foreigners are not sufficiently familiar with domestic economic problems to be able to render sound judgment, especially if their own houses are not entirely in order.

The IMF has set up machinery to analyze economic conditions in participating countries and to suggest remedies for payments imbalances. Before granting loans, it requires prospective borrowers to present an accurate portrait of their payments problems, and what they are doing to correct them. Moreover, all countries retaining some form of exchange control

l to consult with the Fund annually. Even those that are not
engage in such consultations find it highly useful to take advan-
nnual meetings on economic and monetary problems with the
a result, the Fund is always well-informed on national economic
and is in an excellent position to give advice on the basis of
larity with a wide variety of national conditions.

de the IMF, national monetary authorities frequently consult with
other and seek ways to avoid a loss of confidence in one country's
cy and to prevent subsequent destructive capital flows. In addition,
nay attempt to develop some coordination of monetary policy so that
est-rate changes in one country do not exert excessive adverse forces
i the balance of payments of other countries.

\gain, however, the possibilities of moderating the need for international
iidity are limited. In the foreseeable future, dramatic advances should
t be expected from such exports. Often they are only moderately suc-
:ssful, and prospects for monetary integration, as such, seem far off indeed
—with the possible exception of limited regional integration programs.

LIQUIDITY AND ECONOMIC DEVELOPMENT

Even if it were possible to adjust the stock of international liquidity to
meet future world needs for it—within the context of the present international monetary system—there will remain a group of countries chronically
short of foreign exchange. These are the developing nations of the world.
Providing for their needs is a problem quite different from that of insuring
adequate international liquidity.

Students of international finance often confuse the need for international
reserves with the need for development capital. Hence, they sometimes contend that international liquidity will be inadequate as long as the underdeveloped countries are suffering from a paucity of capital. This notion is
far from the truth. Reserves are being confused with capital; they are two
entirely different stocks with entirely different purposes. As the following
chapter will show, however, certain techniques of monetary reform can be
used to help alleviate both problems at the same time.

Underdeveloped countries are underdeveloped partly because they are
in chronic need of productive capital. This physical capital can be supplied
from internal savings or receipts from abroad, such as foreign capital investments or intergovernmental aid. Much of the needed capital equipment,
in any case, must be imported at least in the short run. This results in
an extreme scarcity of foreign exchange. Consequently, while the international reserves of such countries are generally below what these nations
would like, the cost of holding reserves is also very high. This is not the

result of a scarcity of international liquidity in general, but of an inability on the part of developing nations to earn foreign exchange through exports, capital inflows, and foreign-aid receipts sufficient to meet their needs.

The solution to the problem of gold and foreign-exchange scarcity on the part of developing countries may differ substantially from the problem of providing adequate international liquidity. They are two different questions, and we shall address ourselves to the former in later chapters.

26

INTERNATIONAL
MONETARY
ALTERNATIVES

We have seen that balance of payments adjustment depends heavily on the type of international monetary system that prevails. Two questions are critical: (1) How do imbalances in international payments get adjusted? and (2) How do such imbalances get financed? For the past several decades a wide variety of proposals have been put forward to answer precisely these two questions. And, while the international monetary system continues to evolve, there is no sign that the debate will cease anytime soon. In this chapter we shall review each of the major monetary reform proposals and then try to divine where things seem to be going.

WHERE WE WERE: THE BRETTON WOODS SYSTEM

During the last part of World War II, there was already a great deal of planning underway regarding the prospective economic conditions after the war. The nature of the postwar international monetary system naturally was of great concern to those involved. A system had to be devised which would not only facilitate the process of reconstruction, but which would at the same time provide the durability, stability, and flexibility required of a viable monetary mechanism under a wide variety of economic conditions.

A conference was called at Bretton Woods, New Hampshire, in July 1944 to come to grips with this problem. The international monetary system that evolved was called the *Bretton Woods System* and essentially embodied six main ideas.

1. The value of national currencies should be defined in terms of gold, and exchange rates between the currencies of the world should be *fixed*. However, in the event of "fundamental disequilibrium" (subject to interpretation) in its balance of payments, a nation should be permitted to change the par value of its currency accordingly. The idea was to combine short-term stability with long-term flexibility, as the underlying economic conditions change. Exchange rates were permitted to fluctuate only within one per cent of the par value.

2. International reserves of gold and foreign currencies should somehow be increased in such a manner that short-term balance of payments disturbances need not make a country face the potentially damaging necessity of immediately making basic internal or exchange-rate adjustments in order to restore balance. The idea of a "cushion" of this sort implied the establishment of a pool of currencies upon which nations could draw in times of balance of payments crises—the *International Monetary Fund (IMF)*. A nation's available international reserves thus consisted of its stock of gold and acceptable foreign currencies, plus its unconditional borrowing rights at the IMF, to which SDRs were added later.
shall have a great deal more to say about the International Monetary Fund and international reserves later on.

3. Restrictions to international trade and payments should be eliminated to the greatest possible extent in the interest of world economic welfare. The emphasis has been on the avoidance of exchange controls. The attempt to minimize such impediments included the free convertibility of one currency into another and the requirement of prior IMF approval of any new restrictions to convertibility. Violation of this latter rule was punishable by a withdrawal of the offending country's borrowing rights at the Fund.

4. International institutions should be created which, in close cooperation with the IMF, would promote the liberalization of trade, stabilization of employment, rapid growth, and so on. An association of the IMF with agencies of the United Nations, and with the ill-fated International Trade Organization (ITO) was envisaged. Inherent in this was the recognition that nonmonetary forces can and do lead to monetary disturbances, and that measures applied in one sector invariably engender repercussions in the other.

5. International capital flows, especially to the developing areas of the world, should be facilitated by means of an international agency engaging in long-term self-liquidating loans. This was the origin of the *International Bank for Reconstruction and Development (IBRD)*, also called the *World Bank*.

6. Adjustment of the balance of payments, while of more serious concern to deficit countries, was considered to be the responsibility of the surplus countries as well. For every country with a balance of payments surplus, there must be one or more with a payments deficit. If surplus nations deliberately engage in policies tending to enhance

their excess of international receipts over payments even further, they may thereby cause increased deficits for other countries. Restoration of payments balance was considered the *joint* responsibility of both deficit and surplus countries.

These provisions defined the international monetary system that existed until 1971. It was built around fixed rates of exchange and a definition of payments "equilibrium" that focused on long-term stability in a country's international reserves. Maintaining this "equilibrium" required that countries gear their domestic fiscal and monetary policies in part to the needs of the balance of payments, demanding high interest rates and contractionary fiscal measures in time of deficit, and the opposite in time of surplus—even though this might be far from optimal from the standpoint of national economic goals.

It was thus a system of *conflict,* one which often forced countries to resort to otherwise undesirable policy measures—such as direct controls over trade and financial transactions—in an effort to restore payments balance without sacrificing high-priority domestic goals. There were also inherent asymmetries in the system, with surplus countries under no immediate pressure to compromise domestic economic goals to cure their own payments disequilibria, which represented the mirror-image of other countries' payments deficits. And the burden of adjustment almost invariably fell on the latter. Often the tension became too great and a devaluation was undertaken under pressure from one-way short-term capital flows undertaken by speculators who were in a much better position to gain than to lose.

Nevertheless, the system worked surprisingly well for a quarter century, partly because of the existence of reserve currencies, discussed in the previous chapter. The U.S. could run continuous payments deficits for two decades because other countries were willing to hold the dollar in their own international reserves and thereby run quasi-permanent surpluses, pursue export-led economic growth, and augment world liquidity. Both the U.S. and its partners were thus absolved from the full rigors of adjustment nominally required by the system. Countries also became more sophisticated in the assignment of monetary and fiscal measures to goals of internal and external balance, and this may have extended the system's viability.

But once the acceptability of reserve currencies was called into question, once it became apparent that important economic costs were also associated with payments *surplus* and excessive reserve stocks, the system's unique emphasis on *financing* rather than *correcting* imbalances inevitably led to its downfall. The policy prescription required by the system under the new conditions, the discipline and burden-sharing required to make it work, were politically unacceptable.

The Bretton Woods System was finally brought to an end on August

15, 1971, by the action of the United States, which suspended the convertibility of the dollar into gold—in effect "floating" the dollar—and imposed a 10 per cent across-the-board import surcharge to stimulate action on monetary reform. An abortive attempt was made in December 1971 in the so-called *Smithsonian Agreement* to extend the life of the Bretton Woods System. The Agreement, *inter alia,* permitted wider fluctuations of spot exchange rates (2½ per cent instead of 1 per cent on either side of par) and called into being the Committee of 20 (C-20) industrial and developing countries to work out the rules of a new international monetary order.

The Smithsonian Agreement did not last long, with two dollar devaluations in the following two years and a general movement toward managed floating of exchange rates in 1972 and 1973. Nor did the initial experience with floating rates prove to be the disaster some had feared. They had no obvious adverse effects on world trade and payments. Businessmen indicated that they could learn to live with some flexibility in exchange rates, and that this was in many ways preferable to the uncertainty of second-guessing governments as to when and by how much periodic crises would force them to devalue or revalue their currencies. So the world was dragged into effective monetary reform based on increasing flexibility of exchange rates and—once there—seemed to like it. At the same time, it became clear that a *code of behavior* must govern the new system which is as binding as that governing the old system, and it is with this transition that economists and international monetary authorities will be preoccupied for some time to come.

BACK TO GOLD

Since the demise of the true gold standard decades ago, the international monetary system has been the setting for recurring, periodic crises of varying magnitudes. These have been punctuated by political and economic dislocations that inevitably had their impact on the system. A prominent but dwindling group of economists have associated this apparent international financial instability with the demise of gold. They continue to point to a return to gold as the most effective way to cure the system of its ills. By and large, their arguments have found little favor, although by no means all of them can be taken lightly.

Typically, gold-standard advocates begin by proposing the settlement of international payments imbalances exclusively in gold, with the consequent elimination of foreign exchange (key currencies) and SDRs as components of international reserves and, hence, as an element in the international monetary mechanism. Since the present world stock of gold would quite clearly be inadequate under such conditions, gold-standard advocates generally combine this with a suggested revaluation of gold by making it more expensive in terms of each national currency. All outstanding national-currency liabilities to foreign official monetary institutions would have to be settled in gold, if such a system were adopted.

Each currency would be freely and universally convertible into gold, not only for official institutions but for private individuals and organizations as well. This being the case, the domestic money supply of all countries would be governed by the nation's gold stock. A balance of payments deficit thus would mean a gold outflow, contraction of the domestic money supply, increased interest rates, and reduced incomes (and perhaps prices). These effects would presumably result in substantial capital inflows for the deficit country, reduced imports, and expanded exports. Payments balance would be restored along the lines of the classical gold-standard adjustment mechanism outlined in Chapter 21. Adjustment of the balance of payments in surplus countries, of course, would operate in a reverse manner. Both types of adjustments would be characterized by the automaticity supposedly inherent in the system.

If the gold standard is to work, national monetary authorities must not be permitted to counteract international gold flows through offsetting "defensive" monetary actions—such as sterilization of gold inflows and monetary expansion in the case of gold outflows. This means either 100 per cent gold backing of the money supply or a permanently fixed ratio of gold to the money supply.

Gold-standard advocates often cite the weaknesses inherent in the post-war international monetary system and uncertainties under floating exchange rates in support of their own reform proposals. They seriously question the dependence of added liquidity supplies upon payments deficits of reserve-currency countries and the eventual undermining of confidence that seems to characterize this process. Furthermore, they fail to see why some countries should be permitted chronic payments deficits—excess imports or capital outflows—while others are subjected to strict balance of payments discipline. In addition, they point to the relative lack of balance of payments constraints upon economic-policy formulation in reserve-currency countries and to the inflationary pressures—both domestic and worldwide—that could result. Finally, they distrust any reform proposals that leave the creation of international liquidity in the hands of policymakers—national or supranational—preferring the automatic and impartial operation of the gold standard.

Set against the arguments of the gold-standard advocates are a number of cogent considerations that ultimately tend to rule out this alternative as a realistic solution to the problems of the internal monetary system.

First, as was pointed out in Chapter 21, it is doubtful that the old gold standard really was responsible for the international monetary stability that seemed to characterize the pre-World War I era. There is little evidence that the gold standard "rules of the game" were in fact followed. The indications are that other factors, such as the relatively homogeneous structures of the world's advanced economics at the time, comparatively free international factor mobility, as well as generally favorable economic conditions, did much to cause the gold standard to work as well as it did. Hence, the nostalgia often shown by gold-standard advocates rests on a questionable foundation.

Second, a return to the gold standard placed national economies almost completely at the mercy of international forces. If a balance of payments deficit demands a recession in economic activity on the part of the affected country, then the gold-standard rules demand that the recession in fact materialize. Incomes must fall, and so must employment, given that prices and wages are not very flexible in modern economies. From a political standpoint alone, such harsh discipline would be largely unacceptable in today's world. Governments are charged with the responsibility of insuring that unemployment is kept to a minimum, that price levels remain relatively stable, and that the rate of economic growth is satisfactory. Under such conditions, it would be political disaster for any government—except under the direst of circumstances—to submit rigidly to the adjustments required under the gold standard, both in response to a deficit and a surplus. The costs are simply too great. Indeed, it was the economic and human costs involved that led to the abandonment of the gold standard by virtually all of the world's nations during the Great Depression of the 1930's.

A return to gold—and the upward revaluation of gold that would almost certainly accompany it—would result in a redistribution of purchasing power, both nationally and internationally, that is regarded in most quarters as undesirable. A doubling of the price of gold in all countries would mean that the purchasing power of the gold hoarded by individuals, organizations, and governments would be effectively doubled. Meanwhile, those holding assets denominated in national currencies would realize no such windfall. Internationally, countries having elected to hold their international reserves in foreign currencies—precisely those nations helping to make the postwar monetary system work—would be penalized relative to countries predominantly maintaining gold as their international reserves. The political ramifications of such an arbitrary, one-shot redistribution of purchasing power, both internationally and domestically, would be severe indeed.

The case proposed by the advocates of an unequivocal return to gold as the sole component of international liquidity, then, appears vulnerable to attack from many angles. It is fairly safe to say that the gold standard would be disfunctional in today's economic environment. Still, many of those who advocate this path voice legitimate fears. Their fear of inflation induced by the existing monetary system or some of the other alternatives simply exceeds their fear of recession that might be induced by a return to gold. Their attacks on the postwar international monetary system, concentrated on its inherent weaknesses, have served to hasten discussions of other, perhaps somewhat more viable, alternatives.

DEMONETIZE GOLD

Diametrically opposed to those who seek a solution in a return to gold are those militantly opposed to its role in world monetary affairs. They have little regard for the traditional monetary position of gold and see it as a useless carryover from times past, one that impedes progress toward a more workable international monetary system. They seek a phased elimination of gold as an element of international liquidity, and were encouraged by the U.S. suspension of dollar convertability in 1971. They propose a free market for gold, treated as any other commodity market, with both spot and futures trading. International payments would continue to be settled partially in gold during a specified transition period, but in decreasing proportions and gradually supplanted by SDRs. Intergovernmental gold transactions, to the extent that they still occur, would eventually be made at prevailing free market prices.

RESERVE CENTRALIZATION

As early as 1944, John Maynard Keynes proposed what he considered a workable international monetary mechanism that would support trade and payments liberalization on a worldwide scale after the end of the war. He felt that above all a plan was needed that would improve the balance of payments adjustment mechanism and insure monetary stability during the reconstruction era.

Keynes proposed an *International Clearing Union,* which would have the power to create an international money, *bancor.* The value of gold and each national currency would be fixed in terms of bancor. Moreover, each nation would agree to accept bancor for settlement of international payments imbalanced on a par with gold. A deficit country would have the choice of transferring to creditors gold or bancor, or both, at its own discretion, and the surplus countries would be compelled to accept payment in this form. Each participating country would be assigned a quota, based on the volume of its international trade, which set the maximum amount of bancor that it could borrow from the Clearing Union. Once a country incurred a balance of payments deficit, it could simply take advantage of its drawing rights and borrow bancor (*overdrafts*) to finance it. A total of one quarter of its quota could be drawn unconditionally within a given year.

The operation of the Clearing Union would be quite simple. Deficit countries thus would simply transfer bancor to surplus countries, just as an individual writes a check on his account in a commercial bank in favor of a creditor. Countries with chronic deficits would incur negative bancor, while surplus countries would undergo a buildup in bancor balances. As the bancor balances of deficit countries become increasingly negative, and those of the surplus nations positive, *both* would incur a penalty charge varying with the size of the deficiency or surplus in bancor deposits. Hence, both deficit and surplus countries would be tangibly encouraged to restore payments balance and restore their bancor deposits to zero.

As an added penalty on deficit countries, overdrafts in excess of 50 per cent of their normal borrowing quotas would have to be secured by gold, acceptable foreign currencies, or other assets. Moreover, deficit nations would have to obey Clearing Union directives on restoring payments balance—devaluation, internal adjustments, or *ad hoc* payments restrictions—under threat of the ultimate sanction, the refusal of any further bancor loans. An initial 5 per cent devaluation could be taken without Union permission. Similarly, chronic surplus countries would be subject to like, though perhaps somewhat milder, pressure to put their houses in order.

Although gold would continue to play a part in the international-payments mechanism, as a collateral means of payments settlement along with bancor, its role would be diminished. Its *relative* importance would be reduced immediately, although Keynes suggested that its significance be diminished *absolutely* as well. The International Clearing Union would buy gold for bancor deposits in unlimited amounts and at fixed prices, but would not be required to sell gold. Hence, the role of gold was envisioned as a gradually declining one.

In sum, the Keynes plan provided an alternative monetary system which revolved around reserve centralization. Exchange rates would remain fixed, but would be variable through devaluation should circumstances warrant. Each nation would be under continual pressure to adjust its payments balances, hence presumably helping to reduce the need for international liquidity. The supply of liquidity would be variable and able to adjust to changing requirements virtually automatically, as bancor is created and destroyed as overdraft facilities are used. Liquidity creation, however, would still be limited by Union action in granting overdraft privileges, and its power over internal economic affairs in the participating countries would be clearly circumscribed.

Keynes's plan for international monetary reform was received in a decidedly cool manner in 1944, largely because of its revolutionary nature with regard to the prewar system and on account of the American position as a chronic surplus country. Several decades later, a number of variants on his proposal, most of them far more radical, fare substantially better.

Perhaps the most significant reserve centralization plan for monetary reform was proposed in 1960 by Robert Triffin of Yale University in his *Gold and the Dollar Crisis.*[1] Like Keynes, Triffin would create an effective international central bank by expanding the existing IMF into such an institution (XIMF).

Each nation would be required to deposit specified amounts of reserve currencies and gold in the XIMF, in return for which they would receive bancor deposits. The bancor value of both national currencies and gold would be fixed. International settlements would be effected by transfers of bancor, reserve currencies, and gold, although the latter two would eventually be completely replaced by bancor as international means of payment. To achieve this, Triffin proposed that countries be required gradually to convert all of their reserve currency balances to bancor. Since the XIMF would pay interest on bancor deposits, gold eventually would be reduced in importance as a component of international reserves in favor of bancor.

Exchange rates would be fixed, although provision was made for devaluation under appropriate circumstances. In the event of devaluation, the XIMF holdings of the nation's currency would be secured by means of a gold guarantee.

A country with a balance of payments deficit would draw on its bancor deposits to finance that deficit. If the deficits continue and its bancor deposits are depleted, the XIMF would lend it further amounts of bancor on a temporary basis, subject to the initiation of remedial balance of payments action on the part of the borrowing nation. So far the plan is somewhat similar to Keynes's program and the present lending operation of the IMF. The XIMF would also be empowered to control the amount of bancor available. It would be enabled to sell securities in the capital markets of various nations and to issue bancor against the currency received—thereby expanding the supply of liquidity—and to contract international liquidity by repurchasing bancor for the currency so acquired. Or it could purchase securities in these capital markets in direct return for payment in bancor and thus expand the supply of liquidity. In this way, the XIMF would be able to control directly the supply of international liquidity, both over short and long periods of time.

Triffin suggests that the only way to insure that the supply of international liquidity will always parallel the need for it—so that no depressing shortage or inflationary liquidity surplus results—is to endow some supranational agency with the power to create and destroy international reserves as conditions change, much as national central banks are able to vary

[1] Robert Triffin, *Gold and the Dollar Crisis* (New Haven: Yale University Press, 1960).

the money supply as a matter of policy. In order to avoid the inadvertent creation of excess international reserves, and as a concession to some of his critics, Triffin would set an upper limit of 3 to 5 per cent per year on liquidity growth.

Like the Keynes plan, the Triffin proposal's main selling point lies in its ability to add flexibility to payments adjustment and to avoid the payments crises otherwise so common under fixed rates. Yet there is no real improvement in the adjustment mechanism. Some would contend that its ability to press for payments adjustment under threat of suspension of credits constitutes a substantial advance. Others would maintain that such pressure would not be used effectively and by its virtually unlimited reserve-creating ability, chronic deficits would be facilitated and inflationary pressures result from an over-expansion of liquidity. Still others object to the implicit voice such a plan gives to the XIMF in the formulation of monetary and fiscal policies of deficit nations.

Perhaps even more important is the potential direct impact of XIMF purchases and sales of securities in the participating nations. Purchases would effectively increase the bancor deposits of those countries in which they are undertaken, and deficit countries—as well as underdeveloped nations—would certainly hope that their own securities would be the ones purchased. Surplus nations would tend to be opposed to such a development. Moreover, the value of any securities acquired would have to be guaranteed in some way, preferably in gold which is readily marketable, so that the choice of markets is in effect restricted by this requirement alone.

The Triffin plan does not constitute a panacea for the world's monetary problems, since the functioning of the adjustment mechanism itself remains unchanged. But the rigidities of the system would be largely overcome—along with its vulnerability—by increasing the responsiveness of the supply of liquidity to changing needs for it. It constitutes an exercise in multi-national cooperation in which a certain amount of national economic sovereignty would be transferred to an international agency. This is, perhaps, its greatest weakness in a world still beset by the notion of the supremacy of national independence. Also, the system would be operated by managers in a limited discretionary manner. This leaves it open to many of the criticisms voiced by advocates of the gold standard and flexible-exchange rates who prefer automaticity to discretionary control. Finally, there is some question about the operation of such a program in practice, and whether or not it would arouse more international conflicts and problems than it would solve.

These proposals are based on *financing* international payments imbalances, rather than improving the *adjustment* process itself. There is general agreement that the development of SDRs has resolved much of the problem in this area. Together with the continued acceptability of certain reserve currencies and the continued holding of official gold, at least for the time being, SDR allocations are expected to provide the incremental liquidity needed—especially as this need is reduced by improvements in the adjustment mechanism itself.

FLEXIBLE RATES

Many students of international monetary affairs attributed the instability and vulnerability of the postwar system to the pegging of national currency values. Their objections were not aimed specifically at the role of gold, but at the general inability of the exchange rate to adjust to changing supply and demand conditions. With fixed exchange rates and with periodic payments crises and devaluations under pressure, they saw the pegged-rate system as one that by its very nature *fosters* emergencies and instabilities.

To an economist, the advantages of flexible exchange rates are undeniable. The automaticity of the adjustment mechanism under this system (as described in Chapter 21) was appealing in itself. Moreover, it promised, at least partially, to insulate the domestic economy from external forces and to avoid the painful income adjustments, short of devaluation, called for by pegged exchange rate systems. The objectives of domestic economic policy could be freely pursued without being subject to balance of payments considerations. Moreover, the entire problem of international liquidity and reserve adequacy would disappear. Since adjustment is automatic, reserve needs are minimal, and are determined largely by the degree of intervention—if any—that governments decide to undertake for the sake of "orderly" foreign-exchange markets.

It has also been argued that flexible-exchange rates reinforce the effectiveness of monetary policy in maintaining internal balance. Anti-inflationary restrictive monetary policies, for instance, raise domestic interest rates. This will tend to induce capital inflows, increase the supply of foreign exchange, and lower the exchange rate on the spot market. As a consequence, imported goods become relatively cheaper for domestic buyers, and the rise in imports helps to depress the domestic level of economic activity. Working through the impact of restrictive monetary policy on the exchange rate, then, the direct depressing effect of higher interest rates on aggregate demand is reinforced by the effect on imports. The reasoning is equally applicable to expansionary monetary policy; lower interest rates tend to induce increased capital outflows (demand for foreign exchange), which raise the exchange rate and stimulate exports. The latter, in turn, act as an expansionary influence on domestic economic activity, along with the direct effects of monetary ease on aggregate demand.

Those opposing flexible-exchange rates maintained that the very features that make this system so appealing simultaneously render it of limited value from a practical point of view.

First, they argued that by liberating domestic economic policy from external constraints, flexible-exchange rates would give the green light to prodigal, reckless monetary and fiscal measures, ultimately destined to exert a broad, inflationary impact on the economy. Domestic inflation would have no deleterious impact on the balance of payments, since the home currency simply depreciates accordingly. But the depreciation and increased cost of imports may serve to further reinforce the domestic inflationary spiral. Supporters reply that flexible rates may actually assist in combating inflation by serving as a highly sensitive indicator of relative price levels. Moreover, a depreciating exchange rate may be equally, if not more, embarrassing to domestic policymakers than the necessity for a devaluation under pegged rates. Besides, defenders of flexible rates contended, price-level stability is a goal of domestic economic policy—just as is full employment—and there is no reason to believe that governments will abandon this goal just because the possibility of depleting international reserves is removed.

Second, critics maintained that exchange-rate fluctuations under flexible rates would be of much greater amplitude than under pegged rates. This would raise the cost of hedging the foreign-exchange risk and, if forward markets are too narrow, would render forward exchange cover unobtainable for practical purposes. By increasing the cost of covering the foreign-exchange risk on all sorts of international commercial and financial transactions, opponents of flexible rates contend, this system would impede international trade and capital movements.

Defenders of flexible rates countered that exchange rates would *not* be unstable and that any variations that do occur are (a) a reflection of underlying economic conditions, (b) preferable to exchange controls or devaluation in any case, and (c) an alternative to potentially damaging internal adjustments of the national economy. Besides, no matter what variations occur, the international trader or investor would have substantially equal probabilities of gaining as of losing, and there is little evidence to suggest that the opportunities for hedging would, in fact, dwindle.

Third, it was argued by detractors of flexible rates that volatile, short-term capital movements might be destabilizing and tend to widen exchange-rate fluctuations. Political, military, and economic factors, real or imagined, can lead to massive short-term international capital flows that could distort exchange rates far out of line with those that would ordinarily prevail. Simple speculation, too, would be destabilizing to the extent that the speculators' expectations prove to be wrong. Erratic, wild exchange-rate swings would impose huge losses on some and present others with large gains.

Again, defenders of flexible rates raised counter-arguments. They contended that the speculation that does occur will indeed turn out to be stabilizing in nature, with speculators well-informed about the underlying relative currency values. They discussed the possibility of destabilizing speculation as unproven in fact and unfounded in theory, maintaining instead that speculative capital flows will be stabilizing and contribute short-term exchange-rate stability combined with long-term flexibility, much along the lines of the classical flexible-rate model. In any case, they contended that the chance of gains *and* losses under flexible rates is clearly preferable to the one-way speculation that exists under pegged rates. Finally, they maintained that whether speculation turns out to be stabilizing or destabilizing in nature depends largely upon the economic policies adopted by the individual nations involved.

Fourth, critics argued that exchange rates are likely to vary erratically not only over short periods, but also over more extended time spans as economic activity in different countries changes. For instance, a nation's exchange rate is likely to depreciate whenever it is enjoying an economic boom, or whenever its trading partners are undergoing recessions, and appreciate during a slump in economic activity. Since business cycles are not synchronous internationally, the exchange rate will fluctuate cyclically. Resources will be shifted to export and import-competing sectors whenever the home currency depreciates, only to find that they have been misallocated when a subsequent currency appreciation sets in. Since the inter-sectoral shift of economic resources is costly, flexible exchange-rate systems would in this way be a burden on national economies and also impede economic growth.

Supporters of flexible rates retort that periodic inter-sectional misallocation of resources also occurs under fixed exchange-rate systems, characterized by periodic devaluations, and during periods of deflationary policy designed to restore payments balance.

To these arguments on flexible-exchange rates, pro and con, must be added the controversy concerning stability conditions that must be met, as we have detailed in Chapter 21. If the Marshall-Lerner condition is not met, assuming infinitely elastic supply functions, a depreciation of the home currency will simply worsen the balance of payments and bring about further depreciation. The argument thus centers around whether the relevant demand elasticities are sufficiently high to meet the stability condition.

Critics of flexible exchange predictably have argued that elasticities are indeed low and, hence, result in instability. Opinion among economists has varied from low elasticities prevailing in the immediate post-World War II reconstruction years, to sufficiently high elasticities of highly competitive economies in recent times. It has also been shown that even if an exchange rate is unstable, a sufficiently large exchange-rate shift will eventually result in a stable equilibrium, although the required shift may well be excessive.

Arguments for and against flexible exchange rates have gone on for a long time and will certainly continue in the future. They generally pit academic economists against the "practical men"—bankers and businessmen—who must live with and operate under whatever exchange-rate system is in existence. It is an argument of conceptual appeal; neatness and flexibility are set against important practical considerations about the uncertain outcome of such a system. As a result of this impasse, numerous compromise alternatives have been advanced to simultaneously insure flexibility *and* stability.

ADAPTED FLEXIBILITY AND CURRENCY FLOATS

Numerous types of flexible-exchange rates are possible, and unrestricted-exchange-rate variation is only one. They are based on the degree of government intervention that is incorporated in the foreign-exchange markets. Intervention may be unilateral or multilateral (a cooperative effort among a group of nations).

Some of the objections to flexible exchange rates—to the extent that they are valid—can be answered by judicious use of government foreign exchange operations. Exchange-stabilization funds may be set up that can be used to offset those exchange rate fluctuations that are considered harmful or deleterious to the working of the system. Such foreign-exchange pools may be national or multi-national in character, and the very existence of such funds may be a highly important factor in discouraging harmful capital flows from arising in the first place.

Still, the underlying forces of supply and demand remain free to determine the exchange-rate level under such a system. The danger is, of course, that government intervention will be used to maintain disequilibrium rates (i.e., "dirty" floating), thus proving the system to be little better than that of pegged-exchange rates. Under this system, government intervention is instead limited to "smoothing" out short-term exchange-rate fluctuations and insuring orderly foreign exchange markets. It thus represents a relatively "clean" system of floating currencies.

A second adaptation of flexible-exchange rates as a compromise measure is the so-called *band proposal*. This involves the maintenence of "central" exchange rates, but permits fluctuation of the exchange rate about these rates. The Bretton Woods system, as we know, permitted exchange-rate variations of 2 per cent, 1 per cent above and below par. In this plan it is merely necessary to widen this band of permissible variation. The exchange rate would be freely set by forces of supply and demand within the band and small adjustments in the rate would be automatic. When the rate has been maintained at the upper or lower limit for an extended period of time, it is a signal to monetary authorities that income and price adjustments, or a currency revaluation, are in order.

Advocates of this particular plan pointed to its evolutionary, rather than revolutionary, nature, claiming that it represented a readily feasible solution necessitating few basic changes in the international monetary order. Moreover, they emphasized its ability to economize on the world need for liquidity. Much of the payments adjustment burden would fall on exchange-rate variation. The exchange rate, in turn, would indicate the direction of change in a nation's economic and payments situation long before a crisis point is reached. Widened exchange-rate limits would give nations the power to redirect adverse international capital flows by affecting the cost of hedging via operations in the forward markets. Opponents argued that the band proposal continues to run into the problem of one-way speculation, which also plagues pegged rates, once one of the two limits is reached. And the automaticity of true flexible exchange rates would still be sacrificed for chronic debtor or creditor nations which must seek adjustment in the classical manner, or by currency revaluations. As we have noted, a version of the band proposal was tried in the 1971 Smithsonian Agreement, which widened the permissible range of fluctuation to $4\frac{1}{2}$ per cent, without much lasting success as a binding rule of the game.

A third variation on the theme of flexible-exchange rates revolves around exchange-rate flexibility that characterizes only transactions between certain geographical areas of the world. Countries with close economic ties would maintain fixed exchange rates *among* themselves, with rate flexibility prevailing *between* the various groupings. For example, the U.S., Canada, and Latin America might become a dollar bloc, Continental Europe and parts of Africa perhaps a franc bloc, with Great Britain heading up the traditional Sterling Bloc.

Within each bloc the exchange rates between national currencies would remain fixed, This would present few problems since payments imbalances are presumably held to a minimum among such countries. Between blocs, however, exchange rates would be permitted to vary relatively freely. A deficit in the Sterling Bloc's balance of payments with the dollar bloc, for example, would signal a depreciation of the currencies included in the former area relative to those incorporated in the latter.

Bloc flexibility has some advantages in that it would perhaps make it possible to avoid serious payments disequilibria and, hence, cut down on the needs for international liquidity. To the extent that it contributes to world economic divisions and rigidities in the international economic structure, however, it is probably inferior to some of the other monetary reform proposals that have been advanced.

This approach rests on the so-called theory of *optimum currency areas*, which proposes that the economic characteristics of certain geographic areas point to a single currency as the most efficient payments mechanism for that area, but that exchange rates between such areas should ideally be flexible. It is by no means certain, for example, that the United States should ideally be a single currency area, or that the EEC should have eight different national currencies.

An attempt to resolve the latter issue was the EEC attempt to limit member currencies' fluctuations against each other to *half* of the fluctuation permissible under the Smithsonian Agreement. This "snake in the tunnel" technique, discussed earlier, presupposed a high degree of policy coordination among the member countries and a reasonable degree of balance in internal payments. That these conditions were not met was indicated by the fact that the U.K. and Italy failed to join in the first place, and France and Austria dropped out soon thereafter.

FLOATING TOWARD A NEW SYSTEM

As we have indicated, the intellectual debate on international monetary reform provided the preconditions for change, but was overtaken by events in 1971 when a *de facto* floating currency system was initiated. In the mid-1970's, a hodge-podge system exists without explicit rules of the game. As Table 26-1 shows, some countries (e.g., France, Canada, Japan) float freely. Others, such as Belgium and Germany, continue revised Smithsonian central rates measured in SDRs and permit limited variations from these rates, which serve as guidelines only and are themselves subject to change. Still other countries such as the U.S. and Australia, are pegged to SDR par values, but effectively float as other currencies float against them.
Finally, there is a large group of developing countries whose currencies are pegged to the dollar, the French franc, or to sterling, representing the currencies of their main trading partners.

So the search is on for a permanent set of new rules governing the international payments adjustment process. The floating rate system seems to be working well—it surprised many by calmly absorbing the great shocks caused by the oil crises of 1973-1974—and so discussions about formulating a permanent set of rules have proceeded slowly.

There seems to be general agreement among governments that the following seven requirements must be met by the reformed international monetary system:

1. It should conform to the principle of equal rights and obligations of all participating countries.
2. It should have regard for the interests of the developing countries.
3. It should continue to be based on fixed but adjustable parities.
4. It should provide for the effective regulation of the supply of liquidity in the world.

Table 26–1
Examples of Exchange Rates as of April 30, 1974
(currency units per unit listed)

Member	Currency	Par Value SDRs	Central Rate SDRs	U.S. dollar	Pound sterling	French franc	Other	Market Rate U.S. dollar
				Member Maintains Exchange Rate Against				
Afghanistan [2]	afghani			45.00				
*Algeria	dinar	4.93706						
Argentina[2]	peso			5.00				
Australia	dollar	0.810994						
Austria	schilling			3				18.145
*Bahamas	dollar	1.20635						
*Bahrain	dinar	0.476190						
Bangladesh	taka				18.9677			
Barbados	dollar				4.80			
*Belgium[2,4]	franc		48.6572					
*Bolivia	peso		24.1270					
Botswana	rand				0.671141			
Brazil[2]	cruzeiro				6.535			
*Burma	kyat		5.80717					
*Burundi	franc	95.0000						
Cameroon	franc					50.00		
Canada	dollar			3				0.9604
Central African Republic	franc					50.00		
Chad	franc					50.00		
Chile[2]	escudo			550.00				
*China, Republic of	new Taiwan dollar		45.8413					
Colombia[2]	peso			23.35				
Congo, People's Republic of the	franc					50.00		
Costa Rica[2]	colon	10.3384						
Cyprus	pound			3				0.3509
Dahomey	franc					50.00		
*Denmark[1]	krone		7.57831			50.00		
Dominican Republic	peso	1.20635						
Ecuador[2]	sucre		30.1587					
Egypt[2]	pound				0.392479			
El Salvador	colon	3.01587						
Equatorial Guinea	peseta						1.005	
*Ethiopia	dollar	2.50000						
*Fiji	dollar		0.965078					
Finland	markkaa			3				3.667
France	franc			3				4.8750
Gabon	franc					50.00		
Gambia, The	dalasi				4.00			
*Germany, Federal Republic of[4]	deutsche mark		3.21979					
Ghana	cedi			1.15385				
Greece	drachma			3				29.59
Guatemala	quetzal	1.20635						
Guinea	syli						0.0366	
Guyana	dollar				5.2114			
Haiti	gourde	6.03176						
Honduras	lempira	2.41270						
Iceland	krona			3				80.00
India	rupee				18.96777			
Indonesia[2]	rupiah			415.00				
*Iran	rial	82.2425						
*Iraq	dinar	0.357143						
Ireland	pound				1.00			
*Israel	pound		5.06665					
Italy	lira			3				632.125
Ivory Coast	franc					50.00		
*Jamaica	dollar		1.09668					
Japan	yen			3				279.75
*Jordan	dinar	0.387754						
*Kenya	shilling		8.61675					
Khmer Republic[2]	riel			375.00				
Korea	won			398.90				
*Kuwait	dinar	0.357143						
Laos[2]	kip			600.00				
Lebanon	pound			3				2.31
Lesotho	rand				0.671141			

Member	Currency	Par Value SDRs	Central Rate SDRs	U.S. dollar	Pound sterling	French franc	Other	Market Rate U.S. dollar
Liberia	dollar	1.20635						
*Libyan Arab Republic	dinar	0.357143						
*Luxembourg[2,4]	franc		48.6572					
Malagasy Republic	franc					50.00		
Malawi	kwacha	....		3	....			0.8197
Malaysia	dollar	....		3	....			2.3585
Mali	franc					100.00		
Malta	pound	....		3	....			0.3636
Mauritania	ouguiya					10.00		
Mauritius	rupee				13.3333			
Mexico	peso	15.0793						
Morocco	dirham	....		3	....			4.26
*Nepal	rupee		12.7390					
*Netherlands[4]	guilder		3.35507					
New Zealand	dollar	....		3	....			0.6861
Nicaragua[2]	cordoba	8.4447						
Niger	franc					50.00		
*Nigeria	naira		0.793648					
*Norway[4]	krone		6.87145					
Oman	rial Omani			0.345395				
*Pakistan	rupee	11.9428						
Panama	balboa	1.20635						
Paraguay[2]	guarani			126.00				
Peru[2]	sol			38.70				
Philippines	peso			6.78				
Portugal	escudo	....		3	....			23.04
*Qatar	riyal	4.76190						
Romania	leu						0.148112[6]	
*Rwanda	franc		112.00					
*Saudi Arabia	riyal	4.28255						
Senegal	franc					50.00		
Sierra Leone	leone				2.0			
Singapore	dollar	....		3	....			2.4010
*Somalia	shilling	7.51881						
South Africa	rand			0.671141				
Spain	peseta	....		3				57.70
Sri Lanka[2]	rupee				15.60			
Sudan[2]	pound			0.348242				
Swaziland	rand			0.671141				
*Sweden[4]	krona		5.50094					
Syrian Arab Republic	pound			3.675				
*Tanzania	shilling		8.61675					
*Thailand	baht	24.1270						
Togo	franc					50.00		
Trinidad and Tobago	dollar				4.80			
*Tunisia	dinar	....		3	....			0.4167
*Turkey	lira		16.8889					
*Uganda	shilling		8.61675					
United Arab Emirates	dirham	4.76190						
United Kingdom	pound	....		3	....			0.4123
United States	dollar	1.20635						
Upper Volta	franc					50.00		
Uruguay[2]	peso			1,078.50				
Venezuela[2]	bolivar			4.285				
Viet-Nam[2]	piastre			620.00				
Western Samoa	tala		0.719193					
Yemen Arab Republic	rial	....		3	....			4.525
Yemen, People's Dem. Republic of	dinar		0.416667					
Yugoslavia	dinar	....		3	....			14.8148
Zaire	zaire		0.603176					
Zambia	kwacha	0.775509						

* Member is availing itself of wider margins of up to 2¼ per cent on either side of parity relationship based on par values or central rates

[2] As notified to the Fund. Members having par values and central rates may also maintain their exchange rates against another currency or other currencies

[3] Member maintains multiple currency practice and/or dual exchange market.

[4] The member has notified the Fund that its currency is not being maintained within specified margins.

Belgium, Denmark, Germany, Luxembourg, the Netherlands, Norway, and Sweden maintain maximum margins of 2¼ per cent for exchange rates in transactions in the official markets between their currencies and those of the other countries in this group.

[5] Peseta per Spanish peseta.

[6] Grams of fine gold per currency unit. [7] Rupees per pound sterling. Data: MIF Treasurer's Department.

Source: International Monetary Fund.

5. It should be designed to re-establish a general convertibility of currencies.

6. It should provide for securing the necessary adjustments in the balance of payments in participating countries.

7. It should have regard to the need to reduce the de-stabilizing effects of short-term capital flows.

One thing is certain: The kind of international monetary cooperation ultimately forced upon countries periodically by the old system must become a permanent feature of the new one. The co-equal responsibility of surplus and deficit countries for payments disequilibria must be accepted and acted upon. This means that exchange-rate adjustments must be undertaken when necessary by *both* sides and the resulting adjustment costs shared equitably. Above all else, a strong international commitment to burden-sharing is a prerequisite for *any* truly viable system. The problem is how to implement a system that will attain this objective.

The key to this problem is devising a set of rules that will bring about shifts in currency values when these are needed to restore equilibrium. Such rules are necessary whether a system of central rates or dirty floating predominates. One type of arrangement was proposed by the United States in 1973. It held that equilibrating currency value changes ought to be virtually *automatic,* based on an *objective* criterion—namely, changes in a country's international reserves. The process is as follows: Market forces cause a country's currency to appreciate toward the upper limit of flexibility in relation, for example, to the existing central rate. The country intervenes in the foreign-exchange market to keep the rate from exceeding that limit and in the process accumulates reserves. This is a "signal" that the rate *may be* out of line and should be allowed to move up. In reverse, market forces result in a currency's depreciation toward its lower limit, intervention to constrain the depreciation causes reserve losses, and consideration ought to be given at some point to an equilibrating downward movement in the rate.

We have emphasized that exchange rates are closely related to real economic variables—particularly income and employment—with exchange-rate increases tending to depress the level of aggregate economic performance, and decreases tending to stimulate the level of economic activity. This sensitivity is directly related to the importance of the foreign sector in the national economy, and is the source of the basic problem that countries tend to be more willing to see their currencies depreciate than appreciate whenever an "objective" case can be made that such a shift is called for. This asymmetry persists in a reformed international monetary system based on managed flexibility. We would expect countries whose currencies depreciate and which subsequently lose reserves to permit lower exchange rates fairly readily. We would also expect countries subject to currency appreciation and reserve accumulation to resist that upward shift for as long as possible. The greater this asymmetry in motivation and the greater the discretion governments may exercise in deciding *when* it is time for a fundamental exchange-rate change, the more of the vulnerability and crisis-sensitivity of the old international monetary order is retained in the new one.

There are two alternatives for solving this problem. First, governments may agree that surplus and deficit countries are indeed co-equally responsible for alleviating their own payments imbalances, and commit themselves unconditionally to prompt action specifically in the area of exchange-rate changes. The second is to agree *ab initio* to remove exchange-rate changes from government discretion and make them subject to an automatic mechanism based on some generally acceptable formula. Historical experience in the postwar period shows that the first solution will not work. Hence the question is whether the second solution *will* work, whether it is politically feasible, and what compromises might be necessary to render it a viable component of international monetary reform.

United States proposals for a relatively "pure" system of the second type, with parity shifts virtually mandatory triggered by reserve gains or losses, were greeted with skepticism in Europe. In part, the European view was justified, because the simplicity and elegance of using reserves as an automatic trigger is not matched by its conceptual soundness. International reserves are not totally reliable as a trigger because of the wide variety of factors that influence them, some of which are and should be reflected in relative currency values, while others are more transitory in nature. There was also the question of timing: How long do reserve losses or gains have to go on before they can be considered "basic" and grounds for exchange rate shifts? How large do they have to be? What about the fact that national economic structures differ greatly, and that this influences both the real cost of adjustment and the validity of using reserves as the sole criteria in a trigger mechanism.

But the European objections went further than this. They attacked the "automaticity" in concept itself: They insisted that government discretion should *continue* to play a major role in deciding *whether* and *when* currency-value changes should be undertaken and concluded that (a) a number of economic indicators *in addition to* reserves should be considered as relevant signals for possible parity shifts, (b) the operative criteria should be *wide* fluctuations in whatever indicators are finally adopted, and (c) these variations should lead only to automatic *consultations* on whether parity changes are in order, and not to the changes themselves.

As the debate evolved in the mid-1970's, the U.S. became more amenable to a complex trigger mechanism based on several fundamental indicators of economic performance, with reserve changes still playing a major role but with such factors as price-level changes and trends in the balance of trade increasingly important. The Europeans also backed away from an inflexible position that any such triggers constitute no more than an "early warning system" with no compulsion on anyone's part to do anything about emerging payments disequilibria. Agreement seemed to be approaching on a compromise whereby a mutually acceptable trigger mandates the countries involved to undertake positive action in shifting exchange-rates with a specified time, but the precise nature of the policy measure would be subject to high-level consultation and agreement in an appropriate forum such as a strengthened International Monetary Fund. This is only one aspect of the problem of international monetary reform, but probably the most critical one—the one that will ultimately determine whether the new system is truly viable no matter what form it takes.

This is the kind of debate that ultimately will give birth to the new international monetary order. Economic historians twenty years hence, looking back at the early and mid-1970's may well conclude that we were more than halfway there. It was a time of debate, confrontation, and conciliation. There are those who argued that we were on the razor's edge between a new and better system on the one hand, fully supportive of international economic interdependence, and international monetary collapse on the other. Others were confident that the latter was out of the question—that we were already beyond the critical point, and passed it in surprisingly good form.

VI

Economic Interdependence, Growth, and the Multinational Enterprise

27

INTERNATIONAL FACTOR TRANSFERS AND ECONOMIC DEVELOPMENT

Economic growth and the international economy are closely interconnected. Growth depends on increases in the quantity and quality of physical capital, the quality and size of the labor force (human capital) and useful knowledge—technology, broadly defined—which determines the efficiency with which the capital and human resources are used in the productive process. It also depends on access to natural resources, renewable and nonrenewable, and on the ability to achieve economies of scale in production.

Each of these has important international dimensions. International investment flows, both direct and portfolio, permit international reallocation of physical capital. International flows of people (migration) has certainly played a critical role in the economic development of the New World, for example, and more recently has been manifested in the "guest workers" in Western Europe and in the "brain drain" of the 1960's to the United States. We have learned very early in our discussion of international economics that real economic gains can be achieved *either* by international trade or by international factor mobility—that they are in effect substitutes for one another. These gains have certainly been important in historical terms.

International transfers of technology have had no less important a role in the development of individual countries, and international trade and investment permits the efficient exploitation of natural resources—without close ties to the international economy, resource-poor and resource-rich countries would be severely constrained in terms of development prospects. Lastly, particularly small countries are dependent on access to international markets in order to achieve economies of scale in production, thereby attaining some of the efficiencies available to countries with large internal markets.

In this and the following two chapters we shall outline the importance of the international economy for economic development—both on the factor-transfer and trade sides—with particular reference to problems of less-developed countries and the evolution of the multinational corporation. The multinational enterprise trades, invests, and transfers technology in a "package" basis in a transnational logistical pattern, and hence serves as a powerful catalyst shaping the development of the international economy.

MIGRATION

For many countries population pressures represent a positive barrier to economic growth—in absolute as well as per capita terms. Some, such as India, have long been plagued by a population growth that virtually equals the rate of growth in output. The result is stagnant output per capita, a reduced rate of capital formation resulting from the necessity of diverting resources to food production, and large-scale unemployment and perhaps also underemployment. Other countries, such as Australia (and some western European nations during the pre-World War II era) find the rate of population growth too slow in order to use effectively the other productive factors at their disposal. Thus, they find it in their own interest to stimulate population growth.

International migration provides an answer to both of these problems, albeit not always one that is feasible or desirable. Historically, the U.S. was certainly one of the most favored beneficiaries of international migration. During the hundred years between 1830 and 1930, the American economic growth experience as we know it could hardly have been possible without a massive population infusion from abroad. Not only did immigration provide the labor needed to bring the nation's plentiful, high-quality land into production, but it also brought agricultural know-how that made the immigrants immediately useful as contributors to growth. Other immigrants brought with them knowledge that could be applied in nonagricultural pursuits and—certainly not least important—immigration stimulated demand and hastened the process of specialization and industrialization that characterized U.S. growth during this era. At the same time, the withdrawal of this population from Europe probably did little to inhibit growth there, and almost certainly detracted from European economic advance much less than it contributed to American growth.

The economics of migration may be illustrated in terms of Figure 27–1. Given two countries in isolation, A and B, curve AA' depicts the marginal product of labor in A, and BB' represents the marginal product of labor in B. Assume the total labor supply in A is ON_2 and that in B is $O'N_2$. Total national output in the first country will therefore be $OADN_2$, and in the second country $O'BEN_2$. The wage rate in A will be W_3, and in B it will be W_2.

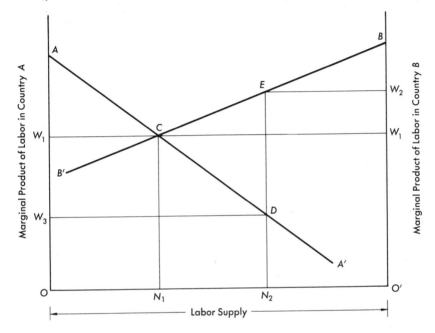

Fig. 27–1.   Economic effects of international migration.

Now suppose we permit labor to move freely between the two countries, and assume that migration is costless and occurs solely in response to wage differentials. Workers will move from A to B until the wage rates are equal at W_1. A total of N_1N_2 workers will migrate. Total output in the country of emigration (A) shrinks from $OADN_2$ to $OACN_1$, and in the country of immigration total output rises from $O'BEN_2$ to $O'BCN_1$. The total production gain in $B(N_2ECN_1)$ outweighs the production loss in $A(N_1CDN_2)$ by the amount DCE, the overall increase in combined production as a result of migration. Wage rates for those who remain in A will rise from W_3 to W_1, and for the original labor force in B wage rates will fall from W_2 to W_1.

Migration will be more beneficial (a) the lower the marginal product of labor in the country of emigration and the faster it falls, and (b) the higher the marginal product of labor in the country of immigration, and the more slowly it falls. Each of these conditions will contribute to raising the gain in combined production (area DCE in Figure 27–1) resulting from migration.

There will also be a redistribution of income from the owners of capital and land to labor in the country of emigration, and a reverse redistribution in the country of immigration. In Country A, of the initial national product $OADN_2$, quantity OW_3DN_2 went to labor and quantity W_3AD to other productive factors. After the migration, of the total product $OACN_1$, quantity OW_1CN_1 goes to labor and the rest (W_1AC) to the cooperant factors. Labor's relative share of the national product is clearly increased. In Country B, of the initial national product $O'BEN_2$, the shares of labor and other productive factors were $O'W_2EN_2$ and W_2EB, respectively. After the inflow of immigrants, the relative shares of the total product $O'BCN_1$ going to labor and other factors are OW_1CN_1 and W_1CB, respectively. The point is that as a result of migration, labor becomes relatively *more* scarce in A and *less* scarce in B, with the result that relative income shares change accordingly—labor gains relatively in A and loses relatively in B.

Migration between nations is of course controlled by a great many non-economic as well as economic variables. Religious, racial, and political oppression have been mentioned as reasons for large-scale international migration in the past, and there is no question but that such considerations have been of substantial importance. But what about *de facto economic* elements affecting the movement of people internationally? This is basically a question of the *costs* versus the *returns* involved. Presumably, migrants envision higher real incomes and, hence, a higher level of living for themselves and their families as a result of moving from one place to another. They move from one set of circumstances under which their productivity is relatively low to one where it is relatively high, perhaps because their services are combined with greater quantities of other inputs. This forms the basis for the benefits to be derived from migration.

But migration also involves a cost. Obviously, it costs something to move yourself, your family, and your worldly possessions from one place to another in transport expenses alone. It also takes time, and no income is generally received in the interim. There is a less apparent cost involved both in the inconvenience of moving and in the social, cultural, and language adjustments that must be made. These may be impossible to measure except in a very implicit way by the individual himself.

The potential migrant must make a choice by comparing all of the explicit and implicit costs of migration with the economic and noneconomic gains he expects. If the latter significantly exceed the costs, clearly the decision will be to migrate. If the individual's roots in his home environment are extremely strong, however, the gains may have to be so great as to virtually preclude movement by these criteria.

Demographically, the most obvious effect of international migration is that it increases the population of the destination country and decreases the population of the country of origin. In reducing population pressures in the latter, it may actually help to lower mortality rates and increase the birth rate—which in the long run may more than offset the initial population reduction. Moreover, in the country of destination, immigration may cause a significant secondary population increase if the immigrants have a higher fertility rate than the indigenous population. Immigration may also change the age composition of the population in the destination country, since immigrants are almost always in the younger age groups. This itself will help to raise the birth rate. The latter consideration does not apply, of course, to migration that involves predominantly males or to nonvoluntary, refugee types of migration.

If the destination country is already heavily populated, these effects may not apply, however. Immigration may in such cases actually lead to a decline in birth rates or increased emigration from that country. Any such reduction in birth rates may be partly attributed to the immigrants' occupying the lowest socioeconomic ranks, and driving the indigenous population up the socioeconomic order where birth rates are generally lower. Whether or not any birth-rate drop attributable to immigration will outweigh the initial population infusion is open to question.

Aside from the demographic question, migration influences economic growth in both countries in numerous ways. For example, the *human-capital* investment above a certain level embodied in a migrant represents an irrecoverable loss to the country of origin and a windfall gain to the country of destination. The term "brain drain" has gained popularity in western Europe during the 1960's; it refers to the migration of highly trained individuals to the U.S. in response to higher wage levels and improved job opportunities. Unlike foreign investments in physical capital a nation rarely earns a return on its exports of human capital unless the remittances of the emigrants assume very sizeable proportions indeed.

Moreover, the character of the migrants is of substantial consequence. Are they young, adventurous, and energetic people or are they merely outcasts who cannot find productive work at home? The more the former characteristics apply, the more beneficial migration will be to the destination country, and the more harmful it will be to the country of origin. The reverse may be true if the latter applies, particularly if both countries are highly populated. Thus, the quality of migrants, as well as the quantity, is significant for both economies.

The question of remittances is interesting in and of itself. Such countries as Italy, Spain, Turkey, and Greece which sent laborers—usually single males—to northern Europe during the 1960's and 1970's benefitted very substantially from high remittances to families remaining behind. Should entire families migrate, however, remittances would usually tend to dwindle until, after a generation or two, they dry up altogether.

The benefit the recipient nation can expect from immigration, therefore, hinges upon the nature of the immigrants themselves, as well as upon the nature of the economy involved. It also is contingent upon the speed with which they are assimilated into the indigenous culture, particularly with respect to language. This will help to determine the extent to which the immigrants are able to participate fully in the productive process and the negative influences they might exert through social disturbances and stratification. The stage of development of the countries of immigration and emigration is also important. Finally, we must look at the endowment in the recipient country of resources compatible with labor. This will determine the productivity of the immigrants and their net contribution to economic welfare. It is clear, for instance, that the labor shortage acted as a brake on western European economic growth during the 1960's, and that this was substantially alleviated through migration.

Immigration *policy* varies widely from one country to the next. Some countries, already suffering from population pressure, discourage immigration altogether. Other countries, suffering from underpopulation, encourage immigration but only on a selective basis, with the notion of attracting primarily high-quality additions to their respective labor forces. Still others encourage immigration, but only on a temporary basis, preferring to retain the right of expulsion should the labor shortage become less acute and unemployment threaten the indigenous work force. Such policies, regulated by *labor permits,* really provide a kind of unemployment insurance for the home labor force, since the guest workers will be let go first in times of economic slack.

Finally, we ought to look briefly at international migration and its relation to trade among countries. The factor-endowments theory of trade teaches that unrestricted international trade under certain conditions tends to equalize factor prices between countries. This is true of wages, and any impediments to the free movement of goods internationally will insure that such equalization does not and cannot occur.

Suppose trade were restricted by tariffs and quotas, and all frontiers were opened to free international migration. Clearly labor would move in response to real wage differentials, everything else being equal, from low-wage to high-wage countries along the lines presented in Figure 27–1. This lowers real wages in the latter and raises them in the former, with the result that differences in relative factor costs diminish. In each instance, output of the import-competing goods rises, production of the export goods falls, and trade dwindles. Carried to the limit, migration will continue until real wages are equalized internationally and trade ceases altogether. It is clear that migration can indeed serve as a substitute for trade, reducing the basis for trade by narrowing differences in relative factor endowments.

In reality, of course, there are other factors to be considered, particularly international differences in production functions, differences in demand patterns between countries, as well as the fact that labor is rarely entirely immobile or entirely mobile internationally. Hence, we can say that migration *may* substitute for trade to a degree, but it is doubtful whether it can replace trade. It is certain, however, that under conditions of restricted trade, migration can do what trade is prevented from doing: expanding world productive efficiency by permitting a more nearly optimum combination of productive resources in output of goods and services.

CAPITAL

Like labor, capital is an element in the productive process that can be expanded to provide a source of growth in two ways: through internal generation and through receipts from abroad. Unlike labor, however, capital is extremely mobile internationally and responds quickly to differences in yields, providing that there are no restrictions and that risk factors pose no obstacle.

In a closed economy, all domestic investment must originate in domestic saving. The nation is limited to its own productive capabilities in providing for consumption needs as well as for investment objectives. A desire on its part to increase the rate of capital formation under conditions of isolation necessarily involves repressing consumption and diverting more of its productive resources to capital formation. What if, however, consumption is already at very low levels (as it is in underdeveloped countries), and very little in the way of saving and investment can be attained in this manner? Is the nation doomed to continuing low rates of capital formation and—to the extent that capital formation is a determining factor in economic growth—continuing unsatisfactory rates of economic progress? The obvious answer in such a case, and one to which developing nations tend to turn very readily, is to import capital from abroad.

Borrowing abroad increases the resources available to an economy by making possible imports that were not possible before. It makes little difference whether the imports (ultimately financed through borrowing) consist of consumption or capital goods, as long as the incremental resources thus made available are eventually channeled into capital formation. For instance, if the necessary capital goods can best be supplied internally, borrowing abroad may be used to import food and other consumer goods which, in turn, liberate domestic resources that can then be channeled into the production of investment goods. If, on the other hand, the capital goods are most advantageously imported, then the receipts from external borrowings can be used directly to finance the imports of investment goods. In either case, the additional resources contribute to capital formation.

On the surface, the most evident need for foreign capital is to make possible imports of capital equipment that is unavailable domestically. Some types of equipment cannot be made available at home, at least in the short run, without a costly and wasteful channeling of resources into lines of production to which they are ill-suited, or into the production of goods which cannot be supplied efficiently on a relatively small scale. But even when the needed equipment *must* come from abroad, foreign borrowing is certainly not the only way to finance such imports. Instead, domestic resources could be channeled into export production, and the resulting foreign-exchange receipts used to secure the necessary imports of capital equipment. Borrowing abroad is rarely the *only* path to increased capital formation, even if the needed capital goods can be secured only from foreign sources.

Foreign borrowing, moreover, must not be considered a substitute for internally generated capital formation. The ever-present danger is that such inflows may be used to finance imports of foodstuffs and other consumer goods, while domestic resources used for the production of similar commodities remain unchanged. This results merely in a temporary rise in domestic consumption levels which, while perhaps desirable in and of itself, contributes nothing to capital formation and very little to economic growth—the possible exception here being an improvement in the quality of labor due to improved nutritional and health levels.

THE TRANSFER PROBLEM

When we speak of capital transfers between countries, we are referring to the transfer of *physical* capital resources. International capital flows, on the other hand, are normally undertaken in *financïal* terms, whether in the form of direct foreign investment, debt instruments, or foreign aid. The physical and financial flows are not necessarily parallel, and when they diverge widely certain difficulties can arise for the source as well as receiving countries which is generally termed the "transfer problem."

Suppose Country *A* invests $1 billion in Country *B*'s financial assets. *B* incurs an obligation to service the capital infusion via interest or dividend remissions, while *A* expects a return in terms of international purchases of real good and services. If there is no real-goods transfer between *A* and *B*, either directly or via third countries, *B*'s productive capacity will not expand commensurately and the debt service may prove difficult. At the same time, *A* may not realize the additional real goods it expects from the savings invested abroad, and inflationary pressures may result. The point is that a certain parallelism must exist between the real and financial flows in order for the transfer problem to be avoided.

Probably the most outstanding example of the transfer problem arose after World War I and the heavy reparations imposed on Germany at the

Peace of Versailles. Financial reparations were coupled with partial industrial dismemberment of Germany and high import barriers on the part of
many of the reparations-receiving countries. As a result, the real transfers
could not be made leading to an eventual reparations moratorium—as chron-
icled in Keynes' classic work *The Economic Consequences of the Peace*.
More recently, interest in the transfer problem has been rekindled by the
massive increase in oil prices and the resulting financial flows.

ABSORPTIVE CAPACITY

If we assume that foreign borrowing will be used entirely to promote
physical-capital formation, we become involved next in questions concerning
the amount of borrowing that a country should logically undertake from
foreign sources. Borrowing abroad necessarily involves a cost in the form
of repayments of interest and dividends. These represent a portion of a
nation's productive resources continually required to service its external
debt. If externally financed capital formation is to contribute to economic
growth, its net contribution to output must at least exceed this amount.

Suppose for the moment that the labor force, technology, and the other
cooperant inputs remain unchanged. Diminishing returns will see to it
that the yield on incremental additions to the physical-capital stock falls
after some point, and, once it has fallen to the level at which the cost
of debt service is just being covered, there is no further justification for
additional foreign borrowings. Under such conditions, which certainly approximate those obtaining in the short run, we say that a nation's *absorptive
capacity* of external capital resources is strictly limited. Even in the long
run there may be limits to absorptive capacity if physical-capital formation
outpaces the growth of cooperant elements in the growth process.

Let us look at this question a little more closely. In Figure 27–2, curve
AM depicts the marginal product of capital corresponding to each and
every level of the national capital stock. Suppose *OH* is the national stock
of productive capital, all of which is owned by domestic residents. Total
national output then comprises the area under the curve, *OACH*, of which
the area *ABC* will be the real wages paid to other productive factors and
the area *OBCH* represents the earnings of the invested capital at a yield
OB.

Suppose, further, that foreign borrowing increases the national capital
stock to *OJ*. Total output becomes *OAGJ*, for an increase of *HCGJ*, with
real wages to cooperant factors rising by *DBCG* to *ADG*. Of the total
capital stock *OJ*, only quantity *OH* is owned by domestic residents, as
before, and hence their earnings fall from *OBCH* to *ODEH*. The remaining earnings on the capital stock, *HEGJ* is paid to foreign investors.

The results of foreign investment? Earnings of domestic investors have fallen by *DBCE*, all of which is transferred to the other factors of production whose relative productivity and employment have risen as a consequence. Total output has risen by *HCGJ*, of which *ECG* goes to noncapital productive factors, and the remainder, *HEGJ*, is paid to foreign investors at a yield of *OD*. Foreign borrowing under conditions of diminishing marginal product of capital thus tends to redistribute real income from the owners of capital to the owners of other productive factors. This assumes, of course that the marginal product of capital curve remains stable.

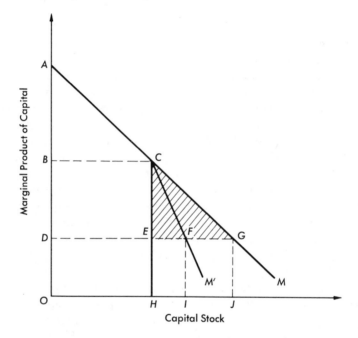

Fig. 27–2.   Capacity to absorb capital.

If foreign investors require a yield of *OD*, the total absorptive capacity of this particular economy is *HJ* of foreign capital. Should the marginal product of capital curve fall more rapidly, for example, *CM'*, absorptive capacity at that particular yield will be correspondingly reduced to *HI*.

Suppose additions to the national capital stock over and above the amount *OH* are completely unproductive and therefore have a zero yield. The capacity of the country to absorb capital is then clearly defined as that amount, *OH*, regardless of how low a rate of return foreign lenders are seeking.

This sort of analysis can be expanded to provide a vehicle for looking at the economics of foreign lending from both the borrower's and the lender's viewpoints. In Figure 27–3, we assume a two-country world composed of an advanced and a backward economy and a total capital stock of *OO'*. Of this total capital endowment, *OC* belongs to the developed country, *A,* and *O'C* resides in the developing economy, *U.* The two curves *XA* and *YU* represent the marginal product of capital at different investment levels for the advanced and underdeveloped economies, respectively.

In isolation, the advanced country would invest its entire capital stock *OC* at home, at a yield of *OK.* Total product is *OXGC,* with *KXG* going to cooperant factors of production, and *OKGC* going to the owners

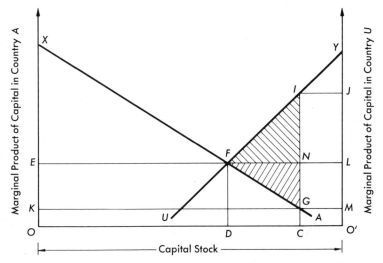

Fig. 27–3. International capital transfers, yields, and income distribution.

of capital. Similarly, the developing country invests all of its capital *O'C* at home at a yield of *O'J,* with total product being *O'YIC* of which *O'JIC* goes to the owners of capital, and the remainder (*YIJ*) to the cooperant productive factors.

Now suppose we opened up the system to free international capital flows. The advanced country, under *ceteris paribus* conditions, would now invest *OD* of its capital at home, and the rest, *DC,* in the underdeveloped economy at a yield of *OE.* Total domestic product is now *OXFD,* to which must be added earnings on the foreign investment in the amount *DFHC* for a total national income of *OXFHC.* Real income with free foreign investment is obviously greater—than that obtaining if all capital had to be invested at home—by the amount *FHG* (*OXFHC — OXGC* = *FHG*), so the lending country gains in this regard. Internally, returns to noncapital productive factors are reduced from *EXG* to *EXF,* and returns to capital are increased from *OKGC* to *OEHC.*

For the borrowing country, the inflow of foreign capital in the amount

DC causes a drop in investment yields from $O'J$ to $O'L$. Total output grows from $O'YIC$ to $O'YFD$ by the amount $CIFD$. ($O'YFD - O'YIC = CIFD$.) Of this increase in output, the amount $DFHC$ must be paid to the foreign investors, so that the net gain in national income accruing to the domestic economy is HIF ($CIFD - DFHC = HIF$). Again, internal returns to domestic owners of capital fall from $O'JIC$ to $O'LHC$, while returns to the owners of noncapital productive factors rise from YIJ to YFL.

From a world standpoint, total production has risen from $OXGC + O'YIC$ to $OXFD + O'YFD$, by an amount $FHG + HIF$ (the shaded area in Figure 27-3). The more rapidly the marginal product of capital falls in the underdeveloped economy (signifying increasingly limited absorptive capacity), and the more slowly the marginal product of capital falls in the developed country, the less will be the amount of foreign lending that is undertaken, and the smaller will be the gains that can be derived. For example, suppose the absorptive capacity of the underdeveloped country is limited to its own capital stock, and its marginal product of capital schedule "breaks" and becomes vertical at point I. There would then be no justification for any international lending at all and no gains to be derived. In this sense, when we talk about capacity to absorb foreign capital, we are concerned with the slope of that segment (IU) of the borrowing country's marginal product of capital curve corresponding to capital stock levels in excess of that available internally.

It would seem logical that the capacity of developing economies to absorb foreign capital is quite limited, with some sort of "break" in the marginal product curve at any given point in time. This can be attributed to a number of factors.

1. The cooperant agents, particularly entrepreneurship and labor possessing the skills and qualities needed, are likely to be extremely scarce or even nonexistent. Whereas it may be argued with reason that enterpreneurial and technological skills can be imported along with the capital, and labor may be trained to meet the needs of the capital infusion, this is certainly not possible in the short run.

2. It takes time to organize a variety of different complementary facilities to render any substantial new investment productive. This particularly involves the creation of efficient transportation, communication, power, and port facilities. If few or none of these already exist or cannot be supplied concurrently, the productivity of foreign capital infusions will be limited indeed. Again, these facilities can be provided, but not in the short run.

3. What about the output provided by foreign-financed capital facilities? There are two possibilities: (a) that it will be exported and (b) that it will be absorbed domestically. If the export market is of sole or overriding importance, as is true for oil wells in Libya,

iron ore mines in Venezuela, or copper production in Zambia, this consideration does not constitute an import obstacle. If, on the other hand, the output is designated for domestic consumption, a market for the particular commodity must be provided. This market may not exist or may be in the early formative stages, and a further limitation will thus be imposed on the capital absorptive capacity of a developing economy.

All of these considerations would seem to indicate that, at least initially, the marginal productivity of capital in developing countries is probably falling very rapidly. If so, their capacity to absorb foreign capital will be strictly limited. In the intermediate or long run, of course, each of these limitations can and probably will be overcome, with consequent increases in their absorptive capacity. This process may be hastened through (a) previous infusions of technical assistance; (b) massive educational and training programs aided by foreign countries or international agencies; (c) temporary importation of key personnel; (d) domestic and foreign promotion of development of social and economic overhead facilities; and (e) concentration on capital projects promising substantial export potential, or for which a viable internal market already exists.

Much public assistance, such as loans by the *International Bank for Reconstruction and Development* (IBRD), or *World Bank*, are negotiated on a *project* basis. A nation must come up with a feasible, specific project that meets the agency's standards and that fits into a long-range, overall development planning strategy. The simple shortage of projects that meet such established criteria is taken to signify limited absorptive capacity on the part of developing economies. Underdeveloped countries typically reply that project loans are certainly not the only type of foreign borrowing that needs to be undertaken, and that the mere *drawing up* of project loan applications is often beyond their capabilities. Moreover, they assert that project financing may give rise to extensive further capital requirements which are difficult to fill.

Whereas the notion of absorptive capacity of developing economies is at least conceptually sound, there is a much larger question related to inflows of foreign capital for economic and especially social overhead facilities. It is hardly possible, for instance, to measure the yield on investments in schools, roads, or sewer systems; yet no one will deny that these facilities are beneficial to economic growth in a variety of different ways. Besides, they help to raise the capacity of the economy to absorb capital for more specific projects. Hence, developing countries argue that foreign governments ought to make available to them grants and liberal long-term loans for these very purposes on an extended-appropriations basis. Advanced nations, for their part, tend to resist this sort of long-term commitment, partly due to the absence of clear guidelines as to the productivity of

the invested capital, partly because of the lack of control over the uses
to which the capital is put.

TYPES OF DEVELOPMENT CAPITAL FLOWS

It might be appropriate at this point to define briefly the kinds of international flows of capital as they apply to developing economies. We can
classify them by economic sectors—governmental and private—and by the
purposes to which the proceeds of the capital inflow are put by the recipient
country.

Perhaps the most obvious type is lending by one government to another
as part of a general economic-assistance or foreign-aid program, and possibly
tied to foreign policy in terms of the evaluation of aid criteria and goals.
Unilateral government-to-government loans and grants of this type take
on all sorts of forms. They range from relatively "hard" project loans, requiring repayment in the currency of the lender or some other convertible
currency and with strict supervision of the uses of funds, to outright grants
with few if any strings attached. Between these two extremes are numerous
other forms of assistance.

For instance, in the latter category general-purpose loans may be made
with few stipulations as to the use of funds. These may be "balance of
payments" loans to provide needed foreign exchange for development.
They may have a variety of interest rates attached and repayment terms
of varying degrees of rigidity. General-purpose and project-type loans may
or may not be "tied" to purchases in the lender country. Most unilateral
government development loans today are tied in this manner. Some countries, particularly in the Communist bloc, make loans at nominal interest
rates under which the developing country receives capital equipment and
repays in primary products over an extended period of time.

Soft loans, repayable in the currency of the borrower (which is usually
inconvertible), are made for a variety of purposes and usually involve
a very small or zero debt-service foreign-exchange cost to the borrowing
nation. Interest and principal payments are credited to a local-currency
account of the lending country. These so-called *counterpart funds* are normally used to pay the local costs that the lending government incurs on
a day-to-day basis, such as operating the embassy and consulates, and even
expenses incurred in the course of junkets by government dignitaries.
Counterpart funds are also returned to the recipient government in the
form of loans or grants to help meet local costs of development programs.

A special type of soft loan involves the sale of agricultural surpluses to developing countries for local currency, as under U.S. Public Law 480. P.L.
480 shipments and similar aid in the form of foodstuffs are supposed to
liberate resources in the recipient economy from agricultural pursuits which,

in turn, are then to be transferred to the export sector or to the domestic investment-goods sector. To the extent that they permit the recipient countries to expand foreign exchange on capital-good imports—foreign exchange that would otherwise have had to be spent on imported foodstuffs—they also yield a direct benefit.

There are a number of technical problems in connection with surplus food shipments. Moreover, their precise impact on growth is hardly clear, with the possible exception of their contribution in avoiding famine during crop shortages. The question is whether the required structural economic readjustments supposed to be triggered by these food shipments actually do occur, and hence whether any positive effect on growth thus comes about.

Apart from Public Law 480, most American development assistance is channeled through the *Agency for International Development* (AID) and the *Export-Import Bank* (Eximbank). AID was organized in 1961 to replace several previous agencies involved in the administration of American foreign aid. AID is charged with making development loans, administering technical-assistance programs, distributing aid in support of U.S. military assistance, and disposing of P.L. 480 counterpart funds for development purposes. Its loans are made to private, public, financial, and business organizations, as well as directly to foreign governments for specific projects. AID loans are made both on a project basis and for more general "balance of payments" purposes. Virtually all AID loans have been tied to purchases in the U.S. Dollar loans are repayable in U.S. currency over extended periods of up to forty years at nominal rates of interest which vary with the nature of the borrower and the type of loan.

The Export-Import Bank in its present form was established in 1945 to help finance American exports. It was supposed to aid in the financing of those transactions that could not secure adequate financing through private sources. Requests for Eximbank credits come from U.S. firms as well as from foreign firms or government agencies wishing to buy U.S. goods. Loans may be made on a project or balance of payments basis and, in addition, are used to finance U.S. agricultural exports. Eximbank resources also stand behind the U.S. export credit guarantee insurance system to facilitate and reduce the cost of private export financing. All repayments of interest and principal must be made in U.S. dollars on terms ranging from five to twenty years at interest rates around 5 to 6 per cent.

A second type of public international development lending activity is carried out by international organizations. Perhaps most important of these is the International Bank for Reconstruction and Development (IBRD). The IBRD was organized at the 1944 Bretton Woods conference to facilitate the flow of capital to developing countries. Using funds garnered from government subscriptions and bond flotations on the world's capital markets, the IBRD engages almost exclusively in hard, project-type loans. The rates of interest charged are only slightly higher than its own cost of capital. A careful study of proposed projects and a close supervision of their execution are IBRD hallmarks.

To provide development capital on less stringent terms for a variety of purposes—especially for social overhead—the *International Development Agency* (IDA) was created to make long-term, low-interest loans to developing countries. Such loans are sometimes extended in conjunction with IBRD project loans and thereby simultaneously (a) increase the profitability of the project loan, (b) extend the average repayment terms of the combined loans, and (c) lower the overall capital cost to the borrower. Another part of the IBRD-IDA system is the *International Finance Corporation* (IFC), which invests equity capital in the private sector of developing economies and eventually liquidates its holdings through sales to indigenous investors. On a hemispheric basis, there is the *Inter-American Development Bank* (IDB), which lends to Latin-American nations on liberal terms, concentrating on economic and social overhead projects. Also to be considered is the *European Development Fund* (EDF), which assists former territories of the Common Market countries and other developing nations as a purely European effort.

The advantages of international lending agencies—as opposed to intergovernmental development assistance in the form of loans and grants—are clear:

1. There is little or no foreign-policy pressure attached to the receipt of foreign capital which obligates the recipient in some way other than the mere servicing of the debt.
2. The loans and grants of international agencies are much less likely to be tied to purchases in any one country or group of countries. This permits the recipients to make their purchasing decisions purely on the basis of price and equality. They can thereby maximize the benefits they receive by reducing the real cost of capital.
3. Repayment obligations (at least on the part of IBRD) are expressed in no uncertain terms, and this promotes a no-nonsense application of the development assistance to the most worthwhile projects available. In addition, there is no connection between international agency loans and one other form of intergovernmental aid—military aid.

Economic and military aid are by no means mutually exclusive. For most developing countries, there is only one source of military equipment and that is imports. If an underdeveloped nation sets an armaments goal and is willing to expend its scarce foreign exchange for this purpose, then receipts of foreign military assistance in the form of war materiel will liberate some foreign exchange for nonmilitary imports. To the extent that these new imports are capital goods, the military aid becomes economic aid. The reverse can happen too, however, with economic assistance being transferred into imports of war materiel by liberating foreign exchange that can be used for this purpose.

Even more directly, military assistance which cuts down manpower or other defense needs internally can result in a transfer of domestic resources into development. Conversely, development assistance may permit the transfer of productive resources into military pursuits. So long as foreign exchange and productive resources can be transferred to consumption, investment and military uses, there is little sense in attempting to draw a strict line between foreign aid of a military and a nonmilitary character.

Finally, we must consider another very important type of capital transfer to developing countries—private direct investments and private lending. The second of these is perhaps the easier to dispose of. National or regional governments and private businesses may borrow abroad on an individual basis, either directly from banking houses or by bond flotations on the world's more developed capital markets. Private firms in developing nations as a rule have a difficult time meeting the normal commercial loan standards that banks impose upon their clients. This is, of course, not true if they are affiliated with a large, international firm that is willing to place its own credit rating on the line. This is good reason for the existence of public national or international lending agencies that service the needs of—or are willing to guarantee private loans to—such firms.

Governments of underdeveloped countries, and sometimes even governmental units below the national level, periodically make use of private borrowings abroad. In the absence of political instability they have easier access to bank loans and to private placements of debt obligations with financial institutions in developed nations than do private businesses in developing countries. They must, of course, be willing and able to pay customary interest rates and submit to stringent repayment schedules. Moreover, the willingness of investors to purchase foreign-government obligations varies markedly from one period to the next. For instance, during the 1920's, foreign bond flotations in New York reached truly impressive levels. The depression put an end to that, and the market in New York for foreign-government bonds did not show signs of life again until the early 1960's—an interval of almost forty years!

Direct private investment in developing countries is quite another matter. Private investment tends to be motivated by the expectation of profit under conditions of greater or lesser degrees of uncertainty. From the developing country's viewpoint, direct foreign investment is a source of capital for the immediate creation of productive facilities and also a simultaneous infusion of technology, entrepreneurship, development-orientation, and sometimes even ancillary economic and social intrastructure investment. To the extent that direct foreign investments yield profits, they serve as reliable sources of government tax revenues—revenues that can then be re-channeled into further capital formation. In many instances, direct foreign investment is made in export production which then serves as a valuable source of foreign exchange for the nation. Necessarily, they also involve a remission of earnings abroad which provide a reasonable return—considering the conditions under which they are made—to the owners of capital. The question is whether the "costs" of earnings remissions to the host economy are more than offset by the benefits that direct foreign investment brings with it.

In some cases, objections to direct foreign investment raised by developing countries are based on its effect upon income distribution. It is charged that foreign direct investment tends to maintain or widen existing income differentials between groups in the society—that it widens the gap between the sectors singled out by foreign investors and the remainder of the economy. For instance, direct investments by foreigners may not coincide with the national government's development plan since they may be predominantly concentrated in the extractive industries, with very little value added to the domestic economy, relatively low manpower requirements, and little infusion of technology into the local economy. Or the investments may be so out of step technologically with the remainder of the national economy that the result is an *enclave*, which is entirely outward-oriented and which holds few benefits for the host country itself.

Charges are often heard, moreover, that direct private investments in underdeveloped countries are primarily exploitive in nature, and that they yield, if not an absolute worsening of economic conditions, at least a suboptimal path to economic advancement. Occasionally, these are unsubstantiated statements made purely for political consumption, either within the affected country itself or internationally, and they are designed to conjure up visions of neo-colonial exploitation. In other cases, such charges represent dissatisfaction with the share of the gains going to the host country. Depending on the strength of its bargaining position, relative to that of the foreign investors, the host country may take measures designed to achieve what it considers a more equitable division of the gains.

For instance, heavier taxes may be imposed, statutory wage rates increased, or export and import regulations altered in favor of the host country. Raising import restrictions on components and materials may be designed to increase the local value added and thus increase the benefits to the economy—both directly and indirectly through a broader dissemination of technology and skills. This second objective may also be approached be requiring or encouraging joint ownership and management by local residents. Joint ventures can have the additional benefit of enhancing indigenous entrepreneurial interest and skills, but these are often approached with extreme caution by foreign investors, especially if they are required to assume a minority ownership interest.

The pros and cons of private direct investment in developing countries are largely unsettled. The gains to the host economy on the surface seem substantial indeed. But they defy measurement, if only because of the impossibility of estimating their educational and technological effects. Meanwhile, the costs to the recipient country are also considerable in earnings remissions alone, although the risks involved (investors would argue) seem to more than justify such returns in many instances. Developing countries also worry about the possible adverse structural side effects of foreign private investments on their economies, and about whether this really represents the best way of going about the task of securing maximum growth. Opinions vary, and will continue to do so for a long time to come. These issues are discussed in greater detail in Chapter 29.

CAPACITY TO SERVICE FOREIGN DEBT

Capital inflows of developing countries—whether in the form of grants, private or public loans, or direct investments—are limited on the supply side (a) by the willingness of foreign governments to provide foreign aid and (b) by the way whatever foreign aid they agree to supply is apportioned among prospective recipients, as well as (c) the alternatives that exist for private loans and investments in the investors' home countries or other developed nations.

On the demand side such capital inflows are limited (a) by the absorptive capacity of the developing economies, as we noted earlier, and (b) by the prospective capacity of these economies to service the debt thus incurred.

With the exception of outright grants, debt service plays a role in all types of foreign capital in two ways:

1. Productive resources must be directed toward repayment of interest, profits, and principal which otherwise could be employed for consumption or further investment.
2. If interest, principal, and dividend payments are stipulated in foreign currencies, a nation must be able to provide the foreign exchange necessary to make these remissions possible.

The second of these considerations makes the capacity to service debt essentially a balance of payments problem. The first consideration would appear to be the more important in the long run.

If foreign-capital inflows are used by developing countries to expand exports or to stimulate output in import-competing industries, the balance of payments problem of debt service presumably takes care of itself. This particular use of foreign capital helps to insure that the foreign exchange required for interest and principal remission will be available. But what of foreign borrowing used for purposes other than export-expansion or import-reduction? What about, for example, investment in economic and social overhead capital? The rationale is that such uses of foreign capital ultimately result in an increased productive capacity of the economy as a whole, including export- and import-competing industries. While the repayment capacity—in terms of foreign exchange—evidently will ultimately materialize as a result of *any* type of investment that enhances the overall productive capability of the economy, this will generally be a long-term proposition in the case of overhead facilities.

In discussing repayment capacity as a criterion for additional foreign borrowing by underdeveloped countries, both short-term and long-term considerations must play a role. A nation's ability to meet the interest, dividend, and principal repayment obligations coming due during a given year depends upon the state of its balance of payments and its international-reserve position. If its current receipts exceed its current expenditures, this excess may be used to make the debt service payments. If, on the other hand, a foreign-exchange earnings surplus is attributable to further capital inflows, it will be using these receipts to service *past* debt. If, finally, the new foreign-capital inflows give rise to equivalent or nearly equivalent imports, so that the balance of payments as a whole is in deficit, the ability to service debt depends on the amount of international reserves the nation has at its disposal.

One test of the capacity to repay in the short run is the so-called *debt-service ratio:* total annual remissions of interest, dividends, and principal amortization divided by total annual foreign-exchange receipts from sales of goods and services abroad. Also used is the *public debt-service ratio,* which places interest and principal repayments on public debt alone in the numerator and total exports of goods and services in the denominator. A high debt-service ratio implies limited capacity of the borrowing country to service its debt, with correspondingly increased chance of default. Indications are, however, that the debt-service ratio is hardly an adequate single guide to either capacity to pay or to danger of default. A great deal depends on the composition of the debt, the access of the country to emergency sources of international reserves and, certainly not least important, its *willingness* to meet its obligations. Hence, we sometimes find countries with extremely high debt-service ratios and a clean record of repayment and others with much lower debt-service ratios and a history of frequent defaults—even on their public debt. Several Latin American countries are notable for falling into the second category.

In the long run, debt-service ratios are of little significance. Only projections of *both* debt-service requirements *and* current foreign-exchange earnings would make them of value. Such projections would certainly possess doubtful validity, which would decline further as the projections were extended. Much more important are (a) the projected economic growth of the borrowing country which ultimately determines capacity to repay in terms of domestic resources; and (b) the channeling of some of the expanded productive capacity into export- and import-competing lines in order to insure the long-run availability of foreign exchange for debt-service purposes. A large volume of foreign debt-service obligations places a constraint on the manner in which productive resources may be allocated during the growth process.

Whether or not the growth path of borrowing countries is satisfactory depends partly on the rate at which additional capital formation is generated through internal savings and investment. This normally means that the marginal savings rate must be sufficiently high and that the rate of population growth must be sufficiently low to permit rapid increases in domestic savings and investment. The rate of growth, as we saw earlier, also depends on increases in the level of technology, both embodied and disembodied with respect to other productive factors, and on improvements in the various other elements that we identified as contributing to economic development. On top of this, however, the rate of growth also is affected by the amount of domestic income that must be transferred to other countries in the form of debt-service remissions. This hinges on the total volume of foreign debt outstanding, the average rate of return that must be paid on this debt, and the required rate of amortization of principal.

Paradoxically, in the case of most developing countries the sustained growth required for long-range debt-service capability depends also on the rate of receipt of new capital from abroad. These countries find that they must remain net capital importers for decades, which means that *gross* capital imports must continue to rise rapidly in order to more than cover the repayments on the outstanding debt and still permit net imports which constitute the real capital transfers. In short, a nation's development path will generally have to be export-oriented in order to cover the rapidly growing import requirements as well as the debt-service. Countries which fail in following such a path eventually find themselves in trouble, having to reduce needed imports in order to service a pool of outstanding foreign debt. It is easy at such a time to talk of foreign exploitation or rationalize the need for default. But this does little to cover up the real problem: the failure to provide the real means for servicing externally held debt under conditions of rapid economic growth and import expansion.

TECHNOLOGY

Having looked at international movements of labor and capital within the context of the needs and capabilities of developing countries, we now turn to international transfers of technology and their contribution to economic progress in the recipient countries.

Technology can be transmitted internationally in a variety of ways.

1. It may be embodied in imports of capital goods.
2. It may accompany foreign direct investment in the form of capital-goods imports that often parallel it and, more directly, in the organization of production and administration.
3. Technology may be embodied in labor and transmitted through immigration.
4. It may be transferred directly—either through the private sector or the public sector—by consulting arrangements, licensing agreements, technical-assistance programs, or simple imitation.

One is tempted to conclude from an examination of the principles of economic growth that any type of technological transfer will be beneficial to the development of the recipient nation. This is hardly true. Just as developing countries have a greater or lesser absorptive capacity for capital from abroad, depending on a variety of factors, so also is their capacity to absorb technology limited. Not only may certain types of technological infusions fail to contribute very significantly to economic progress, but they may have side effects which can actually prove to be detrimental to economic development.

In the years immediately following World War II, Germany and Japan seemed to have an insatiable thirst for technology from abroad, specifically from the U.S. They imitated and assimilated whatever they could, and both reached high levels of technical sophistication very rapidly. In both these nations absorption of foreign technology undoubtedly played an important role in the phenomenal rates of growth that they enjoyed during the first ten or fifteen postwar years. In each case, of course, all of the *prerequisites* for a high rate of technological absorption already existed: highly skilled labor, broadly based demand for industrial goods, appropriate social and economic infrastructure, and so forth. In both instances, the postwar phase of their rapid growth aided by technological assimilation represented "catching up" in a very real sense.

Other countries have not been so fortunate in being able to profitably apply imported technology in their own development efforts. Specifically, technology is most often applied in capital-intensive production. Yet developing countries suffer from a scarcity of capital, a low capital–labor ratio, and hence their production is characterized mainly by labor intensity. The danger is that instead of contributing significantly to output under such conditions, infusions of technology will merely tend to shift factor proportions and result in unemployment by displacing labor. A point of controversy is whether developing countries should opt for the most sophisticated technology available, even though it must be applied in capital-intensive production, or whether they should seek out only the technology directly applicable to the labor-intensive nature of production as it exists within the country at a point in time.

Good arguments can be made for both sides of the question. If, for example, there is very little substitutability of capital for labor in certain lines of production, labor displacement as a result of the adoption of advanced technology would be minimal; both labor and capital would be saved, which could then be redeployed in other sectors of the economy. Even better, if technology of a certain type is primarily capital-saving—which is certainly not out of the question—the overall capital-output ratio would be affected in a positive way. Because capital-intensive industries are likely to be the fastest growing, and hence tend to have a high rate of reinvestment, applications of modern technology to these industries is likely to have the further effect of increasing the overall rate of capital formation.

On the other hand, technology used in capital-intensive industries may, through the expansion of these industries independently of the remainder of the economy, lead to a type of *dual* economy. This may well be unfavorable to overall economic growth, if there is no transfer of knowledge between the two segments. To the extent that broad application of labor-saving technology creates unemployment, even if this occurs in the process of stimulating total production, it may be a politically unacceptable solution. The question then revolves around (a) how rapidly the induced unemployment will be re-absorbed as a consequence of economic growth, (b) the capacity of the existing institutional arrangement to cope with it over extended periods of time, and (c) its effort on the attitudes and expectations of the people.

By and large, it is probably safe to say that technological transfers to developing countries should be such that they are appropriate to the indigenous conditions of production. Developing nations should not, as a general rule, blindly adopt the latest technological methods available abroad. Rather, they should selectively absorb those techniques suitable to their own productive conditions and relative factor endowments, which may mean adopting obsolescent technology, modifying foreign technology, or developing their own. Unfortunately, numerous factors militate against this. Local officials insist on the latest and the best as a matter of national pride. Foreign technical advisors and entrepreneurs tend to transfer intact the technology prevailing in their home countries whether it is appropriate to the developing economy or not. Gradually, however, the realization of adaptive technological transfers is growing, and inappropriate technological infusions promise to be less troublesome in the future.

ENTREPRENEURSHIP

Entrepreneurship—the willingness and ability to marshall the resources and technology that are available for productive employment under conditions of uncertainty—is of crucial significance to economic growth. This task may be given over to private individuals, governments, or a combination of both. In most developing countries there is a distinct scarcity of entrepreneurial qualities in the indigenous population, due perhaps to custom, social statification, religion, collectivism of various sorts, and a variety of other factors. All of these serve to impede innovation and experimentation, either by degrading it or by reducing the obtainable rewards. This is not to say that the potential for entrepreneurial activity does not exist. It may simply be dormant, exercised in innumerable small and localized but certainly not insignificant ways. Indeed, the existing capacity for entrepreneurship may be substantial indeed, but it simply may not yet have been permitted to come to the surface.

Generally, as an economy progresses beyond the primitive, subsistence stages into the market- and money-oriented phase that is a prerequisite for growth, the extent of entrepreneurial activity tends to increase as the obstacles to entrepreneurship recede and the opportunities for it are enhanced. It may well be, however, that the development of entrepreneurial qualities lags behind what is needed to promote satisfactory growth, and that entrepreneurship thus may become a bottleneck. There are several possible remedies for such a situation, prominent among which are increased government participation and increased influence of foreigners. We are concerned here with the second of these two possible ways of breaking the entrepreneurial barrier to growth.

Foreign influences on the entrepreneurial characteristics of the indigenous population typically work through a segment of that population composed of bright, ambitious people and filter down to a more broadly based infusion of entrepreneurship. Foreign-led business and industrial operations provide the local population with examples to follow in the organization of their own activities—examples that can be supplemented in a more formal way through business education.

It is easy to underestimate the role of infusions of entrepreneurial behavior from abroad in the economic development of various countries at various times. The Indians in East Africa, the Chinese in Southeast Asia, and the Jews in Northern Europe are frequently mentioned in this regard. In each case, the outside groups permeated the local economies and infused entrepreneurial behavior into the indigenous groups. They did this on a broad scale by becoming a part of the population, although this process was not without more or less serious conflicts and frictions. They assumed the role of a catalyst, bringing out whatever latent entrepreneurship existed locally and marshalling available resources for economic progress. Their generally superior economic standing promoted additional efforts on the part of the natives, desirous of keeping up with the comparative affluence of the immigrants.

An interesting facet of this question is the entrepreneurial contribution of migrants to an underdeveloped area when the migrants themselves originate in an equally underdeveloped region. Their expectations are not inflated, and initially they live by the same standards as the local population. Yet they have been released from the stultifying, restrictive social and cultural environment of their home countries, and simultaneously they are stimulated by being placed in a new, entirely foreign environment which provides a basic challenge to their ingenuity and instincts for survival. Of course, the idea that primarily the most energetic, forward-looking individuals in a society tend to migrate may also be important in this regard.

The contribution of foreign entrepreneurship is exercised in various ways:

1. Foreigners provide competition for local businessmen and force them to upgrade their methods in order to survive.
2. Foreign entrepreneurs employ local workers who are infused with new values and methods, and who later may employ these independently in their own self-interest.
3. They help to create an active demand for goods and services of all kinds, both by stimulating production complementary to their own and by demonstrating a need and desirability for their own and others' products.

The foreign origins of entrepreneurial activity—whether by immigrant groups or by foreign firms operating in the local economy—often give rise to government subsidies and other assistance to purely indigenous entreprises, thereby helping to eliminate the foreigners' advantage. This can nullify much of the contribution that foreign entrepreneurship can make by rendering emulation and imitation less desirable and necessary. Moreover, the apparent foreign influence may also lead to political and social conflicts that can result in expropriation, nationalization and expulsion, again reducing the contribution that foreign entrepreneurial infusion can make.

28

INTERNATIONAL TRADE AND ECONOMIC DEVELOPMENT

Much has been written about the role of international trade in the process of economic growth, particularly within the context of conditions prevailing in the present-day developing nations of the world. What is the effect of economic growth, in its various forms, on the direction, volume, and composition of trade? Conversely, what does international trade imply with respect to the growth path of an economy? What are the relevant policy alternatives involved? How does a nation's terms of trade behave as its economy—and the economies of its trading partners—grows and change in structure and in form?

The subject of trade and economic growth has been explored at length and the conclusions reached are by no means harmonious. We propose in this chapter to explore some of the ways in which international trade and economic development are interrelated, and to draw from the analysis some inferences concerning appropriate commercial and development policy measures. The discussion will focus on the problems and opportunities international trade holds in store for underdeveloped economies in particular.

The dictates of the theory of comparative advantage, viewed either as a reflection of the classical idea of intercountry differences in the conditions of production or as the Heckscher-Ohlin notion of international variations of factor endowments, are clear in their implications for developing economies. In a static sense and given a two-country, two-commodity model, world economic welfare will be maximized if each nation specializes in those particular goods in which it has a comparative advantage. As economic growth changes relative factor endowments and productivity differentials, trade flows and national economic structure will shift, but the basic conditions of collective welfare maximization will still hold true.

But it also seems to be true that most or all of the assumptions that underlie the traditional formulation of comparative-advantage theory are somewhat limited in their applicability to real world conditions, particularly as they exist in underdeveloped economies. If we agree that comparative advantage is at least partly restricted in this way, then it follows that the policy implications constructed on this theoretical base, centering on free trade, also may be misleading. This has been argued by a great many economists for more than a century, and the arguments have gained significantly in political importance since World War II.

As early as the 1850's, the German economist Friedrich List and the American Henry C. Carey called for restrictions to international trade on essentially developmental grounds, as did some of their contemporaries.[1] List felt that economic growth in all regions in the nontropical part of the world progressed through five stages—savage, pastoral, agricultural, agricultural-manufacturing, and agricultural-manufacturing-commercial— and that government policy should foster rapid progress through these stages. Free trade should prevail in the early stages, but indigenous industries should be protected from competition from more advanced economies as the manufacturing and commercial stages are reached. In order to achieve broadbased, diversified economic progress in developing areas, and in order for these areas to avoid becoming mere suppliers of raw materials to advanced nations, Carey also advocated protection of domestic industry as a superior alternative to free trade.

Much more recently, the arguments against free trade as a universally optimal solution have gained in persuasiveness and sophistication. They are based on a variety of grounds applicable to underdeveloped countries and the problems of maximizing the rate of economic growth under conditions prevailing in this particular context. We shall begin by outlining several of the more weighty arguments, omitting the often cited (and much abused) infant-industry case for protection that was already discussed in some detail in Chapter 8.

[1] Friedrich List, *National System of Political Economy* (New York: Longmans, Green & Co., 1904); Henry C. Carey, *Principles of Social Science* (Philadelphia: J. B. Lippincott, 1858–1859).

THE PREBISCH-SINGER THESIS

What has been the long-range performance of the terms of trade of developing nations? One important set of arguments centers around the notion that over the past century prices of primary goods have fallen substantially relative to prices of manufactures. Since the developing countries primarily import manufactured goods and export primary commodities, this movement must have resulted in a secular deterioration of their collective terms of trade. This means that the developing countries had to export increasing amounts of their products in order to get a given quantity of imports. This loss to the underdeveloped world was the developed countries' gain, since there occurred a simultaneous, secular improvement in their collective terms of trade. It is often referred to as the Prebisch–Singer thesis.[2] The alleged secular deterioration of the developing countries' terms of trade is attributed to a variety of factors:

1. It is stated that the income elasticity of demand for primary products is a good deal less than for manufactured goods, and this, combined with structural and technological raw materials-saving innovations, has led to an overall reduction in the demand for primary goods relative to the demand for manufactures, with the consequent changes in price relationships.
2. It is alleged that the structure of markets for manufactured goods is much more monopolistic than that for primary commodities. The result has been cyclical rises in the price of both manufactured and primary goods in times of economic boom, with primary commodity prices falling farther in recessions than those of manufactures. This downward "stickiness" of industrial-goods prices is attributed to the greater degree of market imperfection involved. Over successive business cycles, of course, the ratchet-type behavior of industrial prices means that they are going to rise relative to those of primary commodities. As a result, the terms of trade of developing nations—exporting primary goods and importing manufactures—tended to deteriorate.
3. Technological change has had its impact upon efficiency in the use of productive resources. In the production of primary goods productivity has risen markedly, and the fruits of this productivity increase have been passed on to purchasers in the form of lower commodity prices. Productivity in industrial activity also has grown, even

---

[2] See Raùl Prebisch, "Commercial Policy in the Underdeveloped Countries," *American Economic Review, Papers and Proceedings,* May, 1959, and also his *The Economic Development of Latin America and Its Principal Problems* (New York: United Nations, 1950); and Hans W. Singer, "The Disbribution of Gains Between Investing and Borrowing Countries," *American Economic Review, Papers and Proceedings,* May, 1950.

more rapidly than that in primary production. However, the gains here are distributed to the owners of productive factors in the form of higher real wages, interest, rent, and profits, with very little of the productivity increase being reflected in lower prices of industrial goods. The result, again, has been a deterioration of the terms of trade of those areas exporting primary goods and importing manufactures. Had all productivity gains—both in primary and in industrial production—been fully reflected in falling prices, industrial-goods prices would have dropped more rapidly than those of primary goods, and the terms of trade of the developing areas would have actually improved.

The Prebisch-Singer thesis maintains that these three sets of reasons have been responsible for the apparent secular deterioration of the terms of trade of the primary-goods-producing areas. Since these happen to include all of the developing areas of the world, there has been a transferral of real income from those least able to afford it to those least in need of it—from the underdeveloped to the developed countries.

The thesis is open to serious question, however, although the emotion inherent in this sort of argument should be ample warning that it is not to be taken lightly. In the first place, the allegation is based largely on movements in the British terms of trade from the late 1800's to the end of the 1930's. During this time, the British commodity terms of trade actually did improve substantially. Apart from the somewhat doubtful reliability of the data itself, is it readily possible to infer that secular movements in the British terms of trade can be used as an accurate indicator of an *opposite* movement in the terms of trade of areas producing primary commodities? This is a questionable proposition at best, since the import-mix of the countries supplying primary goods does not necessarily coincide with the British export-mix. Nor is the commodity composition of Britain's imports necessarily coincident with the export commodity composition of the developing countries, or even representative of the imports of other developed nations. The British import and export composition undoubtedly was unique and not at all ideally suited for computing a secular terms of trade trend designed to serve as an inverse proxy of that facing the developing areas of the world.

Moreover, there is always the question of *quality* change. The quality of primary products tends to remain relatively constant—with some rare exceptions such as the production of naval oranges—simply because such commodities do not lend themselves to extensive quality improvement. Meanwhile, the quality of manufactures has risen substantially; a 1920 automobile is not the same as a 1975 model. If quality changes were taken into account, then, the improved character of the developing areas' imports combined with the relatively unchanging quality of their exports would render any indicated deterioration of their terms of trade much smaller and perhaps negate it entirely.

Even more perplexing is the fact that the composition of trade and output of industrial goods is always changing. Developing countries import goods today that did not even exist ten, fifty, or a hundred years ago; and by the same token commodities imported in some past era may have entirely disappeared from the scene today. How is it possible, under such circumstances, to compute price indexes alleged to show secular deterioration of the terms of trade of developing areas?

Further objections may be applied to the conceptual foundations of the deterioration thesis itself:

1. The income-elasticity of demand for primary goods—especially for foodstuffs—may well be low, but this does not constitute the sole determinant of the terms of trade. Rather, changes in supply conditions are equally important. Hence, although the *demand* for industrial goods may have grown more rapidly than the demand for primary commodities, so has the *supply* of industrial commodities during the process of rapid growth in the industrialized areas.

2. There is some question whether the commodity terms of trade are really what we want to look at. Is it not more significant to regard changes in the amount of imports that a given quantum of productive factors in the primary goods producing areas will buy, i.e., the *single factoral terms of trade?* Clearly, this must have increased as productivity grew in the primary producing regions. True, if productivity growth was more rapid in developed than in underdeveloped areas, as the Prebisch-Singer thesis asserts, then the latter's *double factoral terms of trade* will have deteriorated. But, the overall welfare level must have consistently improved as the single factoral terms of trade improved.

3. The alleged "ratchet effect" of prices in developed countries over the business cycle is subject to question. It is open to doubt, for instance, that imperfections in market structures were such that they prevented downward price movements in recessions. Besides, prices in the *international* marketplace respond to competitive conditions prevailing not in one country, but in many countries. This reduces even further the role of market imperfections in bringing about upward pressure on the developing countries' import prices.

4. We may look at the changes in transport conditions that have occurred during the time the terms of trade deterioration is supposed to have taken place. As we know, most countries value exports at f.o.b. prices and imports on an c.i.f. basis. Increases in transport efficiency— hence reductions in freight charges—during this period would naturally have reduced the c.i.f. values of British imports. Yet it would clearly be fallacious to attribute this reduction to decreasing export prices of the primary-goods-producing areas. That sub-

stantial reductions in transport costs did occur between the late 1800's and the beginning of World War II is a matter of record.

When it is examined in the light of all of these considerations, then, the idea of secular deterioration in the terms of trade of developing nations loses much of its persuasiveness. It seems tenuous, indeed, to draw inferences from this allegation about the course of future events and to employ it as a basis of commercial policy. True, any terms of trade improvements that can be secured for the developing nations by commercial policy are desirable from the standpoint of their level of living and rate of growth. But policy measures undertaken to this end—either singly or collectively be developed or developing nations—should not be regarded as means to right the wrongs of the past. Rather, they should be taken for what they are: conscious efforts to assist the developing areas in their attempts to achieve more rapid economic growth. Still, it is difficult to ignore the Prebisch-Singer thesis, if only on the basis of its emotional content. It is even more difficult to try to negate it with numerous, highly complex arguments.

In recent years the prices of renewable and nonrenewable raw materials have shown a marked tendency to rise, in part because of unprecedented prosperity among the industrial countries and in part because of increasingly evident supply limitations in certain raw-materials sectors. Moreover, particularly in the petroleum field the exporting countries have been successful in cartelization and driving up prices dramatically. For the developing countries as a whole, therefore, a significant improvement in the terms of trade may be underway, resulting in a major transfer of income from the developed countries—as well as some income redistribution among the developing countries themselves.

PREFERENTIAL MARKET ACCESS

The Prebisch–Singer thesis was one of the arguments underlying the idea that developing countries should have preferential—as opposed to most-favored nation—access to the industrial-country markets of the world. A twofold beneficial effect is expected: (1) The terms of trade of the developing nations may improve as duties are preferentially reduced, resulting in a transfer of customs revenues from the importing to the developing exporting countries; and (2) The volume of LDC exports may rise as demand for this export both grows and shifts from developed-country suppliers not receiving preferential market access.

Trade preferences for developing countries are not new, having been embodied in such schemes as the British Commonwealth Preference System, the EEC Overseas Associated States, the U.S. Laurel-Langley Agreement with the Philippines, among others. A new breakthrough in this area come in 1971 when the Generalized System of Preferences (GSP) was implemented by the EEC, Japan, and several other industrial countries. The preferences were negotiated in the United Nations Conference on Trade and Development (UNCTAD). The *horizontal equity* (each supplier nation treated equally) embodied in MFN treatment was thus recognized as being inherently unfair to the developing countries, which can hardly be considered "equal" in competitive terms. By according special trade concessions to the developing countries, the GSP provides an element of *vertical equity* (unequals treated unequally) intended specifically to benefit them.

By accepting the GSP, the developed countries committed themselves to admit a wide variety of manufactures from developing countries on a tariff free or reduced-tariff basis, without demanding reciprocity on the part of the beneficiaries. Generally excluded from the products covered were agricultural commodities and a range of "sensitive" goods which, unfortunately, encompass many of the products in which the developing countries have an immediate or near-term comparative advantage. On top of this, some of the preference offers, including the EEC and Japan, incorporated tight "ceilings" on permissible preferential imports. If a developing country actually succeeds in taking advantage of the preferences by rapid export expansion, the preference is likely to be withdrawn. And since many of the ceilings are predetermined, the bulk of the gains may in fact go to the importers in the developed countries, and not to the preference beneficiary. Lastly, the U.S. did not implement its own scheme of preferences for over four years after the original implementation date, until the summer of 1975.

Although the GSP may appear conceptually attractive its actual implementation is another story altogether, and the net benefits derived by the developing countries may turn out to be quite marginal.

UNSTABLE EXPORT MARKETS

Another argument against free trade and the unrestricted operation of comparative advantage in underdeveloped countries relates to the peculiar nature of the market for their exports.

Developing countries have traditionally been subject to highly unstable export markets. Their exports tend to be concentrated in primary commodities that rise and fall in price on the world markets. Often their exports are limited to a very narrow range of these primary goods, so that the world price of a single commodity, say coffee, can be the determining force in the export receipts of developing nations. Their imports, in contrast, tend to comprise a broad range of manufactured consumer and investment goods, the prices of which tend to be relatively stable over time. With stable import prices and unstable export prices, the terms of trade of these countries naturally are going to fluctuate—because of conditions that are entirely beyond their control. As a result, economic conditions and the rate of economic growth in underdeveloped nations are vitally affected by forces operating on the world markets for primary commodities.

Once a developing country is specialized in this manner—with investments committed in the export sector and with largely import-dependent consumption patterns established—a country is faced with an economy governed by external market conditions. This is true in spite of the fact that it may be conforming perfectly to the dictates of comparative advantage. The question thus arises whether it would not be better to have a lesser degree of specialization and perhaps a lower level of real income, in return for increased stability, the restoration of a semblance of economic control, and reduced uncertainty. But even if this question is answered in the affirmative, there are problems in applying a program which is designed to insure a desired degree of stability.

An underdeveloped country may decide to increase import restrictions in the hope of lowering its import prices, or to raise export restrictions with the intention of raising the price of its exports. Either or both of these measures may result in improved terms of trade. However, the world-market demand for the primary commodity exports of a particular developing country will generally prove to be highly elastic, with a large number of competing countries offering alternative sources of supply. Export restrictions thus are likely to result in a substantial fall in export volumes, with little or no rise in prices. The likely result is that the country will be worse off than before. Similarly, by raising import restrictions, the diminutive size of the typical underdeveloped economy's market itself would tend to indicate a highly elastic import supply, and preclude a fall in import prices. In short, developing nations have little monopoly power in exports, and little monopsony power in imports, and their attempts to influence the terms of trade unilaterally via commercial policy are hardly likely to meet with success.

In more technical terms, the offer curve of a given developing nation's trading partners is likely to be highly elastic. With this type of foreign-offer curve, as we noted in Chapter 8, the optimum tariff will be very low. Whatever improvement trade restrictions bring to the terms of trade is likely to be more than offset by reduced trade volumes, thus placing the nation on a lower welfare level. There is very little scope, then, for a developing country to improve its current welfare position by employing the tools of commercial policy on its own, especially in response to short-run changes in foreign-market conditions. As we shall see a little later, however, this does not necessarily hold true where several countries producing a certain primary commodity organize in order to control supply, or where exporting and importing nations agree on price-stabilization schemes.

PRIVATE AND SOCIAL COSTS AND RETURNS

The terms of trade arguments against free trade as a desirable policy for developing countries—with regard to both long-run and short-run problems—are important and must be reckoned with. This is true even if the cogency of these arguments can be diminished somewhat on theoretical, as well as on empirical, grounds. Along somewhat different lines, it has been proposed that as an industry is established and grows in an underdeveloped setting, it may well present the country with significant external economies that will contribute to economic growth above and beyond the contribution of the industry itself. The existence of such an industry indeed may not be justified on purely individual or private grounds. But the additional *social* returns it yields may well reverse this relationship. Since protection or subsidization may be the only way such an industry can establish itself, a departure from the dictates of comparative advantage may well be justified.

The social returns, upon which this argument for protection hinges, can take on a variety of forms. It is asserted first that returns to labor in a developing country tend to be abnormally low in the largest sector of its economy, agriculture, and that there is extensive *underemployment*. Meanwhile, returns to labor in the manufacturing, usually import-competing, sector are abnormally high and labor is relatively scarce. Protection would result in an absorption of unemployed or underemployed agricultural labor in manufacturing by inducing an expansion of import-competing output. The transfer of labor to manufacturing will presumably lower labor costs in that sector, and enhance the nation's competitive viability by eliminating its disadvantage in this regard. This argument centers around the idea that economic advance historically is almost always associated with industrialization; i.e., labor productivity can be raised above the low level prevailing in agriculture only in this manner. Hence, trade restrictions that result in a redistribution of labor from agriculture to industry—from low-productivity to high-productivity employment—foster economic growth.

The idea that a nation's real income can be raised by transferring productive resources from low-yield to high-yield uses applies also to other factors of production, especially capital. This is true of any significant gap between social and private costs, and there is no guarantee that protection designed to influence the deployment of labor will not simultaneously affect the allocation of other productive factors adversely. The question is whether desirable resource transfers can be brought about selectively, in such a way that the adverse side effects do not outweigh them. In this regard tariffs and other protective devices seem decidedly inferior to policies designed directly to enhance resource mobility.

Besides, there is some question about agricultural underemployment it-self. How significant is it? Is there really a permanent and substantial difference in the productivity of labor between primary and secondary in-dustries—i.e., between agriculture and manufacturing? Labor productivity in the industrial sector may be equally low, or only marginally higher, than in agricultural pursuits. And even if there were significant differences, there is little evidence that agricultural skills are immediately adaptable to industrial tasks, again pointing out that protection by itself is indeed an inferior way of achieving labor transfers effectively. Social barriers must be removed, retraining programs instituted, and the supply of cooperant factors improved in order for unemployed and any existing underemployed labor to shift to more gainful pursuits either in the industrial sector, or in any other area.

There thus appears to be relatively little substance to the case for protec-tion as a means of promoting growth through industrialization in underde-veloped countries. This is so, apart from the fact that industrialization and the de-emphasis of agriculture may really constitute a diversion from the optimum growth path, particularly if agriculture is the prime source of exports. Underutilized resources should be shifted to more productive employments, either in primary or in secondary production, and protection is a very poor way of achieving this. On the other hand, protection may contribute something by reducing the risk factor on private capital investments.

Perhaps a more persuasive objection to free trade under conditions of economic backwardness (again related to the question of economic and social costs and returns), is based on the idea that import-competing indus-tries give rise to significant external economies which benefit other parts of the economy. The total yield of such an industry equals its private returns plus its social returns, and yet the industry is judged solely on its private returns. Since total yields are understated, perhaps protection from foreign competition is justified.

External benefits of protected industries may be realized in several ways. Techniques used in the protected industry may be adopted by other industries, thereby raising their productive efficiency. Output of this indus-try may be used as inputs by other industries with substitution for other inputs at, hopefully, eventually lower costs. Supplier industries evolve as satellites and gain importance in their own right, with the concurrent devel-opment of joint facilities raising the productive efficiency of all firms. All of these external forces, resulting from the protected growth of a significant industry, may well raise the social yield of that industry to very high levels that more than justify the protection granted.

Whether or not this argument for protection can be considered valid depends, naturally, upon the magnitude of the social benefits derived.

These will vary widely from one situation to the next, but the necessary protection must be accorded at the outset. Since protection is based on estimates which have wide margins for error, mistakes will be made—mistakes that may go uncorrected for substantial periods of time. Even if protection is justified on the basis of social returns exceeding private returns, and the protected industry eventually becomes competitive as a result of external and internal cost reductions, there is no assurance that the trade restrictions will then be removed.

Whereas it is not difficult to visualize circumstances under which this argument for protection of import-competing industries in developing countries might apply, the need for careful analysis of the possibilities for external benefits cannot be stressed enough. Moreover, what evidence is there that these same external benefits upon which the protection argument rests are not also applicable to *export* industries? Would not free trade with export-centered development bring substantially the same external benefits with none of the costs engendered by protection? The real question is whether the external gains are greater in the export- or in the import-competing industries. Only if this is true of the latter and import-competing industries possess very substantial advantages over export industries will the case for protection hold up.

ACCELERATING GROWTH

Apart from the above reasons for departing from free trade, both of which are designed to support economic development in specific ways, there are more general arguments against free trade. These arguments also rest on the idea that restriction of imports is one way to speed up the growth process.

In most developing countries the demand for a broad range of consumer goods over and above basic staples is satisfied largely through imports. Increases in incomes tend to spill over more or less directly onto imported goods. Suppose consumer goods that might substitute for imports are not available domestically—which is certainly a reasonable assumption in the case of the majority of underdeveloped economies. Import restrictions then cause people to save a greater proportion of their income, either voluntarily or involuntarily through inflation induced by the restrictions. If import restrictions caused savings to rise, domestic-capital formation may be accelerated and the released foreign exchange can be used to import capital goods from abroad. Even if domestic residents do not materially reduce their *expenditures* on imported consumer goods, as a result of tariffs, for instance, a substantial part of these expenditures go to the government as customs duties, and the savings function is performed in this manner.

Increasing voluntary or involuntary saving at home by means of trade restrictions is one way the tools of commercial policy can be used to raise the rate of capital formation in underdeveloped countries. It is not out of the question, of course, that the capital formation called forth in this manner may largely be channeled into the production of import-substituting consumer goods. Domestically produced consumer goods would then merely substitute for those previously imported and the savings rate might drop to its previous level. The contribution of tariffs to capital formation in such a case would not be a sustained one. The beneficial effect will be even less, the more productive resources are withdrawn from the export sector as a result, thereby reducing the volume of exports.

There is another way in which capital formation can be supported by trade restrictions. Suppose the government lets it be known that after a certain date, a year or two hence, the tariff on finished consumer goods imports will be raised substantially, but the duty on components and raw materials will stay the same or be lowered. If the market is significant, foreign suppliers may set up assembly plants inside the tariff wall, making substantial direct investments in the process. Thereafter, a similar move could be made with regard to components, inducing further investment until the entire manufacturing process (along with the technology, entrepreneurship, managerial know-how, and so forth) has been transferred in. Eventually, the protective tariffs might be lowered and the industries originally attracted in this manner might even end up in the export sector. Precisely this kind of strategy has been used by some of the larger developing nations—with varying measures of success—notably by Brazil, India, and Mexico.

Another way in which trade restrictions may improve capital formation in developing countries is via the terms of trade. To the extent that tariffs or other import barriers—or export restrictions—do in fact result in an improvement in the terms of trade, real income will rise. If part of all of this income rise can be channeled into saving and investment, capital formation in turn will rise. As noted earlier, however, the possibility for developing countries to improve their terms of trade by trade restrictions under normal circumstances is slim indeed. This, combined with the difficulties involved in ensuring that the increased income is indeed devoted to saving and investment in the domestic economy, renders this particular policy of somewhat dubious value.

The desirability of import restrictions, as stimuli to economic growth through increased capital formation, attraction of foreign technology, and so forth, depends largely upon the development path that is chosen by the national policymakers under existing political and economic conditions. The idea of "balanced" versus "unbalanced" economic growth is often discussed in this connection. Those advocating "balanced" growth, contend that a variety of industries should be simultaneously established by underdeveloped countries in a parallel manner. Equally broad demand patterns and internal trade will then presumably evolve and hasten the development process.

Advocates of "unbalanced" growth disagree. They believe, instead, that the intensive development of a few, selected, export-oriented industries will *pull* with them a wide variety of supplier and satellite industries and that this will ensure optimum growth. The ends sought by the advocates of both approaches are the same, with the disagreement centering on the means of achieving these ends.

In either case, arguments are likely to be heard for protection as a way of speeding the balanced or selective, as the case may be, development of industries. Those advocating unbalanced growth may call for infant-industry protection for the "lead" industries on the grounds that they will eventually attain economic viability. A good deal more than protection may be required, and the likelihood that any lead industries will ultimately be in the import-competing sector in any case is relatively slight.

It is more likely that protection will be called for by proponents of balanced growth on the grounds that broadly based growth of domestic demand and supply is necessary for rapid development. This would appear to justify import barriers on a wide variety of commodities, since many of the industries slated for growth will indeed have to be import-competing. Some economists have carried this thesis to the point where protection is demanded on "infant economy" grounds. But there is little reason why balanced growth should have to concentrate on import-competing industries, and the wisdom of extensively protecting these same industries is open to question. The cost in terms of economic inefficiency and distortion of resource allocation may well outweigh whatever benefits are derived.

Perhaps even more fundamentally, one might question whether forced industrialization, either balanced or unbalanced, is an optimal way of attacking the problem of growth in the first place. Will not expansion of the industrial sector through protection siphon off agricultural resources which, to the extent that they are not underemployed, result in impeded agricultural output? Such developments could cause a significant reduction in agricultural exports, which might even be reflected in rising imports of farm commodities. In either case, the tendency would be a lower rate of capital formation and a reduction of the net gains from the industrialization program.

TRADE AS AN AGENT OF GROWTH

The arguments against free trade under conditions of economic backwardness are largely based on the premise that growth must be inward-oriented—i.e., it is based on the domestic market, and dependence on foreign markets is something of a liability. Yet we find countries, such as Japan, New Zealand, Norway, and Denmark, all of which have attained respectable growth rates, that are largely dependent upon foreign trade and seemingly thriving under it. Is it not possible that free international trade, far from being a hindrance to growth, can actually serve as the causative force of rapid economic progress?

An economy concentrating on rapid expansion of export industries along the lines of comparative advantage may indeed insure itself of both the "gains from trade" and the "gains from growth." It need not, as the above arguments for trade restrictions seem to imply, necessarily sacrifice the former in order to attain the latter. By emphasizing export production, the developing economy will be able to take advantage of a wide market— much wider than its own—which enables both capital and labor to be used more effectively in the production process. This, in turn, justifies the application of modern technology and permits internal and external economies of scale to be realized. At the same time, supplier and other industries receive the benefits of technological transfers and other external benefits from the export sector. The concentration upon export industries with wide markets, high efficiency, and rapid growth will also elevate the rate of capital formation—both internally generated and attracted from abroad—while the relatively free importation of foreign products itself has a beneficial "demonstration effect" on the indigenous economy. This last element is particularly important. By stimulating acquisitive motives on the part of the local population, it may induce a certain "growth mentality" and behavior patterns conducive to rapid development, while at the same time inducing new ideas and techniques into local production through imitation.

Such arguments seem to bear some weight. Not only may a country better its static welfare by specializing according to the dictates of comparative advantage, and garnering the gains from international trade, but, by so doing, it also may simultaneously insure improvements in productive efficiency, the rate of capital formation, and various other growth elements. This assumes, of course, that the export industry does indeed undergo rapid growth. Why should not the export sector become the *leading* sector in the economy and pull the other sectors along in its upward path? This touches on a very basic question. Will any growth in the export sector *in fact* be transmitted to the remainder of the economy and thus result in the desired, ultimate, broadly based economic development we are looking for?

The answer depends on the type of export industry that is involved and on the ease with which the decisive linkages with the rest of the economy can be established. This is essentially an institutional question. The nature of the export industry is also important in terms of the vertical supply relationships that exist between it and the rest of the economy, as well as the extent to which its output is, in turn, absorbed—or has the potential of being absorbed—at home. The stronger are these ties, the more likely it is that rapid growth in the export sector will be diffused. Finally, the type of market structure involved, i.e., the nature of existing competitive conditions, may also be of substantial significance in this regard. It is hardly surprising, therefore, that the real benefits to a developing economy of rapidly growing iron ore, copper, rubber, tobacco, tin, and meat export industries differ markedly from one another.

One way in which development policy can help insure that a nation's gains from trade will not preclude possible gains from growth is to encourage—in line with comparative advantage—greater value added in its export industries. Instead of exporting frozen fish, for example, a nation may shift to exports of fish filets, or fully processed and packaged fish products ready for consumption. This insures that more of the final value of the commodity, as it is consumed, is contributed by the exporting as opposed to the importing country.

There is also a question of the productive techniques employed in the export sector compared with those applied in the remainder of the economy. If export-production techniques are identical to those prevailing in the rest of the economy there will be little scope for benefit. It is also true, however, that the more *inappropriate* are these techniques to production in the remainder of the economy, the fewer will be the benefits attainable from rapid growth of the export sector. There is little question, for instance, that the techniques used for extracting, transshipping, and loading iron ore are of little use to an economy that is predominantly agricultural and simple, small-scale manufacturing in nature. If, on the other hand, any such techniques were directly or indirectly applicable on a broad scale, it would be quite another story.

Rapid export growth will tend to raise the real incomes of those engaged in the export sector. If some of this income is saved, this will tend to raise the national rate of capital formation. Some of these additional savings will be re-invested in export production. But it is not at all improbable that some will spill over into investments in the remainder of the economy. Moreover, it appears reasonable to expect that any such infusion of capital into nonexport production will grow as the possibilities for home-produced goods in the domestic market expand.

Of course, rapid income growth of those engaged in export production will also increase their consumption levels. Initially, this consumption may have to be satisfied almost entirely by imports since this is the only probable source of the kinds of goods that will be demanded. As this market grows, it may become increasingly feasible to start local production, first of rather basic consumer goods and then of increasingly sophisticated commodities.

In this way the growth of the export sector can be linked to the rest of the economy via *demand*. As the nonexport sectors grow, their ability to take over productive techniques already in use in export production increases, while some eventually evolve into export industries themselves.

We have already mentioned the vulnerability of export industries to market developments in other parts of the world—developments entirely beyond the control of the underdeveloped economies. This consideration can militate against the export sector's effectiveness in leading economic growth, even if all of the other factors are favorable. The growth rates in the export sector may fluctuate erratically. These variations may then be transferred back to the remainder of the economy and influence incomes, income distribution, employment, capital formation, and the attitudes of entrepreneurial groups toward the prospect of sustained growth. Variations in export growth naturally will also influence export receipts, and it thus becomes partly a balance of payments problem with significant induced variations in the capacity to import. Hence, even if all of the preconditions for export-led economic growth are fulfilled, there is no guarantee that the export sector will be a reliable engine of growth, if only because of the vagaries of the international marketplace.

COMMODITY AGREEMENTS

How may the fluctuations in export prices and receipts be stabilized so that the contribution of the export sector to economic growth can be materially enhanced? There are two sides to this question. They involve the stabilization of demand for and supply of the primary commodities which form the bulk of developing countries' exports. It is abundantly clear that individual underdeveloped nations normally are powerless to bring about such stability by regulating the volume of their exports and output. Generally, individual importing countries also can do little in this regard. Whatever stability is achieved must involve either bilateral agreements, between an exporting and an importing nation, or multilateral schemes, either among the supply nations or among the importing nations or both.

We have already looked at such schemes as long-term purchase commitments, quotas, and buffer stocks in connection with commercial policy. All of these are usually concluded bilaterally between developed and developing countries. Potentially more effective as a general proposition are commodity agreements, which underdeveloped nations almost always view with favor as a desirable solution to their export instability. There is, however, one major problem. Will it be possible for the stabilization schemes to avoid pegging prices at disequilibrium levels and seriously missing long-run price trends? The answer, and even opinions as to the importance of the question itself, are almost always couched in emotional terms. It is clear that any disequilibrium system, such as a commodity agreement, inevitably involves production quotas, disagreements among suppliers, stock-piling problems, and other technical difficulties. In addition, there is the very real possibility that if the agreed upon price is set at a sufficiently high level, substitutes may be developed to shut the affected commodity out of the market entirely. The last eventuality increases, the longer dis-equilibrium prices are maintained. To many economists in developed na-tions, the whole problem of international commodity-price stabilization smacks of their own, often distasteful, agricultural support programs.

Analytically, the operation of commodity agreements is quite simple. In Figure 28–1, curve D represents the demand for a developing nation's

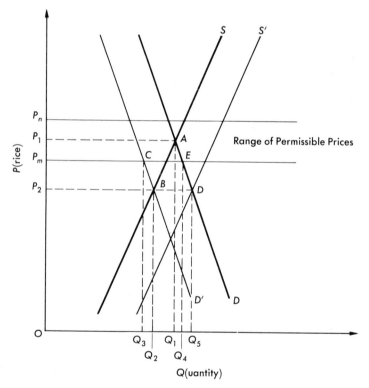

Fig. 28–1. Commodity price stabilization.

exports of a given primary commodity. Curve S, which is likely to be relatively inelastic, represents that country's supply of the commodity for export. Suppose equilibrium price and quantity are initially P_1 and Q_1, re-spectively. A fall in export demand to D' would reduce the price to P_2, quantity exported to Q_2, and export receipts from the original OP_1AQ_1 to OP_2BQ_2. By establishing a *minimum price* of P_m, the commodity agreement prevents export prices from falling below that level. Given an identical demand reduction from D to D', export receipts would fall to OP_mCQ_3, which is substantially above the corresponding receipts under free-market conditions.

In a similar manner, commodity agreements will prevent a drastic price reduction resulting from an inordinate expansion of export supply. Suppose supply grew, perhaps due to unusually favorable crop conditions, from S to S'. With constant foreign demand D price would fall to P_2, and export receipts would be reduced from P_2 and export receipts would be reduced from OP_1AQ_1 to OP_2DQ_5. By limiting the price reduction to P_m, the commodity agreement assures that export receipts fall to only OP_mEQ_4.

It is not difficult to see that commodity agreements will be more effective in preventing a fall in export receipts in response to supply and demand shifts: (a) the more inelastic is the foreign demand, and (b) the more inelastic is the domestic export supply.

In a similar way, an upward limit may be set on prices, P_n in Figure 28-1, in order to prevent erratic short-term price increases with possibly damaging effects on domestic resource allocation.

It is generally accepted that, even if they can be applied successfully, commodity agreements will be able to stabilize prices of only a limited number of commodities. Commodities for which there are competitive, close substitutes can be ruled out from the start as being unsuitable in this regard. Others, especially rice, involve major importing countries that also are underdeveloped and hence price stabilization would involve income redistribution *among* developing economies. Commodities often considered suitable for price stabilization include sugar, tea, coffee, cocoa, and bananas, largely because they are not, within limits, subjected to either of the above constraints.

The problems involved in establishing commodity-price stabilization agreements are manifold, especially if the supplier countries attempt to do it by themselves. Export quotas must be determined and allocated to the participating countries according to some mutually agreeable formula. These nations must then either find ways to reduce production of indigenous suppliers or to finance huge stockpiles, and perhaps both. Output reduction might be attacked by export taxation, alternative crop subsidies, or other measures designed to encourage producers to limit production of the commodity in question.

As is true of all international supply-limiting agreements, commodity price stabilization schemes tend to incorporate severe internal stresses that render them unstable at best. Countries find it economically and politically costly to adhere to such agreements, even if they are successfully negotiated. It is perfectly rational for such countries to attempt to dispose of surplus commodities on the world market if—as will normally be true—marginal receipts exceed marginal cost. This is tantamount to breaking the agreement, and, with more and more of the signatory nations engaging in such underhanded activities, any agreement to stabilize prices by limiting supply is bound to succumb. Politically as well, it is difficult for a nation to accept foreign control over its internal economic affairs and domestic welfare, which is really what multi-national commodity agreements involve. These tensions are similar to those working against the long-run stability of international cartels, for instance.

One way to get around this problem is to form commodity-price stabilization agreements in which *both* supplier and major importing nations are involved. It is much more difficult, under such circumstances, for suppliers to evade the terms of the agreement. This substantially enhances its viability. More likely than not, any such agreements will have to embody an extensive and effective control apparatus, including severe penalities for noncompliance. Provisions for substantial stockpiling, plus some encouragement to agricultural diversification, are also likely to be part of such agreements. In any case, efforts to hold the agreement together through the inevitable crises will have to be energetic indeed. Relatively successful experiments along these lines are the International Coffee Agreement, negotiated in 1962, and on the supply end alone, the West African Cocoa Marketing Board.

And, of course, there is oil. The Organization of Petroleum Exporting Countries (OPEC) in the early 1970's showed that prices could be successfully raised (a) *if* the product is reasonably homogeneous, (b) *if* no good substitutes exist, at least in the short run, (c) *if* a large proportion of incremental supplies are in the hands of cartel members, (d) *if* the cartel itself is cohesive, and (e) *if* some members of the cartel are willing to cut back supplies. In the OPEC case, the latter condition was made possible by a political event in the October 1973 Arab–Israeli war and by the fact that some of the major suppliers (e.g., Saudi Arabia, Kuwait, Libya) were strongly united in a politico-military effort and could in fact cut back supplies without doing significant damage to themselves. Whether these same conditions for unified action exist in the case of other primary commodities is indeed doubtful.

Nobody denies that price instability of primary commodities is deleterious to economic growth in the developing nations. It increases the degree of uncertainty involved in development planning and sets off fluctuations in most of the agents of growth, particularly in capital formation. Whether or not commodity agreements provide the solution is open to question, as experience with the somewhat analogous farm-support programs in developed nations amply testifies. But it does constitute one answer which can be made to work in a reasonably satisfactory manner, albeit only through intense cooperation among those concerned. Alternatives involve internal commercial tax and government-expenditures policies that may well prove to be insufficient and unable to provide the desired degree of stability. This is especially true if the export of primary commodities is of overwhelming importance to the national economy.

TRADE, DEVELOPMENT, AND ENVIRONMENT

One of the interesting questions related to the economic growth process is its impact on the human environment. Many countries have made the political decision that productive resources must be allocated to environmental protection even if this means a reduction in the rate of growth. Aside from the direct growth implications, environmental control has international trade and financial implications as well, particularly if—as seems likely—different countries will approach the problem in different ways, at different rates of speed, employing different techniques, and operating under different environmental conditions.

Some of the international economic consequences are fairly clear-cut. A shift in international competitiveness may develop between environmental leaders and laggards with possible balance of payments implications—although payments dislocations may be largely absorbed by exchange-rate flexibility. Different products have different environmental costs associated with them, so that the structure of trade of individual countries may shift. Investment in new or expanded plants precluded from domestic sites for reasons of pollution may spill over internationally, with implications for both trade and investment flows. Relative prices may shift between natural raw materials and their synthetic substitutes. International transport may become more costly and occasionally disrupted.

These are only some of the possible directions of the effects of environmental control on the international economy, and it is still too early to tell how important they may eventually become. Nevertheless, this is an area that certainly bears watching.

POTENTIAL CONTRIBUTIONS OF TRADE

We have outlined the possible conflicts between trade and growth as sources of gains for developing economies. Few would deny that these are of considerable significance in this context, and this has given rise to numerous arguments against free trade on the part of underdeveloped economies. Of course, we also saw that trade *can* indeed play a leading role in economic development, as it has in many of today's advanced countries. This is true despite allegations of secularly declining terms of trade facing primary-commodity-producing areas. The entire question may boil down to (a) the "penetrative power" of trade vis-à-vis the remainder of the economy and (b) the effectiveness of the linkages between it and the export sector. The latter, we noted, often leave a great deal to be desired.

Along these lines, improvements of economic and social mobility of the population is important, as are reductions in monopolistic and monopsonistic elements in the economy. Disfunctional social, political, economic, and cultural institutions and attitudes should be modified in order to be more attuned to the efficient transmission of forces from the export sector to the remainder of the economy. Much more can be done in this regard through substantial investments in the social and economic infrastructure— in schools, hospitals, vocational training institutes, communications and transportation facilities, stable and enlightened government, and so forth. Government policies toward growth must also be attuned to the conditions at hand, with active encouragement of entrepreneurship, saving, and investment, or even assumption of this role by the government itself should the private sector find it impossible.

With a flexible, adaptable economy able to absorb and productively utilize trade-induced benefits and insure that they are diffused effectively, the preconditions for export-led growth are at hand. It then becomes necessary to insure that *de facto* stability and expansion of export receipts is as strong as possible. This may be approached multilaterally or bilaterally via trade-liberalization agreements with the advanced countries. For the individual developing economy, this means enhanced competitiveness, both with regard to competing primary-products suppliers and to substitute commodities. In this vein, it is also important to insure that export production is carried out as efficiently as possible, with the possibility in mind of eventually expanding the domestic value added over and above existing stages of processing.

Perhaps equally important, developing economies must remain flexible in the sense of being able to shift resources to more rapidly growing exports should the circumstances warrant. In this way a strong export stimulus to growth can be insured, even given the inevitable vagaries of international demand patterns, particularly with a view toward the ever changing makeup of industrial inputs brought about by advancing technology.

We have already mentioned that, despite the relative narrowness of the home market, it is not at all inconceivable that underdeveloped countries may eventually become significant exporters of manufactured goods—even of manufactures largely unrelated to their primary commodity exports. Such exports may be destined for other developing countries at relatively similar stages of economic advance, or even directed to developed nations. None of this precludes temporary, selective import restrictions designed to nurse import-competing industries along to the point where they are able to survive on their own.

Ultimately, the possibilities for export-led growth, as outlined in perhaps somewhat optimistic terms here, hinges largely upon the nature of growth policies that are adopted by the indigenous governments. These should not be underestimated, for they determine the suitability and adaptability of the economy to export-led growth. Structural readjustments and temporary setbacks must be taken into account as being part of the growth process. Policies designed solely to offset such adjustments are merely attacking the *symptoms* of growth in a largely negative way and benefiting overall growth relatively little.

29

TRADE, GROWTH, AND MULTINATIONAL ENTERPRISE

In this, the concluding chapter of this lengthy volume, we shall discuss one of the principal actors on the international economic stage: the multinational corporation (MNC). All of the issues we have examined—trade theory, commercial policy, foreign exchange and the balance of payments, and the international economics of development—are profoundly influenced by the MNC, which actually *does* on a transnational basis all of the things that concern the international economic and financial position of national states. It does them quickly, efficiently, and often effectively and this is where many of the MNC's costs and benefits to the international economy lie.

The multinational corporation did not become a household word until well into the 1960's. A unique combination of factors suddenly propelled it into the public spotlight: (a) balance of payments deficits and persistent unemployment in the United States; (b) inflation, capital inflows, and growing foreign ownership of businesses in Canada and Western Europe; (c) rising nationalism, alleged neo-Colonialism, and faltering economic progress in many developing countries; (d) the instability of an international monetary system increasingly vulnerable to massive short-term capital movements toward the close of the Bretton Woods era; and (e) political turmoil in many parts of the world.

People searched for common threads running through all of these troublesome political and economic trends. Many thought they had found such a common thread in the multinational corporation. It appeared to be something new and exciting, something nobody knew very much about, and hence unknown in its potential for good or evil. Links existed—or were alleged to exist—between the multinational firm and each of the disturbing international developments of the time. And so it was easily concluded that we were faced with an awesome new force, operating outside the confines of national law and national control, which could very well turn out to be a malignancy in the world economic and political order.

Of course, the multinational enterprise has existed during most of this century and, in another form, during the Colonial period. While it is nothing new in concept, the multinational corporation has gradually assumed the role of a central determinant of the future shape of the international economy. Many of the real effects of the multinational firm on income, employment, trade, transfer of technology, and related questions would materialize sooner or later anyway, as a result of shifting economic structures in a relatively open world economy. But now they occur much more *rapidly* and more *dramatically,* accompanied by almost instantaneous applications of entrepreneurship and managerial skill, and this has made the multinational firm an object of intense scrutiny and public debate. Let us outline several of the major issues surrounding the multinational corporation and its influence on the economy and society in which it operates.

WHAT MNC'S DO

The first question is a definitional one: What is a "multinational corporation"? We can define it as a firm that maintains and controls production facilities in two or more national states, and that operates these facilities as part of an integral logistical network. It takes the form of a unified management and planning *system* in which interdependence of costs, competitiveness, technology, procurement, marketing, profitability, and decision-making is clearly recognized. The *behavior* of management and the control of operations are obvious determinants in deciding which firms are indeed multinational and which merely operate foreign subsidiaries as independent profit centers in the form of appendages with substantially separate decision systems. This is one reason why the line between multinational and other firms is rather unclear, and one of the grounds for the confusion that often surrounds the issue. Nor can the definitional question be dismissed as mere semantics, since the impact of the multinational enterprise on national economies is in large measure dependent on its transnational systems-approach to management.

Most often, a multinational firm is identified with a given "home" country in terms of ownership and management—although its equity may be held by individuals and institutions in many countries and a number of foreigners may be found among its top management. Generally, it is identified with the manufacturing sector, although the services sector is increasingly involved as well. Typically, the affiliates of multinational firms will assimilate comfortably into the economy, society, and culture of the "host" country, and frequently will take on the public image of a "domestic" firm. While ultimate control is invariably exercised by corporate headquarters, management ranks are normally filled predominantly by local personnel, often operating with considerable autonomy.

The multinational corporation is closely identified with foreign direct investment, which during the past decade has grown substantially more rapidly than either world trade or world production. To cite some figures, U.S. direct foreign investment in manufacturing during the 1960's increased at an average annual rate of about 11.6 per cent measured by book value and 12.3 per cent measured by sales of foreign affiliates, compared with 9.3 per cent for world trade and 7.0 per cent for world industrial production. The role of the multinational firm in this growth can be seen in the increased share of the manufacturing sector in U.S. foreign direct investment from 32 per cent in 1959 to over 40 per cent in 1970. It can also be seen in a tendency to acquire *existing* foreign firms, which frequently seems to be a characteristic of purposeful corporate planning in a multinational context.

To a significant extent, the competitive advantages that the multinational corporation seems to enjoy can be traced to the fact that it is indeed multinational: It is in a position to make a careful analysis—virtually disregarding political frontiers—of the cost of labor, capital, and other productive resources, labor skills, proximity to markets, and a host of related factors. It then analyzes its present and prospective product-mix, and determines *what* can best be done *where* in the context of a global or regional logistical network. Sometimes it acts in a manner identical to its local competitors in a given host country. Sometimes it assembles or makes components from imported or local materials and sends them to another country for further processing. Often it merely assembles final products for local or third markets. Sometimes it produces nothing at all in the host country and maintains only a marketing operations. Occasionally its local productive operations are limited to a research and development function, for which the firm itself is the sole customer.

The point is that by operating intra-firm logistics on a global scale, the multinational firm can significantly lower costs by taking advantage internally of the traditional gains from international trade discussed in Chapters 4 and 5, allocating productive factors more rationally, and sharing these gains with its customers (in the form of lower prices) and its suppliers of labor, capital, and other resources (in the form of higher prices). One of the symptoms of this process is a tendency for international trade to shift from *finished* products to *intermediate* products, which indeed seems to be taking place.

But the multinational firm can also trace its competitive advantage to the fact that it *itself* creates efficiency. It typically represents a highly effective collector, transferor, and assimilator of information concerning the market—demand, supply, technology, transport, and so forth. In this way it overcomes lack of knowledge, one of the major impediments to competition in the international marketplace. The multinational corporation in addition tends to be an innovator in the development and application of modern management techniques—which it then applies, where appropriate, in each of its operating units. Things that don't work get discarded; those that do work rapidly get adopted globally as a matter of company policy. Not least important, multinationals tend to be highly innovative in production, distribution, and new-product technology—again disseminated rapidly throughout the firm—and this often provides a competitive lead based on know-how in the various markets they serve.

A basic issue is whether the multinational firm's unprecedented capabilities for increasing efficiency in the international economy are always in fact employed in the pursuit of this goal. Or whether it frequently uses these same unique advantages to restrict competition and, by exercising monopoly power, retain for itself many of the benefits that are supposed to accrue to the international economy generally. That this in fact happens is beyond doubt. The extent to which it indicts the multinational firm as an institution potentially inimical to the public interest is still open to question.

From the American vantage point, the multinational firm certainly has not been an unmixed blessing, and has created a number of problems for U.S. trade and for the national economy. It has probably served to increase the average size of business firms and may on occasion inhibit effective competition. It reduced the "technology gap" that served for years as an underpinning of U.S. export competitiveness. And together with increased captive-imports, this phenomenon seems to many to have eroded the U.S. competitive position in merchandise trade and accelerated shifts in national industrial structure that are not in themselves costless. It has strengthened the U.S. position with respect to international trade in services, including earnings on foreign investments, and has reinforced the apparent trend toward a services-oriented economy in the United States. The basic question is whether these adjustment burdens outweigh the undeniable benefits that the multinational firm provides. Perhaps the most sensitive problem of all concerns employment.

EMPLOYMENT EFFECTS AND ECONOMIC ADJUSTMENT

There is the general presumption that employment trends move in much the same direction as direct foreign investment; that countries playing host to multinational firms can expect positive employment effects while the home countries—as capital exporters—must expect some job-displacement.

This is a highly sensitive political issue in the United States and other MNC headquarters countries, giving rise to proposals intended to curb foreign operation of MNC's and impose restrictions on competitive imports linked to MNC operations.

Whether or not job-displacement is a significant burden attributable to the multinational firm is difficult to establish, if only because so many factors affect employment patterns—of which international investment is only one. Besides, even if there has been some job-displacement, it hardly follows that national material welfare is on balance harmed when all of the effects on productivity, terms of trade, earnings on capital, and externalities are considered. But this is not a politically telling argument—aside from basically insoluble problems involved in generating defensible estimates of net welfare effects—and so the employment issue has assumed a high level of significance in its own right.

Proponents of the job-displacement thesis argue that direct foreign investment by the multinational corporation can largely be traced to international differences in labor costs. Through offshore production it eliminates markets previously (or potentially) served by exports, and hence export-dependent jobs. It even serves the home market through captive-imports of goods previously produced domestically. In the process, workers are displaced and must bear the cost of relocating, retraining, and being transitionally unemployed while the firm happily enhances its overall profitability.

The other side argues that very often direct foreign investment is needed to get around other countries' trade barriers, or to overcome prohibitive labor-cost differentials, and thus serves markets that would not have produced exports anyway. It has been demonstrated that multinational corporate operations are highly sensitive to trade barriers in establishing production facilities, in terms of a significant positive correlation between effective rates of protection and the relative volume of production and sales of foreign-owned affiliates going on behind it. International *capital flows* are thus instrumental in securing the gains that otherwise would flow from international *trade* and specialization, and the multinational enterprise is instrumental in promoting this shift. Similarly, rapidly expanding foreign markets sometimes can only be served by on-site production facilities. And if offshore production for subsequent importation into the U.S. were not undertaken by American multinationals, foreign firms would soon capture this market. Besides, exports of capital equipment, parts, and components associated with direct foreign investment—together with administrative personnel needed to oversee foreign operations—probably reduce or eliminate most or all of any job-displacement effect that might otherwise occur.

Who is right? The evidence is contradictory. Some estimates purport to show that a half-million jobs have been *lost* in the U.S. as a result of adverse trade movements, of which a major part can be traced directly to multinational corporate operations. Another set of estimates produced at about the same time shows a *gain* of over half a million U.S. jobs as a result of these same factors. Most other studies conclude that the employment effect has been, on balance, positive but not very significantly so.

The reader who remembers Part I of this book may wonder what all of the excitement is about. After all, isn't labor as a factor of production *supposed* to be affected by trade and capital flows? And isn't the multinational firm to be *congratulated* for helping the process along and accelerating the reallocation of the world's resources in a more rational way? Unfortunately we don't live in a world of theory, and the adjustment process is a socially painful one. By increasing the speed of required adjustment, the multinational firm has become a major target of those who do not wish to adjust—or desire to adjust more slowly. In any case, the debate on employment effects will continue and may even lead to commercial and financial controls in the not too distant future. Fortunately, the employment effects in capital-receiving countries are generally beneficial—although significant labor shortages may develop from time to time. But there is always the risk of an eventual letdown if and when conditions change and the multinational corporation suddenly takes its operations elsewhere.

CAPITAL MARKETS AND INTERNATIONAL PAYMENTS

The impact of multinational firms on capital markets is not as politically sensitive—and perhaps not as visible in terms of serious adjustment burdens—as in the case of labor. Nevertheless, their operations have induced strains on various national capital markets from time to time, particularly in host countries where the generally superior credit rating of such firms may give them an edge over local competitors. And by bringing general corporate resources to bear in a given market, by obtaining capital where it is cheap and using it where it brings the highest return, the multinational firm does contribute to a rational utilization of this particular resource, with commensurate gains for lenders, for consumers, and for the firm itself.

There is a unique problem with regard to the impact of the multinational firm on capital markets in developing countries, where a special incentive to borrow derives from a desire by the firm to reduce its own political risk exposure. The allegation is that local firms are denied competitive access to sources of funds, that this may bias the developing industrial structure toward foreign ownership, and that a balanced and rational growth pattern and coherent development planning will be more difficult to achieve. The evidence available thus far does not lend much support to this thesis. But this hardly denies the potential seriousness of the problem.

Closely related is the impact of the multinational firm on the balance of payments. For the MNC's home country the speed and magnitude of payments disturbances are likely to be greater than if such firms did not exist. International transfers of capital and technology imply an adverse payments shifts due to export-displacement, import-stimulus, and the initial capital outflow itself. Although this shift automatically sets in motion off-setting flows of investment earnings, royalties, exports of components, and so forth, its abruptness can increase pressures on foreign exchange markets and the international payments adjustment process.

Such "basic" payments disturbances are paralleled by short-term insta-bility contributed by multinational firms with large cash balances, receiv-ables, and debt, striving to anticipate shifts in relative currency values. Do they engage in the kinds of "hot money" flows that have made life miserable for central bankers in the last year of Bretton Woods? They would be fools not to. And even if the treasurers of multinational firms operate only *defen-sively* to hedge against possible foreign exchange losses, their actions would contribute substantially to international financial instability. But the fault lies not with them, but with a system of exchange rates that delayed neces-sary adjustments until one-way speculation and the resulting crises are in-evitable. The answer probably does not lie in condemning the multinational enterprise as a culprit, but in changing the rules of international finance to more appropriately govern the nature of the balance of payments adjust-ment process as it exists in the real world.

TECHNOLOGY TRANSFERS

One explanation for the success of multinational firms focuses on techno-logical gaps. Even in the early days of foreign business activity in tropical agriculture and extraction of fuels and raw materials, the justification of such operations was based on the fact that local enterprise had either the capital nor the know-how to exploit available indigenous resources. Con-flicts naturally arose from time to time and sometimes involved serious inter-national political strains, but by and large foreign firms were welcomed in host countries who felt that, all things considered, they had more to gain than to lose.

This pattern of multinational corporate involvement based on flexibility, skill, and know-how carried over into the industrialization era in the devel-oping countries. Foreign firms were welcome to manufacture locally prod-ucts which otherwise would have to be imported, and for which technical capabilities were lacking domestically. Direct foreign investment frequently represented a mandatory component of the national growth strategy, whether based on import substitution or export expansion. This partly ex-plains the active involvement of multinational firms in developing countries which clearly is *not* based on taking advantage of cheap indigenous labor for use in captive-export production.

What happens when the know-how gap narrows? The multinational firm becomes increasingly vulnerable as the apparent benefits to the host country decline; the country may have generated the necessary expertise itself, or can buy it from abroad on a contract basis. The entry of local firms may sharpen the competitive environment, and may cause shifts in public policy biased against the foreign-owned subsidiary. The end result can be a significant diminution of the multinational firm's control over its own operations. As the pressure mounts, the firm is increasingly forced to search for new ways to widen the know-how gap and reestablish its value to the host country. If it cannot provide the new goods or new expertise that would maintain its allure, or if it has no special control over export markets or sources of key imported supplies, it must count on gradual encroachment on its autonomy. The result may be greatly increased governmental participation in its operations, even nationalization or expropriation.

In such cases, multinational firms find themselves constantly striving to keep the technological gap wide enough to justify their own existence in a cost-benefit balance as viewed from the perspective of developing host countries preoccupied with their *current* (not past) contributions to social welfare. At the same time, the firm may try to reduce its risk exposure by increasing the proportion of local debt (but not equity) in its capital structure. It may try to reduce the diffusion of know-how by minimizing the throughput of local employees in critical skill areas. It may tend to concentrate its output for the local market in product lines where the know-how gap is relatively wide. All of these defensive techniques may further erode its position in the local economy and intensify the pressure.

This kind of scenario obviously does not explain the rather successful operation of multinational firms in the industrial countries, where the technological gap is small or nonexistent, without undue pressure from host governments. This is partly explained by the realization by government that vigorous competition is good for local industry; that local firms are themselves involved in foreign ventures and hence are in no position to demand sanctions against foreign subsidiaries; that multinational firms insure rapid diffusion of technology, so that the host country can remain on the cutting edge of technical progress regardless where these innovations are generated. The implication is that rapid growth of market-oriented economies in the less developed countries is fundamentally in the interest of multinational firms by reducing the kind of adverse pressures just mentioned and placing the cost/benefit nexus on an entirely different—and more favorable—footing.

THE POLITICAL ENVIRONMENT

This brings us to the political and legal conflicts surrounding the multinational enterprise, particularly between the firm and the host country. The most difficult is outright nationalism: that firms operating in a given country ought to be staffed, managed, controlled, and owned by nationals of that country. Nationalistic instincts are ubiquitous, and are appealed to whenever political conflicts involving multinational corporations arise—some for entirely legitimate reason.

There is the problem, for example, of foreign subsidiaries being subject to host-country laws yet at the same time having to abide by home-country regulations (legal extraterritoriality) in such areas as antitrust and East–West trade. Carried further, there is often the nagging suspicion that the multinational firm may at times act as a political agent for its home government, either because this is endemic to the system or in return for national political support when the firm gets into trouble. Then there is the problem of taxation: By using imaginative pricing policies, the multinational firm is frequently in a position to minimize its overall tax burden by taking its profits in low-tax countries. When a host country tries to redress what it regards as an inequity, political problems often arise.

Another hot political issue has been extraterritoriality of decision-making: Where decisions fundamentally affecting the local economy—including cessation of operations—are made thousands of miles away at corporate headquarters with little or no regard for their broader impact on the host country. The multinational firm may also exploit its market power to drive local competitors out of business, or dominate large segments of local industry.

To a large extent, political conflicts arise from a misunderstanding of how multinational business *really* operates and how it can best be used in the national interest. Some are convinced that multinational firms will do exactly what they can get away with—no more, no less. In many advanced countries what the firm can get away with is clearly limited—by antitrust laws, by big labor, by national economic policies, by social, environmental, and consumer-oriented measures. When the firm moves into a different environment some of these countervailing forces may not exist or may be poorly developed, and the firm adopts policies that would never be tolerated at home and which sooner or later lead to political difficulties in the host country. Multinational enterprise is by its very nature extremely adept at operating under different sets of rules. It is largely up to the *host country* to make rules that best fit its own social, economic, and political goals. The multinational firm will then indicate whether it wants to play by those rules. If not, the country can seek alternative ways of accomplishing what the firm would have done. If so, the country may be successful in harnessing the unprecedented organizational, technological, and operational capabilities of the multinational corporation to achieve national goals in the most efficient possible manner.

Still missing in national efforts to maximize the benefits provided by the multinational enterprise—to harness its energies in pursuit of maximum economic welfare on a global scale—is some degree of international consistency in the rules governing its operations. As we have seen, rules have more or less dominated international trade and finance for decades, and they have contributed immeasurably to the evolution and maintenance of a viable international economic order. No such rules govern international investment, and this policy vacuum is the source of much uncertainty and conflict both on the part of firms and of governments. Agreement on some basic issues, such as nondiscrimination in national policies affecting foreign and domestic firms, would go a long way toward meeting this need. However, there remains a great deal of disagreement on the nature of such rules—and whether they are desirable at all—so that the prospects for progress in this important area of policy are not at all bright.

The multinational corporation *acts as if* there were not national political frontiers, and in doing so has greatly intensified international economic interdependence. It has eroded national economic sovereignty, much to the discomfort of politicians. But this discomfort may well be a sign that multinational enterprise is doing the job it is supposed to do, that on balance it represents a major contribution to an improved international economic order. There is nothing sacred about it. It is a *tool* to be used by the world for its economic and political betterment, and its effectiveness can be maximized by viewing it as such.

Extensions and Additional Readings

Section E-1

General References and Historical Background

Recommended as collateral reading in conjunction with this volume is J. D. Richardson and R. E. Baldwin (eds.), *Selected Topics in International Trade and Finance: A Book of Readings* (Boston: Little, Brown, 1973). As an alternative, the following two books are highly recommended: Gerald M. Meier, *Problems of Trade Policy* (New York: Oxford University Press, 1973) and Robert Z. Aliber, *The International Money Game* (New York: Basic Books, 1973).

Prominent among the good general texts in international economics are Mordechai Kreinin, *International Economics: A Policy Approach* (New York: Harcourt Brace Jovanovich, 1971); and Charles P. Kindleberger, *International Economics*, 5th Edition (Homewood, Ill., Richard D. Irwin, 1973).

Two good texts at a more advanced level are Murray C. Kemp, *International Trade and Investment* (Englewood Cliffs, N.J.: Prentice-Hall, 1969), and I. F. Pearce, *International Trade* (New York: Norton, 1970). An advanced book relying on geometric presentation is Jaroslav Vanek, *International Trade: Theory and Economic Policy* (Homewood, Ill.: Richard D. Irwin, 1962). For a mathematical presentation, see Akira Takayama, *International Trade* (New York: Holt, Rinehart and Winston, 1972).

Students interested in empirical analysis in international economics should definitely obtain a copy of E. E. Leamer and R. M. Stern, *Quantitative International Economics* (Boston: Allyn and Bacon, 1970). An elaboration, in readable form, of some of the theoretical points contained in this book may be found in M. O. Clement, R. L. Pfister, and K. J. Rothwell, *Theoretical Issues in International Economics* (Boston: Houghton-Mifflin, 1967).

Two volumes of readings present some of the classic articles in the field: Howard S. Ellis and Lloyd A. Metzler (eds.). *Readings in the Theory of International Trade* (Homewood, Ill.: Richard D. Irwin, 1950); and R. E. Caves and H. G. Johnson (eds.), *Readings in International Economics* (Homewood, Ill.: Richard D. Irwin, 1968).

An excellent historical and institutional treatment may be found in John Parke Young, *The International Economy*, 4th ed. (New York: Ronald Press, 1964). Interested students are also referred to J. B. Condliffe, *The Commerce of Nations* (New York: Norton, 1950), which emphasizes the position of Great Britain as an international trader and banker, and to Jacob Viner, *Studies in the Theory of International Trade* (New York: Harper, 1937). See also Gottfried Haberler, "Integration and Growth of the World Economy in Historical Perspective," *American Economic Review*, March, 1964.

An account of Mercantilist ideas is contained in Eli F. Heckscher, *Mercantilism* (London: George Allen & Unwin, 1935) and in Gustav Schmoller, *The Mercantile System and Its Historical Significance* (New York: Peter Smith, 1931), reprinted from the German edition of 1881. Developments during the 1930's are vividly presented by Wilhelm Roepke, *International Economic Disintegration* (London: Stevens, 1942).

Section E-2A

Two-Factor Two-Product Analysis

The isoquant–isocost approach to production theory, as surveyed in Chapter 2, relates to the output of a single good using optimal combinations of two different factors of production. It is now possible to expand this analysis to include output of two different goods using two factor-inputs. In this way we will be able to build a very simplified but nonetheless useful economic model of the behavior of an entire economy. This will prove to be of substantial value in our subsequent analysis of the impact of international trade and commercial policy measures on economic structure, as well as upon the returns earned by the various factors of production.

We shall assume the existence of an economy which possesses only two productive factors, capital and labor, and produces only two types of commodities, A-goods and B-goods. The nation's resource endowments in the form of labor and capital must be fully employed in the production of the two types of goods in order for it to reach its output potential and thereby maximize its economic well-being. This is true no matter whether the emphasis is to be on the production of A-goods or on B-goods.

Referring to Figure E2–1, generally known as an Edgeworth-Bowley box diagram, the total capital endowment of the economy is given by the height of the box—the distance AG or, identically, BH. Similarly, the length of the box is taken to represent the nation's total endowment of labor (AH or BG). In order for both resources to be fully employed, the total labor force AH and capital stock AG must be entirely committed to production.

The use of labor and capital in the production of the A-good is represented by a series of isoquants A_1, A_2, A_3, and so on, signifying successively higher output levels of that particular commodity. Similarly, utilization of the two factors in the production of the B-good is pictured by means of a series of isoquants B_1, B_2, B_3, and so on, beginning at the B-origin and increasing toward the lower left corner of the box. Any output combination of A-goods and B-goods where an A-isoquant crosses, or is tangent to, a B-isoquant will use up all of the available capital and labor. The reader can easily verify for himself that production of the A-good at one point in the box and production of the B-good at another point represents an under-utilization of resources, i.e., less than full employment of all available capital and labor. Factor use will, however, be optimized only where an A-isoquant is *tangent* to a B-isoquant.

This proposition may be easily demonstrated. Suppose it is decided to produce at point T. Output of the A-good is AT and output of the B-good

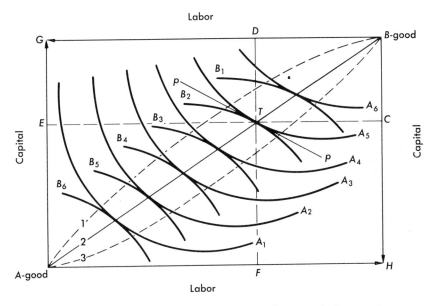

Fig. E2–1. Two-factor, two-product analysis.

is *BT*. At this point, *BC* of capital is used in the production of *B*-goods, and the remainder of the capital stock (*CH* or *AE*) is employed in producing the *A*-good. The amount *BD* of the available labor force is used in producing the *B*-good, and *AF* (or *DG*) in producing the *A*-good. Both resources, labor and capital, are fully employed in production at point *T*, where *A*-isoquant A_5 is tangent to *B*-isoquant B_2. It is impossible to produce more of one good without thereby simultaneously decreasing the production of the other.

But why could not *AT* of the *A*-good be produced at some point along isoquant A_5 other than point *T*? Because at any other point along A_5 it would be possible to increase production of the *B*-good *without* simultaneously reducing output of the *A*-good—by simply moving *along* isoquant A_5 toward point *T*. Hence, in general, the use of available inputs, here labor and capital, will be optimal only whenever an *A*-isoquant is tangent to a *B*-isoquant. This, of course, holds true not only for the tangency of A_5 and B_2 at point *T*, but also for the respective tangencies of $A_6 - B_1$, and $A_4 - B_3$, and so forth. At each individual tangency, different quantities of *A* and *B* will be produced, but optimal efficiency in factor use will nevertheless be maintained. The line 2 in Figure E2–1, connecting all possible tangencies of *A*- and *B*-isoquants, is called the *optimum-efficiency locus*. At each point along the optimum-efficiency locus, labor and capital are being employed to most efficiently produce different quantities of the *A*- and *B*-goods.

Suppose that instead of yielding a linear optimum efficiency locus such as line *2*, the various tangencies had fallen so that curve *3* turned out to represent the locus of all optimum-efficiency production points. It would then be clear that relatively more labor is used under optimum conditions in the production of the *A*-good, and that relatively more capital is used in producing the *B*-good. Commodity *A* would be considered to be *labor-intensive,* and commodity *B* would be termed *capital-intensive*. Exactly the opposite would hold true if curve *1* turned out to be the optimum-efficiency locus; the *A*-good would be deemed capital-intensive and the *B*-good, labor-intensive.

Returning for a moment to point T in Figure E2–1, AE of capital and AF of labor are used in the production of the *A*-good. The capital/labor ratio in the production of that good is therefore AE/AF. In the production of *B*-goods, the relevant capital/labor ratio at point T is BC/BD. In general, *intensity* with which productive factors are employed in the production of a given good is given by the slope of a straight line drawn from the origin assigned to that commodity to the production point. We saw in the previous section that, with optimal factor combinations in the production of any good, the marginal rate of substitution of one factor for the other will equal the ratio of the prices of the two factors. Under perfect competition, the price of labor relative to the price of capital at point T is given by the slope of a common tangent pp.

The effects of changes in factor endowments may also be analyzed by means of the same box diagram. Increases in the nation's capital stock, for instance, would be represented as an expansion of the vertical dimension of the box, while labor force growth would result in an extension of its horizontal dimension. Technological advance, which enhances the productivity of both labor and capital, would cause an increase in both the vertical and the horizontal dimensions of the box. Capital-saving technological change would extend primarily the vertical dimension of the box, while labor-saving technological change would effect primarily its horizontal dimension.

How each of these forces, as well as the existence of different factor endowments internationally, affects national economic structure and international economic relationships is the subject of discussions employing this type of analysis in Chapter 5. At the same time, this method is helpful in observing the impact of commercial policies on relative returns to productive factors as well as on the output-mix of various national economies engaged in international transactions, discussed in Chapters 7 and 8.

Section E-2B

Background Reading in Economic Analysis

One of the best treatments of price theory can be found in Richard H. Leftwich, *The Price System and Resource Allocation,* 5th Edition (Hillsdale, Ill.: Dryden Press, 1973). Somewhat more advanced, but equally good, is Edwin Mansfield, *Microeconomics: Theory and Application* (New York: Norton, 1970). At the introductory level, a first-rate and concise treatment is provided in Joseph P. McKenna, *Logic of Price* (Hillsdale, Ill.: Dryden Press, 1973).

See also Paul A. Samuelson, *Economics,* 9th Edition (New York: McGraw-Hill, 1973), which is recommended as well for an introductory review of macroeconomic theory and policy.

The student can sharpen his skills in national income determination by taking a look at Thomas F. Denburg and Ducan M. McDougall, *Macroeconomics,* 4th Edition (New York: McGraw-Hill, 1973). An efficient way to develop a solid foundation in this area is to work through a text such as William E. Mitchell, John H. Hand, and Ingo Walter, *Exercises in Macroeconomics* (New York: McGraw-Hill, 1973). In the monetary sector, a book that is both enjoyable and educational is Lawrence S. Ritter and William L. Silber, *Money,* 2nd Edition (New York: Basic Books, 1973).

Section E-3

Useful References on International Trade Statistics

Students are often at a loss where to find international trade statistics. These data are provided for the developed market-economy countries—basically, Western Europe, North America, and Japan—in Organization for Economic Cooperation and Development, Statistical Papers, Series C, *Trade by Commodities,* published monthly in Paris. This publication gives imports and export totals, by product according to the Standard International Trade Classification (SITC) scheme, and by country of origin or destination. The same thing can be obtained, for all countries that publish trade statistics, from the United Nations Statistical Office, Statistical Papers, Series D, *Commodity Trade Statistics,* published for each reporting country quarterly (Jan.–Mar., Jan.–June, Jan.–Sept., and Jan.–Dec.). Both publications include trade values in U.S. dollars and trade volumes in physical quantities (tons, units, etc.). Students are warned to make sure they are looking at the correct issue and data set for the information desired. Mistakes in gathering trade data can be the source of exquisite pain!

Both the U.N. and OECD provide summary statistics on exports and imports by broad product groups and by countries in various annual publications. For the European countries, another good source are the statistical offices of the European Communities in Brussels for data starting in the late 1950's. If all else fails, there are always statistics published at the national level, but these often are difficult to obtain and may create unforseen problems. Students intending to work with trade data can avoid grief and save a lot of time by first taking a look at the Leamer and Stern book, cited in Section E–1.

Section E-4

Additional Readings on Comparative Advantage

General surveys of international trade theory may be found in Richard E. Caves, *Trade and Economic Structure* (Cambridge, Mass.: Harvard University Press, 1963); Gottfried Haberler, *A Survey of International Trade Theory* (Princeton, N.J.: International Finance Section, Princeton University, 1961); and Jagdish Bhagwati, "The Pure Theory of International Trade," *Economic Journal,* March, 1964. More detailed presentation of the classical notions are contained in Gottfried Haberler, *The Theory of International Trade* (London: W. Hodge & Co., 1936); and Jacob Viner, *Studies in the Theory of International Trade* (New York: Harper, 1937).

An excellent modern account is presented in Ronald Findlay, *Trade and Specialization* (Baltimore: Penquin Books, 1970). For some of the original writings in convenient form, see William R. Allen, *International Trade Theory: Hume to Ohlin* (New York: Random House, 1965), especially the first half of the book.

The ideas of the early thinkers in international trade theory can be found in Adam Smith, *An Inquiry into the Nature and Causes of the Wealth of Nations* (London: 1799); David Ricardo, *On the Principles of Political Economy and Taxation* (London: 1817); John Stuart Mill, *Principles of Political Economy* (London: 1848); and Francis Y. Edgeworth, "The Theory of International Values," I and II, *Economic Journal,* March, September, and December, 1894.

Also C. F. Bastable, "On Some Disputed Points in the Theory of International Trade," *Economic Journal,* June, 1901; Gottfried Haberler, "The Theory of Comparative Costs Once More," *Quarterly Journal of Economics,* February, 1929; Frank William Taussig, "Wages and Prices in Relation to International Trade," *Quarterly Journal of Economics,* August, 1906; and Jacob Viner, "The Doctrine of Comparative Costs," *Weltwirtschaftliches Archiv,* No. 36, 1932.

Section E-5A

Factor Price Equalization

We can show, rather conveniently, how trade affects returns to the factors of production by applying the Edgeworth–Bowley box diagrams introduced in Section E–2A. Referring to Figure E5–1, the reader will recall that a series of isoquants, or equal-product curves, representing successively higher levels of output, are drawn outward from diagonally opposed origins for each of two commodities, A and B. At any point (such as R) where an A-isoquant touches a B-isoquant the available supply of both factors of production, here labor and capital, is being fully utilized. However, only at the points where an A-isoquant is *tangent* to a B-isoquant (such as at S) are the two productive factors being employed in the most efficient possible manner. All such tangencies of A- and B-isoquants de-

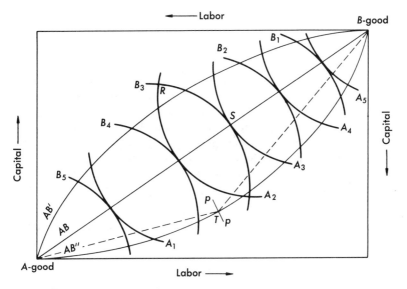

Fig. E5–1. Box diagram of possible national output combinations of two commodities with given factor supplies.

termine the line *AB,* the *optimum efficiency locus.* This optimum efficiency locus describes the set of output alternatives identical to the transformation functions, or production possibilities curves, with which we have worked up to now.

The point along *AB* (or along the corresponding transformation function) at which it is decided to produce hinges entirely upon demand considerations. If more of the *A*-good is demanded, production will be closer to the *B*-origin on line *AB.* If more of the *B*-good is demanded, the reverse will be the case.

Curve *AB* will be linear if both resources are used in the production of both commodities in equal proportions. If the *A*-good is labor intensive and the *B*-good is capital intensive, however, the optimum efficiency locus will be concave and similar to curve *AB″* in Figure E5–1. Conversely, the convex curve *AB′* will apply if the *A*-good is capital-intensive and the *B*-good is labor-intensive. These relationships will naturally also be reflected in the shape of the corresponding transformation function.

The proportions of productive factors used in the output of each of the two goods are given by the slope of a line drawn from the relevant origin to the production point. For example, if the optimum efficiency locus is *AB″,* and it is decided to produce a certain combination of the *A*- and *B*-goods given by point *T,* then the slope of the dashed line *AT* gives the proportions of labor and capital used in the production of the

A-good. With the same output combination at point T the slope of the dashed line BT represents the proportions of labor and capital used in the production of the B-good. The relative prevailing marginal products of the two factors under these circumstances—and hence their relative returns—are given by the slope of the common tangent to the two isoquants at the production point (in this case line pp, a common tangent to A- and B-isoquants, not drawn, at point T).

Note that the relative marginal products and returns of the two factors, as given by the slope of this common tangent, will change as production is shifted along either of the curved optimum efficiency loci. Only if the optimum efficiency locus is linear will the ratio of the marginal product of labor to the marginal product of capital be constant no matter how much of either good is produced.

We can now proceed to use this tool to show how international trade tends to bring about both commodity and factor price equalization by simply superimposing two box diagrams, representing the prevailing factor endowments in two trading nations, upon one another. Figure E5–2 does this. One of the two countries is labor-abundant, $ACB'D$, and the other is capital-abundant, $AEBF$. Both produce capital-intensive (B) goods and labor-intensive (A) goods. Their optimum efficiency loci are, respectively, AB and AB'.

In the absence of international trade, let us assume that the labor-abundant country produces at some point, R, consistent with domestic demand conditions, while the capital-abundant nation similarly produces at point T. Note that relative factor returns (the slopes of lines p and p') differ substantially between the two countries. In the labor-abundant country the returns to labor are low relative to the returns to capital, the scarce factor. The reverse is true in the capital-abundant country, with the marginal product (and returns) of capital low relative to that of labor.

With international trade, the labor-abundant country begins to specialize increasingly in the labor-intensive A-good, moving along its optimum efficiency locus toward B'. At the same time, the capital-abundant nation moves from point T in the direction of increased production of the capital-intensive good B. Trade will grow along the lines presented in the previous chapter, in the absence of transport costs, *until the prices of the two commodities are precisely equal* in the two countries at points V and S, respectively. With identical technologies and all other productive conditions the same, the proportions of labor and capital used in the production of the two commodities are equal for both countries, and the prevailing ratios of the returns of capital to the returns of labor (the slopes of common tangents p^2 and p^3) *must* therefore also be equal. All of this can be easily summarized as follows:

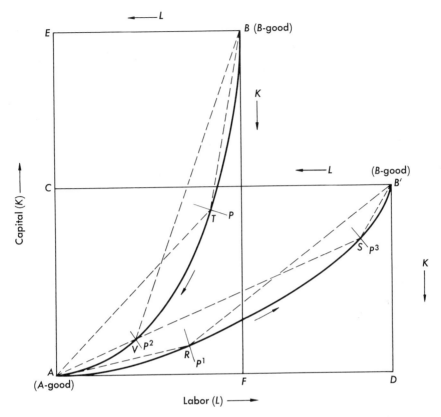

Fig. E5–2. Trade, production, and factor prices: two countries, two commodities, and two productive factors.

	Slope of:
Labor-abundant country, without trade:	
Proportions of labor and capital used in A-good	AR
Proportions of labor and capital used in B-good	B'R
Ratio of return of labor to return of capital	p'
Capital-abundant country, without trade:	
Proportions of labor and capital used in A-good	AT
Proportions of labor and capital used in B-good	BT
Ratio of return of labor to return of capital	p
Labor-abundant country, with trade:	
Proportions of labor and capital used in A-good	AS
Proportions of labor and capital used in B-good	B'S
Ratio of return of labor to return of capital	p^3
Capital-abundant country, with trade:	
Proportions of labor and capital used in A-good	$AV \ (= AS)$
Proportions of labor and capital used in B-good	$BV \ (= B'S)$
Ratio of return of labor to return of capital	$p^2 \ (= p^3)$

In short, commodity prices have been equalized between the two countries. In each case economic structure, in the form of output combinations, has shifted in the direction of increased specialization in the production of that commodity using relatively more of the abundant factor. Simultaneously, returns to the more abundant factor have increased relatively, while relative returns to the scarcer factor have declined in both countries. This has led to an equilization of the ratios of factor returns in the two economies, and the factor proportions (factor intensities) used in the production of both commodities have become identical for both national economies.

Section E-5B

The Stolper-Samuelson Theorem

Does international trade really alter the distribution of income?[1] Figure E5-3 depicts an optimum efficiency locus for production in a relatively capital-abundant, labor-scarce economy producing a capital-intensive, B, and a labor-intensive, A, commodity. Without trade, let us assume production occurs at point T, with the slope of the common tangent, p_1, to the two isoquants, A_2 and B_1, representing the ratio of the returns of labor to the returns of capital.

With international trade, the country naturally begins to specialize in the capital-intensive B-good for which its factor endowments give it a comparative advantage. Production thus shifts from point T to some new equilibrium at R, representing greater specialization in the capital-intensive commodity. In the process, the contracting import-competing industry (A), being labor-intensive, releases relatively small amounts of capital and relatively large amounts of labor. The capital thus released is immediately absorbed in the expanding production of the capital-intensive (B) good, but there is less of an increase in demand for the released labor. As a result, the relative amount of capital used in production increases in *both* industries, and the relative amount of labor used consequently declines in *both* industries. That is, the capital/labor ratio in the production of *both* goods is higher with trade at point R than without trade at point T. Hence, the marginal productivity of labor declines, and that of capital

[1] Wolfgang F. Stolper and Paul A. Samuelson, "Protection and Real Wages," *Review of Economic Studies*, November, 1941, and reprinted in H. S. Ellis and L. A. Metzler (eds.), *Readings in the Theory of International Trade* (Homewood, Ill.: Richard D. Irwin, 1949), pp. 333–57.

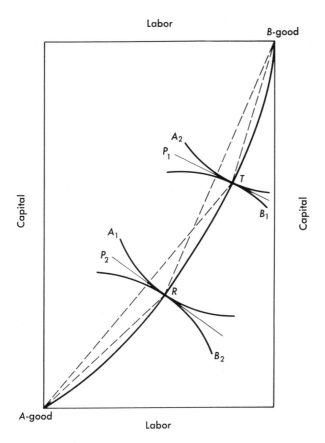

Fig. E5–3. International trade and factor prices.

rises in both industries. If factor prices are an accurate reflection of marginal productivities, it thus follows that real wages will fall, and that the real returns to capital will rise under these conditions, as a result of international trade. This is indicated by the slopes of the common tangents p_1 and p_2 in Figure E5–3.

International trade has under these conditions adversely affected the relative position of labor. It has altered domestic income distribution in favor of the owners of capital. Here, then, is a ready-made argument for protection against imports and a reduction of the volume of international trade. If production can be moved in the *opposite* direction, back toward the pre-trade position at point T in Figure E5–3, then the whole process can be reversed.

We shall explore further the implications of the Stolper–Samuelson theorem later on, in connection with the theory of commercial policy. Thus, we need state here only that this analysis, too, hinges on a large number of more or less restrictive assumptions.

Section E-6

Additional Readings on Traditional Trade Theory

The original work on the factor-endowments approach appears in Eli F. Heckscher, "The Effect of Foreign Trade on the Distribution of Income," *Economisk Tidskrift*, XXI, 1919, which is reprinted in H. S. Ellis and L. A. Metzler, eds., *Readings in the Theory of International Trade* (Homewood, Ill.: Richard D. Irwin, 1949); and Bertil Ohlin, *Interregional and International Trade* (Cambridge, Mass.: Harvard University Press, 1933).

For the geometrical technique, see K. Lancaster, "The Heckscher–Ohlin Trade Model: A Geometric Treatment," *Economica*, February, 1957. A good exposition can be found in Charles P. Kindleberger's text, *International Economics*, 5th ed. (Homewood, Ill.: Richard D. Irwin, 1973).

On trade and factor prices, see Paul A. Samuelson's two articles "International Trade and the Equalization of Factor Prices," *Economic Journal*, June, 1948, and "International Factor Price Equalization Once Again," *Economic Journal*, June, 1949. See also James E. Meade, *Trade and Welfare* (London: Oxford University Press, 1953), chs. 20–22 and appendixes 5 and 6; Lloyd A. Metzler, "Tariffs, the Terms of Trade, and the Distribution of National Income," *Journal of Political Economy*, February, 1949; K. Lancaster, "Protection and Real Wages: A Restatement," *Economic Journal*, June, 1957; Jan Tinbergen, "The Equalization of Factor Prices Between Free-Trade Areas," *Metroeconomica*, July, 1949; and R. F. Harrod, "Factor-Price Relations under Free Trade," *Economic Journal*, June, 1958.

The original writings on reciprocal demand are found in Alfred Marshall, *Money, Credit and Commerce* (London: Macmillan, 1923); and F. Y. Edgeworth, "The Theory of International Values, II," *Economic Journal*, September, 1894.

On the application of indifference analysis, see W. W. Leontief, "The Use of Indifference Curves in the Analysis of Foreign Trade," *Quarterly Journal of Economics*, May, 1933; W. J. Baumol, "The Community Indifference Map: A Construction," *Review of Economic Studies*, Vol. 17, 1949–50; Paul A. Samuelson, "Social Indifference Curves," *Quarterly Journal of Economics*, February, 1956; Tibor Scitovsky, "A Reconsideration of the Theory of Tariffs," *Review of Economic Studies*, Summer, 1942; and N. Kaldor, "Welfare Propositions of Economies and Interpersonal Comparisons of Utility," *Economic Journal*, December, 1939.

The construction of offer curves using community indifference curves in this chapter follows James E. Meade, *A Geometry of International Trade* (London: George Allen & Unwin, 1952), ch. 2. The geometric presentation of general equilibrium follows from his chapter 3. See also J. L. Mosak, *General Equilibrium Theory in International Trade* (Bloomington, Ind.: Principia Press, 1944); S. Mookerjee, *Factor Endowments and International Trade* (New Delhi: Asia Publishing House, 1958); and H. G. Johnson, *Money, Trade and Economic Growth* (London: George Allen & Unwin, 1962), ch. 2.

Some other works of interest are: Gottfried Haberler, "Some Problems in the Pure Theory of International Trade," *Economic Journal*, June, 1950; Abba P. Lerner, "Diagrammatical Representation of Demand Conditions in International Trade," *Economica*, August, 1934; Bela Balassa, "The Factor-Price Equilization Controversy," *Weltwirtschaftliches Archiv*, No. 1, 1961; M. Michaely, "Factor Proportions in International Trade: Current State of the Theory," *Kyklos*, Fasc. 4, 1964; I. F. Pearce and S. F. James, "The Factor Price Equalization Myth," *Review of Economic Studies*, No. 2, 1951–52; T. N. Rybczynski, "Factor Endowment and Relative Commodity Prices," *Economica*, November, 1955; and J. Vanek, "An Alternative Proof of the Factor Price Equalization Theorem," *Quarterly Journal of Economics*, November, 1960.

Excellent surveys are contained in W. M. Corden, *Recent Developments in the Theory of International Trade* (Princeton: International Finance Section, Princeton University, 1965); Gottfried Haberler, *A Survey of International Trade Theory* (Princeton: International Finance Section, Princeton University, 1961); and, in more detail, Richard E. Caves, *Trade and Economic Structure* (Cambridge, Mass.: Harvard University Press, 1960).

For a modern synthesis, see Ronald Findlay, *Trade and Specialization* (Baltimore: Penquin Books, 1970). Also Peter W. Frevert, *Production and Trade* (New York: Holt, Rinehart and Winston, 1972), and Heinz Robert Heller, *International Trade*, 2nd ed. (Englewood Cliffs, N.J.: Prentice-Hall, 1973).

Section E-7

Changing Factor Supplies

Chapter 7 discussed the effects of changing supply conditions—in both the export- and import-competing sectors—as well as demand conditions on the volume and terms of international trade. Supply shifts were attributed to changes in both factor endowments and factor efficiency. In this section, we shall illustrate the underlying relationship between changing factor supplies and changes in national output.

SHIFTS IN ONE FACTOR

Referring back to Figure E5–2 (page 551), it is not difficult to visualize how changes in factor supplies, occurring in one or both of the trading countries, would alter the picture presented there. An increase in the national capital stock would be depicted as an increase in the vertical dimension of the box diagram, and the growth of the labor force represented as an expansion of the horizontal dimension. An example of the impact of changing factor endowments is given in Figure E7–1.

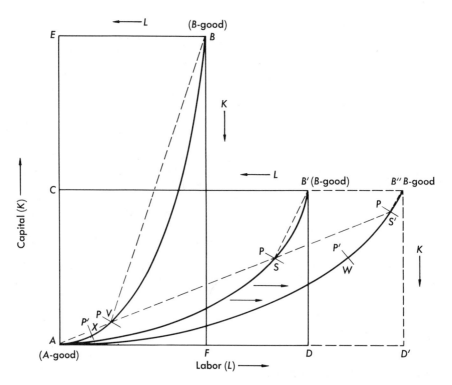

Fig. E7–1. Changing factor supplies and economic structure.

Assume that the labor-abundant country undergoes a sizable expansion of its labor force. The relevant box diagram for that country now changes from *ACB′D* to *ACB″D′*—the horizontal dimension of the box has been extended by the amount of the labor force growth. Presumably, the increased supply of labor will be used to expand output of the labor-intensive good for export. If we assume for the moment that factor proportions in the production of each commodity remain as they were before the change, production in the labor-abundant country will shift from point *S* to *S′*, and the relative wage rate will remain the same as before. Output of the labor-intensive export good rises accordingly, while output of the im-port-competing capital-intensive good shrinks, since some capital must be withdrawn from the latter sector in conjunction with the additional labor. The degree of national specialization in the production of the *A*-good is considerably enhanced, although the production point is un-changed in its capital-abundant trading partner.

Most probably, however, the factor proportions will change as well, resulting in more labor input per unit of output and a lower relative wage rate. In such a case, production would shift from point *S* to some point on curve *AB"*, such as *W*. Specialization in the labor-intensive export good would be enhanced here too, but not by as much as in the earlier case. Also the reduction of import-competing production would not be as great. The new factor proportions line (not drawn) would be flatter, with the capital-abundant country increasing the degree of its specialization in the capital-intensive commodity *B* by moving to production point *X*. In either case, the overall volume of trade between the two countries is likely to grow substantially as a result, with imports and exports of both nations expanding.[1]

Similarly the reader can easily work out for himself the effects of in-creased endowment of capital in the capital-abundant country. Increases in the endowment of the *abundant* factor appear to lead to greater special-ization in the production of the commodity using that particular factor intensively, by one or both of the trading countries. An increase in export supply, and a reduction in import-competing supply tend to occur, and the volume of trade expands.

It follows that an increased relative endowment of the *scarce* factor in one or both countries will lead to decreased specialization and to a reduced volume of international trade via raised import-competing produc-tion. Once the point is reached where the scarce factor of one or both of the countries has grown to such an extent that the box diagrams of the two economies are identical (using the Hecksher–Ohlin assumption that factor productivity, too, is identical and unchanging), the comparative advantage basis for trade will have disappeared.

SHIFTS IN SEVERAL FACTORS

As part of the economic growth process, it is likely that both scarce and

---

[1] A number of assumptions must be made if this result is necessarily to follow. See T. N. Rybezynski, "Factor Proportions and Comparative Advantage," *Economica,* November, 1955.

abundant factors of production will undergo expansion, although perhaps at different rates. On the surface it would seem that, if supplies of the abundant factor grow faster, the volume of trade will increase, while more rapid expansion of the scarce factor will lead to a reduction in the volume of trade.

Figure E7–2 represents increases in endowments of two productive factors via the familiar two-factor, two-commodity box diagram. Initially, the capital endowment of XB and labor endowment of XA prevail. The optimum efficiency locus is the curved line XY. Since this particular country is capital-abundant, it is likely that production takes place close to the Y origin—relatively more of good X than good Y. Good X is likely to be exported in return for imports of good Y.

Suppose that the country undergoes a substantial increase in the stock of capital, with no increase in the size of the labor force. The horizontal

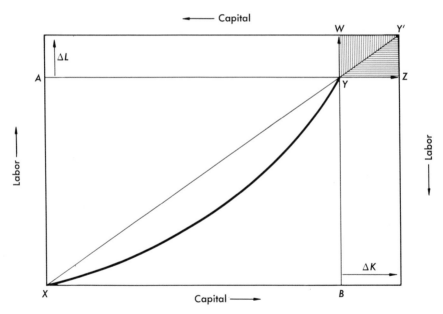

Fig. E7–2. Changing factor endowments: two factors.

dimension of the box diagram thus expands, but its vertical dimension remains unchanged. Hence, the Y-origin moves in the direction YZ, and the optimum efficiency locus XY will also shift to the right. If relative prices remain unchanged, as in the previous example (Figure E7–1), the supply of exports of good X increases, while the supply of import-competing goods (Y) shrinks for the same reason. Again, if the increased capital supplies are to be effectively utilized, they must be combined with some labor. Since this additional labor can be secured only by withdrawing it from production of the import-competing good Y, its production will be reduced. Both capital and labor will be released from import-competing production in the process, but labor at a faster rate than capital since import-competing output is labor-intensive.

With factor-intensities remaining the same as before, a greater quantity of good X and a smaller amount of good Y will be produced as a result of the change in the capital endowment. This is often called *ultra-export-biased* expansion of factor supplies. An increase in the endowment of the abundant factor alone will tend to expand exports of commodities using that factor intensively, and simultaneously lead to an expansion of imports by reducing import-competing production. In short, it increases the volume of trade without influencing the direction of trade, and it reinforces the basis of comparative advantage by enhancing existing differences in relative factor endowments. This is the same conclusion drawn earlier for one factor.

What if, on the other hand, this same country undergoes an expansion of its labor force—the scarce factor of production. The horizontal dimension of the box diagram in Figure E7–2 now stays the same, while the vertical dimension grows from BY to BW. The optimum efficiency locus thus pivots to the left, with the Y-origin shifting in the direction of W. Again assuming that factor intensities remain constant, output of import-competing goods will grow and, as factors are withdrawn from production of good X, output of the export good will contract. The result is a reduction in both imports *and* exports—in the volume of trade.

An increase in the endowment of the scarce factor, the endowment of the abundant factor remaining constant, thus reduces the comparative advantage basis for trade by cutting down international differences in factor endowments. It tends to reduce the volume of trade—both imports and exports—and is termed *ultra-import-biased* factor expansion.

Now, let us suppose that endowments of *both* labor and capital grow proportionately. A new box diagram with increased horizontal *and* vertical dimensions will emerge, and since both factors have increased in the same proportion, a new origin Y' will result on a northeast extension of the diagonal XY. The optimum efficiency locus, maintaining the same shape as before, extends along YY', and if factor intensities remain constant, the output of both export good X and import-competing good Y is increased in proportion. No change occurs in the degree of specialization or the basis for comparative advantage, i.e., relative factor endowments in this case of *neutral* expansion of factor supplies.

Of course, growth in factor supplies does not necessarily entail an increase in the supply of either one factor or the other exclusively, or a proportionate increase in both, as presented in the three cases above. For instance, we may have an increase in both labor and capital supplies, but labor proportionately more than capital, or capital proportionately more than labor. In terms of Figure E7–2 this would place the Y origin in the shaded areas YWY' or $YY'Z$; respectively. What happens in cases such as this?

In the first instance, with supplies of the scarce factor (labor) increasing proportionately more than those of the abundant factor (capital), a new optimum efficiency locus somewhat to the left of the original will result. Output of both goods will grow, but the supply of import-competing products will expand more rapidly than the supply of exports. In the second case, with the supply of the abundant factor growing relatively more than that of the scarce factor, production of the export commodity will grow relatively more than output of the import-competing good. If production of the import-competing commodity is expanded relatively more, imports will be reduced somewhat more than exports grow (*import-biased* factor expansion). A relative increase of export production will lead to a growth of trade (*export-biased* factor expansion). The former reduces the nation's pre-existing comparative advantage and the latter tends to enhance it.

Changes in productive factor supplies, then, may affect the basis for trade if, in fact, trade is founded on intercountry differences in factor endowments. It may expand or contract the volume of trade, depending upon whether changes in factor supplies have a greater bearing on import-competing or export industries. It may even change the direction of trade if it causes a reversal in the nation's relative factor endowments. Note also that, according to the terms of trade analysis presented in the previous section, import-biased change in factor supplies will tend to result in terms of trade improvement, and that export-biased factor supply change may lead to their deterioration.

Section E-8

Readings on the Modern Theory of International Trade

The best surveys of trade theory are contained in Richard E. Caves, *Trade and Economic Structure* (Cambridge, Mass.: Harvard University Press, 1960); Gottfried Haberler, *A Survey of International Trade Theory* (Princeton, N.J.: International Finance Section, Princeton University, 1961); W. M. Corden, *Recent Developments in the Theory of International Trade* (Princeton, N.J.: International Finance Section, Princeton University, 1965); and Jagdish Bhagwati, "The Pure Theory of International Trade: A Survey," *Economic Journal,* March, 1964. With respect to the more recent extensions of the theory and its empirical validity, the best surveys are contained in Raymond Vernon (ed.), *The Technology Factor in International Trade* (New York: National Bureau of Economic Research, 1970), especially the chapter by G. C. Hafbauer; and Robert E. Baldwin, "Determinants of the Commodity Structure of U.S. Trade," *American Economic Review,* March, 1971.

On the opportunity cost approach to comparative advantage, see the relevant chapters in Gottfried Haberler, *The Theory of International Trade* (London: Wm. Hodge & Co., 1936); and also his "Some Problems in the Pure Theory of International Trade," *Economic Journal,* June, 1950.

See also Jacob Viner, *Studies in the Theory of International Trade* (New York: Harper, 1937), chs. 8–9; Chi-Yuen Wu, *An Outline of International Price Theories* (London: Macmillan, 1939); James W. Angell, *The Theory of International Prices* (Cambridge, Mass.: Harvard University Press, 1926); and Carl Iversen, *Some Aspects of the Theory of International Capital Movements* (Copenhagen: Munksgaard, 1936).

On the gains from trade, see Paul A. Samuelson, "The Gains from International Trade," *Canadian Journal of Economics and Political Science,* May, 1939, and his "The Gains from International Trade Once Again," *Economic Journal,* December, 1962; R. E. Baldwin, "The New Welfare Economics and Gains in International Trade," *Quarterly Journal of Economics,* February, 1952; and Murray C. Kemp, "The Gain from International Trade," *Economic Journal,* December, 1962.

Also of interest will be John H. Williams, "The Theory of International Trade Reconsidered," *Economic Journal,* June, 1929; Jan Tinbergen, *International Economic Integration* (Amsterdam: Elsevier, 1954), especially the sections on decreasing opportunity costs; Abba P. Lerner, "The Diagrammatical Representation of Cost Conditions in International Trade," *Economica,* August, 1932; and G. D. A. MacDougall, "Some Practical Illustrations and Applications of the Theory of Comparative Advantage," *Economic Journal,* December, 1951.

On transport costs, see Walter Isard and Merton J. Peck, "Location Theory and International and Interregional Trade Theory," *Quarterly Journal of Economics,* February, 1954; J. N. Wolfe, "Transport Costs and Comparative Advantage," *Journal of Political Economy,* August, 1959; R. A. Mundell, "Transport Costs and International Trade Theory," *Canadian Journal of Economics and Political Science,* August, 1957; and Murray C. Kemp, *The Pure Theory of International Trade* (Englewood Cliffs, N.J.: Prentice-Hall, 1964), ch. 10.

A general introduction to the theory of location may be found in Walter Isard, *Location and Space Economy* (New York: Wiley, 1956), chs. 1 and 2. Also useful in this regard is M. L. Greenhut, *Plant Location in Theory and Practice* (Chapel Hill: University of North Carolina Press, 1956), chs. 1–3.

Some of the pioneering work in the field may be found in Alfred Weber, *Theory of Location* (Chicago: University of Chicago Press, 1928); A. Lösch, *The Economics of Location* (New Haven, Conn.: Yale University Press, 1954); and E. M. Hoover, *Location of Economic Activity* (New York: McGraw-Hill, 1948). Location under imperfect competition is specifically explored by Harold Hotelling, "Stability and Competition," *Economic Journal*, Vol. 39, 1929, pp. 41–57; Arthur F. Smithies, "Optimum Location in Spatial Competition," *Journal of Political Economy*, Vol. 49, 1941, pp. 423–39; and Frank A. Fetter, "The Economic Law of Market Areas," *Quarterly Journal of Economics*, Vol. 38, 1924, pp. 520–29. Useful discussions of the effects of location may also be found in William S. Vickery, *Microstatics* (New York: Harcourt Brace Jovanovich, 1964), pp. 323–34; and in M. L. Greenhut, *Microeconomics and the Space Economy* (Chicago: Scott, Foresman, 1963).

Other important works of interest are Theodore O. Yntema, *A Mathematical Reformulation of the General Theory of International Trade* (Chicago: University of Chicago Press, 1932); Jagdish Bhagwati, "International Trade and Economic Expansion," *American Economic Review*, December, 1958; W. M. Corden, "Economic Expansion and International Trade: A Geometrical Approach," *Oxford Economic Papers*, June, 1956; and Svend Laursen, "Production Functions and the Theory of International Trade," *American Economic Review*, September, 1952.

The evolution of the theory can be traced by consulting such works as Edward S. Mason, "The Doctrine of Comparative Costs," *Quarterly Journal of Economics*, November, 1926; Gerald M. Meier, "The Theory of Comparative Costs Reconsidered," *Oxford Economic Papers*, June, 1949; R. A. Mundell, "The Pure Theory of International Trade," *American Economic Review*, June, 1957; Joan Robinson, "The Pure Theory of International Trade," *Review of Economic Studies*, No. 2, 1946–1947; and Jacob Viner, "The Doctrine of Comparative Costs," *Weltwirtschaftliches Archiv*, Vol. 34, 1932.

General surveys of some of the dynamic aspects of international trade theory can be found in Gerald M. Meier, *The International Economics of Development* (New York: Harper, 1968).

On the effects of supply and demand shifts on the terms and volume of trade, see the Meier work, noted above, Chapter 2; and M. O. Clement, R. L. Pfister, and K. J. Rothwell, *Theoretical Issues in International Economics* (New York: Houghton Mifflin, 1967), ch. 3.

The following will also be of interest in this regard: W. R. Allen, "The Effects on Trade of Shifting Reciprocal Demand Schedules," *American Economic Review*, March, 1952; J. Bhagwati, "Growth, Terms of Trade and Comparative Advantage," *Economia Internazionale*, August, 1959; H. J. Bruton, "Productivity, the Trade Balance and the Terms of Trade," *Economia Internazionale*, August, 1955; and W. M. Corden, "Economic Expansion and International Trade: A Geometric Approach," *Oxford Economic Papers*, June, 1956.

Also, see C. P. Kindleberger, "The Terms of Trade and Economic Development," *Review of Economics and Statistics*, February, 1958; R. Findlay and H. Grubert, "Factor Intensity, Technological Progress, and the Terms of Trade," *Oxford Economic Papers*, February, 1959; M. C. Kemp, "The Relation Between Changes in International Demand and the Terms of Trade," *Econometrica*, January, 1956. and his "Technological Change, the Terms of Trade and Welfare," *Economic Journal*, September, 1955; and A. K. Dasgupta, "The Elasticity of Reciprocal Demand and the Terms of International Trade," *The Indian Journal of Economics*, October, 1941.

Perhaps the best definition of the various types of terms of trade is found in G. Haberler, *Survey of International Trade Theory* (Princeton: International Finance Section, Princeton University, 1961). See also F. C. Benham, "The Terms of Trade," *Economica*, November, 1940.

Some notable empirical studies of the terms of trade are E. Devons, "Statistics of United Kingdom Terms of Trade," *Manchester School*, September, 1954; A. H. Imlah, "The Terms of Trade of the United Kingdom, 1798–1913," *Journal of Economic History*, November, 1950; C. P. Kindleberger, *The Terms of Trade, a European Case Study* (New York: Wiley, 1956); and K. Martin and F. G. Thackeray, "The Terms of Trade of Selected Countries, 1870–1938," *Bulletin of the Oxford University Institute of Statistics*, November, 1948.

On the effects of changes in factor endowments, technology, and demand, the following will prove useful: J. R. Hicks, "An Inaugural Lecture," *Oxford Economic Papers*, June, 1953, and his *Essays in World Economics* (New York: Oxford University Press, 1959); T. M. Rybezynski, "Factor Endowments and Relative Commodity Prices," *Economica*, November, 1955; Harry G. Johnson, *International Trade and Economic Growth* (London: George Allen & Unwin, 1958); J. Bhagwati and H. G. Johnson, "Notes on Some Controversies in the Theory of International Trade," *Economic Journal*, March, 1960; and Staffan Burenstam Linder, *An Essay on Trade and Transformation* (Stockholm: Almqvist & Wicksell, 1961).

Some studies related to the examination of the conventional trade theories are B. Balassa, "An Empirical Demonstration of Classical Comparative Cost Theory," *Review of Economics and Statistics*, August, 1963; T. Balogh, "Factor Intensities of American Foreign Trade and Technical Progress," *Review of Economics and Stat'tics*, November, 1955; S. Clemhout, "Production Function Analysis Applied to the Leontief Scarce-Factor Paradox of International Trade," *Manchester School*, May, 1963; P. T. Ellsworth, "The Structure of American Foreign Trade: A New View Examined," *Review of Economics and Statistics*, August, 1954; and J. C. Ford, "The Heckscher-Ohlin Theory of the Basis of Commodity Trade," *Economic Journal*, September, 1963.

Also, see W. W. Leontief, "Factor Proportions and the Structure of American Trade," *Review of Economics and Statistics*, November, 1956; G. D. A. Mac-Dougall, "British and American Exports: A Study Suggested by the Theory of Comparative Costs," Parts I and II, *Economic Journal*, December, 1951 and September, 1952; R. M. Stern, "British and American Productivity and Comparative Costs in International Trade," *Oxford Economic Papers*, October, 1962; B. C. Swerling, "Capital Shortage and Capital Surplus in the United States," *Review of Economics and Statistics*, August, 1954; S. Valavanis-Vail, "Leontief's Scarce Factor Paradox," *Journal of Political Economy*, December, 1954 and his "Factor Proportions and the Structure of American Trade: Comment," *Review of Economics and Statistics*, February, 1958; and J. Vanek, "The Natural Resource Content of Foreign Trade, 1870-1955, and the Relative Abundance of Natural Resources in the United States," *Review of Economics and Statistics*, May, 1959.

On the human skills issue in trade theory, see Peter B. Kenen, "Nature, Capital, and Trade," *Journal of Political Economy*, October, 1965; Irving B. Kravis, "Wages and Foreign Trade," *Review of Economics and Statistics*, June, 1966; Donald B. Kessing, "Labor Skills and International Trade: Evaluating Many Trade Flows with a Single Measuring Device," *Review of Economics and Statistics*, August, 1965; Donald B. Keesing, "Labor Skills and Comparative Advantage," *American*

Economic Review, May, 1966; Helen Waehrer, "Wage Rates, Labor Skills and United States Foreign Trade," in Peter B. Kenen and Roger Lawrence (eds.), *The Open Economy* (New York: Columbia University Press, 1968); K. W. Roskamp and G. C. McMeekin, "Factor Proportions, Human Capital and Foreign Trade," *Quarterly Journal of Economics,* February, 1968.

On scale economies, see G. C. Hufbauer, *Synthetic Materials and the Theory of International Trade* (London: Weidenfeld & Nicolson, 1966), especially Appendix B; and Donald B. Keesing, "Population and Industrial Development: Some Evidence from Trade Patterns," *American Economic Review,* June, 1966.

The "stages of production" theory is discussed in David Felix, "Beyond Import Substitution: The Latin American Dilemma," in G. F. Papanek (ed.), *Development Policy: Theory and Practice* (Cambridge, Mass.: Harvard University Press, 1968); and Albert O. Hirschman, "The Political Economy of Import-Substituting Industrialization in Latin America," *Quarterly Journal of Economics,* February, 1968.

The technological gap dimension is surveyed in M. V. Posner, "International Trade and Technical Change," *Oxford Economic Papers,* October, 1961; Irving B. Kravis, "'Availability' and Other Influences on International Trade," *Journal of Political Economy,* April, 1956; Donald B. Keesing, "The Impact of Research and Development on United States Trade," *Journal of Political Economy,* February, 1967; and W. Gruber, D. Mehta, and R. Vernon, "The R&D Factor in International Trade and International Investment by United States Industries," *Journal of Political Economy,* February, 1967. The latter is also related to the "product-cycle theory." See also Seev Hirsch, "The United States Electronics Industry in International Trade," *National Institute Economic Review,* November, 1965; and Raymond Vernon "International Investment and International Trade in the Product Cycle," *Quarterly Journal of Economics,* May, 1966.

On preference similarity and international trade, see S. B. Linder, *An Essay on Trade and Transformation,* (Stockholm: Almquist & Wicksell, 1961); H. G. Grubel, "Inter-Industry Specialization and the Pattern of Trade," *Canadian Journal of Economics and Political Science,* August, 1967; and Michael Michaely, *Concentration in International Trade* (Amsterdam: North Holland, 1962).

With respect to the comparative evaluation of trade theories, see Harry G. Johnson, "The State of Theory in Relation to the Empirical Analysis," in Raymond Vernon (ed.), *The Technology Factor in International Trade* (New York: National Bureau of Economic Research, 1971).

Section E-9

Readings on the Political Economy of Trade Policy

In recent years there has been a renewed interest in the political process of trade-policy formation. For a discussion of the American experience, see R. L. Allen and I. Walter, *The Formation of United States Trade Policy: Retrospect and Prospect* (New York: New York University Institute of Finance, 1971). Also Leland B. Yeager and David G. Tuerck, *Trade Policy and the Price System* (Scranton, Pa.: Intext, 1966), and Charles P. Kindleberger, *Foreign Trade and the National Economy* (New Haven, Conn: Yale University Press, 1962). The best available case-oriented volume is Gerald M. Meier, *Problems of Trade Policy* (New

York: Oxford University Press, 1973). See also R. G. Hawkins and I. Walter, *The United States and International Markets* (Lexington, Mass.: D. C. Heath, 1972).

For the political dynamics in action, see U.S. Congress, House Committee on Ways and Means, *Trade Expansion Act of 1962, Hearings Before the Committee on Ways and Means,* 87th Congress, Second Session, 1962. Also Harald B. Malmgren, *Economic Peacekeeping in Phase II* (New York: Quandangle Books, 1973); C. Fred Bergsten, "Crisis in U.S. Trade Policy," *Foreign Affairs,* July, 1971; *Future United States Foreign Trade Policy,* Report to the President by the Special Representative for Trade Negotiations (Washington, D.C.: Government Printing Office, 1969); and *United States International Economic Policy in an Interdependent World,* submitted by the Commission on International Trade and Investment Policy (Washington, D. C.: Government Printing Office, 1971).

Section E-10-11

Readings on Tariffs and Nontariff Barriers

One of the best surveys of barriers to international trade is Robert M. Stern, "Tariffs and Other Measures of Trade Control: A Survey of Recent Developments," *Journal of Economic Literature,* September, 1973. Another *must* is Harry G. Johnson, *Aspects of the Theory of Tariffs* (Cambridge, Mass.: Harvard University Press, 1972).

The pioneering article on the effect of tariffs on the terms of trade is Tibor Scitovsky, "A Reconsideration of the Theory of Tariffs," *Review of Economic Studies,* Summer, 1942. See also W. M. Gorman, "The Effect of Tariffs on the Level and Terms of Trade," *Journal of Political Economy,* June, 1959; R. F. Kahn, "Tariffs and the Terms of Trade," *Review of Economic Studies,* No. 1, 1947–48; R. E. Baldwin, "The Effects of Tariffs on International and Domestic Prices," *Quarterly Journal of Economics,* February, 1960; N. Kaldor, "A Note on Tariffs and the Terms of Trade," *Economica,* November, 1940; L. A. Metzler, "Tariffs, the Terms of Trade and the Distribution of National Income," *Journal of Political Economy,* February, 1949; and W. M. Corden, "Tariffs, Subsidies and the Terms of Trade," *Economica,* August, 1957.

On tariffs and income distribution, see the Metzler article, just noted, and, of course, W. F. Stolper and P. A. Samuelson, "Protection and Real Wages," *Review of Economic Studies,* November, 1941.

On the "optimum" tariff question, the following works will be useful: J. M. Fleming, "The Optimal Tariff from an International Standpoint," *Review of Economics and Statistics,* February, 1956; H. F. Johnson, "Optimum Tariffs and Retaliation," *Review of Economic Studies,* 1953–54; J. de Graaff, "On Optimum Tariff Structures," *Review of Economic Studies,* 1949–50; and H. Giersch, "The Trade Optimum, A Contribution to the Theory of Economic Policy," *International Economic Papers,* No. 7, 1957.

Other works on tariff theory are J. Black, "Arguments for Tariffs," *Oxford Economic Papers,* June, 1959; F. D. Graham, "Some Aspects of Protection Further Considered," *Quarterly Journal of Economics,* February, 1923; E. E. Hagen, "An Economic Justification of Protectionism," *Quarterly Journal of Economics,* November, 1958; A. Henderson, "The Restriction of Foreign Trade," *Manchester School,* January, 1949; H. G. Johnson, "The Cost of Protection and the Scientific Tariff," *Journal of Political Economy,* August, 1960; and I. M. D. Little, "Welfare and Tariffs," *Review of Economic Studies,* No. 2, 1949–50.

Also of interest in this connection is James E. Meade's *Trade and Welfare* (London: Oxford University Press, 1955), especially Part II.

Noteworthy institutional and historical studies are A. Isaacs, *International Trade: Tariffs and Commercial Policies* (Homewood, Ill.: Richard D. Irwin, 1948); F. W. Taussig, *The Tariff History of the United States* (New York: Putnam, 1931); R. Vernon, *America's Foreign Trade Policy and the GATT* (Princeton, N.J.: Princeton University, 1954); and L. W. Towle, *International Trade and Commercial Policy,* 2nd ed. New York: Harper, 1956).

On tariff structure theory, see W. M. Corden, "The Structure of a Tariff System and the Effective Protective Rate," *Journal of Political Economy,* June, 1966; B. Balassa, "Tariff Protection in Industrial Countries," *Journal of Political Economy,* December, 1965; and G. Basevi, "The U.S. Tariff Structure," *Review of Economics and Statistics,* May, 1966.

In recent years a considerable body of literature on nontariff barriers has developed. Some general works of interest are: Robert E. Baldwin, *Nontariff Distortions of International Trade* (Washington, D.C.: Brookings, 1970); Harald B. Malmgren, *Trade Wars or Trade Negotiations?* (Washington, D.C.: The Atlantic Council, 1971); Gerard and Victoria Curzon, *Hidden Barriers to International Trade* (London: International Trade Centre, 1970); International Chamber of Commerce, *Non-Tariff Barriers to Trade* (Paris: ICC, 1969); and Ingo Walter, "Nontariff Barriers and the Free Trade Area Option" *Banca Nazionale del Lavoro Quarterly Review,* March, 1969. See also Chapters 4 and 5 in Robert G. Hawkins and Ingo Walter, *The United States and International Markets* (Lexington, Mass.: D.C. Heath, 1972).

There have been a number of attempts to quantify the affects of NTB's, most of which have been relatively unsuccessful. These include the Baldwin volume, noted above, and Ingo Walter, "Non-Tariff Obstacles and Trade Preferences for Latin America," *Inter-American Economic Affairs,* Spring, 1970: *Idem.,* "Non Tariff Barriers and the Export Performance of Developing Countries," *American Economic Review,* Papers and Proceedings, May, 1971; *Idem.,* and Jae W. Chung, "Non-Tariff Obstacles and Trade Preferences for Developing Countries," *Kyklos,* Fasc. 4, 1971; *Idem.,* and Jae W. Chung, "The Pattern of Non-Tariff Barriers to International Market Access," *Weltwirtschaftliches Archiv* Bd. 108, 1972; and *Idem.,* "Non-Tariff Obstacles to Trade Among Industrial Countries: Some Preliminary Evidence, *Economia Internazionale,* September, 1972.

On the legal issues, see particularly Stanely D. Metzger, *Lowering Nontariff Barriers* (Washington, D.C.: Brookings, 1974). On the border taxes, see Stanley S. Surrey, "The Wonderful World of Taxes," *Columbia Journal of World Business,* May–June, 1968. On customs valuation, see H. Grubel and H. G. Johnson, "Nominal Tariff Rates and United States Valuation Practices," *Review of Economics and Statistics,* August, 1967; and on government procurement, Organization for Economic Cooperation and Development: *Government Purchasing* (Paris: OECD, 1966).

On assessing the affects of various types of trade barriers, see F. D. Holzman, "Comparison of Different Forms of Trade Barriers," *Review of Economics and Statistics,* May, 1969; and Jagdish Bhagwati, *Trade, Tariffs and Growth* (Cambridge, Mass.: MIT Press, 1969). The best available listing of empirical studies of the effects of tariffs and other trade barriers is contained in the Stern survey article, referred to above.

Section E-12

Readings on Trade Liberalization

Two relatively recent books consider the question of trade liberalization from both political and economic perspectives: Gerald M. Meier, *Problems of Trade Policy* (New York: Oxford University Press, 1973), and Robert G. Hawkins and Ingo Walter (eds.), *The United States and International Markets: Trade Policy Options in an Age of Controls* (Lexington, Mass.: D.C. Heath, 1972). On measuring the trade effects of liberalization, see E. E. Leamer and R. M. Stern, *Quantitative International Economics* (Boston: Allyn & Bacon, 1970). See also Bela Balassa, "Tariff Reductions and Trade in Manufactures Among the Industrial Countries," *American Economic Review* June, 1966; Bela Balassa and Mordechai E. Kreinin, "Trade Liberalization Under the Kennedy Round: The Static Effects", *Review of Economics and Statistics*, May, 1967; M. June Flanders, "Measuring Protectionism and Predicting Trade Diversion," *Journal of Political Economy*, April, 1965; L. H. Officer and J. R. Hurtubise, "Price Effects of the Kennedy Round on Canadian Trade," *Review of Economics and Statistics* August, 1969; Robert G. Hawkins, "The Economic Impact on the United States of a U.K.–Canada–U.S. Free Trade Association" in T. M. Franck and E. Weisband (eds.), *A Free Trade Association* (New York: New York University Press, 1968).

On trade liberalization, see W. S. Salant, *Import Liberalization and Employment* (Washington, D.C.: Brookings, 1961); Tibor Scitovsky, "A Reconsideration of the Theory of Tariffs," *Review of Economic Studies,* Summer, 1942, and reprinted in H. S. Ellis and C. A. Metzler (eds.), *Readings in the Theory of International Trade* (Homewood, Ill.: Richard D. Irwin, 1950); and P. B. Kenen, "The Strategy of Trade Liberalization," in Joint Economic Committee, U.S. Congress, *United States Commercial Policy—A Program for the 1960's* (Washington, D.C.: U.S. Government Printing Office, 1961). See also Bela Balassa, *Trade Liberalization* (Baltimore: The Johns Hopkins Press, 1967).

Also useful are H. G. Brainard, "The Trade Expansion Act, 1962," *Lloyds Bank Review,* January, 1963; G. Curzon, *Multilateral Commercial Diplomacy* (London: Michael Joseph, 1965); R. Vernon, *American Foreign Trade Policy and the GATT* (Princeton, N.J.: Princeton University Press, 1954); and J. Wemelsfelder, "Welfare and Tariff Preferences," *Weltwirtschaftliches Archiv,* No. 2, 1960.

For an interesting set of alternative strategies for the post-Kennedy Round era, see Richard N. Cooper, "Trade Liberalization Among Developed Countries," in *The Future of U.S. Foreign Trade Policy,* Hearings before the Subcommittee on Foreign Trade Policy, Joint Economic Committee, 90th Congress, 1st Session (Washington, D.C.: Government Printing Office, 1967). See also Ernest H. Preeg, *Traders and Diplomats* (Washington, D.C.: The Brookings Institution, 1970); Kenneth W. Dam, *The GATT: Law and International Economic Organization* (Chicago: University of Chicago Press, 1970); Michael K. Evans, *The Kennedy Round in American Trade Policy* (Cambridge, Mass.: Harvard University Press, 1971); and Thomas B. Curtis and Stephen B. Vastine, *American Trade Policy and the Kennedy Round* (New York: Praeger, 1971).

On second best theory and welfare effects, see J. E. Meade, *Trade and Welfare* (Oxford: Oxford University Press, 1955), ch. VII and ch. II of the Mathematical Supplement; J. M. Fleming, "On Making the Best of Balance of Payments Restrictions on Imports," *Economic Journal,* March, 1951; I. M. D. Little, *A Critique of Welfare Economics* (Oxford: Clarendon Press, 1950); E. J. Mishan, "A Survey of Welfare Economics, 1938–1959," *Economic Journal,* June, 1960; R. G. Lipsey and K. Lancaster, "The General Theory of the Second Best," *Review of Economic Studies,* No. 1, 1956–57; and H. G. Johnson, "The Cost of Protection and the Scientific Tariff," *Journal of Political Economy,* August, 1960. The Arguments are neatly summed up by W. M. Corden, *Recent Developments in the Theory of International Trade* (Princeton, N.J.: International Finance Section, Princeton University, 1965).

An excellent restatement of the theory of commercial policy, in terms of the impact of trade restrictions on departures from theoretically optimum conditions, is contained in Jagdish Bhagwati, *The Theory and Practice of Commercial Policy: Departures from Unified Exchange Rates* (Princeton, N.J.: International Finance Section, Princeton University, 1968).

Section E-13

Additional Readings on Customs Union Theory

An excellent summary of the statics of customs unions, as well as the best general survey of economic integration, is found in Bela Balassa, *The Theory of Economic Integration* (Homewood, Ill.: Richard D. Irwin, 1961). Also, see Rudolf Sannwald and Jacques Stohler, *Economic Integration* (Princeton, N.J.: Princeton University Press, 1959); M. O. Clement, R. L. Pfister, and K. J. Rothwell, *Theoretical Issues in International Economics* (Boston: Houghton Mifflin, 1967), ch. 4; and R. G. Lipsey, "The Theory of Customs Unions: A General Survey," *Economic Journal,* September, 1960.

The original studies in customs union theory are Jacob Viner, *The Customs Union Issue* (New York: Carnegie Endowment for International Peace, 1950); Jan Tinbergen, *International Economic Integration* (Amsterdam: Elsevier, 1953); Tibor Scitovsky, *Economic Theory and Western European Integration* (Stanford: Stanford University Press, 1958); Franz Gehrels, "Customs Union Theory from a Single-County Viewpoint," *Review of Economic Studies,* No. 1, 1956–1957; and James E. Meade, *The Theory of Customs Unions* (Amsterdam: North Holland, 1955), and his *Problems of Economic Union* (Chicago: University of Chicago Press, 1953).

See also H. Makower and G. Morton, "A Contribution to the Theory of Customs Unions," *Economic Journal,* March, 1953; E. A. G. Robinson (ed.), *Economic Consequences of the Size of Nations* (London: Macmillan, 1960); B. C. Bentick, "Estimating Trade Creation and Trade Diversion," *Economic Journal,* June, 1963; D. D. Humphrey and C. E. Ferguson, "The Domestic and World Benefits of a Customs Union," *Economica Internazionale,* May, 1960; H. G. Johnson, "The European Common Market—Risk or Opportunity?" *Weltwirtschaftliches Achiv,* No. 2, 1957, and also his "The Gains from Freer Trade with Europe," *Manchester School,* September, 1958; R. A. Mundell, "Tariff Preferences and the Terms of Trade," *Manchester School,* January, 1964; and J. Spraos, "The Condition for a Trade-Creating Customs Union," *Economic Journal,* March, 1964.

Some applied studies are L. B. Krause, "European Integration and the United States," *American Economic Review,* May, 1963; P. Streeten, "Common Fallacies about the Common Market," *Weltwirtschaftliches Archiv,* No. 2, 1963; E. Thorbecke, "European Economic Integration and the Pattern of World Trade," *American Economic Review,* May, 1963; A. Lamfalussy, *The United Kingdom and the Six* (Homewood, Ill.: Richard D. Irwin, 1963); I. Walter, *The European Common Market: Growth and Patterns of Trade and Production* (New York: Frederick A. Praeger, 1967); Bela Balassa, *Trade Liberalization Among Industrial Countries* (New York: McGraw-Hill for the Council on Foreign Relations, 1967), and his "Trade Creation and Trade Diversion in the European Common Market," *Economic Journal,* March, 1967.

Perhaps the best review of the many empirical studies of regional trade liberalization is contained in Willy Sellekaerts, "How Meaningful are Empirical Studies on Trade Creation and Diversion?", *Weltwirtschaftliches Archiv,* December, 1973. See also E. M. Truman, "The European Economic Community: Trade Creation and Trade Diversion," *Yale Economic Essays,* Vol. IX; Walton T. Wilford, "Trade Creation in the Central American Common Market," *Western Economic Journal,* March, 1970; and Mordechai Kreinin, "Trade Creation and Diversion by the EEC and EFTA," *Economia Internazionale,* May, 1969.

Section E-14

Additional Readings on Dynamic Gains from Integration

The problems of economic integration covered in this chapter are surveyed in Bela Balassa, *The Theory of Economic Integration* (Homewood, Ill.: Richard D. Irwin, 1961); U. W. Kitzinger, *The Politics and Economics of European Integration* (New York: Praeger, 1963); and Finn B. Jensen and Ingo Walter, *The Common Market—Economic Integration in Europe* (Philadelphia: Lippincott, 1965).

On the dynamic effects of integration, see Chapters 5–8 of the Balassa volume, noted above. Also, see Tibor Scitovsky, *Economic Theory and Western European Integration* (Stanford, Cal.: Stanford University Press, 1958), and his "International Trade and Economic Integration as a Means of Overcoming the Disadvantages of a Small Nation" in E. A. G. Robinson (ed.), *Economic Consequences of the Size of Nations* (London: Macmillan, 1960). Of additional interest will be C. D. Edwards, "Size of Markets, Scale of Firms, and the Character of Competition" in the Robinson volume; James E. Meade, *Problems of Economic Union* (Chicago: University of Chicago Press, 1953), and his *The Theory of Customs Unions* (rev. ed., Amsterdam: North Holland, 1965).

On labor mobility, see Meyer Bernstein, "Labor and the European Communities," *Law and Contemporary Problems,* Summer, 1961; Alessandro Molinari, "Manpower and the Common Market," *Banca Nazionale del Lavoro Quarterly Review,* December, 1958; and P. Lamartine Yates, *Food, Land and Manpower in Western Europe* (London: Macmillan, 1960).

Also of interest will be the following: H. Niehaus, "Effects of the European Common Market on Employment and Social Conditions in Agriculture," *International Labour Review,* April, 1958; Herbert Giersch, "Economic Union Between Nations and the Location of Industries," *Review of Economic Studies* No. 2,

1949–50; R. O. Wilberforce, "Restrictive Practices in the European Common Market," *Journal of Business Law*, April, 1958; Pierre Uri, *Partnership for Progress* (New York: Harper, 1963); Leon N. Lindberg, *The Political Dynamics of European Integration* (Stanford, Cal.: Stanford University Press, 1963).

On integration in underdeveloped areas, see R. L. Allen, "Integration in Less Developed Areas," *Kyklos*, Fasc. 4, 1961; R. S. Bhambri, "Customs Unions and Underdeveloped Countries," *Economica Internazionale*, No. 2, 1962; R. F. Mikesell, "The Theory of Common Markets as Applied to Regional Arrangements among Developing Countries," in R. Harrod (ed.), *International Trade Theory in a Developing World* (London: Macmillan, 1963); Miguel Wionczek (ed.), *Latin American Economic Integration* (New York: Frederick A. Praeger, 1966); and Ingo Walter and Hans C. Vitzthum, *The Central American Common Market: A Case Study on Economic Integration in Developing Areas* (New York: Institute of Finance, New York University, 1967).

See also Angus Maddison, "Industrial Productivity Growth in Europe and the United States," *Economica*, November, 1954; J. M. Blair, "Technology and Size," *American Economic Review: Papers and Proceedings*, May, 1948; Marcus Fleming, "External Economies and the Doctrine of Balanced Growth," *Economic Journal*, June, 1955. R. R. Nelson, "The Simple Economics of Basic Scientific Research," *Journal of Political Economy*, June, 1959; Tibor Scitovsky, *Economic Theory and Western European Integration*, (Stanford, Cal.: Stanford University Press, 1958). Bela Balassa, *Trade Liberalization Among Industrial Countries* (New York: McGraw-Hill, 1967), chapter 5; and E. Mansfield, "Size of Firm, Market Structure, and Innovations" *Journal of Political Economy*, December, 1963.

Also of interest may be W. Beckerman, "Projecting Europe's Growth," *Economic Journal*, December, 1962; A. Lamfalussy, *The United Kingdom and the Six* (Homewood, Ill.: Richard D. Irwin, 1963). J. S. Bain, *Barriers to New Competition* (Cambridge, Mass.: Harvard University Press, 1956); and I. Svennilson, *Growth and Stagnation in the European Economy* (Geneva: United Nations Economic Commission for Europe, 1954).

Section E-15

Additional Readings on Trade and Market Structure

For some evidence on imperfect competition in international trade, see Corwin D. Edwards, "Barriers to International Competition: Interfirm Competitive Behavior," in Robert G. Hawkins and Ingo Walter, *The United States and International Markets* (Lexington, Mass.: D.C. Heath, 1972). Also D. L. McLachlan and D. Swann, *Competition Policy in the European Community* (London: Oxford University Press, 1967); and Herbert G. Grubel, "Intra-Industry Specialization and the Pattern of Trade," *Canadian Journal of Economics and Political Science*, August, 1967.

Cartels and other trade-restricting forms of organization are covered in Don Patinkin, "Multiple-plant Firms, Cartels and Imperfect Competition," *Quarterly Journal of Economics*, February, 1945; C. R. Whittlesley, *National Interests and International Cartels* (New York: Macmillan, 1946); E. Hexner, *International Cartels* (Chapel Hill: University of North Carolina Press, 1945); E. S. Mason,

Controlling World Trade (New York: McGraw-Hill, 1946); and General Agreement on Tariffs and Trade, *Restrictive Business Practices* (Geneva: GATT, 1959).

On dumping and international price discrimination, the classic work is Jacob Viner, *Dumping* (Chicago: University of Chicago Press, 1923); see also G. Lovasy, "International Trade Under Imperfect Competition," *Quarterly Journal of Economics,* August, 1941; O. J. McDiarmid, "Imperfect Competition and International Trade Theory" in H. A. Innis (ed.), *Essays in Political Economy* (Toronto: University of Toronto Press, 1938); and D. B. Marsh, *World Trade and Investment* (New York: Harcourt Brace Jovanovich, 1951), ch. 22. For some recent studies, see Bela Balassa, *Trade Liberalization Among Industrial Countries* (New York: McGraw-Hill for the Council on Foreign Relations, 1967); and Bela Balassa and Associates, *Studies in Trade Liberalization* (Baltimore: The Johns Hopkins Press, 1967).

For analyses of commodity agreements and export controls, see B. C. Swerling, *Current Issues in Commercial Policy* (Princeton, N.J.: Princeton University 1962); J. A. Pincus, "What Policy for Commodities?" *Foreign Affairs,* January, 1964; W. Butler, "Trade and the Less Developed Countries," *Foreign Affairs,* January, 1963; Jan Tinbergen, *Shaping the World Economy* (New York: Twentieth Century Fund, 1962); G. Haberler, *et al., Trends in International Trade* (Geneva: General Agreement on Tariffs and Trade, 1958); and the following United Nations publications: *Commodity Trade and Economic Development* (1954), *International Compensation for Fluctuations in Commodity Trade* (1961), and *Measures for Economic Stability* (1951). See also R. G. Hawkins, J. Epstein, and J. Gonzales, *Stabilization of Export Receipts and Economic Development* (New York: Institute of Finance, New York University, 1966).

Also of interest will be H. C. Wallich, "Stabilization of Proceeds from Raw Materials Exports," in H. S. Ellis (ed.), *Economic Development for Latin America* (New York: St. Martin's Press, 1961); and P. T. Bauer and F. W. Paish, "The Reduction of Fluctuations in the Incomes of Primary Producers," *Economic Journal,* December, 1952.

On state trading, useful references are R. F. Mikesell and J. N. Behrman, *Financing Free World Trade with the Sino-Soviet Bloc* (Princeton, N.J.: Princeton University, 1958); Jacob Viner, *Trade Relations Between Free Market and Controlled Economies* (Geneva: League of Nations, 1943); F. L. Pryor, "Foreign Trade Theory in the Communist Bloc," *Soviet Studies,* July, 1962; N. Spulber, *Economics of Eastern Europe* (Cambridge: Technology Press, 1957); as well as two issues of *Law and Contemporary Problems* devoted to the question of state trading in the spring and summer of 1959.

Section E-16

Glossary of Terms Used in Balance of Payments Analysis*

Autonomous transactions in the balance of payments are those undertaken for their own sake. Their net effect in each period is reflected in the net total of financing transactions. This analytic division of the balance of payments transactions into the two classes, autonomous and financing, though desirable, is difficult in practice. In fact, the final group in a balance of payments table is rarely entitled "financing items," as this would raise more questions than it would answer. A more readily identifiable approximation to such a group is all that is usually possible, for example, "monetary movements" or "net reserves."

Basic balance. Roughly defined as the balance of current and long-term capital transactions, the basic balance is intended to measure longer-term tendencies in the balance of payments and to show a balance that has not been distorted by fluctuating, easily reversible, or speculative factors.

Capital Account. In the earliest published balance of payments statements, the capital account was given prominence as the group of transactions which financed the current account. Although the financing function is now more often attributed to a much smaller group of transactions within the capital group (financing other capital as well as current transactions), the capital account retains analytic interest as the group which comprises the net acquisition of financial assets.

Central monetary institutions, such as the central bank or exchange office and the Treasury or Finance Ministry, play an important role in the balance of payments. They are the national authorities who mobilize finance to meet balance of payments deficits (or surpluses), for which purpose they have control over the national reserves. Alternatively, they may mobilize other means of financing to substitute for the use of reserves. Note that central monetary institutions' transactions cannot always be equated with reserve movements; the institutions may undertake long-term loan transactions or operate bilateral payments agreements that are not normally classed among reserves.

C.i.f. (cost, insurance, freight). The c.i.f. valuation is one of the conventional ways of recording merchandise imports (see also f.o.b.), but is not often applied to exports. Note that "C.i.f. basis" is commonly used to denote that imports are recorded c.i.f., while exports are recorded f.o.b.

At the point of valuation, such as the customs frontier of the importing country, the c.i.f. value of merchandise is recorded as including all international freight and insurance up to that point that has to be met by the importer. It follows that freight and insurance recorded on a c.i.f. basis in the balance of payments do not include these debits for freight and insurance on imports. The entries for freight and insurance on this basis do, however, include credit entries offsetting domestic companies' earnings that have been included in the c.i.f. value of imports (an example of the inclusion in the balance of payments of transactions between residents of the same country).

* This glossary was prepared by John Alves, Assistant Chief of the Research Department of the International Monetary Fund and originally appeared in *IMF Survey,* November 12, November 23, and December 17, 1973 (condensed).

On either the c.i.f. basis or the f.o.b. basis, the net total for merchandise, freight, and merchandise insurance will be the same. The trade balance, however, is different: on the c.i.f. basis the surpluses are lower and the deficits higher than on the f.o.b. basis.

Customs data on imports are published by the great majority of countries on a c.i.f. basis. Statistics on imports based on an exchange record are likely to be on a mixed basis, as actual payments recorded are sometimes c.i.f., sometimes f.o.b.; this may also be true of exports in the exchange record.

Contra-entries (or counterpart entries). Every entry in the balance of payments has its contra-entry, or -entries, explicitly or implicitly in some other item, where they will be of opposite sign. For example, a transaction in goods or services may be reflected in a movement in an international account in a commercial bank and thus give rise to a balance of payments contra-entry in the monetary sector of the capital account. A gift in kind may be recorded under merchandise, with a contra-entry under unrequited transfers.

Credits and Debits. A credit in the balance of payments records the provision of goods or services, a decrease in holdings of an asset, or an increase in liabilities. A debit records the acquisition of goods or services, an increase in assets, or a decrease in liabilities. Credits and debits form the two elements in the simple double-entry system used for recording the balance of payments.

Currency conversion rates. Under a regime of fixed par values, a balance of payments expressed in terms of one currency can readily be converted into another currency by using their par values and disregarding the customary minor fluctuations that are permitted around those values in foreign exchange markets. At the other extreme, when currencies are floating, conversion rates have to be obtained from market averages, and a large measure of approximation has to be accepted, not only in conversions but also in the original compilation of a national balance of payments, since the balance of payments is an aggregation of transactions originally denominated in a variety of different currencies.

Current account. The current account comprises transactions in goods, services, and unrequited transfers, and thus excludes transactions in financial assets and liabilities. This is the widest definition and the one that is generally accepted; at various times and in various countries there have been narrower definitions of the current account, and all or part of the category of unrequited transfers has been excluded; even investment income has been grouped with certain transfers and excluded from the current account. Some analysts prefer to exclude governmental transfers from the current account, while others exclude official aid grants. For this reason, whenever the term "current account" is employed, it should be defined.

Deficit. A deficit in the balance of payments, reflected in a loss of reserves, implies that the economy's international earnings are exceeded by expenditures. Deficit can also be defined in various other ways; deficits (or surpluses) on the trade balance, the current balance, the basic balance, or the overall balance are all of interest in balance of payments analysis (see also the definitions of those balances elsewhere in this glossary).

Direct investment is undertaken to acquire or to extend control over an enterprise. It has proved difficult to find an exact definition of control to use in balance of payments classification; nevertheless, the category has a dominating importance in almost any analysis.

Among the sectors of the capital account, direct investment is something of an exception, being defined functionally rather than institutionally. Even if defined as the sector comprising all direct investment enterprises, it overrides the institutional classification to include governmental direct investment.

Errors and omissions. The net total of errors and omissions is a balancing item that compensates for any excess of recorded credits over recorded debits (or vice versa). The total can be large, where balance of payments statistics are obtained from diverse sources, and can be of importance in analysis by suggesting, for example, a capital outflow (not otherwise recorded) or a wrong valuation of merchandise.

The absence of errors and omissions is more likely to suggest an unambitious balance of payments statement, based solely on self-balancing banking statistics, and is less likely to suggest a comprehensive statement covering all appropriate categories.

F.a.s. (free alongside). A variant of the f.o.b. convention for recording merchandise. The loading charges are excluded from the value recorded, which is otherwise the same as f.o.b.

Financing items. See **autonomous transactions.**

F.o.b. (free on board). The most frequently used method of recording merchandise for the balance of payments (see also **c.i.f.**). On the convention that exports and imports are valued at the customs frontier (or similar point of exit and entry), all international freight and insurance beyond that point is excluded from the value of merchandise and included elsewhere in the balance of payments.

Freight. On the f.o.b. basis of accounting (see **f.o.b.**), international freight is recorded entirely separately from the merchandise on which it is paid and transactions between residents are not included (as is normally the case

for most balance of payments categories). For a given country, freight credits on this basis represent earnings on exports and by carriers of the country on trade between other countries; freight debits mainly represent payments on imports.

On the c.i.f. basis (see **c.i.f.**) freight earnings may be recorded on exports, on imports, and on other shipments. The freight earned (credit) on imports is included to offset the value of that freight which is included in the c.i.f. value of imports (debit) and represents a transaction between residents of the same country, since the importer has paid a resident carrier.

Gold plays two distinct roles in the balance of payments. In one role it is akin to merchandise and may be exported and imported just as any other commodity (nonmonetary gold). In the other role, it is held by a country's monetary authorities to form part of its international reserves; monetary gold may cross international frontiers in settlement of international indebtedness, and in this role it should be excluded from merchandise totals.

Nonmonetary gold enters into the balance of payments not only in a commodity role, but in other instances by the fact of "monetization," when gold is sold by mining companies or other residents to the monetary authorities. An entry is required in the balance of payments to offset an increase in international reserves although there has been no international transaction. The reverse process of "demonetization" also has to be recorded.

Government transactions are grouped together in various areas of the balance of payments. Exports and imports by the government are not often distinguished in the merchandise item, but governmental services (other than transportation, travel, and investment income) form a separate item covering transactions both of the domestic government and of foreign governments. The unrequited transfers of the domestic government form another item, and the central government is one of the sectors of the capital account. Any international reserves held by the domestic government, rather than by central monetary institutions, are classified among "reserves and related items," where the government's holdings are usually specified separately.

Imbalance. Although by definition the total of credit entries is equal to the total of debit entries, there may be trends in certain items in the balance of payments leading to distortion and strains that correspond to imbalance elsewhere in the domestic social accounts and in the balance of payments of one or more other countries.

Insurance. At one time a main item among the services distinguished in the balance of payments, insurance is now more usually separated into merchandise insurance (part of the freight item) and nonmerchandise insurance (a component of the item for miscellaneous services). The merchandise insurance may be recorded (in the same way as freight) on an f.o.b. basis or a c.i.f. basis. On the f.o.b. basis, no amounts of insurance are included in the value of imports, and transactions between residents are excluded. On the c.i.f. basis, import insurance premiums are included in the value of imports, partly offset by credit entries in merchandise insurance representing that part of the premiums which is received by resident companies.

Investment income. Interest on loans, securities, and deposits; dividends on shares; and profits of enterprises are all included in this category. In most balance of payments presentations, investment income is grouped with services.

Balance of payments methodology differs from that for national income statistics by including undistributed

earnings in the total for investment income. The same amounts are entered (with opposite sign) in the item for direct investment, with the result that there is no net impact on the balance of payments as a whole. Certain countries have been unable to collect or estimate figures for undistributed earnings and they omit them from their balance of payments.

Invisibles. The term usually covers services and unrequited transfers and is used to distinguish those categories from visibles (merchandise) in the current account.

Long-term is used in the balance of payments to describe a security or other financial instrument with an original maturity of more than one year; in a few countries the dividing line may be set at two or three years, but one year is the most usual. An analysis of the capital account into long-term or short-term elements is perhaps less interesting than an analysis by sector or by function, but long-term characteristics can sometimes be a useful criterion for choosing the items that enter into the basic balance (see also **basic balance**).

Losses by unprofitable direct investment enterprises are usually entered in the balance of payments as deductions from investment income. Thus negative entries (minus credits or minus debits) can occasionally result when the enterprises in that sector have done badly during a given period. Losses in reserves will normally reflect a deficit in the balance of payments, but they may also result from changes in the par value or market value of currencies held in the foreign exchange reserves. Losses resulting from changes in value have usually been excluded from the balance of payments.

Market values should be used in the balance of payments for recording transactions, but it is necessary to employ some substitute valuation, giving an approximate equivalent, when the market value cannot be established.

In currency conversions, market values are used only in a floating situation, when no effective par value can be quoted.

Merchandise. Almost all of the exports and imports by a given country are entered in the balance of payments in the merchandise account, which also includes goods sold abroad that do not enter the merchant's own country. The criterion for inclusion is an international change of ownership, and the timing of the inclusion should correspond to the time when ownership changes. The small amounts of goods that change ownership but are not covered by the merchandise account include travelers' purchases abroad (which form part of the travel total) and purchases of goods by diplomatic and military personnel (classified under government).

Migration. Effective transfers by migrants are recorded in the balance of payments when the individual moves his residence (or center of interest) from one national economy to another. His having done so may be established under tax laws or exchange control regulations; in the absence of other criteria, his remaining in his new country for one year or more may suggest the probability that he has migrated.

Multilateral settlements. See **regional statements.**

Nonmonetary capital. Although the term sounds contradictory it is commonly used as a short way to describe the category comprising the capital transactions of the nonmonetary sectors (nonbank sectors) of the economy.

Overall balance. The balance that has to be financed by reserves and related items or by net official reserve movements. The overall balance comprises the basic balance and also the short-term, readily reversible transactions normally excluded from the basic balance. In recent Fund presentations the overall balance has been shown in two ways: first, excluding the allocation of SDRs and second, including the allocation of SDRs.

Payments balance. A journalists' term usually used in approximately the same sense as overall balance. Its use indicates the presence of a dangerous wish to quote the single figure that will summarize the balance of payments surplus or deficit for the period. The balance of payments is best understood by considering various cumulative balances, such as trade balance, current account balance, basic balance, and overall balance.

Payments basis (or settlements basis). A balance of payments described as being on this basis is normally taken from an exchange record and is a first approximation to a more comprehensive statement (see **transactions basis**).

Payments imbalance usually means "deficit" but sometimes means "large surplus."

Portfolio investment. As distinct from direct investment (undertaken for the sake of obtaining entrepreneurial income), portfolio investment is undertaken for the sake of investment income or capital gains.

Private sector, the sector most likely to be affected by market forces, is given greatest prominence in the Fund standard presentation in the capital account where the sectors' assets and liabilities (what it owns and what it owes) are the criteria for classification, rather than the transactions initiated by the sector. Thus private sales abroad of government securities will be attributed to the government sector in the capital account in the balance of payments of the seller's country.

The private sector is also distinguished for unrequited transfers and is confined to domestic private transactions. See also **government transactions.**

Regional statements. A regional balance of payments may be difficult to compile and to interpret when multilateral use of currencies is permitted and the currency used for settlement need not be the currency of one of the transacting countries; a reconciliation item is provided in a regional table for each region specified, in the form of an entry against, "multilateral settlements" (or, failing that, by regional net errors and omissions).

Regional balance of payments statements continue to be of interest to analysts, the more so since the emergence of regional groups such as the European Community and the free-trade areas in Latin America.

A regional statement is of greatest interest where trade and payments are on strict bilateral lines, but where such situations exist balance of payments statistics are not often made available for publication.

Reserves and related items. Reserve assets are the actual (spot) holdings of gold and foreign exchange assets, together with IMF positions and SDRs, available to the monetary authorities to meet balance of payments deficits. Changes in reserve assets are usually recorded net in the balance of payments, in the sense that they may be grouped with any liabilities that constitute reserves for other countries.

Certain categories are conventionally excluded from reserves such as long-term loans and payments agreement balances because of their limited availability. Assets held in nominally long-term form are often included, however, if they are readily marketable.

Reserve creation. Reserves can be created by the allocation of SDRs and by the monetization of gold and they can be destroyed by the reversal of those processes. In addition, since reserves are expressed in terms of a currency or of a unit of account, realignments of currencies can change the value of reserves expressed in terms other than those of the currency held.

Reserve gains. See losses.

Residence is an important criterion in deciding which transactions should be included in the balance of payments, as most transactions recorded therein are between residents of different countries. An individual, enterprise, or institution is regarded as resident if the principal center of interest is in the country in question. An individual in a country for less than one year might be regarded as a visitor rather than as a resident (see also **travel**).

Resident-to-resident transactions are included as occasional, necessary exceptions to the general rule that the balance of payments deals with transactions between residents of different countries. For example, an asset in the form of a claim on a foreigner may be traded between, say, the domestic government and a domestic enterprise, and this gives rise to balance of payments entries. Similarly, the offsetting of the domestically paid freight included in the value of merchandise c.i.f. is achieved by recording another resident-to-resident transaction.

Sectors. The sectors distinguished in the IMF's present standard presentation of the capital account in the balance of payments comprise direct investment, the rest of the (nonbank or nonmonetary) private sector, local government, central government, deposit money banks, and the central monetary authorities. Apart from direct investment, this type of sectoring is by the type of institution rather than by the function of the transaction. In recent years, this sectoral division of the capital account has been partly overridden by the introduction of a final group in the presentation, "Reserves and related items," defined functionally rather than institutionally, but in fact almost always referring to the central government and the central monetary authorities.

Services ("invisible services") in the balance of payments are conventionally listed under the principal categories of freight, other transportation, travel, investment income, other governmental, and other private services (including insurance other than the merchandise insurance usually classified with transportation). Services, together with merchandise, nonmonetary gold, private and government unrequited transfers make up the current account in the widest of its usual definitions.

Settlements basis. See payments basis.

Short-term is used in the balance of payments to describe a security or other financial instrument with an original maturity of normally less than one year; see also **long-term.**

Special drawing rights (SDRs) did not fit easily into the existing framework of balance of payments classification. The allocation of SDRs is an act of reserve creation that is not an unrequited transfer, a capital account transaction, or a reserve movement (although the counterpart entry is an increase in reserves). Like monetary gold, SDRs are assets that have no corresponding liability.

The IMF solution to the problem of classifying the allocation of SDRs in the balance of payments has been to create a new separate group immediately preceding the reserves and related items. Holdings of SDRs, of course, form part of reserves, and there is no problem in recording the increases or decreases therein.

At the national level, most central bank balance sheets include SDRs as assets, and they are offset on the liability side by an entry for allocations of SDRs.

Surplus. A surplus in the balance of payments is reflected in a gain in reserves, implying that the economy's international earnings exceed expenditures. See also **deficit** for other possible definitions.

Trade balance. Of the succession of cumulative balances that can be used in analyzing the balance of payments, the trade balance is often the most important as it comprises merchandise, often the largest amounts shown in the statement. Merchandise figures are normally available soon after the end of each month and provide an early indication of balance of payments trends, even though the figures may not have been fully adjusted to fit into a balance of payments framework. The trade balance based on unadjusted customs statistics will include amounts of freight and insurance where imports have been valued c.i.f.; it may include goods such as contractors' equipment entering the country without change of ownership; it may exclude the value of ships and aircraft entering service abroad and never recorded as imports. There are many other differences in coverage, timing, and valuation between customs totals and the fully adjusted balance of payments totals. These differences are often small but can on occasion be large, and the unadjusted trade balance must be used with caution as an indicator of developments.

Transaction value (see also **market value**). In valuing merchandise, where no readily ascertainable market value exists, the compiler will often have to use a transaction value represented perhaps by the value quoted on the invoice or the entry made in intercompany books. Such values may sometimes not be realistic, but they relate to actual changes in company books and thus have the specious attraction of not causing errors and omissions in the balance of payments statement.

Transactions basis. This term, like "economic basis," is sometimes used to denote a balance of payments appropriately compiled to cover the transactions that have taken place rather than the receipts and payments to which they give rise. A simple example of the difference in approach is debt that is due but not paid. Nothing is recorded on the "payments basis," but in the full statement on the transactions basis, repayment is recorded when due, financed by a new liability arising from nonpayment. Similarly, merchandise purchased on credit is recorded, on a payments basis, only when paid for; on a transactions basis the purchaser's goods would be recorded when he obtained them, with an offsetting entry under trade credit. The later settlement of the trade credit would give rise to further entries in the balance of payments.

Transfer payments, transfers, unilateral transfers are all terms that have been used in the past in the sense of unrequited transfers.

Transportation (see also **freight**). In addition to freight on international shipments, transportation in the balance of payments includes, for example, the following categories of services: passenger fares, time-chartering of ships and aircraft, port disbursements (including bunkering, ships' stores, and repairs), airport disbursements, mail fees, salvage earnings, and earnings from foreign costal trade.

Travel as defined for the balance of payments covers visitors' expenditures within the country they are visiting, but it does not cover their transportation expenses to or from that country. The category covers living expenses, entertainment, purchases of goods, and transportation within the country visited. Visitors include tourists, businessmen, government officials, students, pilgrims, and invalids seeking treatment. A visitor staying longer than one year might be considered to become a resident of the country, but the qualifying period varies from country to country according to exchange control and other local regulations.

Undistributed earnings. The investment income earnings of an enterprise, not distributed to shareholders but reinvested in the enterprise, are included in the balance of payments statements of most countries even though the funds will have remained within the enterprise concerned. The advantage of including these earnings (offset by new investment) is that the full amount of the earnings of foreign capital is recorded on the one side, and the full amount of new investment by (or under the control of) nonresidents is recorded on the other side. See also **investment income.**

Unit of account. A balance of payments statement is ideally expressed in terms of a stable unit of account. A series of figures expressed in a currency that has been frequently devalued is meaningless for international comparisons and sometimes even for domestic consideration. Until 1971, the U.S. dollar was the most usual currency of account for balance of payments statements. In IMF publications, the SDR is now normally used as the unit of account.

Unrequited transfers are, broadly, transactions undertaken without a quid pro quo and previously were variously known as transfer payments, unilateral transfers, or donations. The term, unrequited transfers, has been taken from national income accounting (although balance of payments accounts do not often follow the national income accounts in subdividing these transfers into current and capital). In the balance of payments, unrequited transfers are conventionally included in the current account, although in some analyses a part of government transfers may instead be included with certain loans in a total for official aid.

Valuation. A correct valuation basis for merchandise, or securities, or currencies is often a problem for the balance of payments compiler, who should aim to record the market value at the time of each transaction. Approximations often have to be accepted. See also **market value** and **transaction value.**

Visible trade is merchandise trade (see **merchandise**) as distinct from "invisible trade" in services.

Workers' earnings (see also **migration**). Wages and salaries earned by visiting workers should be recorded in full as debits in the services section of the balance of payments, as earnings by nonresidents, and the temporary workers' expenditures should also be re-

corded as credits in the same section (the balance is assumed to have been remitted to the worker's home country). If the worker remains for more than one year, he might be regarded as a resident and his earnings and expenditures would no longer be recorded in the balance of payments. In practice, many countries will be able to record only the net remittance, and there may be various criteria for residence; thus, the statistics for workers' earnings may not be comparable from country to country.

Section E-17

Additional Readings and Sources of Data for Balance of Payments Analysis

On balance of payments statistics, see R. G. D. Allen and J. S. Ely (eds.), *International Trade Statistics* (New York: Wiley, 1953); and U.S. Bureau of the Budget, Review Committee for Balance of Payments Statistics, *The Balance of Payments Statistics of the United States* (Washington, D.C.: U.S. Government Printing Office, 1965).

An extremely worthwhile, but difficult, exposition of the balance of payments may be found in James E. Meade, *The Balance of Payments* (London: Oxford University Press, 1951), chs. 1–3.

The different concepts of balance are surveyed in the Bureau of the Budget Study, cited above, and in Walter R. Gardner, "An Exchange-Market Analysis of the U.S. Balance of Payments," *IMF Staff Paper,* May, 1961; Walther Lederer, "Measuring the Balance of Payments," in Joint Economic Committee, U.S. Congress, *Factors Affecting the United States Balance of Payments* (Washington, D.C.: U.S. Government Printing Office, 1962), pp. 73–86; and Hal B. Lary, *Problems of the United States as a World Trader and Banker* (New York: National Bureau of Economic Research, 1963), ch. 2 and appendix A.

Current balance of payments data for the U.S. may be found in issues of the *Federal Reserve Bulletin* and the *Survey of Current Business.* Both of these periodically publish special tables including the balance of international indebtedness, or international investment position. For the balances of payments of other countries, the best sources are the International Monetary Fund's *International Financial Statistics,* and the United Nations' *Monthly Bulletin of Statistics,* both of which are published monthly. Statistical publications of the individual countries themselves also will be useful, especially statistical yearbooks and the bulletins of the national central banks and treasuries, as well as large national and international commercial banks.

Perhaps the most thorough and instructive analysis of U.S. balance of payments deficits, certainly worth reading from a methodological standpoint alone, is Walter S. Salant, *et al., The United States Balance of Payments in 1968* (Washington, D.C., Brookings Institution, 1963). Another such study is Hal B. Lary, *Problems of the United States as World Trader and Banker* (New York: National Bureau of Economic Research, 1963).

On the balance of payments impact of capital flows, one interesting study is Philip W. Bell, "Private Capital Movements and the U.S. Balance of Payments Position," in Joint Economic Committee, U.S. Congress, *Factors Affecting the United States Balance of Payments* (Washington, D.C.: U.S. Government Printing Office, 1962). Also of interest in the same volume are R. E. Baldwin, "Implications of Structural Changes in Commodity Trade"; and E. M. Bernstein, "The Long-Run Prospect for the U.S. Balance of Payments."

More recent analyses are contained in Benjamin J. Cohen *Balance of Payments Policy* (Philadelphia: Penguin, 1969); David T. Devlin, "The U.S. Balance of Payments: Revised Presentation," *Survey of Current Business,* June, 1971; and John Pippenger, "Balance of Payments Deficits: Measurement and Interpretation," *Federal Reserve Bank of St. Louis Review,* November, 1973.

Section E-18

Additional Readings on Foreign Exchange

An excellent discussion of the foreign-exchange market may be found in Leland B. Yeager, *International Monetary Relations* (New York: Harper, 1966), ch. 2. Also see Paul Einzig, *The Foreign Exchange Market* (London: Macmillan, 1964); Norman Crump, *The ABC of Foreign Exchanges,* 13th ed. (London: Macmillan, 1963); Robert M. Stern, *The Balance of Payments* (Chicago: Aldine, 1973); and Robert Z. Aliber, *The International Money Game* (New York: Basic Books, 1973).

On the mechanics of foreign exchange, the following will be of value: Alan Holmes and Francis H. Schott, *The New York Foreign Exchange Market,* 4th ed. (New York: Federal Reserve Bank of New York, 1972); Morgan Guaranty Trust Company's *Export and Import Procedures* (New York: Morgan Guaranty, 1973); and for those who read German, Helmut Lipfert, *Devisenhandel* (Frankfurt/M: Fritz Knapp Verlag, 1958). An excellent introductory article is Clay J. Anderson, "The Foreign Exchange Market," in F. B. Jensen and I. Walter, *Readings in International Economic Relations* (New York: Ronald Press, 1966).

On forward exchange, see Paul Einzig, *A Dynamic Theory of Forward Exchange* (London: Macmillan, 1961) including the question of interest arbitrage. Also, see Jerome L. Stein, "The Nature and Efficiency of the Foreign Exchange Market," Essays in International Finance, No. 40, (Princeton, N.J.: International Finance Section, Princeton University, 1962); S. C. Tsiang, "The Theory of Forward Exchange and Effects of Government Intervention on the Forward Exchange Market," *IMF Staff Papers,* April, 1959; B. Reading, "The Forward Pound, 1951–59," *Economic Journal,* June, 1960; Robert Z. Aliber, *The International Market for Foreign Exchange* (New York: Frederick A. Praeger, 1969); and Benjamin J. Cohen, *Balance of Payments Policy* (Baltimore: Penguin, 1969).

On Eurocurrency markets, the best available work is Geoffrey Bell, *The Euro-Dollar Market and the International Financial System* (London: Macmillan, 1973).

Section E-19

Additional Readings on International Monetary Standards

A vast literature now exists on alternative international monetary standards and their implications for trade and payments. See, for example, Egon Sohmen, *Flexible Exchange Rates: Theory and Controversy* (Chicago: University of Chicago Press, 1961), and by the same author, *International Monetary Problems and the Foreign Exchanges* (Princeton, N.J.: International Finance Section, Princeton University, 1963); Milton Friedman, "The Case for Flexible Exchange Rates," in his *Essays in Positive Economics* (Chicago: University of Chicago Press, 1953); G. N. Halm, "Fixed or Flexible Exchange Rates," in Joint Economic Committee, U.S. Congress, *Factors Affecting the United States Balance of Payments* (Washington: U.S. Government Printing Office, 1962); R. Z. Aliber, "Speculation in Foreign Exchanges: The European Experience, 1919–1926," *Yale Economic Essays,* Spring, 1962; and R. E. Caves, "Flexible Exchange Rates," *American Economic Review,* May, 1963.

Also of interest will be Fritz Machlup, "The Theory of Foreign Exchanges" in his *International Payments, Debts, and Gold* (New York: Scribner's, 1964), ch. 1; and James E. Meade, *The Balance of Payments* (Oxford: Oxford University Press, 1951), chs. 12, 14, 15, 17, and 20, although much of this may prove a bit complex at this stage.

Section E-20

Additional Readings on International Transmission of Business Conditions

Excellent presentations of foreign-trade multipliers may be found in Charles P Kindleberger, *International Economics,* 5th ed. (Homewood, Ill.: Richard D. Irwin, 1973), ch. 20; and Donald Bailey Marsh, *World Trade and Investment* (New York: Harcourt Brace Jovanovich, 1951), chs. 17–18. Kindleberger uses graphical analysis to particularly good advantage. A somewhat more difficult analysis is presented by Jaroslav Vanek, *International Trade: Theory and Economic Policy* (Homewood, Ill.: Richard D. Irwin, 1962), ch. 7.

On foreign repercussions, it is difficult to surpass Fritz Machlup, *International Trade and the National Income Multiplier* (Philadelphia: Blakiston, 1943) for clarity of exposition. For a graphical presentation, see Romney Robinson, "A Graphical Analysis of the Foreign Trade Multiplier," *Economic Journal,* September, 1952.

Interested students may also wish to consult the following: Herbert Giersch, "The Accelerator and the Propensity to Import," reprinted in International Economic Association, *International Economic Papers,* No. 4 (New York: Macmillan, 1954); F. D. Holzman and A. Zellner, "The Foreign Trade and Balanced Budget Multipliers," *American Economic Review,* March, 1958; J. E. Meade, *The Balance of Payments* (London: Oxford University Press, 1951), chs. IV and V; K. Miyazawa, "Foreign Trade Multiplier, Input-Output Analysis and the Consumption

Function," *Quarterly Journal of Economics,* February, 1960; H. Neisser and F. Modigliani, *National Incomes and Foreign Trade* (Urbana: University of Illinois Press, 1953); J. J. Polak, *An International Economic System* (London: George Allen & Unwin, 1954); and G. L. Rees, "Price Effects and Foreign Trade Multiplier," *Review of Economic Studies,* Vol. 20, No. 3, 1952–53.

In recent years an effort has been made to specify the macroeconomic linkages among economies in much greater detail by tying together short-term macroeconomic forecasting models for the major industrial countries. The best discussion of these efforts may be found in R. J. Ball (ed.), *The International Linkage of National Economic Models* (Amsterdam: North Holland, 1973).

Section E-21

Readings on Fixed Exchange-Rate Payments Adjustment

An excellent presentation of the adjustment process under fixed exchange-rate equilibrium and disequilibrium systems is contained in Robert A. Mundell, "The International Disequilibrium System," *Kyklos,* Fasc. I, 1961. Our analysis of automatic balance of payments adjustment under the fixed- and flexible-exchange rates follows rather closely the exposition in Meade's *The Balance of Payments* (Oxford: Oxford University Press, 1951), ch. 15. His entire section on balance of payments adjustment in the absence of ad hoc restrictions (chs. 11–19) is the most thorough one available, but very difficult reading. Alternatively, see Leland B. Yeager, *International Monetary Relations* (New York: Harper, 1966), chs. 4–6.

On the gold standard and the price-specie flow mechanism, see R. G. Hawtrey, *The Gold Standard in Theory and Practice* (London: Longmans, Green & Co., 1947); W. E. Beach, *British International Gold Movements and Banking Policy, 1881–1913* (Cambridge: Harvard University Press, 1935); A. I. Bloomfield, *Short-Term Capital Movements Under the Pre-1914 Gold Standard* (Princeton, N.J.: Princeton University, 1963); and T. E. Gregory, *The Gold Standard and Its Future* (New York: E. P. Dutton, 1935).

Also, see J. M. Fleming, "Money Supply and Imports," *IMF Staff Papers,* May, 1961; J. J. Polack and L. Boissonneault, "Monetary Analysis of Income and Imports and Its Statistical Application," *IMF Staff Papers,* April, 1960; and W. A. Brown, Jr., *The Gold Standard Re-interpreted, 1914–1934* (New York: National Bureau of Economic Research, 1934).

For an excellent survey, see Anne O. Krueger, "Balance of Payments Theory," *Journal of Economic Literature,* March, 1969.

Section E-22

Readings on Flexible Exchange-Rate Payments Adjustment

For a more extensive bibliography, see the paper by Anne O. Krueger cited in Section E-21.

On adjustments under flexible rates, see Egon Sohmen, *Fluctuating Exchange Rates: Theory and Controversy* (Chicago: University of Chicago Press, 1961); Milton Friedman, "The Case for Flexible Exchange Rates" in his *Essays in Positive Economics* (Chicago: University of Chicago Press, 1953); R. E. Caves, "Flexible Exchange Rates," *American Economic Review*, May, 1963; S. C. Tsiang, "An Experiment with a Flexible Rate System: The Case of Peru, 1950–54," *IMF Staff Papers*, February, 1957; and E. V. Morgan, "The Theory of Flexible Exchange Rates," *American Economic Review*, June, 1955.

On the Marshall–Lerner condition and import elasticities, see Alfred Marshall, *The Pure Theory of Foreign Trade* (1879) as reprinted (London: London School of Economics, 1930); A. P. Lerner, *The Economics of Control* (New York: Macmillan, 1944); C. P. Kindleberger, *International Economics*, 5th ed. (Homewood, Ill.: Richard D. Irwin, 1973), Appendix F; G. H. Orcutt, "Measurement of Price Elasticities in International Trade," *Review of Economics and Statistics*, May, 1950; and P. Streeten, "Elasticity Optimism and Pessimism in International Trade," *Economia Internazionale*, February, 1954.

Also of interest will be W. F. Stolper, "The Multiplier, Flexible Exchanges and International Equilibrium," *Quarterly Journal of Economics*, November, 1950; R. A. Mundell, "The Monetary Dynamics of International Adjustment Under Fixed and Flexible Exchange Rates," *Quarterly Journal of Economics*, May, 1950; R. E. Jones, "Depreciation and the Dampening Effects of Income Changes," *Review of Economics and Statistics*, February, 1960; Ragnar Nurkse, "Conditions of International Monetary Equilibrium," *Essays in International Finance*, No. 4 (Princeton, N.J.: Princeton University, 1945); and W. M. Scammel, *International Monetary Policy*, 2nd ed. (London: Macmillan, 1964), chs. 2–4.

Section E-23

Additional Readings on Balance of Payments Adjustment via Macroeconomic Policy

On questions of internal versus external balance, see James E. Meade, *The Balance of Payments* (London: Oxford University Press, 1951), chs. VII–X; Leland B. Yeager, *International Monetary Relations* (New York: Harper, 1966), ch. 6 and appendix; M. O. Clement, R. L. Pfister, and K. J. Rothwell, *Theoretical Issues in International Economics* (New York: Houghton Mifflin, 1967), chs. 5 and 8; and W. M. Scammell, *International Monetary Policy* (London: Macmillan, 1964), ch. 4.

On balance of payments disequilibria and their causes, see James E. Meade, *The Balance of Payments*, chs. IV–VII; R. Nurkse, "Conditions of International Monetary Equilibrium," in H. S. Ellis and L. A. Metzler (eds.), *Readings in the Theory of International Trade* (Homewood, Ill.: Richard D. Irwin, 1949); Hal B. Lary, *Problems of the United States as World Trader and Banker* (New York: National Bureau of Economic Research, 1963); J. G. Williamson, "Dollar Scarcity and Surplus in Historical Perspective," *American Economic Review*, May, 1963; and Bela Balassa, "Recent Developments in the Competitiveness of American Industry and Prospects for the Future," in Joint Economic Committee, U.S. Congress, *Factors Affecting the United States Balance of Payments* (Washington, D.C.: U.S. Government Printing Office, 1962).

Also of interest is R. N. Cooper, "The Competitive Position of the United States," in Seymour E. Harris (ed.). *The Dollar in Crisis* (New York: Harcourt Brace Jovanovich, 1961); H. G. Johnson, *International Trade and Economic Growth* (Cambridge: Harvard University Press, 1958), and his "Economic Expansion and the Balance of Payments," *Bulletin of the Oxford University Institute of Statistics*, February, 1955; C. P. Kindleberger, *Foreign Trade and the National Economy* (New Haven, Conn.: Yale University Press, 1962); J. M. Fleming and S. C. Tsiang, "Changes in Competitive Strength and Export Shares of Major Industrial Countries," *IMF Staff Papers*, August, 1956; J. H. Furth, "Unbalanced International Accounts: Diagnosis and Therapy," *American Economic Review*, May, 1961; and S. Laursen, "Productivity, Wages, and the Balance of Payments," *Review of Economics and Statistics*, May, 1955.

See also R. A. Mundell, "The Appropriate Use of Monetary and Fiscal Policy for Internal and External Stability," *IMF Staff Papers*, March, 1962; Jan Tinbergen, "International Coordination of Stabilization and Development Policies," *Kyklos*, Fasc. 3, 1959; Ragnar Nurkse, "Domestic and International Equilibrium" in Seymour Harris (ed.), *The New Economics* (New York: Alfred A. Knopf, 1947); F. A. Lutz, *International Payments and Monetary Policy in the World Today* (Stockholm: Almquist & Wiksell, 1961); P. B. Kenen, *British Monetary Policy and the Balance of Payments, 1951–57* (Cambridge, Mass.: Harvard University Press, 1960); and Hal B. Lary, *Problems of the United States as World Trader and Banker* (New York: National Bureau of Economic Research, 1963).

Also of interest will be E. M. Bernstein, *International Effects of U.S. Economic Policy*, Study Paper No. 16 in Joint Economic Committee, U.S. Congress, *Study of Employment, Growth and Price Levels* (Washington, D.C.: U.S. Government Printing Office, 1960); J. H. Furth, "International Developments and Monetary Policy" in Finn B. Jensen and Ingo Walter (eds.), *Readings in International Economic Relations* (New York: Ronald Press, 1966); S. C. Tsiang, "The Role of Money in Trade Balance Stability," *American Economic Review*, September, 1961; Robert A. Mundell, "Capital Mobility and Stabilization Policy Under fixed and Flexible Exchange Rates," *Canadian Journal of Economics and Political Science*, November, 1963, and his "The International Disequilibrium System," *Kyklos*, Fasc. I, 1961.

Policy measures for internal and external balance are reviewed in Marina v. N. Whitman, *Policies for Internal and External Balance* (Princeton, N.J.: International Finance Section, Princeton University, 1970); and Richard N. Cooper, *The Economics of Interdependence* (New York: McGraw-Hill, 1968).

Section E-24

Additional Readings on Disequilibrium Adjustment via Prices and Direct Controls

The best available survey on balance of payments adjustment is Anne O. Krueger, "Balance of Payments Theory," *Journal of Economic Literature*, March, 1969. Especially good on capital controls is Norman S. Fieleke, *The Welfare Effects of Controls Over Capital Exports and the United States* (Princeton, N.J.: International Finance Section, Princeton University, 1971). On the exchange-rate flexibility, see Stanley W. Black, *International Money Markets and Flexible Exchange Rates* (Princeton, N.J.: International Finance Section, Princeton University, 1973).

An excellent survey of disequilibrium in the balance of payments, with particular reference to the post-World War II U.S. experience, is contained in M. O. Clement, R. L. Pfister, and K. J. Rothwell, *Theoretical Issues in International Economics* (Boston: Houghton Mifflin, 1967), ch. 8.

On devaluation and income effects, see S. S. Alexander, "Devaluation Versus Import Restriction as an Instrument for Improving Foreign Trade Balance," *IMF Staff Papers,* April, 1951; his "Effects of a Devaluation on a Trade Balance," *IMF Staff Papers,* April, 1952; and his "Effects of a Devaluation: A Simplified Synthesis of Elasticities and Absorption Approaches," *American Economic Review,* March, 1959; E. M. Bernstein, "Strategic Factors in Balance of Payments Adjustment," *Review of Economics and Statistics,* February, 1958; J. Black, "A Savings and Investment Approach to Devaluation," *Economic Journal,* June, 1959; S. B. Linder and B. J. Cohen, "Balance of Payments Adjustment in a Disequilibrium System," *Kyklos,* Fasc. 1, 1964; Fritz Machlup, "The Terms of Trade Effects of Devaluation Upon Real Income and the Balance of Trade," *Kyklos,* Fasc. 4, 1956, and also his "Relative Prices and Aggregate Spending in the Analysis of Devaluation," *American Economic Review,* June, 1955; and R. E. Jones, "Depreciation and the Dampening Effects of Income Change," *Review of Economics and Statistics,* February, 1960.

Also, see H. G. Johnson, *International Trade and Economic Growth* (London: George Allen & Unwin, 1958); A. C. Harberger, "Currency Depreciation, Income and the Balance of Trade," *Journal of Political Economy,* February, 1950; and Egon Sohmen, "The Effect of Devaluation on the Price Level," *Quarterly Journal of Economics,* May, 1958.

For discussions of the balance of payments effects of exchange control, see J. B. Condliffe, *The Reconstruction of World Trade* (New York: W. W. Norton, 1940); H. S. Ellis, *Exchange Control in Central Europe* (Cambridge: Harvard University Press, 1941); James E. Meade, *The Balance of Payments* (London: Oxford University Press, 1951), part V; and the International Monetary Fund's publication *Report on Exchange Restrictions* (Washington, D.C.: IMF, Annual).

Of interest on clearing arrangements will be J. H. C. de Looper, "Current Usage of Payments Agreements and Trade Agreements," *IMF Staff Papers,* August, 1955; H. H. Schloss, *The Bank for International Settlements* (Amsterdam: North Holland Publishing Co., 1953); Robert Triffin, *Europe and the Money Muddle* (New Haven: Yale University Press, 1957); R. F. Mikesell, *The Emerging Pattern of International Payments,* Essays in International Finance, No. 18 (Princeton: International Finance Section, Princeton University, 1954); L. W. Towle, *International Trade and Commercial Policy* (New York: Harper & Row, 1956); as well as the relevant chapters in W. M. Scammell, *International Monetary Policy* (London: Macmillan, 1963).

Specifically on the Sterling Area, see Philip Bell, *The Sterling Area in the Postwar World* (Oxford: Clarendon Press, 1956); and J. Polk, *Sterling: Its Meaning in World Finance* (New York: Harper & Row, 1956). An excellent survey is contained in Leland B. Yeager, *International Monetary Policy* (New York: Harper & Row, 1966), chs. 18–21.

Multiple exchange rates and their uses are covered in Eugene R. Schlesinger, *Multiple Exchange Rates and Economic Development* (Princeton: Princeton University Press, 1952); E. M. Bernstein, "Some Economic Aspects of Multiple Exchange Rates," *IMF Staff Papers,* March, 1950; as well as in R. F. Mikesell's *Foreign Exchange in the Postwar World* (New York: Twentieth Century Fund, 1954).

On other direct expenditure switching policies for balance of payments adjustments, see M. F. W. Hemming and W. M. Corden, "Import Restriction as an Instrument of Balance-of-Payments Policy," *Economic Journal,* September, 1958; Ragnar Frisch, "On the Need for Forecasting a Multilateral Balance of Payments," *American Economic Review,* September, 1947; and also the relevant chapters in Meade's *The Balance of Payments.*

On the cost of adjustment, see Edward M. Bernstein, "Strategic Factors in Balance of Payments Adjustment," *IMF Staff Papers,* August, 1956; Tibor Scitovsky, *Requirements of an International Reserve System,* Essays in International Finance, No. 49 (Princeton: International Finance Section, Princeton University, 1965); Fritz Machlup, "Real Adjustment, Compensatory Corrections, and Foreign Financing of Imbalances in International Payments," in R. E. Baldwin, *et al., Trade, Growth and the Balance of Payments* (Chicago: Rand McNally, 1965); Benjamin J. Cohen, *Adjustment Costs and the Distribution of New Reserves,* Studies in International Finance, No. 18 (Princeton: International Finance Section, Princeton University, 1966); and Staffan Burenstam Linder, *An Essay on Trade and Transformation* (Stockholm: Almquist & Wiksell, 1961), ch. V.

Section E-25

Additional Readings on International Liquidity

An excellent treatment of the liquidity question is contained in Fritz Machlup, *International Payments, Debts, and Gold* (New York: Scribner's, 1964), chs. 10–13. See also the relevant chapters in W. M. Scammell, *International Monetary Policy,* 2nd ed. (London: Macmillan, 1964); and L. B. Yeager, *International Monetary Relations* (New York: Harper, 1966).

On gold, see M. A. Kriz, "Gold in World Monetary Affairs Today," *Political Science Quarterly,* December, 1960; E. M. Bernstein, "The Adequacy of United States Gold Reserves," *American Economic Review,* Papers and Proceedings, May, 1961; and especially the Federal Reserve Bank of San Francisco publication *The Search for Certainty in an Uncertain World* (San Francisco: Federal Reserve Bank of San Francisco, 1962). Also of interest will be O. L. Altman, "A Note on Gold Production and Additions to International Gold Reserves," *IMF Staff Papers,* April, 1958; F. D. Graham and C. R. Wittlesley, *Golden Avalanche* (Princeton, N.J.: Princeton University Press, 1939); A. P. Lerner, "Let's Get Rid of Our Cross of Gold," *Challenge,* April, 1964; and Robert Triffin, *Gold and the Dollar Crisis* (New Haven, Conn.: Yale University Press, 1960).

On liquidity problems, see J. K. Horsefield, "International Liquidity," *Finance and Development,* December, 1964; Robert V. Roosa, "Balance of Payments Adjustment and International Liquidity," *Journal of Finance,* March, 1964; C. P. Kindleberger, "Balance of Payments Deficits and the International Market for Liquidity," *Essays in International Finance,* Princeton University, May, 1965; F. A. Lutz, "The Problems of International Liquidity and the Multiple-Currency Standard," *Essays in International Finance,* Princeton University, March, 1963;

H. G. Aubrey, *The Dollar in World Affairs* (New York: Frederick A. Praeger, 1964); and S. E. Rolfe, *Gold and World Power* (New York: Harper 1966).

On international monetary cooperation, see Clay J. Anderson, *Defending the Dollar* (Philadelphia: Federal Reserve Bank of Philadelphia, 1962); Charles A. Coombs' periodic articles in the Federal Reserve Bank of New York *Monthly Review* entitled "Treasury and Federal Reserve Foreign Exchange Operations"; and relevant contributions in Joint Economic Committee, U.S. Congress, *Factors Affecting the U.S. Balance of Payments* (Washington, D.C.: U.S. Government Printing Office, 1962).

On the IMF, see H. Aufricht, *The International Monetary Fund* (New York: Frederick A. Praeger, 1964); Shigeo Horie, *The International Monetary Fund* (London: Macmillan, 1964); IMF Staff, "Introduction to the Fund," *Finance and Development,* June, 1964; and G. P. Nicoletopoulos, "Stand-by Arrangements," *Finance and Development,* December, 1964.

The relationship between the supply of international liquidity and reserve country payments deficits is explored in Peter B. Kenen, "International Liquidity and the Balance of Payments of a Reserve-Currency Country," *Quarterly Journal of Economics,* November, 1960. See also IMF Staff, "The Adequacy of Monetary Reserves," *IMF Staff Papers,* October, 1953; Jacques Rueff and Fred Hirsch, "The Role and the Rule of Gold: An Argument," *Essays in International Finance,* Princeton University, February, 1967; and Robert V. Roosa and Fred Hirsch, "Reserves, Reserve Currencies and Vehicle Currencies: An Argument," *Essays in International Finance,* Princeton University, May, 1966.

Also, see Robert Triffin, "The Dollar and International Liquidity Problem Reconsidered," *Kyklos,* Fasc. 3, 1958; N. Kaldor, "The Problem of International Liquidity," *Bulletin of the Oxford University Institute of Statistics,* August, 1964; R. Harrod, "A Plan for Increasing Liquidity: A Critique," *Economica,* May, 1961; O. L. Altman, "The Management of International Liquidity," *IMF Staff Papers,* July, 1964, and his "A Note on Gold Production and Additions to International Gold Reserves," *IMF Staff Papers,* April, 1958; J. M. Fleming, "The Fund and International Liquidity," *IMF Staff Papers,* July, 1964, and his "International Liquidity: Ends and Means," *IMF Staff Papers,* December, 1961; M. O. Clement, "A Functional Approach to the Concept of International Reserves," *Kyklos,* Fasc. 3, 1963; W. M. Brown, "Concept and Measurement of Foreign Exchange Reserves," *Economic Journal,* September, 1955; H. W. Arndt, "The Concept of Liquidity and International Monetary Theory," *Review of Economic Studies,* No. 1, 1947–48; and T. Balogh, "International Reserves and Liquidity," *Economic Journal,* June, 1960.

On Eurodollars, see A. R. Holmes and F. M. Klopstock, "The Market for Dollar Deposits in Europe," Federal Reserve Bank of New York *Monthly Review,* November, 1960; G. L. Bell, "The Eurodollar Market," Federal Reserve Bank of St. Louis *Review,* December, 1963; O. L. Altman, "Foreign Markets for Dollars, Sterling and Other Currencies," *IMF Staff Papers,* December, 1961; and his "Recent Developments in Foreign Markets for Dollars and Other Currencies," *IMF Staff Papers,* March, 1963; Paul Einzig, "Has the Euro-dollar a Future?" *Statist,* October 11, 1963, his "Statics and Dynamics of the Euro-dollar Market," *Economic Journal,* September, 1961, and his *The Euro-dollar System* (London: Macmillan, 1964); and E. Bloch, *Eurodollars: An Emerging International Money Market* (New York: Institute of Finance, New York University, 1966).

Section E-26

Additional Readings on International Monetary Reform

The various types of alternative international monetary systems are surveyed in Fritz Machlup, *Plans for Reform of the International Monetary System* (Princeton: International Finance Section, Princeton University, 1964); R. G. Hawkins and S. E. Rolfe, *A Critical Survey of Plans for International Monetary Reform* (New York: Institute of Finance, New York University, 1965); *International Monetary Arrangements: The Problem of Choice,* Report on the Deliberations of an International Study Commission of 32 Economists (Princeton, N.J.: International Finance Section, Princeton University, 1964); and Leland B. Yeager, *International Monetary Relations* (New York: Harper, 1966), chs. 26–28. For some of the original writings, see Herbert G. Grubel (ed.), *World Monetary Reform: Plans and Issues* (Stanford, Cal.: Stanford University Press, 1963); and Robert G. Hawkins (ed.), *Compendium of Plans for International Monetary Reform* (New York: Institute of Finance, New York University, 1965).

On a return to gold, see Jacques Rueff, "The West is Risking a Credit Collapse," *Fortune,* July, 1961, and also his "Gold Exchange Standard a Danger to the West," in the Grubel volume, cited above. In the same volume, see also the article by M. A. Heilperin, "The Case for Going Back to Gold."

On demonetization of gold, see A. P. Lerner, "Let's Get Rid of Our Cross of Gold," *Challenge,* April, 1964; H. Piquet, "Some Consequences of Dollar Speculation in Gold," in Joint Economic Committee, U.S. Congress, *Factors Affecting the United States Balance of Payments* (Washington, D.C.: U.S. Government Printing Office, 1962); as well as the Machlup survey, above, for his own plan of planned reductions in the gold price.

On flexible exchange rates, see Milton Friedman, "The Case for Flexible Exchange Rates," in his *Essays in Positive Economics* (Chicago: University of Chicago Press, 1953); R. E. Caves, "Flexible Exchange Rates," *American Economic Review,* May, 1963; W. J. Baumol, "Speculation, Profitability, and Stability," *Review of Economics and Statistics,* August, 1957; Egon Sohmen, *Flexible Exchange Rates: Theory and Controversy* (Chicago: University of Chicago Press, 1961); L. G. Telser, "A Theory of Speculation Relating Profitability and Stability," *Review of Economics and Statistics,* August, 1959; F. A. Lutz, "The Case for Flexible Exchange Rates," *Banca Nazionale del Lavoro Quarterly Review,* December, 1954; and R. Nurkse, *International Currency Experience: Lessons of the Inter-War Period* (Geneva: League of Nations, 1966).

Also, see George N. Halm, *The "Band" Proposal: The Limits of Permissible Exchange Rate Variations* (Princeton, N.J.: International Finance Section, Princeton University, 1965); and James E. Meade, "The International Monetary Mechanism," *Three Banks Review,* September, 1964, for a sampling of proposals to widen flexibility limits. On the Canadian experience, see R. Rhomberg, "Canada's Foreign Exchange Market: A Quarterly Model," *IMF Staff Papers,* April, 1960; and H. C. Eastman, "Aspects of Speculation in the Canadian Market for Foreign Exchanges," *Canadian Journal of Economic and Political Science,* August, 1958.

On reserve currency extensions, see the Report of the 32, noted above, as well as F. A. Lutz, *The Problem of International Liquidity and the Multiple Currency Standard* (Princeton, N.J.: International Finance Section, Princeton University, 1963), and his *The Problems of International Equilibrium* (Amsterdam: North Holland, 1962); J. Williamson, "Liquidity and the Multiple Key-Currency Proposal," *American Economic Review*, June, 1963; and Robert V. Roosa, *Monetary Reform for the World Economy* (New York: Harper, 1965).

For the Keynes and Triffin plans for reserve centralization, see Robert Triffin, *Gold and the Dollar Crisis* (New Haven, Conn.: Yale University Press, 1921); J. W. Angell, "The Reorganization of the International Monetary System: An Alternative Proposal," *Economic Journal*, December, 1961; O. L. Altman, "Professor Triffin on International Liquidity and the Role of the Fund," *IMF Staff Papers*, May, 1961; J. M. Fleming, "The Fund and International Liquidity," *IMF Staff Papers*, July, 1964; L. B. Yeager, "The Triffin Plan: Diagnosis, Remedy, and Alternatives," *Kyklos*, Fasc. 3, 1961; Maxwell Stamp, "The Fund and the Future," *Lloyds Bank Review*, October, 1958; and "The Stamp Plan—1962 Version," *Moorgate and Wall Street*, Autumn, 1962.

The best way to keep up on current issues in international monetary reform is to read the *IMF News Survey* (free) and the appropriate sections in the London *Economist*. Current thinking by academics and others is best reflected in the publications of Princeton University's International Finance Section.

Section E-27

Additional Readings on International Factor Transfers and Economic Development

Probably the best general volume in this general field is Gerald M. Meier *The International Economics of Development* (New York: Harper, 1968), which covers virtually all aspects of international economics from the standpoint of the developing countries.

On international migration, see W. A. Lewis, *The Theory of Economic Growth* (Homewood, Ill.: Richard D. Irwin, 1955); H. H. Villard, *Economic Development* (New York: Holt, Rinehart & Winston, 1963); and C. P. Kindleberger, *Economic Development*, 2nd ed. (New York: McGraw-Hill, 1965), ch. 15.

International capital transfers to developing countries are analyzed in G. M. Meier, *International Trade and Development* (New York: Harper, 1963), ch. 5; Ragnar Nurkse, *Problems of Capital Formation in Underdeveloped Countries* (Oxford: Basil Blackwell, 1953); J. R. Hicks, *Essays in World Economics* (New York: Oxford University Press, 1959); P. N. Rosenstein-Rodan, "International Aid for Underdeveloped Countries," *Review of Economics and Statistics*, May, 1961; T. Balogh and P. Streeten, "Domestic versus Foreign Investment," *Bulletin of the Oxford University Institute of Statistics*, August, 1960; D. Mac-Dougall, "The Benefits and Costs of Private Investment from Abroad: A Theoretical Approach," *Economic Record*, March, 1960; and H. W. Arndt, "Overseas Borrowing—the New Model," *Economic Record*, August, 1957.

Also, see D. Finch, "Investment Service of Underdeveloped Countries," *IMF Staff Papers*, September, 1951; R. F. Mikesell, *Public International Lending for Development* (New York: Random House, 1966), and his *United States Private and Government Investment Abroad* (Eugene: University of Oregon Press, 1962); G. M. Alter, "The Servicing of Foreign Capital Inflows by Underdeveloped Countries" in H. S. Ellis and H. C. Wallich (eds.), *Economic Development for Latin*

America (New York: St. Martin's, 1961); and D. Avramovic and R. Gulhati, *Debt Service Problems of Low Income Countries* (Baltimore: Johns Hopkins, 1960).

On lending agencies, see H. Feis, *Foreign Aid and Foreign Policy* (New York: St. Martin's, 1963); R. E. Asher, *Grants, Loans and Local Currencies: Their Role in Foreign Aid* (Washington, D.C.: Brookings, 1961); F. T. Moore, "The World Bank and Its Economic Missions," *Review of Economics and Statistics,* February, 1960; R. F. Mikesell, *United States Economic Policy and International Relations* (New York: McGraw-Hill, 1952); Antonin Basch, *Financing Economic Development* (New York: Macmillan, 1964); J. A. Pincus, "The Cost of Foreign Aid," *Review of Economics and Statistics,* November, 1963; W. Diamond, *Development Banks* (Baltimore: Johns Hopkins, 1957); and Bela Balassa, "The Capital Needs of Underdeveloped Countries," *Kyklos,* Fasc. 2, 1964.

R. D. Robinson, *International Business Policy* (New York: Holt, Rinehart and Winston, 1964), provides a fascinating analysis of private investment in developing countries. Also, on the operations of the IBRD, see the selections in Finn B. Jensen and Ingo Walter, *Readings in International Economic Relations* (New York: Ronald Press, 1966), ch. 13.

On technology and entrepreneurship, see A. O. Hirschman, *The Strategy of Economic Development* (New Haven, Conn.: Yale University Press, 1958); R. S. Eckaus, "The Factor Proportions Problem in Underdeveloped Areas," *American Economic Review,* September, 1955; Chapter 14 of the Kindleberger *Economic Development* text and R. D. Robinson's book, noted above; and W. G. Friedmann anl G. Kalmanoff (eds.), *Joint International Business Ventures* (New York: Columbia University Press, 1961).

Section E-28

Additional Readings on International Trade and Economic Development

For the best overview of trade and development, see Gerald M. Meir, *The International Economics of Development* (New York: Harper, 1968). See also Robert G. Hawkins and Ingo Walter (eds.), *The United States and International Markets* (Lexington, Mass.: D. C. Heath, 1972), especially chapters 3, 4, 5, 12 and 13; as well as Staffan Burenstam Linder, *Trade and Trade Policy for Development* (New York: Frederick A. Praeger, 1967).

On the general subject of trade and growth, see Gerald M. Meier, *International Trade and Development* (New York: Harper & Row, 1963); and also Staffan Burenstam Linder, *Trade and Trade Policy for Development* (New York: Frederick A. Praeger, 1967).

On the terms of trade, see Raùl Prebisch, "Commercial Policy in the Underdeveloped Countries," *American Economic Review,* May, 1959; Hans W. Singer, "The Distribution of Gains Between Investing and Borrowing Countries," *American Economic Review,* May, 1950; P. T. Ellsworth, "The Terms of Trade Between Primary Producing and Industrial Countries," *Inter-American Economic Affairs,* Summer, 1956; R. E. Baldwin, "Secular Movements in the Terms of Trade," *American Economic Review,* May, 1955; W. A. Lewis, "Economic Development with Unlimited Supplies of Labour," *Manchester School,* May 1954; Jagdish Bhagwati, "International Trade and Economic Expansion," *American Economic Review,* December, 1958; Theodore Morgan, "The Long-Run Terms of Trade Between Agriculture and Manufacturing," *Economic Development and Cultural Change,* October, 1959; and Gottfried Haberler, "Terms of Trade and Economic Development," in H. S. Ellis (ed.), *Economic Development for Latin America* (London: Macmillan, 1961).

For other arguments for and against protection, see Albert O. Hirschman, *The Strategy of Economic Development* (New Haven, Conn.: Yale University Press, 1958); Ragnar Nurkse, *Equilibrium and Growth in the World Economy* (Cambridge, Mass.: Harvard University Press, 1961); H. B. Chenery, "Comparative Advantage and Development Policy," *American Economic Review,* March, 1961; Mihail Manoilesco, *Theory of Protection and International Trade* (London: P. S. King, 1931); M. Fleming, "External Economies and the Doctrine of Balanced Growth," *Economic Journal,* June, 1955; and E. E. Hagen, "An Economic Justification of Protectionism," *Quarterly Journal of Economics,* November, 1958.

Also, see Staffan Burenstam Linder, *An Essay on Trade and Transformation* (New York: Wiley, 1961); and Gottfried Haberler, *International Trade and Economic Development* (Cairo: National Bank of Egypt, 1959).

Of additional interest will be A. K. Cairncross, "International Trade and Economic Development," *Economica,* August, 1961; Jacob Viner, *International Trade and Economic Development* (New York: Free Press, 1952); Ragnar Nurkse, "Some International Aspects of the Problem of Economic Development," *American Economic Review,* May, 1952, and his *Problems of Capital Formation in Underdeveloped Countries* (London: Basil Blackwell, 1953); J. R. Hicks, *Essays in World Economics* (New York: Oxford University Press, 1959); United Nations, *Towards a New Trade Policy for Development* (New York: United Nations, 1964); G. Myrdal, *An International Economy* (New York: Harper & Row, 1956); and Hla Myint, "The Classical Theory of International Trade and the Underdeveloped Countries," *Economic Journal,* June, 1958.

On export stabilization, see P. T. Bauer and F. W. Paish, "The Reduction of Fluctuations in the Incomes of Primary Producers," *Economic Journal,* December, 1952; Boris C. Swerling, *Current Issues in International Commodity Policy* (Princeton: International Finance Section, Princeton University, 1962); J. D. Coppock, *International Economic Instability* (New York: McGraw-Hill, 1962); James E. Meade, "International Commodity Agreements," in United Nations Conference on Trade and Development, *Commodity Trade* (New York: United Nations, 1964); R. M. Stern, "International Compensation for Fluctuations in Commodity Trade," *Quarterly Journal of Economics,* May, 1963; R. G. Hawkins, J. Epstein and J. Gonzales, *Stabilization of Export Receipts and Economic Development— International Commodity Agreements and Compensating Financing Plans* (New York: Institute of Finance, New York University, 1966); and J. W. F. Rowe, *Primary Commodities in International Trade* (Cambridge: Cambridge University Press, 1965).

On trade and environmental management, see Ingo Walter, "Environmental Management and the International Economic Order" in C. Fred Bergsten (ed.), *The Future of the International Economic Order* (Lexington, Mass.: D. C. Heath, 1973). The latter volume is also an excellent review of some of the upcoming policy issues in the international economy.

Section E-29

Additional Readings on Multinational Enterprise

A great deal has been written in recent years about the operation of multinational enterprises. See, for example, John M. Stopford and Louis T. Wells, *Managing the Multinational Enterprise* (New York: Basic Books, 1972); Raymond Vernon, *Sovereignty at Bay* (New York: Basic Books, 1971); and Charles P. Kindleberger (ed.), *The International Corporation* (Cambridge, Mass.: MIT Press, 1970). Also John H. Dunning, *Studies in International Investment* (London: Allen & Unwin, 1970); and for a good textbook, see Vern Salera, *Multinational Business* (Boston: Houghton Mifflin, 1969).

For some of the political pressures, see Harold Bamet and Ronald Müller, *Global Reach* (New York: Simon & Schuster, 1975); Harry Magdoff, *The Age of Imperialism* (New York: Modern Reader Paperbacks, 1969); and J. J. Servan-Schreiber, *The American Challenge* (New York: Atheneum, 1968). For a more balanced view, see Jack M. Behrman, *National Interests and the Multinational Enterprise* (Englewood Cliffs, N.J.: Prentice-Hall, 1970).

On investment behavior, see Thomas Horst, "Firm and Industry Determinants of the Decisions to Invest Abroad: An Empirical Study," *Review of Economics and Statistics,* August, 1972; and A. E. Scaperlanda and L. J. Mauer, "The Determinants of U.S. Direct Investment in the EEC," *American Economic Review,* September, 1969.

On employment effects of multinational corporations see especially Robert G. Hawkins, "The Multinational Corporation: A New Trade Policy Issue in the United States," in R. G. Hawkins and I. Walter (eds.), *The United States and International Markets* (Lexington, Mass.: D. C. Heath, 1972). On MNC money management, see R. B. Stobaugh and S. M. Robbins, *Money and the Multinational Enterprise* (New York: Basic Books, 1972).

INDEX